MICHELE STEFANELLI

Due Diligence of a Layer 2

MICHELE STEFANELLI

BITCOIN HYPER · LAYER 2 · DUE DILIGENCE

Due Diligence of a Layer 2

How to evaluate a crypto project in its pre-mainnet phase

The Bitcoin Hyper Case

VOLUME I

Foundations, Architecture, and Security

MICHELE STEFANELLI
Independent Financial Advisor · OCF Register · NAFOP · AIAF
Founder of MS Digital Asset Academy
Executive Education · Saïd Business School, University of Oxford

MS

MS DIGITAL ASSET ACADEMY

Due Diligence of a Layer 2 – The Bitcoin Hyper Case
Volume I – Foundations, Architecture, and Security of a Layer 2 on Bitcoin

MS

Published by MS Digital Asset Academy — Noale (VE), Italy
ISBN 979-12-82708-02-9
ISBN-A (DOI): 10.979.1282708/029
ORCID 0009-0004-3755-1292
First English Edition: July 2026
Complete work in two volumes.
Translated from the Italian original edition: ISBN 979-12-82708-00-5 · ISBN-A 10.979.1282708/005.

Official record of the work and copyright statement

The opinions expressed in this book are exclusively the author's and do not in any way constitute financial, tax, or legal advice. The author declares that, as of the date of publication, he holds no positions in the project under analysis and no economic or consulting relationships with its promoters. The full methodological note is set out in Volume II.

To my wife
and my daughters.

For their quiet presence,
for their silent support,
for having shared with me the time of this book.

TABLE OF CONTENTS

Contents

Preface

Why this book, and why now

When I began studying Bitcoin Hyper, I admit, I did so with the eye of the most scrupulous advisor: the one who is not impressed by promises, but verifies every detail, questions every claim, and looks for coherence between a project's architecture, its numbers, and its sustainability. I wanted to understand whether Bitcoin Hyper truly withstood the test of a rigorous due diligence, whether the presale data told a credible story, and whether the promised architecture rested on concrete technical foundations. It was an exercise I had already done dozens of times, on other projects. I thought it would take a few days.

Months have passed.

What was meant to be a quick analysis turned into a journey inside one of the most fascinating and divisive questions of the contemporary crypto world: **can Bitcoin be extended without betraying it?** It is a question that sounds technical, but is in fact philosophical. Bitcoin is not just a protocol: it is a pact of trust among millions of people who have knowingly chosen a slow, conservative network precisely because slow and conservative is its virtue. Touching it means breaking that pact. Leaving it as it is means giving up everything that modern programmability has made possible elsewhere — decentralized finance, smart contracts, shared-state applications, the parallel execution of thousands of operations per second.

Bitcoin Hyper presents itself as the answer to this dilemma. An architectural answer, not a political one: it does not ask Bitcoin to change, but proposes to build on top of it a fast, programmable execution layer anchored to its finality. It is an elegant idea, at least in principle. The problem — and the reason this book exists — is that between the elegance of the idea and the solidity of the implementation lies an abyss that marketing tends to fill with reassuring words such as "ZK rollup," "Bitcoin security," "decentralization." Words that are half true, or true only in words, and that must be translated, taken apart, and reassembled until one truly understands what they promise and what they do not.

This book is the product of that translation.

What you will find in these pages. A complete technical guide, written so that a reader who is not an engineer can follow it all the way through. I chose a precise method: each chapter is born as a direct answer to a question left open by the previous one. Nothing is included because it "belongs to the subject": every concept enters the stage at the moment it becomes necessary to understand the next one. We start from a problem (Bitcoin is slow), we introduce a solution (a fast layer on top), we discover that the solution generates a new problem (how is security guaranteed?), and from that problem the next chapter is born. It is the same logic by which the Bitcoin Hyper team built its own project, one architectural decision at a time. Following that same logic is the best way to understand the result.

What you will not find. You will not find a fan's enthusiasm, nor a detractor's demonization. Bitcoin Hyper is a project under construction: some of its components already run on devnet, others are still theoretical research, others still are declarations of intent. Writing as if everything were ready would be dishonest. Writing as if nothing existed would be blind. I have sought the middle path: describing what is documented, distinguishing what is implemented from what is designed, and signaling clearly where the public promise diverges from what the whitepaper declares. When the marketing says "ZK rollup" and the technical document describes a trusted sequencer with periodic anchoring, I report both, and I leave the reader the tools to judge.

Who this book is for. Three kinds of readers, and it tries to serve them all without betraying any. **The curious reader** who has heard of Bitcoin Hyper and wants to understand what it is without having to become a blockchain engineer: for them I have built every chapter around concrete analogies — the highway built above the state road, the notary signing the register, the multiple checkout lanes of a supermarket — that translate the technology into everyday images. **The investor** weighing whether to put their money into the project: for them I have dedicated, in Volume II, an entire Part to critical analysis, with the list of questions every serious due diligence should ask, and with the signals to monitor in the months leading up to the mainnet launch. **The developer or researcher** who wants to understand the architectural choices in depth: for them I have added, in every chapter, a section of technical FAQs with precise examples, and in the appendix a reasoned glossary; in Volume II, an annotated reading of the whitepaper.

A note on my position. I am not affiliated with the Bitcoin Hyper team. I have received no compensation for writing this book. Any tokens I may have purchased in the presale are disclosed in Volume II (Appendix E) and do not exceed the threshold that could condition my judgment. I have written as an external observer with a debt of honesty toward those who read me: if I am wrong, I want to be wrong in public, with arguments the reader can check. For this reason every technical claim is anchored to a source — the official whitepaper, the team's updates, the audit reports, independent analyses — and every source is cited so that anyone can verify it.

A note on time. This book was written between the summer of 2025 and the spring of 2026, in parallel with the project's evolution. Some chapters were born as a reaction to a team update; others were rewritten three times because three times the team published new information that changed the picture. The result is a work that photographs Bitcoin Hyper at a precise moment of its history, the one that precedes the mainnet launch. A year from now, some of these pages will have been overtaken by events. That is as it should be: an honest technical book is one that ages well because it told the truth of its own moment, not one that pretends to last forever.

A note on style. I chose prose, not bullet points. I chose the long paragraph, not the slide. I did so for a precise reason: technical concepts are understood only when their causal link is visible, and a causal link needs syntax, not graphics. When one idea generates another, the bond between the two is a conjunction, a comma, a subordinate clause. Breaking that syntax into bullet points shatters it. For those seeking a summary, at the end of every chapter there is a "what to take away" recap. For those seeking understanding, there is the whole chapter.

The book you hold in your hands is the result of this choice. I hope it accompanies you with the same honesty with which it was written.

Michele Stefanelli
Noale, July 2026

⁂

Introduction

Bitcoin Hyper, in two images and one question

Can the slowest, most cautious, most reliable machine ever built be made fast — without touching it?

This is the question around which the cryptocurrency world has revolved for more than a decade, and Bitcoin Hyper is one of the most ambitious answers proposed so far. Whether it is also a solid answer is precisely what this book sets out to establish; but to grasp what is at stake, two images suffice.

The first is that of **Bitcoin today**: a network that has run for seventeen years without ever stopping, that has weathered attacks, forks, market crises, and hostile governments, and that every ten minutes adds a block to its public ledger. It is the most solid truth machine ever built by human beings — and precisely for this reason it is also, deliberately, a limited machine: it processes about seven transactions per second, in moments of heavy traffic its fees reach prohibitive levels, and its internal language, Script, can do almost nothing of what we today call an "application." No automated lending, no decentralized exchanges, no shared-state games. Bitcoin is the perfect vault; but it is, precisely, only a vault.

The second image is that of **Solana**: a network that processes tens of thousands of transactions per second, where fees are measured in fractions of a cent and where developers write applications in Rust and deploy them in minutes. It is fast, programmable, alive — and it is so at the price of a security model different from Bitcoin's, of a history of service outages that its own community has not forgotten, and of a concentration of validating power that some judge an acceptable compromise and others do not.

Keep these two images in mind, because they do not merely open the book: they are the two poles between which every design choice we encounter will swing. Every time Hyper gains something of the second — speed, programmability, minimal costs — we will have to ask how much of the first it is spending to obtain it; and it is in that price, declared or unspoken, that the true nature of a Layer 2 hides.

From here comes the question that gives rise to Bitcoin Hyper: **can one take the solidity of the first image and the speed of the second, and make them coexist** — without asking Bitcoin to change, and without asking Solana's developers to relearn everything from scratch?

The answer the team proposes is a three-layer architecture; it is worth fixing it in mind right away, because the entire rest of the book is nothing but the verification, layer by layer, of this promise.

At the base remains Bitcoin, untouched: slow, conservative, secure, immutable, exactly as it has always been. Nothing new is asked of it — it continues to do its job, recording the truth, at the pace of one block every ten minutes.

Above it sits Bitcoin Hyper, the rollup, and this is where things move: transactions are collected, ordered, and executed in parallel by an engine borrowed from Solana — the Solana Virtual Machine, the SVM — with thousands of operations per second, very low latencies, and minimal costs. At regular intervals, however, this layer pauses for an instant and sends Bitcoin a "compressed photograph" of everything that has happened: a cryptographic signature, a state root, a seal. From that moment — this, at least, is the promise — what happened above becomes as final as what happens inside Bitcoin.

At the top stand the applications: decentralized exchanges, lending protocols, games, social apps, NFTs, wallets — everything developers will be able to build with the same tools they already use on Solana. It is the layer the end user sees and touches, the one in which Bitcoin ceases to be merely "holdable" and becomes "usable."

Described this way, the architecture appears elegant and almost obvious. In reality **every layer hides a question — and every question, in this book, has a precise address.**

We start from the underlying paradox — why the most secure network in the world is also the one that can do the fewest things, and why its custodians want it that way — and from there, from the map of roads already attempted, from payment channels to sidechains to forks (Part I). Having established that one must build *on top of* Bitcoin and not *inside* it, it remains to understand what truly distinguishes a rollup from a sidechain presenting itself as one (Part II); and since a rollup needs an engine, why the team chose Solana's of all engines, inheriting the technology of a rival ecosystem (Part III). An engine that executes must then deliver to Bitcoin a commitment that Bitcoin cannot read: hence the problem of how to formulate it, and of where the data that makes it verifiable by anyone should live (Part IV). But if someone collects and orders those transactions, that someone has power — who are they, and what prevents them from abusing it (Part V)? And if they do abuse it, what defenses kick in, and how does one design a system that under attack does not collapse but degrades in a controlled way (Part VI)? Finally, assuming everything works: who will build on this network, with what tools, and within what ecosystem of services (Part VII)?

There is, however, one question that contains them all, and it is the reason this book takes the form of a due diligence and not of a manual: **how much of all this already exists — and how much is still**

only a promise? Bitcoin Hyper is, as I write, a pre-mainnet project: the definitive network has not yet been launched. And it is precisely in this phase that an analysis of this kind is most needed: decisions — about investing, about building, about simple attention — are made before the facts exist, not after. It is the question that runs through the entire work, and it will find its full answer in the second volume, the volume of judgment; but it cannot even be posed seriously without the work of this first volume, the volume of understanding.

It is worth pausing for a moment on what the words *due diligence* mean here. In the language of finance, it is the preliminary examination by which one verifies the substance of what is being proposed, before committing capital or reputation to it: one reads the documents, checks the numbers, looks for coherence between what a project declares and what it actually is. Applying it to an infrastructure still under construction, however, is a more unusual and more demanding exercise than the customary one, because much of the object does not yet exist in verifiable form: there is an architectural design, there are technical documents, there are announcements — but there is not yet a definitive network on which to measure its real behavior. In such a case the examination cannot limit itself to photographing a result: it must evaluate a project — the coherence of its design, the quality of its choices, the solidity of the path separating the idea from its execution. It is a subtle assessment, to be redone on every page; and it is precisely this continuity that makes the work demanding and, I believe, useful.

And it is worth saying right away: the outcome is not a foregone conclusion, and this book does not presume to anticipate it. If the answer to the opening question turned out to be yes, the largest and most immobile capital in the industry would become programmable without abandoning the security that guards it; if it turned out to be no, Bitcoin Hyper would join the long list of attempts we will encounter from Part I onward. But this is exactly why the title speaks of a "case": Bitcoin Hyper is, beyond being the object of the investigation, the proving ground of a method. The questions we will learn to ask — what truly anchors, who orders, who holds custody, what happens when something breaks — hold for any Layer 2, present or future. Whatever happens to the project, those questions remain with the reader: in an industry where information ages within weeks, they are the part of the investment that does not depreciate.

One clarification, before we begin: to the best of my knowledge, this is the first organic work to subject Bitcoin Hyper to an independent due diligence. It is not a badge of merit; it is a responsibility — and the way I intend to honor it is already written in the preface pages that precede.

But to understand why Bitcoin Hyper exists, one must first understand why Bitcoin, on its own, is not enough. Not because it is a failed project — it is, on the contrary, the most successful in the history of cryptocurrencies — but because it was conceived to do few things, and to do them superbly: its strength is its limitation. Understanding that limitation, and above all understanding why it was chosen deliberately, is the first step toward understanding everything that follows.

And it is from here that Chapter 1 begins.

⁂

⁂

Note to the First Edition

July 2026

This book rests on a precise documentary base, distributed across its chapters and appendices. Among the most relevant factual elements: the **warning of January 19, 2026** issued by the Comisión Nacional del Mercado de Valores (Volume II, §35.9-bis), the **actual scope of the Coinsult and SpyWolf audits** at the time of the presale (§18.6), the **documented trajectory of the staking APY** from over 700% to 36% in twelve months (Volume II, §30.7), a **documentary discrepancy** in the Rewards allocation between the whitepaper and the presale page (Volume II, Appendix D), and the analysis of the legal structure of **Sentinum Ltd** in light of the findings that emerged from public registries (Volume II, Appendices D and E).

In Volume II, **Chapter 28-bis** introduces the comparison with the 2024–2026 generation of Bitcoin Layer 2s — Citrea, BitLayer, BOB, Merlin Chain, Botanix Labs — which today represents the benchmark against which Hyper will be judged. **Appendix F** (in Volume II) documents the recurring editorial pattern in the marketing of pre-mainnet crypto presales, some of whose operating traits Bitcoin Hyper shares, as identified by independent investigations.

For every factual claim I have applied a precise editorial principle: *document the pattern, do not qualify it.* I will never use the terms *scam*, *fraud*, *swindle*. I will use *regulatory warning*, *operating pattern*, *documentary discrepancy*, *documented correlation*. Where only one source is available, the explicit formulation is *"according to X."* All citations point to public sources verifiable at the time of writing; some links may decay over time, in which case I suggest the reader search for the document by title or consult the Internet Archive.

The purpose is not to issue a verdict, but to provide tools of analysis. Bitcoin Hyper is a pre-mainnet project with an ambitious technical vision, exposed to a high risk profile that the prudent reader is called upon to assess with tools of their own. The pages that follow provide those tools.

Michele Stefanelli

Noale, July 2026

Editorial Note on Volume I

Why this work is in two volumes

This work was born as an extended due diligence on the Bitcoin Hyper case. Its breadth, its technical density, and the need to distinguish sharply between architectural understanding and critical evaluation made a two-volume publication natural.

Volume I builds the technical grammar indispensable for reasoning about the project: Bitcoin as a settlement layer, the scalability problem, the rollup model, the Solana Virtual Machine, settlement, sequencing, security, and the developer experience. It is the volume of understanding: its purpose is not to judge, but to put the reader in a position to do so.

Volume II continues the journey by shifting the attention from structure to evaluation: competitive comparison, tokenomics, the state of the ecosystem, documentary gaps, risks, the due diligence method, and pre-mainnet scenarios.

The two volumes are autonomous but complementary. They can be read separately — the first as a rigorous technical introduction, the second as an investment analysis — but they are designed to be traveled in sequence. The chapter numbering is continuous, from 1 to 36, precisely to remind the reader that this is a single work, divided for clarity and not in substance.

PART I

The Problem to Be Solved

Bitcoin is the most solid system of value ever built. It is also, deliberately, slow and limited. To understand why Bitcoin Hyper exists, one must first understand why this slowness is not a flaw — it is the point.

PART I · THE PROBLEM TO BE SOLVED

Chapter 1
Bitcoin as a Settlement Layer

The strength and the limit of its philosophy

⁂

1.1 — The Paradox of the Most Important Network in Crypto

There is a paradox at the heart of Bitcoin that anyone who has never stopped to think about it will struggle to grasp. The most secure, most decentralized, most censorship-resistant network ever built by human beings is also, at the same time, one of the **slowest** and most **limited** networks in crypto. Bitcoin processes roughly seven transactions per second. Visa processes tens of thousands. Solana, a blockchain a decade younger, processes hundreds of times more. Ethereum, though itself considered "slow," still surpasses Bitcoin in computational capacity and flexibility.

And yet Bitcoin is worth, as I write, more than all other cryptocurrencies combined. Not out of inertia, not out of nostalgia, not out of investor laziness: it is worth that much **precisely because** it is slow, **precisely because** it is limited, **precisely because** it does not change. This sentence, which on a first reading sounds contradictory, contains everything one needs to understand about Bitcoin before one can understand Bitcoin Hyper. If you do not grasp the paradox, you do not grasp the reason Bitcoin Hyper exists either.

Let us take it apart slowly.

When Satoshi Nakamoto published the Bitcoin whitepaper in October 2008, the problem he wanted to solve was not "how do I build a fast payment network." It was an entirely different problem: **how do I create digital money that needs no central bank, no private company, no government, and no other trusted authority of any kind in order to function?** It is a deceptively simple question — devastating, in fact — because every form of money humanity had known until that moment, from shells to gold coins, from banknotes to electronic transfers, had always needed **someone** to guarantee its value or its authenticity. Gold coins needed an authority to certify their weight. Banknotes needed a central bank to control their issuance. Bank transfers needed commercial banks to manage the accounts. Even the digital money that existed before Bitcoin — think of PayPal, credit cards, online payment systems — was money that moved on top of private ledgers, run by companies that could freeze accounts, censor transactions, go bankrupt, be seized by governments, be hacked.

Satoshi wanted to create a form of money that **needed no one**. Not a bank, not a government, not a private company, not a central technical authority. A form of money that would exist and function even if every government in the world decided to ban it, even if every bank in the world decided to boycott it, even if every technology company in the world decided to switch it off. This, to be clear, is a radical goal. Not a "technical" goal. A political, philosophical, almost utopian goal.

And here is the point from which everything else follows: **to reach this goal, Satoshi had to deliberately sacrifice speed, flexibility, and programmability.** These were not accidents along the way. They were conscious sacrifices. Every time a blockchain speeds up, every time it becomes more flexible, every time it adds complex functionality, **it introduces some form of compromise on decentralization, on security, or on independence from trusted authorities.** Bitcoin refused those compromises. It chose to be slow and limited because only by being slow and limited could it be truly, radically, profoundly decentralized.

This is the first thing to take away, and to keep firmly in mind for the rest of this book: **Bitcoin's slowness is not a bug. It is a feature.** Its simplicity is not backwardness. It is a choice. Its conservatism is not laziness. It is principle. Understanding this means understanding why any project that wants to "extend" Bitcoin cannot do so by modifying Bitcoin itself. It means understanding why Bitcoin Hyper, and Lightning Network before it, and the earlier scaling attempts before that, all chose the same road: **build on top, not inside**. Let us see, then, with a little patience, where this philosophy comes from and why it is so solid.

⁂

1.2 — The Byzantine Generals Problem, or Why an Invention Was Needed

To understand the genius of Bitcoin, we need to take a small step back into the history of computer science. In the 1970s and 1980s, theoretical computer scientists had run into a seemingly unsolvable problem, formalized in 1982 by three researchers — Lamport, Shostak, and Pease[1] — through a military allegory that became famous: the **Byzantine Generals Problem.***

The allegory is simple. Imagine an army besieging a city. The army is divided into several contingents, each commanded by a general, and each camped at a different point around the walls. To win, the generals must coordinate a simultaneous attack: if they all attack together, they win; if even one fails to attack, the others are decimated. The generals can communicate only through messengers, who cross enemy territory to carry orders from one camp to another. The problem is that some generals might be traitors: they might send false, contradictory, deceptive messages to sabotage the attack. And the messengers themselves might be intercepted, replaced, manipulated. **How do the loyal generals coordinate if they do not know whom to trust?**

Translated into computing terms, the problem becomes this: **how does a network of distributed computers, in which some nodes may be malicious or faulty, reach agreement on a single shared state?** For nearly thirty years, the academic community had accumulated partial results, elegant but impractical solutions, theoretical proofs of the problem's limits. No one had found a solution that actually worked at global scale, in a genuinely open environment, where anyone could participate without permission and where one could not know in advance how many participants there would be, nor who they were.

* The adjective "Byzantine" has no historical connection to the Byzantine Empire: the authors chose it merely as a neutral label for an arbitrary fault, in which a component can behave not just inertly but deliberately deceptively. The classical result of that work establishes that a system can reach agreement only if loyal nodes exceed two thirds of the total: with n participants, at most f malicious ones can be tolerated provided that $n \geq 3f + 1$. Proof of Work, described below, does not remove this limit but reformulates it in terms of computing power rather than number of nodes.

FIGURE 1.1 **FROM THE BYZANTINE GENERALS PROBLEM TO PROOF OF WORK.**

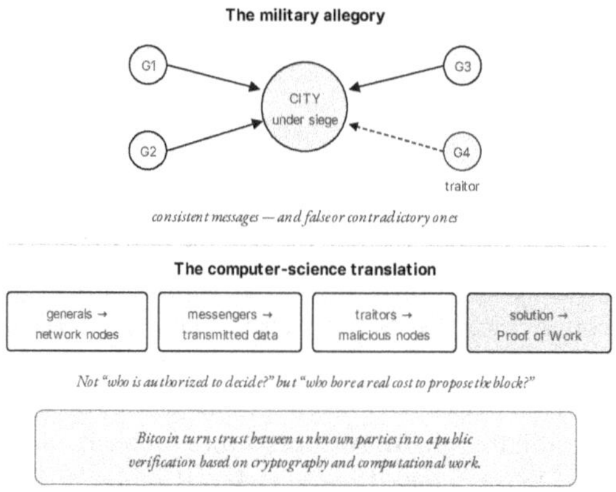

FIGURE 1.2 **BITCOIN'S CONSERVATIVE MINIMALISM: THREE APPARENT LIMITS, THREE STRUCTURAL GUARANTEES.**

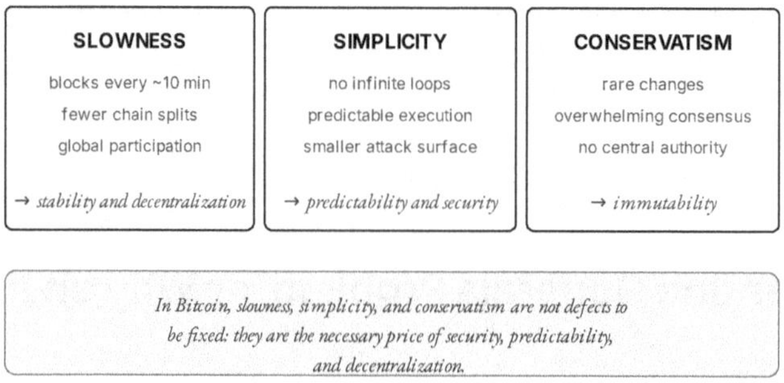

Bitcoin solved the problem with an invention that, seen today, looks almost trivially simple, but that in fact required combining three existing technologies in a way no one had ever put together before: **cryptographic hash functions** to guarantee data integrity, **digital signatures** to authenticate the authors of transactions, and — this is the revolutionary part — a consensus mechanism called **Proof of Work**, which forces whoever wants to propose a new block of transactions to spend real electrical energy to prove they have worked for it.

The idea behind Proof of Work is ingenious in its brutality: instead of asking *who* has the right to write the next block — a question that opens the door to every form of governance and therefore of centralization — Bitcoin asks *how much effort* someone has put into writing it. More effort = more right. And since effort is measured in electrical energy actually consumed, and electrical energy costs real money, and real money is finite, **you cannot cheat**. You cannot pretend to have worked. Either you burned the energy, or you did not. Cryptography is the impartial judge that verifies.

From this architectural choice — apparently just a technical one — everything else follows. **Why is Bitcoin slow?** Because every ten minutes, on average, someone in the world manages to solve the required cryptographic problem and proposes the next block. Could the interval be reduced? Yes, but it would become dangerous: overly frequent blocks increase the probability of chain "forks," increase centralization (because only the miners with the fastest connections would win), and increase vulnerability to attacks. Ten minutes is a compromise chosen deliberately to maximize the stability of the system at global scale, even for nodes with slow connections, even in parts of the world with less developed infrastructure. **Slowness is the price of universal participation.**

Why is Bitcoin limited in its functionality? Because its internal language — Script — was deliberately designed **not to be Turing-complete**. This means Script cannot execute arbitrarily complex programs. It can perform few operations, simple and predictable ones: verifying signatures, checking time conditions, handling basic multisig. No infinite loops, no unbounded recursion, no complex computation. Could Script be made more powerful? Yes, but doing so would introduce enormous risks: contract bugs, resource-exhaustion attacks, unpredictable behaviors, exposure to vulnerabilities that cannot be foreseen in advance. **Limitation is the price of total predictability.**

Why is Bitcoin conservative about change? Because every modification to the protocol requires the approval, in practice, of an enormous portion of the global community: miners, developers, exchanges, wallets, users, companies. Without a central authority, there is no one who can "decree" an upgrade from above. One can only propose it, debate it for years, build consensus, and finally implement it only if the overwhelming majority of the network accepts it. Historical examples such as the long battle over SegWit, or the even longer and often bitter one over block size that led to the Bitcoin Cash fork in 2017[2], show how hard it is to change even the simplest parameters. **Conservatism is the price of having no benevolent dictator.**

And so we are back to the opening paradox. All these limitations — slowness, simplicity, conservatism — are not residual defects of a young project that will improve over time. They are **the very foundations of Bitcoin's value**. If Bitcoin became as fast as Solana, it would lose the decentralization that makes it secure. If it became as flexible as Ethereum, it would lose the predictability that makes it reliable. If it became as upgradable as any ordinary app, it would lose the resistance to evolution that makes it immutable.

This is the **philosophy of conservative minimalism**, and it is the filter through which the community judges any attempt to "improve" Bitcoin. Understanding it well, here, will spare us an enormous amount of confusion in the chapters ahead.

⁂

1.3 — What a "Settlement Layer" Concretely Means

At this point an expression enters the stage that we will use constantly throughout this book, and that deserves careful explanation: the **settlement layer** — the layer where value is **finally and definitively settled**. Bitcoin Hyper, like every serious scaling project, starts from a precise assumption: **Bitcoin is a settlement layer, not an execution layer.** Understanding the difference between the two is the decisive step.

Let us think for a moment about the traditional banking world, because it offers a very useful analogy. When you pay for your coffee at the bar with a credit card, two distinct things actually happen. The first:

the bar receives a near-immediate authorization confirming your payment. You drink your coffee right away; the barista does not wait. The second, which happens behind the scenes and which you do not even notice, is the **actual settlement** of the money between your bank and the bar's bank. That settlement can take hours, days, sometimes more than a week, and it passes through complex interbank systems, clearing houses, end-of-day reconciliations. **The fast payment is execution. The slow movement of real money is settlement.**

FIGURE 1.3 **EXECUTION AND SETTLEMENT: THE FAST PAYMENT AND THE DEFINITIVE TRANSFER OF VALUE.**

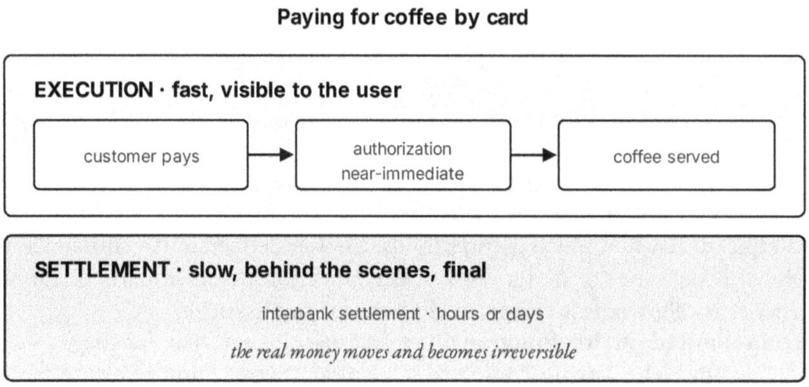

Execution authorizes quickly; settlement makes final what was authorized.

The two functions are kept separate for a precise reason: execution must be fast to serve the user, but settlement must be precise, final, irreversible — and therefore necessarily slower. A "settled" transaction is one that can no longer be undone. A merely "executed" transaction is still reversible, suspended in a gray zone where the authorization exists but the real money has not yet moved. Confusing the two exposes us to enormous risks: think of what would happen if banks declared a payment "settled" merely because it had been authorized, and that payment later turned out to be fraudulent. Settlement exists precisely to make irreversible, once verified, what has been authorized.

Bitcoin is a settlement layer. Once a Bitcoin transaction has been confirmed by a sufficient number of blocks — conventionally six confirmations, about an hour — that transaction is practically impossible to reverse. Not merely difficult, not merely improbable: practically impossible, because reversing it would require redoing all the cryptographic work accumulated by the network from that moment onward, work that grows every ten minutes. This is why Bitcoin is also called "internet money" or, by those who want to emphasize its macroeconomic role, **"digital gold"**: its primary function is not to be fast, but to be **final**. When you receive bitcoin, after the confirmations, **you have truly received bitcoin**. No one can roll back, dispute, freeze, or seize that payment. It is settled.

Bitcoin is not — and does not want to be — an execution layer[a]. It does not want to handle the fast moment of the "payment authorized at the bar." It does not want to run complex smart contracts executing thousands of operations per second. It does not want to be the level on which to build the user experience of a decentralized exchange or an on-chain game. All these things, in principle, *could* be done inside Bitcoin — but doing them would mean giving up what makes Bitcoin the ultimate settler. It would mean speeding up the blocks, complicating the language, broadening the functionality, and in doing so destroying the fundamental property: irreversibility guaranteed by decentralization.

This distinction — fast execution above, slow and final settlement below — is exactly the structure we will find, in all the coming chapters, at the base of Bitcoin Hyper's architecture. **Hyper will be the fast execution layer. Bitcoin will remain the final settlement layer.** The two layers talk to each other through a precise mechanism, which we will examine in detail from Chapter 4 onward, called "anchoring." For now it is enough to keep the idea in mind: Bitcoin does one thing only, and does it with finality. Everything else must be built on top, not inside.

There is an analogy I find particularly useful for explaining this distinction to newcomers, and that I will use often in these pages: **Bitcoin is the land registry; Hyper will be the real-estate agency.** The land registry records definitively who owns what; it does so slowly, with bureaucracy, with stamps, through a process that requires precise formal steps. The real-estate agency is fast and flexible: it shows houses to buyers, handles negotiations, collects offers, arranges appointments. The two functions are different and complementary: no one would ask the land registry to be as fast and flexible as an agency, and no one would trust an agency that presumed to replace the registry in recording ownership. **Both are needed, and they are needed separate.**

---

[a] **Execution layer.** The level where transactions and programs are actually processed and produce their effects: transfers, trades, applications. It is the "doing" — fast and flexible. It is distinct from the settlement layer, which instead records the final outcome slowly and definitively. Bitcoin is designed for the second role, not the first: the choice to entrust execution to an upper level, leaving settlement to Bitcoin, is precisely the architectural principle on which a Layer 2 such as Hyper rests.

FIGURE 1.4 **BITCOIN AS THE SETTLEMENT LAYER, HYPER AS THE EXECUTION LAYER.**

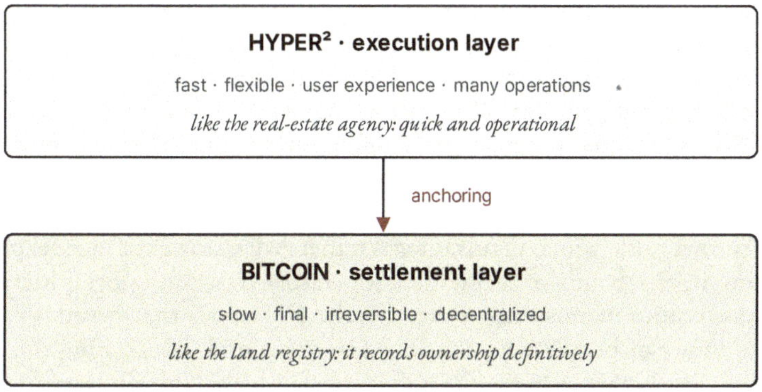

Hyper executes above what Bitcoin settles below: built on top, not inside.

⁂

1.4 — The Technical Limit: Seven Transactions per Second, and Why It Is So

At this point, let us confront Bitcoin's limit numerically, because it is important to be aware of **how** slow it is and of **exactly why** it is that slow. The figures circulating online are often imprecise or exaggerated in both directions — some speak of three transactions per second, some of ten, some of twenty — and understanding where those numbers come from helps you avoid being confused by them.

Bitcoin's theoretical limit is calculated as follows. Every ten minutes a block is added to the chain. Each block has a maximum size of about four megabytes (following the introduction of SegWit in 2017, which effectively quadrupled capacity relative to the original one-megabyte limit, although in a non-linear way for technical reasons beyond the scope of this chapter). Four megabytes hold, on average, between two and three thousand transactions, depending on their complexity. Divided by the six hundred seconds of a block, we get roughly **three to seven transactions per second** under normal conditions, with peaks up to around ten in particularly favorable scenarios. **Seven is the figure conventionally used as the reference.**

Seven transactions per second. For a sense of scale : the Visa network, under normal conditions, processes about 1,700 transactions per second globally, with documented peaks that can exceed 24,000. This means that Visa, in an average second, does more than Bitcoin does in four minutes. Solana, in its most optimistic claims, speaks of over 50,000 transactions per second, although the figures actually sustained are typically lower. Ethereum, before its most recent optimizations, ran at 15–30 per second; with rollups built on top, it can reach far higher numbers.

TABLE 1.1 **THROUGHPUT COMPARED**

Network	Claimed TPS	Sustained TPS	Notes
Bitcoin (L1)	7	3–7	Structural limit: 4 MB blocks every 10 minutes.
Ethereum (L1)	≈ 30	15–25	With L2 rollups it exceeds 2,000 effective TPS.
Solana	65,000	2,000–5,000	Claimed peak vs. actual average operation.
Visa	24,000	1,700	Centralized system; peak vs. global average.

Sources: *Bitcoin Core specifications; Visa public reports; independent Solana Foundation benchmarks (2024); Ethereum.org metrics. "Sustained" figures reflect average operation under realistic load, not simulated peaks.*

The point to understand is that this limit of seven per second **is not a problem of obsolete technology**. Bitcoin could, technically, increase block size and process many more transactions per second. It was debated for years, it was the heart of one of the greatest controversies in Bitcoin's history — the so-called "block size war" of 2015–2017 — and it led to the Bitcoin Cash fork, which did indeed enlarge the blocks. **But the Bitcoin community deliberately refused to go down that road**, and it refused for reasons that are the heart of the philosophy described above.

Increasing block size would have several side effects. **First**: larger blocks require more bandwidth to propagate through the network, which disadvantages miners with slower or more expensive connections, concentrating mining in the hands of a few large operators in a few geographic areas of the world. **Second**: larger blocks require more storage space for the full nodes that maintain the chain's history, which reduces the number of people who can afford to run a node, weakening the decentralization of verification[3]. **Third**: larger blocks increase the risk of "stale blocks," blocks that are produced but then discarded because another miner produced an alternative one in the meantime, generating inefficiencies and potential chain splits. All these effects, taken together, would run against the radical decentralization that is the point of the whole project.

The conclusion the community reached, after years of debate, is clear: **Bitcoin's scalability is not solved by enlarging Bitcoin. It is solved by building layers on top.** This — let us repeat it — is exactly the architectural principle from which Bitcoin Hyper is born, and from which Lightning Network and other earlier attempts were born before it.

But Bitcoin's limit is not only in the transactions-per-second numbers. There is a far more radical limitation to be understood: **Bitcoin cannot execute complex smart contracts.** And here we enter perhaps the most delicate part of this chapter, the one where it becomes truly clear why the idea of Bitcoin Hyper makes sense.

⁂

1.5 — Script, or Why Bitcoin Cannot Do What Ethereum Does

When Vitalik Buterin published the Ethereum whitepaper in 2013, he did so with a precise observation that is worth rereading carefully today. He had spent time in the Bitcoin community and had proposed, without success, extending Bitcoin's language to make it more powerful. The Bitcoin community's answer had been, in essence: "**no.**" So Buterin, frustrated, decided to build a new blockchain from scratch that would have what Bitcoin did not want to have — a Turing-complete language, capable of executing arbitrarily complex programs, which he called **smart contracts.**

What does "Turing-complete" concretely mean? It means the language can express any algorithm we can conceive. It is the same level of expressive power as a traditional programming language like Python or Java. It means loops (repeating an operation N times), recursion (a function that calls itself), arbitrarily nested control structures, complex data manipulation. It means, in short, **being able to write real applications,** not just sequences of elementary operations.

Bitcoin, deliberately, **is not Turing-complete**. Its Script language is what is called a very limited "stack-based" language, supporting few operations, no loops, no recursion, no arbitrary control structures. What can Script do? Simple, well-defined things. **Verify a digital signature**, that is, check that whoever is trying to spend bitcoin actually holds the private key corresponding to the address the funds come from. **Check time conditions**, that is, lock bitcoin until a certain date or a certain number of blocks. **Handle basic multisig**, that is, require that N signatures out of M possible ones be present to authorize a transaction. **Verify hashes**, that is, compare the result of a hash function against an expected value, useful for certain kinds of conditional payments.

FIGURE 1.5 **BITCOIN SCRIPT AND ETHEREUM: TWO PHILOSOPHIES OF PROGRAMMABILITY, AND WHY A HIGHER LAYER IS NEEDED.**

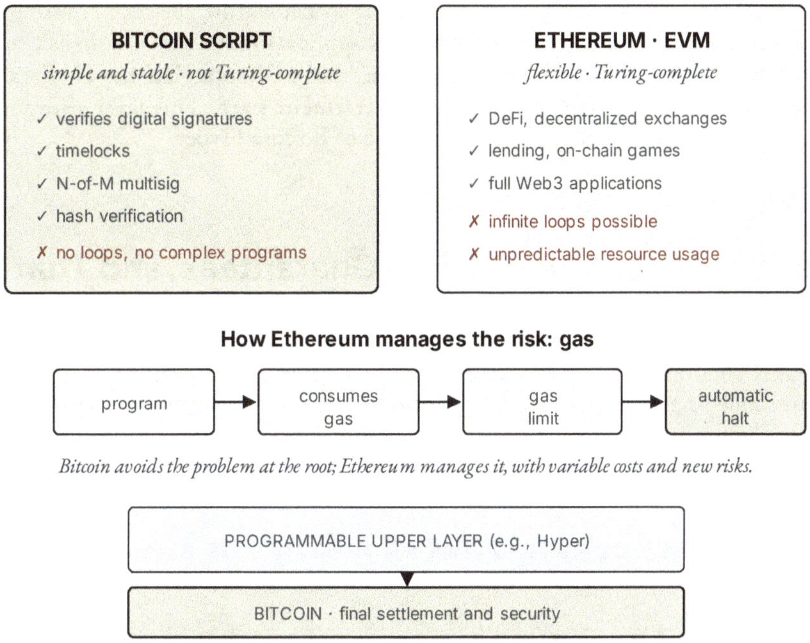

Bitcoin does not give up complex programmability out of technical backwardness, but to protect stability, predictability, and security: Script executes only simple, predictable operations, with no loops and no recursion. Ethereum takes the opposite road, embracing Turing-completeness and managing its risks through gas, which however introduces variable costs and new vulnerabilities. To build advanced applications while keeping Bitcoin as the security base, a programmable upper layer is therefore needed, anchored to Bitcoin for final settlement.

And little else. With these primitives one can still build some interesting things — timelocks for deferred payments, elementary escrow contracts, certain kinds of payment channels that we will see in the next chapter — but **one cannot build applications in the modern sense of the word**. One cannot build a decentralized exchange running thousands of orders per second. One cannot build a lending protocol computing compound interest on a thousand positions at once. One cannot build a game with shared state among multiple players. One cannot build a social network. One cannot build, in short, **anything of what we today call "DeFi" or "Web3."**

Here too, it is crucial to understand that **this limitation is not technical backwardness**. Satoshi could have made Script Turing-complete. He did not, and he did not do so deliberately, for a precise reason worth explaining. A Turing-complete language, by definition, can contain programs that run forever. Think of a `while True: pass` loop that never ends. On an ordinary computer this is not a big problem: you interrupt it, close it, restart. **On a blockchain, where every node must execute every program in order to verify it, an infinite loop is a catastrophe.** It would freeze the network. It would exhaust the resources of every node. It would make the blockchain unusable.

Ethereum solved this problem by introducing the concept of **gas**: every operation costs a small amount of gas, and every transaction has a maximum amount of gas it can consume; when the gas runs out, the program halts automatically, regardless of whether it has completed its work or not. It is an elegant solution, but it carries a series of complications: it makes transaction costs unpredictable (because they depend on the program's complexity), it introduces subtle vulnerabilities ("out-of-gas" attacks), and it makes the system more complex and therefore more prone to bugs.

Bitcoin refused to go down this road. **It chose not to have the problem, instead of managing it.** No Turing-completeness means no infinite loops, no arbitrarily complex programs, no unforeseen bugs, no resource-exhaustion attacks. Bitcoin scripts always terminate, in predictable time, with a defined result. **The limitation of the language is the guarantee of the system's stability.** Once again, it is the principle of conservative minimalism applied all the way down: better to give up potentially useful functionality if that functionality introduces risks that can compromise the system's fundamental property.

From this architectural choice follows a consequence worth stating clearly, because it is the starting point of this entire book: **if we want to build complex applications using Bitcoin as the security base, we cannot do it inside Bitcoin. We must build a layer above Bitcoin that has the flexibility Bitcoin lacks, and that leans on Bitcoin only for the final settlement part.** This layer above is what we will watch take shape, chapter after chapter, under the name of Bitcoin Hyper.

⁂

1.6 — The Three Properties Bitcoin Guarantees, and That Must Be Preserved

Before closing this chapter, and before moving on in Chapter 2 to the question "how do you extend Bitcoin without modifying it?", I want to bring into precise focus **exactly which properties of Bitcoin any extension project must preserve**. This list — which we will call "the three constitutive properties" — will be the yardstick we use in the following chapters to judge every architectural choice made by Bitcoin Hyper.

FIGURE 1.6 **THE THREE CONSTITUTIVE PROPERTIES OF BITCOIN**

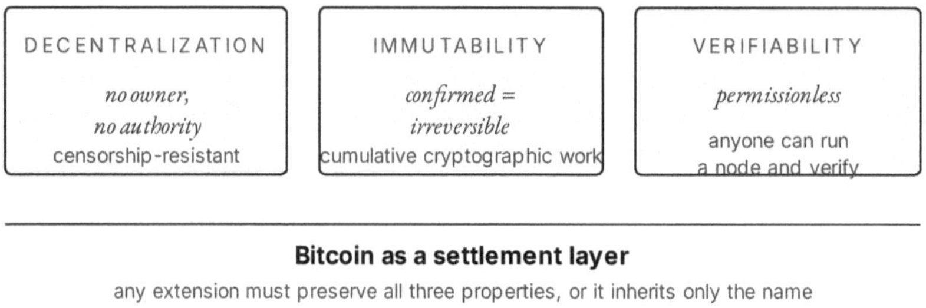

The three pillars are the yardstick for every project "anchored to Bitcoin." If one of them falls, the project does not inherit Bitcoin's security: it merely borrows its name. In the chapters that follow, every architectural choice made by Bitcoin Hyper will be judged by how well it preserves these three.

First property: decentralization. Bitcoin has no owner, no administrator, no controlling authority. No one can decide who may participate and who may not. No one can decide which transactions to accept and which to reject. No one can change the rules without the consent of the overwhelming majority of participants. This property is what makes Bitcoin censorship-resistant: no government, no company, no authority can "switch off" Bitcoin or prevent someone from using it. Any project that leans on Bitcoin for security must preserve, at least tendentially, this property. If the project is run by a company that can decide whose transactions to accept, **it is not inheriting Bitcoin's decentralization: it is merely borrowing its name.**

Second property: immutability. A confirmed Bitcoin transaction cannot be undone. Not by political choice, not by court order, not by community consensus — it is **physically** impossible, because undoing it would require redoing all the cryptographic work accumulated after it, and that work grows every ten minutes, making the cost of reversal exponentially prohibitive. Immutability is the foundation of Bitcoin's function as a settlement layer. Any project that claims to "inherit Bitcoin's security" must be able to demonstrate that the transactions processed within it, once finalized, enjoy the same immutability. If the project's transactions can be altered by an internal decision, a software upgrade, or a governance vote, **they are not inheriting Bitcoin's immutability: they are merely declaring that they do**.

Third property: permissionless verifiability. Anyone, at any time, with a computer powerful enough to run a Bitcoin node, can independently verify the entirety of the blockchain's history, from the very first transaction onward. They need no one's permission, they need to trust no one, they need not pay to access the data. Everything is public, everything is verifiable, everything is reproducible. This property is what makes Bitcoin transparent: trust rests not on someone's word, but on the technical possibility of verifying everything autonomously. Any project that declares itself "anchored to Bitcoin" must in turn be independently verifiable, ideally using only Bitcoin's public data and open-source software. If verification requires trusting a service provided by the project's team, **it is not inheriting Bitcoin's verifiability: it is merely associating its own brand with Bitcoin's brand**.

These three properties — decentralization, immutability, permissionless verifiability — are the **gold standard** against which we will judge Bitcoin Hyper in every subsequent chapter. When the team declares "we inherit Bitcoin's security," our question will always be the same, applied to each of the three properties: **"do you actually do it, or do you merely say it?"** The answer, I anticipate, will often be "you do it partially, you do it with compromises, you do it with a long-term path that has yet to be implemented." And that is fine, as long as one is honest about those compromises. It is not fine when one claims to have all three while in reality holding one out of three.

⁂

1.7 — Questions and Answers: Clarifying the Chapter's Concepts

At this point in the chapter, with the main concepts established, it is worth fixing them through a sequence of questions and answers. These are the questions I hear most often from those who have followed my seminars and consulting work on the subject. Each comes with a concrete example.

Question 1: If Bitcoin is so slow, how do people use it for everyday payments?

In the vast majority of cases, **they don't**. Bitcoin is used as a store of value, not as a means of payment for coffee. When it is used as a means of payment, it is almost always through custodial services (exchanges, centralized wallets) that handle transactions internally at speed, and lean on the blockchain only for final settlement. For example: if you transfer bitcoin from one account to another within the same exchange — say, between two accounts on Coinbase — the transaction is instantaneous, **but it is not a Bitcoin transaction**: it is a write on Coinbase's internal database. When instead you move the bitcoin out of the exchange to a personal wallet, then you have a real Bitcoin transaction, with its confirmation times. **Concrete example:** in El Salvador, where Bitcoin has been legal tender since 2021, most everyday payments go through Lightning Network, not through Bitcoin directly. Lightning is a layer on top of Bitcoin that we will see in Chapter 2.

Question 2: If Bitcoin cannot do smart contracts, how do we explain projects like Ordinals, BRC-20, and Runes running on Bitcoin?

These projects represent **the outer limit of what can be done with Script**, creatively exploiting its capabilities to "inscribe" arbitrary data into Bitcoin transactions. They are ingenious devices, but they are not smart contracts in the Ethereum sense of the term. They execute no complex logic: they merely record data that is then interpreted by external software. **Concrete example:** a BRC-20 token is not a token in the sense of an Ethereum ERC-20. It is a textual inscription inside a Bitcoin transaction saying "here is a token named X in quantity Y," and it is then up to software outside Bitcoin to keep track of who owns what. Bitcoin itself does not know BRC-20s exist: **it sees only arbitrary data inscribed in its transactions.** It is a form of writing on Bitcoin's walls, not an execution of programs inside Bitcoin.

Question 3: Why doesn't Bitcoin simply add the ability to run smart contracts, perhaps as an optional feature?

Because every addition to the base protocol is one more attack surface, one more possible source of bugs, one more complication of the security analysis. Bitcoin's philosophy is that the base protocol must be **maximally simple** precisely in order to be maximally secure. Anything "optional" must still be implemented in every node and validated by everyone, and so it is not truly optional at the protocol level. **Concrete example:** when Taproot was activated in 2021 — an upgrade adding certain more advanced cryptographic capabilities — the debate lasted years, and the upgrade was designed with extreme caution, maintaining full backward compatibility and introducing the new capabilities only as tools for those who wish to use them, without altering the fundamental rules. Even an upgrade considered "minor" like Taproot required an extremely long process of community validation. Adding full smart-contract functionality would be, by comparison, a revolution — and the community would not accept it.

Question 4: Is Bitcoin's conservative philosophy really pure virtue? Doesn't it risk making Bitcoin obsolete compared with more modern blockchains?

It is a legitimate question, and the answer requires nuance. On one hand, yes: conservatism limits what Bitcoin can do directly, and other blockchains can do things Bitcoin cannot. On the other hand, however, **Bitcoin's specialization as a settlement layer is exactly what makes it precious.** One does not ask the notary to be as fast as a courier: one asks him to be precise and definitive. If Bitcoin stopped being conservative to chase the functionality of Ethereum or Solana, it would lose what distinguishes it, and it still could not compete on equal terms with systems designed from the outset for those uses. **Concrete example:** it would be as if the European Central Bank decided to launch its own instant-payments app to compete with PayPal. Even if it succeeded, it would lose its authority as the ultimate guarantor of monetary stability, without managing to beat PayPal on its own ground. Better to do one thing, and do it in a way no one else can do better.

Question 5: What would happen if tomorrow the majority of miners decided to change Bitcoin's rules, say to speed up the blocks?

Technically, miners can modify the software they run, but if they modify the rules in a way that is incompatible with the rest of the network, they produce a **chain split** (a fork): their version becomes a separate blockchain, while the original blockchain continues to exist as long as someone runs the original software. **Concrete example:** this is exactly what happened in 2017 with Bitcoin Cash. A group of miners and developers wanted to increase block size. The majority of the network disagreed. The result was a split: those who wanted bigger blocks created Bitcoin Cash (BCH), which still exists today but is a separate blockchain, with a market value enormously lower than Bitcoin's. **The lesson is that Bitcoin is not changed by a majority of miners, but by the overwhelming consensus of the entire community — users, developers, exchanges, companies, miners.** Without that consensus, the attempted change produces only a fork that the majority community ignores.

Question 6: So any attempt to "make Bitcoin do more" is bound to go through external solutions, like Lightning Network or Bitcoin Hyper?

Yes. **This is the central point of the entire book.** The question is not "how do we modify Bitcoin?" but "how do we build on top of Bitcoin?". Scaling or programmability solutions for Bitcoin can only be external layers that lean on Bitcoin for the security and settlement part, but do everything else elsewhere. **Concrete example:** Lightning Network, the most mature scaling solution for Bitcoin, works exactly like this: you open a "payment channel" with someone through a Bitcoin transaction; within it you can exchange bitcoin back and forth instantly and for free; at the end you close the channel with another Bitcoin transaction that records the final balance. Between the opening and the closing, everything happens off the Bitcoin blockchain. Bitcoin Hyper will do something conceptually similar, but with a different architecture and far broader capabilities. We will discuss it in Chapter 2 and in all the chapters that follow.

⁂

1.8 — WHAT TO TAKE AWAY FROM THIS CHAPTER

Before moving on to Chapter 2, where we will see how Bitcoin's limitation generated, over the years, a series of extension attempts culminating logically in the idea of Bitcoin Hyper, it is useful to fix the key concepts just covered in schematic form.

Bitcoin is a deliberately slow and limited network. Its slowness and its limits are not technical defects but philosophical choices, serving to guarantee maximum decentralization, maximum security, and independence from any central authority.

Bitcoin is a settlement layer, not an execution layer. Its function is to record definitively and irreversibly who owns what. It is not designed to run fast applications or complex programs.

Bitcoin processes about seven transactions per second, and this limit is structural. It cannot be raised significantly without compromising decentralization, and the community explicitly refused that road in the block size battle of 2017.

Bitcoin cannot execute complex smart contracts. Its internal language, Script, is not Turing-complete and supports only simple, predictable operations. This limitation is intentional and serves to guarantee the system's stability.

Bitcoin guarantees three fundamental properties — decentralization, immutability, permissionless verifiability — that any extension project must preserve, on pain of losing its authentic link to Bitcoin's security.

Any project that wants to "extend" Bitcoin to make it faster or more programmable must do so by building layers on top of Bitcoin, not by modifying Bitcoin itself. This is the architectural lesson that leads directly to the concept of the Layer 2, and to the historical evolution we will see in Chapter 2: from Lightning Network, Bitcoin's first Layer 2, to the rollup model on which Bitcoin Hyper is based.

Chapter 1 ends here. We have established Bitcoin's philosophical and technical foundations, and we have understood why any attempt to "make it do more" can only go through external solutions. In ***Chapter 2 — The Question That Generated Hyper: Can Bitcoin Be Extended Without Being Modified?****, we will see how this question was first posed explicitly by Joseph Poon and Thaddeus Dryja in the 2015 Lightning Network whitepaper, how it then traveled through various attempts in the years that followed, and how it has now come to generate the rollup model on which Bitcoin Hyper is based.*

NOTES

1 Leslie Lamport, Robert Shostak, Marshall Pease, *The Byzantine Generals Problem*, in "ACM Transactions on Programming Languages and Systems," vol. 4, no. 3, July 1982, pp. 382–401.

2 On the so-called "block size war," see Jonathan Bier, *The Blocksize War: The battle over who controls Bitcoin's protocol rules*, independently published, 2021. The book reconstructs the technical and political debate that led to the fork.

3 As of today, running a full Bitcoin node requires about 550 GB of storage and a stable asynchronous connection. An 8 MB block (as in Bitcoin Cash) doubles or triples these requirements.

Bitcoin: slow by choice, strong by *design*

Because Bitcoin is a **settlement** layer, not an execution layer. Its strength arises from its limits — and to extend it one builds **on top of** Bitcoin, not inside.

1 The most secure network is also the most limited

Strength

- Security
- Censorship resistance
- Public verifiability
- Decentralization
- Immutability

Limit · BY CHOICE

- About 3–7 TPS
- Non-Turing-complete Script
- Very slow changes
- Blocks every ~10 min
- Little flexibility

Bitcoin's slowness is not a bug. **It is the price of its independence.**

2 From the Byzantine generals to Proof of Work

Unknown nodes — honest, faulty, or malicious → **Proof of Work** — proposing a block costs real work → **Public verification** — everyone checks cryptographically

Bitcoin does not ask «who is authorized to decide?» — it asks **«who has borne a real cost to propose this block?»**

Trust among unknown people is replaced by **verifiable computational work.**

3 Three apparent limits, three structural guarantees

Slowness
Blocks every ~10 minutes.
It reduces forks and favors global participation.

Simplicity
Limited, predictable Script.
It reduces bugs, infinite loops, and attack surface.

Conservatism
Rare, difficult upgrades.
It protects from rushed or centralized changes.

Bitcoin does not chase maximum speed. **It protects maximum predictability.**

4 Bitcoin settles, Hyper executes

Hyper² — EXECUTION LAYER: fast transactions · applications · DeFi · smart contracts · user experience

↓ ANCHORING ↓

B Bitcoin — SETTLEMENT LAYER: final settlement · immutability · security · independent verification · definitive ownership

Bitcoin is the **land registry** — it records definitively who owns what.

Hyper is the **real-estate agency** — it makes operations fast and fluid.

5 The yardstick for judging every Bitcoin Layer 2

Decentralization
no owner, no central administrator, no permission to participate.

Immutability
a settled transaction cannot be annulled or arbitrarily rewritten.

Permissionless verification
anyone must be able to check the system without trusting the team.

(!) If an extension loses these three properties, **it does not inherit Bitcoin's security: it takes only its name.**

THE KEY POINT

Bitcoin is strong precisely because it is limited: it was not born to execute everything, but to **settle value definitively**. To make it faster and programmable without betraying its philosophy one must build **on top of** Bitcoin, not **inside** Bitcoin. It is from this necessity that the idea of **Bitcoin Hyper** is born.

PART I · THE PROBLEM TO BE SOLVED

Chapter 2
The Question That Generated Hyper

Can Bitcoin be extended without being modified?

⁂

2.1 — Where We Start Again

In Chapter 1 we established a point worth repeating at the start of this one, because everything that follows depends on it: **Bitcoin is a deliberately limited network**, and those limitations are the price of its absolute security. We saw that the protocol is not to be touched, that the community consensus required to modify it is effectively unreachable for radical changes, and that the story of the 2017 "block size war" demonstrated concretely what happens to those who try to force the issue: a split, a fork, and the birth of a separate network that the majority community regards, simply, as something else.

From here comes the question that gives this chapter its title, and that is the founding question of the entire history of Bitcoin Layer 2s: **if Bitcoin cannot be modified, but we still want it to do more, where do we build the additional functionality?** It is a question that sounds obvious today, after ten years of attempts and iterations, but when it was first posed in explicit terms — in 2015, in the Lightning Network whitepaper[1] — it was not obvious at all. It was an almost heretical question. Most observers of the crypto world, in those years, took it for granted that scalability would come either by modifying Bitcoin (as the "big blockers" faction wanted) or by building better alternative blockchains (as Ethereum, and then everyone else, was doing). The idea of **leaving Bitcoin as it is and building something else on top** was a third way that did not yet have a clear name, did not yet have an established theory, and had not yet proven that it worked.

This chapter tells the story of how, in ten years, we went from the initial suspicion that "something on top of Bitcoin might be possible" to the architectural certainty that gives life to Bitcoin Hyper today. It is a chapter in the history of ideas, more than in pure technology. But it is an indispensable story, because each of the attempts we will see — Lightning, the federated sidechains, Stacks, Rootstock, Liquid, and finally the rollups — added a brick to the theory, and each left a legacy that we find again in Hyper's architectural choices. Understanding this history means understanding **why Hyper is structured exactly the way it is structured**, and not in any of the thousand other possible ways.

The chapter's guiding thread is a precise causal thread: every solution is born from the limits of the previous one, and every limit of the current solution opens the door to the next. Let us begin at the beginning.

⁂

2.2 — The First Principle: Separating What Must Be Recorded from What Must Be Executed

To understand how one "extends Bitcoin without modifying it," one must first grasp an insight that seems obvious but took years to be formalized: **not all interactions between people need to be recorded on the blockchain**. Some do, some do not. The question then becomes: which ones do, and which do not?

Think about it with an everyday example. If you and a friend exchange money back and forth over the course of an evening — one pays for the pizza, the other pays for the wine, the first pays for the taxi, and at the end you settle up — you do not need to record every single step on your bank statement. It is enough, at the end, to compute the difference and have one pay the other the balance. **If every one of those individual movements had to go through a formal bank transfer, with its delays and fees, it would be absurd.** The bank transfer — the equivalent, in our context, of a Bitcoin transaction — is an instrument of **settlement**, and it should be reserved for situations where a movement of money genuinely needs to be recorded with finality. For everything else, private agreements, promises, notes on a scrap of paper — anything that is enough for the two of you — will do.

The fundamental insight behind all Bitcoin Layer 2s is exactly this, applied to the digital world: **if two or more people interact frequently, they can keep track of their interactions privately, off the blockchain, and use the blockchain only to record the initial opening and the final closing of their relationship.** In between, they can carry out as many interactions as they wish — a thousand per second if needed — without paying any fee and without waiting for any confirmation, because those interactions are their own business, not the business of the public network.

From this insight follows an architectural principle that I will call, for convenience, the **separation principle: what must be recorded (settled) and what must be executed are different things, handled by different layers.** Bitcoin handles settlement. Something else handles execution. The two layers talk to each other at precise, well-defined points — when an interaction begins, and when it ends — but are otherwise independent. This principle is the seed from which Lightning Network, the sidechains, the rollups, and today Bitcoin Hyper have grown. **Every Bitcoin Layer 2 is, at bottom, a different application of the same separation principle.**

But the principle, on its own, is not enough. One must solve a concrete problem that the principle carries with it: **if interactions happen off the blockchain, how do I trust that whoever manages those interactions is honest?** This is the problem that generated ten years of research, and that led to progressively more sophisticated solutions. Let us look at them in the order in which they appeared, because each solves one piece of the problem while leaving the next piece open.

⁂

2.3 — Lightning Network: The First Layer 2 in Bitcoin's History

In January 2016, Joseph Poon and Thaddeus Dryja published a document that many today consider the true starting point of all Layer 2 theory: **"The Bitcoin Lightning Network: Scalable Off-Chain Instant Payments."** It is a dense, technical text that proposes a surprisingly elegant solution to a problem that until then had seemed unsolvable: how do you make millions of Bitcoin payments per second without modifying Bitcoin?

The idea of Lightning Network starts from a simple primitive that Bitcoin, fortunately, supports: the ability to create transactions that are signed by both parties involved and that can take effect only under certain conditions. On this primitive, the concept of the **payment channel** is built. It works like this.

Imagine that Alice and Bob want to exchange payments frequently. Together they do one thing: each puts a certain amount of bitcoin into a special transaction that requires both signatures to be spent. This transaction is recorded on the Bitcoin blockchain, and it is the only "public" record of their relationship: it says "Alice and Bob have jointly locked this much bitcoin in a dual-signature account"[*]. From that moment on, **there is an open channel between Alice and Bob**. They can exchange payments by privately modifying the distribution of the bitcoin within the channel: Alice sends 0.1 to Bob (the channel state is now "Alice has X-0.1, Bob has Y+0.1"), then Bob sends 0.05 to Alice (the state becomes "Alice has X-0.05, Bob has Y+0.05"), and so on. Every exchange is instantaneous. Every exchange is free. Every exchange is private. **Bitcoin knows nothing about it.** What Alice and Bob exchange are signatures on new versions of the initial transaction, each of which invalidates the previous one.

When Alice and Bob decide to close the channel — because they have finished interacting, or because they want their bitcoin back — they publish on the Bitcoin blockchain the **latest** version of the transaction, the one reflecting the final balance. Bitcoin then settles the situation and each gets their share. The Bitcoin blockchain has recorded two transactions in total: the opening and the closing. **In between, Alice and Bob may have made a million payments to each other, and Bitcoin paid no cost to handle them.**

Even at this stage, Lightning Network would be useful but very limited: it only helps if I interact frequently with the same person. The stroke of genius in Poon and Dryja's whitepaper[†] is the next step: **channels can be chained.** If Alice has an open channel with Bob, and Bob has an open channel with Carol, then Alice can pay Carol by going through Bob, even though Alice and Carol have never opened a direct channel. Bob acts as a "bridge," routing the payment, and cryptography guarantees that he cannot steal the funds in the process. At global scale, this means that anyone who has at least one open channel with someone who is in turn connected can reach anyone else in the network. **A network of channels forms — a "Lightning Network," precisely — where payments travel like packets on the Internet, hopping from node to node until they reach their destination.**[‡]

* Dual-signature account (2-of-2 *multisig*): a Bitcoin address whose funds can be spent only with the signature of both parties. It is the primitive that makes the payment channel possible: neither of the two can move the bitcoin alone, and every balance update requires the agreement of both.

† Joseph Poon and Thaddeus Dryja, *The Bitcoin Lightning Network: Scalable Off-Chain Instant Payments*, 2016. It is the document that formally introduces bidirectional payment channels and their chaining; it is not a protocol approved by a central authority, but a technical proposal later implemented by multiple independent software projects.

‡ Multi-hop routing relies on *Hashed Timelock Contracts* (HTLCs): each intermediate node can collect the payment only by revealing a cryptographic secret, and each hop is protected by a time deadline which, if not met, returns the funds to the sender. It is this mechanism — not trust in Bob — that guarantees the funds cannot be siphoned off along the route. The practical limit remains *liquidity*: a payment can transit only if every channel along the path has sufficient capacity in the required direction.

FIGURE 2.3 **THE LIFE CYCLE OF A LIGHTNING CHANNEL AND ITS LIMITS.**

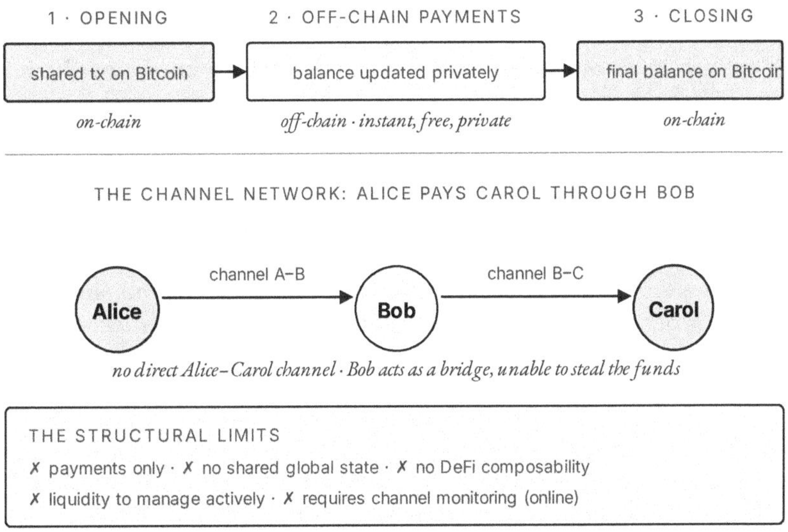

Bitcoin records only two transactions — the opening and the closing of the channel; in between, Alice and Bob can exchange millions of instant, free, private payments by updating the balance off-chain. By chaining channels, a network forms in which Alice pays Carol through Bob, without a direct channel. Lightning solved the problem of fast payments, but not that of complex applications: no smart contracts, no shared global state, no DeFi composability. Hence the search for a new generation of Layer 2s on Bitcoin.

Lightning Network is today an operational reality with years of experience behind it. It works. It is used in production, notably in El Salvador as we mentioned in Chapter 1, and in other countries where Bitcoin is employed as a means of everyday payment. But — and here the cause-and-effect chain that leads us toward Bitcoin Hyper comes into play — **Lightning has structural limits that make it unsuitable for a whole universe of applications that we now consider essential in the crypto world.**

The first limit is that Lightning does **payments only**. It cannot execute complex smart contracts, it cannot host decentralized exchanges, it cannot do automated lending, it cannot handle NFTs natively. Its specialization — fast micropayments between connected people — is also its cage. All the machinery we described above works for exchanges of bitcoin, and for little else.

The second limit is **liquidity management**: to receive payments, you must have open channels with sufficient "inbound capacity," which requires active planning, technical knowledge, and in many cases locked-up capital. For a developer wanting to build a complex application, it is a logistical nightmare.

The third limit is the **need to be online**. Lightning's security model requires participants to monitor their channels, because a channel can be closed fraudulently by a dishonest counterparty who publishes an old version of the state. Solutions exist — "watchtowers," guard towers that do the monitoring for you — but they are a workaround, not a structural solution.

The fourth limit, perhaps the most philosophically significant, is that Lightning **has no shared global state**. Every channel is a story unto itself. There is no publicly verifiable "Lightning ledger" where an application can read the state of all users. This means one cannot build applications that require

composability — the property by which one protocol can read and use another protocol's data, and from which all of modern DeFi springs.

Lightning, in other words, solved **one** problem (fast payments), but left all the others untouched. The question its existence generated is therefore: **can what Lightning did for payments be done for complex smart contracts?** It is an enormous question, because complex smart contracts require a global state, a full virtual machine, a system of addresses and contracts, and a whole set of infrastructure that Lightning does not offer. The answer to this question is what generated the second generation of Layer 2s on Bitcoin, and then the third, and finally, today, Bitcoin Hyper.

⁂

2.4 — Federated Sidechains: The Shortcut You Pay Dearly For

The first serious answer to the question "how do I run complex smart contracts on Bitcoin?" came in the form of an apparently simple idea: **I build a separate blockchain, with all the functionality I want, and I connect it to Bitcoin through a mechanism that allows bitcoin to move back and forth.** This idea took the name **sidechain**, and it had its first concrete implementation with a project called **Liquid**, launched by Blockstream in 2018.

Liquid is a Bitcoin sidechain run by a consortium of some fifteen companies — exchanges, market makers, crypto financial service providers — which together constitute the **federation** that governs the network. When you want to use Liquid, you send your bitcoin to an address controlled by the federation, and in exchange you receive an equivalent amount of **L-BTC**, the version of bitcoin that runs on Liquid. You can use these L-BTC on the sidechain to do things Bitcoin does not allow: faster transactions (one block per minute instead of every ten), confidential transactions (amounts are not public), issuance of native tokens representing other assets. When you are done, you return the L-BTC and the federation unlocks your original bitcoin.*

* This bitcoin ↔ L-BTC exchange is called a *peg* and is bidirectional: *peg-in* when depositing bitcoin to receive L-BTC, *peg-out* in the opposite direction. The ratio is always 1:1, but the correspondence is not guaranteed by the Bitcoin protocol: it depends on the federation actually holding the deposited bitcoin in custody and returning it on request. This is where the trust model discussed in the rest of the section is concentrated: whoever holds L-BTC does not own bitcoin, but a claim on an identified consortium.

FIGURE 2.4 **THE FEDERATED SIDECHAIN: HOW IT WORKS AND ITS COST IN TRUST.**

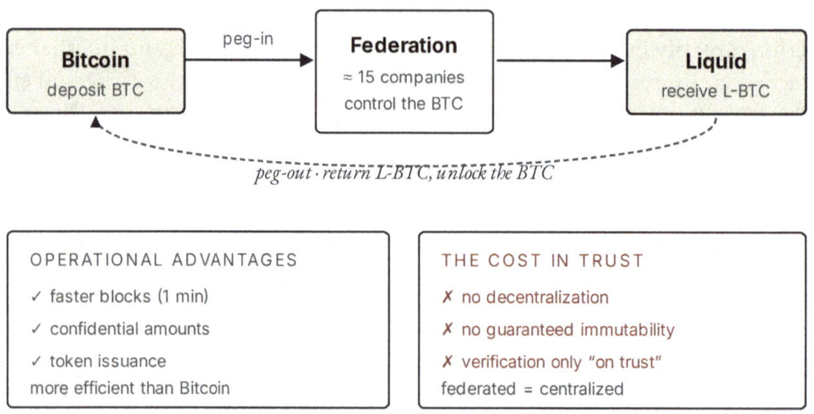

With the peg-in, the user deposits BTC with the federation and receives L-BTC on Liquid; with the peg-out, they return the L-BTC and unlock the original bitcoin. In exchange they get faster blocks, confidential amounts, and token issuance — but the deposited bitcoin is materially controlled by a consortium of identified companies. The federated sidechain is an effective shortcut, but the price to pay is a security model weaker than Bitcoin's: it inherits neither decentralization, nor immutability, nor permissionless verifiability.

The model works, and Liquid has been in production for years. But there is an enormous problem, and it is exactly the one the separation principle had warned us not to underestimate: **who runs the sidechain?** In Liquid, the answer is "a federation of fifteen companies." Those companies have material control of the deposited bitcoin. If five or six of them decided to collude, they could in theory — the system is designed to make it difficult, but not impossible — appropriate users' funds. Even without hypothesizing collusion, the federation **can censor**: it can refuse to process transactions it dislikes, it can exclude addresses, it can decide whom to accept and whom not.

Put more philosophically: **Liquid borrows Bitcoin's name but does not inherit the three constitutive properties we listed in Chapter 1.** It does not inherit decentralization, because the federation is a small, identified group. It does not inherit immutability, because the federation could in theory rewrite history if it decided to do so collectively. It does not inherit permissionless verifiability, because to verify the sidechain's state one must trust the federation's software. Liquid is a **federated sidechain**, and this word — federated — is an elegant euphemism for **centralized in a group of identified entities**.

The federated sidechain model thus has the merit of being relatively simple to implement and of working in practice, but the enormous flaw of **not being a genuine extension of Bitcoin**: it is a parallel blockchain that uses bitcoin as its internal store of value, but that has its own security model — completely different and much weaker. For applications where trust in a consortium of identified companies is acceptable — for example, fast transfers between centralized exchanges — it can be fine. For applications requiring the same guarantee as Bitcoin, it cannot.

The question that federated sidechains leave open is therefore: **can a sidechain be built that does not require trusting a federation?** It is the question that generated the second wave of attempts.

⁂

2.5 — Stacks and Rootstock: Two Different Ways of Really Trying

In the years after Liquid, two projects tried to answer the question "how do I build a sidechain that is not federated[a]?" in profoundly different ways. The first is **Rootstock** (RSK), launched in 2018, and the second is **Stacks**, which has existed in its current version since 2021. They are worth comparing, because they represent two distinct philosophies, both of which informed, in different ways, Bitcoin Hyper's choices.

[a] **Federated sidechain.** A separate blockchain, connected to Bitcoin, in which the movement of funds and the security depend on a defined group of operators — the "federation." It offers efficiency and simplicity, but asks the user for a form of trust: one must be confident that this group behaves correctly and does not act in a coordinated way against users' interests. It is precisely the limit that projects like Rootstock and Stacks tried to overcome, exploring models in which the trust required is reduced or replaced by verifiable guarantees.

TABLE 2.1 **TWO ROADS TO BITCOIN PROGRAMMABILITY.**

Project	Since	Link to Bitcoin	Inspiration
Rootstock (RSK)	2018	Merge mining[b]	Ethereum ecosystem (EVM)
Stacks	2021	Proof of Transfer (PoX)[c]	Proprietary model (Clarity)

Rootstock and Stacks answer the same question — building programmability around Bitcoin without a federation — with two opposite philosophies: inheriting an existing ecosystem on one side, building an original model on the other. Both choices offer useful lessons for evaluating Bitcoin Hyper.

[b] **Merge mining.** A technique by which Bitcoin miners can simultaneously validate, with no significant additional work, the blocks of a second chain such as Rootstock. Security is therefore not inherited automatically: it depends on how many

miners choose to participate, and it always remains a fraction of the computing power protecting Bitcoin.

[c] **Proof of Transfer (PoX).** Stacks' consensus mechanism in which, instead of expending energy, participants transfer already-existing bitcoin to obtain the right to produce blocks on the new chain. It ties Stacks' activity to Bitcoin's, but introduces its own chain and token, distinct from the Bitcoin protocol.

FIGURE 2.1 **ROOTSTOCK AND STACKS: TWO DIFFERENT PATHS, TWO LESSONS FOR HYPER.**

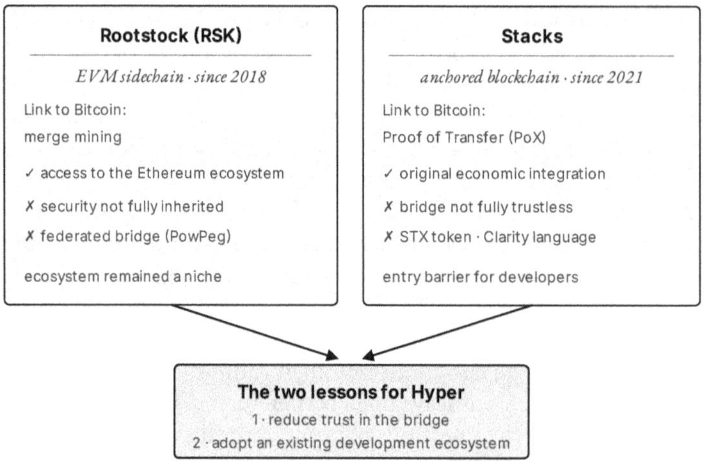

Rootstock chooses EVM compatibility and ties itself to Bitcoin via merge mining, but the security is not fully inherited and the bridge remains federated (PowPeg). Stacks invents Proof of Transfer and a language of its own, Clarity, but the bridge is not fully trustless and the STX token plus the new language raise the entry barrier. Hyper is also born from the lessons of Rootstock and Stacks: reduce trust in the bridge, and adopt an already-existing development ecosystem.

Rootstock tried the most obvious road: building a Bitcoin sidechain that would be compatible with Ethereum's virtual machine (EVM), so as to bring to Bitcoin all the applications and all the developers already working with Ethereum. The idea was seductive: combining Bitcoin's security base with Ethereum's development ecosystem, taking the best of both worlds. For the connection between Bitcoin and Rootstock, a mechanism called **merge mining** was developed: Bitcoin miners can, alongside the work they do for the main blockchain, also mine Rootstock blocks, receiving additional rewards. This, in theory, should anchor Rootstock's security to Bitcoin's computational power.

The problem is that merge mining, in practice, **does not inherit Bitcoin's security**: it inherits it only if a significant percentage of Bitcoin miners participate, and if no group of hostile miners can attack Rootstock specifically without coordination. In practice, the percentage of miners participating in merge mining has always been limited, and Rootstock's security model also depends on a **federation** (called "PowPeg") that manages the bitcoin bridge between the two networks. So even Rootstock, in the end, has a federated component that undermines the claim of "inheriting Bitcoin's security." The ecosystem of applications that developed has remained modest, and Rootstock today is a niche reality compared with its initial ambitions.

Stacks tried a different road, more creative and in some respects bolder. Instead of building a sidechain with independent consensus, Stacks invented a mechanism called **Proof of Transfer** (PoX): to produce blocks on the Stacks blockchain, validators must "transfer" bitcoin to specific addresses on the Bitcoin blockchain. In other words, **to participate in Stacks consensus, one must spend real bitcoin**. This creates a tight economic bond between the two networks: whoever wants to attack Stacks must spend bitcoin to do so, and the bitcoin spent in the process ends up as rewards for other participants in the system.

Stacks also introduced a smart contract language of its own, called **Clarity**[a], and built an infrastructure for decentralized applications anchored to Bitcoin. It underwent a significant evolution with the Nakamoto upgrade, which improved block times and finality. It is a serious project, with an active ecosystem, and with a coherent philosophical basis. But Stacks too has its limits.

The first limit is that, **while anchored to Bitcoin for consensus, Stacks is a separate blockchain with its own state**: its "virtual" bitcoin (sBTC in the most recent versions) still requires a custody mechanism to be linked to real bitcoin, and that mechanism has historically been managed by a federation of "stackers" acting as collective custodians. The latest evolutions have reduced the centralization of this custody, but the structural problem remains: **there is today no perfectly trustless[b] way to move bitcoin back and forth between Bitcoin and Stacks**. All current mechanisms involve some form of multisig or distributed custody, which is still a form of trust in an identified group.

The second limit is that **Stacks uses its own native token (STX) as its internal unit of account**, not bitcoin. Fees are paid in STX, smart contracts operate with STX, and bitcoin enters the picture only as a secondary asset. For those who wanted an extension of bitcoin that was truly bitcoin-centric, this has often been perceived as a significant philosophical compromise.

The third limit — and here we return to why these projects matter in our story — is that **Clarity is not compatible with any of the existing development ecosystems**. Neither with Ethereum's Solidity, nor with Solana's Rust. It means that developers who want to work on Stacks must learn a new language, use new tools, rewrite applications from scratch. It is an enormous entry barrier, and it has slowed adoption.

Stacks and Rootstock, taken together, offer us two precious lessons that Bitcoin Hyper has internalized. **Lesson one**: anchoring consensus to Bitcoin is not enough, if the bridge between the two networks remains a centralized point of trust. **Lesson two**: creating a proprietary smart contract language means giving up an entire ecosystem of already-existing developers, and that is an enormous cost that often goes unrecovered. **From these two lessons flow directly two of Hyper's fundamental choices**: the pursuit of a bridge mechanism as trustless as possible, and the decision to adopt an already-existing language — in this case Solana's — instead of creating a new one.

---

[a] **Clarity.** The programming language in which Stacks smart contracts are written. It was designed to be predictable and harder to misuse, but it is specific to Stacks: those who learn it cannot reuse that code or those tools on other networks.

[b] **Trustless.** Said of a mechanism that works without having to place trust in a specific person or group: correctness is guaranteed by verifiable rules, not by a custodian's honesty. It is the opposite of a system that depends on a federation or an intermediary that must be trusted.

FIGURE 2.2 **A DECADE OF LAYER 2 ATTEMPTS ON BITCOIN, BEFORE THE ROLLUP ERA**

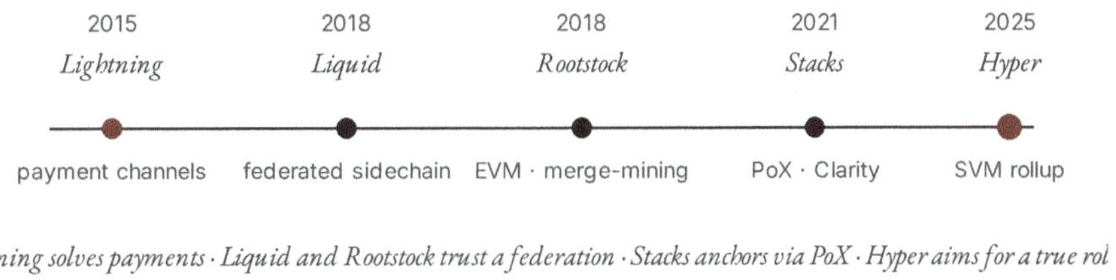

Each stage is born from the limits of the previous one. Lightning extends payments but not programmability; Liquid and Rootstock introduce the smart contract but at the cost of a trusted federation; Stacks anchors consensus to Bitcoin but with a proprietary language. Bitcoin Hyper presents itself as the next link: a rollup that inherits Bitcoin's security without giving up an already-existing developer ecosystem.

⁂

2.6 — The Turning Point: The "Rollup" Idea Arrives from Ethereum

At this point in our story, we are around 2020–2021. Lightning Network is in production but confined to payments. Liquid works but is federated. Stacks and Rootstock have shown the feasibility of more ambitious extensions but with significant compromises on decentralization and on the development ecosystem. The question — how do you build a true extension of Bitcoin that preserves its three constitutive properties? — is still open.

And here an idea comes into play that, in one of history's ironies, **was born not in the Bitcoin world but in the Ethereum world**. It is the idea of the **rollup**, and its maturation between 2019 and 2022 was one of the most important chapters in the recent history of blockchains. To understand why Bitcoin Hyper exists today in the form it exists, we must understand what a rollup is, and why Ethereum adopted it as its central scaling strategy.

Ethereum, like Bitcoin, had its years of "scalability war." There too the question was: how do we scale the network without compromising decentralization? The initial answers were all versions of the "shard" model — dividing the network into many sub-networks working in parallel — but they were complicated, slow to implement, and introduced new security problems. Then, around 2019–2020, a group of researchers — including Vitalik Buterin himself, but also teams such as Optimism, Arbitrum, StarkWare, and Matter Labs — began developing a different idea: **the rollup**.

The rollup insight is devastatingly simple once grasped. It works like this. **Transactions are executed on a secondary blockchain optimized for speed.** But it is not a sidechain with independent consensus: it is a "rollup chain" that, periodically, takes a compressed summary of everything that has happened within it and **publishes it on the main blockchain**. That summary includes two fundamental things: a mathematical "photograph" of the final state (the state root), and enough raw data to allow anyone to independently **reconstruct** what happened.

The stroke of genius is here: **the raw transaction data is published on the main blockchain, but the execution is not.** The main blockchain does not have to execute the transactions — an expensive operation — but only to store their data, a much cheaper operation. It means the main blockchain can "host" hundreds or thousands of rollup transactions in the same space where it previously hosted a single one, because the direct verification of transactions happens elsewhere, and what is stored on-chain is only the data needed to reconstruct what happened if necessary.

From this basic insight follow two main variants, which it is important to distinguish because they are often presented in a confused way in marketing materials.

FIGURE 2.2 **THE ROLLUP INSIGHT: EXECUTION HAPPENS OFF-CHAIN, VERIFIABLE TRUTH STAYS ON-CHAIN.**

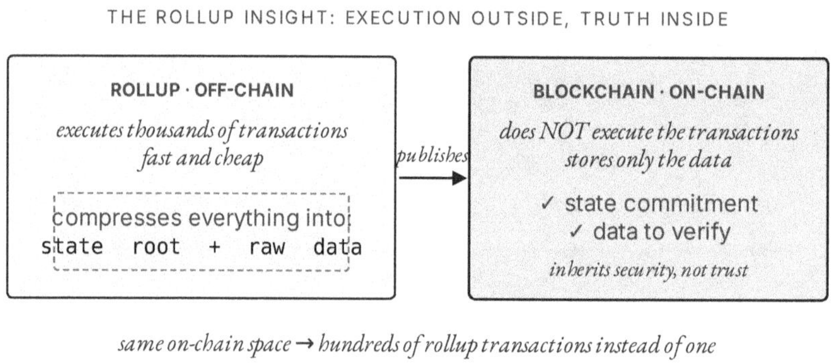

The rollup moves execution off the main blockchain, but keeps on the main blockchain the verifiable truth of the state. Transactions run on a fast, cheap secondary chain; onto the main chain go only the state commitment and the raw data needed to reconstruct what happened. The main chain executes nothing — an expensive operation — but stores the data — a cheap operation — thus hosting, in the same space, hundreds of rollup transactions instead of one. Here lies the difference from the sidechain: the rollup does not rely on a trusted consortium, it structurally inherits the security of the main chain.

Optimistic rollup. The sequencer publishes the state commitment and the transaction data on the main blockchain, but **provides no direct mathematical proof that the state is correct**. It is assumed to be — hence the name "optimistic" — and anyone is given the opportunity, during a predefined time window (typically seven days on Ethereum), to publish a **fraud proof** demonstrating that the sequencer cheated. If no one raises objections within the allotted time, the state is considered final. If someone raises a valid objection, the state is rejected and the sequencer punished. Optimism, Arbitrum, and Base are Ethereum's main optimistic rollups.

Zero-Knowledge rollup (ZK-rollup). The sequencer publishes the state commitment **together with a mathematical proof** — a zk-SNARK or zk-STARK — certifying that the state is the correct result of executing certain transactions starting from the previous state. The proof is verifiable in a few milliseconds by anyone, and requires no challenge window: either it is valid, or it is not, and the mathematics decides. zkSync, Starknet, Polygon zkEVM, and Linea are Ethereum's main ZK-rollups. ZK-rollups are conceptually more powerful, but mathematically much more complex to implement; optimistic rollups are simpler but have the challenge window that delays full finality.

FIGURE 2.3 **THE TWO ROLLUP VARIANTS COMPARED: OPTIMISTIC VERSUS ZERO-KNOWLEDGE.**

Variant	What it publishes on-chain	How correctness is guaranteed	Examples (Ethereum)
Optimistic rollup	State commitment + transaction data	Assumed correct; challenge window (≈7 days) for a *fraud proof*	Optimism, Arbitrum, Base
ZK-rollup	State commitment + mathematical proof (zk-SNARK / zk-STARK)	The proof is verifiable in milliseconds; no waiting: the mathematics decides	zkSync, Starknet, Polygon zkEVM, Linea

Both variants share the same principle — execution outside, truth on-chain — but differ in how the state is proven correct. The optimistic variant assumes correctness and relies on a fraud proof within a challenge window (on Ethereum typically seven days): simple to implement, but with delayed finality. The ZK variant publishes a cryptographic proof verifiable in milliseconds, with immediate finality, at the price of far more complex mathematics. In neither case does the main blockchain trust a consortium or a team: it either has the proof (ZK), or it has the data to verify after the fact (optimistic).

Both variants, however, share the fundamental architectural principle: **execution happens outside, but the ultimate truth — the data and the state commitments — is recorded on the main blockchain, inheriting its security structurally, not through federation.** The main blockchain trusts no one: it either has the mathematical proof (ZK)[*], or it has the data to verify after the fact (optimistic)[†]. In no case does it trust a consortium of companies or an identified team.

This is the qualitative leap that separates rollups from federated sidechains. **It is not a matter of efficiency: it is a matter of trust model.** And the trust model of a well-designed rollup is extraordinarily close to the trust model of the main blockchain, **far** closer than any federated sidechain can be.

[*] **Mathematical proof (ZK).** In "zero-knowledge" rollups, a cryptographic proof is published together with the state, mathematically demonstrating the correctness of the computations without having to redo them. The main blockchain verifies it and, if valid, accepts the state with immediate certainty: trust is placed in the mathematics, not in a time interval for challenges.

[†] **After-the-fact verification (optimistic).** In "optimistic" rollups the state is initially accepted "on trust," but remains challengeable for a certain period: anyone with the data can demonstrate its possible incorrectness (via a fraud proof) before it becomes final. Security thus rests on data availability and a time window, not on an immediate proof.

Between 2020 and 2024, rollups on Ethereum went from academic idea to dominant infrastructure. Today most of Ethereum's activity no longer happens on the mainnet, but on the rollups. It is an enormous success, and a case study in how a solid architectural idea, well implemented, can change the trajectory of an entire ecosystem. **After the success of rollups on Ethereum, it was inevitable that someone would ask: can the same be done on Bitcoin?**

⁂

2.7 — Why Bringing Rollups to Bitcoin Is Harder than on Ethereum

The short answer is: **yes, but it is much harder.** The reasons are interesting because they take us straight into the architecture of Bitcoin Hyper, and they explain why many of Hyper's choices differ from those of Ethereum rollups.

On Ethereum, building a rollup is relatively "simple" — relatively, to be clear, because we are still talking about advanced cryptography and distributed-systems engineering — because the Ethereum blockchain has everything needed to support a rollup in its base protocol. It has complex smart contracts that can verify fraud proofs. It has cryptographic primitives that can verify validity proofs. It has data storage space designed specifically for rollups (the "blob space" introduced with the EIP-4844 upgrade in 2024). In other words, **Ethereum has been progressively modified to be a good settlement layer for rollups.**

Not Bitcoin. Bitcoin is not modified. Bitcoin has no complex smart contracts. Bitcoin has no cryptographic primitives for verifying zk-SNARKs. Bitcoin has no data space optimized for rollups. **Bitcoin, from the point of view of a rollup wanting to lean on it, is an extremely minimal settlement layer that offers only a few things**: the ability to record small amounts of arbitrary data (via OP_RETURN[a] or similar techniques), the ability to build scripts that lock funds under certain conditions, and the guarantee of immutability of the recorded data. That is all.

The problem of building a rollup on Bitcoin then becomes: **how do you build a rollup when the underlying layer can do none of what rollups traditionally require?** It is a non-trivial question, and the answer requires architectural creativity. The main roads that research has explored in recent years are several, and Bitcoin Hyper is combining them in an original way.

---

[a] **OP_RETURN.** An instruction of Bitcoin's script that allows a small amount of arbitrary data to be attached to a transaction, without affecting the movement of funds. It is one of the few "legitimate" ways to write information onto Bitcoin, and for this reason it is studied as a possible channel for anchoring rollup data. The available space, however, is very limited and the cost non-negligible: an ingenious but narrow solution, far from the abundant data space Ethereum introduced specifically for rollups.

FIGURE 2.4 **WHY A ROLLUP IS "EASY" ON ETHEREUM AND HARD ON BITCOIN.**

What a rollup needs	Ethereum	Bitcoin
On-chain proof verification	✓ complex smart contracts + cryptographic primitives	✗ Script cannot verify zk-SNARKs
Data space for rollups	✓ blob space (EIP-4844, 2024)	✗ only a few bytes via OP_RETURN
Conditional scripts on funds	✓ fully programmable	~ limited to a few conditions
Immutability of recorded data	✓	✓ (the only thing it offers in full)
Philosophy	modified specifically for rollups	not modified, on principle

Ethereum has been progressively modified to be a good settlement layer for rollups: it has smart contracts that verify proofs, cryptographic primitives, and dedicated data space. Bitcoin, on principle, is not modified: it offers only the ability to record a feu bytes, limited conditional scripts, and the immutability of the data. It is a minimal settlement layer. Building a rollup on top of it therefore means reinventing, with architectural creativity, everything that on Ethereum is already in the protocol.

FIGURE 2.5 **THE FOUR ROADS TO ROLLUPS ON BITCOIN, WITH TRADE-OFFS AND STATE OF MATURITY.**

#	Road	In short	Trade-off	Maturity
1	Minimal anchoring	Only the state root on Bitcoin; the data lives elsewhere	Moves the data availability problem elsewhere	In use today
2	Proofs verified outside Bitcoin	The proofs are verified on another chain; on Bitcoin only the result	External dependency: not "purely Bitcoin"	In use today
3	New opcodes (OP_CAT)	Proof verification directly on Bitcoin	Requires a soft fork: touches Bitcoin	Future proposal
4	BitVM-style mechanisms	Simulates complex smart contracts without modifying Bitcoin	Brilliant but with many open details	Experimental

On Ethereum the rollup model is mature; on Bitcoin it is still under construction, and every solution carries specific trade-offs. Minimal anchoring and off-chain proof verification are practicable today — but the first moves the data availability problem elsewhere, and the second introduces an external dependency. New opcodes such as OP_CAT would verify proofs directly on Bitcoin, but require a soft fork that touches the protocol. BitVM promises to simulate complex smart contracts without modifying anything, but it is experimental. Hyper combines the first two for now, with the idea of evolving toward BitVM as the technology matures.

First road: minimal anchoring. The rollup publishes on Bitcoin only the strictly necessary datum — typically the state root, a 32-byte string that is the mathematical "photograph" of the rollup's state at a given moment. This datum is slipped into a Bitcoin transaction via OP_RETURN or via Taproot, and from that moment it is immutably recorded. The transaction data is not published on Bitcoin, because Bitcoin has no space to host it. The transaction data lives elsewhere — on a network of rollup nodes, on specialized "data availability layers," or on other blockchains designed specifically to host data (such as Celestia or EigenDA). This approach is cost-efficient, but it moves the data availability problem elsewhere, where it requires solutions of its own.

Second road: proof execution outside Bitcoin. The validity proofs of a ZK-rollup cannot be verified inside Bitcoin, because Script lacks the cryptographic capabilities to do so. So what does one do? They are verified elsewhere — typically on Ethereum, or on another blockchain capable of it — and on Bitcoin only the result of the verification is recorded. This road is elegant but introduces an external dependency: the rollup's security depends not only on Bitcoin, but also on the blockchain where the proofs are verified. For projects that want to be "purely Bitcoin," this is a significant compromise.

Third road: new Bitcoin opcodes. There is a movement, within the Bitcoin community, to introduce new opcodes (operations of the Script language) that would allow certain forms of cryptographic proofs to be verified directly on Bitcoin. The most discussed proposal is **OP_CAT**, which is apparently an extremely simple operation — concatenating two strings — but which, combined with other existing primitives, would enable the verification of complex cryptographic proofs directly on Bitcoin. It is a road that requires a modification of the Bitcoin protocol (a soft fork), and therefore runs against the principle of not touching Bitcoin that we described in Chapter 1. For now it remains a future possibility, not an operational reality.

Fourth road: BitVM-style mechanisms. This is a more recent approach, proposed in 2023 by Robin Linus, that uses a highly sophisticated combination of cryptography and game logic to "simulate" complex smart contract capabilities on Bitcoin without modifying it. It is a brilliant idea but still in the experimentation phase, with many technical details to be resolved before it becomes practical.

Each of these roads has merits and flaws. **Bitcoin Hyper has chosen, for now, a combination of the first two**, with the idea of being able to evolve toward more decentralized roads (such as BitVM) as the technology matures. We will see the details in the coming chapters, but it is important that the reader arrive at those chapters aware that **there is no obvious or standardized road for building rollups on Bitcoin**: every project is making different choices, each with specific trade-offs, and none of those choices has yet consolidated as "the industry standard." The rollup model on Ethereum is mature. The rollup model on Bitcoin is still under construction.

⁂

2.8 — The Choice of the Solana Virtual Machine: A Decision That Changes Everything

There is one last architectural decision we must address in this chapter, because it is the choice that differentiates Bitcoin Hyper from almost all its predecessors, and it deserves to be understood before proceeding. **Bitcoin Hyper does not use Ethereum's virtual machine. It uses Solana's virtual machine.** This choice was publicly declared by the team in a specific post of June 2025, where it is justified with precise technical arguments worth reconstructing.

When designing a Layer 2 — whatever the base blockchain — one of the first problems that arises is: **which execution environment to adopt for smart contracts?** It is a choice that conditions everything else: the developers who will be able to build on the layer, the kinds of applications that will be possible, the actual performance of the system, the compatibility with other ecosystems.

The most obvious choice, in 2024–2025, would have been Ethereum's EVM. It is the de facto standard of the crypto world. Thousands of existing applications could be ported with minimal changes. Hundreds of thousands of developers already know Solidity and the tools of the EVM ecosystem. All the main Ethereum rollups — Optimism, Arbitrum, Base — use the EVM. Even Bitcoin projects such as Rootstock chose the EVM precisely to benefit from this existing ecosystem. It would seem the natural, almost obligatory choice.

Bitcoin Hyper rejected this choice. The motivation the team gave publicly is **technical**: the EVM has architectural characteristics that make it ill-suited to a system designed to scale massively. **The EVM is single-threaded and serial**[a], which means transactions are executed one at a time, in line, without being able to exploit parallel execution. **The EVM has a heavy and relatively inefficient gas system**, which limits the complexity of economically sustainable operations. **The EVM was not designed for high-performance environments**: it was designed for maximum decentralization of execution, and from that choice follow its throughput[b] limitations.

The SVM, the Solana Virtual Machine, was designed from scratch with a different objective: **maximizing performance**. SVM transactions declare in advance which accounts they will touch, and this allows the runtime to execute in parallel all the transactions that do not touch each other. The execution system, called **Sealevel**, exploits all the CPU's cores and reaches throughput levels the EVM cannot even approach. SVM programs are written in Rust or C, compiled into efficient native binaries, and run at much higher speeds than EVM contracts.

---

[a] **Single-threaded and serial.** It means the system processes one transaction at a time, in line, even when the operations are independent of one another. It is the opposite of "parallel" execution, in which multiple transactions that do not affect each other are processed simultaneously, fully exploiting the processor's power.

[b] **Throughput.** The amount of work a system can dispatch in a given interval of time — here, the number of transactions processable per second. Higher throughput means more capacity; it is a measure distinct from "latency," which instead concerns how long the individual transaction takes.

TABLE 2.2 **EVM AND SVM COMPARED.**

Aspect	EVM	SVM

Execution	Serial, one at a time	Parallel across multiple cores
Languages	Solidity, EVM bytecode	Rust or C, native binaries
Accounts	Not declared in advance	Declared in the transaction
Objective	Compatibility, adoption	Throughput, performance

The decisive difference is execution: the EVM processes transactions one at a time, whereas the SVM, knowing in advance which accounts each will touch, can execute the independent ones in parallel. It is this architectural choice that explains the throughput gap, and it is the reason Bitcoin Hyper preferred the SVM despite its narrower adoption compared with the EVM.

FIGURE 2.6 **THE ARCHITECTURAL FORK: EVM VERSUS SVM.**

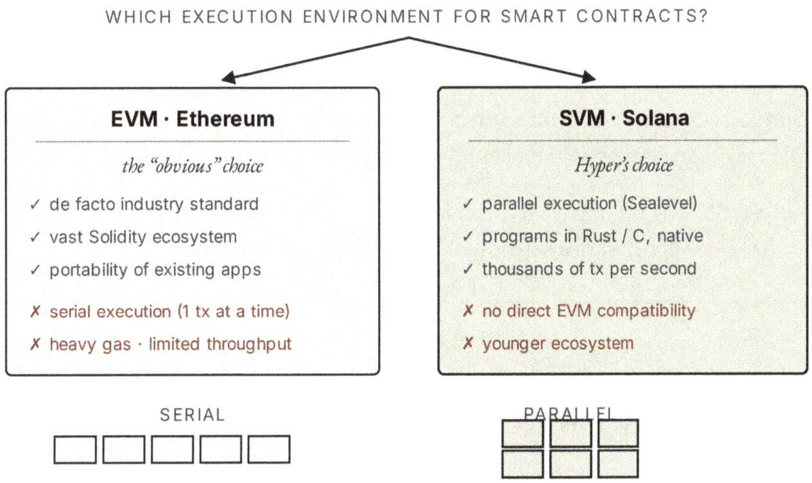

The choice of execution environment conditions everything else: developers, possible applications, performance, compatibility. The EVM is the de facto standard, with a vast ecosystem and portable applications, but it executes transactions one at a time. The SVM, with the Sealevel runtime, executes them in parallel and reaches far higher throughput, at the price of giving up direct compatibility with Ethereum. Hyper chose the second road.

The choice of the SVM carries three important consequences that the investor or the developer must weigh carefully.

Positive consequence one: Bitcoin Hyper, if the implementation lives up to the promises, can actually reach throughput on the order of thousands of transactions per second, enabling use cases that would have been impossible with an EVM rollup on Bitcoin — real-time on-chain games, decentralized exchanges with order books, high-frequency shared-state applications.

Positive consequence two: Solana's development ecosystem — which in terms of number of developers and existing applications is second only to Ethereum's — can be brought onto Bitcoin Hyper with minimal changes. A developer who writes Solana applications today can, in principle, deploy them on Hyper using the same commands (`solana program deploy`), the same tools (the Anchor framework), the same languages. It is the "zero friction" strategy for developers that the team has explicitly declared.

Negative consequence: Bitcoin Hyper is not compatible with the EVM ecosystem. All existing Solidity applications — the majority of today's DeFi universe — cannot be ported directly. They would require rewrites in Rust, or an EVM compatibility layer built on top of Hyper, which however would add complexity and could introduce vulnerabilities. For now, the choice is clear: **Hyper is an island compatible with Solana, not with Ethereum**. Those coming from Ethereum will have to rebuild, not merely port.

This choice is a bet, and it must be recognized as such. If it proves right, Bitcoin Hyper will have an enormous performance advantage over any Bitcoin rollup using the EVM, and will be able to attract a distinct developer ecosystem. If it proves wrong, it will be because the Solana ecosystem turns out to be smaller or less migratable than hoped, and because the inertia of the EVM ecosystem was underestimated. **It is a decision that time will judge**, and it is worth keeping in mind as one of the key points on which to evaluate the project in the coming years.

IN BRIEF · THE SVM BET

Performance advantage: parallel execution and throughput on the order of thousands of transactions per second, enabling use cases impossible for an EVM rollup on Bitcoin.

Ecosystem advantage: lower friction for Solana developers, who can port their applications with minimal changes.

Limit: no direct compatibility with the Solidity applications of the EVM universe — those coming from Ethereum must rebuild, not merely port.

Risk: the Solana ecosystem could turn out to be smaller or less migratable than expected, and the EVM's inertia may have been underestimated.

The choice of the SVM is not merely technical: it is the strategic bet that can turn Hyper into a high-performance Bitcoin rollup, but that separates it from the EVM ecosystem.

⁂

2.9 — Questions and Answers: Clarifying the Chapter's Concepts

As in Chapter 1, let us fix the concepts through a sequence of questions I have frequently been asked when explaining this material informally.

Question 1: If Lightning Network has existed for almost ten years and works, why do we need Bitcoin Hyper?

Because Lightning does payments only, and we need much more. The crypto world of recent years has shown that people want to do with their digital money everything they used to do with traditional finance: lending, trading, derivatives, tokenized assets. And they also want to do new things that traditional finance cannot: automated liquidity, decentralized governance, NFTs, on-chain games. **Lightning can do none of this.** Lightning is specialized in micropayments, and in that role it is excellent, but it is not a substitute for a general-purpose Layer 2. **Concrete example:** if you want to take out a fixed-rate loan using bitcoin as collateral, you cannot do it on Lightning. You can do it on Aave or Compound[*] (on Ethereum), or you could do it on Hyper if Hyper ends up having the equivalent protocols. Lightning and Hyper are not in competition: they are complementary solutions to different problems.

---

[*] **Aave and Compound.** Two of the main decentralized finance (DeFi) applications born on Ethereum: they allow crypto assets to be lent and borrowed automatically, through on-chain programs and without a banking intermediary. They are cited here as an example of functions — collateralized lending — that Lightning cannot offer and that a general-purpose Layer 2 like Hyper could instead host.

Question 2: What technically distinguishes a rollup from a federated sidechain? They seem like similar things.

The difference is the **security model**. In a federated sidechain, the security of your funds depends on the honesty of a consortium of identified companies: if they decide to steal your funds, all you can do is sue them in court (hoping you know who they are and where they sit jurisdictionally). In a well-designed rollup, the security of your funds depends on the mathematics and on the main blockchain: if the rollup's sequencer tries to steal your funds, you (or anyone else) can publish a fraud proof or a validity proof demonstrating the theft, and the main blockchain will reject the fraudulent transaction automatically, without anyone having to "decide" anything. **Concrete example:** if Liquid (a federated sidechain) decided tomorrow not to give you back your bitcoin, you would have to sue Blockstream and the members of the federation in different jurisdictions, hoping to win. If Optimism (an optimistic rollup) tried not to give you back your ether, you could publish a fraud proof and the system would return your funds automatically, regardless of the Optimism team's will. **It is an enormous difference in the trust model, even if the end user might not notice it in everyday use.**

Question 3: Is Bitcoin Hyper an optimistic rollup or a ZK-rollup?

This is a question where the project's communication has been, let us say, ambiguous. The initial marketing spoke of a "ZK rollup." The whitepaper, read carefully, describes an architecture that has more of the characteristics of an optimistic rollup — there is a trusted sequencer, there is periodic anchoring, there is no validity proof on every batch — while mentioning the use of zero-knowledge techniques for other purposes (privacy, compression). The team's most recent updates, in particular those of 2026, have become more cautious in their terminology, speaking of "commitment models," "anchoring cadence," "approaches inspired by both optimistic and validity-based rollups." **In essence: Hyper is a hybrid rollup still being defined**, where the specific choices between optimistic and ZK are still the subject of research and implementation. We will see in Chapter 19 the implications of this hybridity for the security model.

Question 4: Why does Bitcoin Hyper not wait for the new opcodes on Bitcoin (such as OP_CAT) to be introduced, so as to build something more trustless?

For two reasons, one practical and one strategic. **Practical**: introducing new opcodes requires a soft fork, which in turn requires community consensus. The debate around OP_CAT and similar proposals has been going on for years, and there is no certainty it will ever be approved, let alone approved quickly. Waiting means potentially waiting forever. **Strategic**: whoever builds something functional today, even with compromises, can accumulate ecosystem, experience, infrastructure, and will be able to evolve toward more trustless models when they become available. Whoever waits arrives late. **Concrete example:** Lightning Network was launched before all the Bitcoin upgrades that would have made it more efficient were available (Taproot in particular, which arrived in 2021). Lightning's creators built what they could with what there was, and integrated the improvements afterward. Hyper appears to be following the same philosophy.

Question 5: How realistic is it that Solana developers will migrate to Hyper?

It depends on many factors, and honestly it is one of the hardest points to predict. **Pro**: the technical compatibility is high (same tools, same language, same libraries), the Bitcoin brand is powerful at attracting interest, and Solana developers are used to working with high throughput and might appreciate an environment combining performance and Bitcoin security. **Con**: developers are notoriously sensitive to the existing ecosystem — to liquidity, to users, to partners — and Solana already has a mature ecosystem that Hyper will have to build from scratch. If Hyper fails to attract a critical mass of applications in the first 12–24 months after the mainnet launch, it risks remaining a technically interesting but economically irrelevant island. **Concrete example:** Sui and Aptos, two blockchains with technical characteristics similar to Solana's launched in 2022–2023, struggled to attract developers from the Solana ecosystem precisely because the liquidity and the users were already elsewhere. Hyper could face the same challenge.

Question 6: If Hyper fails, what happens to the bitcoin users have deposited in the bridge?

This is the most important question a prudent investor should ask, and the answer depends critically on the bridge's architecture. **In an ideal scenario**, the bridge is designed so that, even if the Hyper team disappeared tomorrow, users could recover their bitcoin through automatic mechanisms based on the Bitcoin blockchain. **In a real-world scenario**, most current bridges have some form of dependence on specific operators, and in the event of the project's abandonment or malfunction, recovering the funds could be difficult or impossible. The documentation available on Hyper is not yet detailed enough to clarify this point one hundred percent, and it is one of the main open technical questions about the project. We will address it in depth in Chapters 11 and 21, when we discuss the Canonical Bridge and the forced exit mechanisms. For now it is enough to know that **this is one of the areas where the investor's due diligence must be most rigorous**, and where the marketing promises must be scrupulously checked against the technical documentation.

⁂

2.10 — WHAT TO TAKE AWAY FROM THIS CHAPTER

Before moving on to Chapter 3, where we will see in detail the map of solutions — sidechains, forks, rollups — and why the rollup model is the one Bitcoin Hyper chose, let us fix the key points.

Bitcoin Layer 2s are scaling solutions that lean on Bitcoin without modifying it. They are based on the separation principle between the execution layer (fast, above) and the settlement layer (slow and final, below — that is, Bitcoin).

The history of Bitcoin Layer 2s runs from Lightning Network (2016) to Bitcoin Hyper (today), passing through Liquid, Stacks, Rootstock, and other attempts. Each solution solved one piece of the problem while leaving the next piece open, and the trajectory moved progressively toward ever more trustless and general-purpose models.

Lightning Network is Bitcoin's first successful Layer 2, but it is limited to payments. It cannot support complex smart contracts or general-purpose decentralized applications.

Federated sidechains (such as Liquid) work but do not inherit Bitcoin's properties: they are parallel blockchains run by identified consortia, with a trust model very different from Bitcoin's.

Stacks and Rootstock tried to go beyond the federated model, with mixed results. They showed the feasibility of more ambitious extensions, but with significant compromises on the development ecosystem (proprietary languages) and on the decentralization of the bridge.

Rollups are the most mature evolution of the Layer 2 model, initially developed for Ethereum starting in 2019–2020. They are distinguished from federated sidechains by the security model: trust is placed not in a consortium of companies, but in mathematics and in the main blockchain.

Building rollups on Bitcoin is harder than building them on Ethereum, because Bitcoin offers far more limited primitives. Current research is exploring several roads, and Bitcoin Hyper is combining some of them in an original way.

Bitcoin Hyper chose the Solana Virtual Machine* as its execution environment, a decision that sets it apart from most existing Bitcoin rollups. It is a bet on performance and on the Solana ecosystem, with compromises on compatibility with the Ethereum universe.

Chapter 2 ends here. We have seen where the idea of extending Bitcoin without modifying it comes from, and we have followed the historical-causal thread that led from Lightning Network's initial insight to the rollup model adopted today by Bitcoin Hyper. In ***Chapter 3 — Sidechains, Forks, Rollups: The Map of Possible Solutions****, we will go into detail on the three main architectural approaches, comparing them on precise criteria (decentralization, security, programmability, developer experience), and we will understand why the Hyper team specifically chose the rollup model and not the other two.*

---

[*] **Solana Virtual Machine (SVM).** The execution environment introduced by Solana, capable of processing multiple transactions in parallel to achieve high performance. Bitcoin Hyper adopts it as the engine of its rollup: it is the choice that sets it apart from the other projects built on Bitcoin.

NOTES

1 Joseph Poon, Thaddeus Dryja, *The Bitcoin Lightning Network: Scalable Off-Chain Instant Payments*, draft 0.5.9.2, January 2016. Available at lightning.network.

Extending Bitcoin without *modifying it*

From Lightning to rollups: the path that leads to Bitcoin Hyper. Bitcoin's strength is the stability of the protocol — so one builds **on top**, separating execution and settlement.

1 If Bitcoin is not to be touched, where does one build?

Upper layers — WHERE ONE BUILDS: fast payments · smart contracts · DeFi · applications · fast UX

↓ BUILDING ON TOP, NOT INSIDE ↓

₿ Bitcoin L1 — STABLE FOUNDATION: settlement · security · immutability · public verification · conservative protocol

Bitcoin's scalability does not arise by changing Bitcoin: **it arises by separating what must be settled from what must be executed.**

2 Recording little, executing much

Opening on Bitcoin — initial state anchored → **Thousands of off-chain / Layer 2 interactions** — frequent, fast activity → **Closing / anchoring** — final truth on Bitcoin

Like friends on a night out: **not a bank transfer for every expense** — the accounts are done at the end and only the balance is settled.

Bitcoin settles the result. **The Layer 2 handles the activity.**

3 Ten years of attempts: every solution leaves a lesson

2015/16	**Lightning Network** · PAYMENT CHANNELS — Instant off-chain payments. **Limit:** payments only, no global state or composable DeFi.
2018	**Liquid** · FEDERATED SIDECHAIN — Faster and more flexible, with L-BTC. **Limit:** trust in a federation of operators.
2018	**Rootstock** · EVM + MERGE MINING — Ethereum-style smart contracts around Bitcoin. **Limit:** security not fully inherited, federated bridge.
2021	**Stacks** · PROOF OF TRANSFER + CLARITY — A chain economically anchored to Bitcoin. **Limit:** its own token and language, a bridge not entirely trustless.
2025	**Bitcoin Hyper** · SVM ROLLUP ON BITCOIN — Fast execution above, settlement on Bitcoin below. **Challenge:** bringing the rollup model to Bitcoin, which was not born to verify it.

Every stage is born from the limit of the previous one — *they are not equivalent solutions.*

4 The rollup leap: execution outside, verifiable truth inside

Rollup / L2 — EXECUTION: executes transactions · updates the state · compresses the result · produces the state root

↓ PUBLISHES COMMITMENT + DATA / PROOFS ↓

₿ Settlement — VERIFICATION + FINALITY: keeps the commitment · makes the reference immutable · allows verification

Optimistic Rollup
valid unless contested: a window for the fraud proof is needed.

ZK Rollup
valid only with a mathematical proof: more complex, cryptographic verification.

The rollup does not ask for trust in a federation: **it brings verification onto the settlement level.**

5 On Bitcoin it is harder — and why Hyper chooses SVM

Ethereum · ADAPTED TO ROLLUPS
complex smart contracts · on-chain proof verification · blob space · mature rollups

Bitcoin · MINIMAL TOOLS
limited Script · OP_RETURN / Taproot · little data space · no native ZK verification · very strong immutability

Minimal anchoring
state root on Bitcoin, data elsewhere.

Proofs verified outside
verification elsewhere, result anchored.

New opcodes
a possible future, but it requires a soft fork.

BitVM-like
promising, but still experimental.

Hyper bets on the **SVM**: **more performance and less friction for Solana developers**, *at the price of direct compatibility with the EVM.*

THE KEY POINT | Bitcoin is not to be modified to become faster or programmable: it is to be used as a **settlement foundation**. Lightning showed that

PART I · THE PROBLEM TO BE SOLVED

Chapter 3
Sidechains, Forks, Rollups

The map of possible solutions

⁂

3.1 — Three Families, Three Philosophies, Three Different Fates

In Chapter 2 we followed the historical thread that led, over ten years, from the insight of Lightning Network[a] to the rollup model adopted by Bitcoin Hyper. But that account was chronological, linear: one solution after another, each born from the limits of the previous one. In this chapter we do something different, and in some ways more important: **we place the three main families of solutions side by side**, compare them on precise criteria, and see why Bitcoin Hyper specifically chose the third family — the rollups — discarding the other two. This is not an academic exercise. It is the foundation for judging with full knowledge any Bitcoin Layer 2[b] project you will come across in the future, because the vocabulary of crypto marketing is rich in words — "extension of Bitcoin," "anchored to Bitcoin," "Bitcoin-compatible," "inheriting Bitcoin's security" — that mean very different things depending on which family the project actually belongs to.

The three families are: **forks**[c], **sidechains**[d] (in all their variants, from federated to merge-mined), and **rollups**[e]. They are three radically different approaches to the problem "how do I make Bitcoin do more," and each carries a distinct philosophical compromise. The fork says: "let us modify Bitcoin, even at the cost of creating a separate version of it." The sidechain says: "let us leave Bitcoin as it is, and build a parallel blockchain that connects to Bitcoin through a custody mechanism." The rollup says: "let us leave Bitcoin as it is, and build a layer on top that executes fast but writes its conclusions onto Bitcoin in a verifiable way." Three different answers, three different fates, and — let us see it right away — only one compatible with the philosophy we described in the preceding chapters.

Let us look at them one at a time, patiently, because understanding them well is the basis for everything you will read in the next three hundred pages.

---

[a] **Lightning Network.** A network of payment channels built on top of Bitcoin to settle fast, low-cost transactions without writing every payment on the main blockchain. It is historically Bitcoin's first scaling solution, but with functions limited to payments.

[b] **Layer 2.** A generic expression for a system built on top of a main blockchain (the Layer 1) in order to increase its capacity or functions, leaning on the base layer for final security. Sidechains and rollups fall within this logic; the fork, which gives rise to a separate network, is instead a case apart.

[c] **Fork.** A modified copy of Bitcoin's code that gives rise to a separate network, with rules of its own. Historical examples are Bitcoin Cash and Litecoin: they do not extend Bitcoin, they create an autonomous variant of it.

[d] **Sidechain.** A parallel blockchain connected to Bitcoin through a custody mechanism (a federation or merge mining). It leaves Bitcoin intact, but introduces trust assumptions of its own.

[e] **Rollup.** A layer that executes transactions outside Bitcoin and publishes their results in verifiable form on the main blockchain. It is the family chosen by Bitcoin Hyper.

FIGURE 3.1 **FORKS, SIDECHAINS, AND ROLLUPS: THREE ANSWERS TO THE SAME QUESTION.**

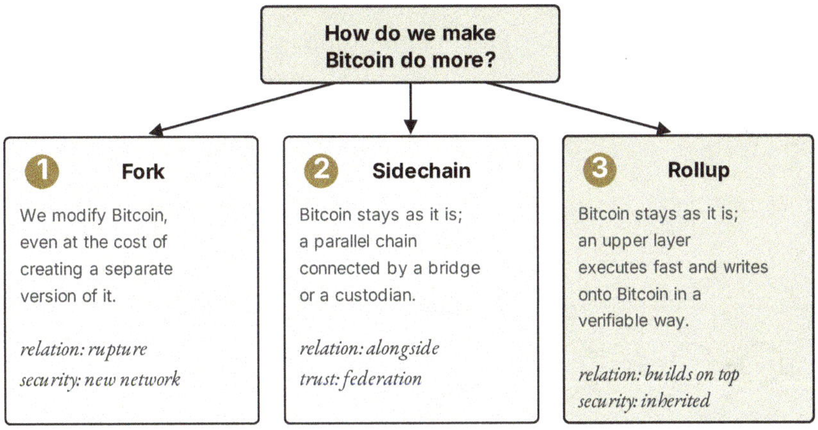

Same question · three philosophies · three different fates

Only the third family is compatible with Bitcoin's philosophy

Forks, sidechains, and rollups all answer the question "how do we make Bitcoin do more?", but they follow three different philosophies and produce three different fates. The fork modifies the protocol and risks a split; the sidechain places alongside Bitcoin a parallel chain connected by a custodial bridge; the rollup builds an upper layer that executes quickly but records verifiable conclusions on Bitcoin. Only this last family structurally inherits Bitcoin's security.

⁂

3.2 — The Fork Family: Changing Bitcoin at the Cost of Splitting It

The first family is also the simplest to understand conceptually, and it is the one the Bitcoin community most radically rejects. A **fork**[*] is a modification to Bitcoin's protocol which, if not accepted by all participants in the network, produces a **split**[†]: from a certain block onward, two separate blockchains exist, one with the old rules and one with the new. From that moment on they are in effect two different networks, with two different tokens, two different communities, two different histories.

---

[*] **Hard fork and soft fork.** Not all modifications cause a split. A soft fork introduces more restrictive, backward-compatible rules: non-upgraded nodes continue to accept the new blocks. A hard fork introduces incompatible rules and, if not adopted unanimously, separates the chain in two. It is to this latter case that the paragraph refers.

[†] **Split (chain split).** The best-known historical example is the birth of Bitcoin Cash in August 2017, originating from the disagreement over block size. From that block onward the two chains proceeded independently, with distinct coins, rules, and communities: a concrete demonstration that an unshared fork does not upgrade Bitcoin, but creates a divergent copy of it.

FIGURE 3.2 **SOFT FORK AND HARD FORK: TWO WAYS OF CHANGING BITCOIN, TWO OPPOSITE OUTCOMES.**

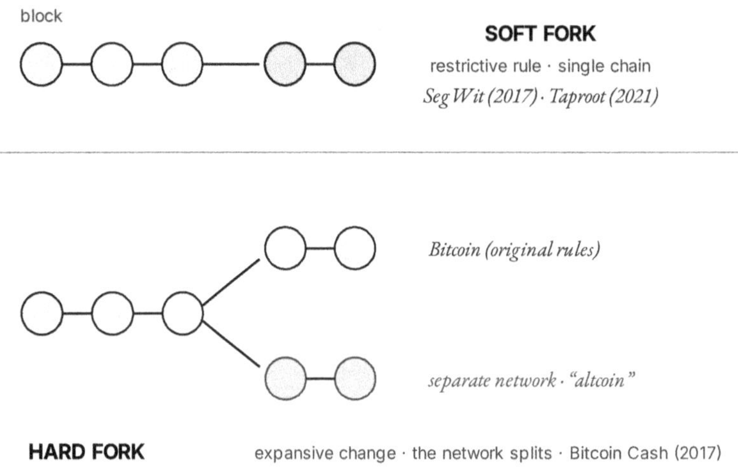

A soft fork introduces restrictive rules compatible with non-upgraded nodes and keeps the network united, like SegWit and Taproot. A hard fork introduces expansive rules that old nodes reject: if not everyone upgrades, the network splits into two separate blockchains, as happened with Bitcoin Cash. Extending Bitcoin with advanced computational capabilities would require modifications so invasive as to impose a hard fork the community would not accept. Proposals such as OP_CAT seek a way through targeted soft forks, but they remain future hypotheses: this is why Hyper chooses to build on Bitcoin as it is today.

Forks fall into two technical categories, **soft forks** and **hard forks**, and the difference matters. A soft fork is a **restrictive** modification: it adds new rules that nevertheless remain compatible with nodes running the old software. Non-upgraded nodes continue to work and to see the new version's transactions as "valid," because the new rules are a subset of the old ones. SegWit in 2017 and Taproot in 2021 were Bitcoin soft forks: they added functionality without splitting the network, because everyone could keep participating even without upgrading immediately. A hard fork, by contrast, is an **expansive** modification: it adds things that old nodes would reject, and therefore requires everyone to upgrade the software simultaneously, otherwise the network divides. Bitcoin Cash in 2017 was a hard fork: those who wanted bigger blocks upgraded, those who did not want them did not, and from that moment two blockchains existed.

Soft forks, in principle, can be accepted by the community if well designed and cautious. Hard forks, on the other hand, are practically impossible in the Bitcoin world: the community has repeatedly shown that it regards them as an assault on the founding pact, and those who have tried to force them have always produced separate networks considered "altcoins" relative to the original Bitcoin. **The history of Bitcoin is the history of a protocol that changes rarely, and when it changes, it does so through the least destructive instruments possible.**

For our purposes, there is a fundamental practical consequence: **the fork road is closed to any project that wants to "extend" Bitcoin by adding significant computational capabilities.** The modifications needed to make Bitcoin Turing-complete, or even just to allow it to verify complex cryptographic proofs, would be so invasive as to require a hard fork, and no community would accept a hard fork of that magnitude. Those who tried — Bitcoin Cash with its limited smart contracts, Bitcoin SV with its more extreme ambitions — produced separate networks that survive today as minority projects, immensely far from Bitcoin's market value and relevance. **The fork, as an extension strategy, does not work.**

There is, however, a subtler variant of this road, worth naming for completeness: there are projects proposing targeted soft forks to **enable** Layer 2 functionality without modifying Bitcoin's basic operation. The most discussed proposal in this direction is OP_CAT,* which we touched on in the previous chapter: a soft fork that would add an apparently innocuous operation (the concatenation of strings) but which, combined with other primitives, would enable the direct verification of complex cryptographic proofs. If OP_CAT were approved — and the debate has been going on for years without resolution — it would become possible to build rollups on Bitcoin with characteristics similar to Ethereum's, with proof verification directly on the base layer. It is an interesting future possibility, but for now it remains on paper. **Bitcoin Hyper, as we have seen, chose to build something that works with Bitcoin as it is today**, without depending on soft forks that might never arrive.

Let us set the fork family aside and move to the second, which is where most Bitcoin extension projects have positioned themselves over the last ten years: the sidechains.

⁂

3.3 — The Sidechain Family: Parallel to Bitcoin, but with Rules of Their Own

A **sidechain** is, literally, a "side chain": a blockchain separate from Bitcoin, with its own consensus[†] and its own rules, connected to Bitcoin through a mechanism that allows bitcoin to move back and forth between the two networks.[‡] The architectural principle is simple to explain, but the implications are complex and must be analyzed carefully, because the word "sidechain" covers realities that differ greatly from one another.

---

[*] **OP_CAT.** An instruction of Bitcoin's Script language, disabled since the beginning, which merely joins (concatenates) two strings of data. Taken alone it seems trivial; combined with other operations, however, it would make it possible to verify complex cryptographic proofs directly on Bitcoin. Its reintroduction would require a soft fork and, as of this writing, it remains a debated, unapproved proposal.

[†] **Consensus.** The mechanism by which the nodes of a blockchain agree on a single shared version of the transaction history, without a central authority. A sidechain has its own consensus, separate and independent from Bitcoin's: this is what makes it a "parallel" chain and not part of Bitcoin.

[‡] **Two-way peg.** The mechanism that "moves" bitcoin between Bitcoin and a sidechain: the bitcoin does not really move, but is locked on the main chain and represented by an equivalent on the sidechain, then unlocked on the way back. The degree of trust this passage requires — who holds custody of the locked funds — is what distinguishes one type of sidechain from another.

FIGURE 3.1 **HOW A SIDECHAIN WORKS: BITCOIN LOCKED IN THE PEG, REPRESENTATIVE TOKENS ON THE SIDE CHAIN.**

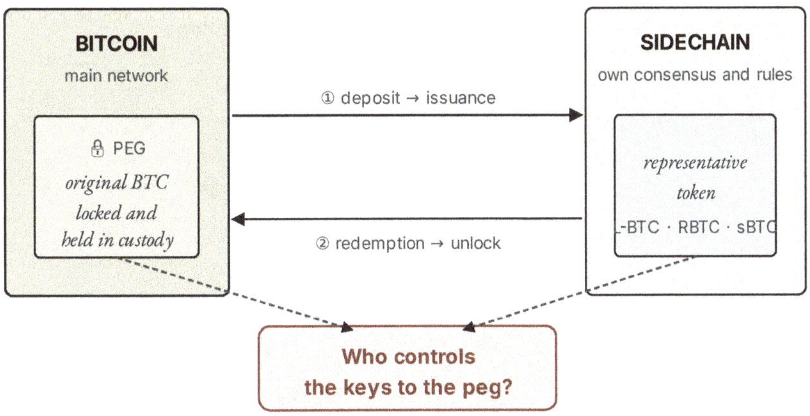

Bitcoin and the sidechain are two separate blockchains: the first remains the main network, the second operates in parallel with a consensus of its own. The user sends BTC to a locking address, the original bitcoin remains in custody in the peg, and on the side chain an equivalent token is issued (L-BTC, RBTC, sBTC); to go back, they return the token and receive the BTC again. The entire security model hinges on a single question — who controls the keys to the peg? — because the sidechain offers flexibility and speed, but does not automatically inherit Bitcoin's security: whoever holds custody of the funds controls access to the locked bitcoin.

The basic operation is as follows. The sidechain has its own consensus mechanism — it may be Proof of Stake, it may be Proof of Authority, it may be a federated variant, it may even be a form of Proof of Work merge-mined with Bitcoin — and this consensus decides which transactions to accept, in what order, and with what final state. When you want to use the sidechain, you send your bitcoin to a special address controlled by whoever runs the sidechain (the "peg")[a]. The bitcoin is "locked" there, and in exchange an equivalent amount of a token representing your bitcoin on the new network is credited to you on the sidechain. This token may be called different things — L-BTC on Liquid, RBTC on Rootstock, sBTC on Stacks — but the mechanism is conceptually the same: **real bitcoin locked on one side, representative token on the other**[b]. When you want to go back, you return the token on the sidechain, someone (the custodian of the peg) unlocks the original bitcoin, and you recover it on the main network.

The decisive question, the one that separates a "good" sidechain from a "bad" one, is: **who controls the peg?** Who holds the keys that can unlock the bitcoin in custody? On how this question is answered depends the sidechain's entire security model, and here the variants are many.

[a] **Peg.** The mechanism that ties the bitcoin locked on Bitcoin to the corresponding tokens on the sidechain: by depositing BTC one receives tokens on the side chain (peg-in), by returning them one unlocks the original BTC (peg-out). The security of the whole system depends on who holds the keys to the peg.

[b] **Representative token.** The unit issued on the sidechain against the deposited bitcoin (for example L-BTC, RBTC, sBTC). It is not native bitcoin: it holds value as long as whoever holds custody of the peg guarantees one-to-one convertibility with the locked BTC.

FIGURE 3.2 **THE FOUR SIDECHAIN VARIANTS COMPARED: IN ALL OF THEM, THE DECISIVE KNOT REMAINS THE CUSTODY OF THE PEG.**

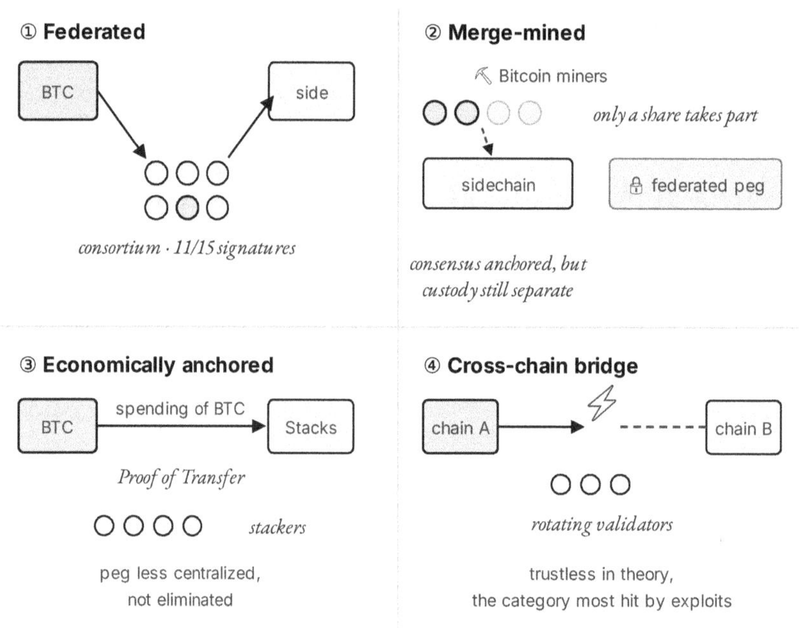

Variant one: the federated sidechain. It is the model adopted by Liquid and, in a similar form, by the first versions of Rootstock. The peg is controlled by a consortium of identified companies, typically ten or fifteen entities. To unlock the bitcoin, the signature of a qualified majority of these companies is needed — for example, eleven signatures out of fifteen. The model works, and is relatively simple to implement, but it carries an enormous dependence on this consortium. If the qualified majority of the companies decides to collude, it can steal all the bitcoin in custody. If even one of these companies is compromised or seized by a government, the model wobbles. **The security is the federation's, not Bitcoin's.** And that is an enormous difference.

Variant two: the merge-mined sidechain[a]. It is the model originally attempted by Rootstock. The idea is that Bitcoin miners, in addition to mining blocks on the main network, can simultaneously mine blocks on the sidechain with the same computational work. In theory, this should anchor the sidechain's security to Bitcoin's computational power: to attack the sidechain, one would need a significant percentage of Bitcoin's total hashpower, which is very costly. **In practice, the model has worked poorly.** For reasons beyond the scope of this chapter, most Bitcoin miners did not participate in Rootstock's merge mining, and the sidechain's security in fact depended on the minority of miners who joined — a much smaller and more attackable base. Moreover, even where merge mining works, **the bitcoin peg between the two networks remains a separate point**, and almost always still requires a federation of custodians to manage the unlocking of funds. Merge mining anchors the *consensus* to Bitcoin, but does not solve the problem of *custody*.

---

[a] **Merge mining.** The technique by which Bitcoin miners can, with the same computational work, produce blocks on a second blockchain as well. The idea is to "borrow" Bitcoin's computing power to protect the sidechain. It works, however, only if a sufficient share of miners chooses to participate: if a minority joins, the inherited security is much weaker than Bitcoin's. Moreover, it protects the consensus, that is, the ordering of blocks, but not the custody of the funds transferred between the two networks, which remains a separate problem.

[b] **Proof of Transfer (PoX).** Stacks' consensus mechanism: instead of consuming energy like traditional mining, participants commit real bitcoin to obtain the right to produce blocks. The spending of BTC creates an economic bond with Bitcoin and an incentive toward honesty. It is an original approach, but it must be distinguished from Bitcoin's security in the strict sense: it anchors consensus to an economic cost, it does not directly inherit the Layer 1's computing power.

Variant three: the sidechain with independent, economically anchored consensus. It is the Stacks model, with its Proof of Transfer[b]. Here the security comes not from merge mining but from an economic mechanism: to validate blocks on Stacks one must spend real bitcoin, and this creates a structural incentive toward honesty. The model is more sophisticated and in some respects more solid than plain merge mining, but here too the bitcoin peg between the two networks is managed by a distributed mechanism (the "stackers") that is an evolved form of federated custody. The centralization of the peg is reduced compared with Liquid, but not eliminated.

Variant four: the "decentralized" cross-chain bridge. It is the model many more recent projects have attempted, often with disastrous outcomes. The idea is that the peg is managed by a set of distributed validators, perhaps selected via staking, perhaps rotated periodically, so as to minimize trust in any single party. The recent history of the industry — from Wormhole to Ronin, from Multichain to Nomad — has shown that these models, **when implemented badly, are the most vulnerable of all**: cross-chain bridges have been the category of crypto infrastructure hardest hit by exploits in recent years, with cumulative losses in the billions of dollars. Building a genuinely trustless bridge between two blockchains with different consensus models is an extremely difficult technical problem, and no fully satisfactory solution has yet been implemented at scale.

TABLE 3.1 **THE FOUR SIDECHAIN VARIANTS AND THE DECISIVE QUESTION: WHO CONTROLS THE PEG?**

Variant	Example	Who controls the peg?
Federated	Liquid	An identified group of custodians (a federation)
Merge-mined	Rootstock	A federation, with security tied to Bitcoin miners
Independent consensus	Stacks	Stackers, with reduced but not eliminated custody
Cross-chain bridge	Recent projects	Distributed validators: historically the weakest point

All sidechain variants share the same underlying question: who holds custody of the locked bitcoin. The degree of trust required changes, but no solution entirely eliminates the custody problem. It is precisely this limit that explains why the rollup model represents a distinct family.

FIGURE 3.3 **THE FOUR SIDECHAIN VARIANTS, DISTINGUISHED BY THE DECISIVE QUESTION: WHO CONTROLS THE PEG?**

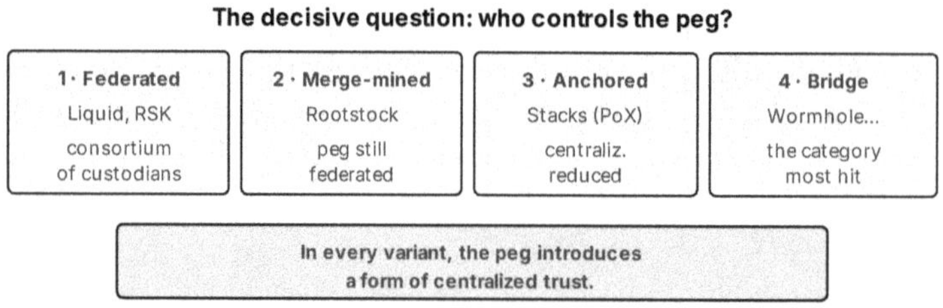

The word "sidechain" covers very different realities, separated by a single question: who holds the keys that unlock the bitcoin held in the peg? In the federated variant, the security is that of a consortium of companies; in merge mining it depends on the hashpower that actually joins, but the peg remains federated; in Stacks an economic incentive reduces — without eliminating — the centralization; "decentralized" cross-chain bridges promise to zero out trust but have been the category of infrastructure hardest hit by exploits. In every variant implemented so far, the peg introduces some form of centralized trust: it is the model's structural weak point.

To sum up. **Sidechains have the merit of offering full flexibility in functionality — they can have complex smart contracts, fast transactions, whatever their designer wants — but the structural flaw of depending on a peg mechanism that, in all its currently implemented variants, introduces some form of centralized trust.** This centralized trust is the model's weak point, and it is the reason the most rigorous part of the Bitcoin community regards sidechains as "altcoins that use bitcoin as an internal asset," rather than "true extensions of Bitcoin."

There is a formulation I like to use to clarify the difference, and that I would like to leave you with: **a sidechain borrows the Bitcoin brand, but builds on a security model of its own.** When the project goes well, the marketing says "anchored to Bitcoin"; when the project goes badly, users discover that the security was not Bitcoin's at all, but the far more fragile security of the federation or bridge that managed the peg. **The rollup, as we shall now see, attempts something profoundly different.**

⁂

3.4 — The Rollup Family: The Difference That Changes Everything

At this point we can address the third family, the one Bitcoin Hyper chose, and understand **why** it is structurally different from the other two. A rollup, as we anticipated in Chapter 2, looks at first sight like a sidechain: there is a separate blockchain executing transactions quickly, there is a mechanism for moving bitcoin back and forth, there is a representative token[a]. From the outside, the user experience can be almost identical. **But under the hood, the security model is radically different**, and this difference is the reason rollups are considered the natural evolution of sidechains rather than simply "another way of doing them."

The rollup's architectural principle can be summed up in one sentence worth memorizing: **a rollup does not ask Bitcoin to trust it; it gives Bitcoin the tools to verify it**[b]. Let us see what that means concretely.

---

[a] **Representative token.** A token that is worth, within the Layer 2, an equivalent amount of bitcoin deposited elsewhere. It allows the value of one's BTC to be used in a faster environment, without moving the original bitcoin. The decisive question is always the same: what guarantees that each token is really backed by a real bitcoin, and that it can be converted back whenever one wishes?

[b] **Verifying instead of trusting.** It is the principle that distinguishes a rollup from a sidechain. In a sidechain, the user must place confidence in whoever runs the system; in a rollup, at least in principle, anyone can independently check that the published state is correct, thanks to the data and the proofs made available. Personal trust is replaced by the possibility of verification: this is precisely the conceptual shift that makes rollups interesting for Bitcoin.

FIGURE 3.4 **SIDECHAIN AND ROLLUP: FROM TRUST IN CUSTODY TO CRYPTOGRAPHIC VERIFICATION.**

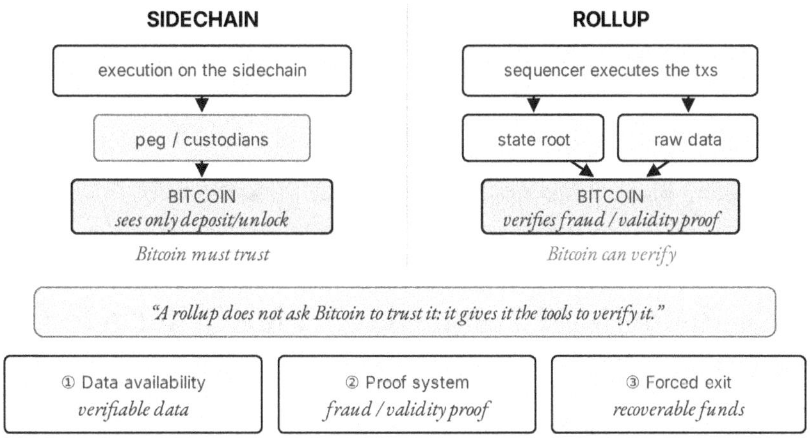

In a sidechain, the execution of transactions happens on the sidechain itself, and Bitcoin **does not know** what went on in there. Bitcoin knows only one thing: that at a certain point funds were deposited to the peg's address, and that at another certain point someone (the federation, the stackers, whoever it may be) will ask to unlock them. The verification of what happened inside the sidechain — of who paid whom, of how the tokens moved — is entrusted entirely to the sidechain itself and to whoever runs it. Bitcoin **has no way to verify** whether the sidechain acted honestly. It trusts.

In a rollup, things are different. The rollup executes transactions internally, yes, but then it does two things the sidechain does not do. **First**: it publishes on Bitcoin a compressed mathematical summary of everything that happened, a so-called "state root," which is a short string yet mathematically bound to every single transaction processed. **Second**: it publishes, somewhere (we will see where in the coming chapters — it is a delicate part), the **raw data** of the transactions, enough to allow anyone to recompute the state root and check whether it is correct.

At this point the architectural magic that distinguishes the rollup from the sidechain happens. **If the rollup's sequencer publishes a wrong state root** — because it cheated, because it made a mistake, for whatever reason — anyone in the world, reading the public data, can notice it and produce a **fraud proof** demonstrating the error. This proof is presented in a form the main blockchain is able to verify, and at that point the blockchain automatically rejects the wrong state root and punishes the sequencer. Or, if the rollup is of the **zero-knowledge** type, the sequencer directly publishes a mathematical proof demonstrating that the state root is correct, and that proof is verified immediately by the main blockchain, with no need for any challenge window.

In both cases — fraud proof or validity proof — **the trust is not in the sequencer, but in the mathematics and in the main blockchain**. The sequencer is not a custodian we ask to be honest; it is an executor we compel to demonstrate its own correctness, or to be publicly refuted by anyone able to do so. This is the fundamental philosophical difference, and it is the reason **a well-designed rollup inherits the security of the main blockchain structurally**, not "marketing-wise."

There is one more point to clarify before proceeding, because it is a subtlety that crypto marketing tends to obscure. **The rollup inherits the security of the main blockchain only if certain precise conditions are satisfied**, and if even one of these conditions fails, the rollup is no longer really a rollup but a sidechain in disguise.

The conditions are three, and they must be kept firmly in mind because they will return constantly throughout the rest of the book. **First condition**: the transaction data must be available and verifiable by anyone (the "data availability" problem we will see in Chapter 14). **Second condition**: there must be a working mechanism for producing and verifying proofs (fraud proofs or validity proofs, depending on the model). **Third condition**: there must be a "forced exit" mechanism allowing users to recover their funds even if the sequencer misbehaves or disappears.

If even one of these three conditions is missing, the rollup is not truly inheriting the security of the main blockchain: it is **declaring** that it does so without the technical structure to support the declaration. It is in this zone — between the declaration and the technical reality — that most serious evaluations of rollup projects are played out. Bitcoin Hyper, as we will see in the dedicated chapters, is explicitly addressing these three conditions in its most recent updates, but the level of maturity of each is different, and an honest evaluation must take that into account.

Note. The three conditions — data availability, a proof mechanism, and the possibility of forced exit — are not abstract formal requirements: they are the technical boundary that separates a real rollup from a sidechain that calls itself one. In the chapters devoted to Bitcoin Hyper, each condition will be taken up individually and assessed against its actual state of progress, always distinguishing what is declared from what is already operational and verifiable.

⁂

3.5 — The Head-to-Head Comparison: Five Criteria for Judging the Three Families

At this point we have described the three families. Let us place them side by side and compare them on precise criteria, because only in this way does it emerge clearly why Bitcoin Hyper chose the third. The criteria we will use are five, and they are the ones that, in my view, a serious investor or developer should always keep in mind when evaluating a Layer 2 project.

FIGURE 3.5 **FORKS, SIDECHAINS, AND ROLLUPS: THREE PHILOSOPHIES COMPARED ON FIVE CRITERIA.**

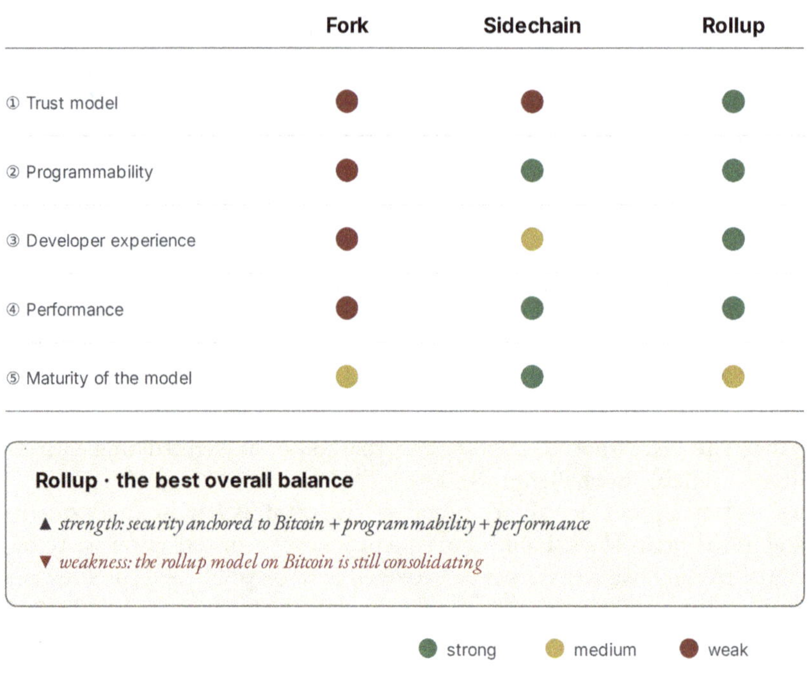

First criterion: the trust model. On whom does the security of your funds depend once you have deposited them into the system? For forks, it depends on the consensus of the forked network, which is typically much smaller and more attackable than that of the original Bitcoin. For sidechains, it depends on the consortium or federation managing the peg, which are identified companies with their jurisdictional vulnerabilities. For rollups, it depends — if the rollup is well designed — on the mathematics and on the main blockchain. **On this criterion, rollups win decisively, provided the three conditions we listed are actually satisfied.**

Second criterion: programmability. What can you build on the layer? Bitcoin forks with extended Script (such as Bitcoin Cash and Bitcoin SV) have limited smart contract capabilities, far from

Ethereum's or Solana's. Sidechains have full freedom to choose their own execution environment, and can be arbitrarily powerful. Rollups can do the same, choosing whatever execution environment they prefer — EVM, SVM, custom environments, anything. **On this criterion, sidechains and rollups are even, and forks lose.**

Third criterion: the developer experience. How easy is it for a developer to port their applications or build new ones? Forks with extended Script require working with a little-used programming language and immature tools. Sidechains with proprietary languages (such as Stacks' Clarity) require learning something new. Sidechains or rollups compatible with existing environments — EVM or SVM — allow the use of tools, libraries, communities, and applications that are already mature. **On this criterion, the projects that adopt an existing environment win, regardless of whether they are sidechains or rollups.** Bitcoin Hyper, by choosing the SVM, places itself in this category.

Fourth criterion: performance. How many transactions per second can be processed, and with what latency? The original Bitcoin does seven transactions per second. Bitcoin forks with bigger blocks can do a few dozen TPS. Sidechains depend on their internal architecture; some are fast, others less so. Rollups, if well implemented, can reach performance comparable to that of the fastest native blockchains, because execution happens outside the main blockchain and is therefore not limited by its speed. **On this criterion, optimized sidechains and well-designed rollups are even, and forks and the original Bitcoin lose.**

Fifth criterion: the maturity of the model. How consolidated is the model from a theoretical and practical standpoint? Bitcoin forks are conceptually simple and well understood, but their historical failure makes them a road hardly worth taking. Federated sidechains are conceptually simple and have worked in production for years, albeit with the compromises we have described. Rollups on Ethereum are by now a mature model, with years of operational experience. **Rollups on Bitcoin, by contrast, are still a model in a consolidation phase.** Bitcoin Hyper is exploring the model while building it, and this is a reality the investor must honestly acknowledge: **the first mover is not only the one who can reap the competitive advantage; it is also the one who bears the cost of discovering the problems not yet known.** On this criterion, one must distinguish between models consolidated on Ethereum (mature rollups) and models still in the research phase on Bitcoin (rollups still theoretical, at least in part).

Putting the five criteria together, a clear picture emerges. **Rollups are the model that, if well implemented, offers the best possible compromise**: a trust model similar to Bitcoin's, complete programmability, an excellent developer experience (if they adopt existing environments), high performance. Their weak point is the maturity of the model specifically for Bitcoin, and it is this weak point that projects like Bitcoin Hyper must confront over their three to five years of roadmap execution.

TABLE 3.2 **FORKS, SIDECHAINS, ROLLUPS: A SUMMARY COMPARISON**

Criterion	Fork	Sidechain	Rollup
Decentralization	Inherited from Bitcoin	Its own, often reduced	Inherited from Bitcoin
Security	Bitcoin's (partial, on a split chain)	Its own, independent	Bitcoin's, via cryptographic anchoring
Programmability	Does not increase	Maximal	Broad, constrained by the proof system
Liquidity	Fragments between original network and fork	Parallel and isolated	Shared through a cryptographic bridge
Cost of access	None: a new autonomous asset	Custodial or federated bridge	Trustless bridge (canonical bridge)

How to read it: *the rollup is the only model that simultaneously maintains Bitcoin's security and broad programmability. Sidechains give up inherited security; forks give up the cohesion of the ecosystem.*

⁂

3.6 — Bitcoin Hyper's Choice: A Rollup, with Honest Compromises

Having understood the three families, we can now place Bitcoin Hyper with precision. **Bitcoin Hyper declares itself a rollup, and architecturally it is one — with some compromises that it is important to recognize.** Let us look at the project's main traits through the lens of this chapter, anticipating some themes we will explore in the dedicated chapters.

Bitcoin Hyper executes transactions outside Bitcoin, on its own infrastructure based on the Solana Virtual Machine. Periodically, it anchors to Bitcoin a compressed state commitment, a mathematical "photograph" of the rollup's state. This is the first characteristic that distinguishes it from pure sidechains: **there is structured anchoring toward Bitcoin**, not a mere custody peg. We already introduced it in Chapter 2 and we will see it in detail in Chapters 11, 12, and 13 of Part IV.

FIGURE 3.6 **BITCOIN HYPER: ROLLUP ARCHITECTURE AND STATE OF MATURITY OF THE CRITICAL COMPONENTS.**

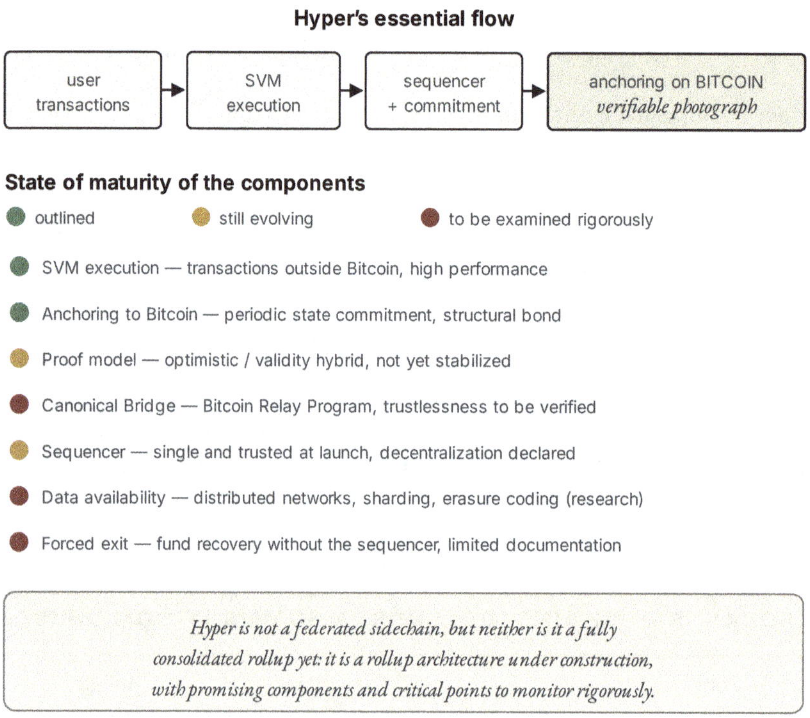

Bitcoin Hyper, the team declares, is exploring mechanisms both of the optimistic type (with fraud proofs) and of the zero-knowledge type (with validity proofs), in a hybrid combination the documentation calls "approaches inspired by both optimistic and validity-based rollups." The term "ZK rollup" used in the initial marketing has been progressively softened into more cautious formulations in recent updates. This is the second important characteristic: **the proof model is not yet fully defined**, and the investor should expect it to clarify progressively over the months and years to come.

As for the bridge between Bitcoin and Hyper — the critical point in any Layer 2 project — the team speaks of a non-custodial **Canonical Bridge** based on a Bitcoin Relay Program, a smart contract that verifies Bitcoin block headers and transaction proofs. This is the mechanism that should make it possible to deposit bitcoin onto Hyper and withdraw it without depending on a trusted federation. As we have hinted, **the actual level of trustlessness of the Canonical Bridge is one of the points on which the documentation is least detailed**, and where the investor's due diligence must be most rigorous. We will see the available details in Chapter 11.

As for sequencing, the team has explicitly declared that **it will launch with a single, trusted sequencer**, with a planned path toward the progressive decentralization of the sequencer. This is a pragmatic choice that recurs in many rollups at launch (Optimism and Arbitrum, too, had single sequencers for years), and it is an honest one if accompanied by a credible path toward distribution. The transparency with which the team communicated this point — a specific post in January 2026 devoted to future sequencing models — is a positive signal, but the actual path will have to be monitored over time.

On data availability — the first of the three conditions of a true rollup — the team published in March 2026 a document exploring the possible strategies, speaking of distributed data networks, erasure coding, sharding, cryptographic commitments. **Here too we are in the exploratory research phase, not in consolidated implementation.** It is an area where the project is writing its strategy in public, and where the specific choices will be decisive for the final security model.

On forced exit* — the third condition — the current documentation is the scarcest. There is no detailed mechanism for how users could recover their funds if the sequencer disappeared or misbehaved. This is probably the area where critical analysis must be most rigorous, and where the promises of "Bitcoin security" must be weighed with the greatest rigor. We will address it specifically in Chapter 21.

Summing up honestly. **Bitcoin Hyper is a rollup in its intentions and in its architectural setup, but it is a rollup under construction** where some of the central mechanisms — data availability, forced exit, sequencer decentralization — are still the subject of research and implementation. Calling it a "ZK rollup," as the more aggressive marketing does, is simplistic and partially misleading. Calling it a "federated sidechain," as some critics do, is unfair, because the architectural setup is different and the anchoring is structural. The correct description is **"a rollup in a consolidation phase, with optimistic and zero-knowledge elements still evolving, and with a declared path toward the progressive decentralization of all its critical components."** A description less seductive than the marketing, but closer to the documented reality.

* **Forced exit.** The mechanism which, in a rollup, should allow the user to recover their funds directly from Bitcoin even if the sequencer stops working or refuses to process their transactions. It is considered one of the guarantees that distinguish a "true" rollup from a sidechain: in its absence, the custody of funds remains in effect entrusted to the operator. For Bitcoin Hyper, as of this edition, it is stated as an objective but not yet detailed in the technical documentation.

⁂

3.7 — A Visual Map of the Architectural Choices

Before moving on to the FAQs, it is useful to leave you with a conceptual map you can keep in mind in the chapters ahead. **Think of the landscape of Bitcoin Layer 2s as a Cartesian plane with two axes.**

On the horizontal axis is **programmability**: on the left, the solutions with limited smart contract capabilities; on the right, those with complete capabilities. Lightning Network sits on the left (it does payments only). Sidechains with EVM or SVM sit on the right. Rollups like Hyper sit fully on the right (total programmability).

On the vertical axis is the **trust model**: at the bottom, the solutions that require trust in identified entities (federations, custodians, multisigs); at the top, those that depend only on the mathematics and on the main blockchain. Lightning sits high (its security depends on the channel's mathematics and on Bitcoin). Liquid sits low (it depends on the federation). Stacks and Rootstock sit in the middle (they reduce trust but do not eliminate it). Well-designed rollups on Ethereum sit very high. **Rollups on Bitcoin, today, sit in a variable zone**: high in their aspirations, in the middle in current reality, because some critical components of the security model are still under construction.

The top-right corner of the plane — high programmability, high trustlessness — is the industry's "grail": a solution that allows any complex application with the same security as the original Bitcoin. No project is fully there yet. **Bitcoin Hyper aspires to position itself in that corner**, and its evaluation depends on believing that the path from where it stands today to where it wants to arrive is credible, well designed, and achievable within the declared timeframe. This is, in the end, the question every investor must ask.

TABLE 3.3 **THE SOLUTIONS ON THE PROGRAMMABILITY / TRUST PLANE.**

Solution	Programmability	Trust model

Lightning	Limited (payments only)	High: depends on the channel's mathematics
Liquid	Partial	Low: depends on a federation
Stacks · Rootstock	Broad (EVM / SVM)	Intermediate: custody reduced but present
Bitcoin Hyper	Complete (SVM)	High, but some components still to be built

The "grail zone" is the top-right corner: high programmability and high trustlessness. No project fully occupies it yet. Bitcoin Hyper declares that it wants to position itself there, but its actual placement will depend on how far the critical components of the security model are built and verified.

FIGURE 3.2 **THE MAP OF ARCHITECTURAL CHOICES: PROGRAMMABILITY VERSUS TRUSTLESSNESS.**

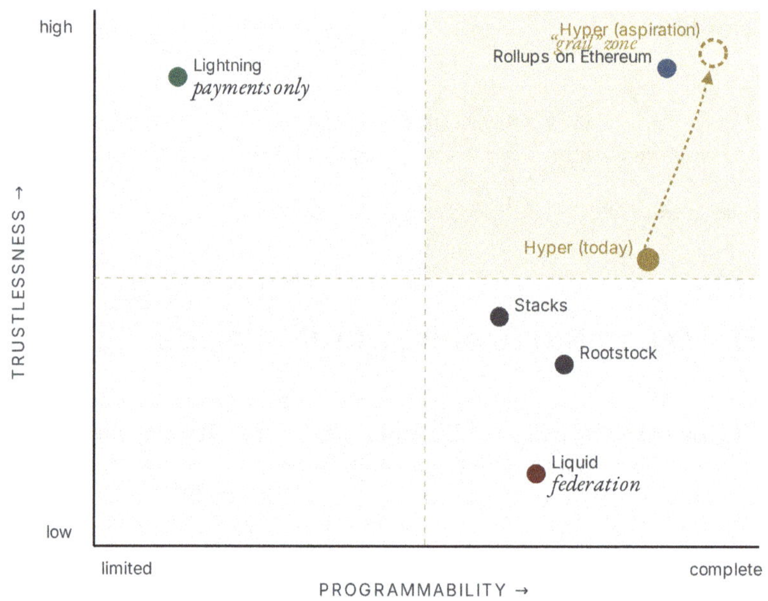

The plane crosses two axes: programmability (horizontal) and trust model (vertical). Lightning occupies the corner of pure security but without smart contracts; Liquid reaches programmability at the cost of a trusted federation; Stacks and Rootstock sit in the middle. The top-right corner — high programmability and high trustlessness — is the "grail" no project has yet fully reached. The distance between the solid dot (Hyper today) and the dashed dot (Hyper in its aspirations) is exactly what the investor is called upon to assess.

⁂

3.8 — Questions and Answers: Clarifying the Chapter's Concepts

Question 1: Why is Bitcoin Cash, which is a fork of Bitcoin, worth so much less than Bitcoin if it has more smart contract capability and bigger blocks?

Because the value of a blockchain does not come primarily from its technical capabilities, but from its **security network**, its **trust network**, and its **social network effect**. When Bitcoin Cash separated from Bitcoin in 2017, the majority of miners, developers, exchanges, services, and users stayed on the original chain. Bitcoin Cash found itself with a tiny fraction of all this, and therefore with enormously lower security (a 51% attack on Bitcoin Cash would cost orders of magnitude less than one on Bitcoin) and with enormously lower market appeal. **Technical capabilities are not enough if the critical mass of participants that gives them value is missing.** Concrete example: in 2024, at certain moments, the entire hashpower of Bitcoin Cash was equal to less than 1% of Bitcoin's. This means that, had someone wanted to attack Bitcoin Cash, they could have done so with a tiny investment compared with what would be needed for Bitcoin. **A blockchain with superior technical capabilities but inferior security is less valuable, not more valuable.**

Question 2: If Liquid is a federated sidechain and has all the problems you describe, why does it exist and why is it used?

Because in some use cases the compromise is acceptable. Liquid is used mainly by centralized exchanges and professional market makers for fast bitcoin transfers among themselves. For these actors, trusting Blockstream and its federated partners is a reasonable compromise: they already trust Blockstream for other things, and in exchange they get transfers much faster and more private than on-chain ones. **The problem with federated sidechains is not that they do not work technically: it is that they do not offer the security model many users think they have.** Concrete example: if you are a professional trader who needs to move 100 BTC between Coinbase and Kraken in a few minutes, Liquid is perfect for you. If you are an individual user who wants to hold their bitcoin definitively for the next twenty years, **Liquid is not what you are looking for**, and holding it in self-custody on the original Bitcoin is the right choice. The product is right for the right audience, wrong for the wrong one.

Question 3: What exactly does "fraud proof" mean, and how does it work in practice?

A fraud proof is a mechanism that allows anyone to **demonstrate mathematically** that a rollup's sequencer committed fraud by publishing an incorrect state commitment. It works as follows. The sequencer publishes a state root, declaring "here is the rollup's state after executing these transactions." Anyone in the world can take the raw transaction data (which must be publicly available — this is the data availability condition), re-execute the transactions in their own copy of the system, compute the real state root, and compare it with the published one. If they differ, that person can construct a fraud proof — a small piece of data pinpointing exactly the point of divergence — and publish it on the main blockchain. The main blockchain then verifies the fraud proof (a much simpler operation than re-executing all the transactions), and if the fraud proof is valid, it rejects the sequencer's state commitment and applies an economic penalty to it. Concrete example: this is exactly the mechanism Optimism uses on Ethereum. The time window for publishing a fraud proof is seven days; if no one raises objections within those seven days, the state commitment is considered final. It is the reason why, on Optimism, withdrawing funds to Ethereum requires a seven-day wait.

Question 4: And what does "validity proof" mean, and how does it differ from the fraud proof?

The validity proof is the "mathematically assertive" version of the fraud proof. Instead of giving anyone the chance to refute the sequencer after the fact, the sequencer is required to provide in advance a mathematical proof — typically a zk-SNARK or a zk-STARK — demonstrating that the state commitment is correct. This proof is verified immediately by the main blockchain, and if it is valid, the state commitment is final on the spot, with no challenge window whatsoever. **The merit is immediate finality.** The flaw is the technical complexity: producing validity proofs at scale is computationally expensive, and designing systems that do so efficiently is one of the industry's most active research frontiers. Concrete example: zkSync and Starknet on Ethereum are ZK-rollups. On zkSync, withdrawing funds to Ethereum typically takes a few hours (the time the sequencer needs to produce the proof and have it verified), not seven days as on Optimism. For applications where fast finality is critical — for example in exchanges between protocols — this difference is enormous. Bitcoin Hyper, according to the current documentation, is exploring a combination of the two families, but the implementation detail is not yet fully public.

Question 5: If rollups on Ethereum are already mature, why not simply build an Ethereum rollup that uses bitcoin as its asset?

In fact, projects doing something similar exist, and Bitcoin Hyper itself has traits that move in this direction (the $HYPER token is an ERC-20 on Ethereum, remember?). But building "an Ethereum rollup that uses bitcoin" means having **two security dependencies**: Ethereum's security (for the rollup model) and the security of the bridge between Bitcoin and Ethereum (to bring the bitcoin into the system). This is in some ways worse than building a rollup directly on Bitcoin, because it adds one more point of fragility. The philosophy of a Bitcoin-centric project is to **minimize external dependencies**, ideally having Bitcoin as the only source of security. Concrete example: a rollup like Arbitrum hosting "wrapped Bitcoin" (WBTC) inherits Ethereum's security for internal operations, but the value of the WBTC depends on the custody of the BitGo consortium, which is a centralized federation. The cumulative risk is the sum of the two risks. Bitcoin Hyper aspires to be "Bitcoin all the way down," even if in practice the transitional ERC-20 still introduces a temporary dependence on Ethereum.

Question 6: Summing up, how do I judge whether a Bitcoin Layer 2 project I come across is a "true rollup," a "sidechain in disguise," or a "camouflaged fork"?

The key questions to ask are five, and they correspond to the criteria we have seen. **One**: where are the state commitments anchored, and with what cadence? If it anchors nothing on Bitcoin, it is a sidechain. If it anchors something, let us see what kind of anchoring. **Two**: who controls the bridge between Bitcoin and the Layer 2? If it is a federation, it is a federated sidechain. If it is a verifiable cryptographic mechanism, it can be a true rollup. **Three**: is the transaction data publicly available so that anyone can verify the state? If not, data availability is missing and the rollup is merely nominal. **Four**: does an implemented and operational fraud proof or validity proof mechanism exist? If not, the security model is not that of a rollup. **Five**: what happens if the sequencer disappears? Does a forced exit mechanism exist? If not, users depend on the sequencer to recover their funds, and the rollup is not really trustless. Concrete example: apply these five questions to Bitcoin Hyper, today, and you will get partial answers — the project is working on all five points, but not all of them are yet fully implemented. Apply them to Liquid and you will get clear but not very reassuring answers — it is a federated sidechain, and honestly so. Apply them to any new project you come across tomorrow, and you will get the real picture of its security model, regardless of what the marketing says.

⁂

3.9 — WHAT TO TAKE AWAY FROM THIS CHAPTER

There are three main families of solutions for extending Bitcoin: forks, sidechains, and rollups. Each has a distinct philosophy and produces very different results in terms of security model, programmability, and user experience.

Forks modify Bitcoin directly, and in practice produce separate blockchains. They have failed historically as an extension strategy, because the Bitcoin community rejects radical hard forks and because the split networks lose the critical mass of security and adoption that gives the original network its value.

Sidechains are blockchains parallel to Bitcoin, connected through a peg. They work and are in production, but in all their currently implemented variants they depend on some form of centralized trust in the peg mechanism, be it a federation of companies or an independent consensus with compromises.

Rollups are the most mature and architecturally solid Layer 2 model. They are distinguished from sidechains because they execute outside Bitcoin but anchor state commitments to Bitcoin in a structured way, and because their security model depends on mathematics and on the main blockchain, not on identified custodians.

A rollup is truly such only if it satisfies three conditions: data availability, the existence of proofs (fraud or validity), and a forced exit mechanism. If even one of these is missing, the project is a rollup in name but a sidechain in disguise in fact.

Bitcoin Hyper declares itself a rollup and is set up as one architecturally, but it is in a consolidation phase where some critical components are still in research or implementation. An honest evaluation recognizes both the project's ambition and the distance between the marketing promises and the current technical maturity.

Judging any Bitcoin Layer 2 project takes five criteria: trust model, programmability, developer experience, performance, maturity of the model. Applying them systematically protects against marketing confusion and makes it possible to position every project relative to the others objectively.

Chapter 3 ends here. We have built a solid conceptual map of the three families of Layer 2 solutions for Bitcoin, and we have understood why Hyper places itself specifically in the rollup family, with all the merits and uncertainties that follow. In ***Chapter 4 — Anatomy of a Rollup: The Four Components Every Rollup Must Have****, we will go inside the rollup model to understand how it is structurally made: execution, sequencing, settlement, data availability. These are the four pillars that will return constantly throughout the rest of the book, and understanding well what each one does is the basis for all the technical chapters to come.*

Forks, sidechains, rollups: three roads for extending *Bitcoin*

Only the rollup tries to build **on top of** Bitcoin without breaking it and without relying on central custody. Three families, **three different trust models**.

1 How to make Bitcoin do more? The same question, three answers

Fork
We modify Bitcoin. If the network does not accept, a new chain is born.

Sidechain
We place a chain beside Bitcoin. A parallel chain uses BTC represented through a peg.

Rollup
We build on top of Bitcoin. Fast execution outside, verifiable results on Bitcoin.

The same question, three philosophies: **three different trust models** *— not three names for the same thing.*

2 Fork: changing Bitcoin means risking a split

Original Bitcoin — existing rules < **Fork** — new rules, new asset, new community

Soft fork
more restrictive, backward-compatible rules · e.g. SegWit, Taproot.

Hard fork
incompatible rules: if not everyone upgrades, the network splits.

(!) A hard fork does not extend Bitcoin: **it creates an autonomous variant.** Changing Bitcoin radically almost always means leaving it.

3 Sidechain: more flexibility, but trust in the peg

BTC locked on Bitcoin L1 → **peg / bridge** → **Sidechain** (representative token (L-BTC / RBTC / sBTC)) → **BTC unlocked**

The central question: who controls the keys of the peg? — a representative token is not native BTC

Federated
a consortium controls the peg.

Merge-mined
the miners participate, the peg is often separate.

Anchored (PoX)
it reduces trust, it does not eliminate it.

Cross-chain bridges
flexible, but historically exposed to exploits.

4 Rollup: execution outside, verification on Bitcoin

Rollup / L2 — EXECUTION: user transactions · sequencer · fast execution · updated state · state root

↓ ANCHORING ↓

₿ Bitcoin L1 — SETTLEMENT: commitment · immutability · verifiable reference · final settlement

1 Data Availability
available, verifiable data.

2 Proof system
fraud proof or validity proof.

3 Forced exit
recovering the funds even if the sequencer censors.

The rollup does not ask Bitcoin to trust: **it gives it tools to verify**. *Without these three conditions, it is only* **a sidechain in disguise**.

5 Where Bitcoin Hyper sits: a rollup under construction

users → transactions → SVM → sequencer → state commitment → ₿ Bitcoin

Better defined
SVM execution · periodic anchoring · rollup architecture · Solana dev experience

Evolving
proof system · data availability · sequencer decentralization · Canonical Bridge · forced exit

To be evaluated rigorously
effective trustlessness · audits · documentation · observability · behavior on mainnet

Hyper is not a federated sidechain, **but neither is it an already fully consolidated rollup**: *it is a rollup under construction.*

THE KEY POINT

Forks, sidechains, and rollups are not three names for the same thing. The **fork** breaks Bitcoin's continuity; the **sidechain** introduces trust in the peg; the **rollup** builds on top of Bitcoin with a **verifiable** bond with the Layer 1. Bitcoin Hyper chooses this third road, but its credibility will depend on data availability, proofs, bridge, forced exit, and progressive decentralization — not on the name used in the marketing.

PART II

The Rollup Model Applied to Bitcoin

If Bitcoin cannot be modified, one must build on top of it. This is the story of an idea that starts from a 2015 whitepaper, passes through the maturation of the rollup model on Ethereum, and arrives at the architecture proposed by Bitcoin Hyper.

PART II · THE ROLLUP MODEL APPLIED TO BITCOIN

Chapter 4
Anatomy of a Rollup

The four components every rollup must have

⁂

4.1 — Why an Anatomy Is Needed

In the three preceding chapters we built the context. We know why Bitcoin is limited, we know why any extension must be built on top of it without modifying it, we know why the rollup model is the one that today represents the most solid architectural compromise. Now, however, comes the moment to take this "rollup model" apart piece by piece, to see what it really contains. **Without this operation, all the chapters that follow would become a sequence of technicalities without a frame of reference.** With this operation, instead, every technical detail we encounter from here on will find its place on a map we already know.

FIGURE 4.1 **THE FOUR COMPONENTS OF A ROLLUP**

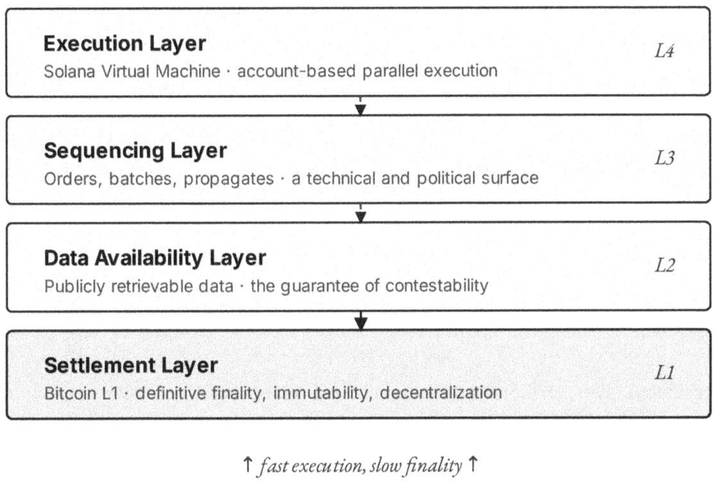

How to read it: *the rollup is a modular stack. The execution layer is fast and flexible, the sequencing orders, the data availability guarantees public verifiability, the settlement anchors everything to Bitcoin. The separation of roles is what makes it possible to scale without sacrificing Bitcoin's fundamental properties.*

The idea of this chapter is simple: **there is a structure common to all rollups**, regardless of whether they are built on Ethereum or on Bitcoin, whether they use the EVM or the SVM, whether they are optimistic or zero-knowledge. That structure has four components, and each has a precise role. Understanding the four components means understanding, in one stroke, 80% of what there is to know about any existing or future rollup. It is like learning human anatomy: once you know where the heart, the lungs, the stomach, and the brain are, any medical textbook you read afterward will have a point of reference to latch onto.

The four components are: **execution**, **sequencing**, **settlement**, and **data availability**. We will use these four names constantly in the chapters that follow, so it is worth introducing them with care, understanding what each does, understanding how they talk to one another, and understanding why every serious rollup — including Bitcoin Hyper — must solve the specific problems of each of them. I begin with a concrete image that helps me hold everything together, and that I will propose you carry forward as a mental reference for the whole book.

⁂

4.2 — The Logistics Company Metaphor

Imagine an international logistics company that has to handle thousands of shipments a day between different cities. This company cannot, for obvious reasons, record every single movement of every parcel directly in the government's official registries: it would be too slow, too costly, and the government offices simply would not know where to put all that stuff. But at the same time, at the end of the day, the company must be able to demonstrate that what it did was done correctly, and customers must have the certainty that their parcels reached their destination and were not lost or stolen.

How does such a company organize itself? Typically with a four-level structure. **First level: there is a central warehouse where the parcels are actually worked**: opened, checked, sorted, repacked, shipped. It is the place of concrete physical action, where things happen. **Second level: there is a logistics coordinator** who decides in what order to process the parcels, which trucks leave first, which routes to use, how to manage priorities. It is the organizational mind that makes the operational decisions moment by moment. **Third level: there is an administrative office that, periodically, prepares a summary of everything that has been done** and presents it to the government notary for official registration. It does not bring him all the details — that would be needlessly verbose — but a signed summary certifying the overall results of the day. **Fourth level: there is a company archive where the detailed records of every single shipment are kept**, accessible to anyone entitled to them: the customers who want to track their parcels, the inspectors who want to check the company's work, the notary himself who in turn might want to check the specific entries of the summary he registered.

These four levels are called, in the rollup world: the **execution layer** (the warehouse), the **sequencing layer** (the coordinator), the **settlement layer**[1] (the notary), and the **data availability layer**[2] (the archive). They are exactly the four parts that make up any well-designed rollup. If even one of the four is missing, the system does not work or works badly: without the warehouse, no work gets done; without the coordinator, chaos; without the notary, no official proof; without the archive, no possibility of independent verification.

---

[1] **Settlement layer (the notary).** The level that periodically anchors onto Bitcoin the fingerprint of the rollup's state (the state root), making its conclusions verifiable and hard to alter. It does not execute the transactions: it records their seal on the base layer.

[2] **Data availability layer (the archive).** The level that keeps the raw transaction data publicly retrievable, so that anyone can recompute the state and contest it if wrong. Without this data, independent verification is not possible, even when the seal is correctly anchored.

FIGURE 4.1 **THE LOGISTICS COMPANY METAPHOR AND THE FOUR LEVELS OF THE ROLLUP.**

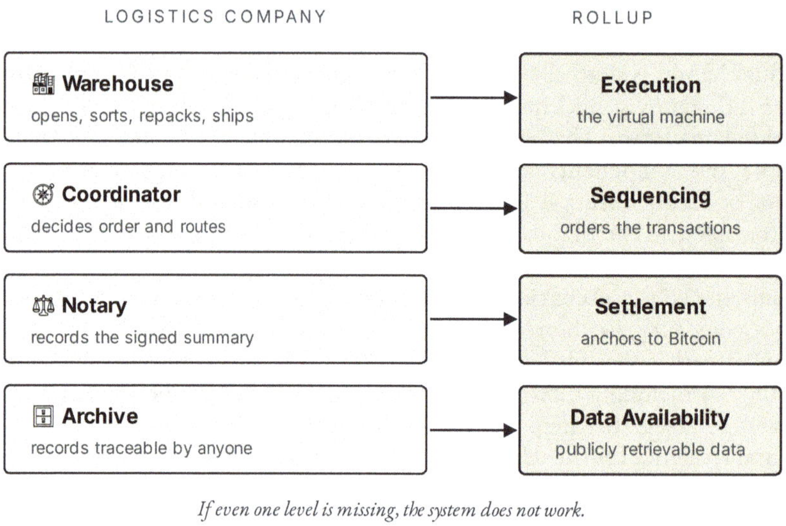

Every function of the logistics company corresponds to a component of the rollup. The warehouse, where the parcels are worked, is the execution layer; the coordinator who decides order and routes is the sequencing; the notary who records the signed summary is the settlement, which anchors the results to Bitcoin; the archive consultable by anyone is the data availability layer. The metaphor holds for the whole book: faced with a technical detail, it is enough to ask which of the four levels it belongs to.

Keep this image in mind, because we will use it repeatedly. Every time you get confused about where a certain technical detail sits in the architecture, **ask yourself: is this a warehouse thing, a coordinator thing, a notary thing, or an archive thing?** The answer will orient you immediately. Now let us go into the individual components, one at a time.

⁂

4.3 — The First Component: The Execution Layer, or the Warehouse

The execution level is the place where transactions are actually processed. Every rollup needs a computational environment capable of taking an incoming transaction, reading the current state of the system, applying the changes the transaction requires, and producing the next state. This computational environment has a technical name — the **virtual machine**[*] — and it is the heart of the rollup, because it is where the applications actually live and where everything users perceive as "activity" on the network happens.

The choice of the virtual machine is one of the most important architectural decisions for any rollup, and we already touched on it in Chapter 2 when we discussed Bitcoin Hyper's choice of the SVM. Let us recall the essential points. The virtual machine is essentially a language: it defines what can be done and how. Ethereum's EVM is a serial, single-threaded language, rich in historical compromises but with an enormous developer ecosystem. Solana's SVM is a parallel language, optimized for performance, with a smaller but more modern ecosystem. Other virtual machines exist — Move, CosmWasm, and others still — each with its merits and flaws, but EVM and SVM are today the two great families into which the industry divides.

To understand concretely what the execution layer[‖] of a rollup does, let us take an example. Suppose Alice wants to send 100 units of a certain token[¶] to Bob, within a rollup. The transaction Alice signs and sends contains a few essential pieces of information: who the sender is, who the recipient is, which token, how much. When this transaction reaches the execution layer, the virtual machine does several things in sequence. **It verifies Alice's signature**[†] to make sure it is really she who is sending the transaction and not someone else passing themselves off as her. **It reads Alice's balance in the current state**[‡] of the rollup to check that she actually has 100 units of that token. **It subtracts 100 from Alice's balance and adds 100 to Bob's balance**, writing the new state. **It records the event** so that any applications or users can see it. All of this happens in milliseconds, and produces a new result: the rollup's state has changed, there is a new version of the ledger reflecting the payment that occurred.

This example is simple, but the same operations apply to arbitrarily complex transactions. If Alice is not simply sending tokens to Bob but is interacting with a smart contract[§] — say, depositing collateral into a lending protocol — the sequence is the same, only more articulated. The virtual machine verifies the signature, reads the state, executes the contract's code (which in turn can read and write other pieces of state), produces the new state. **The execution layer is the mind that runs the applications**, and its speed and capacity define what can be built on the rollup.

---

[*] **Virtual machine.** The computing environment that executes the rollup's transactions and programs: it takes the current state, applies the requested changes, and produces the next state. Different families exist — for example EVM and SVM — which define different languages and performance.

[†] **Digital signature.** Every transaction is signed with the sender's private key; anyone can then verify its validity with the corresponding public key, without knowing the private key. It is this that guarantees that only the owner of the funds can dispose of them, and that the signature is valid only for that specific transaction.

[‡] **State.** By "state" we mean the set of all the balances and application data at a given moment: a sort of photograph of the ledger. Every valid transaction modifies it, producing a new version; it is a compact synthesis of this state (the state root) that the rollup periodically anchors to Bitcoin.

[§] **Smart contract.** A program recorded on the network that automatically executes pre-established rules when it receives a transaction (for example locking collateral or issuing a loan). For the virtual machine it is a transaction like any other, only more articulated.

‖ **Execution layer.** The component of the rollup that concretely processes the transactions: it reads the state, applies the rules, computes the new state. It is the "mind" that runs the applications, distinct from the levels that order the transactions, make them available, and anchor them to Bitcoin.

¶ **Token.** A unit of digital value recorded and transferable on the network, whose balance is held in the system's state. In the example it represents what Alice transfers to Bob; more generally, tokens are the objects on which the rollup's applications operate.

Note. The "read, modify, record" sequence described in the example is deliberately simplified. In a real environment every step is accompanied by additional checks — verification of authorizations, computation of fees, error handling, and cancellation of the entire operation if a single phase fails. Atomicity, that is, the principle by which a transaction is executed in full or not executed at all, is what prevents inconsistent intermediate states and is an essential property of any execution layer.

FIGURE 4.2 **HOW THE EXECUTION LAYER PROCESSES A TRANSACTION: THE EXAMPLE OF ALICE AND BOB.**

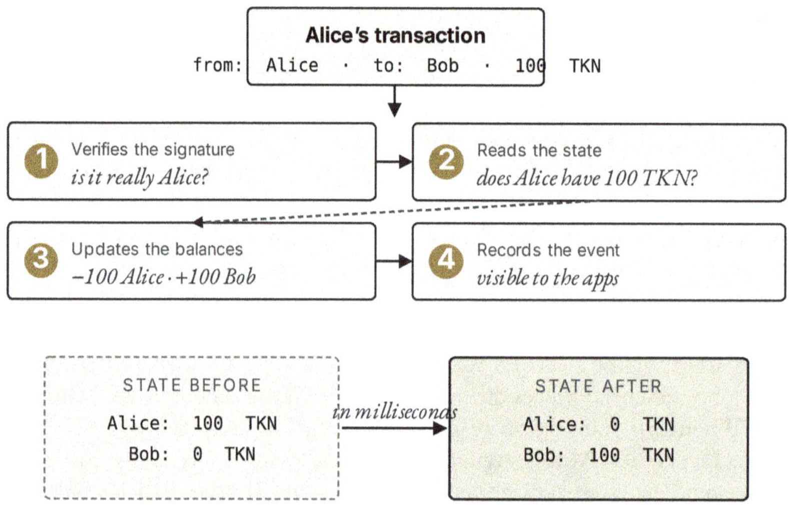

The virtual machine takes Alice's signed transaction and performs four operations in sequence: it verifies the signature, reads the state to check the balance, updates the balances by subtracting from one and adding to the other, and records the event so the applications can see it. The result is a new state of the rollup — a new version of the ledger reflecting the payment. The same sequence holds for arbitrarily complex transactions: only the code executed at the intermediate step changes.

For Bitcoin Hyper, as we have seen, the execution layer is based on the SVM. This means the applications are written in Rust or C, compiled into BPF format (an efficient binary format), and run on a runtime that allows parallel execution through the declared-accounts model. **In theory, this should allow Hyper to reach higher performance than an EVM rollup**, although in practice the actual performance will depend on the specific implementation and will have to be measured when the system is operational at scale. The team explicitly mentioned, in a post of November 2025, that the publication of realistic benchmarks is one of its declared transparency objectives. We will see in the coming chapters which variables contribute to a rollup's actual performance, and how the numbers should be read when they arrive.

There is a subtle aspect of the execution layer worth touching on already now, even though we will explore it in Chapter 10: the problem of **determinism**. A rollup's virtual machine must have a non-negotiable property: given the same input, it must always produce the same output, regardless of who is running it, on what hardware, at what moment. It sounds obvious put like that, but when working with parallel execution and high performance, guaranteeing perfect determinism is one of the hardest engineering challenges. **Without perfect determinism, the rollup cannot be verified independently**, and therefore the entire security model we described in Chapter 3 collapses. Bitcoin Hyper devoted a specific post to this problem (December 2025) precisely because the SVM, being parallel, needs additional measures to guarantee the determinism that the EVM, being serial, has automatically. It is a technical detail that becomes important later on.

⁂

4.4 — The Second Component: The Sequencing Layer, or the Coordinator

Once we have a warehouse capable of processing transactions, we need someone to decide **in what order** the transactions enter the warehouse. It sounds trivial, but it is one of the most consequential decisions in a rollup, and for this reason we will address it in depth in Chapter 15. For now, it is enough to understand what the sequencing layer does and why it exists.

Let us think about what happens in a system with thousands of users sending transactions simultaneously from all over the world. Transactions reach the rollup in different orders depending on who sent them, from where, through which network path. Without a centralized ordering mechanism, two users could see the same transactions in different orders, and therefore compute different final states. **Someone must decide a canonical order, and this order must be the same for everyone.** That someone is the sequencer.

Concretely, the sequencer[a] does three things. **It receives the transactions** from users and their wallets. **It orders them into a canonical sequence**[b] according to certain criteria (typically by time of arrival, but it can also take into account the fees offered or other rules). **It groups them into batches**[c] which are passed to the execution layer to be processed. From the outside, the sequencer is the point of contact between the world of users and the internal world of the rollup: it is there that transactions "enter" the system.

The sequencer has enormous power, and here lies the delicate part. By ordering the transactions, it can **favor** some over others. It can **censor** transactions it does not like simply by not including them. It can **extract value** from advance knowledge of incoming transactions, a practice known as MEV (Maximal Extractable Value) which has generated an entire strand of research and practice in the industry. All of these are possibilities that depend on who controls the sequencer and under what rules it operates.

---

[a] **Sequencer.** The component that receives incoming transactions and fixes their official order before they are executed. It is a powerful role: whoever controls it decides which transactions enter and in what sequence. In most rollups it is initially run by the team, with decentralization planned over time.

[b] **Canonical sequence.** The single ordering of transactions considered valid by the whole network. It is needed because, receiving transactions in different orders, different nodes would compute different states: a shared order guarantees that everyone arrives at the same result.

[c] **Batch.** A group of already-ordered transactions that the sequencer passes together to the execution layer for processing and, subsequently, for anchoring. Grouping them reduces costs and makes publication on Bitcoin more efficient.

Note. MEV (Maximal Extractable Value) is not a phenomenon exclusive to rollups: it exists on any blockchain in which one actor decides the order of transactions, and on networks like Ethereum it has given rise to a genuine market. In the chapters devoted to the sequencer we will see how the initial centralization of this role — common to nearly all rollups at launch — is a point of attention to be weighed together with the decentralization roadmap declared by the project.

FIGURE 4.3 **THE SEQUENCER: WHAT IT DOES, WHAT POWER IT HAS, AND WHAT LIMIT IT CANNOT CROSS.**

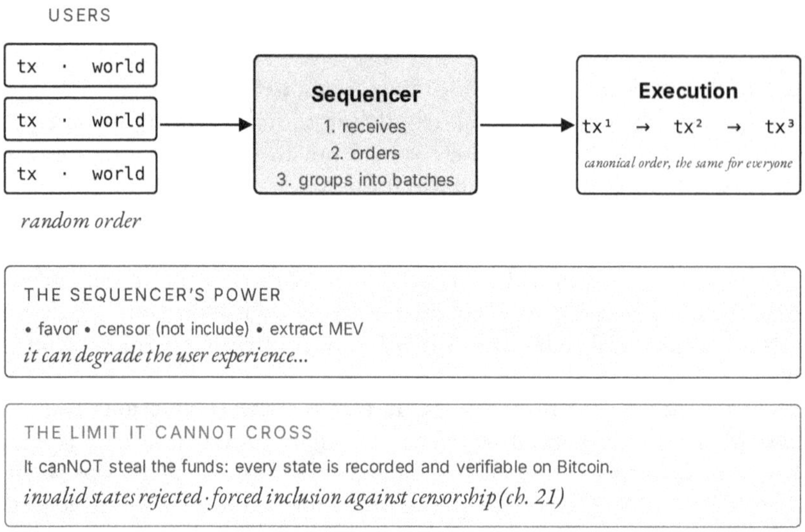

The sequencer receives the transactions arriving in random order from all over the world, orders them into a canonical sequence that is the same for everyone, and groups them into batches for the execution layer. This role gives it real power — it can favor, censor, extract MEV — but it meets a limit it cannot cross: it cannot steal the funds, because every state it produces is recorded and verifiable on Bitcoin. It is the distinction that separates a rollup from a federated sidechain: the sequencer is a service provider that can degrade the experience, not a custodian that can take the money.

As we already hinted in Chapter 3, most rollups today start with a **single sequencer**, run by the team developing the project. It is a pragmatic choice: a single sequencer is simple, fast, predictable, and allows the team to iterate rapidly on features without having to coordinate a distributed system. Optimism, Arbitrum, Base have all operated with a single sequencer for years, and in some cases continue to do so. **Bitcoin Hyper will do the same at launch**, with a single sequencer run by the core team, and with a planned path toward progressive decentralization in the months and years that follow.

This initial centralization of the sequencer is one of the points at which critics of rollups often point their finger, and it must be addressed honestly. Yes, a single sequencer is a point of centralization. Yes, in principle the sequencer could censor or manipulate. But — and this is the crucial point — **the sequencer cannot steal users' funds**, because everything it does is recorded on the main blockchain and independently verifiable. If the sequencer produced invalid states, the system would reject them; if it censored transactions in an evident way, users could theoretically force inclusion through forced inclusion mechanisms (a topic we will see in Chapter 21). **The sequencer is a service provider that can degrade the user experience, not a custodian that can steal the funds.** This distinction is crucial, and it separates rollups from federated sidechains, where the custodian of the peg actually can steal the funds.

That said, **the decentralization of the sequencer remains an important objective**, and serious rollups are actively working to get there. The possible strategies are various — rotating leadership, auctions of sequencing rights, validator committees, systems based on BLS or other cryptographic schemes — and Bitcoin Hyper is exploring them in the research phase. We will return to this in Chapter 17.

⁂

4.5 — The Third Component: The Settlement Layer, or the Notary

We come to the third component, the one that gives the rollup its fundamental property: the bond with the main blockchain. The settlement layer is the point where the rollup "presents itself to the notary" and has the results of its work officially registered. For Bitcoin Hyper, the notary is Bitcoin. For

Ethereum's rollups, the notary is Ethereum. In both cases, the function is the same: **to make the rollup's state commitments immutable and publicly verifiable**, leveraging the security of the main blockchain.

The conceptual operation is the one we already introduced in the preceding chapters, but now we can look at it with more precision. Periodically — the cadence is a variable we will see in Chapter 13 — the rollup takes the current state of its system and computes a compressed mathematical summary of it. This summary is called the **state root**, and it is a string of 32 bytes (256 bits) that is mathematically bound, through a Merkle tree,* to every single datum of the rollup's state. Changing even a single bit of the state would completely change the state root: it means the state root is a unique, unforgeable fingerprint of the state.

This state root is then published on the main blockchain through a special transaction. For Bitcoin Hyper, the team is exploring several publication modes — OP_RETURN,† Taproot‡, timelocked structures — which we will explore in Chapter 12. All these modes share the purpose of **inserting the state root into Bitcoin's immutable data**, so that from that moment on it is impossible to modify it retroactively without rewriting all of the subsequent Bitcoin blockchain, a practically impossible operation.

---

* **Merkle tree.** A data structure that summarizes a large set of information in a single final fingerprint, combining the data in pairs and repeating the operation up to the top. The apex of this tree is the state root: comparing it is enough to know whether even a single datum has changed, without having to walk through the entire state.

† **OP_RETURN.** An instruction that allows a small amount of arbitrary data to be attached to a Bitcoin transaction, without that data representing spendable funds. It is one of the most direct ways to anchor an external piece of information — such as a rollup's state root — into the chain, leaving a permanent trace of it.

‡ **Taproot.** An upgrade of the Bitcoin protocol activated in 2021, which introduces more flexible signatures and greater efficiency and privacy in transactions. It also offers richer ways to insert and structure data anchored to the chain, and for this reason it is listed among the technical avenues through which a rollup can publish its state root on Bitcoin.

Once the state root is anchored on Bitcoin, **the rollup's state is crystallized**. Everything that happened before the state root is final: no one can go back, modify the transactions, alter the balances. The rollup inherits, on that specific state root, Bitcoin's immutability. And that is exactly what we want: the speed of the rollup combined with the finality of Bitcoin.

FIGURE 4.4 **THE SETTLEMENT LAYER: BITCOIN AS NOTARY, AND THE DISTINCTION BETWEEN IMMUTABILITY AND CORRECTNESS.**

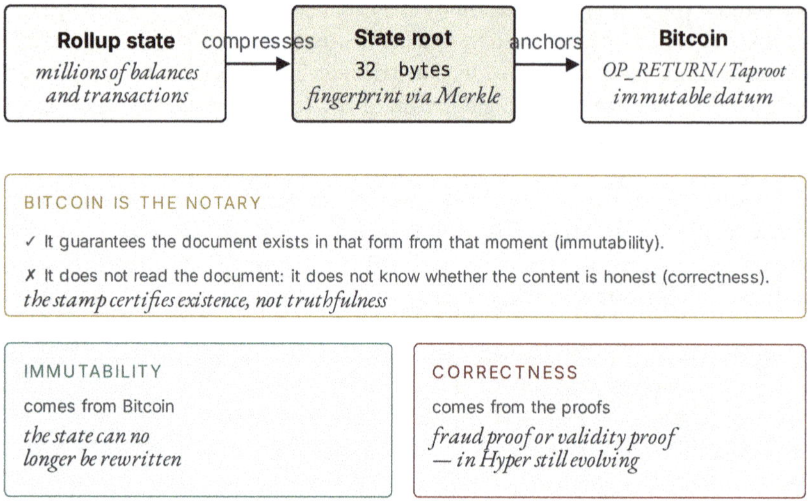

Periodically the rollup compresses its state into a 32-byte state root and anchors it to Bitcoin through a special transaction. From that moment the state is crystallized. But Bitcoin is a notary who applies the stamp without reading the document: it guarantees that the state root exists in that form — immutability — not that the content is honest. Correctness comes from another source, the proof mechanism. Confusing the two is the ambiguity that less transparent marketing leverages when it declares "Bitcoin security" meaning only immutability; in Hyper the proof model is still evolving.

There is, however, an important point that must be grasped well, because it distinguishes true settlement from apparent settlement. **Bitcoin, by anchoring a state root, does not know whether that state root is correct.** It anchors a datum, yes, but it does not verify that the datum actually corresponds to a legitimate execution of the transactions. Bitcoin is the notary who puts the stamp on the document, but does not read the document to check whether the content is truthful. The stamp guarantees that the document exists in that form from that moment; it does not guarantee that the content is honest.

From this observation follows the need for the proof mechanism — fraud proof or validity proof — which we discussed in Chapter 3. **Bitcoin guarantees immutability, but correctness comes from elsewhere**: from the mathematics of cryptographic proofs or from anyone's ability to raise a fraud proof. **The settlement layer alone is not enough; it must be accompanied by a validity mechanism.** It is the point where the marketing of the less honest projects tends to be most ambiguous: they declare "Bitcoin security" implying immutability, while neglecting to specify that correctness depends on other mechanisms that might not yet be fully operational.

In the case of Bitcoin Hyper, as we have already anticipated, the proof model is still evolving. The team speaks of "approaches inspired by both optimistic and validity-based rollups," which means the definitive system will combine fraud proofs and validity proofs in ways that will be clarified over the coming months of development. This hybridity is interesting and potentially powerful, but it is also an area where the technical documentation must mature further before it can give definitive answers.

⁂

4.6 — The Fourth Component: The Data Availability Layer, or the Archive

We come to the last of the four components, and perhaps the subtlest, because it is the one many people — even insiders — tend to underestimate. The data availability layer is the archive where the **raw data** of the rollup's transactions is kept, not just their compressed summaries. Without this archive, the rollup's security model collapses, even if all the other components work perfectly. Let us see why.

Let us recall what the settlement layer does: it anchors the state root* on Bitcoin. A state root is a string of 32 bytes. But to **verify** that this state root is correct — a crucial operation for the rollup's security model — one must have the data of the transactions that led to that state root. **Without the raw data, one cannot recompute the state root and compare it with the one anchored on Bitcoin.** Without this possibility of comparison, no one can notice if the sequencer† has published a wrong state root.

In other words: the raw transaction data is **the raw material of verification**. Without it, even if in theory a fraud proof‡ or validity proof§ mechanism existed, no one could use it concretely because the basic information would be missing. **Data availability is the precondition of everything else.**

The problem, and here lies the technical difficulty, is that the raw transaction data of an active rollup is **a lot**. Thousands of transactions per second mean gigabytes of data per day. Publishing all this data directly on Bitcoin is impracticable: Bitcoin has very limited space for arbitrary data in its blocks, and using it for the rollup's raw data would be enormously expensive. So the raw data must live elsewhere. But where?

---

* **State root.** A short cryptographic fingerprint (32 bytes) that summarizes the entire state of the rollup at a given moment, a bit like a seal that changes if even a single datum changes. It is this fingerprint, not the complete data, that the rollup anchors on Bitcoin.

† **Sequencer.** The component that collects users' transactions, orders them, executes them, and publishes the result (the state root) on Bitcoin. In today's rollups — Bitcoin Hyper included, at least in the initial phase — it is often a single party: this is why the proof mechanisms serve to prevent a possible error or abuse on its part from going without remedy.

‡ **Fraud proof.** A mechanism typical of "optimistic" rollups: the state published by the sequencer is taken as good, but anyone, within a time window, can present a proof demonstrating a fraud and have it annulled. It works only if the raw data is available to whoever wants to perform the check.

§ **Validity proof.** The opposite approach, used by ZK-rollups: each update is accompanied by a cryptographic proof attesting in advance to the correctness of the state, with no need for waits or challenges. It is more efficient to verify, but more complex to generate.

Note. Data availability — the guarantee that the raw data remains actually retrievable — is today one of the most discussed themes in rollup design. The solutions adopted by other ecosystems range from full publication on the Layer 1 to separate dedicated layers, all the way to committees of guarantors. Each choice shifts the balance between cost and trust: where the data is kept, and who guarantees that it remains available, is a decisive question for any Layer 2, Bitcoin Hyper included.

FIGURE 4.5 **THE DATA AVAILABILITY LAYER: WHY RAW DATA IS THE RAW MATERIAL OF VERIFICATION.**

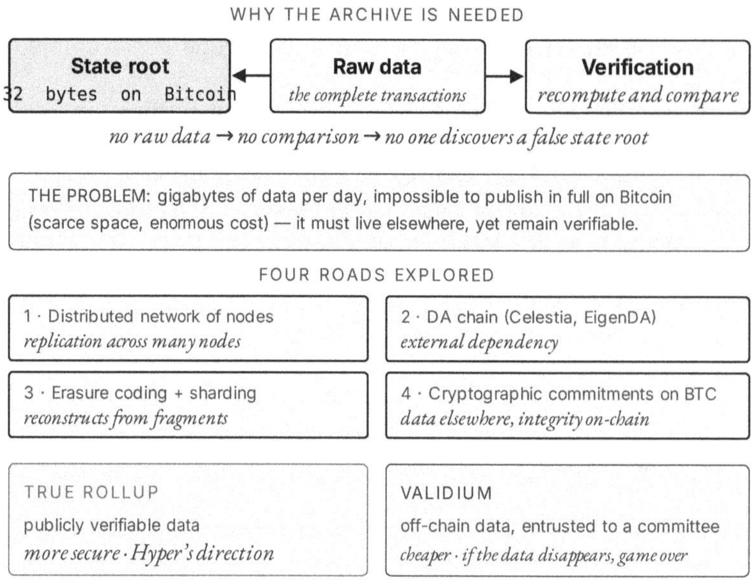

The state root alone is not enough: to check that it is correct, one needs the raw transaction data from which to recompute and compare it. Without the archive, no one can notice a false state root. But the data of an active rollup is gigabytes per day, impossible to publish in full on Bitcoin: it must live elsewhere while remaining verifiable. The four roads explored range from a distributed network of nodes to cryptographic commitments on Bitcoin. The choice determines whether the system is a true rollup — publicly verifiable data, more secure — or a validium — off-chain data entrusted to a committee, cheaper but fragile. Hyper is oriented toward the true rollup, with details still to be consolidated.

The possible solutions are various, and Bitcoin Hyper published a specific exploratory document (March 2026) that reviews them. **First solution**: a distributed network of rollup nodes that replicate the data among themselves. It works if the nodes are numerous and geographically distributed, but it depends on their operational continuity. **Second solution**: blockchains specialized in data availability, such as Celestia or EigenDA. They are designed precisely for this purpose and offer solid cryptographic guarantees, but they introduce an external dependency that Bitcoin Hyper might want to avoid in order to remain "Bitcoin-centric." **Third solution**: erasure coding and sharding, mathematical techniques that make it possible to reconstruct complete data from partial fragments, reducing the need for every node to keep everything. **Fourth solution**: publishing on Bitcoin only "cryptographic commitments" to the data, so that anyone can verify the integrity of the raw data kept elsewhere.

The model Bitcoin Hyper is exploring combines elements of these different strategies. The exact direction is not yet fully clarified, but the team has publicly acknowledged that **data availability is a first-order architectural challenge**, to be tackled alongside settlement and execution. It is a correct and honest position. **The risk that must be monitored is that, at launch, the data availability solution may be centralized or semi-centralized** (for example, run entirely by the team's nodes), and that the actual decentralization of this function may take years to be achieved. It is a nuance that changes the real security model a great deal, even if not the declared one.

There is a piece of terminology worth introducing here, because it comes up often in technical debates. A distinction is made between **true rollups**[a] and **validiums**[b]. A true rollup publishes the raw transaction data in some place verifiable by anyone, so that data availability is publicly guaranteed. A validium, by contrast, keeps the raw data off-chain in a way that is not publicly verifiable, trusting a committee or a service provider that stores it. **A validium is cheaper but has a weaker security model**, because if the data disappears, there is no longer any way to verify the state. The distinction between rollup and validium is a parameter every serious project should clarify explicitly, and Bitcoin Hyper seems oriented toward a true rollup model, but with implementation details still to be consolidated.

[a] **True rollup.** A rollup that makes the raw transaction data publicly retrievable, so that anyone can reconstruct and verify the state independently. It is the model with the strongest security guarantees, because it asks no one to be trusted for data availability: the price to pay is the higher cost of publishing that data.

[b] **Validium.** A variant that keeps the raw data off the main chain, entrusting its storage to a committee or a provider. It costs less and goes faster, but introduces a point of trust: if that data becomes unretrievable, no one can any longer demonstrate what the correct state is. It is the classic trade-off between economy and robustness that every project should declare clearly.

⁂

4.7 — How the Four Components Talk to One Another

Now that we have described the four components separately, it is important to understand how they **work together**, because a rollup is a system where each piece is useful only in the context of the others. Let us look at the complete flow of a transaction, from beginning to end, through the four components.

TABLE 4.1 **THE FOUR COMPONENTS OF A ROLLUP AND THEIR ROLE.**

Component	What does it do?	Critical question
Execution	Executes the transactions and updates the state	How fast and expressive is it?
Sequencing	Establishes the order of the transactions	Who controls the ordering?
Settlement	Anchors the results to Bitcoin	With what cadence and what finality?
Data availability	Keeps the raw data for verification	Where is it published and who can reconstruct it?

The four components are not independent modules: each acquires meaning only in the context of the others. A rollup is solid when all four operate in a coordinated and verifiable way; the weakness of a single one reflects on the entire system.

TABLE 4.2 **THE FOUR COMPONENTS OF THE ROLLUP: ROLE AND MUTUAL DEPENDENCE.**

Component	What does it do?	Whom does it depend on?
1 · Sequencer	Receives the transactions, orders them, and groups them into batches.	Useless without the execution that processes what it orders.
2 · Execution	Computes the new state by applying the transactions in the SVM environment.	Receives the order from the sequencer; its state must be demonstrated.
3 · Proofs	Cryptographically attest that the execution is correct.	They rest on the execution; they must be verified on the Layer 1.

4 · Settlement	Publishes commitments and proofs on Bitcoin, anchoring the state.	Without proofs and data it could crystallize nothing.

No component has value in isolation: the sequencer orders, the execution computes, the proofs attest, and the settlement anchors the result to Bitcoin. The rollup's strength comes from the way the four pieces depend on one another.

FIGURE 4.2 **THE FOUR COMPONENTS OF A ROLLUP AND THEIR INTERACTIONS**

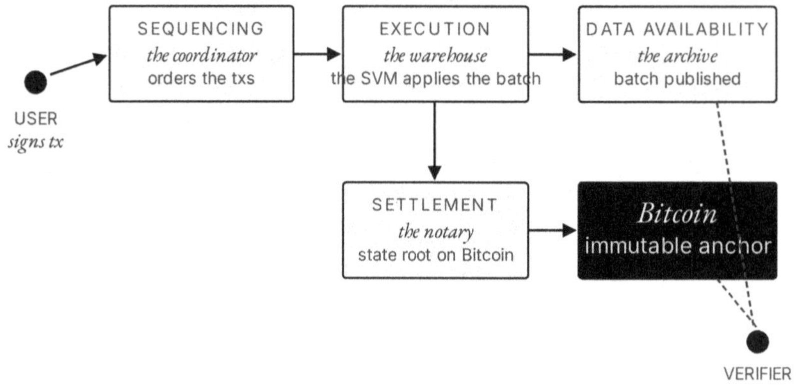

The user signs a transaction, the sequencing orders it, the execution applies it producing the new state. From there the flow forks: the settlement anchors the state root on Bitcoin (immutable finality), while the data availability publishes the raw data of the batch. The verifier, finally, can re-examine both — data and anchor — and independently ascertain that the declared state is correct. It is the choreography that makes the rollup verifiable without trust.

Alice signs a transaction and sends it to the rollup. The message reaches the **sequencer** (the coordinator), which receives it together with hundreds of other transactions coming from other users. The sequencer orders these transactions into a canonical sequence and groups them into a batch. When the batch is ready, it is sent to the **execution layer** (the warehouse), where the virtual machine applies the transactions one by one to the current state, producing the next state. At this point the rollup has a new state, but that state lives only within the rollup itself: users see their balances updated, applications react, but nothing is yet anchored on Bitcoin.

Periodically, the rollup performs two operations in parallel. **First operation**: it computes the state root of the new state and publishes it on Bitcoin through the **settlement layer** (the notary). From that moment, the state corresponding to the state root is crystallized and no longer modifiable. **Second operation**: it publishes the raw data of the batch's transactions in the **data availability layer** (the archive), where anyone can access it and verify the state independently.

Together, these four operations — sequencing, execution, settlement, availability — form the rollup's complete cycle. **Every transaction passes through all four levels**, each of which contributes essentially to the functioning and security of the system. If even a single component is missing, the system does not work or works in a degraded way.

FIGURE 4.6 **THE FOUR LEVELS OF THE ROLLUP IN THE DAILY NEWSPAPER METAPHOR.**

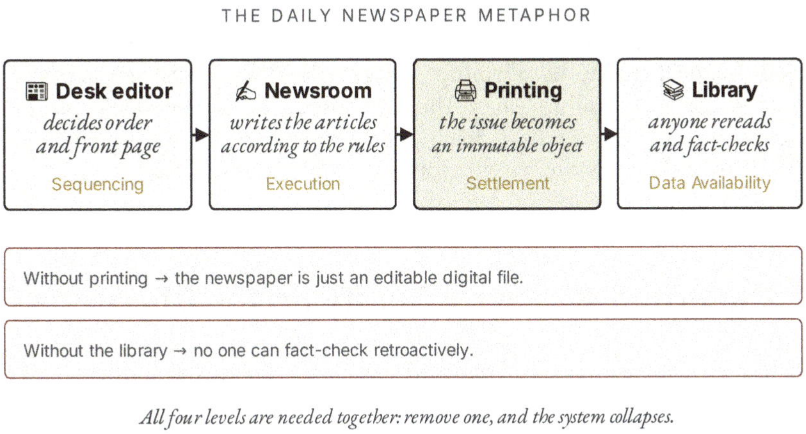

The desk editor who decides order and front page is the sequencing; the newsroom that writes the articles is the execution; the printing, which makes the issue an immutable, archived object, is the settlement; the library where anyone can reread every edition and verify that the summaries correspond to the complete articles is the data availability. Without printing, the newspaper remains an editable file; without the library, no one can fact-check after the fact. The four levels work only together.

There is a metaphor I like for this flow. Think of a daily newspaper. **The sequencer is the desk editor** who decides which stories go on the front page and in what order. **The execution layer is the newsroom** that actually writes the articles applying the rules of journalism. **The settlement layer is the printing**, the moment when the issue of the newspaper physically becomes an immutable object archived in libraries. **The data availability layer is the possibility for anyone to go to the library and read all the previous editions** and verify that the summaries the newspaper published actually correspond to the complete stories of the articles. Without printing, the newspaper is just an editable digital file. Without the library, no one can fact-check retroactively. **All four are needed together.**

⁂

4.8 — Modularity as a Design Principle

There is an important idea I want to introduce before the FAQs, because it governs the way modern rollups are designed and because Bitcoin Hyper embraces it explicitly. **The four components can be modular**, that is, separate and potentially replaceable. This idea, developed in recent years in the Ethereum world under the name of the "modular blockchain thesis," has profound implications for how rollups can evolve over time.

Think about it. Historically, monolithic blockchains like the original Bitcoin or the original Ethereum do everything in a single level: execution, sequencing, settlement, and data availability are fused together in the main protocol. This is simple and robust, but it limits the possibilities of evolution: if you want to improve one aspect, you have to modify the entire protocol. **A modular blockchain, by contrast, separates the levels and allows each to evolve independently**, perhaps replacing one with a better solution without having to touch the others.

For a rollup, modularity translates like this. **The execution layer** can be SVM, EVM, or any other virtual machine, and in principle one could even change environment over time (although it is not trivial). **The sequencing layer** can be single, distributed, based on auctions, on rotation, or on any other model, and it can evolve from one to another. **The settlement layer** can be Bitcoin, Ethereum, or even both simultaneously in a "dual settlement" model. **The data availability layer** can be an internal distributed network, or a specialized blockchain like Celestia, or a system of cryptographic commitments, and different solutions can coexist.

This modularity is a philosophical characteristic of Bitcoin Hyper's design, which the team made explicit in a specific post of March 2026 devoted to the "future-proof" architecture. The idea is that, **by**

rigorously separating the four levels, the system can evolve over time: improving the performance of the execution layer without touching the settlement, decentralizing the sequencer without touching data availability, changing the anchoring cadence without touching the execution. It is a far-sighted design choice, but it also carries operational complexities that must be managed with care.

For the investor or developer evaluating the project, modularity offers an additional criterion of judgment: **a well-designed rollup is a rollup where the four levels are actually separate and individually improvable**, not a rollup where they are fused into a monolithic block that is hard to upgrade. Bitcoin Hyper appears to have been set up according to this principle, although full verification will require seeing how the system evolves in its first years of life.

⁂

4.9 — Questions and Answers: Clarifying the Chapter's Concepts

Question 1: If the sequencer is centralized, why do people still speak of the rollup as "decentralized"? Is that not a contradiction?

It is an excellent question, and it must be addressed with honesty. **The centralization of the sequencer is real, but the decentralization of the overall system does not depend on the sequencer alone.** Think of the system as a joint-stock company. The sequencer is the CEO, certainly, and its centralization matters. But there is also a board of directors (the network's operators), a board of auditors (those who can raise fraud proofs), a shareholders' meeting (the community), and above all there is a public ledger (the main blockchain) that anyone can consult. **Even if the CEO is a single person, the decisions taken are public, verifiable, and contestable.** This is very different from a federated sidechain, where the CEO is a consortium of CEOs deciding together over a private ledger. Concrete example: in 2023, Optimism suspended its sequencer for a few hours due to a technical problem. Transactions stalled, but no funds were lost, because the security model did not depend on the sequencer's continuous activity. It is exactly the proof that the sequencer's centralization is a problem of service availability, not of the security of funds.

Question 2: How is it possible that the state root, a string of 32 bytes, can represent the state of a system with thousands of accounts and millions of transactions?

Thanks to the mathematical magic of **Merkle trees**, a data structure that makes it possible to "compress" any quantity of data into a single fingerprint, in such a way that modifying even a single bit of the original data would completely change the fingerprint. It works like this. Take all the data of the state (balances, contracts, events). Divide the data into small pieces. For each piece, compute its cryptographic fingerprint (hash). Then take the fingerprints in pairs, and for each pair compute the fingerprint of the concatenation. Keep going up, halving the number of fingerprints each time, until you are left with a single final fingerprint: that is the state root. **A fundamental property is that the state root also makes it possible to demonstrate the existence of a single datum without having to transmit all the data**: it is enough to provide the datum's fingerprint and the "path" of intermediate fingerprints up to the root. This structure is one of the masterpieces of modern computer science, and it underlies Bitcoin itself as well as all rollups. Concrete example: if the rollup has a million accounts and you want to demonstrate that your balance is 100, there is no need to transmit all the millions of other balances. About 20 intermediate fingerprints suffice (the base-2 logarithm of a million), for a total of a few hundred bytes. This property makes efficient demonstrations possible on arbitrarily large states.

Question 3: What happens if the data availability layer goes down while the settlement layer keeps working?

This is precisely the worst-case scenario for a rollup, and it is the reason data availability is considered a fundamental security condition. **If the state roots keep being anchored on Bitcoin, but the raw data has disappeared, users find themselves in a paradoxical situation**: they know the rollup's state has been crystallized in some specific value, but they do not know what that value is. It is like having a notarial certificate saying "document X exists" without ever being able to read document X again. In such a situation, the network becomes effectively unreadable: no one can any longer know who owns what, no one can build applications any longer, no one can withdraw funds to Bitcoin any longer because the proof of one's balance can no longer be constructed. **This is why data availability is a structural condition, not an option.** Concrete example: in 2022, some gaming sidechains had temporary data availability problems, and users found themselves momentarily unable to access their in-game NFTs. They were protected by the main blockchain (they knew the assets existed), but they could not use them until the data was restored. For a serious rollup, such a situation is unacceptable, and the data availability mechanisms must be designed to withstand even the disappearance of significant parts of the infrastructure.

Question 4: Is Bitcoin Hyper building all four components from scratch? Or is it reusing existing solutions?

It is combining both approaches. **For the execution layer, it is reusing the SVM**, avoiding the enormous cost of building a virtual machine from scratch. This is a wise choice: the SVM is a complex, mature piece of software, tested in production on Solana, and building an alternative one would have been a strategic mistake. **For the sequencing layer, it is developing its own implementation**, because the specific needs of a rollup anchored to Bitcoin are different from Solana's, and the coordinator must be designed specifically for the context. **For the settlement layer, it is developing the Bitcoin Relay Program and the anchoring mechanisms**, here too an original piece of work specific to Bitcoin. **For the data availability layer, it is exploring various roads** that combine elements of distributed networks, erasure coding, and cryptographic commitments. **In essence: Hyper reuses the piece most worth reusing (the SVM) and custom-builds the pieces that require adaptation to the Bitcoin context.** It is a correct engineering choice that reduces implementation risk.

Question 5: How much time typically passes between a transaction and its final anchoring on Bitcoin?

It depends on the anchoring cadence chosen by the rollup, which is a configurable variable (we will see the details in Chapter 13). Ethereum's rollups typically anchor every few minutes, although "complete finality" arrives only after the anchoring transaction has in turn been confirmed by a certain number of subsequent blocks. For a rollup on Bitcoin, the timings are longer by nature, because Bitcoin has blocks every ten minutes and conservative finality arrives after six blocks (one hour). **So: if the anchoring cadence is every ten minutes, and Bitcoin finality requires six blocks, the total time between the execution of a transaction on the rollup and its complete finality on Bitcoin is on the order of one hour.** For most users, however, this complete finality is not the one they perceive: the user perceives the transaction as "done" when it is processed on the rollup (milliseconds or seconds), because the system acts as if the state were already definitive. Bitcoin finality is the insurance of last resort, which protects against catastrophic scenarios but which users do not experience directly in everyday life. Concrete example: when you pay by credit card, you perceive the payment as instantaneous, even though the actual bank settlement takes days. The same holds for rollups: the user experience is instantaneous, the Bitcoin settlement is long-term, and the separation of the two is a positive characteristic of the design.

Question 6: If the four components are separate, where exactly does the "rollup" as an entity sit? In which of the four?

The rollup is not one of the four components; it is the **system** that puts them together and makes the end-to-end flow work. Think of it as a restaurant: the kitchen is a component, the maître is a component, the cash register is a component, the tax records are a component. But "the restaurant" is none of these: it is the organization that coordinates them. Bitcoin Hyper as a project is exactly this: the coordination of the four components, the definition of their interfaces, the management of their evolutions over time. **The value of a rollup project lies in no single component, but in the quality of the coordination among all of them.** It is an important point for investors: the judgment on a rollup is not made by looking at one thing alone (the virtual machine, or the bridge, or the sequencer), but by looking at the overall integration. Concrete example: Optimism and Arbitrum both use the EVM as their execution layer, both anchor on Ethereum, both had a single sequencer for years. And yet they are different projects, with different cultures, different choices on the details, different evolutions. The difference lies not in the individual components, but in the way they are integrated and in the way they evolve. The same logic will apply to the evaluation of Bitcoin Hyper against other Bitcoin rollups that may emerge in the coming years.

⁂

4.10 — WHAT TO TAKE AWAY FROM THIS CHAPTER

Every rollup has four fundamental components: the execution layer, the sequencing layer, the settlement layer, and the data availability layer. They are the "four pillars" that will return constantly throughout the rest of the book.

The execution layer is the virtual machine that runs the transactions and the applications. For Bitcoin Hyper it is the SVM, chosen for performance and compatibility with the Solana ecosystem. The choices about the virtual machine condition everything that can be built on the rollup.

The sequencing layer is the coordinator that orders the transactions and groups them into batches. It is typically centralized at a rollup's launch, and its progressive decentralization is one of the long-term objectives. The sequencer's centralization is a problem of service availability, not of the security of funds.

The settlement layer is the anchoring point on the main blockchain, where the state commitments are crystallized. For Bitcoin Hyper it is Bitcoin, and the anchoring mechanism is the subject of active research among various modes (OP_RETURN, Taproot, timelocks).

The data availability layer is where the raw transaction data lives, necessary for the independent verification of the rollup's state. It is the most underestimated component but one of the most crucial for the security model.

The four components talk to one another in a continuous cycle: transactions pass from the sequencer to the execution, the state commitments are anchored to the settlement, the raw data ends up in the data availability. If even a single component is missing, the system does not work or works in a degraded way.

Modularity is a design principle that allows the four components to evolve independently, replacing one without having to touch the others. Bitcoin Hyper has explicitly embraced this principle, which facilitates the "future-proofing" of the architecture.

Bitcoin Hyper, evaluated through these four components, is at different stages of maturity for each: the SVM is a mature, reused component; the sequencing is clear in its intentions with a declared decentralization path; the settlement is in a prototyping phase with specific choices to be consolidated; data availability is in a more exploratory phase. This diversity of maturity is physiological for a pre-mainnet project, but it must be acknowledged honestly.

---

*Chapter 4 ends here. We have built the anatomy of the rollup, understanding how it is structurally made, and we have introduced the four names we will use constantly throughout the rest of the book. In **Chapter 5 — Off-Chain Execution, On-Chain Settlement: The Basic Choreography**, we will go inside the rollup's fundamental movement, seeing in detail how transactions move from the fast execution above to the definitive anchoring below, and how this choreography produces the combination of speed and security that is the model's central promise.*

NOTES

1 The term became established in the post-2020 Ethereum debate thanks to the work of Mustafa Al-Bassam (Celestia) and John Adler (Fuel). See Al-Bassam, *Fraud and Data Availability Proofs*, arXiv:1809.09044.

Anatomy of a *rollup*

Execution, sequencing, settlement, and data availability: the four pillars of Bitcoin Hyper. If even one level is missing, the system **does not work — or works in a degraded way**.

1 A rollup is a modular stack

L4	**Execution** · the virtual machine	executes transactions and applications.
L3	**Sequencing** · the coordinator	orders the transactions and creates the batches.
L2	**Data Availability** · the archive	keeps the raw data for verification.
L1	₿ **Settlement** · Bitcoin	crystallizes state commitments and finality.

Fast execution above. **Slow, definitive finality below.**

2 The logistics metaphor

Warehouse = Execution
works the parcels → executes transactions and smart contracts.

Coordinator = Sequencing
decides order and priorities → orders the transactions.

Notary = Settlement
records the official summary → anchors the state root on Bitcoin.

Archive = Data Avail.
keeps the complete records → makes the raw data available.

Without the warehouse there is no work · without the coordinator there is chaos · without the notary there is no finality · **without the archive there is no verification.**

3 What each level does, one by one

Execution Layer
reads the state, applies the rules, produces the new state.
FOR HYPER
SVM, Rust/C, parallel execution, account model.

Sequencing Layer
receives, orders, and groups into batches: a single canonical sequence.
FOR HYPER
single sequencer at launch, decentralization to be verified.

Settlement Layer
publishes the state root on Bitcoin and makes the commitment immutable.
FOR HYPER
Bitcoin L1 via OP_RETURN, Taproot, or other anchorings.

Data Availability
keeps the raw data: without it, no one can reconstruct the state.
FOR HYPER
an area to consolidate: distributed networks, sharding, erasure coding.

4 The complete flow: from the wallet to settlement on Bitcoin

user signs the tx → **sequencer** orders, batches → **execution / SVM** updates the state → **state root** fingerprint of the state → ₿ **settlement** immutable commitment

IN PARALLEL **data availability** publishes the raw data of the batch → **independent verifier** reconstructs the state and compares the root

The state root gives the **seal**; *the raw data allows the* **check**. *The immutability of the commitment does not by itself demonstrate the correctness of the state.*

5 Modularity and maturation: evaluating level by level

Execution
Most mature
SVM already existing and tested in Solana.

Sequencing
Centralized at launch
a roadmap toward more operators is needed.

Settlement
In prototyping
frequency, method, and finality to be clarified.

Data Availability
Most exploratory
where the data lives and who reconstructs it.

(!) The strength of the rollup does not lie in a single component, **but in the coordination among all of them** — modular, verifiable, improvable level by level.

THE KEY POINT

A rollup is a four-level choreography: the **sequencer orders**, the **execution computes**, the **settlement anchors on Bitcoin**, the **data availability** makes independent verification possible. Bitcoin guarantees **immutability, not automatically correctness**: proofs and available data are needed. Hyper will inherit security and credibility only if all four components work together, transparently and progressively decentralized.

PART II · THE ROLLUP MODEL APPLIED TO BITCOIN

Chapter 5
Off-Chain Execution, On-Chain Settlement

The basic choreography

⁂

5.1 — The Dance That Holds Everything Together

If in Chapter 4 we dissected the rollup into four separate components, in this chapter we perform the reverse operation: we set the pieces back in motion. Because a rollup is not a static collection of parts — it is a **choreography**, a continuous cycle in which execution, sequencing, settlement, and data availability talk to one another in a precise rhythm. Understanding this rhythm means understanding how the rollup manages to do two things at once that at first sight seem contradictory: **to go as fast as Solana and to be as immutable as Bitcoin**. These are statements that, put like that, sound like marketing slogans. And yet, at the technical level, they are both true — provided one understands that they do not live in the same moment, but in two different beats of the same dance.

FIGURE 5.1 **THE CHOREOGRAPHY: OFF-CHAIN EXECUTION, ON-CHAIN SETTLEMENT**

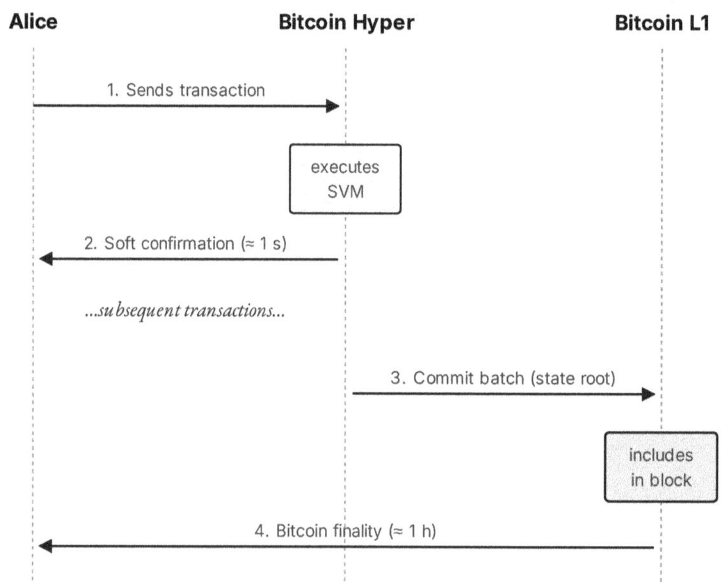

Two times, two speeds: *the user sees the fast confirmation (step 2); the irreversible finality arrives later, when Bitcoin includes the batch (step 4). The separation of user experience and finality is the architectural heart of every rollup.*

The key point of this chapter is a distinction worth repeating from the outset, because it is the thread that will hold the whole discussion together: **speed and finality are not the same thing**, and a well-designed rollup exploits exactly this difference to offer both. Speed is the experience the user perceives while interacting with the system: they click, confirm, see the result in a few seconds. Finality is the moment when what happened becomes irreversible, carved into the stone of Bitcoin, impossible to modify even for whoever runs the rollup. Between the first moment and the second, time passes — minutes, perhaps an hour — but in that time the user does not wait idly: they use the system, do other things, live their digital life as if everything were already definitive. **The rollup sells them an instantaneous experience and gives them, behind the scenes, a delayed but iron-clad guarantee.** Let us see how.

⁂

5.2 — Two Times, Two Speeds: The Separation That Changes Everything

To understand the choreography of a rollup, one must first accept an idea that, in the world of traditional finance, is familiar to us but that in the crypto world is sometimes forgotten: **many sophisticated payment systems work thanks to the separation between the moment when something "happens" and the moment when that something becomes "definitive."** We touched on this in Chapter 1, when we distinguished between the execution layer and the settlement layer. Now we can pick up that reasoning in a more operational way.

Think of the credit card payment you make at a restaurant. When the waiter runs the card through the POS, something nearly instantaneous happens: the system verifies that your card is valid, that there is enough credit available, that there are no suspicions of fraud. In a few seconds, the payment is "authorized." You sign, say goodbye, leave the restaurant. For you, and for the restaurateur, **the payment has happened**. But it is not yet definitive. In the following days, behind the scenes, a far more complex process takes place: the transaction is processed by the card network, the banks involved exchange the real funds, any disputes are handled, and only after a few days (or even more, in the case of a chargeback) does the movement of money become truly irreversible.

Note. The distinction between authorization and definitive settlement is not a detail of traditional finance: it is exactly the concept that, transferred to the world of rollups, separates the fast confirmation on the Layer 2 from the finality anchored to Bitcoin. Recognizing this difference is essential in order not to confuse the speed perceived by the user with the actual security of an operation — a misunderstanding that crypto marketing often feeds, presenting speed as if it were already irreversibility.

FIGURE 5.2 **TWO TIMES, TWO SPEEDS: IMMEDIATE AUTHORIZATION AND DEFINITIVE SETTLEMENT.**

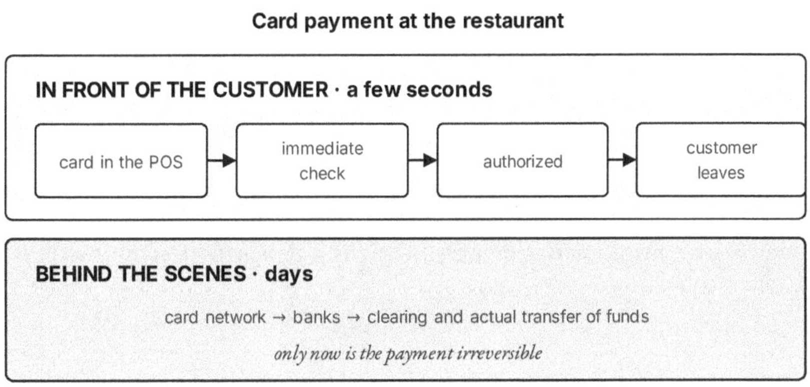

The user experience is immediate; the definitive settlement happens behind the scenes.

This separation — fast authorization, slow but definitive settlement — is not a flaw of the credit card system, it is its strength. It allows millions of people to make billions of payments a day without having to wait each time for physical money to move between the banks. **The user experience and the final guarantee are separate**, and this allows the system to scale to dimensions that would otherwise be impossible.

Rollups apply exactly the same architectural principle to the blockchain world. **The execution of transactions happens quickly on the rollup**: the user signs, the sequencer orders, the execution layer processes, and in a few seconds (or fractions of a second) the rollup's state is updated. From that moment, the user sees their balance modified, the applications react, the transaction is "done" for any practical purpose. **Settlement, by contrast, happens more slowly, periodically, on Bitcoin**: the rollup collects a certain number of transactions, computes the state commitment, and publishes it on Bitcoin at regular intervals. Only at that point, when the commitment is anchored and confirmed, does the transaction become truly irreversible.

Between execution and settlement, time passes. How much time depends on architectural choices we will see in Chapter 13 when we discuss the anchoring cadence. For now it is enough to know that we are talking about an interval that can range from a few minutes to a few tens of minutes, depending on the configuration. **In that interval, the rollup's state exists in a gray zone**: it is already definitive from a practical standpoint (users treat it as such, applications rest on it, balances are modified), but it is not yet crystallized on Bitcoin in an immutable way. It is a gray zone managed very well by well-designed rollups, because in that zone the risks are limited and well defined: the sequencer could censor, could stall, could in extreme cases attempt fraud — but none of these things can take funds away without the system reacting.

FIGURE 5.3 **THE ROLLUP'S CHOREOGRAPHY: EXECUTION, GRAY ZONE, AND ANCHORING ON BITCOIN.**

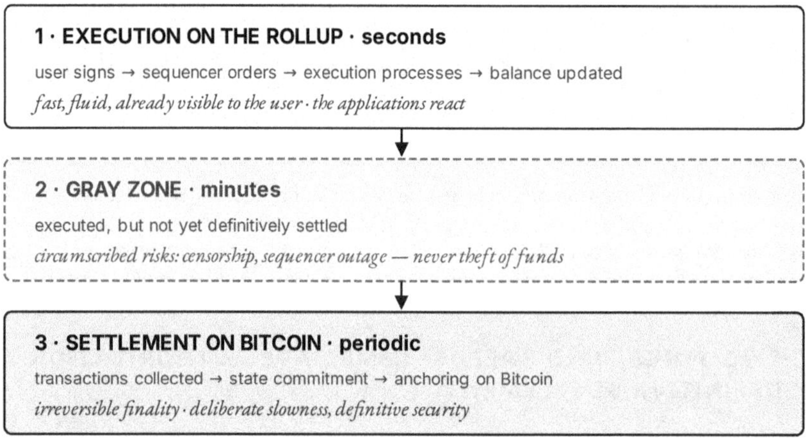

The rollup offers the fast experience; Bitcoin makes the truth of the state definitive.

And it is precisely here that the elegance of the rollup model can be appreciated. **The instantaneous experience is sold to the user, the deferred security is guaranteed behind the scenes, and the two planes do not step on each other's toes.** The user experiences the rollup as if it were Solana — fast, fluid, responsive. But they know that, behind it, there is Bitcoin which every X minutes signs the ledger and makes any retroactive manipulation impossible. It is a design that combines two virtues which, taken separately, are incompatible.

⁂

5.3 — The Journey of a Transaction: A Day in the Life of Alice

To make the choreography concrete, let us follow a transaction from beginning to end, with an eye on the timing details and on the responsibilities of each component. Our protagonist will be Alice, who wants to send 50 units of a token on Bitcoin Hyper to her friend Bob.

FIGURE 5.4 **THE COMPLETE JOURNEY OF A TRANSACTION: A DAY IN THE LIFE OF ALICE.**

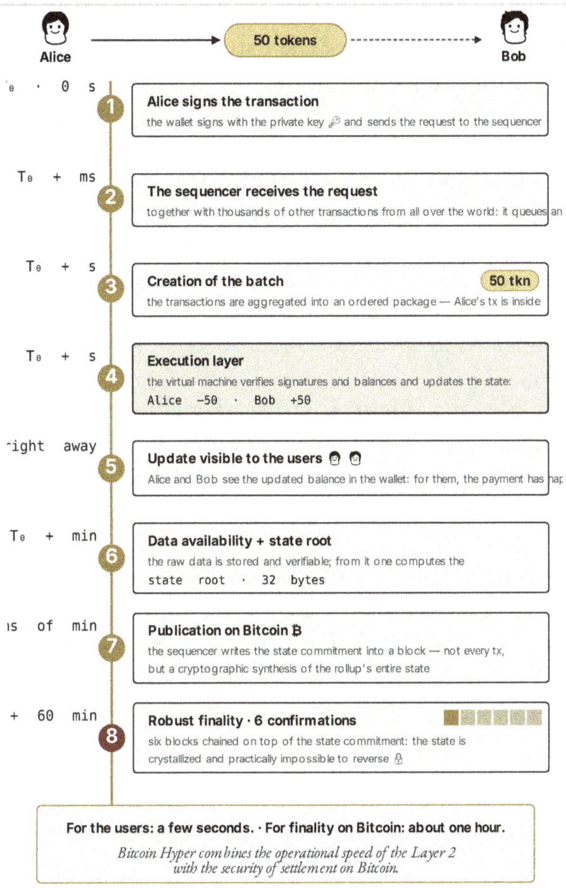

The same transaction — the 50 tokens Alice sends to Bob — passes through eight phases on a single timeline: in a few seconds the signature is ordered, executed, and the balances updated (for Alice and Bob the payment has already happened), while the anchoring on Bitcoin makes the state irreversible after about one hour.

Phase 1 **Time zero, second zero: Alice signs the transaction.** On her wallet, Alice sees her balance, decides to send 50 to Bob, confirms the operation. The wallet constructs a transaction formatted according to the rollup's rules, signs it with Alice's private key, and sends it to the sequencer. **At this point, from the rollup's standpoint, the transaction exists but has not yet happened**: it is only a request the sequencer will have to process.

Phases 2-3 **Time zero plus a few hundred milliseconds: the sequencer receives the transaction.** Together with Alice's transaction, the sequencer is receiving hundreds or thousands of other transactions coming from users all over the world. The sequencer queues them, orders them according to its own criteria (typically by order of arrival or by the fees offered), and when it has accumulated a certain number of transactions or when a certain amount of time has passed, it constructs a **batch**, a package containing the transactions in a specific sequence.

Phase 4 **Time zero plus a few seconds: the batch enters the execution layer.** The virtual machine takes the batch and applies the transactions one at a time to the rollup's current state. For each transaction, it verifies the signatures, checks the balances, applies the changes, records the events. When Alice's turn comes, it subtracts 50 from her balance and adds 50 to Bob's balance. **At this point, the rollup's state has changed.** Alice sees the updated balance on her wallet (minus 50), Bob sees his updated balance (plus 50). For them, the transaction has happened. The whole system acts as if it were definitive.

Phase 5 **Time zero plus a few seconds: the rollup's nodes propagate the new state.** All the nodes monitoring the rollup — the explorers, the indexers, the applications resting on it — receive the update and reflect it in their interfaces. The applications that depend on Alice's or Bob's balance react accordingly. If Alice and Bob are using a chat application, they can see immediately that the payment has happened. If they are using a DeFi application, the application can immediately take the next action that depends on that payment.

Phase 6 **Time zero plus a few minutes: the batch is included in the data for settlement.** The rollup does not anchor every single transaction on Bitcoin — it would be enormously inefficient. It waits to accumulate a significant number of transactions over a period of time, and then prepares a larger batch for settlement. Alice's transaction is part of this broader batch. **During these minutes, the rollup's state exists only in the rollup's own nodes and in the availability data**, not yet on Bitcoin.

Phase 7 **Time X (configurable, typically tens of minutes): the sequencer publishes the state commitment on Bitcoin.** The sequencer computes the state root corresponding to the rollup's new state, constructs a Bitcoin transaction containing this state commitment (via OP_RETURN or another mechanism we will see in Chapter 12), and sends it to the Bitcoin network. At the same time, it publishes the raw data of the batch in the data availability layer, so that anyone can verify that the state root is indeed the correct one.

Phases 7–8 **Time X plus ten minutes: the settlement transaction is included in a Bitcoin block.** A Bitcoin miner includes the sequencer's transaction in a block and adds it to the blockchain. **From this moment, the state commitment is recorded on Bitcoin**, but with the finality typical of a single confirmation, which the Bitcoin community considers sufficient only for payments of limited amount.

Phase 8 **Time X plus sixty minutes: six confirmations on Bitcoin.** After five more blocks have been added on top of the block containing the state commitment, finality is considered robust by Bitcoin standards. **At this point, the state commitment is practically impossible to reverse**: to do so, someone would have to redo all the cryptographic work accumulated over the last six blocks, an economically prohibitive operation. The rollup state corresponding to that state commitment is officially crystallized.

Summing up: for Alice and Bob, the transaction happened in a few seconds. For the system, complete finality arrived about an hour later. Between the two moments, the transaction existed in a gray zone, but a gray zone managed so that users did not notice it and their funds were protected all the same.

This journey is the basic flow of every transaction on Bitcoin Hyper. **Every element of this flow can be optimized — the sequencer's speed, the cadence of the batches, the settlement mechanism, the structure of data availability — but the conceptual structure is this.** Keep it in mind, because it will return constantly.

⁂

5.4 — The Four Phases of Settlement: From the Batch to Immutability

Now that we have followed a single transaction, let us zoom in specifically on the most complex part of the flow: the settlement proper, that is, the process through which the rollup's state is crystallized on Bitcoin. This process, seemingly simple ("publish a state commitment on Bitcoin"), hides four distinct phases worth articulating with care, because each has specific security implications.

FIGURE 5.5 **THE FOUR PHASES OF SETTLEMENT: FROM THE RAW TRANSACTIONS TO BITCOIN'S IMMUTABILITY**

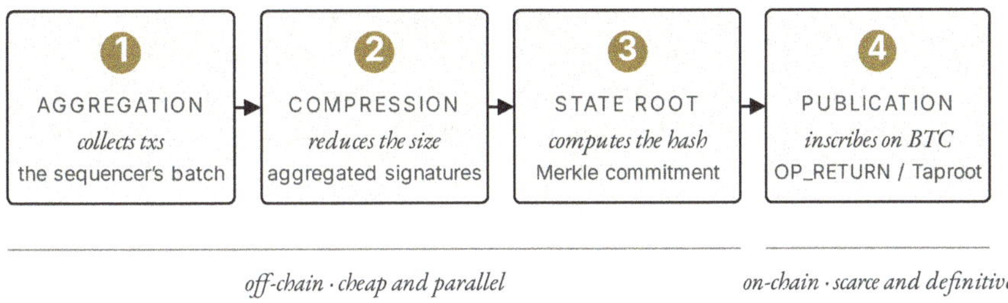

The first three phases happen off-chain — in the rollup — where computation is cheap and parallel. Only the fourth phase touches Bitcoin, where space is scarce and confirmations definitive. The rollup's economic key is precisely this asymmetry: aggregate hundreds of transactions on the outside, inscribe a single compact commitment on the inside.

First phase: aggregation. The sequencer collects the transactions processed over a certain period and aggregates them into a batch. This batch may contain hundreds or thousands of transactions, depending on the chosen anchoring cadence and the rollup's traffic. Aggregation is the moment when it is decided what goes into the "document to be signed" that will go onto Bitcoin. **If a transaction is excluded from the batch, it will not be anchored, and this is one of the ways a dishonest sequencer could censor.** This is why forced inclusion mechanisms (which we will see in Chapter 21) matter: they allow users to force the inclusion of transactions even if the sequencer tries to ignore them.

Second phase: compression. The data of the batch's transactions is compressed through various techniques. Signatures are aggregated, redundant data is eliminated, structures are optimized. The goal is to reduce the occupied space to a minimum, because space on the Bitcoin blockchain is scarce and costly. **Compression is the rollup's economic key**: it is what makes it possible to "summarize" hundreds of transactions in a few bytes, cutting the cost per transaction by orders of magnitude compared with what one would have writing directly on Bitcoin.

Third phase: computation of the state commitment. The sequencer computes the state root corresponding to the rollup's new state after the application of all the batch's transactions. As we saw in the previous chapter, this is a 32-byte value that is mathematically bound to every element of the state. Together with the state root, the sequencer also prepares any proofs or attestations required by the validation model (fraud proof or validity proof, depending on the model).

Fourth phase: publication on Bitcoin. The sequencer constructs a Bitcoin transaction containing the state commitment (and potentially a reference to the raw data published elsewhere) and sends it to the Bitcoin network. From this moment, the commitment is waiting to be included in a block. After inclusion, the countdown of confirmations begins that will lead to complete finality.

These four phases represent the "bridge" between the rollup and Bitcoin. It is on this bridge that the difference between a well-designed rollup and a badly designed one is played out. **A well-designed rollup manages every phase with care**: it aggregates in a predictable, non-censorious way, compresses in a verifiable way, computes state commitments with robust proofs, publishes on Bitcoin with regularity. A badly designed rollup leaves room for manipulations, errors, or worse still, security fragilities.

For Bitcoin Hyper, the available documentation leaves some elements clear and others still evolving. **Aggregation is managed by the sequencer according to rules the team has announced** but which in the initial phase depend on the single sequencer. **Compression is the subject of active research**, especially as regards the balance between reducing costs and maintaining verifiability. **The computation of the state commitment uses standard structures** for the SVM with adaptations specific to Bitcoin. **Publication on Bitcoin** is exploring various modes (OP_RETURN, Taproot, timelocks), as we have seen. It is an architecture in a consolidation phase, where the specific decisions on each phase will be clarified in the months preceding the mainnet launch.

⁂

5.5 — Anchoring as the System's "Heartbeat"

There is an image I like for describing the relationship between the rollup and Bitcoin in the settlement process: **anchoring as the system's heartbeat**. Think about it. The rollup, during the interval between one anchoring and the next, lives in a sort of apnea. It is doing things, processing transactions, updating balances, but its state is still "suspended" relative to Bitcoin. Then, periodically, the system takes a "breath": it computes the state commitment, publishes it on Bitcoin, and with that breath everything that happened in the preceding apnea becomes part of the official, immutable history. Then another apnea begins, and so on, in a continuous cycle.

This heartbeat has a cadence, and the cadence is a central variable in the rollup's design. **Frequent beats** (for example, every ten minutes) mean that every state is anchored early, that the risk window is short, that users can trust finality quickly. But frequent beats also mean **high anchoring costs**: every anchoring is a Bitcoin transaction that pays fees, and making many of them costs a lot. **Rare beats** (for example, every hour) cut costs but lengthen the risk window: the rollup's state stays in apnea longer, and any problem during that time becomes potentially more serious.

The Bitcoin Hyper team explicitly addressed this trade-off in a specific post (January 2026), declaring that the anchoring cadence will be a **configurable parameter**, not a fixed rule. This is a wise choice: it means the system will be able to adapt its own heartbeat to the conditions of the moment — more frequent when Bitcoin fees are low and activity is high, less frequent when fees are high and activity is low. It is an adaptive design that reflects the team's mature understanding of the problem.

FIGURE 5.6 **THE SYSTEM'S HEARTBEAT: THE ROLLUP'S FLOW ABOVE, ANCHORING ON BITCOIN BELOW**

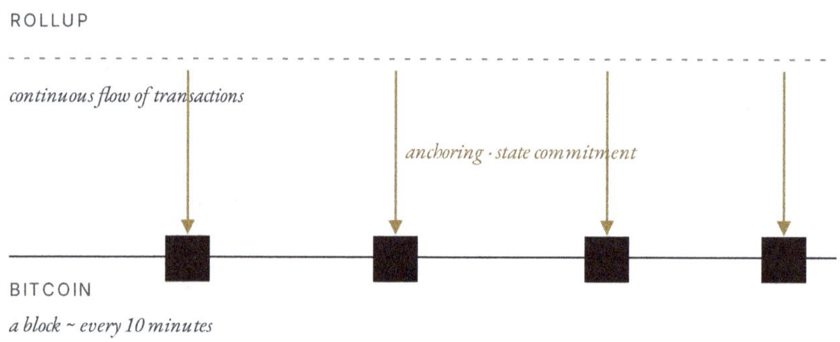

The upper line is the rollup, where transactions flow continuously (the dots). The lower line is Bitcoin, where the blocks arrive at regular intervals (the rectangles). Between the two, the vertical arrows are the "beats" — the moments when the rollup computes a state commitment and inscribes it on a Bitcoin block. Frequent arrows mean short risk windows and high anchoring costs; sparse arrows the opposite. The configurability of the cadence is what allows the system to breathe at the right rhythm for the moment.

There is, however, a subtle point worth touching on. **Even with frequent beats, complete finality is not instantaneous**, because Bitcoin itself needs a certain number of confirmations to consider a transaction definitive. So the process is actually two-layered: first one publishes on Bitcoin (the beat), then one waits for Bitcoin's confirmations (the consolidation of the beat). For most users, this double layer is invisible, because they live in the rhythm of the rollup's instantaneous experience. But for applications where finality has particular value — for example, withdrawals to Bitcoin for large amounts — the double layer becomes relevant and can require significant waits.

Here one sees an interesting difference from Ethereum's rollups, worth touching on. On Ethereum, finality is faster (Ethereum has block times of a few seconds and complete finality in a few minutes), but the cost per anchoring is historically higher (although it dropped drastically with the introduction of blob space in 2024). On Bitcoin, finality is slower (block times of ten minutes, complete finality in one hour), but the space for arbitrary data is scarcer, and so more compression and attention to costs are needed. **The two models optimize for different trade-offs**, and each has its own strengths and weaknesses.

5.6 — Perceived Speed vs. Guaranteed Finality: The Dual Nature of the User Experience

A point I want to underline with particular care, because it is often a source of confusion both among new users and among some critics of rollups, is the **dual nature of the user experience**: perceived speed and guaranteed finality are not the same thing, and understanding the difference makes it possible to appreciate correctly what a well-designed rollup offers.

Perceived speed is what the user experiences directly. They click confirm on the wallet, and within a few seconds (at most a few tens of seconds, rarely more) they see the result of their transaction. The updated balance. The confirmation of the send. The response of the application that depended on the transaction. For the user, **the transaction is "done" from that moment**: the whole system acts accordingly, everything reacts as if that transaction were a definitive part of history.

Guaranteed finality, by contrast, is what comes into play in pathological situations. If the sequencer misbehaved, if the rollup had a technical problem, if there were an attack, if something went wrong — **until the state commitment is anchored and confirmed on Bitcoin, there is in theory a possibility that the transaction could be invalidated**. Not because someone will erase it, but because in the absence of anchoring there is not yet an "official truth" crystallized on Bitcoin that could be used to reconstruct the state in case of problems.

FIGURE 5.6 **THE TWO NATURES OF THE USER EXPERIENCE.**

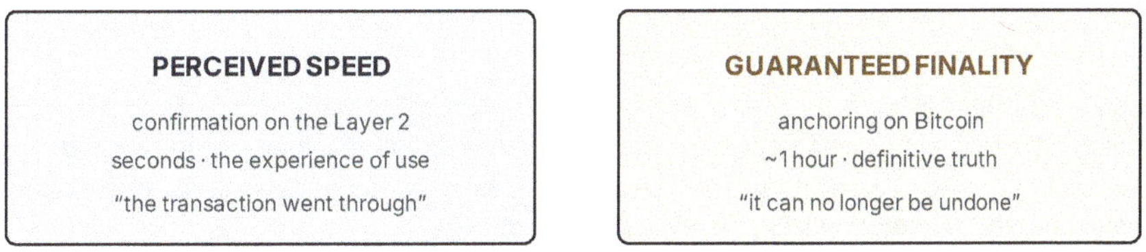

Two different times of the same operation.

The user experiences the transaction as instantaneous, but its definitive irreversibility matures more slowly, when the state is anchored and confirmed on Bitcoin. Perceived speed and guaranteed finality are not in contradiction: they are two distinct moments of the same operation, and confusing them is one of the most common sources of misunderstanding about rollups.

TABLE 5.1 **PERCEIVED SPEED AND GUARANTEED FINALITY COMPARED.**

Aspect	Perceived speed	Guaranteed finality[*]
When it manifests	Right after the click in the wallet	When the state is anchored on Bitcoin
Timing	Seconds	From minutes to hours, depending on the cadence
What it guarantees	The operation has been processed on the L2	The operation is irreversible
Residual risk	Possible invalidation in pathological cases[†]	None, once confirmed

The two dimensions are not in contradiction: they describe different moments of the same transaction. The user perceives the speed, but it is the finality anchored to Bitcoin that makes it definitive. Confusing the two leads to overestimating the security of an operation just confirmed on the Layer 2.

TABLE 5.2 THE TWO NATURES OF THE USER EXPERIENCE COMPARED.

Aspect	Perceived speed	Guaranteed finality
When it acts	In ordinary use, at every transaction.	In pathological situations: failures, attacks, errors.
Timing	A few seconds, rarely more.	After anchoring and confirmation on Bitcoin.
What it guarantees	An immediate result the user can use.	Truth crystallized on Bitcoin, reconstructable.
Residual risk	Theoretical reversibility until anchoring.	None once confirmed on the Layer 1.[‡]

The two dimensions are not in contradiction: perceived speed makes the rollup usable in everyday experience, while guaranteed finality steps in as a safety net in exceptional situations. A well-designed rollup offers both, distinguishing clearly what is already usable from what is already definitive.

[*] **Settlement finality.** The moment when an operation becomes irreversible and can no longer be undone. Unlike traditional payment systems, where finality is a legal guarantee, here it is a technical property: it kicks in when the rollup's state is anchored on Bitcoin and inherits the immutability of the underlying chain.

[†] **Pathological cases.** This expression denotes the anomalous situations — sequencer malfunction or dishonesty, technical failures, attacks — in the window between execution on the Layer 2 and definitive anchoring. It is the only interval in which an operation already "seen" by the user could still be invalidated; once confirmed on Bitcoin, the risk vanishes.

[‡] **Layer 1.** The base blockchain — here Bitcoin — which provides fundamental security and immutability. The systems built on top of it to increase its performance are called "Layer 2": a transaction is truly definitive only when it is recorded and confirmed on the Layer 1.

FIGURE 5.7 FROM PERCEIVED SPEED TO GUARANTEED FINALITY: THE DUAL NATURE OF THE TRANSACTION.

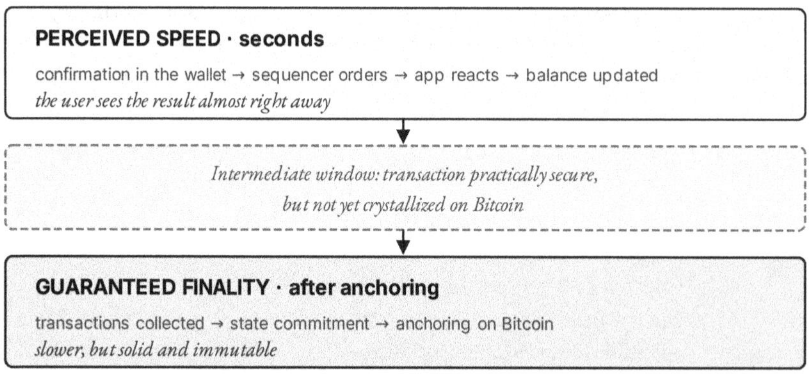

Speed is a soft guarantee; anchoring on Bitcoin turns it into a hard one.

Put like that, the system sounds risky. It is not, and the reason is that **the risks in the window between execution and finality are limited and well defined**. Let us see which ones. The sequencer cannot invent transactions that were not signed by users, because transactions are cryptographically signed and the sequencer does not possess the private keys. The sequencer can order the transactions as it pleases (with potential MEV implications), but it cannot alter their content. The sequencer can censor some transactions, but forced inclusion mechanisms exist to counter censorship (although in Bitcoin Hyper's initial phase these mechanisms have yet to be fully specified). The sequencer could publish a wrong state commitment, but in that case the system would reject it through fraud proofs or validity proofs.

In other words: **in the window between execution and finality, there are risks, but they are risks over which we have structural control**. The speed perceived by the user is "practically safe" for any normal use, and the guaranteed finality then arrives to confirm immutably what was already practically safe. It is not a system where speed is a lie disguised as apparent security; it is a system where speed is a "soft" guarantee that becomes "hard" after anchoring.

The only situation in which the difference between perceived speed and guaranteed finality becomes critical is for **operations of very high value or very long duration**. If you are moving a million dollars in bitcoin, it is prudent to wait for complete finality before considering the operation concluded. If you are buying a coffee, perceived speed is more than sufficient. **The typical experience of traditional finance is exactly the same**: for micropayments one trusts the fast authorization, for large transactions one waits for complete bank settlement. Rollups reproduce this same logic in the blockchain world, and they do so structurally and transparently.

FIGURE 5.8 **MICROPAYMENTS AND LARGE TRANSFERS: WHEN TO WAIT FOR COMPLETE FINALITY.**

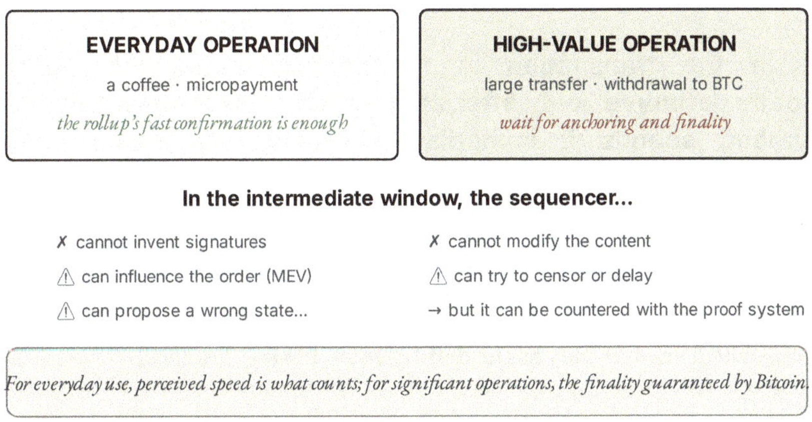

⁂

5.7 — What Happens Between One Anchoring and the Next: The Managed Gray Zone

To close the description of the basic choreography, I want to touch explicitly on a point that often remains implicit: **what exactly happens in the gray zone between the execution of a transaction and its definitive anchoring?** Understanding this gray zone is fundamental for evaluating a rollup's real security model.

The gray zone is the period during which the rollup's state has already been modified by the recent transactions, but that new state has not yet been crystallized on Bitcoin. During this gray zone, the system works like this. Transactions are **ordered** by the sequencer and are processed by the execution layer. The resulting state is **communicated** to all the rollup's nodes, which replicate it in their own databases. The applications built on the rollup read this state and rest on it for their own logic. **Everything works as if the state were definitive**, but technically it is still "awaiting confirmation."

In this gray zone, there are guarantees and there are risks. The **guarantees** are: that the transactions were actually signed by the legitimate owners of the funds (cryptography cannot be bypassed); that the computed state is mathematically correct with respect to the transactions applied (the determinism of the execution layer guarantees it); that the data is available to all the rollup's operators. The **risks** are: that the sequencer reorders the transactions in a way that is suboptimal for the users (extracting MEV); that the sequencer censors some transactions by not including them; that the sequencer stalls temporarily due to technical problems, delaying the anchoring.

Notice what is **not** a risk in this gray zone: that someone steals the funds. The sequencer cannot steal, because it does not have the private keys. No other operator of the system can steal, because they do not have the private keys. Cryptography remains the insurmountable wall even during the gray zone. **The risks are of efficiency and experience, not of the security of the funds.**

When the anchoring finally arrives, and when the anchoring is confirmed by Bitcoin finality, the gray zone closes. The state that was "practically definitive" becomes "mathematically definitive." From that moment, even the few residual risks are swept away: the state commitment is crystallized, the history is written, and no one — not the project's team, not the sequencer, not an attacker with unlimited resources — can modify it retroactively.

This "closing of the gray zone" is the moment when the rollup keeps its deepest promise: **Bitcoin security transferred to Hyper's state**. The fact that the closing happens periodically, and not instantaneously, is the small price the model pays to obtain the execution speed that makes it useful. It is an acceptable price, and accepting it consciously is part of using the system well.

⁂

5.8 — Questions and Answers: Clarifying the Chapter's Concepts

Question 1: If the transaction is "practically definitive" right away but "mathematically definitive" only after an hour, what happens if Bob, who received Alice's payment, spends it immediately? Is his subsequent payment also "practically definitive," or does it inherit the uncertainty of Alice's?

It inherits it. It is a subtle but important point. If Bob immediately spends the 50 tokens Alice sent him, before Alice's transaction is anchored, then his new transaction is valid only if Alice's transaction is valid. If for some pathological reason (a dishonest sequencer, a technical problem) Alice's transaction were then not anchored, Bob's transaction could also be invalidated. **This creates what is called a "chain of dependencies," which resolves only at the definitive anchoring.** For most practical uses, this is not a problem, because the risks in the gray zone are limited. But for applications where the value at stake is high, or where speed is critical and the operators cannot afford even the small risk of the gray zone, it is prudent to wait for Bitcoin finality before considering a chain of transactions concluded. **Concrete example:** it is the same logic as the "confirmations" in native Bitcoin transactions. When you receive bitcoin, some services ask you to wait 1 confirmation for small amounts, 3 confirmations for medium amounts, 6 confirmations for large amounts. The logic in rollups is analogous: the more value is at stake, the more confirmations (here, waits toward Bitcoin finality) it is prudent to await.

Question 2: What exactly happens if the sequencer goes offline? Are all the queued transactions lost?

It depends on what you mean by "lost." The transactions users have signed and sent to the sequencer, but which the sequencer has not yet processed, are waiting in the sequencer's queues. If the sequencer goes offline, these transactions remain there but are not processed until the sequencer comes back online. **They are not "lost" in the sense that the signatures are still valid and users can potentially resend them**, but they are not "included" in the rollup's state until someone processes them. If the sequencer stays offline for a long time, in principle forced inclusion mechanisms should exist that allow users to force inclusion directly through Bitcoin transactions, but these mechanisms must be implemented in the specific rollup. **For Bitcoin Hyper, the existence and details of the forced inclusion mechanism are one of the points future documentation will have to clarify.** Concrete example: Optimism had documented sequencer outages in 2023, during which transactions accumulated in the queue but were then processed when the sequencer came back online, without loss of funds. For Bitcoin Hyper, one would expect analogous behavior, but it is a point that deserves attention.

Question 3: Why is it said that the rollup "inherits Bitcoin's security" if in the gray zone there is nevertheless a period of non-finality?

Because the inheritance of security refers to **ultimate finality**, not immediate finality. Once the state commitment is anchored and confirmed on Bitcoin, the rollup's state is just as immutable as Bitcoin's own state. Retroactively modifying an anchored state commitment would require redoing all the proof-of-work accumulated after it, exactly like modifying an original Bitcoin transaction. **In this sense, and only in this sense, the rollup inherits Bitcoin's security.** The gray zone between execution and anchoring is a structural characteristic of the rollup model, not a violation of the security inheritance. Think of a parallel: when you send a registered letter, there is a period during which the letter is in transit and could in theory be lost. Once delivered and signed for, the delivery is definitive and protected by the postal system. The fact that there was a period of travel does not mean the postal system is unreliable: it only means that finality arrives at delivery, not at the moment of sending. The same holds for rollups. Concrete example: in an extreme case, suppose the Hyper team disappeared tomorrow with all the sequencer's keys lost. The transactions already anchored on Bitcoin remain valid, and the corresponding funds can be recovered through emergency mechanisms (if well designed). The transactions in the gray zone at the moment of disappearance would be the only ones at risk, and they could be resent or, in the case of well-designed forced inclusion, forced into the final state.

Question 4: Is there a way to see in real time where the anchoring process stands for my specific transaction?

Yes, and it is one of the essential features of a well-made explorer. A good rollup explorer shows for each transaction at least three pieces of timing information: when it was accepted by the sequencer (execution on the rollup), when the batch containing the transaction was published on Bitcoin (the anchoring), and how many Bitcoin confirmations the anchoring transaction has received (the finality). Bitcoin Hyper, according to the available documentation, is developing an integrated explorer that will show this information in real time. **For advanced users, this visibility matters not just out of curiosity, but for risk management**: it makes it possible to know exactly when a transaction entered complete finality, and therefore when it can be considered definitive for any purpose. Concrete example: an Ethereum rollup explorer like Etherscan shows for each transaction "L2 confirmed" (the transaction has been processed on the rollup), "L1 batch submitted" (the batch has been published on Ethereum), "Finalized" (complete finality has been reached). For Bitcoin Hyper one expects an analogous visualization, adapted to the longer timings of Bitcoin finality.

Question 5: Is the anchoring cadence the same for all rollups, or does it vary from project to project?

It varies significantly. On Ethereum, some rollups anchor very frequently (every few minutes) while others anchor less often (every few hours) to optimize costs. The choice of cadence is one of the most important parameters of a rollup's design, and it depends on factors such as: the rollup's transaction volume, Bitcoin fees at the moment, users' finality expectations, the project's economic strategies. **Bitcoin Hyper, as we have seen, has declared that it wants to treat the cadence as an adaptive parameter**, modifiable according to network conditions. This is a modern choice that reflects the industry's maturation. In recent years, on Ethereum too, it has become clear that fixed cadences are inefficient, and the best rollups implement adaptive logic that balances costs, finality, and performance according to context. Concrete example: during a period of high Bitcoin congestion, with high fees, Bitcoin Hyper could choose to anchor less frequently (for example every hour instead of every half hour), accepting a slightly longer risk window in exchange for sustainable costs. When Bitcoin fees are low, it could anchor more often, reducing the risk window and improving the user experience.

Question 6: If I need to withdraw bitcoin from Hyper to Bitcoin, do I have to wait for the complete finality of a certain state commitment?

Yes, and this is probably the most important case of concrete application of finality. When you request the withdrawal of bitcoin from the rollup to the Bitcoin blockchain, the system must generate a proof of your balance that can be verified by the Canonical Bridge on the Bitcoin blockchain. This proof rests on an anchored state commitment, and until that state commitment has reached complete finality, the withdrawal cannot be processed. **In practice, this means that withdrawing bitcoin from Bitcoin Hyper takes on the order of an hour or more**, even though the request transaction on the rollup is instantaneous. It is a structural characteristic of all rollups and not a limitation specific to Hyper. Concrete example: on Optimism, withdrawing to Ethereum takes seven days because of the fraud proof challenge window. On zkSync (a ZK-rollup), withdrawal takes hours instead of days because validity proofs eliminate the challenge window. For Bitcoin Hyper, given the hybrid model, withdrawal times will probably be in the range of hours, but the definitive details will depend on the final implementation of the proof model. This wait is a positive characteristic, not a flaw: it is the price of complete security for the most important operations.

⁂

5.9 — WHAT TO TAKE AWAY FROM THIS CHAPTER

The basic choreography of a rollup is the separation between fast execution and slow but definitive settlement. The user perceives speed, the system guarantees finality, and the two planes coexist in a way that completes each other without interference.

A transaction on Bitcoin Hyper passes through a journey in several stages: the user's signature, reception by the sequencer, ordering and batching, execution in the virtual machine, propagation of the new state, aggregation for settlement, publication of the state commitment on Bitcoin, confirmation and finality. All this takes time, but the user experiences only the first part as "direct experience."

Settlement happens in four phases: aggregation of the transactions into batches, compression of the data, computation of the state commitment, publication on Bitcoin. Each phase has specific security implications, and a well-designed rollup manages each with care.

Anchoring is the system's "heartbeat," and its cadence is a central design parameter. Frequent beats mean fast finality but high costs; rare beats cut costs but lengthen the risk window. Bitcoin Hyper has declared that it wants to treat the cadence as an adaptive parameter.

Perceived speed and guaranteed finality are not the same thing, and the well-designed rollup exploits this distinction. For most uses, perceived speed is "practically safe" and enough. For operations of high value or long duration, it is prudent to wait for guaranteed finality.

The gray zone between execution and finality presents limited, well-defined risks: censorship, suboptimal ordering, sequencer delays. It is not a zone where someone can steal the funds, because cryptography remains impassable. It is a zone where the user experience might degrade, but the security of the funds is preserved.

The inheritance of Bitcoin security refers to ultimate finality, not instantaneous finality. Once anchored and confirmed, the rollup's state commitment is as immutable as a Bitcoin transaction. The preceding gray zone is a structural characteristic of the model, not a violation of the inheritance.

For applications that require complete finality — in particular withdrawals to Bitcoin — waiting for the definitive anchoring is structurally necessary. This wait is the price of full security, and it is a positive characteristic of the design, not a flaw.

Chapter 5 ends here. We have understood the fundamental choreography that holds the rollup's four components together, and we have seen how the separation between perceived speed and guaranteed finality allows the system to offer both without compromising either. In ***Chapter 6 — Why a Rollup Does Not Fragment the Ecosystem (and a Sidechain Does)****, we will take a philosophical-technical deep dive into the difference between the inheritance of Bitcoin security and independent trust, going deeper into the reason the rollup model is structurally different from federated sidechains.*

Off-chain execution, settlement *on-chain*

The choreography that unites Layer 2 speed and Bitcoin finality. The fast confirmation on the L2 is a **soft guarantee**; the irreversibility on Bitcoin is a **hard guarantee**.

1 Fast above, definitive below: two times, two speeds

Bitcoin Hyper L2 TIME: SECONDS	signature → sequencer → execution → updated balance
₿ Bitcoin L1 TIME: MINUTES / ~ONE HOUR	state commitment → Bitcoin block → confirmations → finality

The user perceives **speed**. *Bitcoin guarantees* **finality**.

2 A transaction's journey: from signature to settlement

- ① **Signature** — Alice signs from the wallet.
- ② **Sequencer** — receives, orders, puts into batches.
- ③ **Execution** — the SVM verifies signatures, balances, rules.
- ④ **Updated state** — balance visible immediately (soft).
- ⑤ **Data Availability** — raw data available for verification.
- ⑥ **State root** — cryptographic fingerprint of the state.
- ⑦ **Bitcoin** — the state commitment is published.
- ⑧ **Finality** — after the confirmations: irreversible (hard).

For the user: **a few seconds**. *For Bitcoin finality:* **the time of the confirmations**.

3 The four phases of settlement: from the batch to immutability

- ① **Aggregation** — the sequencer gathers many txs into a batch.
- ② **Compression** — data optimized to reduce space and costs.
- ③ **State commitment** — the state root of the state is computed.
- ④ **Publication ₿** — commitment on Bitcoin via OP_RETURN / Taproot.

(!) The economic key is the asymmetry: **many transactions outside, a single compact commitment inside Bitcoin.**

4 Anchoring as the heartbeat that links Hyper to Bitcoin

Frequent beats — faster finality, a shorter risk window — but higher Bitcoin costs.

Spaced-out beats — lower costs, larger batches — but slower finality.

The anchoring frequency is the **rollup's heartbeat** — *a compromise between costs and timing, not a defect.*

5 Soft guarantee and hard guarantee

Perceived speed (SOFT GUARANTEE) — a few seconds · updated balance · reactive apps · sufficient for daily use

Guaranteed finality (HARD GUARANTEE) — after the anchoring · Bitcoin confirmations · immutable state · necessary for withdrawals and large amounts

GRAY ZONE · BETWEEN EXECUTION AND FINALITY

THE SEQUENCER CAN delay · temporarily censor · affect the order — IT CANNOT invent signatures · modify signed txs · directly steal the funds

Speed *is what the user experiences.* **Finality** *is what Bitcoin makes irreversible.*

THE KEY POINT

Bitcoin Hyper separates the **time of use** from the **time of finality**. On the **Layer 2** the transaction is fast, visible, and operational; on **Bitcoin** it becomes definitive, immutable, and verifiable. The rollup's choreography is this: executing off-chain, compressing the state, anchoring on-chain, and turning a **soft guarantee** into a **hard guarantee**.

PART II · THE ROLLUP MODEL APPLIED TO BITCOIN

Chapter 6
Why a Rollup Does Not Fragment the Ecosystem

(and a sidechain does)

6.1 — A Distinction That Changes the Nature of the Project

In Chapter 3 we distinguished the three families of Layer 2 solutions — forks, sidechains, rollups — comparing them on technical criteria. In Chapter 4 we dissected the rollup into its four components. In Chapter 5 we followed the choreography that sets them in motion. Now, before descending into the implementation details specific to Bitcoin Hyper starting with the next chapter, I want to pause on a question that has a more philosophical flavor but enormous practical consequences: **why does a rollup, done well, not fragment the Bitcoin ecosystem, while a sidechain, even done well, fragments it structurally?**

It is a question that at first sight seems rhetorical. It seems the answer must be "because the rollup anchors to Bitcoin and the sidechain does not." But that answer is too simple. Sidechains too "anchor" to Bitcoin in the sense that they use bitcoin as an internal asset and have peg mechanisms that rest on the Bitcoin blockchain. The difference is not in the fact that there is a bond with Bitcoin, but in the **type** of bond. It is a subtle point, and it is exactly in this subtlety that the difference between a legitimate extension of Bitcoin and a parallel blockchain that uses its brand is played out.

In this chapter I want to slow down and address the question with the calm it deserves, because understanding this distinction well changes the way you will evaluate any crypto project you come across in the future. It will protect you from the most aggressive marketing, it will help you recognize the promises that have technical substance from those that have only rhetoric, and it will give you the tools to judge Bitcoin Hyper not on the basis of what it says but on the basis of what it is structurally built to be.

The thread of the chapter is this. I begin with the notion of "fragmentation," because it is a word often used confusedly. Then I show why a sidechain, even designed with good intentions, is structurally a separate blockchain of which Bitcoin knows nothing. Then I show why a rollup, even with its current compromises, is structurally an extension of Bitcoin of which Bitcoin has actual knowledge. Finally I return to the specific case of Bitcoin Hyper and we see how it places itself exactly on this spectrum, with honesty about the points where the project's current reality is still distant from the pure theory of the rollup model.

6.2 — What "Fragmenting an Ecosystem" Means

Let us begin with the word that gives the chapter its title, because it is a word used vaguely and it deserves a precise definition. **Fragmenting a crypto ecosystem means breaking it into parts that do not really communicate with one another, each with its own security model, its own community of validators, its own history, and which lean on one another only through bridges that are points of fragility more than of true union.**

Think about what has happened in the crypto world over the last ten years. Hundreds of blockchains were born. Each with its own native token, its own community, its own applications, its own developer ecosystem. In theory, these blockchains "talk" to one another through cross-chain bridges. In practice, cross-chain bridges[a] have been the category of crypto infrastructure hardest hit by exploits[b] in recent years: billions of dollars stolen from Wormhole, Ronin, Multichain, Nomad, Harmony, and dozens of other projects. Every time they are compromised, they show that the blockchains they were supposed to connect were in fact separate universes, where trust in one universe did not transfer to the other.

The result is a fragmented crypto ecosystem. Bitcoin on one side, with its enormous security but its limited functionality. Ethereum on another, with its mature DeFi ecosystem but its historically limited scalability. Solana on yet another, with its speed but with its distinct security model. Hundreds of other blockchains each on its own island. **The user who wants to move value or applications from one island to another must pass over bridges that, in fact, are the weak point of the entire system.**

In this context, building an extension of Bitcoin that was another separate blockchain would mean **aggravating the fragmentation problem**, not solving it. It would mean creating another island, perhaps connected to Bitcoin through a new bridge, with its own security model, its own community, its own applications that do not really talk with the rest. A sidechain, even done well technically, is exactly this: another island.

---

[a] **Cross-chain bridge.** An infrastructure that makes it possible to move value or messages between two different blockchains, which on their own do not "talk" to each other. To work, it must lock the assets on one network and represent them on the other: it is precisely in this passage that the risk is concentrated. Historically, bridges are the most fragile point of the crypto ecosystem, because whoever manages to violate their rules can take the funds held in the link.

[b] **Exploit.** The exploitation of a flaw — in the code, in key management, or in a system's rules — to obtain an unintended result, usually the taking of funds. It is not necessarily a "break-in" in the classic computing sense: often the code works exactly as written, but that behavior contains a logical defect the attacker uses to their advantage. The great bridge thefts (Wormhole, Ronin) are examples of exploits of this kind.

A well-designed rollup is instead something different. **It is not another island; it is an extension of the same island.** Its applications, even though they live outside the main blockchain for performance reasons, are still part of the same security model, the same history, the same "truth" guaranteed by the main blockchain. Let us see why in a structured way.

⁂

6.3 — The Sidechain as a Separate Island: The Problem of the Origin of Truth

To understand why a sidechain is structurally a separate island, we must ask an apparently simple question: **when I look at the state of a sidechain, where does the assurance come from that that state is correct?** The answer is the key to everything.

In a sidechain, the correct state is the one approved by the internal consensus of the sidechain itself. If the sidechain has a federation of fifteen validators signing the blocks, the correct state is the one signed by a qualified majority of these validators. If the sidechain has a Proof of Stake[*] mechanism, the correct state is the one produced by the validators who have staked. If the sidechain has a merge-mined mechanism, the correct state is the one produced by the miners participating in the merge mining. **In every case, the authority that decides what is "correct" sits inside the sidechain itself**, and Bitcoin has no way to verify it.

Bitcoin, from a sidechain's point of view, is simply another blockchain where there is a peg script locking some bitcoin. Bitcoin does not know what happens inside the sidechain. It does not know whether the sidechain's validators are doing their work honestly. It does not know whether the federation is colluding to steal the funds. It does not know whether the consensus algorithm is working correctly. **Bitcoin sees only the deposits and withdrawals at the peg**, and it trusts (because it can do nothing else) that whoever runs the sidechain is doing things well.

This is exactly fragmentation.[†] The sidechain has its own truth, generated internally, with its own security system. Bitcoin has its own truth, generated internally, with its own security system. The two truths touch only through the peg, which is a fragile point where one trusts the other without being able to verify it. **They are two islands connected by a bridge, not a single extended island.**

TABLE 6.1 **WHERE THE TRUTH COMES FROM: SIDECHAIN AND ROLLUP COMPARED.**

Question	Sidechain	Anchored rollup
Who decides the correct state?	The sidechain's internal consensus.	The state demonstrated and anchored on Bitcoin.
Bitcoin's role	An external blockchain with a peg script.	The layer that crystallizes the truth of the state.

Point of contact	The peg: one side trusts the other.	Commitments and proofs verifiable on the Layer 1.
Result	Two separate truths, two islands.	A single truth, an extended island.

The decisive difference is not about speed, but about the origin of truth: in a sidechain the state is born from a separate consensus; in an anchored rollup the truth is crystallized on Bitcoin.

[*] **Proof of Stake.** A consensus mechanism in which the right to validate blocks does not depend on computing power, as in Proof of Work, but on the amount of currency a validator locks up as a guarantee (stake). Whoever acts dishonestly risks losing the locked capital. It is a security internal to the chain, distinct and independent from Bitcoin's.

[†] **Fragmentation (of security).** The condition whereby a chain connected to Bitcoin does not inherit its guarantees, but rests on its own separate security system. Trust is therefore not single and shared, but divided into several independent perimeters that communicate only through the peg — the most fragile point of the entire architecture.

FIGURE 6.2 **THE SIDECHAIN AS A SEPARATE ISLAND: TWO TRUTHS CONNECTED BY A FRAGILE BRIDGE.**

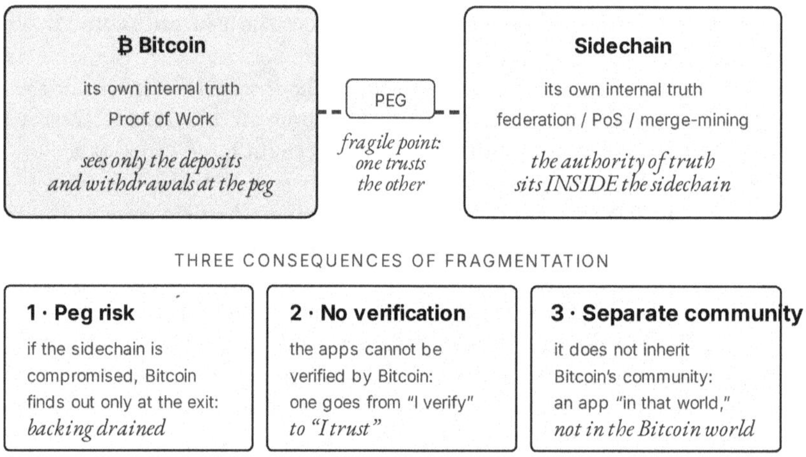

Bitcoin and the sidechain each generate their own truth with their own security system: the authority that decides what is "correct" sits inside the sidechain, and Bitcoin cannot verify it. The two islands touch only through the peg, a fragile point where one trusts the other. From this structure follow three consequences: the risk that the peg is drained without Bitcoin noticing until the exit; the impossibility of verifying the applications from the Bitcoin side, with the shift from the "I verify" model to the "I trust" model; the separation from Bitcoin's community. Even when everything works, structurally the sidechain remains something else.

There are concrete consequences to this structure. The first is that, **if the sidechain is compromised, Bitcoin knows nothing about it until the moment someone tries to bring bitcoin back through the peg.** At that point, if the sidechain has generated "wrapped" bitcoin without real backing, the last ones to try to exit discover that the peg no longer has sufficient backing. This is exactly what happened in various bridge exploits of recent years: the bridge generated tokens on a destination blockchain, someone found a way to "inflate" those tokens without corresponding backing on the origin blockchain, and when too many users tried to go back, it turned out the peg was drained.

The second consequence is that **the applications built on the sidechain cannot really be verified by those on Bitcoin.** If you are a Bitcoin user who wants to interact with a DeFi protocol on Liquid or Stacks, you must trust that the protocol is working as declared, because Bitcoin cannot verify the correctness of the protocol's execution. **You are moving from a system where everything is verifiable**

to a system where you must trust. It is a transition of trust model that many users make without realizing it.

The third consequence, perhaps the most philosophical, is that **the sidechain does not inherit Bitcoin's community**. Building applications on a sidechain means building for the sidechain's community, which is inevitably smaller and different from Bitcoin's. Liquid has its community, Stacks has its own, Rootstock has its own. They are legitimate communities, but they are separate from the main Bitcoin community. An application on a sidechain is an application "in that world," not "in the Bitcoin world."

Summing up. A sidechain fragments because it creates a separate island with its own security model, its own authority of truth, its own community. Even when it works perfectly, even when the validators are honest, even when the peg is never compromised — structurally it is something other than Bitcoin. **The brand borrows from Bitcoin, but the technical substance is elsewhere.**

⁂

6.4 — The Rollup as an Extension: The Origin of Truth Remains Bitcoin

Now let us see why a rollup is structurally different. Here too we start from the fundamental question: **when I look at the state of a rollup, where does the assurance come from that that state is correct?** The answer changes radically.

In a well-designed rollup, the correct state is the one that has been derived deterministically from the transactions whose data is publicly available and whose state commitment has been anchored and confirmed on Bitcoin. Notice that in this sentence there appear no sidechain validators, no federations, no signing committees. There appears only: **public data, deterministic execution, anchoring on Bitcoin.** Three elements all verifiable by anyone, without having to ask anyone's permission and without having to trust anyone.

The public data can be seen by anyone, because it lives in the data availability layer accessible to all. The deterministic execution can be re-run by anyone, because the rollup's virtual machine is open-source software anyone can download and run. The anchoring on Bitcoin can be verified by anyone, because Bitcoin is the most verified public blockchain in the world. **Putting these three pieces together, any observer — equipped with time and skills, but with no special permission — can independently reconstruct the correct state of the rollup and compare it with the state declared by the sequencer.**

This property changes everything. It means that **the authority that decides what is correct does not sit inside the rollup.** It sits in the public data and in the mathematics. The sequencer is not an authority that declares the truth; it is an executor that proposes a version of the truth anyone can verify. If the sequencer proposes something wrong, any observer can notice it and demonstrate it. If the sequencer disappears tomorrow, the rollup's state remains verifiable and reconstructable from the public data and the anchoring on Bitcoin. **The truth does not depend on the sequencer; it depends on Bitcoin and on the mathematics.**

From this property follow consequences opposite to those of sidechains. The first is that **if the rollup's sequencer is compromised, Bitcoin knows**, in the sense that the state commitment anchored on Bitcoin will not correspond to the publicly available data, and this discrepancy will be visible to anyone. The system self-corrects through fraud proofs or validity proofs: the wrong state is rejected, the sequencer punished, and users continue to operate on the correct state. **There is no way for the sequencer to steal the funds without the event being immediately visible and contestable.**

The second consequence is that **the applications built on the rollup can be verified by those on Bitcoin**, at least in principle. If you are a Bitcoin user who wants to interact with a DeFi protocol on Bitcoin Hyper, in theory you can verify the protocol's execution by downloading the public data and re-running it. You do not have to trust the protocol's team or the rollup's team. You have to trust the data and the mathematics. **It is exactly the same trust model as original Bitcoin**: anyone can verify the blockchain's state by downloading the software and processing the data. The rollup maintains this fundamental property.

The third consequence is that **the rollup inherits Bitcoin's community** in a structural sense. The applications built on a Bitcoin rollup are applications "of the Bitcoin world," even though they live in a higher execution layer. A Bitcoin user who uses a rollup is not entering another world; they are using an extension of the world they already know, with the same basic guarantees, the same currency, the same philosophy. **The rollup's community is a subcommunity of Bitcoin's, not a separate community.**

There is an image I like for illustrating the difference. **Think of Bitcoin as a fortified city. Sidechains are colonies outside the city, with their own walls, their own guards, their own government. They are connected to the mother city by roads, but they are other cities.** Rollups, by contrast, **are new districts of the same city**: they have wider streets, more modern buildings, more efficient transport systems, but they are inside the same walls, protected by the same guards, governed by the same laws. When you enter a new district, you are not entering another city; you are simply entering a more modern part of the city you already knew.

FIGURE 6.1 **TWO ARCHITECTURAL METAPHORS: THE EXTERNAL COLONY AND THE INTERNAL DISTRICT**

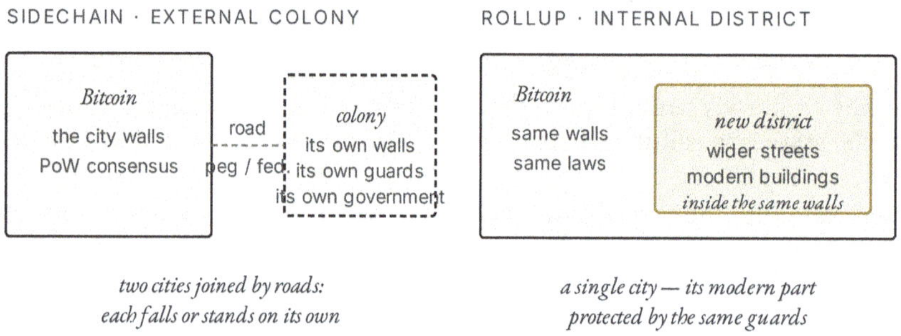

On the left: the sidechain is another city, joined to Bitcoin by roads. Even when the bridge holds, the two have separate defenses. On the right: the rollup is a district of the same city — modern, denser, faster — but inside the same walls and protected by the same guards. The architectural difference is not aesthetic, it is structural: the rollup inherits the city's defenses from within.

⁂

6.5 — The "What Remains If the Team Disappears" Test

To grasp this structural distinction better, there is a mental test I find particularly useful, and which I propose to you as a permanent instrument for evaluating any Layer 2 project. The test is simple: **imagine that the team running the project disappears tomorrow with all the resources, the keys, the infrastructure. What remains?**

For a federated sidechain, the answer is bleak. If the federation disappears, the bitcoin held in the peg becomes inaccessible (the signing keys are in the federation's hands). The sidechain's state stops evolving (the validators no longer sign blocks). The applications freeze (there is no longer anyone processing the transactions). Users lose everything. **The only thing that remains is the sidechain's past history, but it is a history that can no longer be used operationally.** It is as if the colony-city were abandoned: the ruins remain, but those who lived there must go elsewhere.

For an ideal rollup, the answer is completely different. If the team disappears, the rollup's state is nonetheless crystallized in the state commitments anchored on Bitcoin. The raw transaction data is nonetheless available in the data availability layer. **Anyone in the world can download the rollup's open-source software, download the data, and reconstruct the current state.** At that point, any group of volunteers can take over the sequencer and keep the rollup running. Users, if the system is well designed, can withdraw their funds to Bitcoin through the forced exit mechanism, even without the collaboration of the original team. **The rollup survives its team**, because its essential infrastructure does not depend on the team.

This test, in its simplicity, reveals the structural difference. A system where the team's disappearance means the system's death is, fundamentally, a centralized system that uses Bitcoin as a brand. A system where the team's disappearance is manageable and the system remains recoverable is a genuinely decentralized system that inherits Bitcoin's security.

Now let us honestly apply the test to Bitcoin Hyper, on the basis of what the current documentation reveals. **The answer is that Hyper today sits in an intermediate zone**, and it must be acknowledged honestly. On one hand, the architecture is set up so that the team's disappearance does not mean immediate loss of funds: the state commitments anchored on Bitcoin remain valid, and the general idea is that the system survives its team. **On the other hand, in the initial phase, some critical components still depend on the team in a non-replaceable way**: the sequencer is single and run by the team; the data availability layer's nodes are predominantly operated by the team; the forced exit mechanisms are still being specified. **If the team disappeared today, in the pre-mainnet phase, the situation would be complicated.** If the team disappeared in a few years, after the progressive decentralization path had been completed, the situation would be much better.

This is an honest assessment every investor should make. **It does not mean Hyper is a bad project: it means that, today, Hyper is in an initial phase where dependence on the team is still significant**, and that the promise "it survives its team" holds only if the announced progressive decentralization path is actually executed in the declared times and ways. Monitoring this path over the coming years is one of the main criteria for judging whether the project is keeping its promises.

⁂

6.6 — The Deep Meaning of "Inheriting Security"

There is an expression that recurs constantly in the marketing of Bitcoin Layer 2s, and it deserves to be taken apart with the same care with which we took apart the concept of fragmentation: **"inheriting Bitcoin's security."** It is a powerful, suggestive expression, and it is used by practically every project, from the most centralized sidechains to the most decentralized rollups. Yet its meaning changes radically depending on who uses it. Understanding well what it means is another instrument of defense against misleading marketing.

Let us begin with what it does **not** mean. It does not mean that the project generically leans on Bitcoin for something. Practically all Bitcoin-related projects lean on Bitcoin for something, often just to use bitcoin as an internal asset. This is not "inheriting security"; it is simply "using bitcoin as money." Liquid uses bitcoin as its internal currency, but Liquid's security comes from the federation, not from Bitcoin. Stacks uses bitcoin as an anchor for its consensus, but the security of its smart contracts depends on its validators, not on Bitcoin. **Using bitcoin as an asset does not amount to inheriting security.**

FIGURE 6.3 **USING BITCOIN IS NOT ENOUGH: THREE DIFFERENT LEVELS OF RELATIONSHIP WITH THE NETWORK'S SECURITY.**

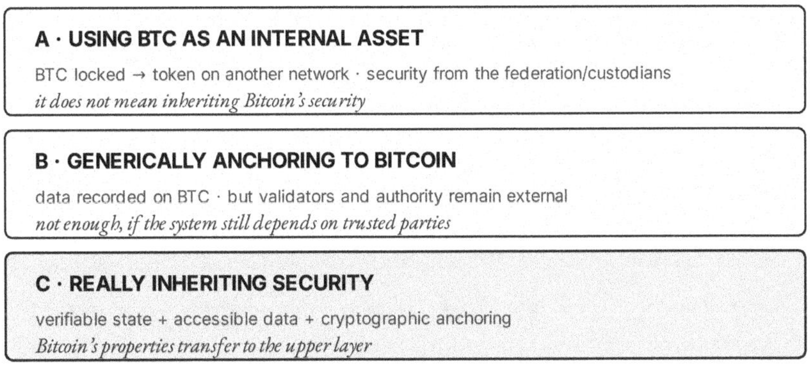

Security is inherited only when Bitcoin's fundamental properties pass to the upper layer.

What does inheriting security mean, then? It means that Bitcoin's fundamental properties — those three constitutive properties we identified in Chapter 1: decentralization, immutability, permissionless verifiability — are transferred to the system built on top. Let us see what it means concretely for each.

Inherited decentralization. The system above Bitcoin must not depend on a centralized entity for its functioning. If there is an operational centralization (like the single sequencer at rollups' launch), this centralization must be temporary and with a credible path toward decentralization, and above all **it must not be a centralization that can touch the security of the funds.** In a federated sidechain, the federation's centralization structurally touches the security of the funds (the federation could steal). In a well-designed rollup, the sequencer's centralization does not touch the security of the funds (the sequencer cannot steal). **The difference is enormous**, even though the marketing tends to confuse them.

Inherited immutability. The state of the system above Bitcoin, once finalized, must be just as immutable as the state of original Bitcoin. Retroactively modifying the state must be practically impossible, exactly like retroactively modifying a confirmed Bitcoin transaction. This is the sense of anchoring the state commitments: it is not just "writing something on Bitcoin," it is writing something in such a way that, from that moment on, the corresponding state is protected by the same computational power that protects Bitcoin itself. **In a sidechain, the immutability is the sidechain's, which depends on its validators; in a rollup, the immutability of the anchored state commitments is Bitcoin's, which is enormously more robust.**

Inherited permissionless verifiability. Anyone in the world, with an adequate computer and without asking anyone's permission, must be able to verify the system's state. For original Bitcoin, anyone can download a full node and verify the entire history of the blockchain. For a well-designed rollup, anyone must be able to download the raw transaction data, re-execute it deterministically, compute the state root, and compare it with the one anchored on Bitcoin. **This entire procedure must be possible without having to go through services controlled by the project's team.** If verification requires using an API run by the team, then verifiability is not fully inherited: it is subordinated to the availability of a centralized service.

Applying these three criteria rigorously, we discover that very few Bitcoin Layer 2 projects today fully inherit Bitcoin's security in the full sense of the term. Most sit in an intermediate zone: they inherit some properties but not all, or they inherit them partially, or they declare that they inherit them but in practice still depend on centralized components. **This is the reality of the industry, and it is important to be honest about this reality instead of passively accepting the marketing declarations.**

FIGURE 6.4 **THE THREE PILLARS OF INHERITED SECURITY AND HYPER'S MATURATION PATH.**

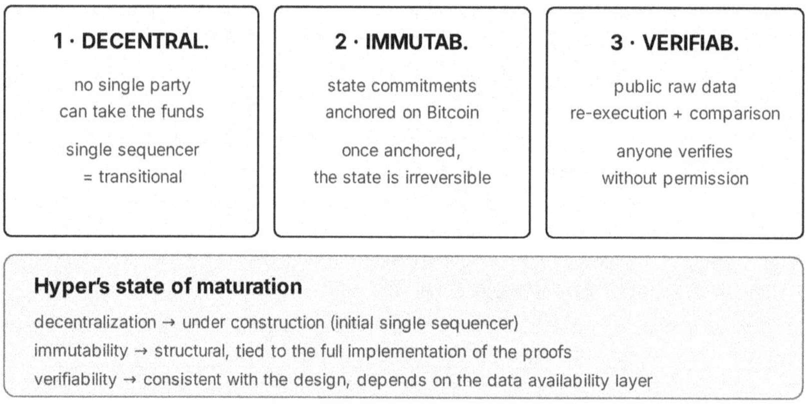

Hyper is designed to inherit Bitcoin's security: full realization depends on its critical components.

For Bitcoin Hyper specifically, the honest judgment is the following. **The architecture is set up to inherit Bitcoin's security in all three dimensions**, and this is what distinguishes it from federated sidechains. But **the full inheritance is not yet realized**, because some critical components of the model are still in a consolidation phase. Decentralization is still under construction (single sequencer at launch). Immutability is already structurally provided for but depends on the actual implementation of the proof model. Permissionless verifiability is theoretically guaranteed by the public data but depends on the maturity of the data availability layer. **In short: the promise of security inheritance is serious and consistent with the design, but the concrete realization is evolving.** Whoever invests in Hyper invests in the credibility of this path, not in a state already reached.

⁂

6.7 — Composability: The Rollup's Hidden Advantage

There is another aspect of the difference between sidechains and rollups that the marketing tends not to emphasize but that is enormously important for anyone thinking about the ecosystem's long-term development: **composability**. It is a technical term, but the concept is simple: it means the capacity of different applications to interact with one another like Lego pieces, where the output of one can become the input of another without friction.

In the Ethereum world, composability is one of DeFi's main engines. On Ethereum, you can take bitcoin (in the form of wrapped Bitcoin), deposit it in Aave as collateral to obtain stablecoins, swap the stablecoins on Uniswap, deposit the result in a Yearn vault, and all this in a single atomic transaction where, if one step fails, the whole sequence is undone. **This atomicity across different applications is what makes composable finance possible**, and it is structurally different from what can be obtained when working through bridges between separate blockchains.

FIGURE 6.5 **COMPOSABILITY AS MODULAR CONSTRUCTION: ONE APPLICATION'S OUTPUT IS THE NEXT ONE'S INPUT.**

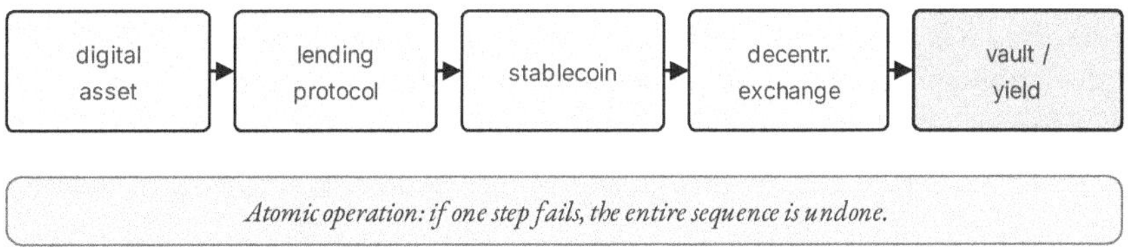

Composability turns separate applications into a single integrated financial ecosystem.

Now, let us apply the concept to the sidechain–rollup comparison. In a world where applications live on separate sidechains, composability is enormously limited. You can use an application on Liquid, and an application on Stacks, and an application on Rootstock, but these applications do not talk to one another directly. To move value from one to another, you must exit the origin sidechain, cross the bridge to return to Bitcoin, cross another bridge to enter the destination sidechain. Each passage costs time, costs fees, exposes you to bridge risks, and above all **it is not atomic**: if one step fails, the others have already happened and you must handle the consequences separately. **The sidechain is an island also from the standpoint of composability: its applications talk to one another internally, but they do not talk with those of the other islands.**

In a world where applications live on a rollup, composability is instead native and atomic within the rollup itself. All the rollup's applications share the same global state, and can interact with one another in complex atomic transactions. **Bitcoin Hyper, by choosing the SVM as its execution layer, also inherits Solana's composability model**, which is one of the most sophisticated in the crypto world. It means that, once the Hyper ecosystem is populated with applications, these applications will be able to interact with one another in ways that sidechain applications cannot.

FIGURE 6.6 **SIDECHAINS AS ISLANDS, THE ROLLUP AS AN INTEGRATED ECOSYSTEM.**

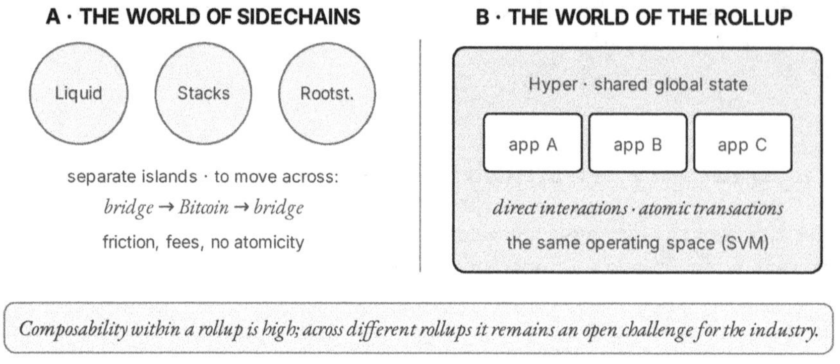

The rollup's advantage is not only security: it is an integrated, modular ecosystem capable of evolving.

There is a point to flag for honesty: **composability between different rollups is a problem not yet perfectly solved across the whole industry.** On Ethereum, composability within each rollup is excellent, but composability between different rollups (for example between Optimism and Arbitrum) is still evolving. For Bitcoin, where rollups are still few and in an initial phase, the problem is even more embryonic. Hyper, in this sense, is betting on being the main rollup for Bitcoin for a certain period, so that internal composability is enough to populate the ecosystem. If other important Bitcoin rollups emerge in the coming years, the problem of composability between rollups will become relevant.

Be that as it may, **for applications living inside the same rollup, composability is structurally much better than that offered by sidechains,** and this is one of the strategic advantages of rollups that less technical marketing tends not to communicate. For a developer or an entrepreneur thinking about building complex applications on Bitcoin, choosing a rollup over a sidechain is not only a matter of security — it is also a matter of flexibility and of future integration possibilities.

⁂

6.8 — The Community as a Structural Effect, Not as Marketing

The last point I want to touch on in this chapter is one that often goes unnoticed but that carries enormous weight in the long run: the effect of the architectural choice on the project's **community.** It sounds like a sociological topic more than a technical one, but in fact it is strictly tied to the technical structure, and understanding it makes it possible to foresee certain dynamics that the marketing does not tell.

In a sidechain, the community is inevitably separate from Bitcoin's. Even when the project is well intentioned, even when the founders are serious people, even when the product works — the sidechain's participants are **the investors and users specific to that sidechain,** not Bitcoiners who have extended their horizon. They have their own Telegram, their own Discord, their own Twitter. They discuss their own metrics, their own applications, their own challenges. They take a marginal interest in what happens to Bitcoin, because technically Bitcoin for them is just the internal asset or the consensus anchoring point, not their main ecosystem.

This separation of communities has concrete consequences. **The project's political and cultural strength is limited to its subcommunity**; it does not benefit from the broader push of the Bitcoin ecosystem. When a crisis arrives — a bug, an attack, a regulatory problem — the sidechain must handle it with its own community resources, which are inevitably smaller. When an opportunity arrives — a technological novelty, a new category of applications — the sidechain must seize it with its own resources, without being able to count on the creativity and energy of the whole Bitcoin world.

In a well-designed rollup, the dynamic is different. The rollup's community is structurally a subcommunity of Bitcoin's, because whoever uses the rollup is using an extension of Bitcoin, not another blockchain. **The Bitcoiners who lean on the rollup do not feel they are "leaving" Bitcoin to**

go into another world; they feel they are extending their possibilities within the same world. Their identity remains primarily Bitcoin, and the rollup is a tool.

This dynamic has very concrete effects on adoption. **A well-positioned rollup can attract attention and resources from the entire Bitcoin ecosystem**, not just from its own subcommunity. Bitcoin developers who would never have considered building on a sidechain (because philosophically they consider it "elsewhere") can consider building on a rollup (because philosophically they consider it "here"). Bitcoin investors who would reluctantly diversify toward a sidechain can allocate toward a rollup as "an extension of their Bitcoin portfolio." Companies and projects that want to enter the Bitcoin world can do so through the rollup without feeling they are betraying the original philosophy.

For Bitcoin Hyper, this dynamic is crucial for long-term success. **The project needs to be perceived as "Bitcoin extended," not as "a new blockchain that uses Bitcoin,"** and this perception depends both on the technical quality of the architecture and on the communication culture the team manages to build. If Hyper manages to position itself as a legitimate extension of Bitcoin, it can attract the energy of the whole Bitcoin ecosystem that wants DeFi without betraying its own identity. If it is perceived as another chain among many, it will be forced to compete in the saturated market of alternative blockchains, where the marketing is ruthless and attention fragmented.

⁂

6.9 — Questions and Answers: Clarifying the Chapter's Concepts

Question 1: If Liquid and Bitcoin Hyper both offer smart contracts, why should I choose one over the other?

Because they offer structurally different products under the same appearance. Liquid offers smart contracts with the security of the Liquid federation: if you trust the members of the federation (Blockstream, Bitfinex, BitMEX, and thirteen other companies), the product is valid for you. Bitcoin Hyper offers smart contracts with a declared path toward complete Bitcoin security: if you believe in the credibility of the progressive decentralization path, the product is valid for you. **They are products for different audiences.** Liquid is for those who accept trusting an identified consortium in exchange for functionality that is immediately available and mature. Hyper is for those who want to tend toward a more trustless model but are willing to accept the compromises of the initial phase and the risk of the consolidation phase. Concrete example: an institutional trader operating between centralized exchanges might find Liquid perfectly suitable, because they already trust the companies involved. An ideological Bitcoiner who wants to extend Bitcoin with DeFi without betraying the decentralized philosophy might find Hyper more aligned, accepting the temporal compromises.

Question 2: Is the composability you speak of really so important for the average user?

For the average user in the initial phase perhaps not, but for the ecosystem's evolution yes, and that is what ultimately determines the rollup's value in the long run. Think about it. DeFi on Ethereum grew from 2018 to 2021 precisely thanks to composability. Aave, Uniswap, MakerDAO, Yearn — all these protocols developed and grew because they could integrate with one another. Sophisticated yield farming strategies, complex derivatives, structured products — all this became possible because the protocols were composable. Without composability, DeFi would have remained a collection of isolated applications. **The same principle applies to any crypto ecosystem: composability is the value multiplier.** For Bitcoin Hyper, the composability inherited from the SVM is one of the most important strategic assets, even if in the first months/years it will not be directly visible to the user. Concrete example: a user who uses a single application on Hyper will not notice composability. But when the applications become five or ten, and it becomes possible to combine them into complex strategies, then the value of composability will emerge. It is a long-term investment of the ecosystem, not an immediate benefit.

Question 3: Can the "what remains if the team disappears" test also be applied to original Bitcoin?

Yes, and it is an illuminating exercise. Original Bitcoin passes the test practically perfectly. If Satoshi Nakamoto and all the Bitcoin Core developers disappeared tomorrow, Bitcoin would keep working. There are thousands of independent nodes running the protocol, hundreds of developers of alternative implementations, thousands of miners distributed around the world. **Bitcoin is designed from the beginning not to depend on any single entity**, and the disappearing-team test is the living proof of this property. For rollups, the test is a maturity metric. A new rollup like Bitcoin Hyper passes the test in a limited way today, because the team is still central to many operational functions. A mature rollup like Optimism passes the test better, because the sequencer still has some dependencies on the team but many components are already distributed. A completely decentralized rollup (which does not yet fully exist, not even on Ethereum) would pass the test perfectly, like original Bitcoin. **The test measures how much a system has grown in its decentralized maturity**, and it is a tool we should apply regularly to any project, also to measure its progress over time.

Question 4: If Bitcoin Hyper's community is a subcommunity of Bitcoin, then why does the project have its own $HYPER token instead of simply using bitcoin?

It is an important question that deserves an articulated answer. Rollups typically have their own token for reasons of governance and incentives. Governance: in a system where the sequencer decentralizes progressively, it is useful to have a token representing voting rights on protocol parameters, on upgrades, on economic decisions. Incentives: to incentivize participants to run nodes, validators, sequencers, it is useful to have a token that can be distributed as a reward. Moreover, in the initial phase, the token is a mechanism for financing the project's development through the presale. **Nonetheless, the fact that a $HYPER token exists does not mean the project is separate from Bitcoin in the same way an alternative blockchain would be.** Bitcoin remains the main asset used to pay fees, for DeFi applications, for withdrawals to the L1. $HYPER is a service token for the rollup's functioning, not the main asset of the ecosystem. It is a subtle but important distinction. Concrete example: on Optimism the OP token is for governance, but Optimism's DeFi applications mainly use ETH, USDC, and other standard assets. On Bitcoin Hyper the dynamic will be analogous: $HYPER for governance, bitcoin (in wrapped form) as the main asset for the applications.

Question 5: What would happen if other Bitcoin rollups emerged in the coming years, perhaps with different technical characteristics? Would Bitcoin Hyper remain relevant?

It is an important strategic question, and it is one of the main factors to monitor in the coming years. The situation on Bitcoin today is similar to Ethereum's in 2020–2021, when rollups were emerging and the competition between different solutions was open. On Ethereum the result was that several rollups found their own space (Optimism, Arbitrum, Base, zkSync, Starknet), each with specific characteristics and its own community, without a single absolute winner. **For Bitcoin, the dynamic is likely to be similar**: several rollups with different architectural choices will emerge, and each will find its segment. Bitcoin Hyper, by choosing the SVM, positions itself in a specific segment — that of developers and applications coming from the Solana world. Other Bitcoin rollups might choose the EVM (to attract developers from Ethereum) or custom environments (to optimize for specific use cases). **Hyper will remain relevant if it manages to build a solid ecosystem in its segment before the competition becomes intense.** The first mover's advantage is significant in the crypto world, but it is not infinite, and it must be exploited with fast execution and technical quality. Concrete example: in the Ethereum world, Optimism kept its place despite the emergence of Arbitrum and Base because it built a solid ecosystem and a differentiated proposition. Hyper will have to do something similar for Bitcoin.

Question 6: Is the difference you describe between rollups and sidechains really so sharp in practice, or are there many intermediate shades in the real world?

In practice there are many shades, and they must be acknowledged honestly. The sharp distinction I drew in this chapter is a conceptual distinction that holds for the ideal models. In the real world, there are projects that call themselves "rollups" but have significant centralized components (like all current rollups on Ethereum, at least in the sequencer), and projects that call themselves "sidechains" but have sophisticated decentralized components (like Stacks with its Proof of Transfer). **The real world is a spectrum, not a dichotomy**, and Bitcoin Hyper currently sits in an intermediate zone of this spectrum. That said, **the conceptual distinction remains useful as a compass for orientation**, because it makes it possible to assess in which direction a project is going and how far along it is on its maturation path. Concrete example: apply the distinction to Optimism. Optimism today has a single sequencer run by the Optimism Foundation, has a fraud proof mechanism that was implemented only partially and recently, has an OP token that is largely centralized. And yet Optimism is considered a rollup, not a sidechain, because its architecture is set up so that all these components can evolve toward more decentralized models without having to rebuild the system. The rollup/sidechain distinction is not an instantaneous state; it is an architectural trajectory.

⁂

6.10 — WHAT TO TAKE AWAY FROM THIS CHAPTER

Fragmenting an ecosystem means breaking it into parts that do not really communicate with one another, each with its own security model and its own community, connected only by bridges that are points of fragility.

A sidechain, even done well, structurally fragments the Bitcoin ecosystem, because it creates a separate island with its own internal authority of truth. Bitcoin knows only what enters and exits the peg, but does not know what happens inside the sidechain.

A rollup, done well, does not fragment: it extends Bitcoin with a new execution layer, but keeps Bitcoin as the ultimate source of truth, through the anchoring of the state commitments and the public availability of the transaction data.

The "what remains if the team disappears" test is a powerful tool for assessing the decentralized maturity of any project. A federated sidechain fails this test dramatically; a well-designed rollup passes it, at least in principle.

"Inheriting Bitcoin's security" means specifically transferring Bitcoin's three constitutive properties — decentralization, immutability, permissionless verifiability — to the system on top. It does not mean simply using bitcoin as an internal asset. The distinction is crucial, and the marketing tends to confuse it.

Composability is a strategic advantage of rollups over sidechains, because the applications of the same rollup can interact atomically, while those of different sidechains must pass through non-atomic bridges.

A rollup's community is structurally a subcommunity of Bitcoin's, while a sidechain's community is a separate community. This difference has enormous effects on adoption and on the attraction of resources over the long run.

Bitcoin Hyper, evaluated through these criteria, sits in an honestly recognizable intermediate zone: the architecture is set up to inherit Bitcoin's security in all its dimensions, but full realization requires the execution of the announced progressive decentralization path. Investing in Hyper is investing in the credibility of this path.

Chapter 6 ends here. We have understood why a rollup does not fragment the ecosystem while a sidechain does, and we have built the conceptual tools to evaluate any Layer 2 project through lenses more rigorous than those of the marketing. From here, Part II of the book closes: we have the foundations of the rollup model, and we are ready to enter Part III, where we will explore specifically Bitcoin Hyper's execution layer.

*In **Chapter 7 — The Choice of the Solana Virtual Machine: A Decision Against the Current**, we will examine in detail why the Hyper team chose the SVM instead of the EVM, what the specific trade-offs of this choice are, and what it means concretely for the project's developers and users.*

Rollup or sidechain: island or *district* of Bitcoin?

Because the type of bond with Bitcoin decides whether the ecosystem **fragments** or **extends**. A rollup is not automatically perfect: it depends on data, proofs, forced exit, and verification.

1 Fragmenting means creating islands

₿ Bitcoin · BRIDGE · FRAGILE · Ethereum · BRIDGE · FRAGILE · Solana · BRIDGE · FRAGILE · sidechain · BRIDGE · FRAG

When every network has its own truth, the user **crosses bridges of trust** *instead of staying within the same system.*

2 The sidechain sits alongside Bitcoin, but does not live inside Bitcoin

₿ Bitcoin
Proof of Work · settlement · its own security · sees only deposit and withdrawal

PEG / BRIDGE
who controls the keys?

Sidechain
federation / PoS / merge mining · internal state · applications · rules of its own

1 **Peg risk**
if the peg is compromised, the locked BTC are at risk.

2 **Limited verification**
Bitcoin does not verify the sidechain's applications.

3 **Separate community**
an ecosystem of its own, not a full extension.

3 The rollup extends Bitcoin from within

Sidechain · external colony
its own walls, its own guards, its own government.

Rollup · internal district
faster streets, modern buildings — but inside Bitcoin's walls.

L2 transactions → deterministic execution → public data → state commitment → ₿ Bitcoin

The sidechain builds another city. **The rollup builds a new district inside Bitcoin's walls.**

4 Inheriting Bitcoin's security: using BTC is not enough

Decentralization
no one can control or block the system definitively.

Immutability
the finalized state is protected by the anchoring on Bitcoin.

Permissionless verification
anyone checks data, state, and commitments without trusting the team.

A · Using BTC
BTC as an internal asset.
NOT ENOUGH

B · Anchoring to Bitcoin
writing data/references on Bitcoin.
NOT ENOUGH WITHOUT VERIFICATION

C · Inheriting security
public data, verifiable state, commitments on Bitcoin.
THE REAL GOAL

Security is inherited **only when Bitcoin's properties become verifiable in the upper layer as well.**

5 The decisive test: what remains if the team disappears?

Federated sidechain · strong dependence on the operator
if the federation disappears: peg frozen · validators halted · apps paralyzed · funds potentially inaccessible

Mature rollup · recoverable system
commitments on Bitcoin · raw data available · open-source software · reconstructable state · forced exit possible

HYPER TODAY
single sequencer · data availability maturing · forced exit to be clarified · still significant dependence on the team

GOAL
decentralized sequencer · redundant data · independent verifiability · documented forced exit · an ecosystem that does not depend on the team

A true rollup must survive its own team.

THE KEY POINT

A sidechain fragments because it creates a new island with a truth of its own and a trust model of its own. A rollup, if designed correctly, extends Bitcoin because it keeps Bitcoin as the ultimate source of truth: anchored state, available data, independent verification. Bitcoin Hyper places itself on this trajectory, but the full inheritance of security will depend on the maturation of the sequencer, data availability, the proof system, and forced exit.

PART III

The Execution Layer

The fast heart of the system. Why the Solana Virtual Machine, how Sealevel works, and what it means to run SVM programs anchored to Bitcoin.

PART III · THE EXECUTION LAYER

Chapter 7
The Choice of the Solana Virtual Machine

A decision against the current

⁂

7.1 — When a Technical Choice Becomes a Strategic Choice

Every crypto project, sooner or later, must make a choice that will define its identity for years to come: **which virtual machine to adopt?** It is a decision that seems purely technical — which software we will use to execute the smart contracts — but in fact it is one of the decisions most loaded with strategic consequences a team can take. It determines who the project's developers will be, which applications can be ported, which communities can be addressed, which ecosystem of tools will be inherited, and ultimately what the project's adoption trajectory will be in its crucial first years.

The Bitcoin Hyper team, facing this choice, did something unexpected. It rejected the industry's de facto standard — Ethereum's virtual machine, the EVM, adopted by practically all the Bitcoin Layer 2s that preceded it — and chose instead the Solana Virtual Machine, the SVM. **It is a decision against the current**, and the very fact of having taken it says something about the project's philosophy: the team preferred to optimize for performance and technical modernity rather than for maximum compatibility with the existing ecosystem. Understanding why it made this choice, and what its real trade-offs are, is the guiding thread of this chapter.

I begin with an observation that deserves to be made explicitly, because it often goes unnoticed. **In the crypto world, the choice of the virtual machine is almost never purely technical.** Even when it is presented as such, behind it there are always considerations of market positioning, of strategic alliances, of bets on the ecosystem's future. The choice of the EVM, which today seems "obvious" to many, is in fact a strategic decision: it means "I want to attract Ethereum's developers and applications, I want to belong to that macro-world." The choice of the SVM is a different strategic decision: it means "I want to attract Solana's developers and applications, I want to belong to that other macro-world." And the choice of a completely new virtual machine (like Move for Sui and Aptos, or Clarity for Stacks) is yet another decision: "I want to build something of my own, I accept the cost of starting from zero in exchange for specific technical properties."

In this chapter I want to take Bitcoin Hyper's SVM choice apart on three levels. **First level, technical**: what the SVM does differently from the EVM, and why these differences matter. **Second level, ecosystemic**: what choosing the SVM means from the standpoint of developers, tools, existing applications. **Third level, strategic**: what bet Hyper is making with this choice, and what the risks and opportunities are. By the end, you should have the tools to assess whether the choice was wise or reckless, and on which premises its success depends.

⁂

7.2 — What a Virtual Machine Is, Really

Before comparing the EVM and the SVM, it is worth taking a step back and understanding what a virtual machine is, because it is a concept often used vaguely. A virtual machine, in the blockchain context, is essentially **a simulated computer that executes programs in a deterministic and controlled way**. Let us see what that means concretely.

Think of your physical computer. It has a processor (the CPU) that executes instructions, a memory that stores data, an operating system that manages the resources, and applications that use all of this to do things. When you launch an application, the operating system assigns it a portion of memory, the processor executes its code, the application does its work. All good.

A blockchain's virtual machine is similar, but with additional constraints deriving from the context in which it operates. **First constraint: it must be deterministic[a].** On a normal computer, an application might behave differently depending on the system clock, on network availability, on the state of the memory shared with other applications. On a blockchain, none of this is allowed: given a transaction, the result must be identical on any node, regardless of the hardware, the operating system, the moment of execution. **Second constraint: it must be terminating[b].** On a normal computer, a program can run forever; on a blockchain, where every node must execute every transaction, an infinite program is a catastrophe. The virtual machine must guarantee that every program finishes in predictable time. **Third constraint: it must be secure.** The blockchain's applications are potentially hostile (anyone can deploy arbitrary code), and the virtual machine must isolate each application so that it cannot interfere with the others or with the underlying system.

[a] **Deterministic.** An execution is deterministic when, given the same input, it always produces the same result — on any computer and at any moment. It is an essential condition for a blockchain: thousands of nodes must be able to re-execute every transaction and all arrive at the same conclusion, otherwise they could not agree on what the correct state is. Everything that introduces variability (clock, network, randomness) must therefore be banned or made controlled.

[b] **Terminating.** A program is terminating if it is guaranteed to finish sooner or later, without being able to run forever. On a blockchain this is crucial: since every node must execute every transaction, a program that does not terminate would freeze the entire network. This is why blockchain virtual machines impose explicit limits — for example a cost for every operation — that ensure the execution concludes in a predictable time.

TABLE 7.1 **THE THREE CONSTRAINTS OF A BLOCKCHAIN VIRTUAL MACHINE.**

Constraint	What does it impose?	Why is it necessary?
Deterministic	Same input, same result on every node.	All nodes must agree on the same state.
Terminating	Every program finishes in predictable time.	An infinite program would freeze the entire network.
Secure	Every application is isolated from the others.	The code is potentially hostile and not vetted.

Determinism, termination, and isolation are not optimizations, but necessary conditions for a distributed network of independent nodes to agree on the same result.

FIGURE 7.1 **WHAT A BLOCKCHAIN VIRTUAL MACHINE REALLY IS: THREE CONSTRAINTS AND FOUR COMMON ELEMENTS.**

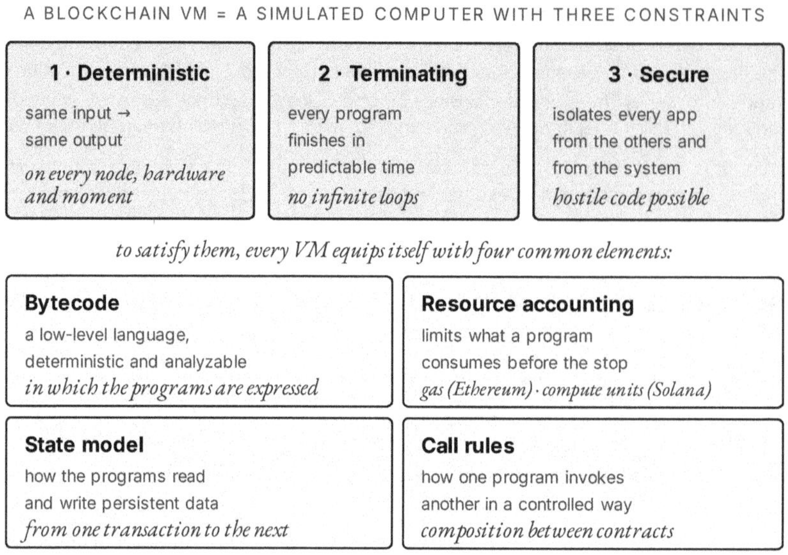

A blockchain virtual machine is a simulated computer that, unlike a normal computer, must respect three non-negotiable constraints: being deterministic (same input, same output on every node), terminating (every program finishes in predictable time), and secure (every application is isolated from the others). To satisfy them, every VM equips itself with four common elements: a deterministic bytecode, a resource accounting system, a state model, and rules for calls between programs. The EVM and the SVM share all these elements: they diverge — deeply — only in the implementation details, which is what the rest of the chapter compares.

To satisfy these three constraints, blockchain virtual machines have very specific architectures. **They have a low-level language (the bytecode) in which the programs are expressed**, designed to be deterministic and statically analyzable. **They have an accounting system for the resources used by the programs** (the "gas" on Ethereum, the "compute units" on Solana), which makes it possible to limit how much a program can consume before being forcibly terminated. **They have a state model** describing how programs can read and write persistent data from one transaction to the next. **They have rules for calls between programs**, describing how one program can invoke another in a controlled way.

All blockchain virtual machines share these basic elements. The differences lie in the details of how each is implemented, and those details, accumulated, produce very different performance and development characteristics. The EVM and the SVM are both virtual machines in the sense we have described, but their implementations diverge deeply, and now we will see how.

⁂

7.3 — The EVM: The Machine That Defined DeFi, and Its Limits

The Ethereum Virtual Machine was introduced in 2015 with the launch of Ethereum, and it is the virtual machine that practically invented the concept of the programmable smart contract on a blockchain. For a decade it was the de facto standard, and still today it is the base on which most of the world's DeFi runs. Understanding its merits and its limits is important because they constitute the reference point against which the SVM measures itself.

FIGURE 7.2 **THE EVM: A SINGLE EXECUTION LANE FOR A VIRTUAL MACHINE DESIGNED BEFORE THE MULTICORE ERA.**

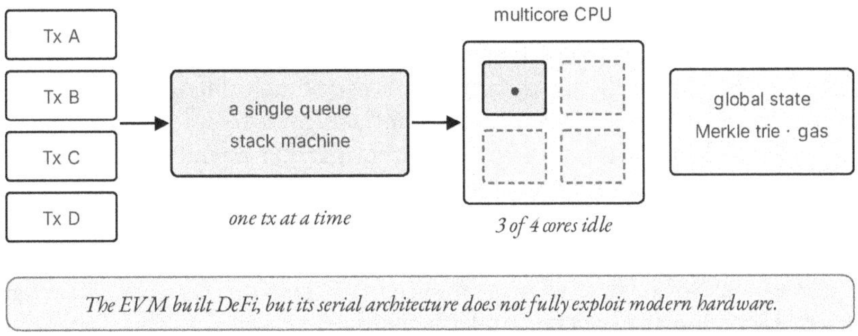

The EVM's merits are significant, and they must be honestly acknowledged before speaking of its limits. **First merit: it is simple and well understood.** The EVM has a relatively direct conceptual architecture: a stack machine that executes instructions one at a time, with a state model based on accounts and key-value maps. Its simplicity has allowed a vast community of developers, researchers, and auditors to study it in depth, developing a shared understanding that is one of the Ethereum ecosystem's most precious assets. **Second merit: it has a mature ecosystem.** Solidity, the main language for writing EVM smart contracts, is today known by hundreds of thousands of developers. Hardhat, Foundry, Truffle, and other development frameworks are mature. OpenZeppelin offers libraries of well-audited standard contracts. Etherscan and similar explorers offer visibility. All this constitutes a development platform that is hard to replicate from scratch. **Third merit: it has become a standard.** It means that applications written for the EVM can be ported from one blockchain to another (from Ethereum mainnet to the various Layer 2s, to compatible blockchains like Polygon, BNB Chain, Avalanche) with minimal changes. EVM portability has been one of the main engines of the crypto ecosystem's growth in recent years.

FIGURE 7.3 **THE TWO FACES OF THE EVM: DEFI'S HISTORICAL STANDARD AND THE ARCHITECTURE THAT TODAY SHOWS ITS LIMITS.**

Merits · why it became the standard	**Limits · why it is dated today**
Simple and well understood — a stack machine studied in depth by developers, researchers, auditors	**Serial execution** — transactions one at a time, even when they touch different data: it wastes modern cores
Mature ecosystem — Solidity, Foundry, Hardhat, OpenZeppelin, consolidated explorers	**Rigid gas** — predefined costs often far from the real cost: inefficiencies and abuses
A portable standard — the apps run on Ethereum, L2s, Polygon, BNB, Avalanche with minimal changes	**Inefficient state** — the global trie makes reads/writes costly and blocks optimizations
A decade of accumulated adoption and trust	**Solidity has traps** — overflow, reentrancy, memory: years of costly hacks in DeFi

The Ethereum Virtual Machine practically invented the programmable smart contract and for a decade was the de facto standard: simple, with a mature ecosystem and a portability that fed the growth of the entire industry. The same advantages, however, rest on architectural choices from 2014–2015 that today weigh as limits: serial execution, a rigid gas system, an inefficient state model, a language — Solidity — full of dangerous corners. This is why projects like Bitcoin Hyper choose not to build on top of it: the bet is that the technical advantage of a more modern architecture will compensate over time for the initial loss of ecosystem compatibility.

The merits stated, let us look at the limits. They are limits deriving from the architectural choices made in 2014–2015, when Vitalik Buterin and the Ethereum team were designing the first smart contract virtual machine in history, in a context where many things we take for granted today were not yet clear. **First limit: execution is serial.** The EVM executes transactions one at a time, in line, even when it would be possible to parallelize them because they touch different data. This is a structural limit of its architecture: the virtual machine was not designed to know in advance which data a transaction will touch, and so it cannot schedule them in parallel safely. On a modern computer with dozens of cores, this means wasting the vast majority of the available computational power. **Second limit: the gas system is rigid.** Every EVM operation has a predefined cost in gas units, calculated to prevent abuse but often far from the real computational cost. This creates inefficiencies: some operations are "too expensive" relative to what they actually cost the network, others are "too cheap" and can be abused. **Third limit: the state model is inefficient.** Access to the global state (the Merkle Patricia trie that stores all the smart contracts' states) requires costly reads and writes, and the fact that all accounts sit in a single shared space prevents sophisticated optimizations. **Fourth limit: the Solidity language has traps.** Solidity is an expressive language but with many dangerous corners: integer overflow (fixed only in recent versions), reentrancy problems, complex memory management, unintuitive compiler behaviors. Years of costly hacks in DeFi were caused by Solidity bugs that developers wrote inadvertently.

These limits, taken together, mean that the EVM today is **a mature but dated virtual machine.** It works, it has an enormous ecosystem, but its performance and its security are significantly below what is theoretically possible with today's technical knowledge. **It is exactly for this reason that some projects, including Bitcoin Hyper, have decided not to build on top of it**, choosing more modern architectures instead. The bet is that the technical advantage will compensate over time for the initial loss of ecosystem compatibility.

⁂

7.4 — The SVM: The Machine Designed for Performance

The Solana Virtual Machine was designed from scratch starting in 2017–2018 by the Solana team, with a very specific goal: **to maximize performance by fully exploiting modern hardware**. The SVM's architectural choices are deeply different from the EVM's, and these differences produce distinctive performance and development characteristics. Let us look at them.

First characteristic: parallel execution through the declared-accounts model. It is the heart of the SVM, and it deserves a careful explanation. On the EVM, a transaction is a sequence of operations that can read and write any part of the global state: the system does not know in advance what the transaction will touch, so it cannot execute it in parallel with others without risking conflicts. On the SVM, the model is different: **every transaction must declare in advance which accounts it will read and which it will write**. The system, knowing this information, can analyze a batch of transactions and understand which are "independent" of one another (they touch different accounts) and can therefore be executed in parallel. Transactions that touch the same accounts are serialized, but those working on different data run in parallel on the CPU's different cores. The result is a throughput potentially orders of magnitude higher than the EVM's, on identical hardware.

FIGURE 7.4 **FROM A SINGLE LANE TO MULTIPLE PARALLEL LANES: THE SVM'S EXECUTION MODEL.**

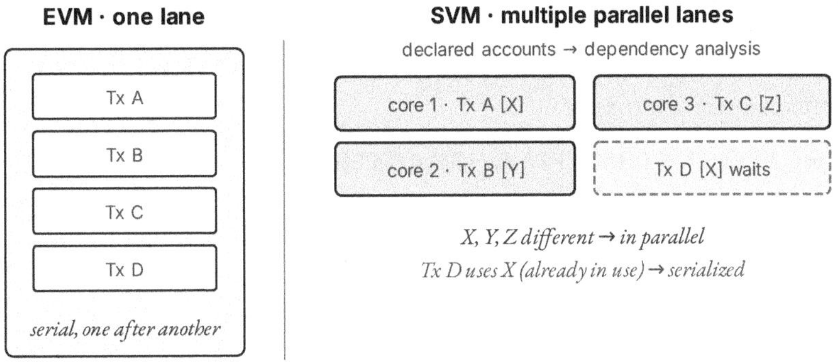

The SVM distributes the work across the cores because it knows in advance the accounts each transaction involves.

Second characteristic: the compute units system. The SVM has an accounting system for computational resources that is more granular and accurate than the EVM's. Instead of the "gas" that approximates the computational cost of each operation, the SVM measures "compute units" that more directly reflect the use of CPU resources. The system is more efficient at rewarding well-optimized code and penalizing inefficient code, and it allows developers and network operators to have a clearer idea of what a program will cost in real terms.

Third characteristic: the account-based state model. This too is different from the EVM. On the EVM, every smart contract has its own internal "storage space," and accessing other contracts' data requires complex cross-contract calls. On the SVM, **the state is organized into separate accounts**, each of which can be owned by a program and contain arbitrary data. A program can read and modify its accounts more easily, and the spatial organization of the state is clearer. Moreover, accounts are "rent-paying": whoever wants to keep data in the state must pay a fee proportional to the space occupied, which creates natural incentives to use space efficiently (although in the modern SVM model there are variants with respect to the original form of rent).

Fourth characteristic: the Rust[a] language. The SVM does not have a proprietary development language like Solidity. It uses Rust, one of the most modern and safest programming languages in existence, originally developed by Mozilla and today adopted in contexts requiring performance and reliability (the Linux kernel, high-scale web services, embedded systems). Rust has characteristics that make it particularly suitable for developing secure smart contracts: the ownership system prevents many memory bugs that are common in Solidity, the type system is expressive and catches errors at compile time, and the library ecosystem is enormous. **Developers coming from Rust find SVM programming much more natural than the transition to Solidity**, even though Rust's initial learning curve is steep.

Fifth characteristic: the Anchor framework. On top of Rust, the Solana ecosystem has developed a framework called Anchor that enormously simplifies the development of SVM programs. Anchor provides macros that automatically generate the repetitive code (account validation, data deserialization, error handling), standard patterns for the most common contracts, and a higher-level syntax that reduces the amount of code the developer must write. It is the equivalent of OpenZeppelin for the Ethereum world, but more integrated into the development process. **Anchor is today the standard tool for those developing on the SVM[b]**, and Bitcoin Hyper inherits it directly in its development environment.

---

[a] **Rust.** A modern programming language, known for combining high performance and strong safety: its compiler prevents at the root many memory-management errors that, in other languages, are a source of vulnerabilities. This is why it has become the standard in the development of SVM programs. The trade-off is a steeper learning curve: writing in Rust requires more discipline, but it eliminates entire categories of defects before the code is even executed.

[b] **Anchor.** A framework built on top of Rust that simplifies the development of programs for the SVM environment, automatically generating the repetitive code and providing ready-made patterns for the most common cases. It plays for the SVM a role similar to the one libraries like OpenZeppelin have had for Ethereum: it reduces manual work and errors. Its

availability on a new Layer 2 is a concrete indicator of the development environment's maturity, but the actual compatibility must always be verified in the field.

Putting these characteristics together, the SVM appears as a virtual machine **more modern, more performant, and safer than the EVM**, at least on paper. The performance is dramatically superior thanks to parallelism. The Rust language reduces entire categories of bugs. The organization of the state is more rational. All this is the technical package Bitcoin Hyper has chosen to adopt. Now let us see what it means concretely for the project.

TABLE 7.2 **THE FIVE DISTINCTIVE CHARACTERISTICS OF THE SVM.**

Characteristic	Main advantage
Parallel execution	Multiple transactions processed together: much higher throughput
Account-based state	Data organized in distinct accounts: efficient, parallelizable access
Compute units	Resources measured with granularity: more predictable costs
Rust language	Safe memory and errors caught at compile time
Anchor framework	Less repetitive code and standardized checks for the developer

None of these characteristics, on its own, defines the SVM: it is their combination that composes the technical package Bitcoin Hyper declares it wants to inherit. The advantages indicated, however, remain "on paper" until they are verified in production.

FIGURE 7.5 **THE SVM TECHNICAL PACKAGE ADOPTED BY HYPER.**

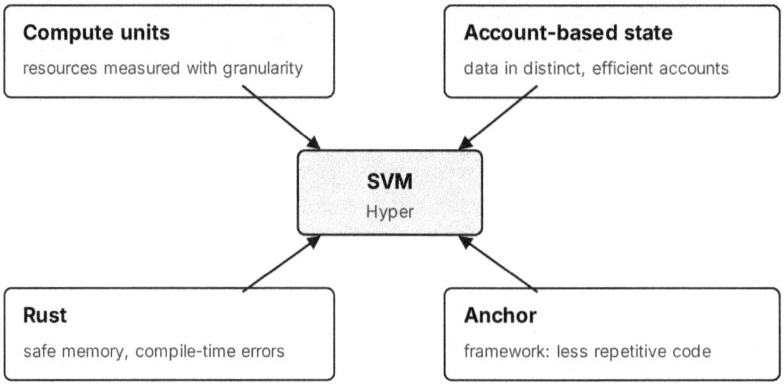

The four elements are not independent: they converge toward a single execution environment. The compute units measure with precision the resources consumed by each operation; the state organized in distinct accounts enables parallel execution; Rust reduces at the root entire categories of memory errors; Anchor takes the repetitive code away from the developer and standardizes the checks. It is the combination of these choices — not a single component — that defines the technical profile Bitcoin Hyper declares it wants to inherit from the Solana ecosystem.

> *A terminological clarification useful for the reader: in this context "SVM" denotes the execution model, that is, the set of rules by which programs are processed, and not a single piece of software. Hyper declares that it adopts this model; the verification will concern how faithfully the actual implementation reproduces its behavior.*

TABLE 7.3 **THE EVM AND THE SVM COMPARED, ON SIX DESIGN DIMENSIONS**

Dimension	EVM (Ethereum)	SVM (Solana, Hyper)
Execution	Serial — one tx at a time	Parallel, through declared accounts
Resource accounting	Gas, rigid and approximate	Compute units, granular
State model	Shared Merkle Patricia trie	Account-based, isolated
Throughput	Tens of TPS	Thousands of TPS
Main language	Solidity	Rust + Anchor
Ecosystem	The largest, the most mature	The second, the fastest growing

How to read it. *The EVM has the ecosystem; the SVM has the architecture. Hyper's bet is that the technical advantage will compensate, over time, for the initial loss of compatibility with Solidity contracts.*

⁂

7.5 — What Changes for Developers

A virtual machine choice is not only a matter of theoretical performance: it is also, and perhaps above all, a matter of **who will choose to develop on the project**. Different worlds of developers have different languages, tools, habits, libraries. Moving an application from one world to the other is not impossible, but it takes time and creates frictions that can determine an initiative's success or failure.

For Bitcoin Hyper, choosing the SVM means **addressing primarily the world of Solana developers**. This includes several categories of developers. Those working on DeFi on Solana — protocols like Jupiter, Raydium, Marinade, Kamino — know the SVM, know Anchor, know how to write efficient code. Those developing gaming applications on Solana — a particularly active sector — know how to exploit the SVM's performance for real-time games. Those working in the Solana NFT world — Magic Eden, Tensor, and other marketplaces — know the specific development patterns. **All these developers, in principle, can bring their applications to Bitcoin Hyper with relatively contained changes**, because the execution environment is nearly identical.

The Bitcoin Hyper team made this strategy explicit in a specific post (October 2025) devoted to developer workflows. The promise is that whoever knows how to use the standard Solana CLI can deploy programs on Hyper without learning anything new: the same commands (`solana program deploy`, `solana call`, `solana logs`) work identically, one just points the client to a Hyper endpoint instead of a Solana endpoint. **This is a drop-in compatibility characteristic that is exceptionally valuable for reducing adoption friction.** A Solana developer who wants to "try" Hyper can do so in a few minutes, without significant investments of time.

Note. The drop-in compatibility described here is a project promise, formulated in an October 2025 update: it indicates the goal of making the Solana tools work by simply pointing to a different endpoint. The decisive verification will come only with the mainnet, when it will be possible to measure how truly "without changes" the compatibility is and which differences emerge in practice. Reducing adoption friction is a real advantage, but it remains one only if confirmed by actual deployments.

FIGURE 7.8 **FROM SOLANA TO HYPER: FAMILIAR TOOLS AND OPERATIONAL COMPATIBILITY.**

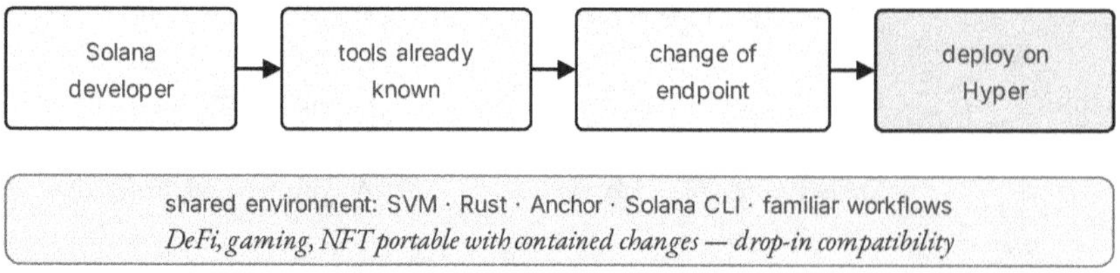

For a Solana developer, trying Hyper means changing destination, not working environment.

But there is the other side of the coin, and it must be faced honestly. **Choosing the SVM also means excluding the world of EVM developers**, which is significantly larger than the SVM one. Existing Solidity[a] applications — the vast majority of the world's DeFi universe — cannot be ported directly. Rewrites in Rust would be needed, which are costly and risky operations: even a simple application can require weeks or months of work to be ported, and every rewrite potentially introduces new bugs. For complex applications like Aave, Compound, Uniswap, a complete rewrite is practically out of the question: the Hyper team cannot expect Ethereum's great DeFi protocols to redo everything from scratch just to support Hyper.

This creates a precise strategic dynamic. **Hyper is betting that it will manage to build a DeFi ecosystem of its own**, mainly through the porting of Solana applications and through the development of new protocols specific to the Bitcoin Hyper environment. It is an ambitious bet, because it means duplicating to some degree the work Solana did in five years, in a much shorter time. If the bet works, Hyper will have a differentiated ecosystem with superior technical characteristics. If it does not work, Hyper risks remaining a technically interesting but economically marginal island.

An intermediate compromise some projects attempt is to **build an EVM compatibility layer on top of the SVM**, so as to be able to execute Solidity contracts as well. Research projects in this direction exist, and in principle it is possible. But it is a complex addition that introduces performance overhead and potential vulnerabilities, and it is not clear whether Hyper will pursue it in the medium term. The team, in its updates, has always presented the SVM as a primary and definitive choice, with no hints of a future EVM layer. Whoever invests in Hyper is investing, at least for now, in an SVM-only world.

[a] **Solidity.** The language in which most smart contracts for Ethereum and for EVM-compatible networks are written. Applications written in Solidity do not run directly on an SVM virtual machine: to be ported, they must be rewritten, normally in Rust.

FIGURE 7.9 **THE SVM BET: LESS FRICTION FOR SOLANA, GREATER DISTANCE FROM THE EVM ECOSYSTEM.**

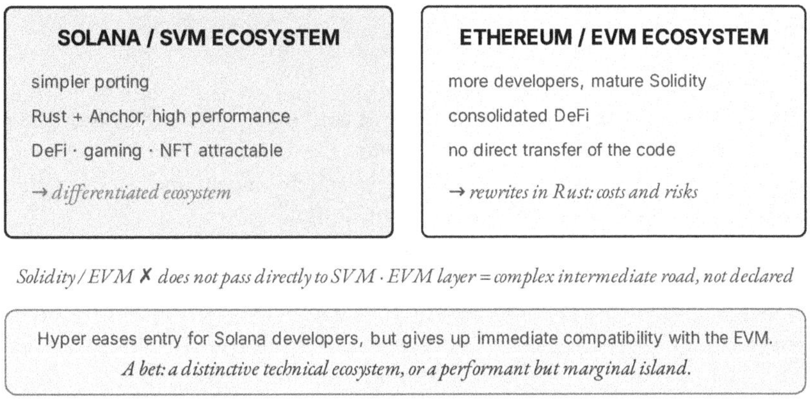

⁂

7.6 — The Delicate Point: The SVM Was Designed for Solana, Not for Bitcoin

There is an aspect that deserves particular attention, because it is an important technical nuance and because the Hyper team explicitly addressed it in a research post (December 2025) devoted to the topic of determinism. **The SVM was originally designed for Solana, a blockchain with characteristics very different from Bitcoin's.** Adapting it to a rollup anchored to Bitcoin requires adjustments that are not trivial, and understanding these adjustments gives an idea of the project's technical complexity.

Let us look at the main differences between the SVM's original context (Solana) and the context in which Hyper is using it (a Bitcoin rollup).

FIGURE 7.6 **THE SAME VIRTUAL MACHINE, TWO DIFFERENT CONTEXTS: WHAT CHANGES BRINGING THE SVM FROM SOLANA TO A ROLLUP ANCHORED TO BITCOIN.**

Dimension	SVM on Solana (original context)	SVM on Hyper (Bitcoin rollup)
Finality	A few seconds, its own consensus	Tens of minutes, inherited from Bitcoin
Block rhythm	~400 ms per block	Fast execution, slow anchoring
Throughput	Enormous target, immediate validation	Also limited by anchoring costs and rhythm
Determinism	Critical, but within Solana's consensus	Even more critical: different nodes must agree on the same state
VM evolution	Upgrades decided by Solana	Open choice: follow Solana or fork

The SVM was designed for Solana, a blockchain with its own consensus, finality in a few seconds, and blocks every 400 milliseconds. Bringing it into a rollup anchored to Bitcoin changes the context on five dimensions: finality becomes Bitcoin's slow one, throughput is also constrained by anchoring costs, and determinism in parallel execution becomes even more critical, because different nodes must reconstruct the same final state from the same transactions — if they diverge, the rollup breaks. There also remains an open strategic choice: follow Solana in the VM's upgrades, maintaining compatibility but depending on its decisions, or fork and diverge. Hyper does not simply "use" the SVM: it adapts it, and the success of this adaptation is a key variable of the project.

On Solana, the SVM runs in a context of independent consensus, where the validators produce blocks every 400 milliseconds and reach finality in a few seconds. On Hyper, the SVM runs in a rollup context, where execution is fast but finality on Bitcoin arrives in much longer times (tens of minutes or more). **This difference in timing changes several things in the design.**

On Solana, the target throughput is enormous (tens of thousands of transactions per second) and all transactions are validated immediately. On a Bitcoin rollup, the actual throughput also depends on the costs and limits of anchoring, and so it can be different. On Solana, the applications assume a certain model of consensus and block propagation. On Hyper, the applications will have to take into account that ultimate finality is Bitcoin's, and this has implications for certain types of logic that depend on finality.

But the most technically interesting point is that of **determinism in parallel execution**. The SVM on Solana executes in parallel thanks to the declared-accounts model, and exploits specific hardware to maximize performance. In a rollup, where different nodes must be able to agree on the same final state starting from the same transactions, determinism is even more critical than it is on Solana itself. **If two nodes of the rollup execute the same batch of transactions and obtain different final states, the rollup breaks.** This means that every detail of the SVM that could introduce non-determinism (the execution order of parallel transactions, the precision of numerical operations, the handling of edge cases) must be locked down rigorously.

The Hyper team, in the December 2025 post, explicitly acknowledged that this is an active research and development problem. It spoke of "rigid limits on execution order, on account access, and on visibility during execution" that must be imposed to guarantee that every transaction produces a single verifiable output. **This work is ongoing, not completed**, and it represents one of the areas where Hyper is innovating with respect to the original SVM.

There is also a practical aspect tied to the fact that the SVM is continuously evolving on Solana. Solana itself releases regular upgrades of its virtual machine, and every upgrade can introduce changes Hyper must consider. A strategic choice arises: **follow Solana in the updates** (maintaining compatibility with the Solana ecosystem but depending on Solana's decisions) **or fork and diverge** (maintaining its own control but progressively losing compatibility). Hyper's current documentation is not yet fully explicit about which of these two roads will be followed, and it is one of the points that will be clarified in the coming months.

All this does not mean the SVM choice was wrong. It means the choice carries with it **non-trivial adaptation costs** the team must bear, and which impose additional original technical work compared to "taking the SVM and using it." Hyper is not simply using the SVM: it is performing a more sophisticated operation of adapting the SVM to the rollup-on-Bitcoin context, and the success of this operation is an important variable for the success of the overall project.

⁂

7.7 — The Strategic Bet: Two Plausible Scenarios

At this point in the chapter, we have enough elements to assess the SVM choice from the strategic standpoint. Let us see how it could develop over the coming years, in two plausible scenarios, so as to understand which variables to monitor.

FIGURE 7.7 **THE TWO POSSIBLE OUTCOMES OF THE SVM BET AND THE VARIABLES THAT WILL TELL WHICH ONE IS COMING TRUE.**

THE STRATEGIC CROSSROADS OF THE SVM CHOICE

SCENARIO 1 · IT WORKS	SCENARIO 2 · IT STRUGGLES
→ *porting of protocols from Solana* → *the developer community grows* → *high-performance apps (gaming, DEXs with order books)* → *use cases impossible on the EVM*	→ *slow developer attraction* → *Solana remains more attractive* → *competition from EVM rollups* → *ecosystem below critical mass*
"the high-performance Bitcoin rollup"	isolation, not differentiation

VARIABLES TO MONITOR (12–24 months from launch)

deployed apps · TVL · unique developers · porting time from Solana · stability under load

a dozen apps = a bad signal · a few hundred = on track · over a thousand = excellent

The SVM choice is bold and technically defensible, but its success will depend on Hyper's capacity to turn the architectural advantage into a real ecosystem. In the favorable scenario, porting from Solana, a growing community, and applications impossible on the EVM make Hyper the high-performance Bitcoin rollup. In the unfavorable one, slow adoption and competition from EVM rollups relegate the project to technical isolation without critical mass. The real scenario will probably be intermediate: to understand which side it is leaning toward, one observes five variables — number of deployed apps, TVL, unique developers, porting time from Solana, stability under real load — in the 12–24 months following the mainnet launch.

Scenario one: the bet works. In this scenario, Hyper manages to build an active ecosystem of SVM applications, attracting portings of protocols from Solana and the development of new protocols specific to it. The Solana developer community recognizes in Hyper an opportunity to work in a Bitcoin-secured environment with familiar tools, and several important teams choose to deploy on Hyper as well as on Solana. The SVM's superior performance over the EVM translates into use cases that on Bitcoin's EVM rollups (or on Ethereum's rollups) are not possible: real-time games, decentralized exchanges with order books, high-frequency shared-state applications. **In this scenario, Hyper becomes the "high-performance Bitcoin rollup," differentiated and competitive in its segment.** The SVM choice turns out to be a far-sighted decision that made it possible to position uniquely.

Scenario two: the bet struggles. In this scenario, the attraction of Solana developers to Hyper turns out slower than expected. The reasons can vary. Perhaps Solana itself remains more attractive to its ecosystem's developers, because it has more liquidity and users. Perhaps the difference between "Bitcoin-secured" and "Solana-secured" is not important enough for many use cases to justify the porting. Perhaps other Bitcoin rollups emerge in the meantime with EVM choices and attract more attention because they have access to the much larger pool of Ethereum developers. **In this scenario, Hyper remains a technically solid but economically marginal project**, with an ecosystem of applications that does not reach the critical mass to generate significant network effects. The SVM choice turns out to be a factor of isolation more than differentiation.

Between these two extreme scenarios there are obviously intermediate scenarios, which are probably the most realistic. **The most likely scenario, in my assessment, is one in which Hyper manages to build a decent but not dominant ecosystem**, with some valuable applications that justify its existence and a certain number of dedicated users, but without becoming the "home" of all DeFi on Bitcoin. In this scenario, Hyper's success depends not only on the SVM choice but on many other factors: the quality of the team's execution, the management of governance, progressive decentralization, the capacity to form strategic partnerships, resilience to any technical problems.

FIGURE 7.9 **THE SPECTRUM OF POSSIBLE SCENARIOS FOR HYPER.**

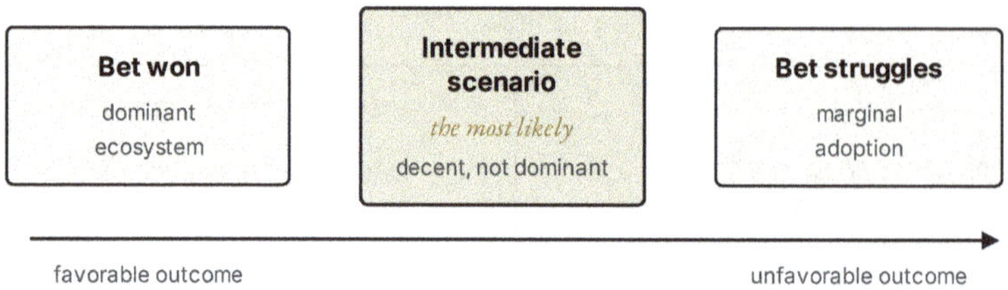

Between the two extreme outcomes — a dominant ecosystem or marginal adoption — the realistic scenario sits in the middle: a useful but not hegemonic network. The actual position will depend not only on the choice of the SVM, but on the quality of execution over time.

The variables to monitor to understand which scenario things are heading toward are several. **Number of applications deployed on the mainnet** once launched: a dozen would be a bad signal, a few hundred in line with expectations, over a thousand an excellent signal. **Total value locked** (TVL) in the DeFi applications: a good indicator of users' real interest as opposed to mere technical curiosity. **Number of unique developers** contributing to projects on Hyper: it measures the health of the development community. **Average time to port an application from Solana**: if it is weeks, excellent; if it is months, problematic. **Performance stability** under real load: comparing the declared benchmarks with those actually sustained in production.

TABLE 7.4 **THE FIVE VARIABLES TO MONITOR AFTER THE MAINNET LAUNCH.**

Variable	What does it measure?	Favorable signal
Applications on the mainnet	Developers' interest in building	From a few hundred up
Total value locked (TVL)	Users' real interest, not just technical	Stable growth over time
Unique developers	Health of the development community	Contributors on the rise
Porting time from Solana	Actual SVM compatibility	Weeks, not months
Performance stability	Endurance under real load	Benchmarks confirmed in production

None of these variables, taken in isolation, is decisive. It is their joint evolution in the twelve to twenty-four months following the launch that indicates whether the bet on the SVM environment is translating into a real ecosystem or remains a technically elegant but little-adopted choice.

These are the parameters that, in the 12–24 months after the mainnet launch, will tell whether the SVM choice was well judged or not. For now, it is too early to give a definitive judgment. **It is fair and honest to say that the choice was bold, technically defensible, but strategically not without risks.** Whoever invests in Hyper is betting, in part, also on the success of this architectural choice.

⁂

7.8 — Questions and Answers: Clarifying the Chapter's Concepts

Question 1: If the SVM is more modern and performant than the EVM, why do all of Ethereum's Layer 2s keep using the EVM instead of switching to the SVM or other virtual machines?

For reasons of ecosystem compatibility, and this is exactly the dilemma the Hyper team faced. Ethereum's Layer 2s (Optimism, Arbitrum, Base, zkSync) chose to maintain EVM compatibility because this allows Ethereum's developers and applications to move to the Layer 2 without changes. **Sacrificing the SVM's superior performance for EVM compatibility is a different strategic choice**, one that privileges the network effect over technical excellence. For Ethereum's Layer 2s this choice makes sense, because their purpose is to scale Ethereum and so they must be accessible to Ethereum developers. For Bitcoin, where a "native" EVM ecosystem does not exist (there is no Bitcoin EVM to extend), the choice is more open. Hyper assessed that the SVM's performance advantage justifies the cost of addressing a different ecosystem. **Concrete example:** Optimism in 2022 seriously considered switching to a modified EVM implementation with parallelism characteristics, but in the end decided to remain fully EVM-compatible. The decision was based entirely on compatibility considerations: all the Ethereum DeFi protocols could deploy on Optimism without changes, and this was considered the decisive factor. Hyper made the opposite choice, accepting not to have access to the pool of EVM applications in exchange for other properties.

Question 2: Can I develop on Bitcoin Hyper if I only know Solidity and not Rust?

In principle yes, but with a learning cost. Rust is significantly different from Solidity, and it is a language known for being hard to learn for those coming from more permissive languages. **The learning curve for a Solidity developer who wants to move to Rust is weeks, not days.** One must learn the ownership system, lifetimes, advanced types, idiomatic patterns, and how all this applies to the smart contract context. Nonetheless, once the curve is overcome, many developers report finding Rust more productive than Solidity in the long run, because the compiler catches more errors at compile time and because the patterns are clearer. For a gradual transition, frameworks like Anchor exist that reduce part of the Rust boilerplate and make the code more similar to what one would write in Solidity. **Concrete example:** a Solidity developer with two years of experience who decides to start developing on the SVM typically becomes productive in 4–8 weeks, with the first small projects deployed in the first month and complex projects after a few months. It is not a trivial transition, but it is feasible. The Hyper team has mentioned the intention to publish teaching material specific to this passage, but at the moment most of the existing learning resources are the general ones of the Solana world.

Question 3: What happens if Solana introduces an SVM upgrade that changes the behavior? Does Bitcoin Hyper have to follow it?

It is exactly the strategic question of "follow or fork" I mentioned in the chapter. The options are several and each has trade-offs. **Option one: Hyper follows Solana.** Every time Solana releases an SVM upgrade, Hyper integrates the same upgrade into its environment. Pros: compatibility with Solana remains complete, the ported applications keep working. Cons: Hyper does not control its own technical roadmap, it depends on the Solana team's decisions, and it might have to integrate changes that are not optimal for the rollup-on-Bitcoin context. **Option two: Hyper forks the SVM and diverges.** Hyper takes the SVM at a certain point and develops its own evolution of it, independent of Solana. Pros: complete control over the roadmap, the possibility of optimizing for the rollup context. Cons: compatibility with Solana progressively erodes, and developers must do extra work to support both platforms. **Option three: hybrid.** Hyper maintains compatibility for the basic functionality but diverges for the rollup-specific functionality. It is probably the most realistic road in the medium term. Hyper's current documentation is not explicit about which strategy the team will adopt, but it is a decision that will become ever more relevant as Solana evolves. **Concrete example:** Solana has already released several significant versions of the SVM (Token Extensions in 2024, various runtime upgrades). Bitcoin Hyper, launching in 2026, inherits a specific version of the SVM and will have to decide what to do with future upgrades. It is an important technical-management variable for long-term success.

Question 4: Does the SVM's parallelization really work in practice, or is it only a theoretical characteristic?

It works in practice, but with nuances. On Solana, the SVM's parallelization produces throughputs effectively much higher than the EVM's, even though the exact numbers depend on the type of transactions and the network's load. Solana has sustained throughputs on the order of thousands of TPS in production, though not always the 50,000+ sometimes mentioned in marketing materials. **The point is that the parallelization is there, it is real, but it is not free.** Applications must be designed to exploit it: if an application always touches the same global accounts, parallelization does not help because the transactions are serialized anyway. The applications that parallelize well are those where different users touch different data (for example, transfers between distinct accounts). **For Bitcoin Hyper, the challenge will be obtaining effective parallelization in the specific rollup context**, where the anchoring cadence and data availability introduce additional constraints. It is an area where the real benchmarks, once available, will say much more than the theoretical benchmarks. Concrete example: a DeFi application like a global lending protocol with a single shared "pool" has limited parallelization on the SVM, because all transactions touch the same pool. An application like a payments system between users, where every user has their own account, parallelizes excellently. Designing applications in a "parallel-friendly" way is a specific skill that SVM developers learn over time.

Question 5: Do native Bitcoin Hyper applications already exist, or is everything still theoretical?

On the basis of the documentation available up to spring 2026, Hyper has a working devnet where developers can experiment with deploying SVM programs. The team has confirmed that the standard Solana commands work, and has mentioned having tested basic components like SPL tokens, escrow contracts, and multisig logic. However, **there is not yet a mainnet open to the public, and therefore there are no applications in production with real users.** Alignment with partner teams is in an initial phase, with a small group of selected builders testing the environment. **This is a normal phase for a pre-mainnet project**, and it is important not to confuse it with a finished-product state. The applications developers are building today are prototypes and proofs of concept; the "real" applications will emerge in the months following the mainnet launch. Concrete example: compare with Ethereum Layer 2. Optimism did its public mainnet in 2021, but it is only in 2022–2023 that significant applications began generating real value. For Hyper, one would expect a similar trajectory: mainnet launch, then 12–18 months of active ecosystem building before applications of significant value emerge.

Question 6: If the SVM choice is a bet, how do I know whether I should bet along with the project?

It is a question that requires an honest approach to risk. The choice to invest in or build on a pre-mainnet project is always a bet, and with Hyper the bet has more variables than an EVM-standard Layer 2 project. There are some criteria that can help with the assessment. **First criterion: the quality of the team's execution.** Are they meeting the announced deadlines? Do they publish regular, substantial updates? Do they respond to technical criticism competently? **Second criterion: the quality of the developer community that is forming.** How many expert SVM developers are showing interest? Are there quality technical discussions on Discord or forums? **Third criterion: the evolution of Solana's standing.** Solana has had historical stability problems (service outages); if these get resolved, the SVM ecosystem becomes more attractive. If they persist, Hyper's appeal as "a more secure SVM" can grow. **Fourth criterion: the competitive situation on Bitcoin Layer 2.** Are other Bitcoin rollups emerging with different choices? Which ones are gaining traction? **Fifth criterion: your own technical understanding.** Do you really understand what the SVM means compared to the EVM, and why this changes the nature of the investment? If there are too many question marks in your assessment, it is reasonable to wait for the picture to become clearer before committing. Concrete example: a prudent investor might decide to observe Hyper for the first 6–12 months after the mainnet launch, assessing the real adoption metrics, before deciding whether to invest significantly. It is a slower approach but it reduces the risk compared to a massive allocation in the pre-mainnet phase.

⁂

7.9 — WHAT TO TAKE AWAY FROM THIS CHAPTER

The choice of the virtual machine is a strategic decision, not only a technical one, because it determines which ecosystem of developers the project will attract and which applications it will be able to host.

Bitcoin Hyper chose the SVM, going against the dominant current that uses the EVM. It is a decision that privileges performance and technical modernity over compatibility with the larger ecosystem.

The SVM is a more modern virtual machine than the EVM, with parallel execution through the declared-accounts model, a more granular compute units system, and the modern, safe Rust language. Its theoretical performance significantly exceeds the EVM's.

The EVM has merits that must not be underestimated: an enormous ecosystem, a standardization that has enabled application portability, a conceptual simplicity that has favored analysis and auditing.

Choosing the SVM means addressing the world of Solana developers, and excluding that of EVM developers at least until a possible compatibility layer. It is a specific bet on the differentiated value the SVM can bring to the Bitcoin context.

Adapting the SVM to the rollup-on-Bitcoin context requires original technical work, in particular as regards determinism in parallel execution. It is an active research area of the Hyper team, not a simple operation of "taking the SVM and using it."

The strategic bet can develop into different scenarios, and the variables to monitor are the number of deployed applications, the total value locked, the number of active developers, the time to port applications from Solana, and performance stability under real load.

For EVM developers, moving to Hyper requires an investment in learning Rust that is significant but feasible. For Solana developers, the passage is nearly instantaneous thanks to tool compatibility.

The success of the SVM on Hyper depends on multiple factors: the quality of the team's execution, the evolution of Solana itself, the competitive situation of Bitcoin's Layer 2s, the capacity to build a differentiated ecosystem of applications.

Chapter 7 ends here. We have understood why Bitcoin Hyper chose the SVM, what the specific trade-offs of this choice are, and which variables will determine whether the bet will work. In ***Chapter 8 — Parallel Execution and the Account Model: How Sealevel Works****, we will descend into the technical details of the SVM's parallelization mechanism, which is the heart of the system's performance advantage, and we will understand concretely how the SVM manages to do in parallel things the EVM is forced to do in sequence.*

NOTE

1 The SVM inherits the "Sealevel" model introduced in Anatoly Yakovenko's whitepaper, *Solana: A new architecture for a high performance blockchain*, 2017. The account model is the central difference with respect to the EVM.

Why Hyper chooses *SVM*

Performance, parallelism, and the Solana developer experience versus immediate EVM compatibility. A choice against the current: **more architecture, less ready-made ecosystem**.

1 The virtual machine decides the project's identity

The EVM road — THE ECOSYSTEM
Solidity · Ethereum · mature DeFi · maximum compatibility · the larger ecosystem

The SVM road — THE ARCHITECTURE
Rust · Anchor · Solana · parallel execution · high performance

The EVM has the ecosystem. The SVM has the architecture. **Hyper bets on the architecture.**

2 A blockchain VM: a simulated computer with rigid rules

Determinism
same input, same output on every node.

Termination
every program finishes in predictable time.

Security / isolation
every application is isolated from the others.

SHARED ELEMENTS: bytecode · resource accounting · state model · cross-program call rules

A blockchain cannot afford unpredictable programs: **every node must arrive at the same result.**

3 EVM vs SVM: a single lane versus multiple parallel lanes

EVM — A SINGLE LANE
one tx after another · Solidity · huge ecosystem · mature tooling · performance limits

SVM — MULTIPLE PARALLEL LANES
declared accounts · parallel execution · Rust · Anchor · compute units · potential throughput

IN PARALLEL
Tx A → account X · Tx B → account Y · Tx C → account Z

MUST WAIT
Tx D → account X again

The SVM does not accelerate by magic: **it accelerates because it knows in advance which data each transaction will touch.**

4 What Hyper inherits from the Solana world

Solana / SVM — FAMILIAR WORKFLOWS
Rust · Anchor · Solana CLI · SDKs · SPL programs

→ ENDPOINT SWITCH

Bitcoin Hyper — L2 ON BITCOIN
SVM execution · settlement on Bitcoin · bridge · data availability · L1 finality

DOES NOT CARRY OVER DIRECTLY: Solidity · EVM smart contracts · already-written Ethereum DeFi · Uniswap / Aave / Compound without a rewrite

For a Solana developer, trying Hyper is **changing destination, not trade** *— but the apps must be adapted, and Rust/Anchor reduce the friction, they do not guarantee security.*

5 The SVM bet: opportunities and risks, to be verified in production

Favorable scenario
porting from Solana · active developers · DeFi, gaming, NFT · high-performance DEXs · apps hard to build on the EVM

Difficult scenario
few developers · Solana remains more attractive · competing EVM rollups · slow porting · below critical mass

TO MONITOR: deployed apps · TVL · unique developers · porting time · stability under load · real benchmarks · doc quality

The SVM choice is **technically defensible***; the performance advantage* **has not yet been demonstrated on mainnet**. *The market will tell whether it becomes a competitive advantage or isolation.*

THE KEY POINT

Bitcoin Hyper chooses SVM for a high-performance Bitcoin Layer 2: parallelism, Rust, Anchor, compute units, and the Solana developer experience. But it gives up **immediate EVM compatibility** and requires rigorous adaptation to the rollup-on-Bitcoin context. Success will depend on real applications, active developers, **stability in production**, and the capacity to turn technical superiority into an ecosystem — to be measured after the mainnet.

PART III · THE EXECUTION LAYER

Chapter 8
Parallel Execution and the Account Model

How Sealevel works

⁂

8.1 — The Technical Heart of the Performance Advantage

In the previous chapter we introduced the SVM as Bitcoin Hyper's architectural choice, and we hinted at the fact that its main performance advantage over the EVM comes from the capacity to execute transactions in parallel. Now let us descend inside this mechanism, because it is the technical detail that justifies Hyper's entire bet on the SVM, and it is also one of the most misunderstood concepts in the industry. **The SVM's parallelism is not "magic"**: it is the result of a precise architectural choice that has concrete consequences on how developers write code and on how applications behave. Understanding this mechanism means understanding something fundamental: the SVM's advantage is not free. It is an advantage obtained by asking developers to work differently, and by rewarding those who structure applications the right way.

FIGURE 8.1 **SEALEVEL: ACCOUNT-BASED PARALLEL EXECUTION**

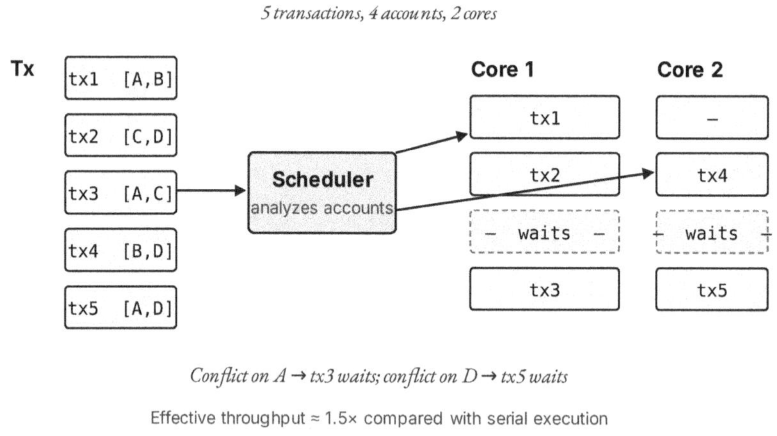

How to read it: *the account model allows Sealevel to execute in parallel the transactions that do not touch one another. The scheduler analyzes the accounts declared by each tx and assigns them to the free lanes. The higher the non-overlap, the higher the effective throughput.*

The system that makes all this possible is called **Sealevel**, and it is the execution runtime that sits underneath the SVM. The name is a marine metaphor — every transaction is a wave traveling down its own independent *lane*. It is a name little known to the general public but famous among blockchain engineers, because it represents one of the most significant architectural innovations of the last decade. The Solana team developed it starting in 2018, and today it is considered one of the elements that most clearly differentiates Solana from first-generation blockchains. Bitcoin Hyper, by choosing the SVM, inherits Sealevel along with everything else, and to a large extent builds its own performance advantage on this runtime.

In this chapter I want to perform an operation that requires patience but pays off: explaining concretely, with simple examples, how Sealevel works. I want you to finish the chapter with a clear intuition of what "parallel execution" means, **how it differs from the EVM's serial execution**, why some applications draw enormous advantage from this characteristic and others do not, and what the practical implications are for developers building on Bitcoin Hyper. They are technical details, but they are details that make the difference between truly understanding the project and stopping at the surface of the marketing.

⁂

8.2 — The Problem of Serial Execution: The EVM Case

To appreciate what Sealevel does, we must first understand the problem it solves. The problem is simple to state: **how does one get a blockchain to execute thousands of transactions per second, exploiting modern hardware?** The EVM, designed in 2014, gave this question an answer that today appears conservative: transactions are executed one at a time, in line. Let us see why.

The EVM treats the blockchain's state as one large shared space. All the smart contracts, all the accounts, all the persistent data live in this single space, and any transaction can, in principle, read and modify any part of the state. **This is a philosophical characteristic of the design**: smart contracts are "composable[a]" because they can interact freely with any other contract, without having to declare in advance whom they will touch. It is elegant, it is flexible, but it has an enormous cost in performance terms: execution remains **serial**[b].

---

[a] **Composability.** The capacity of smart contracts to call and combine with one another freely, like interlocking bricks: an application can use another's functions without prior agreements. It is one of DeFi's strengths, because it makes it possible to build complex services by assembling existing components. It has a price, however: if every transaction can touch any part of the state, it becomes hard to execute them in parallel without risking conflicts.

[b] **Serial execution.** It means processing transactions one at a time, in sequence, even when they have nothing to do with one another. It is the EVM's approach: simple and predictable, but incapable of exploiting modern processors, which have many cores capable of working simultaneously. It is exactly the limit the SVM, with its parallel execution, tries to overcome.

TABLE 8.1 **THE EVM'S SHARED STATE: THE MERIT AND ITS PRICE.**

Characteristic	The merit	The price
A single shared space	Every contract can interact with any other	Impossible to know in advance what a tx will touch
Free composability	The applications combine without declarations	Risk of conflicts between concurrent transactions
Guaranteed determinism	Same result on every node	Execution necessarily serial

The flexibility of the shared state is what makes the EVM so expressive, but it is also the reason it cannot parallelize: not knowing in advance which data each transaction will read or modify, it is forced to execute them one at a time.

FIGURE 8.2 **SHARED STATE AND POTENTIAL CONFLICTS: WHY THE EVM SERIALIZES TRANSACTIONS.**

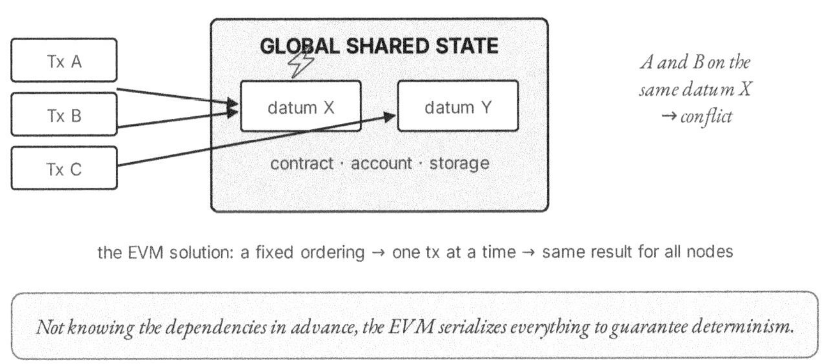

The cost emerges from the fact that, **not knowing a priori what a transaction will touch, the EVM cannot execute different transactions in parallel without risking conflicts.** Think about it. If two transactions could both read and modify the same datum, and if the system executes them in parallel on two different cores, the order in which the changes are applied becomes unpredictable, and different nodes of the network could obtain different final states. This violates the fundamental property of determinism. To avoid it, the EVM executes everything in sequence: one transaction at a time, in a well-defined order, so that the result is always the same regardless of who performs the computation.

On a computer with a single core, this choice would not be a big problem. But modern computers typically have eight, sixteen, thirty-two cores[a], and the most powerful server machines have hundreds. **The EVM, executing everything in line on a single logical core, wastes the vast majority of the available computational power[b].** It is like having an eight-lane highway and using only one. The whole machine is there, idle, waiting for the lane in use to finish its work before it can start again.

---

[a] **Core.** A computing unit inside a processor. Modern processors contain many, and each core can carry out a task independently of the others, simultaneously. A program capable of distributing its work across several cores is much faster than one using only one: it is the difference between putting an entire team to work and a single person. The EVM, executing in sequence, effectively exploits a single core.

[b] **Parallelism.** The capacity to execute several operations at the same instant, distributing them across several cores. On a blockchain it makes it possible to process together all the transactions that do not interfere with one another, enormously increasing the number of operations per second. It is the principle on which the SVM is founded: to make it possible, however, every transaction must declare in advance which data it will touch, so the system knows which ones can proceed simultaneously without conflicts.

TABLE 8.2 **WHY THE EVM SERIALIZES: THE TRADE-OFF BETWEEN DETERMINISM AND PARALLELISM.**

Aspect	Serial execution (EVM)	Consequence
Dependencies between transactions	Not known in advance	Impossible to know which txs are in conflict
Execution order	One transaction at a time	Identical result on every node
Determinism	Guaranteed by construction	The network always agrees on the same state
Use of cores	A single logical core	The multicore power remains unused

The EVM's choice is not a design error, but a compromise: it gives up parallelism to obtain a determinism that is simple to guarantee. The price is structural and becomes evident on modern hardware, where most of the computing capacity remains idle.

FIGURE 8.3 **A SINGLE LANE ON A MULTICORE HIGHWAY: THE STRUCTURAL COST OF SERIAL EXECUTION.**

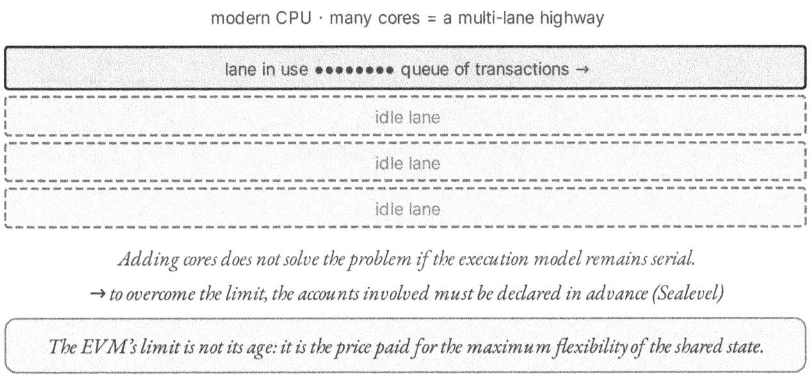

This limit is structural, not implementational. It cannot be solved by writing the EVM better or using better hardware: it derives from the initial philosophical choice of not asking transactions to declare what they will touch. To overcome the limit, the philosophy must change. And that is exactly what Solana did with Sealevel, and what Hyper is now bringing to Bitcoin.

There is an important point I want to emphasize before moving to the SVM model, because it is often misunderstood. **The EVM's limit is not "the EVM is slow because it is old."** The limit is "the EVM is serial because it chose maximum programming flexibility." It is a trade-off choice, not incompetence. The Ethereum team of 2014 knew perfectly well that parallelization was possible, but chose not to do it because it thought flexibility was more important. In 2018–2019, when the Solana team made the opposite choice, the blockchain world had changed and the performance requirements had become much more stringent. **Every era has its design choices**, and understanding the historical motivations behind the choices helps not to judge them anachronistically.

⁂

8.3 — Sealevel's Breakthrough: Declaring What Will Be Touched

Sealevel solves the parallelization problem with an apparently simple but profound idea: **if the transactions declare in advance which parts of the state they will touch, the system can understand which are independent of one another and schedule in parallel only those that do not step on each other's toes.** Put like that, it sounds trivial. Let us see why it is in fact an architectural revolution.

FIGURE 8.4 **SEALEVEL: FROM DECLARED ACCOUNTS TO THE DEPENDENCY GRAPH AND TO MULTICORE EXECUTION.**

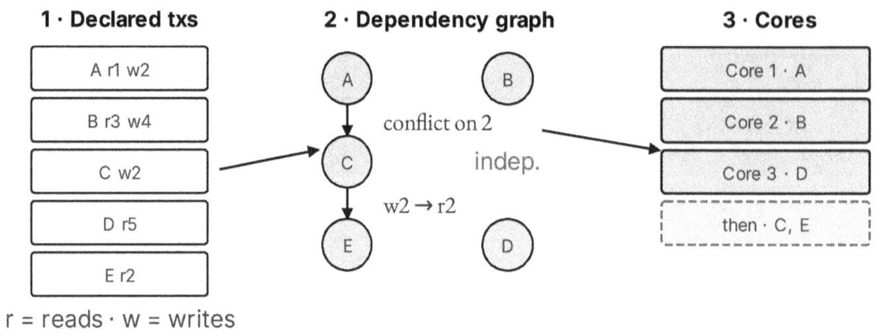

Sealevel does not execute everything in parallel indiscriminately: it uses the declared accounts to parallelize only the independent transactions and serialize the conflicting ones.

On Sealevel, every transaction has a specific structure. In addition to the standard data one expects — who is signing, which program is called, which parameters are passed — the transaction includes an **explicit list of the accounts it will touch**, and for each account it specifies whether it will only be read, or written. This is information provided by the user (or, more typically, by the wallet or the application that constructs the transaction on the user's behalf) before the transaction is sent to the rollup.

When Sealevel receives a batch of transactions to execute, it does something the EVM cannot do: **it analyzes the declared account lists** and builds a dependency graph. Two transactions are independent if their lists do not overlap in a conflicting way: either they touch no account in common, or those accounts in common are only read, not written. Two transactions are dependent if at least one of them wants to write an account the other wants to read or write.

The independent transactions can be executed in parallel on the CPU's different cores, simultaneously, without risk of conflicts. The dependent transactions must be executed in sequence, in a well-defined order. **Sealevel automatically builds this parallel scheduling for every batch**, exploiting all the available cores. On a CPU with sixteen cores, in theory up to sixteen independent transactions can run at the same time.

FIGURE 8.5 **THE EXECUTION MODELS OF THE EVM AND THE SVM, SIDE BY SIDE.**

EVM SERIAL	**SVM** PARALLEL
STATE *a single shared space*	**STATE** *granular: every datum is an account*
TX SHAPE *opaque: any path may write*	**TX SHAPE** *declares the accounts it will use*
SCHEDULER *strict order, one tx at a time*	**SCHEDULER** *dependency graph; non-conflicts in //*
CORES USED *one logical core, whatever the hw*	**CORES USED** *all the machine's cores*
TRADE-OFF *maximum programming flexibility*	**TRADE-OFF** *more rigid contract structure*

The two columns describe the same five aspects of execution. The EVM optimizes for flexibility at the cost of throughput; the SVM shifts the cost onto the developer (in the form of an explicit declaration of the accounts) and repays it in the form of parallelism that scales with the hardware.

Let us think through a concrete example to fix the concept. Imagine a batch of one hundred transactions, of which:

- 50 are transfers between different users (Alice sends 10 tokens to Bob, Carlo sends 5 tokens to Diana, and so on), each touching only two specific accounts
- 30 are interactions with a single large shared DeFi pool
- 20 are mixed operations

On the EVM, these 100 transactions are executed in line, one at a time. If each transaction requires 1 millisecond, the batch requires 100 milliseconds in total.

On Sealevel, the dependency analysis produces this result. **The 50 transfers between different users are completely independent of one another**: each touches two specific accounts, and since different users have different accounts, there are no overlaps. They can all be executed in parallel. **The 30 interactions with the DeFi pool are dependent on one another**: they all want to write the same account (the pool), so they must be serialized. **The 20 mixed operations have partial dependencies** that depend on the specific details.

Sealevel's optimal scheduling would process the 50 transfers on 16 cores in parallel (requiring about 50/16 ≈ 4 milliseconds), simultaneously with the 30 pool interactions on another core (requiring 30 serialized milliseconds), simultaneously with the 20 mixed operations on other cores with their dependency constraints. The batch's total time would be about 30 milliseconds, dominated by the serialized portion of the DeFi pool. **Three times faster than the EVM**, in this specific example, and the ratio can be much higher in batches where the share of independent transactions is even greater.

This is the principle. Sealevel does not perform miracles: it uses the information declared by the transactions to parallelize what is parallelizable, and serialize what is not. The performance gain depends on the **structure of the workload**, not on magic. Workloads with many independent transactions scale excellently. Workloads with concentrations of writes on the same accounts scale worse. Understanding this dynamic is essential for designing applications that truly exploit parallelism.

TABLE 8.3 **A BATCH OF 100 TRANSACTIONS: SERIAL (EVM) VS SCHEDULED BY SEALEVEL (SVM)**

Workload class	Tx	EVM (serial)	SVM (Sealevel)
User-to-user transfers	50	50 ms	~ 4 ms
Shared DeFi pool	30	30 ms	30 ms
Mixed operations	20	20 ms	~ 8 ms
Total batch time	**100**	**100 ms**	**~ 30 ms**

How to read it. *Assumption: 1 ms per transaction, a 16-core CPU. The 50 transfers are fully independent and parallelize almost linearly. The 30 pool interactions all write the same account and serialize. The total time on the SVM is dominated by the serialized portion, not by the number of transactions.*

⁂

8.4 — The Account Model: How State Is Organized in the SVM

To understand fully how Sealevel works, one must understand how the SVM organizes its state, because the account model is the conceptual base on which parallelism rests. Here too the differences with the EVM are deep, and they deserve attention.

FIGURE 8.6 **TWO WAYS OF ORGANIZING STATE: THE EVM'S SHARED STORAGE VERSUS THE SVM'S GRANULAR ACCOUNT MODEL.**

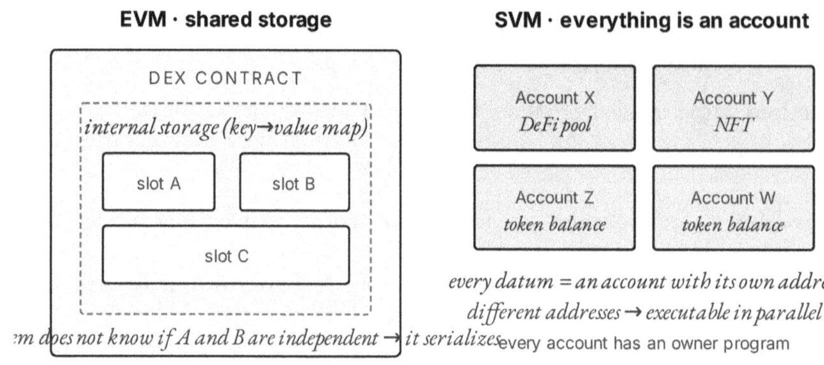

The EVM keeps a contract's state in a single internal storage and, not knowing whether two writes are independent, serializes them. On the SVM every datum is an account of its own, with its own address: if the addresses are different, execution is parallel. Moreover, only the owner program can modify the account — a native permission system.

On the EVM, state is organized like this. There exists one large global space where all the accounts live. Accounts can be of two types: user accounts (controlled by private keys, containing only balances and nonces) or smart contract accounts (containing code and an internal storage space, organized as a key-value map). When a contract wants to store data, it writes it in its own internal space. When a contract wants to read another contract's data, it must make a cross-contract call, which is a costly operation.

On the SVM the model is different and more granular. **Everything is an account.** Not only the users and the contracts, but also every single "piece" of persistent data is an account in its own right. A DeFi liquidity pool is not "the storage of the pool's contract": it is a dedicated account, owned by the pool's program, with its own unique address. An NFT is not "an entry in the NFT contract's storage": it is a dedicated account containing that NFT's specific data. Users' token balances are dedicated accounts for every user-token combination. **Everything that has a persistent state lives in a specific account, identified by a specific address.**

This granularity is crucial for parallelism. When a transaction declares "I will write account X," it is declaring a very small, specific unit of state. Two transactions writing "account X" and "account Y" are completely independent if X and Y are different accounts, even if both are owned by the same program. **On the EVM, where storage is global within a contract, two transactions writing "two different slots in the same contract" could in theory be independent, but the system does not know it, so it serializes them for safety.** On the SVM, the information is explicit and granular, and the system can exploit it.

There is another aspect of the account model worth mentioning: **accounts have an owner**, which is a specific program. Only the owner program can modify an account's data. This creates a natural "permission" system that simplifies security. When a transaction wants to modify an account, the system verifies that the called program is actually the owner, and rejects the modification if it is not. This prevents entire classes of vulnerabilities that on the EVM require developers' explicit attention.

For developers coming from the EVM, the account model requires a change of mindset. One must think about how to structure data into separate accounts instead of putting everything in shared storage. One must think about dependencies between transactions explicitly. **One must design applications to exploit parallelism instead of taking it for granted.** It is extra work at the beginning, but once the model gets into your bones, many developers report finding it clearer and more rational than the EVM model.

For developers coming from Solana, all this is already natural, because it is exactly how they have always worked. And it is here that Hyper's strategic advantage is played out: **whoever already knows how to develop for the SVM brings to Hyper not only the code, but also the design mindset that exploits parallelism.**

IN BRIEF · THE SVM'S ACCOUNT MODEL

EVM — shared storage. A contract's state lives in a single internal space; the system serializes out of prudence because it does not know which writes are independent.

SVM — everything is an account. Every piece of state (pool, NFT, token balance) is an account with its own address: the dependencies are explicit and granular.

Parallelism. Transactions touching accounts with different addresses can be executed in parallel without ambiguity — it is the base on which Sealevel rests.

Security. Every account has an owner program; only that program can modify it. A native permission system that prevents entire classes of vulnerabilities.

Change of mindset. Whoever comes from the EVM must learn to structure state into separate accounts; whoever comes from Solana already does — and that is Hyper's strategic advantage.

⁂

8.5 — Parallelism in the Context of a Rollup: Constraints and Advantages

Now let us apply the discussion to the specific case of Bitcoin Hyper. Sealevel[a] works very well on Solana, where the operating environment is designed around its characteristics. On Hyper, which is a rollup anchored[b] to Bitcoin, there are additional constraints and necessary adaptations, but also specific advantages. Let us look at them.

[a] **Sealevel.** The SVM's execution engine, that is, the part that actually runs the programs. Its peculiarity is executing in parallel all the transactions that do not touch one another, exploiting the many cores of modern processors. It is what allows the SVM to reach performance far superior to serial execution. Bitcoin Hyper inherits Sealevel by adopting the SVM environment, but will have to demonstrate its functioning in its own context.

[b] **Anchored rollup.** A Layer 2 that executes transactions on its own, but periodically "anchors" the result to a main blockchain — here Bitcoin — by publishing a synthetic imprint of its own state there. Anchoring is what ties the Layer 2's security to that of the underlying level: until the state is anchored and confirmed, it does not yet enjoy Bitcoin's definitive finality. It is the characteristic that distinguishes a rollup from a blockchain merely "near" Bitcoin.

TABLE 8.4 **PARALLELISM IN A ROLLUP ANCHORED TO BITCOIN: CONSTRAINTS AND ADVANTAGES.**

Constraints and adaptations	Specific advantages
The data must still be published and anchored to Bitcoin	High throughput thanks to parallel execution
The sequencer must coordinate the order of the transactions	More contained per-transaction costs
Finality depends on the periodic commitments on the Layer 1	Compatibility with Solana tools and developers

Bringing Solana's parallel execution model to a rollup anchored to Bitcoin is not automatic: it requires adaptations tied to data availability, sequencing, and anchoring. In exchange, however, it offers performance and a development ecosystem that traditional sidechains do not make available.

FIGURE 8.7 **PARALLELISM IN THE ROLLUP: MORE LANES, MORE BALANCE.**

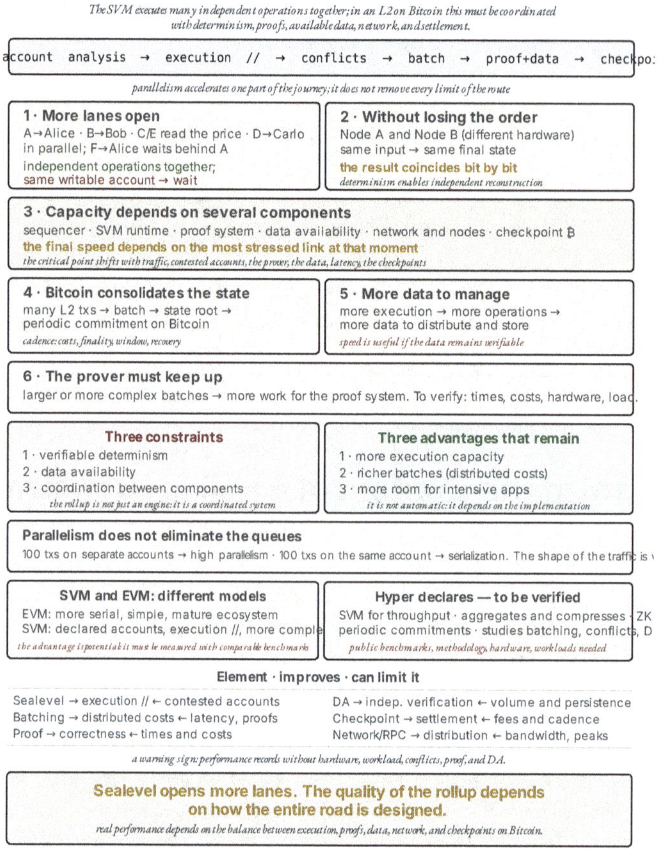

Sealevel makes it possible to execute in parallel the transactions that do not conflict on the same accounts. In the context of a rollup connected to Bitcoin, the advantage remains relevant but must be coordinated with determinism, the proof system, data availability, the network, and periodic checkpoints. Overall performance does not depend on a single bottleneck: it emerges from the balance of the entire architecture.

First constraint: determinism, as a requirement of independent verifiability. On Solana too the validators must execute the same rules and converge on the same state: a transaction's instructions are executed atomically and, if one fails, the entire transaction fails and the changes to the state are undone. In a rollup anchored to Bitcoin, determinism becomes even more visible as a requirement, because nodes and observers must be able to reconstruct the same state from the published data. **Hyper's official page devoted to the topic states that the research concerns rigorous limits on execution order, on account access, and on runtime visibility.**

Second constraint: throughput depends on several components, not on a single bottleneck. If Hyper periodically publishes a compact root, the anchoring does not necessarily contain all the data of the individual transactions: the checkpoint cadence influences above all settlement costs, the rhythm of the checkpoints, finality times toward Bitcoin, the interval between two consolidated states, and the recovery procedures. **Operational throughput can also be limited by the sequencer's capacity, by conflicts between accounts, by proof generation, by data availability, by bandwidth, by network latency, by node performance, and by the RPC infrastructure.** The critical point can shift from one moment to the next.

Third constraint: data availability, distinct from anchoring. The commitment is a compact cryptographic synthesis of the state, published periodically on Bitcoin; data availability is the availability of the data needed to reconstruct and verify what that synthesis represents. **The more transactions Sealevel processes, the more data must remain publicly retrievable for independent verification.** As the industry's documentation makes clear, the complete data is necessary for verification, and the scalability problem consists in guaranteeing its availability without forcing every participant to download and store everything.

The constraints stated, let us look at the advantages the rollup-Sealevel combination can retain. **First advantage: richer batches and amortized checkpoint costs.** Fast execution makes it possible to process more activity between two checkpoints and to distribute the anchoring cost over a greater number of operations. It is not a matter of "saturating" Bitcoin, but of using the interval between two consolidated states more efficiently.

Second advantage: more design space for transaction-intensive applications. Parallelism can widen the space for markets with many operations, frequent payments, games, and social applications. **These applications can also be built in EVM ecosystems, with different architectures and trade-offs**: the SVM's potential advantage consists in providing more capacity for workloads with many independent, frequent operations, not in holding a monopoly on them. Concrete feasibility will in any case depend on proofs, data availability, latency, and infrastructure.

Third advantage: efficient composition between applications. When transactions declare in advance the accounts they touch, it is easier to build patterns in which several applications interact without creating unnecessary bottlenecks. Making the dependencies explicit enables optimizations that, in many cases, reduce the costs of the interactions.

Putting constraints and advantages together, the picture is this. **The SVM offers a potential performance advantage over more serial execution models, but the real magnitude of the advantage will have to be measured through public, reproducible benchmarks.** Sealevel on Hyper will operate in a context different from Solana's, and overall performance will emerge from the balance between execution, proofs, available data, network, and the rhythm of checkpoints on Bitcoin — not from a single transactions-per-second number.

⁂

8.6 — What It Means Concretely for Applications

To close the technical part of the chapter, I want to do a concrete exercise: let us see how four categories of applications behave under Sealevel's parallel execution, and what implications this has for developers and users.

FIGURE 8.8 **FOUR APPLICATIONS, FOUR SHAPES OF TRAFFIC.**

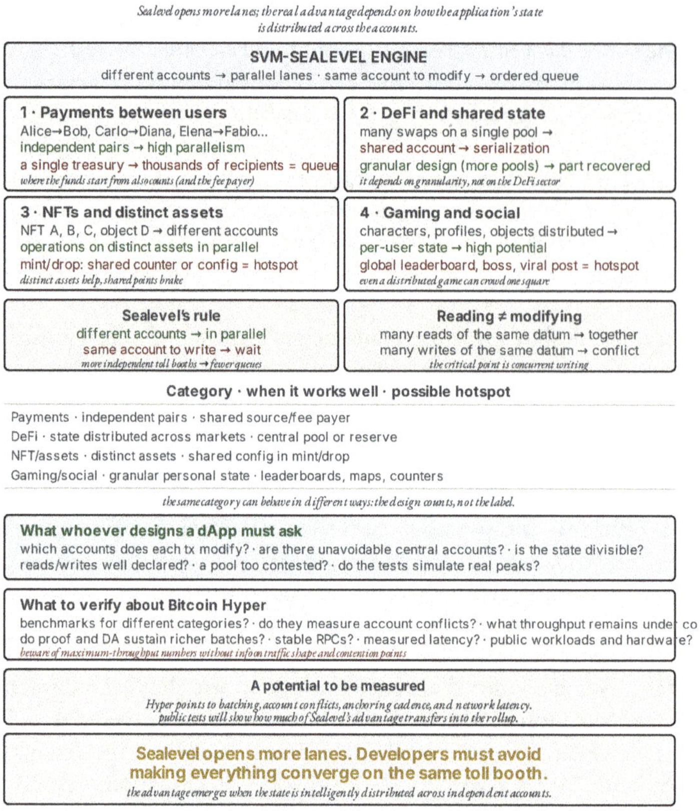

Sealevel's advantage depends on the distribution of the state. Transactions modifying different accounts can proceed in parallel; those that must update the same account come into conflict and require ordered handling. Payments, DeFi, NFTs, gaming, and social apps can therefore obtain very different results depending on how they are designed.

TABLE 8.5 **FOUR CATEGORIES OF APPLICATIONS AND SEALEVEL'S PARALLELISM.**

Category	Potential	When it works well	Where the bottleneck can arise
Transfers between users	High	Independent pairs of senders and recipients	A single source account, shared fee payer, or central account
DeFi with shared state	Variable	State divided across several markets, pools, and positions	Heavily used pools, reserves, or central accounts
NFTs and distinct assets	High in many cases	Operations on different assets	Shared counters, authorities, or configurations in mints and drops
Apps with per-user state	Potentially very high	Distributed profiles, characters, and objects	Global leaderboards, crowded maps, common counters, viral content

The advantage of parallelism does not depend only on the application's category: it depends above all on how many accounts are modified at the same time and on how distributed the state is.

First category: transfers between users. They are often a case favorable to parallelism. When Alice sends tokens to Bob and simultaneously Carlo sends tokens to Diana, the two transactions involve independent accounts and Sealevel can execute them together. **A transfer, however, does not touch only two accounts:** it modifies the source account and the recipient one, it has a fee payer that must be writable, and it can involve mints or other accounts. The correct point is that transfers between independent pairs can benefit greatly from parallelism; if instead thousands of payments start from a single central account — as in a mass distribution — that account becomes a contention point and part of the operations serializes.

Second category: DeFi applications. The result depends on the design. **The advantage decreases when many transactions modify the same pool or the same reserve; it increases when the state is distributed across several markets, positions, and independent accounts.** An AMM with a single heavily used pool creates a contested account and approaches serial behavior; a more granular architecture can recover a good part of the parallelism. It is therefore not correct to say that "all DeFi is serial": what counts is the granularity of the architecture, not the sector's label.

Third category: NFTs and distinct digital assets. Operations on different assets can benefit greatly from parallelism, because each asset normally lives in a separate account and the program's code is distinct from the modifiable data. **During a mint or a drop, however, shared accounts can exist** — the collection's configuration, counters, authorities, distribution mechanisms — that reduce the effective gain. Distinct assets favor parallelism; shared points brake it.

Fourth category: applications with per-user state, like games and social apps. When the state is distributed across characters, objects, areas, and profiles, these applications can draw a significant advantage from Sealevel. **The benefit decreases when many interactions converge on the same objects, the same areas, or the same global counters:** a global leaderboard, a shared boss, a very crowded map, a viral post, or a common inventory can become hotspots. The potential is high, but it is not an automatic guarantee.

You can see how nuanced the picture is. **The correct question is not "which category is fast or slow?", but "how distributed is the state the transactions must modify?".** A simple transfer can become serial if thousands of payments start from the same account; a DeFi application can recover capacity if it avoids concentrating every operation on a single account; a game scales well as long as the players modify personal states, but slows down if everyone updates the same leaderboard at the same time. Designing applications for parallelism is a specific skill.

For Bitcoin Hyper, Sealevel therefore offers an important potential advantage for applications characterized by many independent operations; the concrete magnitude of the benefit will have to be measured with comparable benchmarks. **The project declares that it models the effect of batching, account conflicts, anchoring cadence, and network latency on throughput**, and indicates wallets, financial instruments, and social applications among the areas it intends to make possible. If the architecture keeps its promises, Hyper could prove particularly suitable for applications in which the state is distributed across numerous independent accounts — but sufficient independent benchmarks have not yet been published to assert definitive quantitative superiority.

⁂

8.7 — Questions and Answers: Clarifying the Chapter's Concepts

Question 1: If parallelism requires transactions to declare in advance what they will touch, what happens when a smart contract must do dynamic things where it is not known in advance which account will be referenced?

It is a real limitation of Sealevel, and it must be faced honestly. On the EVM, a smart contract can, during execution, compute the address of another contract to call and then call it. On the SVM, this flow is more rigid: all the accounts the transaction might touch must be declared in the transaction itself. **When the application requires dynamic flexibility, SVM developers use specific patterns**: they declare "all the potentially touched accounts" even if only some will actually be used in a particular execution, or they restructure the logic to first perform an on-chain computation (which reveals the account to touch) and then a separate transaction that touches that account. It is a limitation that requires different design, but it is manageable, and the patterns are by now consolidated in the SVM community. **Concrete example:** an AMM on the EVM can dynamically "discover" the best pool for a swap during execution and use it. On the SVM, the user (or their wallet) typically computes off-chain which pool is best, constructs the transaction that explicitly declares that pool, and sends it. It is a slightly different pattern, but it works.

Question 2: The SVM's account model seems very granular to me — every token, every NFT, everything is an account. Does it not become heavy to have so many separate accounts?

It is an intelligent question, and yes, the model has overhead implications. Having many separate accounts means more data to manage, more addresses to keep track of, more administrative operations (creation, rent, deletion). **Solana managed this cost by introducing the concept of "rent" on accounts**: whoever wants to keep an account in the state must pay a fee proportional to the space occupied, and this creates a natural incentive not to create useless accounts. Empty or no-longer-used accounts can be closed and the funds recovered. Bitcoin Hyper inherits this model, although the specific details of how to manage rent in a rollup context may differ. **The trade-off is: more granularity = more administrative overhead, but also more parallelism = more performance.** For most applications the balance is positive. Concrete example: on Solana, every user who owns a certain token has a dedicated account for that token. If you own 50 different tokens, you have 50 associated accounts. Each of these accounts has a small rent cost. But in exchange, operations on different tokens are completely parallelizable between different users, something that on the EVM requires passing through a single shared ERC-20 contract that becomes a bottleneck.

Question 3: If Sealevel is so advanced, why has Solana had historical stability problems, with consensus outages and other incidents?

It is an important point that deserves to be addressed without hypocrisy. Yes, Solana has had significant service outages, particularly in 2021–2022, when the network froze for hours or days in some cases. The reasons were various: transaction overload during specific events (NFT drops, intense speculative activity), consensus bugs, block propagation problems. **These outages are not directly tied to Sealevel as a component**, but to the overall complexity of the Solana system, which does many optimized things together and therefore has more points of possible failure. Solana has invested significantly in stabilization, and in 2024–2025 the outages became much rarer, though not eliminated. For Bitcoin Hyper, the important point is that **adopting the SVM means adopting Sealevel as an execution component, not the entire Solana stack.** Hyper's consensus is different (it is a rollup anchored to Bitcoin), block propagation is different, the network model is different. So Hyper does not necessarily inherit Solana's stability problems, even though it inherits Sealevel. **This is a positive characteristic of the modular model**: one can take Solana's good pieces without taking all the pieces.

Question 4: How does Sealevel know whether two transactions declaring the same accounts are actually in conflict, or whether they simply "overlap" harmlessly?

The rule is simple and conservative: **if two transactions declare the same account in a way that includes writing, they are considered in conflict and serialized.** Specifically, two transactions are independent only if: (a) they share no account, or (b) the accounts they share are declared as "read-only" by both. If even just one of the two transactions wants to write an account the other touches (even just to read), Sealevel serializes them for safety. **This is a conservative rule**: there are cases where two writes on the same account would in fact be compatible (for example, writing different fields of the same structure), but Sealevel does not analyze at that level of granularity. Sealevel's granularity is the account, not the individual fields within the account. Concrete example: if two transactions want to modify two different fields of a "global configuration" account, on Sealevel they will be serialized even if in theory they could be parallelized. This is a limitation of the model, and it is one of the areas where SVM researchers are exploring future optimizations.

Question 5: How realistic is it to expect Bitcoin Hyper to reach Solana's performance, given that it is a rollup and has all the additional constraints you mentioned?

Realistically, Bitcoin Hyper will not reach the performance of Solana mainnet, at least in the first years. The reasons are structural: Solana has an independent consensus with 400-millisecond block times, while Hyper must coordinate with the Bitcoin anchoring, which has much longer times. The anchoring cadence and anchoring costs limit Hyper's sustainable throughput to levels below Solana's, all else being equal. **That said, Hyper does not need to reach Solana to be useful.** It needs to be significantly faster than Bitcoin's EVM rollups, and that is more realistic. Probably, in optimistic scenarios, Hyper could sustain thousands of transactions per second in favorable cases (parallel workloads), and hundreds in less favorable cases. These are numbers that, if confirmed in real benchmarks, would position Hyper as the Bitcoin rollup with the highest performance, and that is the strategic point. Concrete example: for applications like mass payments in BTC, gaming with tokenized economies, decentralized exchanges, Hyper's performance would be more than sufficient, even if below Solana's. The "Solana-grade" level is not strictly necessary for most use cases.

Question 6: For a developer weighing whether to build on Hyper or on another Bitcoin Layer 2 with the EVM, what are the main practical considerations?

They are several, and they depend a lot on the type of application. **If the application draws strong advantage from parallelism** (gaming, NFTs, mass payments, on-chain social), Hyper offers performance an EVM rollup cannot match, and this is a decisive advantage. **If the application is traditional DeFi with shared state** (AMMs[a], lending, yield farming), the performance difference is less marked, and EVM compatibility with all the oracles, libraries, and auditors becomes more important. In that case, a Bitcoin EVM rollup might be preferable. **If the application requires porting from existing Solidity code**, the EVM is obviously the natural choice, and migrating to Hyper would require a complete rewrite. **If the application comes from Solana**, Hyper is almost a natural choice for extending one's addressable market toward the Bitcoin world. Moreover, there are long-term considerations: the ecosystem's maturity, the quality of the development tools, the available liquidity, the community. Hyper, being new, will start with all these parameters below a more established EVM rollup. For a prudent developer, it can make sense to wait 6–12 months after Hyper's mainnet launch to see how the ecosystem evolves, before committing to building significant applications. Concrete example: a team that wants to build a real-time multiplayer game with a tokenized economy would find Hyper potentially the best choice among Bitcoin's Layer 2s, because parallelism is essential for that use case. A team that wants to port a lending protocol from Ethereum would find a Bitcoin EVM rollup simpler.

---

[a] **AMM** (Automated Market Maker). The mechanism that makes it possible to swap tokens in a decentralized way without a traditional order book: prices are determined automatically by a mathematical formula and by the amount of assets deposited in a liquidity "pool." It is the heart of much of decentralized finance. Since every swap modifies the pool's shared state, the transactions tend to interfere with one another: this is why AMMs draw less advantage from parallel execution than applications in which the operations are mostly independent.

⁂

8.8 — WHAT TO TAKE AWAY FROM THIS CHAPTER

Sealevel is the SVM's execution runtime, and it is the component that enables the parallelism differentiating the SVM from the EVM. It is a 2018–2019 architectural innovation that today represents one of the most modern elements in the industry.

The SVM's parallelism works because the transactions declare in advance which accounts they will touch. Sealevel analyzes these declarations, builds a dependency graph, and schedules in parallel the transactions that do not step on each other's toes.

The SVM's account model is more granular than the EVM's. Every persistent datum is a separate account, with its own address and its own owner. This granularity enables parallelism but requires more structured application design.

The EVM is serial by architectural choice, not by technical limitation. The 2014 choice privileged flexibility over parallelization. Today that choice appears conservative, but it was reasonable in its historical context.

Sealevel's parallelism on Hyper has specific constraints due to the rollup-on-Bitcoin context. Determinism must be absolutely perfect, anchoring limits sustainable throughput, data availability introduces additional constraints.

The performance advantage is not uniform across applications. Transfers, NFTs, gaming, and applications with per-user personal states benefit enormously. DeFi applications with large shared pools benefit in a limited way.

Hyper, if it keeps its promises, will be able to host classes of applications that Bitcoin's EVM rollups cannot host. Real-time games, exchanges with high-frequency order books, on-chain social media. It is the project's strategic differentiation point.

Realistically, Hyper will not reach the performance of Solana mainnet, but it will be significantly faster than Bitcoin's EVM rollups. For most use cases, that is sufficient.

Developing for Sealevel requires a different mindset from Solidity. One must think in terms of separate accounts, explicit dependencies, parallelism as a design parameter. It is extra work at the beginning, but the SVM ecosystem has developed consolidated patterns that reduce the learning curve.

Chapter 8 ends here. We have understood how Sealevel's parallelism works, why it is an architectural revolution with respect to the EVM, and what the concrete implications are for Bitcoin Hyper. In ***Chapter 9 — SVM Programs Running Natively on Bitcoin Hyper****, we will see how all this translates into practice in Hyper's environment, examining in detail what happens when a developer deploys an SVM program on the rollup, which tools they use, and how the experience differs from Solana's.*

NOTE

1 The name "Sealevel" is a marine metaphor: every transaction is a wave traveling down its own independent lane. The model is described in the *Solana Docs, Transaction Processing* section.

CHAPTER 8 · PARALLEL EXECUTION AND THE ACCOUNT MODEL · SUMMARY

MICHELE STEFANELLI

Sealevel: more *lanes* for blockchain execution

How the SVM uses the **account model** to execute transactions **in parallel**.

1 The EVM's serial model

The EVM executes transactions **one at a time**, because it does not know in advance which parts of the state will be read or modified.

Maximum flexibility, but limited throughput.

IN USE

IDLE

IDLE

IDLE

one transaction at a time → simple determinism, but little parallelism

2 Declaring in advance what will be touched

Every SVM transaction **declares the accounts** it will read and those it will modify. The scheduler thus distinguishes independent operations from conflicting ones.

different accounts → **parallel execution**
same writable account → **wait / serialization**

DIFFERENT ACCOUNTS — in parallel ✓

TX-A → X | TX-B → Y | TX-C → Z

SAME ACCOUNT — wait · serialized

TX-D → X | TX-A → X | conflict on X

3 On the SVM, everything is an account

ACCOUNT	ACCOUNT	ACCOUNT	ACCOUNT	ACCOUNT
Token balance	**NFT**	**DeFi pool**	**User profile**	**Gaming object**
acct·X1	acct·N2	acct·P3	acct·U4	acct·G5

The more granular the state, **the more visible the dependencies.**

4 The advantage depends on the traffic

Payments — HIGH
High parallelism if senders and recipients are independent.

NFTs / distinct assets — HIGH
Good parallelism when every asset has its own account.

Gaming / social — POTENTIAL
Great potential if profiles, objects, and characters are separate.

DeFi — VARIABLE
A shared pool can become a bottleneck.

ⓘ **It is not only the application's category that counts. What counts is how distributed the state is.**

5 More speed, but inside a rollup

Bitcoin Hyper inherits the SVM's advantage, but must coordinate it with the **constraints of a rollup anchored to Bitcoin**.

transactions → **account analysis** → **execution //** → **batch** → **proofs / data** → **checkpoint ₿**

• Determinism • Sequencer • Proof system • Data availability • Network and RPC • Settlement on Bitcoin

Sealevel accelerates execution, but **real performance depends on the entire architecture.**

THE KEY POINT

Sealevel opens more lanes, but **does not eliminate the queues**. Independent transactions run in parallel; those competing for the same account must **wait**. The advantage comes from **intelligent state design**.

PART III · THE EXECUTION LAYER

DUE DILIGENCE OF A LAYER 2 · VOL. I

PART III · THE EXECUTION LAYER

Chapter 9
SVM Programs Running Natively on Bitcoin Hyper

When the promise becomes a demo

9.1 — The Moment an Idea Stops Being an Idea

In the world of crypto projects, there is a thin but decisive line separating **an architectural promise** from **a working implementation.** Countless projects have described, in their whitepapers, sophisticated architectures that on paper look revolutionary, and that then never came to work in practice. The industry's recent history is full of examples: "next-generation" blockchains launched with great fanfare and then quietly dying, Layer 2s that were supposed to change the world and instead struggled to deploy even the most basic functionality, systems that promised universal interoperability and then collapsed under their own technical weight.

For this reason, **the moment when a project can demonstrate that its architecture really works, even just at the prototype level, is one of the most important moments of its journey**. It is not yet market success, it is not yet operational maturity, but it is the first concrete step that shows ideas can become code, and that the code can run. For Bitcoin Hyper, this moment was August 2025, when the team publicly announced that standard SVM programs were running natively on the rollup's devnet. It is an announcement worth understanding in depth, because it marks the project's transition from "theoretical research" to "experimentable infrastructure." And because it lets us, finally, concretely see what "SVM rollup on Bitcoin" means when it stops being a marketing phrase.

In this chapter I want to do two things. First, to recount in detail what was demonstrated working, and what it means concretely for developers and for the project's evaluation. Second, to honestly discuss the limits of what was demonstrated — because a working devnet is not the same thing as a mainnet ready for launch, and understanding the difference is essential to correctly assess the project's state. I begin with the positive part, because it is the one that deserves to be appreciated first.

9.2 — What "Native Execution" Means

When the Bitcoin Hyper team announced the native execution of SVM programs, the key word I want to dwell on is exactly that: **native.** It is a term that in the crypto world is used often, and that risks going unnoticed if one does not pay attention to its precise meaning. Let us look at it.

In the context of a Layer 2, "native execution of X" means that X runs **directly on the Layer 2's runtime**, without layers of translation, emulation, or intermediate interpretation. It is different from "compatible execution" or "emulated execution." A blockchain that declares EVM compatibility, for example, can do several things: it can actually have the EVM as its runtime, or it can translate EVM bytecodes into another runtime's instructions, or it can execute EVM contracts in an interpreted sandbox. The three options have very different performance and security characteristics. Only the first is "native" execution in the full sense of the term.

For Bitcoin Hyper, the announcement was that SVM programs run natively, that is, that the rollup actually has Solana's virtual machine as an execution component, not an emulator or a translator. This means concretely several things. **SVM programs compiled in the same format Solana accepts are loaded without changes and run on Hyper's runtime.** The Solana instructions are executed with the same semantics and tendentially with the same performance characteristics. The Solana development tools produce output that works directly on Hyper. **There is no translation layer that could introduce bugs, inefficiencies, or unexpected behaviors.**

The team made it clear that this is real execution, not simulation. In the specific August 2025 post, it mentioned the fact that the standard Solana commands — `solana program deploy`, `solana call`, `solana logs`, `solana config get` — work natively on Hyper's devnet. They are the commands every Solana developer uses daily to deploy and interact with their programs. Seeing them work against a Hyper endpoint, without changes, is the concrete demonstration that the system really executes the SVM in the strong sense of the term.

Think about it from a developer's practical standpoint. You have written a program for Solana, you have tested it, you are distributing it on the standard Solana network. Now you want to try it on Bitcoin Hyper. What do you do? **You open your Solana configuration file, change the endpoint from the**

Solana one to the Hyper one, run the same commands. The program is compiled in exactly the same way, deployed in exactly the same way, runs in exactly the same way. Your developer experience does not change. **What changes is where the program runs**: no longer on the Solana blockchain, but on a rollup anchored to Bitcoin.

This "drop-in compatibility" characteristic is exactly what makes the SVM on Hyper potentially attractive to developers from the Solana world. It does not ask them to learn anything new, it does not ask them to adapt tools, it does not ask them to rewrite code. It asks only that they point to a different endpoint. **It is a radically different value proposition compared with that of other Bitcoin rollups requiring proprietary languages or dedicated development environments.** From this standpoint, the choice not to build something new but to adopt and adapt what already works is a strategically intelligent choice.

⁂

9.3 — What Was Demonstrated Working: The July–August 2025 Devnet

Now let us enter the details of what, exactly, was demonstrated working on Hyper's devnet. The team published two key updates on this theme: one on July 4, 2025 ("Devnet Is Live (Quietly)") and one on August 4, 2025 ("SVM Programs Running Natively"). Together, these two updates tell the story of the project's first concrete step.

The July update was an announcement made "quietly" — the team explicitly chose not to make a big fanfare, but to reveal that the devnet had been operational for a few weeks. This communication choice deserves to be noted, because it is unusual in the crypto world, where typically every small step is celebrated with bombastic announcements. **The Hyper team chose instead to first test, then announce**, and to do so with a measured tone. It is a small signal of an engineering approach rather than aggressive marketing, and it should be appreciated.

What did the devnet support in July 2025? The team explicitly listed these capabilities. **Deployment of programs via the Solana CLI**: developers could compile and upload programs to the rollup using the standard Solana tools. **Contract calls and transaction flows through the web console**: there was a web interface that made it possible to interact with the deployed programs without necessarily having to use the command line. **Account state management and instruction tracking**: the system correctly managed the persistent state and made it possible to track transaction execution. **Real-time visibility of transactions through the explorer**: there was an explorer showing the transactions happening on the devnet, similar to Solana Explorer or Etherscan but adapted to Hyper.

The August update added specific confirmations. The team confirmed full support for the standard Solana commands (`solana program deploy`, `solana call`, `solana logs`, `solana config get`), and stated that they worked "as expected within the Bitcoin Hyper runtime environment," connecting directly to the devnet node and applying real changes to the on-chain[a] state that were "confirmed and verifiable." The language used in the post is precise: "there are no simulations or slapped-together compatibility here: this is real SVM execution on a rollup anchored to Bitcoin."

The team also mentioned having concretely tested some specific components. **Basic equivalents of SPL tokens**: SPL is the standard Solana program for managing tokens, and it is the one typically used to issue tokens on Solana. Seeing the same program work on Hyper is an important test, because it demonstrates that the virtual machine correctly supports one of the most used components of the Solana ecosystem. **Escrow contracts and multisig logic**: common patterns in DeFi, which require the coordination of multiple signatures and conditional custody of funds. **Initial DeFi components**: the team did not specify which, but declared that "everything works flawlessly."

All this, put together, tells a concrete story. **Bitcoin Hyper actually has a working SVM runtime**, on which real programs can be deployed, real transactions made, real states seen. It is not yet the mainnet, it is not yet open to the general public, it is not yet ready to sustain production applications with real value. But it is a concrete demonstration that the architecture is not only a nice idea on paper, it is code that runs.

[a] **On-chain.** Said of a datum or an operation recorded directly on the blockchain and therefore publicly verifiable and no longer modifiable after the fact, as opposed to what happens off-chain, outside the chain.

⁂

9.4 — The Crucial Distinction: Devnet, Testnet, Mainnet

Now, however, we must make a passage that is essential in order not to confuse what exists with what does not yet exist. In the blockchain world, there are different types of "environments" in which a system can run, and understanding the difference is fundamental to correctly assessing a project's state of maturation.

The devnet (development network) is the most experimental environment. It is intended for the project's own developers and for close partners, and it is characterized by intentional instability: the team can deploy radical changes, can reset the state, can change the rules, can break things, because it is exactly there that things should break before reaching production. **On the devnet no real value runs.** The tokens and assets used are "fictitious," without economic value. The transactions that happen are experimental. The state can be erased at any moment. Bitcoin Hyper's devnet, according to the July 2025 update, is exactly this: an internal test environment with selective access for builders.

The testnet (test network) is the next level. It is a more stable environment, where the team commits to not making radical changes and not resetting the state. It is intended for broader development: developers can make more serious prototypes, test applications in conditions that approach real ones, integrate external services. **On the testnet too no real value runs**, but the system is more mature than the devnet. The testnet is typically the intermediate stage between "internal experimentation" and "public production."

The mainnet (main network) is the production environment. It is the one where real value runs, where end users interact, where the applications serve real use cases. The mainnet requires guaranteed stability, tested security, mature operational processes, user support. **Launching the mainnet is an operation that clearly separates the projects that have reached maturity from those still maturing.**

TABLE 9.1 **THE THREE ENVIRONMENTS OF A BLOCKCHAIN PROJECT, AND WHERE BITCOIN HYPER STANDS TODAY**

Stage	Audience	Real value?	Stability guarantee	Hyper status (early 2026)
Devnet	Internal team, selected partners	No (test assets)	Intentional instability; the state can be reset	**Active since Jul–Aug 2025.** Selective access via the team.
Testnet	Public developers	No (test assets)	No radical changes; state preserved	Not yet announced.
Mainnet	End users	Yes (real BTC)	Production grade; contractual uptime	Not yet launched.

Confusing the three rows is the most common error in evaluating a young rollup. Hyper has passed the first row. Each subsequent rou typically requires months of additional engineering — audits, hardening, decentralization — before it can be reached.

Bitcoin Hyper, as of the writing of this book, has a working devnet*. It has not yet publicly announced an open testnet †, let alone a mainnet. ‡ **This is an important point that must be understood without ambiguity.** When the team speaks of "native SVM execution on Bitcoin Hyper," it speaks of execution working on the devnet, in an experimental environment with limited access. It does not speak of execution already running in production with real users and real value.

This clarification is not an attack on the project, it is due honesty about the current state. **The devnet is a concrete and significant result**, it cannot be belittled. But it is also a preliminary result, which precedes the true mainnet launch by months or years, and in the meantime many things can change. The system can reveal scalability[§] problems under real load that do not emerge in internal tests. Security vulnerabilities[‖] can emerge that require rethinking components. Organizational or market challenges can arise that slow down the journey. All serious projects have experienced this, and Hyper will be no different.

The prudent investor or developer, therefore, should distinguish clearly between what has been demonstrated (SVM execution works on the devnet) and what has not yet been demonstrated (SVM execution works in production on mainnet, with real users, with real value, with all the system's components integrated and mature). **They are two statements of very different strength, and mixing them leads to wrong evaluations.**

⁂

9.5 — What Is Still Missing from the Complete Picture

Having appreciated what has been demonstrated, let us see what has not yet been demonstrated, because it is just as important for a balanced evaluation. Hyper's working devnet is a first step, but a rollup's complete system requires many more components, and several of these are still in development or research.

---

[*] **Devnet.** A reserved development environment, used by the team to try out the software under controlled conditions. Access is limited, the data can be wiped, and no real value circulates in it: it serves to demonstrate that a function is technically possible, not that it withstands public use.

[†] **Testnet.** A test network open to external developers and users, which replicates the operation of the definitive network but with valueless tokens. It is the phase in which the system is put to the test by many independent parties, before the actual launch.

[‡] **Mainnet.** The main network, operational and public, where real value and real users circulate. It is the only environment in which one can say a system "really works": it is also the one Bitcoin Hyper, as of this text, has not yet activated.

[§] **Scalability.** A system's capacity to maintain acceptable performance and costs as transactions and users grow. A system can behave well in internal tests and reveal bottlenecks only under the real load of the public network.

[‖] **Vulnerability (security).** A defect in the code or the design that an attacker can exploit to steal funds or alter the system's operation. It often emerges only under real load or after in-depth reviews, and it is one of the reasons the transition to mainnet takes time.

FIGURE 9.1 **BITCOIN HYPER'S PICTURE IN EARLY 2026: WHAT WORKS AND WHAT REMAINS TO BE BUILT**

DONE DEMONSTRATED ON DEVNET	**OPEN** STILL TO BE BUILT
RUNTIME *native SVM programs, no emulation*	**BRIDGE** *production-grade Canonical Bridge, audited*
CLI *standard Solana commands on the Hyper endpoint*	**SEQUENCER** *sustained throughput under real load*
TOKEN *SPL-equivalent token program tested*	**PROOFS** *fraud or validity proofs integrated*
PATTERNS *escrow and multisig logic tested*	**DA LAYER** *mature, decentralizable data availability*
EXPLORER *real-time visibility of devnet txs*	**ECOSYSTEM** *real applications, real users, real value*
	DECENTRALIZ. *distributed sequencer, DA, and governance*

The left column is what an SVM developer can already touch. The right column is what separates the "experimental infrastructure" from the "production rollup with security guarantees." Each item on the right is the subject of one or more later chapters of the book.

The Canonical Bridge in production. The system for depositing and withdrawing bitcoin between L1 and L2 is the project's most critical component from the users' standpoint, because it is the one that concretely holds the value. On the devnet, the team may have simulated the bridge using "fictitious" bitcoin, but the bridge that will manage real bitcoin with real value requires a level of security rigor, auditing, and testing that is orders of magnitude higher. The Canonical Bridge in production has not yet been demonstrated working, and it is one of the components that will require the most time and attention before the mainnet launch. We will address it in Chapter 11 in detail.

The production sequencer with sustained throughput. The devnet probably operates with a sequencer in a relatively light mode, processing test transactions in limited numbers. The production sequencer will have to handle the real traffic of an active mainnet, with all the peaks and anomalies of real traffic. The performance characteristics of a production sequencer are only partially predictable from tests. When launch time comes, there will in all likelihood be surprises — some positive, some negative — that the devnet could not show.

The proof system (fraud proofs or validity proofs) integrated. In the previous chapters we saw how the proof model is central to a rollup's security model. On the devnet, the team is probably operating in "trust the sequencer" mode, without active proofs, because the proofs are still in development. A rollup running on the devnet without proofs is not yet a full rollup: it is experimental infrastructure that demonstrates execution, but does not yet demonstrate the complete security model. The transition from "trust the sequencer" to "trustless via proofs" is one of the most technically challenging passages, and probably one of those that will determine the real timing of the mainnet launch.

The mature data availability layer. Here too, on the devnet the transaction data is probably managed simply, with replication among the team's nodes or publication on an internal system. The production data availability layer, which will have to manage availability for anyone in the world who wants to verify the state, and do so in a decentralized way, is still the subject of research. The team's updates on the topic (in particular the March 2026 one) describe explorations of various strategies, not a completed system.

The application ecosystem. Having the SVM runtime working is a necessary but not sufficient condition for the project's success. Without real applications, built by external teams, used by real users, the rollup is infrastructure without a purpose. On the devnet there are prototypes and tests, not a true ecosystem. The ecosystem's construction will happen in the months and years after the mainnet launch, and will depend on many factors outside the team's technical control.

The decentralization path. The devnet's single sequencer is a pragmatic choice for the initial phase, as we saw in Chapter 4. But progressive decentralization — the transition to a distributed sequencer, the opening of the data availability layer to external operators, the transition of governance toward the community — is a process that takes years and that is still entirely to be done. What exists today is the promise of a path, not a path traveled.

Putting these points together, the picture is clear. **The working devnet demonstrates that the architectural choice of the SVM on Bitcoin is technically feasible, at least in its basic execution components.** It does not yet demonstrate that the complete project, in all its dimensions, will be ready and working at mainnet. The distance between the two statements is where Hyper's future is played out, and it is the distance the prudent investor must monitor in the coming months.

⁂

9.6 — The Practical Deployment Experience: What Really Happens

To conclude the technical part of the chapter, I want to do a concrete exercise: describing step by step what happens when a developer deploys an SVM program on Bitcoin Hyper's devnet. This exercise is useful because it transforms abstract statements about "SVM support" into a sequence of concrete actions that anyone, with the appropriate skills, could replicate.

FIGURE 9.2 **FROM RUST CODE TO DEPLOYMENT ON HYPER: THE SVM DEVELOPER'S OPERATIONAL FLOW.**

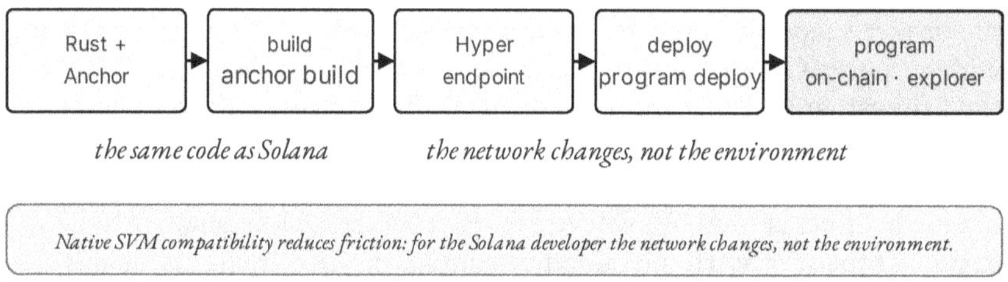

The developer starts from their own program, written in Rust using the Anchor framework.[*] The code is exactly what they would write for Solana: no Hyper-specific modification. They compile the program with `anchor build`, obtaining a binary file in BPF (Berkeley Packet Filter) format, which is the SVM's executable format. This file is exactly what one would obtain compiling for Solana.

At this point, they configure their Solana CLI to point to the Hyper devnet endpoint, which is a URL provided by the team. The command is something like `solana config set --url https://devnet.bitcoinhyper.com` (the exact URL depends on the team's configuration). This single change makes all the subsequent Solana CLI commands talk to Hyper instead of Solana.

The developer runs `solana program deploy ./target/deploy/programma.so`. The CLI takes the binary file, divides it into manageable pieces (because programs can be large), sends each piece as a separate transaction to the rollup, and finally sends a last transaction that "activates" the program. **This entire process is identical to what one would do on Solana.** The Hyper rollup receives the transactions, executes them, and in the end the program is deployed and accessible at a certain on-chain address.

At this point the developer can interact with their program. They can call its functions with `solana call`, read the logs with `solana logs`, inspect the state of the accounts the program manages. **Everything works as on Solana.** The only visible difference is the rollup's relative slowness compared with Solana mainnet — the devnet probably has less aggressive throughput characteristics — and the fact that one is interacting with a system in an experimental phase, where things can behave unexpectedly.

When the developer wants to verify what happened, they go to Hyper's explorer, which shows transactions and states in a way similar to Solana Explorer. They see their program deployed. They see their calls recorded. They see the accounts they modified. **The mental model is exactly Solana's.**

This experience, repeated dozens of times by different developers, is the proof that the technical level of "native SVM on Hyper" works. It is not marketing, it is code that runs. **For those with Solana experience, the friction of starting to experiment with Hyper is minimal.** A few minutes of configuration and you are operational. This is the strategic advantage of drop-in compatibility, and it is one of the project's most precious assets.

---

* **Anchor.** The most widespread development framework for programs in the SVM environment: it provides tools and conventions that simplify writing, testing, and publishing code, reducing repetitive work. The fact that the same framework used on Solana works without changes is the technical foundation of the so-called drop-in compatibility mentioned on this page.

FIGURE 9.3 **FROM DEVNET TO MAINNET: IMMEDIATE COMPATIBILITY AND PROGRESSIVE TESTING.**

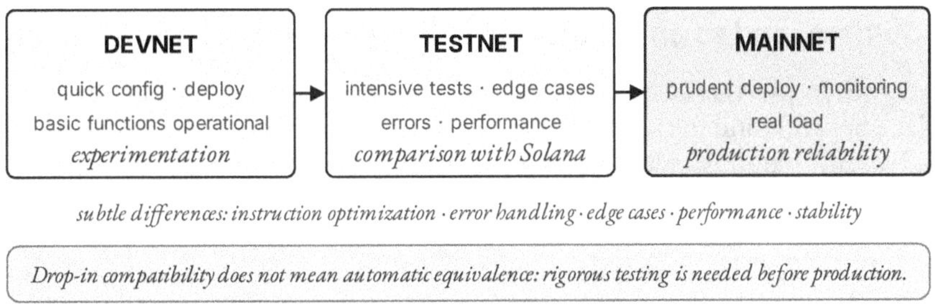

There is an important consideration to make, however, concerning the robustness of the experience in the transition toward production. The fact that the basic commands work on the devnet does not mean that every corner of the SVM's behavior is identical on Hyper compared with Solana. There can be subtle differences — in the way certain instructions are optimized, in the way errors are reported, in the exact behavior of some edge cases — that emerge only through intensive testing. **For production applications, developers will have to do careful testing on Hyper's testnet and then mainnet; they cannot take for granted that "it works on Solana = it works on Hyper" in every detail.** It is an additional commitment, but it is normal for any new system.

⁂

9.7 — Questions and Answers: Clarifying the Chapter's Concepts

Question 1: If the devnet has been working since July 2025, why has the mainnet not been launched yet? What is missing?

Many things are missing, and it is normal that it be so. Launching a mainnet requires bringing all the system's components to maturity, not only the execution layer. It requires the Canonical Bridge in production version, with complete audits and intensive testing. It requires the proof system integrated and working. It requires the data availability layer infrastructure in a decentralizable version. It requires the explorer in a robust version, the RPC ecosystem, the monitoring tools, the operational procedures, user support. It requires emergency plans to manage unforeseen problems. It requires coordination with the partners who will have to integrate the system. **All this requires much more time than simply "running SVM programs."** How much time? It depends on the quality with which the team wants to arrive at the mainnet. Serious projects typically take 12–24 months between the first working devnet and the mainnet launch, and it is a timeline that protects quality at the expense of haste. Concrete example: Optimism had the first working prototypes in 2019–2020, but the "true" mainnet with decent security characteristics arrived only in 2021, and the fraud proofs were fully implemented only in 2024–2025. For Bitcoin Hyper, one can expect a similar trajectory, where the devnet is only the first chapter of a long story.

Question 2: Can I access Bitcoin Hyper's devnet as an external developer? How?

According to the team's communications, access to the devnet is "selective" — it is not completely open to the public, but the team accepts access requests from serious builders who have something to build. The team mentioned being "happy to grant selective access" to those working on something early and wanting to test it. The contact route is via the email address contact@bitcoinhyper.com and via the administrators of the official Telegram channels. It is a typical model for the devnet phase: the team wants to control who accesses in order to avoid excessive load and to concentrate on the partners who are actually building, not just browsing. Those with Solana experience and a serious project in mind have good chances of obtaining access. Those who just want to "try it out" will probably have to wait for the next phases (testnet or mainnet). Concrete example: this is the same dynamic Solana itself had in its early days, and that Ethereum's first rollups had. It is a natural iteration of the process: first internal access, then that of close partners, then the public testnet, then the mainnet.

Question 3: If SVM programs run natively on Hyper, can I use the same wallets (Phantom, Solflare, and so on) to interact with Hyper as I use with Solana?

In principle yes, but in practice adaptations may be necessary. Standard Solana wallets are designed to talk to the Solana network, and to talk to Hyper they must be configured to point to the right endpoint. For users, this typically requires adding a custom "network" in the wallet, a feature most Solana wallets support. The Hyper team is probably working with the main wallets to provide native integration, but as of the writing of this book, complete details on which wallets will support Hyper out of the box are not publicly available. For the devnet, developers probably use manually configured wallets. For the mainnet, the expectation is that integration with the main wallets will be complete at launch or shortly after. Concrete example: when Optimism was launched, MetaMask had to be configured manually to support the network. Within a few months, the integration became automatic in the main wallets. For Hyper a similar trajectory is expected.

Question 4: What types of applications are currently being tested on the devnet, beyond simple SPL programs?

Public information is limited, because many of the partner teams testing the devnet probably prefer not to reveal details about their products before launch. What the Hyper team has mentioned includes standard SPL tokens (to test the token functionality base), escrow contracts and multisig logic (to test the conditional custody patterns common in DeFi), and unspecified "initial DeFi components." It is reasonable to expect that various DeFi, gaming, and infrastructure projects are experimenting on the devnet, but the details will emerge in the months following the mainnet launch. **Ecosystem alignment is one of the points the team has explicitly worked on** (the November 2025 post is devoted to this theme), but for competitive reasons not all the partners have announced their presence. Concrete example: before the launch of an important Layer 2, it is normal for there to be dozens of teams in "stealth mode," working on the infrastructure without giving much visibility. They usually reveal themselves around the mainnet launch, when they have something ready to show the public. For Hyper, this same dynamic is likely.

Question 5: What happens if a critical bug is discovered in Hyper's SVM runtime during devnet use?

It is exactly for this that the devnet exists. The discovery of bugs during the devnet phase is the desired outcome, not a failure. When a developer or a team member finds a critical bug, they typically follow this process. **First: the bug is communicated privately to the Hyper team**, ideally through a dedicated security channel. Communicating it publicly right away would be reckless, because it could allow malicious actors to exploit it before it is fixed. **Second: the team assesses the bug, reproduces the**

problem, develops a fix. This can take hours, days, or weeks depending on the complexity. **Third: the fix is deployed on the devnet** (which, remember, can be modified and reset without problems, being experimental). **Fourth: if the bug has broader implications**, perhaps on the architecture or the design, it can require deeper rethinking that delays other things. **For serious projects, there is typically a bug bounty program** that rewards those who find critical bugs, incentivizing responsible disclosure. Hyper has mentioned the intention to have security audits before the mainnet launch, but the specific details of a public bug bounty program have not yet been communicated. Concrete example: all of Ethereum's Layer 2s have had critical bugs discovered in the devnet/testnet phase, and some even after the mainnet launch. Optimism, Arbitrum, zkSync have all had public incidents. The difference between a serious project and an improvised one is how it manages these bugs: with transparency, timely fixes, and clear communication. Hyper will have to demonstrate the same approach when its turn comes.

Question 6: If the devnet works, why can't real bitcoin already be used instead of fictitious tokens?

For fundamental security reasons. The devnet is an experimental environment where the team can make radical changes, where bugs causing state losses can emerge, where the operational procedures are not yet consolidated. **Allowing real bitcoin in such an environment would mean exposing users to almost guaranteed losses.** This is why devnets always use fictitious assets, and this is why the transition to "real bitcoin" requires not only that the system work, but that it work with levels of reliability and security the devnet cannot yet give. The Canonical Bridge in particular must have been audited in depth, tested under simulated attacks, validated in edge-case scenarios, before real value can be accepted. These processes take months, not weeks. **The day Hyper accepts real bitcoin will be the day of the mainnet launch, not a moment sooner.** Concrete example: Optimism's bridge for ETH was available right from the mainnet launch, but it required a level of auditing and testing of months before being considered ready. There have nonetheless been minor incidents over time, but the system was designed to be recoverable. For Hyper, the same philosophy: no haste in handling real value, and when it begins, it begins with adequate safety margins.

⁂

9.8 — WHAT TO TAKE AWAY FROM THIS CHAPTER

Bitcoin Hyper publicly demonstrated, in July–August 2025, the native execution of SVM programs on its own devnet. It is a concrete result marking the project's transition from "theoretical research" to "experimentable infrastructure."

"Native execution" means the rollup actually has the SVM as a runtime component, not an emulator or a translator. Programs compiled in the same format Solana accepts run directly, without changes.

The standard Solana commands — `solana program deploy`, `solana call`, `solana logs`, `solana config get` — work natively on Hyper's devnet. This is the concrete proof of drop-in compatibility with the Solana ecosystem.

The devnet supports program deployment, contract calls, account state management, visibility through the explorer. Standard components like SPL tokens, escrow contracts, multisig logic were tested successfully.

The devnet is an experimental environment with selective access, not a production system. No real value runs on it, the state can be modified by the team, the operational procedures are still being consolidated.

Between the working devnet and the ready mainnet there is a significant distance requiring months or years of additional work. Missing are the Canonical Bridge in production, the integrated proof system, the mature data availability layer, the application ecosystem, the actual decentralization path.

The practical deployment experience for a Solana developer is practically identical on Hyper. A few minutes of configuration are enough to start experimenting, and this is one of the project's main strategic advantages.

The distinction between what has been demonstrated (a working devnet) and what has not yet been demonstrated (a ready mainnet) is essential for a balanced evaluation. Mixing the two statements leads to wrong judgments.

The transparency with which the team communicated the devnet's progress is a positive signal of an engineering approach. Announcing quietly, after testing, is unusual in the crypto world and should be appreciated.

Chapter 9 ends here. We have seen what "native SVM on Bitcoin Hyper" concretely means, and we have clearly distinguished between what has been demonstrated and what still must be built. In ***Chapter 10 — Determinism: the invisible constraint of speed****, we will descend into one of the project's most technically subtle aspects, the one the team explicitly addressed in a dedicated research post: how to guarantee that the SVM, born for high-speed parallel execution, maintains the perfect determinism a rollup requires. It is a technical chapter, but essential for understanding why certain architectural choices were made, and where something can still break.*

CHAPTER 9 · SVM PROGRAMS RUNNING NATIVELY ON BITCOIN HYPER · SUMMARY MICHELE STEFANELLI

From the whitepaper to the devnet: when the promise becomes *code*

Native SVM programs on Bitcoin Hyper: **what has been demonstrated** and **what remains to be built**.

1 The promise becomes a demo

Bitcoin Hyper has shown working SVM programs on its own devnet. It is not yet mainnet, but it is a first concrete demonstration: the architecture does not stay on paper, **it becomes executable code**.

WHITEPAPER → CODE → DEVNET LIVE

2 Native execution, not emulation

SVM programs run directly on **Hyper's runtime**, with no translators, emulators, or intermediate layers. The Solana developer uses **already familiar** tools and commands.

SOLANA CLI → SVM RUNTIME → BITCOIN HYPER

```
$ solana program deploy
$ solana call
$ solana logs
$ solana config get
```

3 Functionality already observed on devnet

- ✓ **Program deployment** — Uploaded via Solana CLI
- ✓ **Contract calls** — Interaction with the programs
- ✓ **Account state** — On-chain state management
- ✓ **Devnet explorer** — Visibility of the transactions
- ✓ **Initial DeFi patterns** — SPL tokens, escrow, multisig

4 Devnet does not mean mainnet

DEVNET — REACHED
Experimental environment · selective access · no real value.

TESTNET — TO COME
More stable environment · public tests · no real value.

MAINNET — TO COME
Real production · real users · real BTC · full security.

TO MONITOR BEFORE THE MAINNET

- Canonical Bridge audited
- Proof system integrated
- Ecosystem of applications
- Sequencer under real load
- Mature data availability
- Progressive decentralization

THE DEVNET DEMONSTRATES
The **technical feasibility** of SVM execution on Bitcoin Hyper.

THE MAINNET WILL HAVE TO DEMONSTRATE
Operational maturity, **security**, and the capacity to sustain **real value**.

PART III · THE EXECUTION LAYER DUE DILIGENCE OF A LAYER 2 · VOL. I

PART III · THE EXECUTION LAYER

Chapter 10
Determinism

The invisible constraint of speed

⁂

10.1 — A Property Nobody Sees but Everything Depends On

There is a property of blockchains that almost nobody talks about, even among insiders, but on which the very possibility of the system working literally depends. It is not speed, it is not security, it is not decentralization — those are all important but derived properties. The one I am talking about is **execution determinism**: the guarantee that, given a certain input, the system will always produce exactly the same output, regardless of who executes it, on what hardware, at what moment, in what order. It sounds trivial. It sounds obvious. **And yet it is one of the hardest properties to guarantee in modern distributed systems**, and when it breaks, the system collapses.

FIGURE 10.1 **EXECUTION DETERMINISM: THE SAME INPUT ALWAYS PRODUCES THE SAME OUTPUT, WHATEVER THE NODE, THE HARDWARE, OR THE MOMENT. IF THE PROPERTY BREAKS, THE NODES DIVERGE AND THE ROLLUP CANNOT ANCHOR A SHARED STATE.**

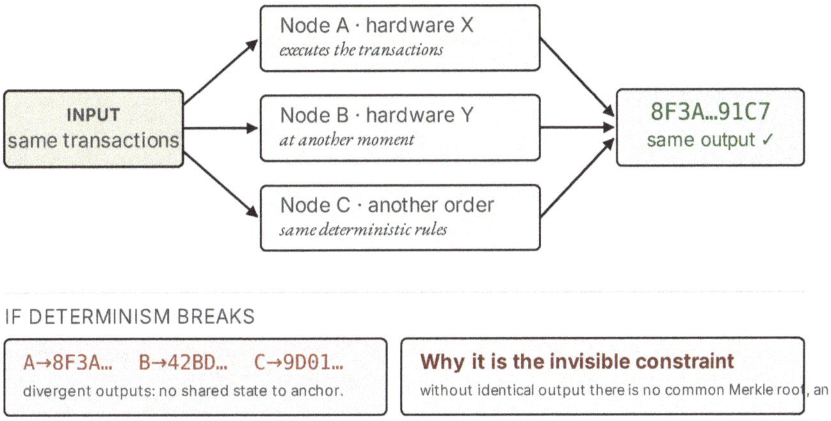

In this chapter I want to explain why determinism is the invisible constraint behind all of Bitcoin Hyper's architectural choices, why the SVM — born to be fast and parallel — poses specific determinism challenges the team must solve, and why a research post published in December 2025 by the Hyper team treated this theme explicitly as one of the project's open points. It is a technical chapter, I admit, and it requires patience. But it is also one of the chapters that will give you the most tools for seriously evaluating the maturity of any Layer 2 project you come across in the future. When a project talks about "speed" and "scalability" and ignores the theme of determinism, it is probably hiding something under the rug. When a project addresses determinism openly, as Hyper has done, it is showing an engineering maturity many competitors do not have.

I begin with a story that clarifies what "determinism" means and why without it a rollup cannot exist. Then we go inside the SVM's specific problem, and finally we see how Hyper is addressing the matter.

⁂

10.2 — The Story of the Two Diverging Nodes

Imagine that two nodes[a] of a blockchain — let us call them Node A and Node B — simultaneously receive the exact same batch[b] of transactions to process. There are ten transactions, in a well-defined order, signed by different users, with precise instructions. **Both nodes have the same software, the same starting data, the same execution rules.** The expectation, in the blockchain world, is trivial: after executing the ten transactions, both nodes must have exactly the same final state. Same balance for every user, same value in every storage[c] cell, same event log[d], same identical everything. If it were not so, the entire system could not work.

And yet, in a world where engineers have not worried enough about determinism,[e] this can happen. Node A finishes processing the batch and obtains a final state we call "state Alpha." Node B finishes processing the exact same batch and obtains a slightly different final state, which we call "state Beta." Maybe the difference is minimal — a balance differing by one satoshi[f], a timestamp[g] different by a microsecond, a slightly different order of the events in the log. But it exists. **And when it exists, even minimally, the entire system collapses.**[h]

---

[a] **Node.** A computer participating in the blockchain network by keeping a copy of it and verifying transactions and state on its own. For the network to work, all the nodes must recompute the same identical result.

[b] **Batch.** A set of transactions grouped and processed together, in the same order, as a single unit of work. In rollups, transactions are processed and anchored in batches, not one at a time.

[c] **Storage.** The blockchain's persistent memory, where programs keep their own data (balances, variables) from one transaction to the next.

[d] **Event log.** An ordered record of the actions produced by the execution of the transactions (for example, transfers or a program's updates). It is part of the state: two nodes must produce the same log, in the same order, for the network to remain in agreement.

[e] **Determinism.** The property whereby the same input always produces, everywhere, exactly the same output. In a blockchain it is an absolute requirement: every node must recompute the state identically from the same transactions, otherwise the network cannot agree on a single truth.

[f] **Satoshi.** The smallest unit into which a bitcoin can be divided: one bitcoin equals one hundred million satoshis. It takes its name from Satoshi Nakamoto, Bitcoin's anonymous creator. In the text's reasoning it is cited to give the measure of the problem: even a discrepancy of a single satoshi between two nodes — that is, of an infinitesimal fraction of value — is enough to break the agreement on the state.

[g] **Timestamp.** The time marker associated with an event or a block. Even a minimal timestamp difference between two nodes is enough to make the final state diverge.

[h] **Divergence and consensus.** If two nodes arrive at even minimally different states, the network no longer has a single valid chain but two competing versions: it is what technically produces a split (fork). Consensus therefore requires the computation to be not only correct, but rigorously reproducible by anyone.

FIGURE 10.2 **WHEN TWO NODES DIVERGE: WHY DETERMINISM IS NEEDED.**

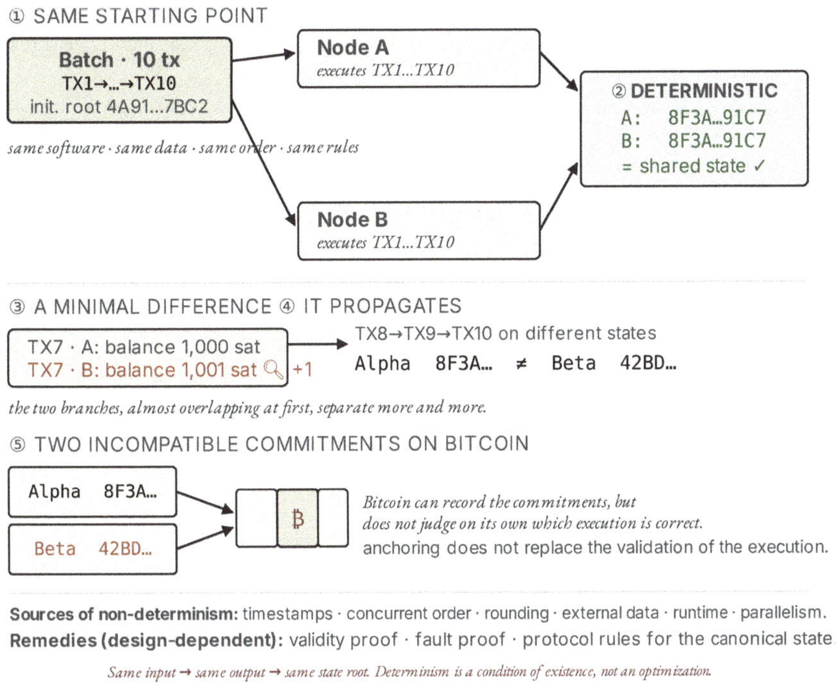

Two nodes receive the same batch and start from the same state: in a deterministic environment they produce the same root; if a source of variability introduces a minimal difference, the states diverge until they generate incompatible commitments. Bitcoin records the roots, but a rule for validating the execution is needed.

It collapses because Node A and Node B will not agree on what the correct state is. When they compare notes to propagate the new state, each will defend its own version. When a third node, Node C, has to choose which version to accept, it will have no criteria for doing so: both were obtained by running the same software on the same data. **The network fragments.** Some nodes follow state Alpha, others state Beta, and from that moment on the two branches diverge forever, because every subsequent transaction will rest on one or the other, widening the difference.

On a traditional proof-of-work blockchain like Bitcoin, consensus recomposes itself because in the end the chain with the most accumulated work prevails, and the nodes on the minority chain are "cut off" and must start again. But it is a costly, slow mechanism, and it still assumes there is a moment of initial non-determinism that then gets resolved. **In a rollup, this mechanism does not exist.** The rollup has no proof-of-work consensus of its own; it relies on the anchoring on Bitcoin for finality. If two nodes of the rollup diverge in state, and each publishes its own state commitment on Bitcoin, Bitcoin does not know which of the two is "right" — it only sees two different commits. The system has no way of resolving the conflict internally.

This is the reason **perfect determinism is not optional for a rollup**. It is not a desirable property, it is a condition of existence. Without perfect determinism, the rollup cannot work. All the rollup's nodes, given the same input, must always, always, always produce the same output. Bit by bit. Not "roughly the same," not "almost always the same": exactly the same, every time.

Put like that, it sounds like an easy demand. In practice, as we shall see, it is one of the hardest demands to satisfy in modern software systems, and it becomes particularly hard when one wants to exploit parallelism for performance.

TABLE 10.1 **TWO NODES, SAME INPUT: THE OUTCOME WITH AND WITHOUT DETERMINISM.**

Aspect	Deterministic execution	Non-deterministic execution

Final state	Identical on every node	Can diverge between the nodes
Published state root[a]	One only, shared	Conflicting versions
Independent verification	Possible for anyone	Without a single reference, not practicable
Outcome for the rollup	Coherent consensus and anchoring	Consensus stalled, anchoring not verifiable

With the same sequence of transactions and the same rules, a deterministic execution produces the same state root on every node. In the absence of determinism the nodes can diverge and, lacking a shared reference, the rollup can neither reach consensus nor anchor a verifiable state on Bitcoin.

⁂

10.3 — The Hidden Sources of Non-Determinism

To understand why determinism is hard, one must know where non-determinism[b] can spring from in software systems. The possible sources are numerous, and some are particularly insidious. The six that follow do not exhaust every risk, but they make it possible to understand the main categories of variability a blockchain runtime[c] must discipline.

---

[a] **State root.** A short imprint (a few dozen bytes) that summarizes the blockchain's entire state at a given moment. Two nodes executing the same transactions deterministically must produce the same state root; it is this imprint the rollup periodically anchors to Bitcoin.

[b] **Non-determinism.** The property whereby the same input can produce different results depending on incidental factors — the order in which the computer performs the operations, the hardware, the moment of execution. In a blockchain it is a defect to be eliminated: if the nodes do not obtain the same result from the same transactions, the network cannot agree on a single truth.

[c] **Runtime.** The software environment that actually executes the blockchain's programs, applying the rules to every transaction. It is the runtime that must guarantee that execution remains deterministic on every node.

FIGURE 10.3 **THE SIX DOORS OF NON-DETERMINISM AND THE COUNTERMEASURES.**

Same initial state + same ordered batch + same rules → same state root.

DOOR	DANGER (example)	COUNTERMEASURE
① **Clock**	*A 14:32:18.245 ≠ B ...251*	*time from the protocol (slot/block)*
② **Randomness**	*A→472981 ≠ B→813604*	*disciplined, verifiable randomness*
③ **Concurrency**	*TX-A,TX-B on the same Account X*	*declared accesses, locking, canonical ord*
④ **Floating-point**	*A 0.3000000 ≠ B 0.3000001*	*integers / fixed-point in critical computa.*
⑤ **Memory/host**	*addresses 0xA41F... ≠ 0x7C92...*	*isolated VM, stable serialization*
⑥ **Toolchain**	*compiler v1 vs v2 → different binaries*	*reproducible builds, pinned versions*

all doors closed →
A = B = 8F3A...91C7 ✓

one open door is enough →
A 8F3A... ≠ B 42BD... ⊘

THE SVM'S CHALLENGE · parallelizing without breaking determinism

TX-A→Account X · TX-B→Account Y
independent → in parallel

TX-C→Account X · TX-D→Account X
in conflict → scheduling and locking

Declaring in advance the accounts read/modified makes it possible to parallelize the independent operations and discipline the conflicts. → Next step: how to reconcile parallelism and determinism in the SVM.

Determinism is not a single feature: it is a discipline applied to the entire stack, at every update too.

Each source, on its own, would be enough to break a rollup. The engineering work of a serious chain is closing all six doors at the same time, and keeping them closed at every update. The classification is illustrative, not exhaustive; the countermeasures indicated depend on the protocol's specific design. The discipline required recalls, in rigor and continuity of controls, that adopted in software systems intended for critical applications.

Source one: the system clock. If a program reads the computer's current time, it obtains a different value every time. Two nodes executing the same code at different moments will have slightly different clocks. **A blockchain cannot allow programs to read the system time**, because it would destroy determinism. Blockchain runtimes cannot let the result depend on the individual computer's local clock: this is why they expose shared temporal information according to protocol rules — for example, timestamps associated with blocks, chain height, slots, or dedicated system accounts — identical for all the nodes.

Source two: random numbers. Generating a random number, by definition, produces different results every time. If a program uses the operating system's randomness, every node will obtain different numbers. **Blockchains cannot allow uncontrolled randomness.** They must use sources defined by the protocol. A value derived from on-chain data can guarantee determinism, but it is not automatically unpredictable or resistant to manipulation. When security really depends on randomness, mechanisms designed specifically for that use case are needed.

Source three: concurrency. When several operations run in parallel, the order in which they complete depends on uncontrollable factors: CPU speed, memory availability, the operating system's load. **If two concurrent operations modify the same datum, the order in which the modifications are applied determines the final state.** On parallel systems without explicit constraints, this is an enormous source of non-determinism. And it is precisely here that the SVM with its parallel model must be careful, as we shall see.

Source four: floating-point numeric operations. On different computers, computations with decimal numbers (so-called "floating point") can give slightly different results due to different hardware precisions, different libraries, compiler optimizations. **This is why, in computations affecting the shared state, integers or fixed-point representations are generally preferred**, with explicit rounding rules. Some runtimes support a limited set of floating-point operations, but their use requires caution. Every program using floating point in critical computations is a potential source of non-determinism.

Source five: memory allocation. The exact memory address where a program allocates its data can differ between different executions, due to techniques like ASLR (Address Space Layout Randomization). If a program uses these addresses in its computations (for example, in hashing), it can produce different results. **Blockchain virtual machines must abstract this variability away**, providing a deterministic memory model.

Source six: build reproducibility and update governance. A distinct but closely related matter concerns the process by which the software is compiled and distributed. Different versions of the compiler, the dependencies, or the flags can produce different artifacts. **This does not necessarily mean the same already-distributed binary is executed non-deterministically**; it does mean, however, that the compilation, deployment, and update process must be rigidly controlled, verifiable, and reproducible.

Putting these sources together, one understands why guaranteeing perfect determinism is an enormous, continuous job. It is not enough to say "let us be careful." The entire stack — from the runtime, to the compiler, to the build tools, to the deployment policies — must be built to systematically exclude every possible source of variation. **It is engineering work comparable to what companies producing software for aviation or medical applications do**, where the same constraints apply with the same severity.

Now let us see what happens in the specific case of the SVM, where the problem of determinism intertwines with the choice of parallelism, creating a technically very interesting situation.

⁂

10.4 — The SVM's Paradox: Parallelism and Determinism in the Same Runtime

We saw in Chapter 8 that the SVM's[a] performance advantage comes from parallel execution[b] through Sealevel[c]. Transactions declaring different accounts can run in parallel on the CPU's different cores[d], exploiting the power of modern hardware. Now, however, let us add the other piece of the puzzle: **this parallel execution must be perfectly deterministic.** The rollup's different nodes, executing the same batch[e] of transactions with their own Sealevel, must obtain bit by bit the same result.

Here lies the apparent paradox. Parallelism increases performance, but it cannot be left to chance. The order in which the operations are processed internally can depend on the hardware and on the system's load; what cannot vary is the observable result of the execution[i]. If two transactions modify truly independent portions of the state, they can proceed simultaneously without altering the final coherence. If instead they compete for the same writable account[f], the runtime[l] must recognize the conflict and discipline its execution.

Sealevel addresses the problem by having every transaction declare in advance the accounts it will need to read or modify. Thanks to this information, the runtime can identify compatible operations, execute in parallel those that do not interfere with one another, and apply locking and scheduling[g] rules when there is contention on the same writable account. Several transactions can also consult a read-only account[h] at the same time.

TABLE 10.2 **HOW SEALEVEL RECONCILES PARALLELISM AND DETERMINISM.**

Situation	Runtime behavior
Transactions on different accounts	Executed in parallel: no conflict possible
Contention on the same writable account	Locking and scheduling: disciplined order[g]
Account consulted read-only	Concurrent access allowed to several transactions

The key is the advance declaration of the accounts: knowing in advance what each transaction will read or write, Sealevel obtains parallelism without giving up determinism. Given the same initial state and the same order, the result remains identical on any hardware.

[a] **SVM (Solana Virtual Machine).** The execution environment that processes transactions according to the model introduced by Solana and adopted by Bitcoin Hyper. It is what makes it possible to execute programs and transactions in parallel rather

than one at a time.

[b] **Parallel execution.** The capacity to process several transactions at the same instant, on different cores of the processor, instead of one after another. It is the source of the SVM's speed advantage, but it works only if it does not alter the final result.

[c] **Sealevel.** The SVM's parallel execution engine: it organizes the transactions so that the independent ones run simultaneously, while keeping the result identical on every node.

[d] **Core.** Each of the independent computing units of a modern processor. More cores make it possible to execute more transactions at the same instant, provided they do not touch the same data.

[e] **Batch.** A set of transactions grouped and processed together, in the same order, as a single unit of work. All the nodes must process the same batch and obtain the same result from it.

[f] **Writable account.** A portion of state a transaction declares it wants to modify. Two transactions that want to write the same account cannot proceed in parallel: the runtime puts them in line.

[g] **Locking and scheduling.** The mechanisms by which the runtime manages transactions competing for the same datum: it prevents simultaneous access (locking) and fixes their execution order (scheduling), so that the result is always the same, on any node.

[h] **Read-only account.** A portion of state a transaction declares it wants only to read, without modifying it. Several transactions can read the same account at the same time without conflict.

[i] **Observable result (determinism).** The final outcome of the execution — the balances, the state — which must be identical on every node. A system is deterministic when, given the same input, it always produces the same result: it is the property that allows all the nodes to agree, even if internally they processed the transactions in parallel and in slightly different orders.

[l] **Runtime.** The engine that actually executes the transactions at processing time, applying the system's rules. It is the runtime that recognizes when two transactions are in conflict and decides how to discipline their execution, so that the result remains coherent on all the nodes.

FIGURE 10.4 **SEALEVEL USES THE ACCOUNTS DECLARED BY THE TRANSACTIONS TO IDENTIFY COMPATIBLE OPERATIONS: THOSE NOT COMPETING FOR THE SAME WRITABLE STATE GO IN PARALLEL, THE CONFLICTING ONES ARE DISCIPLINED. THE INDIVIDUAL TRANSACTION REMAINS ATOMIC AND THE FINAL RESULT MUST REMAIN COHERENT ON DIFFERENT HARDWARE.**

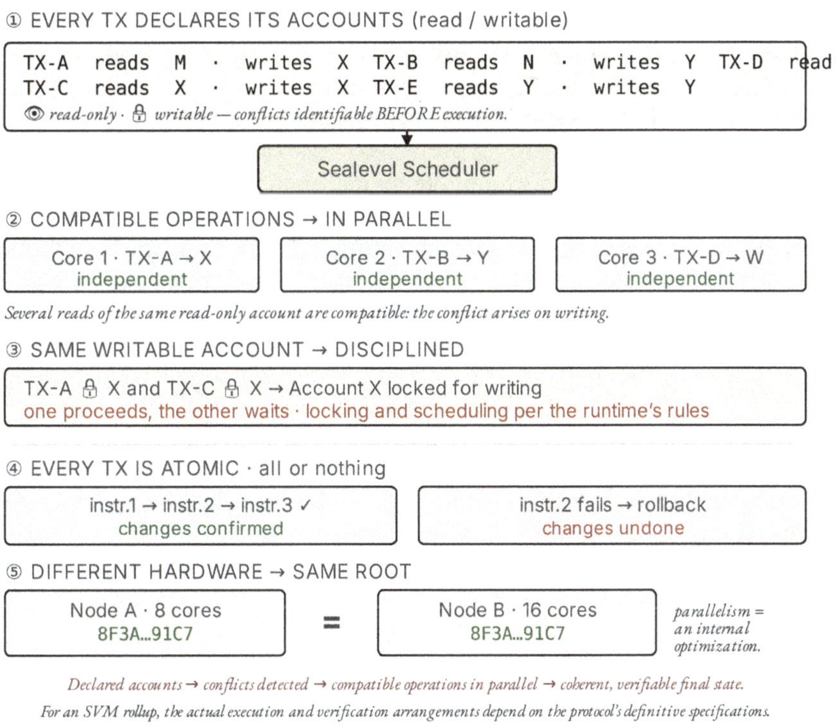

The result is controlled parallelism. The speed comes from the simultaneous execution of the independent operations; the determinism comes from the fact that the dependencies on the state are declared and governed. The nodes can use different hardware and distribute the work internally in different ways, but they must obtain the same final state from the same inputs and the same protocol rules.

The official documentation moreover confirms that every Solana transaction contains one or more instructions, which are treated atomically: if one instruction fails, the entire transaction fails and the state changes are undone.

In practice, making this scheme work well is hard: every detail of the execution must be controlled, the system libraries used by the programs must be deterministic, the cryptographic primitives must produce identical output on different hardware, the internal data structures must behave identically even under different loads. **By adopting an SVM, Bitcoin Hyper can benefit from an execution model designed to exploit the parallelism of modern hardware.** It must, however, integrate this model into its own specific rollup context, precisely defining the runtime, the sequencing, the data availability, and the mechanisms by which the execution is verified. The actual guarantees will depend on the protocol's definitive technical specifications.

⁂

10.5 — Hyper's Research Post on Determinism (December 2025)

The Hyper team, in December 2025, published a research post specifically devoted to determinism in high-performance SVM execution. It is a document worth reading carefully because it demonstrates a technical awareness of the problem that many competitor projects do not show. Let us look at the key points.

The post begins by explicitly acknowledging that **"deterministic execution is the invisible backbone of a credible rollup."** It is a strong and technically correct statement. Without determinism, "there is no shared state, there is no reproducibility, and there is no possibility of challenging a malicious actor." This is exactly the connection we described in the previous sections: without determinism, the rollup model does not work.

The post then addresses the SVM's specificity. It acknowledges that **"the Solana Virtual Machine was not designed for Bitcoin"** and that its Solana-optimized properties — the account-based model, parallel execution — must be adapted to the rollup context. The account model, declared explicitly in the transactions, is a property that facilitates parallelization, but it is not enough on its own: it is also necessary to make sure that the execution of independent transactions, once parallelized, produces canonical results.

Here is the post's central passage, which I quote for its technical significance: **"The design challenge is guaranteeing that parallelism never violates determinism."** To achieve this, "every execution path must be deterministic, regardless of the node executing it." The team spells out that the research explores "how the nodes can impose rigid limits on execution order, on account access, and on runtime visibility." In other words, even if the transactions are executed in parallel internally, **the system imposes explicit constraints that make the final result identical across the nodes**.

The post then addresses the problem of proofs. If a sequencer submits a state root that does not match the deterministic expectations, "a challenge mechanism must exist." Here Hyper explores "several strategies: reproducible proofs, fraud-proof challenges, or deterministic replay logs." Each of these strategies has merits and defects, and the team has not yet publicly committed to which one will be adopted in production. But the fact that the problem has been spelled out and discussed publicly is a signal of maturity.

The post closes with an important philosophical consideration: **"Ultimately, determinism is what makes trust minimization real. Users do not have to believe the sequencer; they can verify the work themselves."** It is exactly the point we have emphasized throughout this book. Permissionless verifiability — one of the three constitutive properties of Bitcoin the Layer 2s try to inherit — depends structurally on determinism. Without determinism, independent verification is impossible. **Guaranteeing determinism is the technical precondition for honoring the philosophical promise.**

What to take away from this post? Three things. First: the Hyper team knows the problem in depth and addresses it explicitly. Second: the solution is under active research, not yet finalized. Third: the final solution will depend on specific choices the team must still complete. **It is not a solved problem; it is a recognized problem being worked on.** For a prudent investor, this is one of the points to monitor in the coming months: when the team releases more detailed technical documentation on how it has implemented determinism in the SVM-Hyper, more precise evaluations will be possible.

TABLE 10.3 **DETERMINISM IN HYPER: WHAT TO TAKE AWAY.**

Point	Status
Awareness of the problem	The team addresses it explicitly
Solution	Under active research, not yet finalized
Technical choices	To be completed and documented
Judgment	A recognized problem, not yet solved

Determinism is not a detail: it is the precondition that makes the entire rollup verifiable. For Hyper it is today a problem addressed seriously but not yet closed; the decisive test will be the publication of a detailed technical specification, which will make it possible to move from declared intentions to verifiable results.

Note 1. "Minimization of trust" (trust minimization) does not mean the total absence of trust, but the progressive reduction of the number of parties the user must trust. Determinism contributes to this goal because it allows anyone to recompute the state and independently verify the sequencer's work, without having to accept it on trust.

Note 2. The transition from "active research" to a definitive technical specification is precisely the type of milestone a due diligence must monitor: until the implementation details are published and verifiable, the claim that determinism is "guaranteed" remains a declared objective, not a demonstrated result.

Note 3. Among the strategies cited, the deterministic "replay log" (deterministic replay log) is an ordered record of all the operations executed: anyone can retrace it step by step and obtain, if the system is truly deterministic, exactly the same final state. It is one of the tools with which an external observer can verify the sequencer's work without having to trust it.

Note 4. "Fraud-proof challenges" (fraud proofs) treat the state published by the sequencer as valid until someone demonstrates, within a time window, that it is wrong: they are the typical mechanism of optimistic rollups.

Note 5. By "reproducible proofs" is meant the possibility for anyone to rerun the computation and obtain exactly the same result as the sequencer: it is the most direct form of verification, and it depends entirely on determinism.

Note 6. "Permissionless verifiability" is the possibility, for anyone and without authorizations, to check the correctness of the state on their own: it is one of the constitutive properties of Bitcoin the Layer 2s try to inherit, and it rests on determinism.

⁂

10.6 — The Three Main Strategies for Guaranteeing Determinism

Hyper's post mentions three families of strategies[a] for managing determinism. It is worth describing them in a bit more detail, because they help to understand what the team might choose and what the implications of each option are.

---

[a] **Validity proof and fault proof.** The two big approaches with which a rollup demonstrates that its state is correct. With the validity proof, every update is accompanied by a cryptographic proof attesting its correctness in advance: nobody has to trust, it is enough to verify the proof. With the fault proof, the state is instead taken as good unless challenged: a time window opens in which anyone can report an error and have it corrected. The first model is more secure but technically complex; the second is lighter but introduces a wait before definitive finality.

FIGURE 10.5 **THREE TOOLS FOR CHECKING THE ROLLUP'S STATE.**

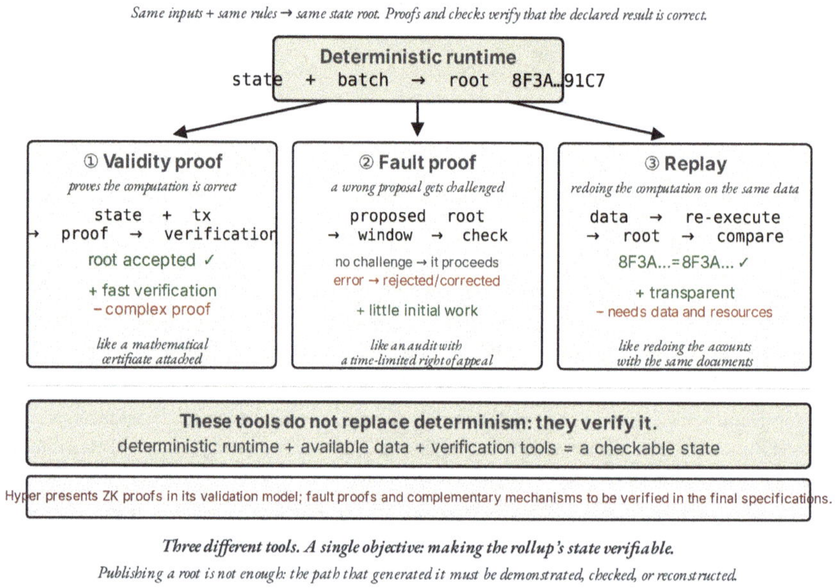

Three tools for verifying the correctness of the execution. Validity proofs mathematically certify a state transition; fault proofs make it possible to challenge a wrong proposal within a preset window; independent replay makes it possible to re-execute the transactions starting from the same data. They do not create the runtime's determinism, but they contribute to making the state published by the sequencer verifiable.

FIGURE 10.5 **THE THREE FAMILIES OF STRATEGIES FOR THE PROOF OF DETERMINISM**

Strategy	How it works	Strengths	Weaknesses
Reproducible proofs *(validity proof)*	The sequencer publishes a zk-SNARK/STARK demonstrating the correctness of every batch.	Fast independent verification; finality is mathematical.	Generating the proofs is computationally costly; zk on the SVM is still maturing.
Fraud-proof challenges	The state is assumed correct; anyone can publish a fraud proof within a window.	Minimal overhead for the sequencer; a well-understood model.	Delayed finality during the challenge window (7 days on Optimism).

Deterministic replay logs	The raw transaction data is published; anyone re-executes and compares the state roots.	Simple and direct; low cryptographic complexity.	Requires full data availability and the cost of re-execution on the verifier.

Hyper has not yet chosen a single row. The current direction reads as a hybrid: deterministic replay logs as the base layer, integrated with elements of fraud or validity proofs for the complete security model. The specific mix will determine finality times, infrastructure costs, and the verifier's hardware requirements.

First strategy: reproducible proofs. The idea is that, every time the sequencer publishes a state commitment, it also provides a "proof" demonstrating how that state commitment was obtained from the previous state and the executed transactions. Anyone, on receiving the proof, can verify it mathematically without having to re-execute the whole batch. The validity proofs of the zero-knowledge world are a sophisticated example of this strategy: a zk-SNARK certifies that the execution was correct, and the verification is fast. **The advantage**: verification is efficient and does not require re-executing the entire batch. **The disadvantage**: producing the proofs is computationally costly, and correctly implementing zk proof systems is one of the industry's hardest technical challenges. For now, complete zk systems on the SVM are not yet available in production, although there are active research projects.

Second strategy: fraud-proof challenges. The idea is that the sequencer publishes the state commitments without providing proofs a priori, and that anyone in the world, seeing the public data, can challenge a wrong state commitment by producing a "fraud proof" demonstrating the problem. If a fraud proof is accepted, the state commitment is rejected and the sequencer punished. **The advantage**: the sequencer does not need to produce costly proofs; it is enough that the data is available and that someone exists to verify it. **The disadvantage**: finality is delayed by a "challenge window," during which the state commitment can still be rejected. On Optimism, this window is seven days; for Hyper it could be different, but significant in any case. It is the model Optimistic Rollups use, and it is well understood but with its limits.

Third strategy: deterministic replay logs. The idea is of a simpler approach: the sequencer publishes the raw transaction data so that anyone can re-execute it and verify the state commitment. There are no sophisticated proofs; there is the complete publication of the data and the invitation to independent verification. **The advantage**: it is simple and direct. **The disadvantage**: it requires the data to always be available (the data availability problem we addressed in Chapter 4 returns), and independent verification requires actually re-executing the transactions, which is costly for whoever wants to verify.

Hyper, according to the current documentation, is exploring a combination of these strategies. Probably the final system will use some form of deterministic replay logs as a base, integrated with elements of fraud proof or validity proof for the complete security model. **The specific choice will have important consequences on the system's characteristics**: finality times, costs, implementation complexity, hardware requirements. When the team clarifies the choice, it will be one of the decisive moments for evaluating the project's technical maturity.

⁂

10.7 — What It Means Concretely for Developers

All this talk about determinism, however important, can seem abstract to developers wondering: "but what do I have to do differently when writing a program intended for Hyper compared with when I work on Solana?" The most prudent answer is that the objective declared by the project consists precisely in reducing the differences to a minimum. Bitcoin Hyper presents its runtime as SVM-compatible and oriented toward the use of the tools familiar to Solana developers. The actual arrangements will naturally have to be verified in light of the definitive technical specifications, but the principle is clear: not reinventing the developer experience, but rather leveraging an ecosystem that already exists.

This does not mean, however, that determinism concerns only the runtime and requires no attention from whoever writes the program. The runtime applies fundamental rules, but the quality of the execution also depends on the design choices of the application code. Some precautions therefore deserve to be remembered.

FIGURE 10.6 **THE SVM DEVELOPER'S CHECKLIST.**

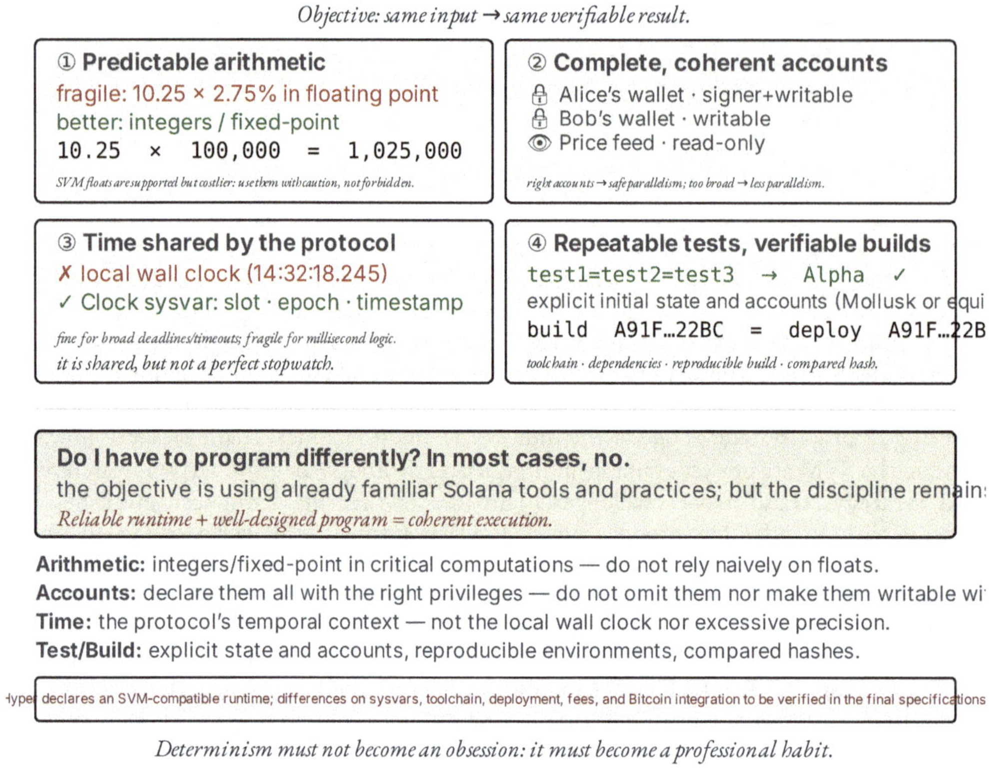

The first concerns numeric computations. Rust supports the f32 and f64 floating-point types, and the SVM allows a limited set of operations of this kind. However, floating-point computations are generally more costly than their integer-based equivalents and can make the rules of precision and rounding less transparent. For amounts, percentages, prices, and rates it is normally preferable to adopt a fixed-point representation: instead of working directly with decimals, one uses integer minimum units and an explicit scale factor. A value of 10.25 can be represented, for example, as 1,025,000 units of one hundred-thousandth. This way, every step of the computation remains controllable.

The second precaution consists in correctly declaring the accounts involved in the instructions. In the SVM model, state lives in the accounts and each instruction indicates the accounts it will need to interact with, specifying which are signers, which are read-only, and which can be modified. The runtime also uses this information to identify the transactions compatible with parallel execution. An incomplete or incoherent declaration can prevent the program from working correctly; an excessively broad declaration can needlessly reduce parallelism. Being explicit does not mean listing superfluous accounts: it means declaring precisely the ones really needed and assigning each the correct privilege.

The third precaution concerns time. Solana makes available the Clock sysvar, which provides information shared by the cluster, such as the current slot, the epoch, and the Unix timestamp. It is a source disciplined by the protocol, not the local clock of the computer on which the program is executed. This information too, however, must be used with judgment. It can be appropriate for timeouts, time windows, or sufficiently broad deadlines; it is more fragile when the application logic requires absolute precision or depends on minimal timestamp variations. In Hyper's context, where the SVM runtime will have to dialogue with the rollup architecture's timings and with Bitcoin's, this aspect deserves specific verification in the definitive documentation.

The fourth precaution concerns testing and deployment. The fact that the runtime is designed to be deterministic does not eliminate the possibility of application bugs. Tests must start from explicitly defined initial accounts and states, apply known instructions, and verify the expected outcomes precisely. Dedicated SVM tools make it possible to build repeatable testing environments. For programs intended for production it is moreover important to use verifiable builds: the source code is compiled in a controlled environment and the hash of the resulting artifact is compared with that of the program actually distributed.

Developers therefore should not experience determinism as an abstract problem to be solved from scratch every day. They must turn it into a professional discipline: preferring predictable arithmetic, declaring the accounts correctly, treating time with prudence, testing the relevant scenarios, and distributing verifiable artifacts. For those coming from the Solana ecosystem, many of these practices are already familiar. For those coming from other environments, they constitute an essential part of the transition toward programming on an SVM runtime.

⁂

10.8 — Determinism as a Precondition for the Security Model

I want to close this chapter by bringing the discussion back to a more philosophical level, because it is important to understand how determinism ties into the rollup's overall security model. It is a link Hyper's post mentions but that is worth developing.

Let us recall the rollups' security model as we have described it in various previous chapters. The rollup executes transactions off-chain at high speed. It publishes state commitments on Bitcoin to inherit its immutability. The raw transaction data is publicly available in some verifiable place. The system works because anyone can, in principle, verify that the published state commitments actually correspond to the correct execution of the transactions.

Notice the key word: "verify." The entire security model depends on the possibility of independent verification. Without verification, the sequencer could publish any state commitments whatsoever, and nobody would know whether they are correct or not. Verification is the mechanism that keeps the sequencer honest; it is what allows the rollup not to ask for trust but to give it to whoever checks.

FIGURE 10.7 **DETERMINISM IS THE INVISIBLE FOUNDATION OF THE ROLLUP'S SECURITY MODEL: THE AVAILABLE DATA FEEDS THE VERIFICATION, VALIDITY OR FAULT PROOFS CHECK THE TRANSITION, THE STATE COMMITMENT SYNTHESIZES THE RESULT, BITCOIN MAKES THE ANCHORING IMMUTABLE. NO ELEMENT, ON ITS OWN, EXHAUSTS SECURITY.**

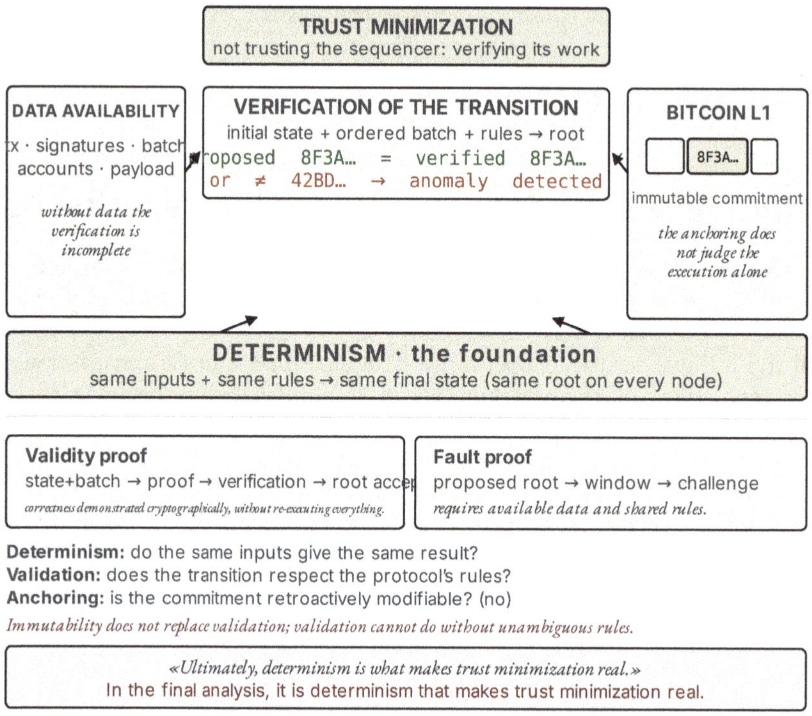

Now think about what verification requires. **One must take the raw transaction data, execute it locally, and compare the resulting state commitment with the published one.** If the two coincide, the sequencer is honest. If they do not coincide, there is a problem. But this procedure has a presupposition: **whoever verifies must obtain the same result as the sequencer by executing the same transactions.** Without perfect determinism, the presupposition collapses. Whoever verifies could obtain a slightly different state commitment not because the sequencer cheated, but because the system is non-deterministic and the results vary.

Without determinism, verification becomes ambiguous. **And without unambiguous verification, the rollup's security model does not work.** The sequencer could publish anything, and whoever verifies could legitimately obtain different results without it being possible to establish who is right.

This is why determinism is a precondition of the security model, not an addition. **Without determinism, all the other properties — anchoring on Bitcoin, fraud proofs, validity proofs, decentralization — have no grip.** One would have a system where everyone agrees there must be a state commitment, but nobody agrees on what it must be.

It is exactly this that Hyper's post acknowledges when it says that "determinism is what makes trust minimization real." Without determinism, trust minimization is an empty promise. With determinism, it becomes a technically guaranteed property.

For Bitcoin Hyper specifically, the prudent investor should therefore carefully monitor how the team concretely solves the determinism problem. **If the team produces detailed technical documentation, independent audits, reproducibility tests across different hardware, it is a positive signal of maturation.** If instead the theme remains in the limbo of "ongoing research" without visible progress, it is a risk signal. Determinism is the invisible constraint, but it is also the most reliable thermometer of the project's engineering seriousness.

⁂

10.9 — Questions and Answers: Clarifying the Chapter's Concepts

Question 1: If determinism is so hard, how have Bitcoin and Ethereum guaranteed it for years without problems?

Both Bitcoin and Ethereum were designed from the start with determinism as an absolute priority, and they made specific choices to obtain it. Bitcoin has an extremely limited Script language that excludes by construction many sources of non-determinism: no loops, no complex operations, no calls to external functions. Ethereum has a more complex language but one nonetheless designed deterministically from the origins: the EVM is serial, time is virtual (it derives from the current block), randomness is derived from hashes, the execution order is strictly defined. **The EVM's choice of serial execution is also, in part, a choice of ease in guaranteeing determinism**: without parallelism, many sources of non-determinism disappear. Solana and Hyper, choosing parallelism for performance, accept a harder technical challenge, but in exchange they obtain higher throughput. Concrete example: in Bitcoin, determinism is guaranteed trivially by the fact that Script can do almost nothing. In Solana, determinism requires sophisticated engineering because the system is much more complex. More capability = more challenges in guaranteeing the properties.

Question 2: If even Solana mainnet has historically had outages, is it because determinism does not work?

No, Solana's outages were caused by other problems (overload, consensus bugs, propagation problems), not by determinism problems in the execution. **The determinism of SVM execution on Solana works**: Solana's validators obtain the same final state by executing the same transactions. If it were not so, Solana simply would not manage to reach consensus, and the problem would be far more visible than the outages it has had. The outages are "liveness" problems (the network stops) and not "safety" problems (the network diverges). They are serious problems but of a different nature. For Hyper, one expects to inherit the determinism that works on Solana, but the rollup context poses additional constraints (as we have seen) that require specific attention. Concrete example: during a Solana outage, the validators agree on what the correct state would have been, but they cannot propagate the blocks fast enough to keep the network active. Determinism works; it is the coordination that fails. They are different problems with different solutions.

Question 3: What would happen in practice if Hyper's determinism broke after the mainnet launch?

It would be a very serious situation, but not an unrecoverable one, and it would depend on how early the problem is detected. If the problem is immediately visible (the nodes diverge openly), the team would intervene immediately: probably with a pause of the rollup, a software correction, and a coordinated restart. Users would temporarily lose access to the system, but the funds should be recoverable. If instead the problem were insidious (rare divergences that are hard to detect), it could accumulate over time before being discovered, making the repair more complex. In extreme cases, it might be necessary to "re-found" the rollup's state at an earlier point, with the loss of some intermediate transactions. **This is why serious projects invest heavily in determinism testing before launch**, including long-term simulations, tests on heterogeneous hardware, and fuzzing to unearth edge cases. Concrete example: in the pre-launch tests of a rollup, it is normal to run dozens of nodes in parallel on different hardware and different configurations, for thousands of hours, and automatically compare their states at every step. Every divergence, even of a single bit, must be investigated and understood before considering the system ready for production. For Hyper, this work is ongoing and will have to be completed before the mainnet.

Question 4: Does the determinism problem apply only to the execution of transactions, or also to other parts of the system?

It applies to the whole system, but with nuances. **The execution of transactions is the most critical part**: without determinism here, nothing works. But other parts must also be deterministic, although less stringently. The generation of batches by the sequencer, for example: the sequencer must produce batches that different nodes of the rollup interpret in the same way. The generation of the state commitment: given the same state, the state root must be bit-for-bit identical. The management of rent (the cleanup of empty accounts): the decisions about which accounts to close must be taken identically by everyone. **Even small problems in these areas can cause divergences.** For Hyper, guaranteeing determinism across the whole stack is work that permeates every component of the system, not only the execution layer. Concrete example: an insidious bug I saw in another project (not Hyper) was in the generation of a transaction's identifier: two nodes computed the identifier in slightly different ways, and this propagated into the system logs, causing divergences in metadata. It was hard to unearth because the "main" state seemed correct, but the metadata did not. Bugs of this kind require careful testing and continuous monitoring to be prevented.

Question 5: If the Hyper team has not yet finalized the determinism strategy, is it prudent to invest in the project?

It is an assessment everyone must make for themselves, but let us look at some elements. On one hand, **the fact that the problem has been publicly recognized and that there is active research is a positive signal**: it shows the team understands the challenge and is addressing it seriously. Many competitor projects do not even talk about determinism. On the other hand, **the fact that the solution is not yet finalized means there is implementation risk**: the chosen strategy could prove harder than expected, problems requiring rethinking could emerge, timelines could stretch. Whoever invests in the pre-mainnet phase is accepting this risk. A prudent strategy could be monitoring the team's updates on the specific theme of determinism in the coming months: if detailed technical documentation is published, if independent audits are completed, if reproducibility benchmarks are published, they are all signals that the problem is on its way to resolution. If instead the theme remains in limbo, it is an alarm bell. Concrete example: for Optimism, the transition from the initial "trust assumptions" to true fraud proofs required years of development, with various false starts and course corrections. The determinism problem is less publicly visible than that of the fraud proofs, but it required analogous work. For Hyper, a similar trajectory is expected: continuous but non-linear progress, with iterations in the design.

Question 6: Is determinism the only hard technical property of a rollup, or are there others just as critical you have not talked about?

There are several, but determinism is probably the subtlest and least discussed. Other critical properties include: **liveness**, that is, the system's capacity to keep processing transactions even under attacks or problems (a system can be deterministic but stop, and liveness guarantees it does not stop); **consensus safety**, that is, the capacity not to accept two contradictory state commitments (correlated with determinism but with additional nuances); **the robustness of the economic incentives**, that is, the guarantee that whoever operates components of the system (sequencer, validators, nodes) has incentives aligned with correct operation; **cryptographic security**, that is, that the cryptographic primitives used are not vulnerable. All these properties must be satisfied simultaneously to have a working, secure rollup. **Determinism is one of them, particularly subtle because invisible and hard to test**, but not the only one. Serious projects work on all these dimensions in parallel. Concrete example: a checklist of properties a well-run rollup team sets itself typically includes dozens of items, each with its own tests and verification procedures. Determinism is one item; there are dozens of others. For Hyper, monitoring progress on all these dimensions is the way to evaluate the project's overall technical maturity, not only that of a single property.

⁂

10.10 — WHAT TO TAKE AWAY FROM THIS CHAPTER

Determinism is the property whereby, given the same input, the system always produces exactly the same output, regardless of who executes it, on what hardware, at what moment.

For a rollup, perfect determinism is not optional: it is a condition of existence. Without determinism, the nodes diverge and the system collapses. Without determinism, independent verification is impossible, and the entire security model does not hold.

The sources of non-determinism in software systems are many and insidious: clocks, randomness, concurrency, floating point, memory allocation, compiler bugs. Guaranteeing perfect determinism requires controlling every level of the stack.

The SVM with its parallel model poses specific determinism challenges. Parallelism by definition introduces non-determinism in the execution order, and the system must be designed to "canonically order" the final effects.

Sealevel solves the parallelism-determinism paradox by separating the execution (parallel) from the application of the effects to the state (canonical). The parallelism is internal and not observable; the final result is ordered and deterministic.

Bitcoin Hyper publicly recognized the determinism challenge in a December 2025 research post. The team is addressing it explicitly as an open problem, with multiple strategies being explored.

The three main families of strategies are: reproducible proofs (validity proof), fraud-proof challenges, deterministic replay logs. Hyper is exploring combinations of these, with the final choice still to be defined.

For developers, determinism is managed mainly by the runtime, but some precautions are important: avoiding floating point, declaring the accounts correctly, avoiding dependencies on precise timestamps, testing on different hardware.

Determinism is a precondition of the rollup's security model. Without determinism, independent verification is impossible, and the promise of "trust minimization" does not translate into a technically guaranteed property.

To evaluate the technical maturity of a rollup project, monitoring how it addresses the determinism problem is one of the most reliable criteria. Detailed documentation, independent audits, reproducibility tests are all positive signals.

Chapter 10 ends here. We have addressed one of the technically subtlest and most important aspects of rollups, understanding why determinism is the invisible constraint on which everything else depends, and how Bitcoin Hyper is addressing the specific challenge of guaranteeing perfect determinism on a parallel architecture. From here on, Part III of the book (The Execution Layer) closes. We are ready to enter Part IV, where we will specifically explore the settlement layer: how the rollup talks to Bitcoin, how the state commitments are anchored, and what the Canonical Bridge's specific technical choices are.

In ***Chapter 11 — State Commitments: the language in which Hyper speaks to Bitcoin****, we will see in detail how the mechanism works that translates the rollup's state into a "compressed photograph" Bitcoin can host, and why this translation is a remarkably sophisticated engineering exercise.*

Determinism: the invisible constraint of *speed*

Why an SVM rollup can be fast only if it **always produces the same result**.

1 Same input, same output

In a rollup, every node must obtain the **same result** starting from the same data. If the final state changes even slightly, the network no longer has a shared truth.

same initial state + same batch + same rules → **same state root**

Node A · hw X
Node B · hw Y
Node C · another order
→ SAME ROOT 8F3A…91C7 ✓

2 A minimal difference breaks the rollup

If two nodes produce **different state roots**, Bitcoin can record the commitments, but does not decide on its own which execution is correct.

Anchoring does not replace validation.

Node A → ROOT ALPHA 8F3A…
Node B → ROOT BETA 42BD…

incompatible commitments
Bitcoin does not judge the execution

3 The six doors to close

01	**Clock**	Local time differs per node
02	**Randomness**	Uncontrolled random
03	**Concurrency**	Order not guaranteed
04	**Floating point**	Different rounding
05	**Memory / host**	Variable environment
06	**Toolchain**	Non-reproducible builds

⚠ **One open door is enough** to obtain divergent roots.

4 Parallelism without losing determinism

The **SVM** is born to execute transactions in parallel. The critical point is doing it without letting the hardware's internal order change the final result.

The parallelism is internal. **The state root must remain one.**

COMPATIBLE OPERATIONS — in parallel ✓
TX-A → X | TX-B → Y | TX-D → W

CONFLICTING OPERATIONS — locking + scheduling
TX-C → X | TX-A → X

5 Verification, not trust

Validity proof
A mathematical proof of the batch's correctness.

Fault proof
The possibility of challenging a wrong state.

Deterministic replay
Anyone re-executes the transactions and compares the root.

Hyper is exploring these strategies: the final choice will have to be documented and verifiable.

THE KEY POINT

Determinism makes the rollup **verifiable**. Without determinism, *trust minimization* remains a promise. With determinism, users do not have to **believe** the sequencer: they can **check it**.

PART IV

The Settlement Layer

The dialogue between Hyper and Bitcoin: state commitments, three roads for anchoring, cadence, data availability. It is here that the promise of "Bitcoin security" becomes a technical choice with precise trade-offs.

PART IV · THE SETTLEMENT LAYER

Chapter 11
State Commitments

The language in which Hyper speaks to Bitcoin

⁂

11.1 — The Translation Problem

Let us open this chapter with a question that, at first sight, seems to have an obvious answer but that in reality hides one of the subtlest engineering challenges of the entire Bitcoin Hyper project. The question is: **how does the rollup, which runs on the SVM and holds inside itself thousands of accounts, millions of potential transactions, complex programs, articulated states, manage to "tell" Bitcoin what has happened inside it?**

FIGURE 11.1 **STATE COMMITMENTS AS A MERKLE ROOT**

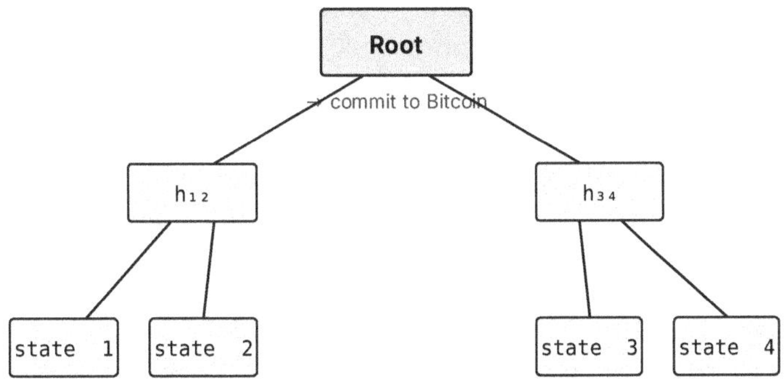

A single signature anchors millions of states: the root is the seal of the entire tree

How to read it: *Hyper does not write every transaction on Bitcoin — it writes only the root. Every client can then cryptographically verify that its own state is included in the tree, by presenting an "inclusion proof" of a few hashes. This is how the rollup reduces the cost of anchoring by orders of magnitude.*

Bitcoin, as we have seen since Chapter 1, is a deliberately minimal network. Its language is poor. Its data space is scarce and expensive. It does not understand complex smart contracts, it cannot manage parallel accounts, it cannot execute arbitrary code. And yet the rollup must, periodically, write on Bitcoin something that allows anyone to verify the state of the rollup itself. Something compact enough to fit in the few bytes available in a Bitcoin transaction, but at the same time expressive enough to capture everything that has happened in the rollup between one anchoring and the next.

It is a problem of translation between two profoundly different languages, and it is the central problem of this chapter. On one side we have a rich, fast language — the SVM with its accounts, its programs, its parallel transactions. On the other we have a poor, slow language — Bitcoin with its few opcodes, its rare blocks, its limited data space. The solution Bitcoin Hyper is developing — the **state commitments**, or simply **commitments** — is the linguistic bridge that allows the two worlds to talk to each other without betraying the identity of either.

In this chapter I want to do three things. First, understand what a state commitment is from the conceptual point of view, because without this basis everything else remains confused. Second, see how state commitments are built technically, through a mathematical structure called the Merkle tree, which is one of the pillars of all blockchain cryptography. Third, examine the specific choices the Hyper team is making for its own state commitment model, based on the research post it published in December 2025 specifically on this theme. It is a chapter technically denser than others, but it is also one of those that will give you the most concrete tools for evaluating the project.

⁂

11.2 — What a State Commitment Is, in Plain Language

Let us begin with a definition I want to build step by step, because it is important for it to settle well into your intuitions before tackling the technical details. **A state commitment[a] is a mathematical fingerprint[b] of a system's state at a specific moment.** I repeat: a mathematical fingerprint. It is a short string — typically 32 bytes, that is, 256 bits[c] — which has the property of being uniquely tied to the state it represents, in such a way that if even a single bit of the state changes, the fingerprint changes completely.

To understand intuitively what this means, think of an analogy with the physical world. Imagine having a book of a thousand pages, written by hand. You want to be able to prove to someone, in the future, that at a certain moment the book was in exactly a certain form. One solution would be bringing them the whole book to check, but it is cumbersome and impractical. A much more elegant alternative is taking the book and submitting it to a process[d] that produces a kind of "seal"[e] — a small alphanumeric code of fixed length — that depends on every single character, on every single comma, on every single detail of the book. If even one letter changes, the seal changes in an unpredictable and profoundly different way. **Then it is enough to archive the seal, not the whole book, and at any moment you can prove that the book was exactly "that one," simply by recomputing the seal from the current book and verifying that it matches the archived one.**

---

[a] **State commitment.** The public, synthetic, unforgeable pledge about what the rollup's state was at a given instant. In practice it coincides with the state root already encountered: the value that summarizes the entire state and that is anchored on Bitcoin so that nobody can modify it after the fact.

[b] **Mathematical fingerprint.** A short value computed from a set of data, which identifies it almost uniquely: like a fingerprint for a person. If the data changes even minimally, the fingerprint changes completely, and this makes it possible to detect any alteration.

[c] **32 bytes (256 bits).** The fixed length produced by the cryptographic hash functions most used today (such as SHA-256): whatever the size of the input data — a few characters or gigabytes — the result is always a string of this size. It is what makes the "seal" compact to archive and immediate to compare.

[d] **Hash function.** The mathematical procedure that transforms any quantity of data into that fingerprint of fixed length. It has two key properties: from the same input it always gives the same result, but from the result it is practically impossible to trace back to the starting data or construct other data giving the same fingerprint.

[e] **Seal.** In the book analogy, it is the intuitive name given to the fingerprint produced by the hash function: a small code that "seals" the content at a given moment. By reapplying the same procedure one can verify that nothing has been modified.

FIGURE 11.2 **FROM THE ROLLUP'S COMPLETE STATE TO A 32-BYTE FINGERPRINT ANCHORED ON BITCOIN.**

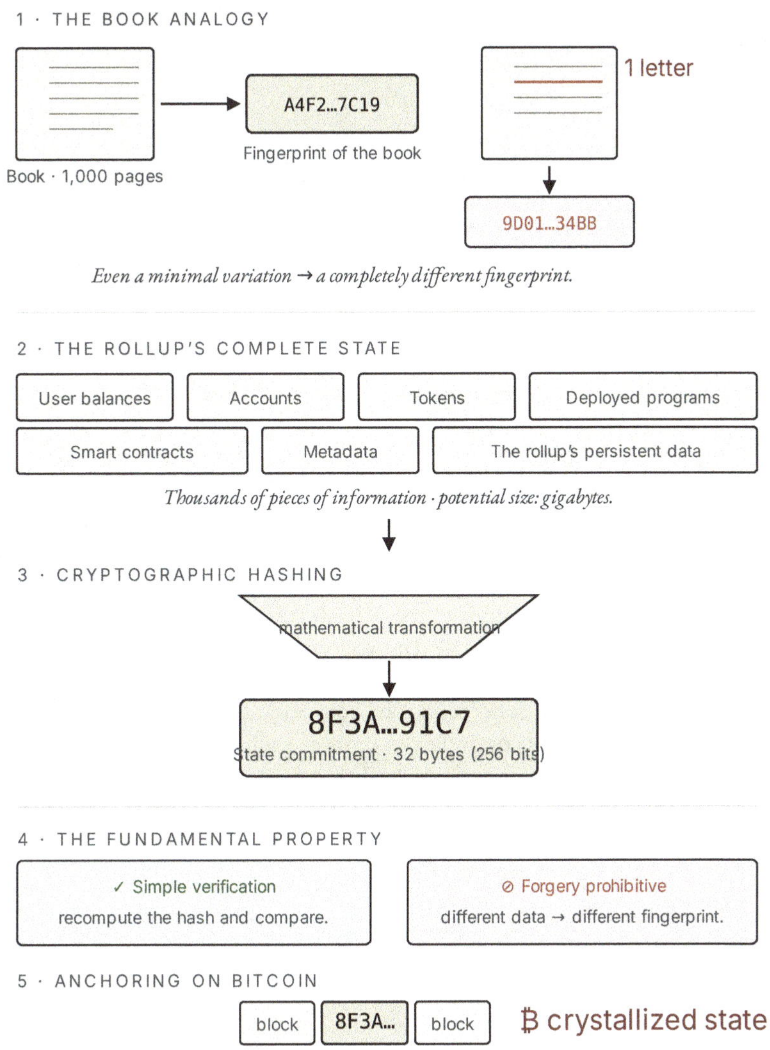

The state commitment is exactly this, applied to the digital world. The state of Bitcoin Hyper at a certain moment contains thousands of pieces of information: all the users' balances, the state of all the deployed programs, the metadata of all the accounts, every persistent datum living on the rollup. This state, as a whole, can be enormous — gigabytes of data. But through a mathematical process called **cryptographic hashing**, all this state is reduced to a single string of 32 bytes. That string is the state commitment, and it is what the rollup publishes on Bitcoin at every anchoring.

There is a property of these fingerprints worth emphasizing, because it is the key to how they work: **they are very easy to verify but practically impossible to forge.** What this means concretely. Given a state and its state commitment, anyone can redo the computation and verify whether the commitment is correct: a few milliseconds of computation are enough. But given a commitment, trying to construct a different state that produces the same commitment is computationally prohibitive: it would require an unrealistic amount of computation, incompatible with any concretely available computational capacity. **This asymmetry — easy verification, impossible forgery — is what makes state commitments a security tool usable in practice.**

Now let us apply this concept to the rollup. The rollup, at every anchoring, computes the state commitment of its current state and publishes it on Bitcoin. Bitcoin records the commitment in the blockchain, where it remains immutable forever. From that moment, the rollup state corresponding to that commitment is "crystallized": anyone in the world, downloading the raw transaction data from the data availability layer, can reconstruct the state and verify that the commitment anchored on Bitcoin is coherent. If someone wanted to retroactively rewrite the rollup's history, they would also have to modify the commitment on Bitcoin, but that is impossible to modify because of Bitcoin's own properties. **The state commitment is the invisible thread that ties the rollup's state to the immutability of the Bitcoin blockchain.**

⁂

11.3 — Merkle Trees: the Structure That Makes All This Possible

At this point you might ask yourselves: "but how, concretely, does one compute a fingerprint of gigabytes of data and obtain only 32 bytes?" The answer is that one uses a mathematical structure called a **Merkle tree**, after the cryptographer Ralph Merkle who proposed it in 1979. It is a structure as elegant as it is fundamental to the functioning of practically every modern blockchain, and it deserves to be understood because it comes back constantly in the crypto world.

Let us begin with the basic idea. A **cryptographic hash function** — famous examples are SHA-256 used by Bitcoin, or Keccak-256 used by Ethereum — is a function that takes any input (of any length) and produces an output of fixed length, typically 256 bits. Hash functions have three important properties: **they are deterministic** (the same input always produces the same output), **they are one-way** (given the output, it is practically impossible to trace back to the input), **they are collision-resistant** (it is practically impossible to find two different inputs producing the same output). These properties make hash functions one of the most powerful tools of modern cryptography.

The Merkle tree is a structure that combines many hash functions to produce a fingerprint of a large collection of data. It works like this. Take all the data you want to summarize — say, a thousand elements — and compute the hash of each. You obtain a thousand hashes. Now take these hashes in pairs, and for each pair compute the hash of their concatenation: you obtain five hundred hashes. Continue: take these five hundred hashes in pairs, and compute the hash of each pair, obtaining two hundred and fifty. Continue again, halving each time, until a single hash remains. **That single final hash is the "Merkle root,"[1] the root of the Merkle tree**, and it is a fingerprint of the entire initial collection.

FIGURE 11.3 **HOW A MERKLE TREE WORKS: FROM THOUSANDS OF DATA ITEMS TO A SINGLE 32-BYTE FINGERPRINT.**

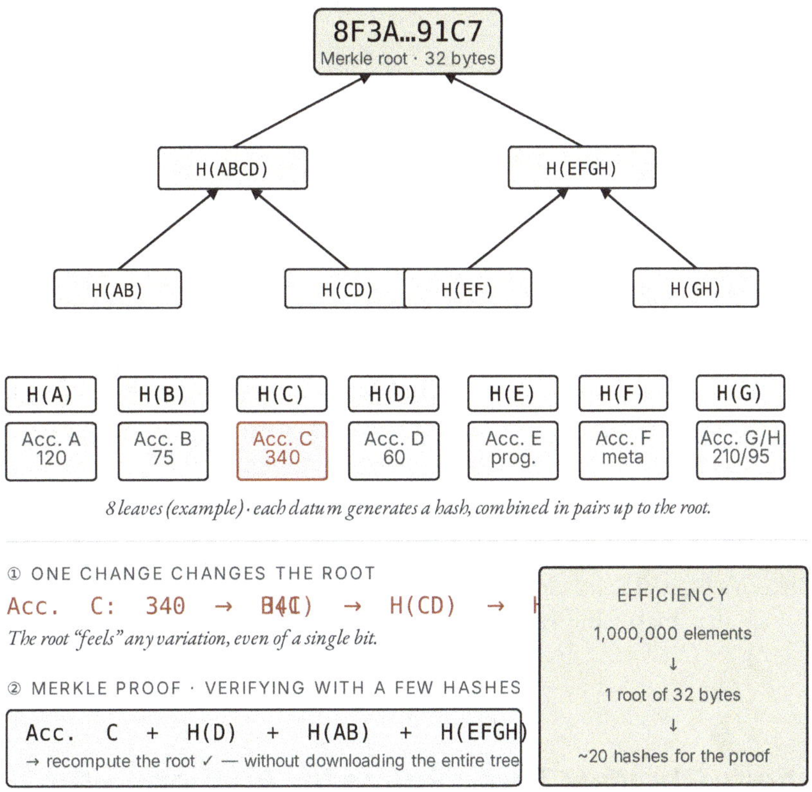

The elegance of this construction lies in two properties that make it useful in practice. **First property: the root changes if even a single original datum changes.** If you modify a single element of the initial thousand, its hash changes, so the hash of the pair including it changes, so the hash of the next layer changes, and so on up to the root. The root "feels" any modification. **Second property: the existence of a single element can be proven without having to transmit all the elements.** To prove that element number 347 was actually in the collection, it is enough to provide the element, its hash, and the "neighboring" hashes along the path up to the root. It is a few hashes, a few hundred bytes, yet they make it possible to verify inclusion with mathematical certainty.

This second property is particularly powerful, and it deserves a small concrete demonstration. Imagine a Merkle tree with a million elements. The root is a single 32-byte hash. To prove that a certain element was in the collection, you need the element plus the "Merkle path" — about twenty hashes, because the base-two logarithm of a million is about twenty. All told, a proof of a few hundred bytes. Compare it with the alternative: to prove inclusion without Merkle trees, you would have to transmit all the million elements. **The ratio is millions to one**, and this is what makes blockchains practical from the bandwidth point of view.

FIGURE 11.4 **A MERKLE TREE COMPRESSES AN ENTIRE STATE INTO A SINGLE 32-BYTE ROOT**

Tree level	Number of hashes	What resides at this level
Leaves	N (e.g. 1,000,000)	Hash of every single account / state element.
Level 1	N/2	Hash of every pair of concatenated leaves.

Level 2	N/4	Hash of every pair of level-1 hashes.
...	...	Every subsequent level halves the count.
Root	1	The 32-byte state commitment anchored on Bitcoin.

Any change in a leaf propagates upward and modifies the root. To prove that a single leaf belongs to the tree, only the leaf and the $log_2(N)$ sibling hashes along the path to the root are transmitted — for a million leaves, about twenty hashes, a few hundred bytes in all.

Now let us apply the Merkle tree to our rollup case. The rollup's state is a large collection of accounts — balances, programs, metadata. The rollup organizes these accounts into a Merkle tree, computing the Merkle root as the state commitment. When the commitment is anchored on Bitcoin, what is anchored is these 32 bytes. Then, **if someone wants to prove that a certain account had a certain balance at a certain moment**, they can provide the account and its Merkle path, and anyone can verify the inclusion by comparing the computation with the Merkle root anchored on Bitcoin. All this without needing to download the rollup's entire state, only a few hundred bytes of proof data.

This is the mathematical structure that allows Bitcoin Hyper to "speak to Bitcoin" efficiently. **Without Merkle trees, state commitments would not work in practice**: either they would be too large to fit in Bitcoin's limited space, or they would not allow efficient verifications. Merkle trees are the piece of technology that makes the entire architecture possible, and this is why they deserve to be understood.

⁂

11.4 — Hyper's Choices: Three Roads for Anchoring the State Commitments

Having understood what a state commitment is and how it is built with a Merkle tree, we can tackle Bitcoin Hyper's specific question: **how, exactly, are these commitments anchored on the Bitcoin blockchain?** This is an important technical choice, because Bitcoin offers several ways to insert data into its transactions, and each has specific characteristics of cost, expressiveness, and visibility.

The research post published by the Hyper team in December 2025 specifically on this theme explores three main roads, corresponding to three techniques available on the Bitcoin blockchain. Let us look at them one at a time.

TABLE 11.1 **THREE ROADS FOR ANCHORING THE STATE COMMITMENTS ON BITCOIN.**

Road	Bitcoin technique	In brief
Compact publication	OP_RETURN[a]	Inserts the commitment[b] as a small on-chain[c] datum
Rich structures	Taproot[d]	Allows more articulated, verifiable commitments
Temporal security	Timelock[e] / challenge window[f]	Leaves an interval for challenging a wrong state

The first two roads concern how to publish the commitment on Bitcoin; the third concerns the security model. They are not necessarily alternatives: an architecture can combine them. Hyper's definitive choice is one of the technical elements still to be finalized.

---

[a] **OP_RETURN.** An instruction that makes it possible to attach to a Bitcoin transaction a small quantity of arbitrary, unspendable data. It is the most direct and proven way to write a commitment into the chain, but it offers very limited space.

[b] **State commitment.** A synthetic fingerprint that summarizes and "seals" the rollup's state at a given moment, published on Bitcoin so that anyone can verify it. It is the datum that the three roads described here serve to anchor to the chain.

[c] **On-chain.** Said of a datum or an operation recorded directly on the Bitcoin blockchain, and therefore public, permanent, and verifiable by anyone. The opposite is "off-chain," what happens outside the chain.

[d] **Taproot.** An upgrade of Bitcoin activated in 2021 that makes transactions more flexible and efficient. It makes it possible to hide articulated spending structures behind a single key, and therefore to anchor richer commitments without weighing down the chain.

[e] **Timelock.** A constraint preventing an operation from being spent or considered definitive before a certain time (or a certain number of blocks) has passed. Applied here, it opens the "challenge window" within which anyone can report a wrong state before it becomes irreversible.

[f] **Challenge window.** The interval of time during which a newly published state can still be challenged by anyone detecting an error, before it becomes definitive. It is the heart of the time-based security model.

First road: state commitments based on OP_RETURN. OP_RETURN is a Bitcoin opcode that makes it possible to include up to 80 bytes of arbitrary data in a transaction, so that they are recorded immutably on the blockchain but do not represent spendable bitcoin. It is the equivalent of writing a note in the margin of a transaction: the note is worth nothing economically, but it stays there forever. For Hyper, OP_RETURN is the simplest way to insert a state root: a standard Bitcoin transaction is published with a specific OP_RETURN containing the 32 bytes of the Merkle root, and from that moment the commitment is anchored. **The advantage**: it is simple, it is well understood by everyone, it is supported by the entire existing Bitcoin ecosystem. **The disadvantage**: the space is limited to 80 bytes (although it is more than sufficient for a single state commitment), and the cost per byte of OP_RETURN can be high if Bitcoin fees rise.

Second road: state commitments based on Taproot. Taproot is a Bitcoin upgrade activated in November 2021 that introduced new possibilities for Bitcoin scripts, in particular the capacity to hide complex structures — like Merkle trees of spending conditions — in a single compact signature. For Hyper's commitments, Taproot offers the possibility of encoding structures richer than a simple OP_RETURN. **Not only the Merkle root can be included, but also structured metadata, cryptographic proofs, or references to other off-chain structures.** When someone wants to verify the commitment, they can "reveal" the hidden structure by mathematically demonstrating that it was actually committed in the signature. **The advantage**: it is more expressive than OP_RETURN, it allows more structured commitments, and in many cases it is more space-efficient. **The disadvantage**: it is technically more complex, it requires more sophisticated tools to build and verify the structures, and the supporting ecosystem is still evolving.

FIGURE 11.5 **THREE ROADS FOR ANCHORING THE STATE COMMITMENTS ON BITCOIN: OP_RETURN AND TAPROOT CONCERN HOW THE COMMITMENT IS PUBLISHED, THE CHALLENGE WINDOW WHEN IT BECOMES DEFINITIVE.**

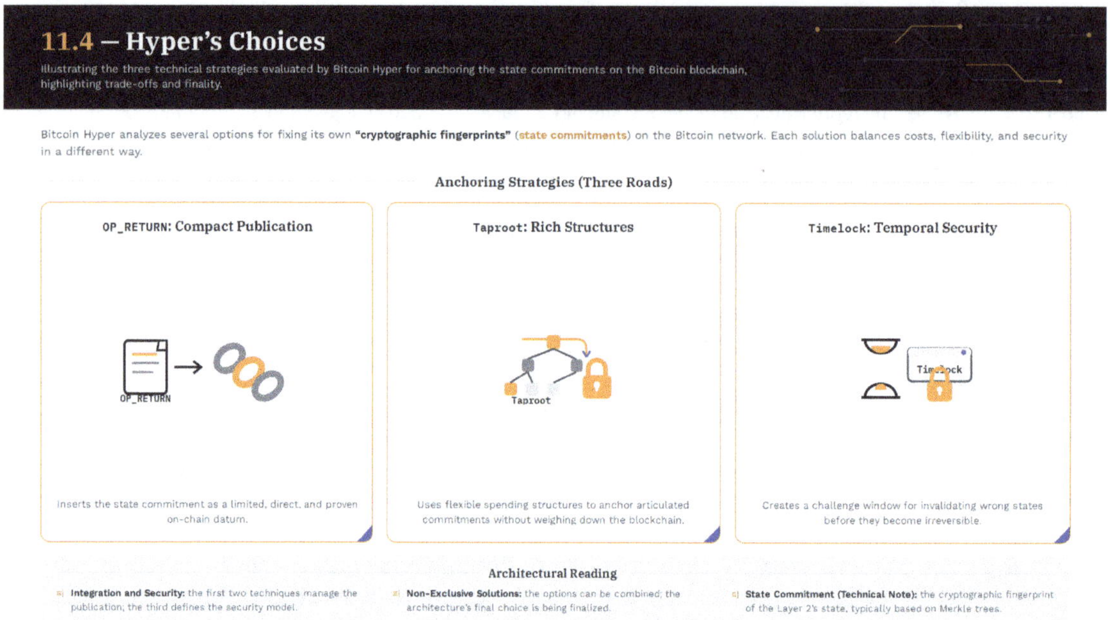

Third road: timelocked state commitments. This is a more sophisticated approach that combines commitments with temporal mechanisms. The idea is that the commitment is published with a "maturation time" during which the community has a way of challenging it if it is wrong. Only after the challenge window does the commitment become definitive. **This is the pattern used by optimistic rollups like Optimism**, where the challenge window is seven days. For Hyper, an analogous approach would make it possible to combine speed (users can operate immediately on the state) with security (there are days during which any problems can be raised). **The advantage**: it offers an explicit security mechanism without requiring complex cryptographic proofs. **The disadvantage**: full finality is delayed, and withdrawals toward Bitcoin require waiting for the challenge window (days instead of hours).

Hyper's post does not publicly commit to which of these three roads will be definitively adopted. On the contrary, it suggests the final system might use combinations of these techniques, perhaps different ones for different types of operations. It is a design choice still open, and one of the most important the team will have to finalize before the mainnet launch. **Understanding the trade-offs of each option helps you correctly interpret the choices the team will announce in the coming months.**

Note 1. OP_RETURN and Taproot are not in competition with the timelock: they belong to different planes. The first two establish how the commitment is written on Bitcoin; the timelock defines for how long a state remains challengeable. This is why a real architecture can adopt them together.

Note 2. The "challenge window" is the distinctive trait of optimistic rollups: the state is considered valid unless proven otherwise within a preset interval. It reduces costs compared with immediate verification, but lengthens withdrawal times — a compromise to be evaluated according to the use case, not in the absolute.

FIGURE 11.6 **THREE ROADS FOR ANCHORING THE STATE COMMITMENTS ON BITCOIN, COMPARED.**

Road	Capacity	Strength	Limit

OP_RETURN	Up to 80 bytes of arbitrary data per transaction.	Simple, mature, supported everywhere.	The cost grows with Bitcoin fees; a rigid byte budget.
Taproot	A commitment tree hidden in a single signature.	Expressive; structured commitments and proofs.	More complex tooling; an ecosystem still maturing.
Timelocked	Commitment + explicit challenge window (days).	An explicit security model, without heavy cryptography.	Delayed finality; withdrawals wait for the window.

The Hyper team has not publicly committed to a single row. The final design will probably be a hybrid — different techniques applied to different operations — with the trade-offs above guiding which combination wins in each case.

⁂

11.5 — The Cadence of the Anchorings and the Problem of Costs

Once the technical modality for anchoring the commitments has been chosen, there is another important architectural decision the Hyper team must make: **how frequently to publish the state commitments on Bitcoin?** This decision, as we have mentioned in previous chapters and as we will explore in Chapter 13, has enormous implications on the system's costs, security, and user experience.

Think of it as a choice of tempo between two extremes. **On one side, anchoring very frequently** — say every five minutes, or at every new Bitcoin block.[a] Advantages: the rollup's state becomes crystallized[b] quickly, the vulnerability window[c] is short, users have finality[d] guarantees in rapid times. Disadvantages: every anchoring is a Bitcoin transaction that pays fees;[e] if Bitcoin fees are high, anchoring frequently becomes very costly for the system, and this cost is passed on to the rollup's users. **On the other side, anchoring rarely** — say once an hour, or even less. Advantages: the anchoring costs are amortized[f] over many more rollup transactions, reducing the cost per transaction. Disadvantages: the rollup's state stays "pending" longer, the vulnerability windows are more extended, users must wait longer for full finality.

[a] **Bitcoin block.** Bitcoin groups transactions into blocks produced, on average, every ten minutes. This rhythm fixes the minimum cadence with which a rollup can anchor its state: one cannot go below the time of one block.

[b] **Crystallized.** Said of the rollup's state when it is fixed and made stable by anchoring it to Bitcoin: once "crystallized," it can no longer be modified or rewritten.

[c] **Vulnerability window.** The interval between the moment an operation is executed on the Layer 2 and the moment it is anchored on Bitcoin and made definitive. In this span of time the state is not yet protected by Bitcoin's immutability: anchoring more often shortens the window, but costs more.

[d] **Finality.** The moment from which a transaction is considered definitive and irreversible. On a rollup anchored to Bitcoin, full finality is reached when the state is recorded on the mother chain.

[e] **Fees.** Every transaction on Bitcoin pays a fee to the miners, whose amount varies with network congestion: when the demand for block space is high, fees rise. For a rollup that anchors frequently, this cost is recurring and is reflected on the users.

[f] **Amortized.** An economic term: an "amortized" cost is distributed over many operations, so that the weight per single transaction becomes small. Anchoring rarely spreads the anchoring cost over more transactions.

[g] **Adaptive parameter.** A value the system does not fix once and for all, but regulates automatically as conditions vary. Here the anchoring frequency rises or falls depending on the cost of Bitcoin fees and the rollup's traffic, instead of staying locked on a preset interval.

[h] **Transaction volume.** The quantity of operations the rollup processes in a given period. When it is high, the fixed cost of each anchoring is distributed over many more transactions, making it convenient to anchor more often; when it is low, it is

convenient to space out the anchorings.

[i] **Fixed frequency.** An anchoring cadence established in advance and kept constant regardless of conditions. It is the opposite of the adaptive parameter: simpler to manage, but it risks proving too costly when fees rise or too slow when more rapidity would be needed.

[l] **Dynamically.** Said of a choice the system makes in real time, adapting it case by case to the circumstances, instead of following a rule decided once and for all. Here it indicates that the anchoring frequency is not programmed in advance, but computed moment by moment based on costs and traffic.

The Hyper team, in the specific post on anchoring frequency (January 2026), explicitly declared it wants to treat frequency as an **adaptive parameter**[g], not a fixed rule. It means the system can decide dynamically[l], based on the conditions of the moment, how frequently to anchor. When Bitcoin fees are low and the rollup's transaction volume[h] is high, it can anchor more often. When Bitcoin fees are high and volume is low, it can slow down. **It is a sensible approach, because it avoids committing to a fixed frequency[i] that could prove wrong under conditions that change over time.**

FIGURE 11.7 **THE CADENCE OF THE ANCHORINGS IS A COMPROMISE BETWEEN RAPIDITY OF CONSOLIDATION, OVERALL COST, AND AVERAGE COST PER TRANSACTION; AN ADAPTIVE STRATEGY CAN REGULATE IT BASED ON BITCOIN FEES, VOLUME, AND FINALITY.**

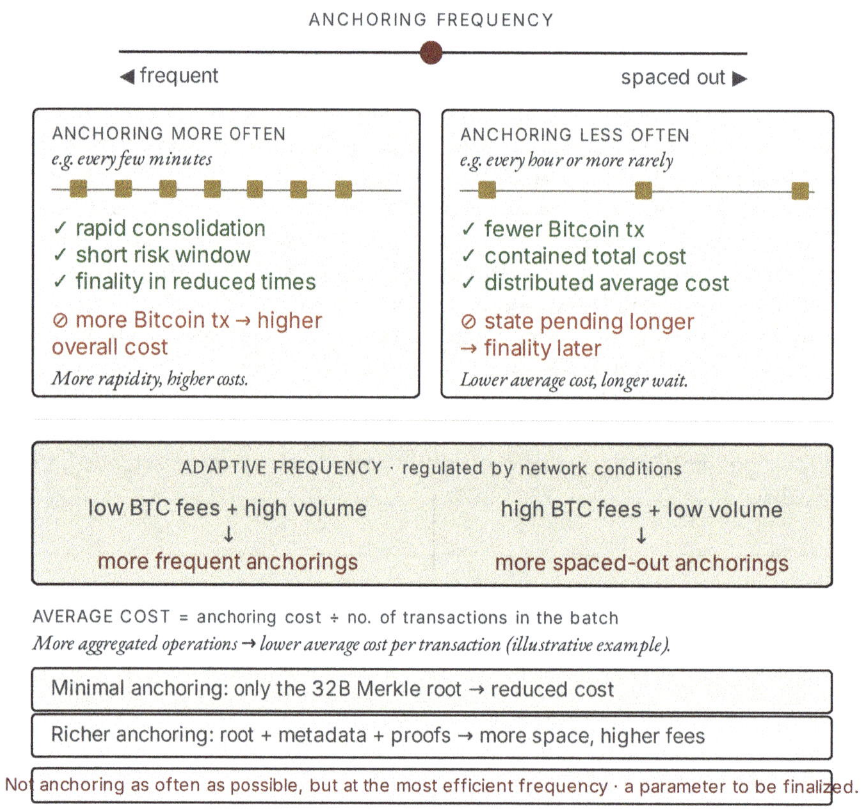

There is another cost dimension worth considering: **not all anchorings must contain only a Merkle root**. They can also include additional data, such as metadata, references to off-chain data, cryptographic proofs. The more information is included, the more the anchoring costs. Hyper, according to the post's indications, is exploring minimal anchorings (only the Merkle root, a few dozen bytes) for most situations, with the possibility of richer anchorings in specific cases (for example, when a problem to report is detected).

Putting these elements together, the system's economic picture is the following. Bitcoin Hyper must bear a continuous cost to anchor its commitments to Bitcoin. This cost is proportional to the frequency of the anchorings and to Bitcoin's fees at the moment. The total cost is amortized over the rollup's transactions, and it is what users pay (in some form) as the "cost of settlement." **The more efficient the**

rollup is at compressing and anchoring, the less it costs per transaction, and the more competitive it is against alternatives.

To give an order of magnitude, consider this. If an anchoring costs, say, a few dollars in Bitcoin fees (a realistic figure in periods of moderate traffic), and the rollup anchors every 30 minutes, the hourly cost of the anchorings is a few dollars. Over an hour, the rollup can process thousands or tens of thousands of transactions. The cost per transaction, due to the anchorings, is fractions of a cent. **This is a very low cost, comparable to that of Ethereum's rollups, and dramatically lower than the cost of a transaction directly on original Bitcoin.** It is exactly the type of value proposition that justifies the rollup's existence.

⁂

11.6 — The Separation between Commitment and Data: the Role of Availability

I want to close the technical part of the chapter by taking up a point we have already touched on before but that is worth reinforcing in the context of state commitments, because it is a subtlety that often confuses. **The state commitment anchored on Bitcoin does not contain the raw transaction data; it contains only the fingerprint of the resulting state.** This is a structural characteristic of the model, not a limit of the system.

Think about it. If Hyper tried to anchor on Bitcoin all the raw transaction data — all the senders, the recipients, the amounts, the signatures, the programs' payloads[a] — the volume would be enormous. Thousands of transactions a day, each with hundreds or thousands of bytes of data, would produce monthly gigabytes that simply cannot fit in Bitcoin without saturating the network. **The anchoring model works only because the synthesis (the commitment) is anchored and the raw data is left to live elsewhere.**

That "elsewhere" is the **data availability layer**[b] we introduced in Chapter 4 and will explore in Chapter 14. It is the system for archiving and distributing the raw data, separate from Bitcoin but critical for the rollup's functioning. When someone wants to verify the rollup's state, they do two things: they download the raw data from the data availability layer, and they download the anchored commitment from Bitcoin. They compare the two: they reconstruct the state from the raw data, compute the Merkle root[c], verify that it matches the anchored commitment. **If it matches, the commitment is honest; if it does not match, there is a problem.**

This two-level model — commitment on Bitcoin, data elsewhere — is what allows the rollup to scale. Bitcoin provides immutability to the compact commitments; the data availability layer provides the space for the voluminous raw data. **Together, the two levels provide the rollup's complete security model.** If either is missing, the system collapses: without Bitcoin, immutability and finality are missing; without the data availability, the data for verifying the commitments is missing.

---

[a] **Payload.** The "useful" content of a transaction: the data indicating which instructions to execute and with which parameters, in addition to sender, amount, and signature. In on-chain programs the payload can be substantial, and it is one of the reasons the raw data becomes too voluminous for Bitcoin.

[b] **Data availability layer.** The system that archives and makes accessible the raw data of the rollup's transactions, separate from Bitcoin but indispensable: without it nobody could reconstruct the state and verify that the anchored commitment is honest. It is explored in Chapter 14.

[c] **Merkle root.** The 32-byte fingerprint that summarizes the rollup's entire state. Recomputing it from the raw data and comparing it with the one anchored on Bitcoin is the gesture with which anyone can verify, independently, that the declared state is authentic.

FIGURE 11.8 **THE STATE COMMITMENT ANCHORED ON BITCOIN IS A COMPACT SYNTHESIS OF THE STATE; THE RAW DATA NEEDED FOR VERIFICATION LIVES IN A SEPARATE LAYER. SECURITY DEPENDS ON BOTH.**

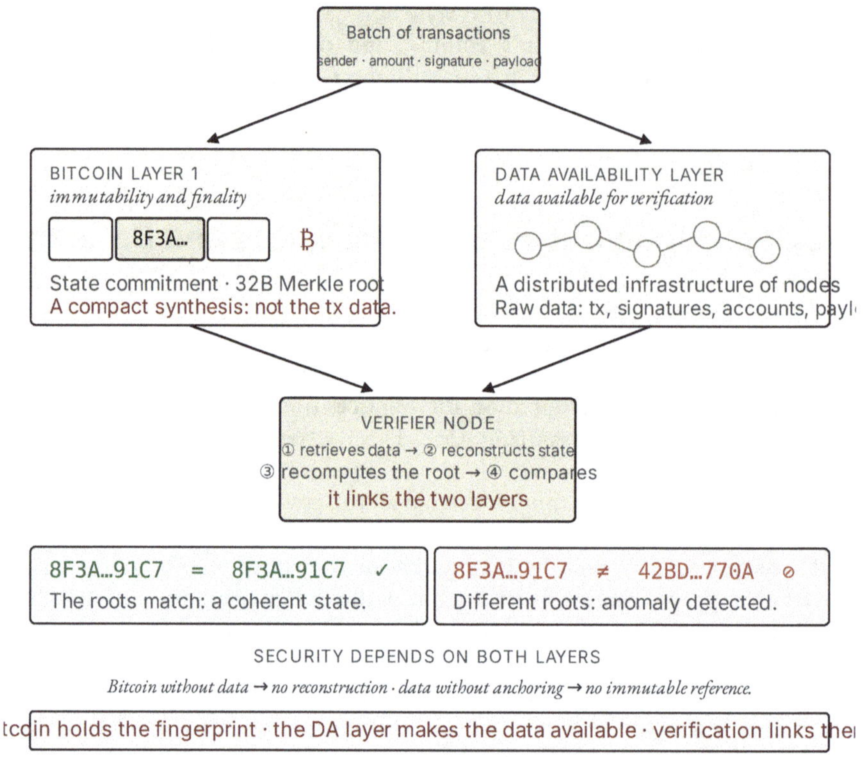

There is an important consequence worth emphasizing. **The rollup's security is the security of the weakest link between the two layers.** If Bitcoin is extremely secure but the data availability layer is centralized and fragile, the overall system is fragile. If the data availability layer is well distributed but the anchorings on Bitcoin are done poorly, the overall system is poor. This is why Hyper must tend to both layers with the same attention, and this is why the research post on data availability is as important as the one on commitments.

For the rollup's users, this separation is largely invisible: applications and wallets abstract away the details, and the user experiences the rollup as if it were a single system. But for those seriously evaluating the project, the separation is important to understand. **When the marketing talks about "Bitcoin security," one must always ask whether it is talking about the immutability of the anchorings (which is effectively Bitcoin-grade) or about the security of the entire system (which also depends on the data availability and the other components). They are two different claims, and the marketing tends to merge them.**

⁂

11.7 — Questions and Answers: Clarifying the Chapter's Concepts

Question 1: If the state commitment is only 32 bytes, how does it "know" the state of a rollup with thousands of accounts and millions of transactions?

It does not "know" it in the sense of containing the data. It "knows" it in the sense of being mathematically tied to that data through the Merkle tree. The metaphor I like to use is that of human fingerprints. Your fingerprint is small — a few square millimeters — yet it is uniquely tied to you: nobody in the world has the same fingerprint. Knowing your fingerprint, someone can verify whether it is you by comparing it with the one you leave on an object. **The state commitment does the same thing with data: it is small but uniquely tied to the state.** To "reconstruct" the state from the commitment something else is needed (the raw data of the data availability layer), but to verify that the state is the right one, the commitment is enough. Concrete example: if I give you a 32-byte commitment and show you a certain state, you can in a few milliseconds compute the state's fingerprint and compare it with the commitment. If they match, the state is the one committed by the commitment. If they do not match, there is a discrepancy. Verification is fast; reconstruction requires the raw data.

Question 2: The Merkle trees you describe seem a simple structure, but I imagine in practice they are more complex. What are the real complications?

Yes, in practice there are several subtleties. I list them briefly. **First**: the choice of the hash function. SHA-256 is the one used by Bitcoin, but other blockchains use other functions (Keccak-256 in Ethereum, BLAKE3 in some recent projects). Hyper must choose which to use, considering trade-offs of security, speed, and compatibility with Bitcoin. **Second**: the tree's specific structure. There are variants of Merkle trees (binary, sparse, Patricia, Verkle) with different efficiency characteristics for insertion, removal, and proofs. The choice depends on the rollup's access pattern. **Third**: how to manage states that change. When a state changes, a portion of the tree must be rebuilt; efficient structures allow incremental updates instead of complete reconstructions. **Fourth**: how to manage accounts that are created or removed over time. The rollup's state is dynamic, and the tree must be able to grow and contract. Concrete example: Ethereum uses a structure called the "Merkle Patricia Trie," which is a more sophisticated variant of the standard Merkle tree, optimized for the dynamic state pattern of blockchains. Hyper could adopt a similar structure or a variant of its own. The specific choice influences performance and proof size, and it is one of the technical details the team will finalize.

Question 3: What happens if two different state commitments are anchored on Bitcoin in a conflicting way?

In principle, on a well-functioning system this should not happen: the sequencer publishes one commitment at a time, each coherent with the previous one. But let us imagine pathological scenarios. **If the sequencer is dishonest and tries to publish two alternative commitments**, the system must have mechanisms to recognize the conflict and resolve it, typically through fraud proofs demonstrating which of the two is coherent with the public data and which is not. **If two competent sequencers produce different commitments** (a situation that could emerge in a distributed sequencing phase), a coordination mechanism resolving the divergence is needed. **If Bitcoin itself has a temporary fork during which both commitments are included in different branches**, the system must wait for Bitcoin itself to resolve the fork before considering either one definitive. In all these cases, the base system managing the state commitments must be robust to conflict situations. Hyper, according to the available documentation, is developing the specific mechanisms for each of these scenarios, although the implementation details are not yet completely published. Concrete example: on Optimism, if a wrong commitment is detected, there is a formal "challenge" mechanism leading to a resolution procedure through fraud proofs. For Hyper an analogous mechanism is expected, adapted to the Bitcoin context.

Question 4: If Hyper is still evaluating between OP_RETURN, Taproot, and timelock, how realistic is it that the final decision will arrive in time for the mainnet launch?

It is a decision the team must finalize before the launch, and it is probably already further along than the public documentation suggests. Research posts typically lay out options and trade-offs in a balanced way, but internally the team almost certainly already has a preferred direction. **The publication of implementation details tends to come later in the development cycle**, close to the mainnet launch, when the choices are consolidated and the team is ready to defend them publicly. For those evaluating the project, the lack of a definitive choice today is not in itself a problem: it is normal for a pre-mainnet project. It would become a problem if the choice were not communicated and implemented in time for the launch, because it would mean the team is trying to postpone hard decisions. Concrete example: Optimism had various state commitment models over its years of development, evolving them as its own technical capabilities matured. For Hyper, the flexibility in the current research is an advantage: it makes it possible to choose the best solution in light of everything that is learned, instead of being locked into decisions made too early.

Question 5: As a user, should I worry about the technical choice between OP_RETURN, Taproot, and timelock?

Largely no, because the choice is invisible to the end user. The rollup's user experience — transaction speed, costs, perceived finality — is influenced by the choice only in indirect ways: some schemes can give faster finality (timelock with short windows), others can be cheaper (OP_RETURN), others more efficient for certain advanced operations (Taproot). But for everyday operations (sending tokens, interacting with applications), the difference is invisible. **The user must worry about other things**: the security of the wallet they use, the quality of the applications they interact with, the system's overall fees. The choice of the commitment mechanism is a concern for the team and for investors evaluating the project's technical maturity, not for end users. Concrete example: a Bitcoin user today does not know which exact opcode is used behind the scenes for their transactions; they care that they work. The same holds for Hyper's users: the technical choice is important for the system's health, but not for everyday use.

Question 6: If state commitments are so powerful, why not anchor the raw data on Bitcoin too, instead of on the separate data availability layer?

For pure questions of scale, as I mentioned in 11.6. Bitcoin has a limited total capacity: in a 4-megabyte block every ten minutes, it can host at most a few megabytes of arbitrary data over time. **If Hyper anchored the raw transaction data too,** even with aggressive compression, it would rapidly saturate Bitcoin with data that has no intrinsic value for the Bitcoin network. It would be an enormously inefficient use of the scarce resource "Bitcoin space," which should be reserved for native Bitcoin transactions and compact commitments. **The two-level model is therefore a necessity, not a choice of convenience.** The commitment goes on Bitcoin because eternal immutability is needed there; the raw data goes elsewhere because only verifiable availability is needed there, and there are more efficient solutions for that. Concrete example: by the same logic, companies do not archive all their emails on their most expensive security servers; they archive only the metadata and signature certificates on high-security systems, and the contents on cheaper but still reliable systems. Hyper applies the same logic to the blockchain context: choosing the right security level for each type of data.

⁂

11.8 — WHAT TO TAKE AWAY FROM THIS CHAPTER

The state commitment is a mathematical fingerprint of the rollup's state, a short string (typically 32 bytes) uniquely tied to the state it represents. It is the "compact language" in which the rollup speaks to Bitcoin.

Merkle trees are the mathematical structure that makes state commitments possible. They make it possible to summarize arbitrarily large collections of data in a single compact fingerprint, and to prove the inclusion of individual elements without transmitting all the data.

Bitcoin Hyper can anchor the state commitments on Bitcoin in three main ways: through OP_RETURN (simple and well understood), through Taproot (more expressive), through timelocked structures (with explicit challenge windows).

The specific technical choice is not yet public, and it will probably be a combination of the three techniques. The Hyper team explored the trade-offs in a specific research post (December 2025).

The frequency of the anchorings is an adaptive parameter, not a fixed rule. Hyper proposes to anchor more frequently when Bitcoin's conditions allow it, less frequently when costs are high.

The state commitment anchored on Bitcoin does not contain the raw transaction data, but only the fingerprint of the resulting state. The raw data lives in the data availability layer, separate but essential for verifiability.

The two-level model — commitment on Bitcoin, data elsewhere — is a necessity of scale, not a choice of convenience. The rollup's security is the security of the weakest link between the two layers.

The cost of the anchorings is amortized over the rollup's transactions, and it contributes to the total cost per transaction. Even with frequent anchorings, the cost per single rollup transaction is fractions of a cent, dramatically lower than the cost of a transaction directly on Bitcoin.

For end users, the specific technical choices on the commitments are largely invisible. The user experience is influenced indirectly, but everyday decisions (sending tokens, using applications) do not depend on these choices.

For those evaluating the project, the clarity with which the team addresses the theme of the commitments is a thermometer of technical maturity. A team that cannot answer clearly the questions about how it anchors to Bitcoin is probably hiding problems.

Chapter 11 ends here. We have understood what state commitments are, how they are built through Merkle trees, and what the specific technical options are that Bitcoin Hyper is evaluating for anchoring its state to Bitcoin. In ***Chapter 12 — Three Roads for Anchoring: OP_RETURN, Taproot, Timelock****, we will go down into the specific details of each of these three techniques, seeing concretely how they work from the cryptographic point of view, what their advantages and disadvantages are, and how they integrate with the rest of the rollup's architecture.*

NOTES

1 After the cryptographer Ralph Merkle, who patented the structure in 1979 (U.S. Patent 4,309,569). The Merkle tree is today at the basis not only of Bitcoin and rollups, but also of Git, of IPFS, and of numerous distributed verification systems.

State commitment: the *seal* with which Hyper speaks to Bitcoin

How an entire rollup state is compressed into a **cryptographic root** that can be anchored on Bitcoin.

1 Two different languages

Hyper is a fast, complex rollup, with accounts, programs, and dynamic state. Bitcoin is minimal, slow, secure, and with little data space.

The rollup must say a lot, using very few bytes.

Bitcoin Hyper · SVM
accounts, programs, batches, complex state

→ CRYPTOGRAPHIC TRANSLATION

₿ Bitcoin L1
blocks, finality, immutability, limited space

2 The state's fingerprint

A state commitment is a short string, typically 32 bytes, mathematically tied to the rollup's state at a precise moment.

A minimal variation in the state completely changes the fingerprint.

THE ROLLUP'S COMPLETE STATE
user balances · accounts · programs · metadata · app state

↓ CRYPTOGRAPHIC HASHING

8F3A…91C7
STATE COMMITMENT · 32 BYTES

3 From the big state to a single root

Merkle trees summarize millions of data items in a single root and verify the inclusion of a single element with **a few hashes**.

☰ 1,000,000 elements → 1 root of 32 bytes

✓ Inclusion proof → a few hashes

The root **"feels" every modification** *of the state.*

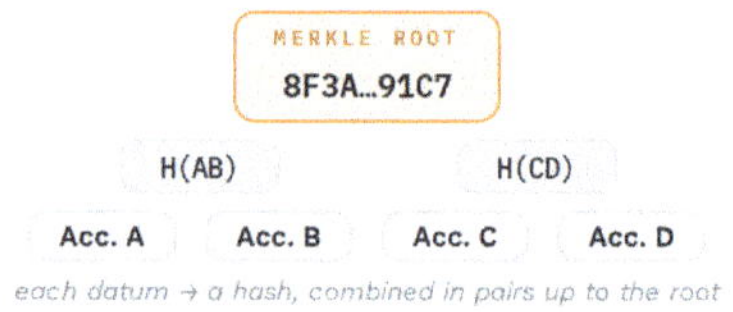

4 How to publish the commitment

HOW **OP_RETURN** Simple, mature, direct. Inserts the root as a small on-chain datum.	HOW **Taproot** More flexible and expressive. Allows more articulated commitment structures.	WHEN **Timelock** A challenge window: time to verify and challenge. Optimistic models.

ⓘ **OP_RETURN and Taproot** concern *how* to publish. **The timelock** concerns *when* a state becomes definitive.

The final model can be **hybrid**.

5 Bitcoin holds the fingerprint, not all the data

₿ BITCOIN L1	**state commitment** · 32B Merkle root · **immutable finality**
DATA AVAILABILITY	transactions, signatures, accounts, payloads — **the raw data of the verification**
VERIFIER NODE	downloads the data → reconstructs the state → recomputes the root → **compares with Bitcoin**

available data + immutable commitment = independent verification

Bitcoin without data is not enough. **Data without anchoring is not enough.**

THE KEY POINT

The state commitment is the cryptographic seal of the rollup's state. **Bitcoin** makes it **immutable**; the data availability layer makes it possible to **verify it**. Security is born from the link between the two layers.

PART IV · THE SETTLEMENT LAYER

Chapter 12
Three Roads for Anchoring

OP_RETURN[1]*, Taproot*[2]*, timelock*

⁂

12.1 — From the Theory to the Practice of Anchoring

In the previous chapter we understood what a state commitment is and why a mechanism is needed to "write" it on Bitcoin immutably. Now let us go down into the concrete details of how this writing technically happens. It is a chapter that requires entering Bitcoin's technology at a level we have so far only skimmed — the Script opcodes, Taproot transactions, timelocks — but I assure you it is an incursion that pays off. **Understanding how Hyper anchors the commitments to Bitcoin means understanding a fundamental thing: the rollup is not "magically talking" to Bitcoin, it is using specific primitives that Bitcoin has offered for years or only recently, each with precise technical characteristics that condition what is possible and what is not.**

FIGURE 12.1 **FROM THE MERKLE ROOT TO THE ANCHORING ON BITCOIN: OP_RETURN PUBLISHES A COMPACT DATUM, TAPROOT COMMITS SCRIPT STRUCTURES WITH SELECTIVE REVELATION, TIMELOCKS ADD TEMPORAL CONDITIONS TO SPENDABILITY.**

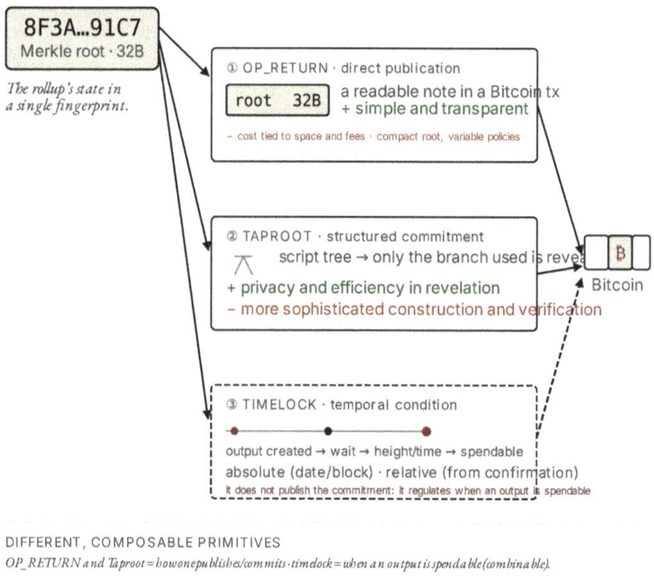

The three roads Hyper's December 2025 research post explores — OP_RETURN, Taproot, timelock — are not inventions of the project. They are techniques available on the Bitcoin blockchain, developed over the years for other purposes, that are now being adapted for the specific case of anchoring rollups. Each has a history, a scope of application, limits, costs. Understanding these three roads well will give you a look inside the "fabric" of Bitcoin that few marketing documents offer, and it will put you in the position of evaluating in an informed way whatever final choice the Hyper team makes.

I want to organize the chapter this way. First I talk about OP_RETURN, because it is the simplest road and the one that will probably be used for the first anchorings. Then I move to Taproot, which is more modern and powerful. Finally I tackle timelocks, which add a temporal dimension that deserves separate attention. For each technique I explain how it works inside Bitcoin, how Hyper would use it, what the pros and cons are, and where it sits in the overall landscape. At the end, we see how these three techniques can be combined, because that is probably what Hyper will do.

TABLE 12.1 **THREE ROADS FOR ANCHORING A STATE TO BITCOIN**

Method	Data space	Cost	Privacy	Adoption

op_return	≈ 80 bytes per output	Medium: pays standard fees	Low: data in the clear on-chain	High: used by Stacks, Counterparty, Omni
Taproot (script-path)	Flexible, up to hundreds of bytes	Low-medium: optimized with commit/reveal	High: the commit does not reveal the content	Growing: the standard of recent rollups
Timelock (indirect covenant)	Indirect reference	Low	Medium	Niche, specific escrow cases

How to read it: *Bitcoin Hyper leans toward a Taproot + op_return mix, exploiting commit-reveal for frequent states and op_return for public checkpoints. The choice is coherent with a rollup that optimizes for scalability without giving up public verifiability.*

⁂

12.2 — OP_RETURN: Bitcoin's Note in the Margin

Let us begin with the simplest and the oldest of the three techniques. **OP_RETURN is an opcode**[a] — that is, an instruction of Bitcoin's Script language — which has existed practically forever in the blockchain, but which in 2014 was formally "promoted" as the official tool for inserting arbitrary data into transactions. Before that date, developers used various tricks to insert data on Bitcoin, some elegant, others very problematic. With the standard adoption of OP_RETURN, Bitcoin Core gave a "clean" way to do this operation.

Let us see what it does concretely. When a Bitcoin transaction contains an output marked with OP_RETURN, that output becomes **deliberately unspendable**. It is like saying "this part of the transaction does not exist as spendable bitcoin, but serves only to carry data with it." That data can be arbitrary — text, hashes, identifiers, anything — up to a limit of 80 bytes per output (a limit that was raised from the original 40 bytes). Once the transaction is included in a block, the OP_RETURN data becomes permanently recorded on the blockchain, immutable like any other part of Bitcoin.

To use a concrete analogy: **OP_RETURN is like the "memo" line of a bank transfer**. When you make a transfer, you can write a memo describing the reason for the payment — "March rent," "birthday gift," "expense reimbursement." That memo is recorded together with the transfer, but it is not the transfer itself: it is additional information accompanying the payment. OP_RETURN works the same way, but for Bitcoin: it carries data that is not monetary value but that is recorded permanently together with the transaction.

For Bitcoin Hyper, OP_RETURN offers the most direct route for anchoring a state commitment. The rollup builds a standard Bitcoin transaction, adds an OP_RETURN output containing the 32 bytes of its state's Merkle root, and sends the transaction to the Bitcoin network. When the transaction is included in a block, the state commitment is anchored. From that moment, anyone in the world can read the OP_RETURN datum from that block and verify that the rollup's commitment is exactly the one declared.

TABLE 12.2 **THE BANK-TRANSFER ANALOGY FOR OP_RETURN.**

Element	Bank transfer	OP_RETURN
Main datum	Amount transferred	A movement of bitcoin[b]
Annotation	Payment memo	Merkle root (32 bytes)[c]

Effect on the balance	None: it is only text	None: an unspendable output[d]
Function	Explaining the operation	Anchoring the rollup's state

As the memo of a bank transfer accompanies a payment without altering its amount, OP_RETURN attaches to the transaction a small annotation — the fingerprint of the rollup's state — without moving funds. It is the simplest way to write the commitment on Bitcoin, making it readable and verifiable by anyone.

[a] **Opcode.** A single elementary instruction of Bitcoin's internal language (Script), with which the network is told what to do with a transaction. OP_RETURN is the opcode that signals: "this part does not move money, it serves only to record data."

[b] **A movement of bitcoin.** To write on Bitcoin, the rollup must still create a transaction, and every transaction moves a minimal quantity of coin (often the technical minimum, called dust).[e] The purpose is not to transfer value, but to bring into existence the transaction that carries the annotation.

[c] **Merkle root.** The 32-byte fingerprint that summarizes the rollup's entire state: comparing it is enough to know whether even a single datum has changed. It is the value actually written in the OP_RETURN annotation.

[d] **Unspendable output.** A Bitcoin transaction is made of outputs, each of which represents funds that someone will be able to spend in the future. An OP_RETURN output is instead marked as unspendable: it can never be reused and serves solely to record data in the chain.

[e] **Dust.** The minimum quantity of bitcoin it makes sense to include in an output: smaller amounts would cost more in fees than they are worth. Anchoring transactions often use precisely this minimum, because their purpose is to carry a datum, not to transfer value.

FIGURE 12.2 **ANATOMY OF A TRANSACTION WITH AN OP_RETURN ANCHORING.**

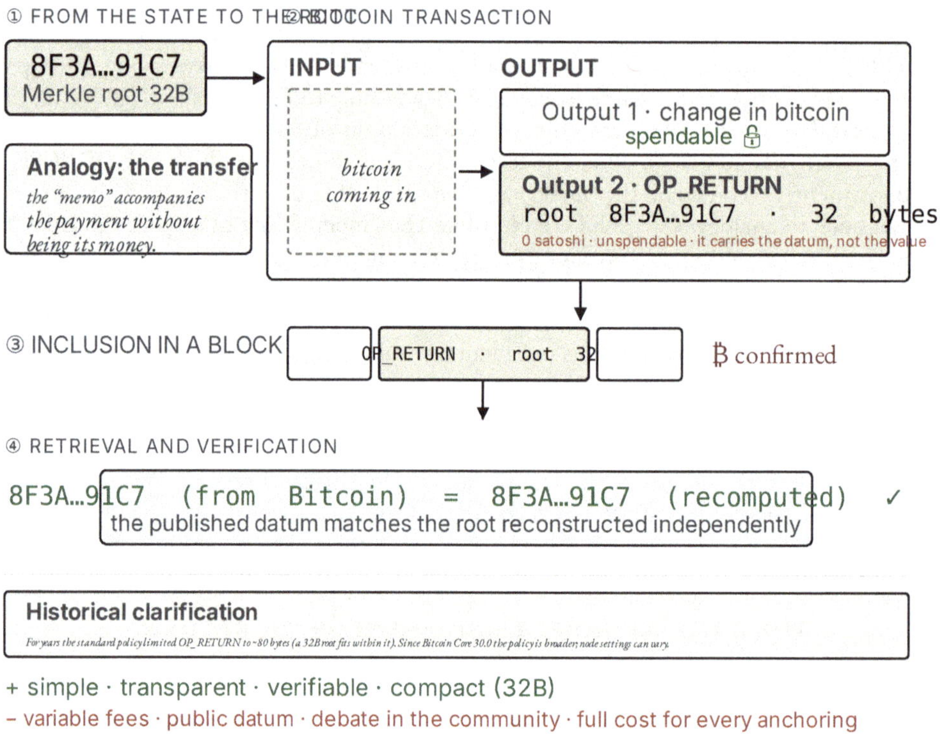

OP_RETURN is like the "memo" line of a bank transfer: it accompanies the transaction without being its value. Hyper adds an OP_RETURN output, deliberately unspendable, which carries the 32 bytes of the Merkle root; when the transaction enters a block the commitment becomes immutable and anyone, with a Bitcoin node, can reread and verify it. The definitive choice of Hyper's anchoring mechanism will depend on the protocol's final specifications.

The **advantages of OP_RETURN** are significant. **First: it is extremely simple to implement.** All Bitcoin development tools support it, all wallets know how to build transactions with OP_RETURN, all explorers know how to display the data. Nothing exotic is needed. **Second: it is universally verifiable.** Anyone with a full Bitcoin node can read the OP_RETURN data without any additional information. **Third: it has a predictable cost.** The cost of an OP_RETURN transaction is that of a standard Bitcoin transaction, plus a small surcharge for the additional bytes.

The **disadvantages** exist and deserve honesty. **First: the 80-byte limit is tight.** For a single 32-byte state commitment it is more than sufficient, but if Hyper wanted to include other metadata — versions, references, identifiers — the space becomes scarce. **Second: the Bitcoin community historically does not love the use of OP_RETURN for purposes not strictly Bitcoin.** A decade-long debate exists on the appropriateness of "polluting" the blockchain with external applications' data, and proposals to further restrict the use of OP_RETURN periodically emerge. **Third: every anchoring is a separate transaction, with its full cost.** There is no way to amortize costs across multiple anchorings in the same transaction, at least not with pure OP_RETURN.

For Hyper, OP_RETURN is probably the sensible choice for the **project's initial phase**. It is simple, it is proven, it is universally understandable. It allows the team to concentrate on other, more complex challenges of the project without first having to solve sophisticated anchoring problems. When the system is more mature, and when specific needs for efficiency or expressiveness emerge, the transition to more advanced techniques can be evaluated.

FIGURE 12.3 **OP_RETURN IS THE SIMPLEST AND MOST DIRECT WAY TO ANCHOR DATA ON BITCOIN: A NATURAL CHOICE FOR HYPER'S INITIAL PHASE.**

Advantages	Limits
Simplicity — supported by every Bitcoin wallet, explorer, and tool: nothing exotic to implement	**Reduced space** — 80 bytes: enough for a 32-byte root, tight for additional metadata
Universal verifiability — anyone with a Bitcoin node reads the datum without additional information	**Debate in the community** — the use of OP_RETURN for non-Bitcoin data is historically contested
Predictable cost — that of a standard transaction plus a small surcharge	**Full cost per anchoring** — every commitment is a separate transaction, not amortizable

The advantages of OP_RETURN — simplicity, universal verifiability, predictable cost — make it the most direct road for anchoring a state commitment on Bitcoin. The limits exist and deserve honesty: the 80-byte space is sufficient for a Merkle root but tight for other metadata, the use of OP_RETURN for external applications' data is the subject of a decade-long debate in the Bitcoin community, and every anchoring costs as much as a full transaction. On balance, however, for Hyper's initial phase OP_RETURN remains the most sensible choice: proven, understandable, and capable of freeing the team for the project's more complex challenges.

⁂

12.3 — Taproot: the Qualitative Leap of 2021

The second road is significantly more modern and deserves a more articulated explanation, because Taproot is probably the most important upgrade Bitcoin has received in the last ten years, and understanding its capabilities is essential for understanding the future of Bitcoin's Layer 2s.

Taproot was activated in Bitcoin's mainnet in November 2021, after years of proposals, debates, revisions. Its design unites the work of various researchers — Pieter Wuille, Anthony Towns, Jonas Nick, Tim Ruffing — and introduces several refined cryptographic innovations. For our purposes, the relevant characteristics of Taproot are two: **Schnorr signatures** and the **Tapscript script trees**.

Schnorr signatures are a type of digital signature alternative to the ECDSA algorithm Bitcoin used previously. They have elegant mathematical properties, in particular the possibility of **aggregating multiple signatures into one**: if several people must sign a transaction together, their signatures can be combined into a single compact signature that is indistinguishable from a single signature. This property has important implications for privacy and efficiency, but for our discussion it matters for other reasons: it makes it possible to build complex transactions that look simple from the outside.

The Tapscript script trees are even more relevant to our theme. The idea is that a Taproot transaction can **hide inside itself a tree of possible spending conditions**, and reveal to the public only the one actually used. Think of it as a contract with many alternative clauses: the contract is signed and posts collateral, but when it is executed, only the specific clause that applies to the case is revealed, not all the others. **This capacity for "commitment and selective revelation" is exactly what is needed for the rollups' state commitments.**

Note 1. Schnorr signatures make it possible to aggregate multiple signatures into one: beyond the efficiency and privacy advantage cited in the text, they reduce the space occupied on-chain and therefore the cost of publishing a commitment. It is a relevant detail for a rollup, which must write on Bitcoin with the maximum possible compactness.

Note 2. "Commitment and selective revelation" is the rendering of the commit-reveal principle: one binds oneself in advance to a set of possibilities by publishing only its fingerprint, and later reveals solely the element actually used. On this property of Taproot rests the possibility of anchoring complex structures without exposing them entirely on the blockchain.

FIGURE 12.4 **ANATOMY OF A TAPROOT OUTPUT: THE INTERNAL KEY AND THE MERKLE ROOT OF THE SCRIPT TREE FORM A COMPACT 32-BYTE OUTPUT KEY. THE KEY PATH CAN KEEP THE ENTIRE TREE HIDDEN; THE SCRIPT PATH REVEALS ONLY THE CONDITION USED AND ITS MERKLE PATH.**

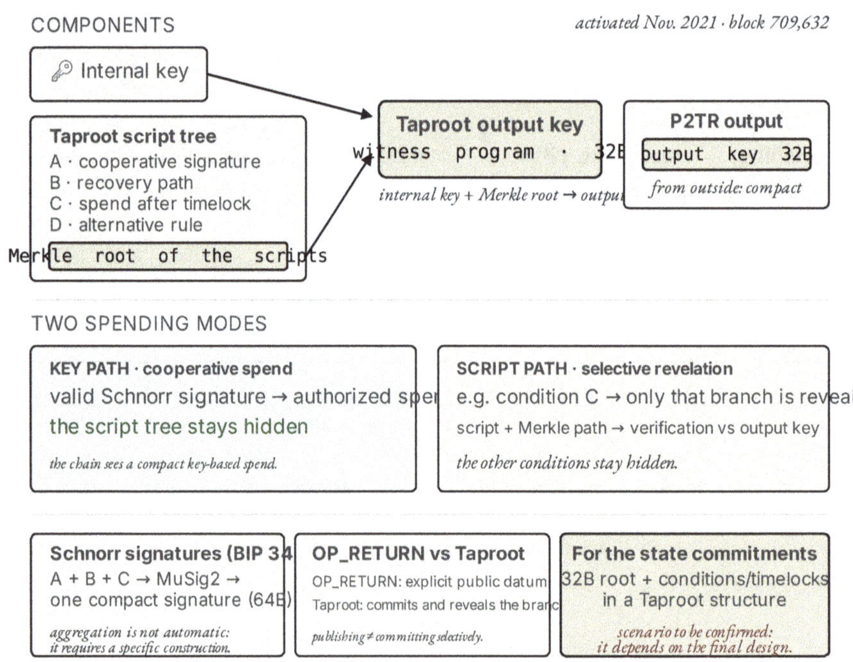

A compact output on the outside · a tree of possibilities on the inside · only the necessary path is revealed.

Let us see how Hyper could use Taproot. When the rollup wants to anchor a state commitment, it builds a Taproot transaction where the output contains a tree structure committing many pieces of information: the state's Merkle root, references to the raw data, any cryptographic proofs, metadata. The tree is "compressed" into a single 32-byte Taproot signature, which is what appears on-chain in a standard way. **Externally, the transaction looks like any Taproot transaction.** But in reality it has committed a whole series of pieces of information that can be "revealed" and verified when necessary.

The **advantages of Taproot** over OP_RETURN are manifold. **First: it is more expressive.** It makes it possible to commit structures much richer than a simple 32-byte value. References, proofs, structured metadata can be included, all in a transaction that is externally compact. **Second: it is more efficient.** The 32 bytes of the Taproot signature potentially commit megabytes of structured data, while OP_RETURN commits only its explicit 80 bytes. **Third: it is privacy-friendly.** The hidden structures actually stay hidden until there is a need to reveal them, reducing the quantity of information exposed on the public blockchain. **Fourth: it lends itself to advanced constructions.** If in the future Hyper wanted to implement sophisticated mechanisms like on-chain fraud proofs, Taproot is the most suitable primitive for building them without modifications of Bitcoin.

The **disadvantages** are above all of complexity. **First: implementing Taproot correctly is significantly more complex than OP_RETURN.** Building the structures, computing the commitments, managing the revelations requires specialized tools and attention to cryptographic details. Bugs in this area would be very dangerous. **Second: the supporting ecosystem is still evolving.** While all Bitcoin tools have supported OP_RETURN for years, advanced support for Taproot is less widespread, especially for non-standard use cases. **Third: verification by external observers requires understanding the rollup's specific structures**, not just "reading a datum." It means explorers and verification tools must be developed specifically for Hyper; using Bitcoin's standard ones is not enough.

For Hyper, Taproot is probably the choice the team aims to use in the **medium term**, once the system is mature and there are specific reasons for obtaining the efficiency and expressiveness it offers. It is an investment in technical complexity that pays off at scale, but that would be excessive for the project's first anchorings.

⁂

12.4 — Timelock Structures: Adding the Time Factor

The third road introduces a dimension the first two do not have: **time as an active part of the anchoring mechanism**. Timelocks are Bitcoin primitives that make it possible to bind an output's spendability to temporal conditions — "this transaction can be spent only after time X" or "only if it has not already been spent by time Y." They are primitives available on Bitcoin for a long time, and they are at the basis of many advanced mechanisms such as the Lightning Network and conditional escrow contracts.

Note. Bitcoin distinguishes two types of timelock: those with an absolute deadline, which fix a precise moment (a block height or a date) before which the output is not spendable, and those with a relative deadline, which measure an interval starting from the transaction's confirmation. The distinction is technical but not secondary: in the anchoring context it determines when a state can be challenged or considered definitive, and therefore directly affects the withdrawal times perceived by the user.

FIGURE 12.5 **TIMELOCKS TRANSFORM TIME INTO A SPENDING CONDITION OF BITCOIN OUTPUTS: CLTV FIXES AN ABSOLUTE DEADLINE, CSV A RELATIVE INTERVAL. COMBINED WITH TAPROOT SCRIPTS, AVAILABLE DATA, AND MONITORING, THEY CONTRIBUTE TO MORE ARTICULATED SECURITY CONSTRUCTIONS. ON THEIR OWN THEY NEITHER VERIFY NOR INVALIDATE A STATE COMMITMENT.**

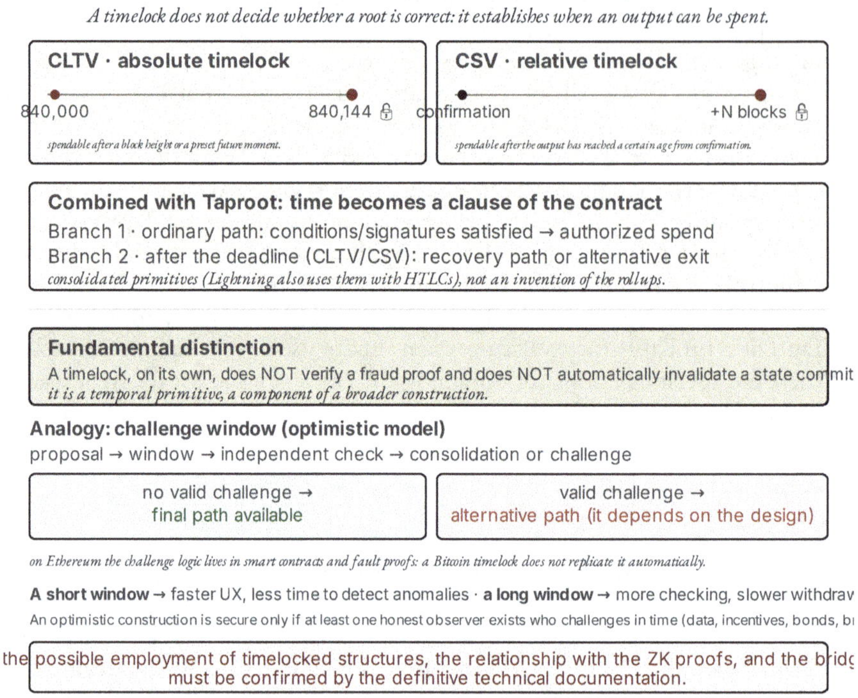

For rollups, the interesting use of timelocks is in combination with the challenge mechanisms. The idea works like this. The rollup publishes a state commitment, but with a timelock structure that says: "this commitment becomes definitive after X time, **unless someone publishes a valid challenge during this interval.**" If nobody challenges, after X time the commitment is crystallized. If someone challenges by demonstrating that the commitment is wrong, the commitment is rejected and the sequencer punished.

This is exactly the pattern used by the **Optimistic Rollups** on Ethereum, like Optimism and Arbitrum. The term "optimistic" derives precisely from this: the system **optimistically assumes the sequencer is honest**, but gives anyone the time to refute the assumption if they have contrary evidence. On Optimism, the challenge window is seven days; for Hyper, it could be different, but the principle is the same.

Implementing timelocks on Bitcoin for Hyper's state commitments requires combining several primitives. Typically a Taproot output committing the state commitment is used, with alternative spending paths that activate temporal and challenge conditions. If the timelock expires without challenges, the state commitment is "validated" through a specific script. If instead a valid challenge arrives before the deadline, it activates an alternative path that rejects the commitment.

The **advantages of the timelock model** are significant for the system's security. **First: it introduces an explicit security mechanism** that does not require complex cryptographic proofs like ZK-proofs. Security comes from the possibility for anyone to challenge wrong commitments. **Second: it is well understood from the experience of Optimism and Arbitrum.** These are patterns proven in production for years, with billions of dollars of value in custody. **Third: it integrates naturally with the data availability model.** If the data is publicly available, anyone can re-execute the transactions, compute the correct state commitment, and challenge wrong commitments during the timelock window.

The main **disadvantages** are two. **First: finality is delayed by the challenge window.** On Optimism, withdrawing funds toward Ethereum takes seven days precisely for this reason. For Hyper, a similar window would mean that withdrawing bitcoin from the rollup toward the Bitcoin blockchain requires waiting days instead of minutes. **Second: it requires active monitoring infrastructure.** For the system to work, there must be at least one active party checking the published commitments and producing challenges when necessary. Without active monitors, the system could accept wrong commitments. Typically this monitoring is done by specialized nodes, but the system must create adequate incentives for those operating these nodes.

For Hyper, timelocks could be used as a **component of the hybrid security model**, perhaps for certain types of operations or as a backup of other mechanisms. The December 2025 research post explicitly mentions "timelocked structures" as one of the three families explored, suggesting the team considers them among the serious options for the final system.

⁂

12.5 — Combining the Primitives: a Possible Hybrid Model

At this point we have analyzed OP_RETURN, Taproot, and timelocks separately. It might seem natural to imagine that the Bitcoin Hyper team must choose a single road and exclude the others. In reality, the distinction is not so sharp. The three primitives[a] do not perform exactly the same function and, precisely for this reason, can be considered as modules potentially composable within a broader architecture.

OP_RETURN offers a simple and transparent modality for publishing a compact datum in a Bitcoin transaction. A 32-byte Merkle root[b] can be recorded on-chain as a public checkpoint,[c] easily readable and verifiable. Taproot answers a different need: it makes it possible to cryptographically commit a tree of possible spending conditions[d] and to reveal only the path actually used. Timelocks, finally, neither publish nor validate the state commitment: they introduce time into the spending conditions, making certain paths available only after an absolute deadline or after a relative interval.

These primitives could therefore contribute, with different roles, to the construction of a modular model[g]. For certain essential checkpoints, the protocol could use a direct, readable publication of the Merkle root. For particular outputs or paths of the bridge,[e] it could provide more articulated Taproot conditions. In specific withdrawal, recovery, or security procedures, it could additionally use temporal constraints based on CLTV or CSV[f].

---

[a] **Primitive.** In cryptography and in protocols, a basic element — an elementary, proven "brick" — with which more complex mechanisms are built. Here the three primitives (OP_RETURN, Taproot, timelock) are the Bitcoin tools combinable to anchor the rollup.

[b] **Merkle root.** The single fingerprint that summarizes an entire Merkle tree, and with it all the data it contains. 32 bytes are enough to represent and verify the entire state it refers to.

[c] **Checkpoint.** A control point: a rollup state published and fixed on Bitcoin at intervals, serving as a certain reference for everyone. Once recorded it becomes a cornerstone no longer modifiable, from which to restart for subsequent verifications.

[d] **Spending conditions.** The rules establishing how and by whom a bitcoin fund can be spent (for example a signature, multiple signatures, or the expiry of a time). Taproot makes it possible to define them in an articulated way, revealing only the one actually used.

[e] **Bridge.** The "bridge" connecting two chains — here Bitcoin and the rollup — making it possible to move value from one to the other with deposits and withdrawals. It is one of the most delicate parts of the architecture, because it holds the funds during the passage: its spending conditions must be protected with particular care.

[f] **CLTV and CSV.** Two instructions of Bitcoin's script that introduce the time factor into transactions. CLTV (CheckLockTimeVerify) locks funds until a precise date or block height — an absolute deadline; CSV (CheckSequenceVerify) locks them for an interval running from the moment the transaction is confirmed — a relative deadline. They are the bricks with which withdrawal and emergency procedures are built: for example, leaving a window of time within which to challenge an operation before it becomes definitive.

[g] **Modular model.** An architecture built by combining distinct, interchangeable components, each with a precise task, instead of relying on a single monolithic solution. Here it means using OP_RETURN, Taproot, and timelocks together, each where it performs best, instead of choosing only one.

TABLE 12.3 **THE THREE PRIMITIVES IN A MODULAR ANCHORING MODEL.**

Primitive	Role in the modular model	When it is used
OP_RETURN	Direct, readable publication of the Merkle root	Essential, public checkpoints
Taproot	Commitment of script structures with selective revelation	More articulated bridge outputs and paths
Timelock (CLTV/CSV)	Temporal conditions on spendability	Withdrawal, recovery, and security procedures

The three techniques do not exclude one another: in a modular model they can coexist, each in the role for which it is most efficient. The actual combination Hyper will adopt is one of the design choices still to be finalized before the launch.

FIGURE 12.6 **A POSSIBLE HYBRID ANCHORING MODEL.**

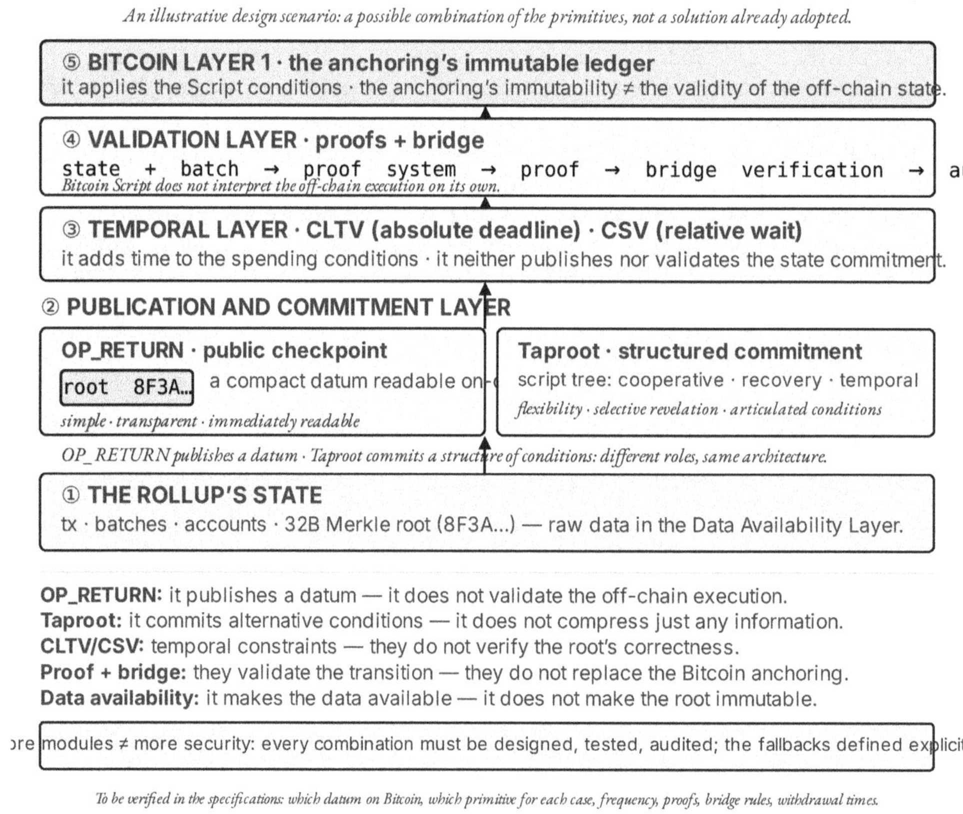

OP_RETURN can publish a compact root, Taproot commit alternative conditions, CLTV/CSV add temporal constraints; proofs and the bridge validate the operations' effects; Bitcoin makes the anchoring immutable. An illustrative configuration, not already adopted.

A simplification must however be avoided. A timelock does not demonstrate that a root is correct and does not automatically invalidate a wrong state commitment. Bitcoin Script applies the spending conditions submitted to it, but it does not autonomously interpret the rollup's entire off-chain execution. The state's correctness must be guaranteed separately by the validation model provided by the protocol.

In the public documentation, Bitcoin Hyper declares that it aggregates and compresses the Layer 2's transactions, uses ZK proofs to guarantee their validity, and periodically commits the state on Bitcoin Layer 1. For withdrawals toward Bitcoin, the project describes a procedure in which the state is verified and a proof is submitted to the canonical bridge before the release of the BTC. It will therefore be important to understand what actual role OP_RETURN, Taproot, and any temporal structures will have within this model.

A modular architecture can offer significant advantages. It makes it possible to use simple tools in ordinary cases and more articulated conditions when the operation requires it. It additionally allows new functionality to be introduced progressively, without weighing down every single anchoring with the maximum possible level of complexity.

Modularity, however, does not automatically guarantee resilience. Every combination must be designed, implemented, tested, and audited. Any fallback paths must also be defined explicitly: they do not arise spontaneously from the availability of alternative primitives.

The most important question is therefore not establishing in advance whether Bitcoin Hyper will adopt a "hybrid" model in a generic sense. What will have to be evaluated is the concrete way in which the team will assign each primitive a precise function: which datum will be published on Bitcoin, with what frequency, through which structure, with which proofs, according to which bridge rules, and with what withdrawal times. The level of detail of the technical specifications will be one of the most significant indicators of the project's engineering maturity.

⁂

12.6 — The Economic Dimension: How Much Anchoring Costs

I want to close this chapter with a consideration I have mentioned in previous chapters but that deserves a dedicated treatment: **how much does it concretely cost to anchor the state commitments to Bitcoin?** It is a question with important economic implications for the rollup's sustainability, and understanding the order of magnitude of the numbers helps in evaluating the project's viability.

Let us begin with the base costs. A standard Bitcoin transaction, today, has a cost varying between a few cents and a few tens of dollars, depending on the network's traffic and the transaction's size. A transaction with OP_RETURN adds only a few cents of cost compared with a standard transaction. A Taproot transaction has similar or slightly lower costs, thanks to the efficiency of Schnorr signatures. **Under normal conditions, anchoring a single state commitment costs a few dollars at most.**

Now let us apply this cost to the system. If Hyper anchors every 30 minutes, that is 48 anchorings a day, for a daily cost of a few hundred dollars under normal conditions. Over a month, that is a few thousand dollars. **It is a significant but sustainable cost**, especially if the rollup processes tens or hundreds of thousands of transactions a day: the final cost per transaction is fractions of a cent.

The complications emerge in extreme scenarios. **If Bitcoin enters a period of high congestion**, fees can rise dramatically — we have seen historical periods with fees of 50 or 100 dollars per standard transaction. Under these conditions, every anchoring would cost hundreds of dollars, and the system's daily cost would become thousands of dollars. Hyper must be designed to withstand these scenarios, perhaps dynamically reducing the anchoring frequency or accumulating more transactions per anchoring.

If the rollup has low transaction volumes, the final cost per transaction rises because the anchorings' fixed cost is amortized over fewer transactions. In an initial phase of the project, where the volume is still low, this can be significant. Hyper must find a balance between anchoring frequently (to offer users good finality) and anchoring less (to keep costs down when volumes are low).

If the system grows successfully and processes millions of transactions a day, the anchoring costs will become negligible relative to the volume, and the rollup will be economically very efficient. But until that volume is reached, the team must bear the anchoring costs even when the volume is still low, and this requires a sustainable economic model for the initial phase.

There is also an important strategic dimension. **The choice of the anchoring technique influences costs not only directly but also through the optimal frequency.** More efficient techniques make it possible to anchor more frequently at the same cost, offering better finality. Techniques with timelocks lengthen the vulnerability window but reduce unit costs. The Hyper team must balance these dimensions according to the project's priorities and the users' needs.

For those evaluating the project, the cost analysis is one of the aspects the team will have to clarify publicly before the mainnet launch. **Transparent cost models, simulated scenarios for different market conditions, contingency plans for adverse scenarios are all elements a prudent investor must be able to evaluate.** Without this information, it is difficult to judge the system's long-term economic sustainability.

⁂

12.7 — Questions and Answers: Clarifying the Chapter's Concepts

Question 1: Why does Bitcoin allow OP_RETURN if it is of no use to Bitcoin itself? Does it not slow down the network?

OP_RETURN exists as a compromise between two opposing needs. On one side, developers have always needed to insert small quantities of data into Bitcoin transactions for various applications — colored coins, document timestamps, Layer 2 applications, and today also projects like Bitcoin Hyper. On the other side, the Bitcoin community wants to prevent the blockchain from being flooded with non-monetary data that inflates the blocks' size without bringing value to the main network. The compromise solution is OP_RETURN: it gives an "official," limited channel for inserting data (a maximum of 80 bytes per output, a single OP_RETURN output per transaction), so that it does not turn into a mechanism of abuse. **The OP_RETURN data is in any case paid for by its creators through transaction fees**, so it does not represent a net cost for the network. The community has periodically discussed whether to restrict OP_RETURN further, but for now the consensus is that the current level is acceptable. Concrete example: every day thousands of transactions with OP_RETURN pass over the Bitcoin blockchain, used for applications ranging from the timestamping of legal documents to Ordinals inscriptions. Hyper would join this family of users, contributing to the traffic but paying its own fair cost.

Question 2: Taproot seems much more powerful than OP_RETURN to me; why do not all projects use Taproot directly?

Taproot is more powerful but also more complex to implement correctly, and this complexity has costs. **First cost: development requires specific competencies.** Building advanced Taproot transactions requires understanding elliptic-curve cryptography, hash trees, aggregated signature schemes. It is specialist knowledge not all teams possess. **Second cost: the risk of bugs is higher.** In complex cryptographic systems, even small errors can create serious vulnerabilities. The sector's history is full of projects that had bugs in apparently correct cryptographic implementations. **Third cost: the tooling ecosystem is less mature.** While OP_RETURN is supported everywhere, Taproot's advanced functionality requires specialized tools that are still evolving. For many projects, the rational choice is to start with OP_RETURN and migrate to Taproot when the system is mature and there are specific reasons for the change. Hyper seems to follow this philosophy: the research post explores Taproot but does not present it as the sole choice for the initial phase. Concrete example: the Lightning Network started without Taproot and is gradually integrating it in the more recent versions. It is a progressive migration requiring coordination among many actors of the ecosystem. For Bitcoin's Layer 2s, a similar trajectory can be expected.

Question 3: If timelocks introduce challenge windows of days, do they not make the system too slow to be usable?

It is a legitimate concern, and it must be addressed with nuance. The challenge window delays **definitive finality**, but it does not delay the everyday **user experience**. As we saw in Chapter 5, the rollup's users experience transactions as instantaneous because they operate on the current state, and definitive finality is a long-term guarantee protecting from the pathological case. **The case where the challenge window really counts is the withdrawal toward original Bitcoin.** If I want to withdraw my bitcoin from the rollup toward the Bitcoin blockchain, I must wait for the withdrawal's state commitment to have passed the challenge window, because only then is it truly definitive. On Optimism this wait is seven days, and users accept it as a necessary trade-off for security. For Hyper, a similar window would be acceptable for non-urgent withdrawals. For urgent withdrawals, "fast bridge" services have emerged in the Ethereum world that advance the funds to the user in exchange for a fee, taking on the risk during the challenge window. Hyper could have similar services for those needing immediate liquidity. Concrete example: today on Optimism there are numerous services allowing one to "withdraw quickly" by paying a fee of 0.1–0.5%. The service advances the funds to the user, and then collects its own capital after the challenge window. It is a healthy market that mitigates the waiting problem for those needing speed.

Question 4: How does Bitcoin "verify" a timelock? If Bitcoin does not understand complex smart contracts, how can it understand a timelock structure?

Bitcoin understands a restricted set of timelock operations through specific opcodes in Script. **OP_CHECKLOCKTIMEVERIFY** verifies that a certain timestamp has been reached. **OP_CHECKSEQUENCEVERIFY** verifies that a certain number of blocks has passed since the transaction's creation. These opcodes are standard Bitcoin primitives, supported by the main protocol, and they do not require "smart contracts" in the Ethereum sense of the term. Bitcoin verifies the timelocks through these primitives, without having to understand the rollup's broader logic. **In practice, a timelock structure for Hyper would be built by combining these opcodes with other elements (Taproot signatures, hashes, and so on)** in such a way that the spending conditions respect the required temporal constraints. Bitcoin validates the conditions in the standard way; Hyper leans on Bitcoin for the verification. Concrete example: the Lightning Network extensively uses OP_CHECKSEQUENCEVERIFY to build its payment channels. It is the mechanism that makes it possible to unilaterally close a channel after a certain time, even if the counterparty is offline. The same family of primitives can be used to build a rollup's challenge windows.

Question 5: If the hybrid model you describe is probable, how can I predict which specific combination Hyper will choose?

You cannot predict it with certainty, but you can observe the signals the team communicates in the coming months. **First signal: the research posts subsequent to the December 2025 one.** The team will probably publish updates deepening specific techniques, and those updates will gradually reveal the design choices. **Second signal: the announcements of partnerships with infrastructure services.** If Hyper announces partnerships with services specialized in Taproot, it is an indicator of technical direction. **Third signal: the published benchmarks.** When the team releases numbers on costs and performance, the specific characteristics will make it possible to deduce the underlying model. **Fourth signal: the security audits.** When the pre-mainnet audits are published, they will describe the architecture in detail, and the combination of techniques will be explicit. **Fifth signal: the content of the open-source code**, if and when it is released. For developers, reading the code is the most direct way to understand the technical choices. Concrete example: Optimism, before launching its own fraud proofs, published dozens of research documents that gradually clarified the architecture. For Hyper a similar trajectory can be expected: progressive clarity through successive communications, with the final combination made explicit close to the mainnet launch.

Question 6: What happens if in the future Bitcoin introduces new opcodes or capabilities that would make the current techniques obsolete?

It is a real possibility and it must be considered. The Bitcoin community has been debating for years the introduction of new opcodes that could enable more powerful rollup mechanisms. **OP_CAT, in particular, is a proposal that would concatenate strings in Script and that — combined with other primitives — would enable the direct verification of complex cryptographic proofs on Bitcoin.** If OP_CAT were approved, it would be possible to build fraud proofs verifiable directly by Bitcoin, eliminating the dependence on timelocks and significantly improving the rollups' security model. **Hyper should be able to integrate new Bitcoin capabilities into its own model when they emerge.** The March 2026 research post on "multi-decade scalability" explicitly emphasizes the importance of a modular architecture that can evolve over time. So, even if Hyper were launched with a certain anchoring model, it should be able to migrate to better models when Bitcoin allows it. **The risk is that migrations of this kind still require time and coordination.** If OP_CAT were approved two years after Hyper's launch, the system would have to manage the transition while maintaining operations during the change. It is a change-management risk, not a fundamental security one, but it must be considered. Concrete example: Ethereum has introduced various upgrades over time (London, Shanghai, Cancun) that significantly modified the environment for rollups. Well-designed rollups managed to integrate the changes, some even drawing advantage from them. For Hyper, similar resilience is expected, but it is a factor to monitor.

⁂

12.8 — WHAT TO TAKE AWAY FROM THIS CHAPTER

Bitcoin offers three main families of techniques for anchoring state commitments: OP_RETURN (the simplest), Taproot (the most powerful), timelock structures (with a temporal dimension). Each family has specific technical characteristics and natural scopes of application.

OP_RETURN is Bitcoin's "note in the margin," simple and universally understandable, with a limit of 80 bytes per output. It is suited for simple anchorings and for the initial phase of projects like Hyper.

Taproot is the qualitative leap of 2021, with Schnorr signatures and script trees enabling complex commitments in externally compact transactions. It is more expressive but requires greater implementation complexity.

Timelock structures add the time factor, enabling challenge windows that allow the community to refute wrong commitments. They are the pattern used by Ethereum's Optimistic Rollups.

The hybrid model Hyper will probably use will combine elements of the three families, with OP_RETURN or Taproot for regular anchorings, timelocks for the security model, and advanced Taproot for special cases.

The anchoring costs are amortized over the rollup's transactions, and under normal conditions they represent a small fraction of the cost per transaction. But costs can rise significantly in periods of high Bitcoin congestion.

The choice of the specific techniques is still open within the Hyper team. The December 2025 research post explores the options without committing to a definitive choice. The progressive transparency in the coming months will reveal the final direction.

For end users, the technical anchoring choices are largely invisible. The experience is influenced indirectly through costs and finality, but everyday decisions do not depend on these details.

For those evaluating the project, the clarity with which the team describes the anchoring choices is a thermometer of maturity. Detailed technical documentation, independent audits, transparent benchmarks are the signals to look for.

Bitcoin could in the future introduce new opcodes making more sophisticated anchoring mechanisms possible. Hyper must be designed to integrate them when they emerge, according to the philosophy of "multi-decade scalability" the team has made explicit.

Chapter 12 ends here. We have understood the three main techniques available for anchoring state commitments to Bitcoin, the characteristics of each, and how Hyper will probably combine them in a hybrid model. In ***Chapter 13 — The Anchoring Frequency: the Rhythm That Decides Costs and Finality****, we will go down into the detail of the temporal dimension, seeing how the choice of the anchorings' frequency is one of the system's most impactful parameters, and how Hyper is treating it as an adaptive parameter instead of a fixed rule.*

NOTES

1 OP_RETURN makes it possible to write up to 83 bytes of arbitrary data as an unspendable output. Introduced in Bitcoin Core 0.9 (2014), it is today the most used tool for the protocols anchored to Bitcoin.

2 Taproot is the Bitcoin upgrade activated on November 14, 2021 (BIP 340, 341, 342). It introduces Schnorr signatures and script-path semantics that make it possible to hide the content until the moment of the spend.

Three *roads* for anchoring Hyper to Bitcoin

OP_RETURN, Taproot, and timelock: different primitives for **publishing**, **committing**, and **timing** the rollup's state.

1 The state becomes a root

The rollup compresses its own state into a **32-byte Merkle root**. This root must be anchored on Bitcoin immutably and verifiably.

The rollup must write little, but commit a lot.

ROLLUP STATE
accounts · batches
programs · data
→ 8F3A…91C7
MERKLE ROOT 32B
→ ₿
BITCOIN L1

2 OP_RETURN: publishing a compact note

OP_RETURN inserts a small datum into a Bitcoin transaction, like **an unspendable annotation**.

ADVANTAGES simple transparent readable by everyone public checkpoints

LIMITS limited space public datum variable fees 1 tx per anchoring

It is the **most direct** *road for writing a Merkle root on Bitcoin.*

BITCOIN TRANSACTION	
INPUT	the tx's funds
OUTPUT	spendable
OP_RETURN	8F3A…91C7

3 Taproot: committing richer structures

Taproot hides script structures behind a compact output and reveals only the necessary branch when needed.

ADVANTAGES more expressive compact (cooperative case) selective revelation

LIMITS complex implementation specialist tooling accurate audits

Taproot does not publish just a datum: **it commits a structure of possibilities**.

TAPROOT OUTPUT KEY
internal key + Merkle root script

Cooperative signature · Recovery path · Temporal condition · Alternative rule

4 Timelock: adding the time factor

Timelocks do not publish the commitment and do not verify the root on their own: they establish **when an output can be spent**.

CLTV
absolute deadline

CSV
relative wait from confirmation

USES challenges withdrawals recovery bridge security

proposed commitment → checking window → finality / challenge

ⓘ A timelock **does not decide whether a root is correct**: it serves within a broader construction. *Time becomes a security condition.*

5 Composable primitives, not stark alternatives

The rollup's state — batches, accounts, Merkle root, data in the DA layer

↓

Publication / commitment — OP_RETURN + Taproot

↓

Temporal layer — CLTV / CSV: waits, withdrawals, recovery

↓

Validation and bridge — proofs, protocol rules, BTC release

↓

₿ Bitcoin L1 — the anchoring's immutability

PRIMITIVE	ROLE
OP_RETURN	publishes a compact root
Taproot	commits structured conditions
Timelock	regulates when an output is spendable
Proof / Bridge	validates the transition
Data Avail.	makes the raw data available

More modules do not automatically mean more security: **every combination must be designed, tested, and audited.**

THE KEY POINT

OP_RETURN publishes. Taproot commits. The timelock times. But the rollup's security is born only when these primitives are **integrated with proofs, bridges, available data, and verifiable rules.**

PART IV · THE SETTLEMENT LAYER

Chapter 13
The Anchoring Frequency

The rhythm that decides costs and finality

⁂

13.1 — The Beat That Ties Two Worlds

In Chapter 5 I introduced an image I want to take up again and develop in depth: **the anchoring as the rollup's heartbeat.** A beat that, periodically, synchronizes the fast world of internal execution with the slow, immutable world of Bitcoin. Between one beat and the next, the rollup lives in a kind of controlled apnea: it processes transactions, updates states, keeps applications running, but its work is still "pending" with respect to Bitcoin. When the beat arrives, everything that happened in the previous apnea is crystallized on the Bitcoin blockchain, becomes part of the immutable history, and the rollup begins another apnea.

TABLE 13.1 **ANCHORING FREQUENCY: CHOICES AND CONSEQUENCES**

Frequency	Cost (per month)	Bitcoin finality	UX latency
Every BTC block (≈ 10 min)	High: ≈ 4,380 commits / month	≈ 1 hour (six confirmations[1])	Low: the user sees rapid confirmation
Every 6 blocks (≈ 1 h)	Medium: ≈ 730 commits / month	≈ 7 hours	Medium: reasonable for most cases
Every 144 blocks (≈ 1 day)	Low: ≈ 30 commits / month	≈ 25 hours	High: heavy for UX, acceptable for batch settlement
On-demand (forced exit)	Variable: the user pays	Variable	Controlled by the user requesting the exit

Central trade-off: *frequent anchorings cost more but offer rapid finality; rare anchorings reduce costs but lengthen settlement times. The choice depends on the mix of applications running on top: active DeFi requires high frequency, enterprise settlement can tolerate low frequency.*

This image, which works well at the intuitive level, hides one of the design decisions richest in consequences of the entire Bitcoin Hyper project: **how long must each apnea last?** Put in more technical terms, **how frequently does the rollup publish the state commitments on Bitcoin?** It is a question that seems to have an obvious answer — "as often as possible, to maximize security" — but that in reality hides a three-dimensional compromise where every choice pays a price. Frequency, costs, and finality are three vertices of a triangle, and one cannot optimize on all three simultaneously: moving toward one vertex means moving away from the others.

In this chapter I want to go down inside this triangle. First, describe the three constraints and why they interact in a non-trivial way. Then, see how Bitcoin Hyper has chosen to face the decision, treating frequency as an adaptive parameter instead of a fixed rule, according to what the team made explicit in the January 2026 research post. Finally, understand what it concretely means for users, for the system's economic model, and for the long-term judgment on the project. It is a chapter that has much to say also for those who will judge other rollups in the future, because the choice of the anchoring frequency is one of the most revealing parameters of the technical and economic maturity of any Layer 2 system.[a]

⁂

13.2 — The Three Dimensions of the Compromise

Let us begin with a rigorous analysis of the three forces pulling at each other when the anchoring frequency[b] is chosen. Understanding them separately is the prerequisite for understanding them together, and it is the prerequisite for understanding why a single "optimal" choice does not exist.[c]

TABLE 13.2 **THE THREE DIMENSIONS OF THE COMPROMISE ON THE ANCHORING FREQUENCY.**

Dimension	Frequent anchoring	Rare anchoring
Finality[d]	Rapid	Slower
Costs on Bitcoin	Higher	Lower
Operational security[e]	Greater	Lesser

The three dimensions move in opposite directions: improving finality and security with frequent anchorings raises the costs on Bitcoin, while reducing costs lengthens the finality times. It is this conflict that makes an "optimal" frequency valid for every case impossible.

[a] **Layer 2.** A network built "on top of" a main blockchain (here Bitcoin, the Layer 1) to process transactions more rapidly and cheaply, while however periodically anchoring its own results to the underlying chain to inherit its security. A rollup is a type of Layer 2.

[b] **Anchoring frequency.** How often the rollup publishes ("anchors") on Bitcoin the consolidated state of its own transactions. Anchoring often means consolidating sooner and more frequently; anchoring rarely means doing it at longer intervals. It is the variable around which the entire compromise described in this chapter revolves.

[c] **Trade-off.** A situation in which improving one objective necessarily worsens another, so that a perfect solution does not exist but only different balancings depending on the priorities. Here the three objectives — rapid finality, low costs, and security — cannot all be maximized together.

[d] **Finality.** The moment from which a transaction is considered definitive and no longer reversible. In a rollup anchored to Bitcoin, full finality is reached when the state is recorded on the mother chain: the more frequent the anchoring, the more rapidly transactions become irreversible.

[e] **Operational security.** The degree of protection of the system in everyday functioning, tied to how long the state remains not yet anchored on Bitcoin. Frequent anchorings reduce this exposed interval, and with it the margin within which a fault or an attack could take effect.

FIGURE 13.1 **THE COMPROMISE TRIANGLE OF THE ANCHORING FREQUENCY.**

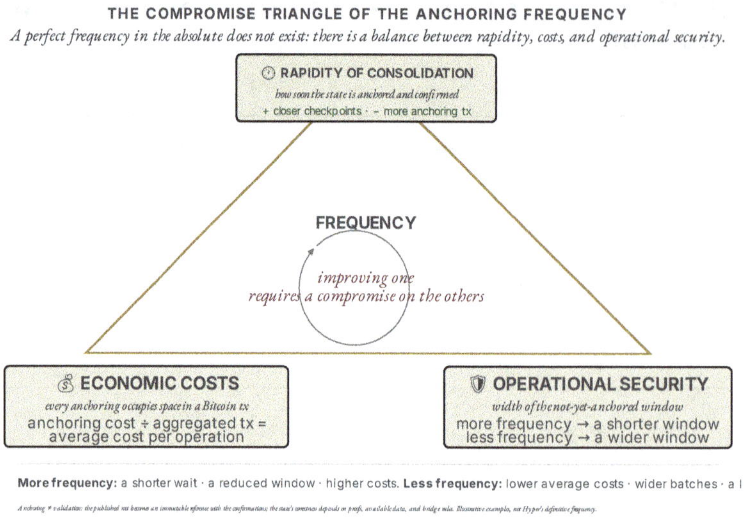

The choice of the anchoring frequency is born from the tension among three forces. The rapidity of consolidation measures how soon transactions are crystallized on Bitcoin: it affects, for example, the times for withdrawing funds. The economic costs grow with the number of anchorings, because each one is a Bitcoin transaction that pays network fees, costs then transferred to the users. Operational security depends on the width of the not-yet-anchored window between one commitment and the next: the shorter it is, the smaller the operational exposure and the complexity of certain recovery procedures — without this eliminating the risks tied to the sequencer, to censorship, or to ordering. The three forces pull in opposite directions: improving one means yielding on at least one other. The concrete choice depends on Bitcoin fees, transaction volume, the proof system, the bridge rules, and the protocol's priorities.

First dimension: the security perceived by users, expressed through finality. When a state commitment is anchored on Bitcoin, the corresponding rollup state becomes effectively immutable. Everything that happened before that commitment is crystallized forever. Between one anchoring and the next, however, the rollup's state is in a gray zone: alive in the sequencer's machines and in the data availability layer's nodes, but not yet sealed by Bitcoin's power. **The more frequent the anchorings, the smaller the window during which the system is in the gray zone. The smaller the window, the more rapidly users reach full finality for their own transactions.** It is intuitive: anchoring every five minutes means all transactions are crystallized within a few minutes of execution. Anchoring every hour means waits of up to an hour before finality.

For certain categories of operations, this difference is crucial. **The most important case is the withdrawal of bitcoin from the rollup toward the Bitcoin blockchain.** To withdraw their bitcoin, the user must wait for the state commitment relating to their own withdrawal to be anchored and to have reached Bitcoin's full finality (six confirmations, about an hour). If the rollup anchors every five minutes, the complete withdrawal takes a little more than an hour from execution. If it anchors every hour, the complete withdrawal takes at least two hours. **For exchanges between exchanges, for movements of capital, for any operation where time counts, the anchoring frequency translates directly into waiting time for the users.**

Second dimension: the economic costs borne by the system. Every anchoring is a Bitcoin transaction that pays network fees. Under normal conditions, a standard transaction costs a few dollars. Under conditions of high congestion, it can cost tens or hundreds of dollars. **The more frequent the anchorings, the higher the system's total costs.** It is direct mathematics: 48 anchorings a day (one every half hour) cost ten times more than 4–5 anchorings a day (one every five hours), at the same cost per transaction.

These costs are in some form passed on to the rollup's users, through the fees they pay for their own transactions. **A rollup with low anchoring costs can offer lower user fees, and be more competitive against alternatives.** A rollup with high anchoring costs must necessarily transfer those costs to the users, and this makes it less attractive. In a market where several Bitcoin Layer 2 solutions exist, the structure of the anchoring costs becomes an important competition factor.

Third dimension: the system's technical security, expressed through the vulnerability window. Between one anchoring and the next, the rollup's state is still "modifiable" in the sense that, if the sequencer misbehaves or if something goes wrong, there are potential risks. A shorter vulnerability window means less time for problems to manifest. A longer window means more exposure to adverse scenarios.

This point has important nuances worth explaining. **It is not that during the vulnerability window the system is "insecure" in an absolute sense.** As we saw in Chapter 5, even during the gray window there are significant guarantees: the sequencer cannot steal the funds, the transactions signed by the users cannot be forged, the state is verifiable by anyone with access to the raw data. **But some things are more vulnerable during the window**: the possibility of censorship by the sequencer is at its maximum, potential MEV is more extractable, the effects of system bugs are wider if they manifest. A shorter window reduces these minor vulnerabilities, even if it never completely eliminates the dependence on the sequencer during the apnea.

The three dimensions — finality for users, economic costs, technical security — interact in a non-trivial way. **Improving one means worsening at least one of the other two.** High frequency = rapid finality + high technical security + high costs. Low frequency = low costs + slow finality + weaker technical security. A choice that optimizes everything does not exist. **Only the choice that best balances the compromise according to the project's priorities and the users' preferences exists.**

⁂

13.3 — Hyper's Choice: the Adaptive Frequency

Having understood the three constraints, we can appreciate the direction indicated by the Hyper team: not fixing forever a single interval between the anchorings, but providing a system capable of adapting to the conditions of the moment. The objective is to find, case by case, a reasonable balance among rapidity, security, and costs.

In the simplest models, the anchorings are published according to a preset rhythm: for example every thirty minutes or every hour. This solution is easy to understand and to manage, but it presents an evident limit: it uses the same interval even when the network's conditions change profoundly.

FIGURE 13.2 **HIGH FREQUENCY VERSUS LOW FREQUENCY: WHAT IS GAINED AND WHAT IS GIVEN UP.**

Dimension	More frequent anchorings	More spaced-out anchorings
Rapidity	The next checkpoint arrives sooner	The next checkpoint arrives later
Costs	The transactions published on Bitcoin increase	Costs can be distributed over wider batches
The user's wait	Generally shorter	Generally longer
The system's balance	More rapidity, but greater costs	More savings, but less speed

The adaptive solution tries to avoid both extremes, regulating the rhythm of the anchorings according to the network's conditions.

An adaptive approach tries instead to observe what is happening on the network. When Bitcoin fees are contained and the rollup is processing many transactions, it can be convenient to publish the anchorings more often. When fees rise and traffic is reduced, it can be more sensible to wait a little longer and gather a greater number of operations in the same cycle.

To work well, this mechanism will have to follow clear, understandable rules. It will be important to know within what limits the frequency can vary, in what situations the system can modify its own rhythm, and who can intervene on the parameters over time. These aspects will have to be explained precisely in the definitive specifications.

The advantages are intuitive. The system can avoid excessive costs when the Bitcoin network is congested and can increase the rhythm of the anchorings when conditions are favorable. In this way, the frequency is not chosen once and for all, but is regulated seeking the best possible balance between economic sustainability and the user's experience.

Naturally, a more flexible system is also more delicate to design. The rules must be public, stable, and verifiable. Users must be able to understand why the rhythm of the anchorings changes and what consequences it produces on waiting times. Flexibility is useful only if it does not turn into unpredictability.

For Hyper, the adaptive frequency therefore represents an interesting direction. It does not automatically guarantee the best result, but it allows the protocol to avoid an overly rigid rule and to react to the network's real conditions. The system's quality will depend on the clarity of the rules, on the transparency of the parameters, and on the team's capacity to demonstrate that the adaptation works in a stable, predictable way.

⁂

13.4 — Concrete Scenarios: How the System Would Behave under Different Conditions

To give concreteness to the concept of adaptive frequency, let us imagine how Hyper would behave in different market scenarios. These are obviously speculations, because the system is not yet in production and the specific parameters are not public, but they are useful for building intuition on how adaptivity translates into concrete behavior.

Scenario one: normal conditions. Bitcoin is having a calm market, fees are in the range of a few dollars per standard transaction, the rollup has a sustained but not exceptional volume. Under these conditions, Hyper probably anchors every 20–30 minutes, keeping a good balance between reasonable finality and sustainable costs. Users see their withdrawals toward Bitcoin completed in about an hour, the fees on the rollup are low, the system runs smoothly. **It is the "base" case for which the system is designed, and probably the one in which it will spend most of its time.**

FIGURE 13.3 **HOW THE ADAPTIVE FREQUENCY RESPONDS TO FIVE MARKET SCENARIOS.**

Scenario	Conditions	Hyper's response	It optimizes for
1 · Normal	Low Bitcoin fees, sustained volume	Anchors every 20–30 min; withdrawals in ~1 hour	Balance
2 · High BTC congestion	Fees at $50–100 per transaction	Slows to every 1–2 hours; withdrawals in 2–3 hours	Economic sustainability
3 · Low rollup volume	A few hundred tx/day, normal fees	Slows to ~1 hour to amortize costs	Per-transaction economics
4 · Demand for finality	High-value apps, critical finality	Accelerates to every 10–15 min; higher fees	User experience
5 · Network stress	Anomaly or suspect sequencer	Accelerates temporarily; reduced window	Security

Hyper does not use an ideal fixed frequency: it adapts its behavior to the conditions of the moment, optimizing case by case for finality, costs, or security. Under normal conditions it seeks balance; when Bitcoin fees explode it slows down to stay sustainable; with little volume it reduces the cadence so as not to let the cost per transaction rise; when an application demands rapid finality it accelerates, accepting greater costs; and faced with an anomaly it tightens the frequency to reduce the vulnerability window. The scenarios are illustrative — the system is not yet in production — but they make concrete the idea of a behavior that changes with the context.

Scenario two: high Bitcoin congestion. For some reason (a market event, a controversial fork, a new wave of Ordinals), Bitcoin fees rise dramatically, reaching $50–100 per standard transaction. Under these conditions, anchoring every 30 minutes becomes prohibitively expensive: the system would spend thousands of dollars a day in fees alone, and the costs would end up on the users. **Hyper would probably react by slowing the frequency**, anchoring perhaps every 1–2 hours. Finality for users would lengthen (withdrawals in 2–3 hours), but the system remains economically sustainable. It is a necessary compromise under adverse conditions.

Scenario three: low rollup volume. The rollup is in its initial phase, with a few hundred transactions a day. Bitcoin fees are normal. Under these conditions, anchoring every 30 minutes means the anchoring cost is amortized over few transactions, making the final cost per transaction rise. **Hyper could slightly slow the frequency** (anchoring every hour instead of every half hour) to improve the economics, accepting a small increase in finality times. When the volume grows, the frequency can rise again automatically.

Scenario four: high demand for rapid finality. A large financial application on the rollup is processing high-value transactions where rapid finality is critical. The community could demand, through the governance mechanism, a higher anchoring frequency to satisfy this need. **Hyper could anchor every 10–15 minutes**, accepting higher costs in exchange for rapid finality. The rollup's fees would rise slightly, but the user experience would improve for the applications that need it.

Scenario five: network stress. An anomaly is detected in the rollup's functioning, perhaps a suspect behavior of the sequencer or an emerging bug. **Hyper could temporarily increase the anchoring frequency** to reduce the vulnerability window, even if the cost rises. It is an automatic response to conditions of elevated risk, similar to how a security system "tightens" when it detects threats.

These scenarios are illustrative, but they make concrete the idea of adaptivity. **The system does not always behave the same way: it behaves in the best way given the conditions of the moment.** When conditions are favorable, it optimizes for rapid finality. When they are unfavorable, it optimizes for economic sustainability. When they are critical, it optimizes for security. **It is intelligent behavior that requires a whole infrastructure of observability, decision, and actuation**, and it is one of the points where Hyper's engineering design will be judged.

⁂

13.5 — The Relationship with Bitcoin's Blocks: a Necessary Synchronization

A technical detail deserving attention is the relationship between the rollup's anchoring frequency and the frequency of Bitcoin's blocks. **They are not independent things**: one leans on the other, and understanding the synchronization helps in understanding the system's real times.

Bitcoin produces a block every 10 minutes on average. This is a fixed parameter of the protocol, regulated by the "difficulty adjustment" that keeps the block time stable independently of the network's total computational power. **Bitcoin's block time is the "base beat" on which any anchoring must synchronize.**

A Bitcoin transaction containing a Hyper state commitment must be included in a block to be recorded. Typically, a transaction is included in the first or second block after being sent, although in periods of high congestion it can take more blocks. **So, from the moment Hyper sends an anchoring transaction, about 10–20 minutes pass before the commitment is recorded in a Bitcoin block.**

But "recorded in a block" does not yet mean "definitively anchored." The Bitcoin community considers finality robust only after six confirmations (six blocks subsequent to the block containing the transaction), which correspond to about an hour. For lower value levels fewer confirmations can suffice, but for full finality the standard number is six.

Putting these times together: **a commitment anchored by Hyper reaches full Bitcoin finality about an hour after being published.** This is a structural time cost, independent of the frequency with which Hyper chooses to anchor. If Hyper anchors every 30 minutes, the commitment of moment T reaches finality at moment T+1 hour approximately. If it anchors every hour, the commitment of moment T reaches finality at moment T+1 hour approximately, but only if that commitment has been published; the previous ones have similar times.

FIGURE 13.4 **FROM THE COMMITMENT TO FINALITY: THE CADENCE OF BITCOIN'S BLOCKS DOMINATES THE ROLLUP'S TIMES.**

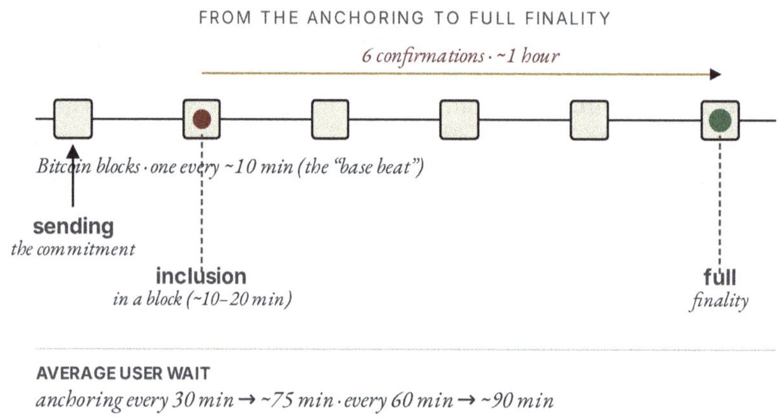

Hyper can optimize the moment of the anchoring, but it cannot compress Bitcoin's finality time: it is the structural price to pay for inheriting its security. Bitcoin produces a block every ~10 minutes — the base beat. Once the commitment is sent, the transaction enters a block within ~10–20 minutes, but robust finality arrives only after six confirmations, about an hour. The anchoring frequency does not shorten the finality of the single commitment: it reduces the user's average wait (≈75 min anchoring every 30 minutes, ≈90 min every 60). Synchronizing the sending right after a new block minimizes the inclusion time, but Bitcoin's confirmation hour remains incompressible.

The anchoring frequency does not reduce the finality time for the single commitment, but it reduces the user's average waiting time. Let us see it concretely. If Hyper anchors every 30 minutes, a user transaction executed at the beginning of an apnea (right after an anchoring) must wait 30 minutes for the next anchoring, plus an hour for Bitcoin finality: a total of 90 minutes. A transaction executed at the end of an apnea (shortly before the next anchoring) waits only a few minutes plus an hour: a total of about 60 minutes. **On average, the total wait is 75 minutes.** If Hyper anchored every 60 minutes, the average wait would rise to 90 minutes.

To optimize further, Hyper could synchronize the anchorings with Bitcoin's blocks, anchoring right after every new block to minimize the inclusion time. But even with this optimization, **the full finality time remains dominated by Bitcoin's confirmation hour**, and this is a parameter Hyper cannot control. **It is the structural price of leaning on Bitcoin, and it is a price worth paying to obtain Bitcoin security on one's own states.**

⁂

13.6 — Implications for Users: What Changes in the Practical Experience

All this technical discussion has concrete implications for the user experience, and it deserves to be translated into practical scenarios to understand what changes in the everyday use of the system.

FIGURE 13.5 **WHO PERCEIVES THE ANCHORING FREQUENCY, AND WHO DOES NOT.**

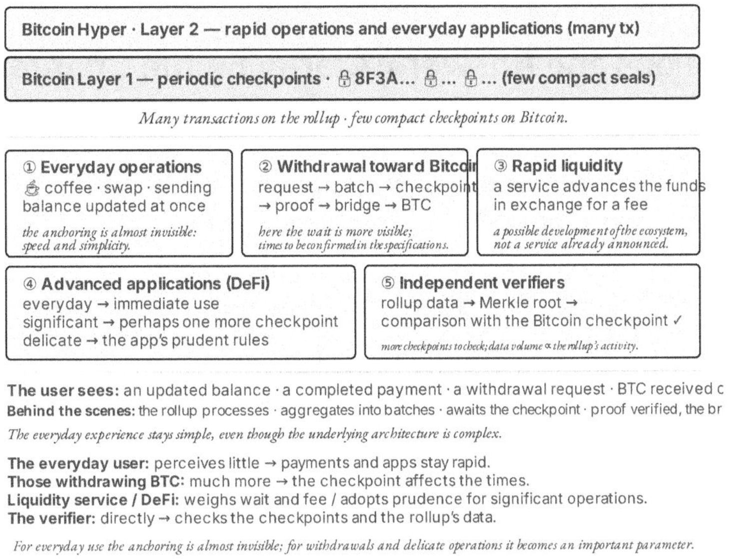

The frequency of the anchorings stays almost invisible in the everyday operations on the Layer 2, but it can affect the times of withdrawals toward Bitcoin, the rapid-liquidity services, the cautions of financial applications, and the work of independent verifiers.

For the everyday transactions on the rollup — payments, exchanges, interactions with applications — the anchoring frequency is almost invisible. The user experiences transactions as instantaneous because they act on the rollup's current state. Bitcoin finality is a long-term guarantee that does not influence the immediate experience. **Buying a coffee, sending a payment to a friend, doing a swap on a DEX — all these operations feel the same regardless of the anchoring frequency.**

For withdrawals toward original Bitcoin — the case most sensitive to frequency — the difference is significant. If Hyper anchors every 30 minutes, a user requesting the withdrawal must wait on average 75 minutes for full finality. If it anchors every hour, the average wait is 90 minutes. If it anchors every 5 minutes (under favorable conditions), the average wait falls to about 65 minutes. **For most users, these differences are acceptable**: anyone familiar with Bitcoin knows that "real" operations require waits on the order of the hour. But for applications requiring speed (cross-chain arbitrage, high-frequency trading), the difference can be important.

For the fast bridges that advance funds — services giving immediate liquidity in exchange for a fee, taking on the risk during the wait for finality — the adaptive frequency creates complications. If the frequency is predictable, the fast bridge can calculate its own cost of capital precisely. If it is adaptive, the cost varies, and the fast bridge must be designed to adapt. Probably the fast bridges that will emerge on Hyper will have dynamic pricing models reflecting the current anchoring frequency.

For sophisticated DeFi applications — lending protocols, derivatives, oracles — the anchoring frequency influences certain technical risks. A longer vulnerability window means more time during which sophisticated attacks based on the gray zone could occur. Applications will have to be designed keeping the predictable window in mind, perhaps implementing additional safeguards for operations of particularly high value.

For node operators and independent validators — those wanting to verify the rollup's state independently — the frequency determines how much activity there is to monitor. A high frequency means more anchorings to verify, more data to download, more operational load. A low frequency reduces these loads. For the system's progressive decentralization, the optimal frequency is the one that allows more independent operators to participate without requiring excessive resources.

In short, the anchoring frequency is not just an internal technical parameter of the rollup. **It is a parameter that propagates through the entire ecosystem**, influencing the user experience, the economic models of the related services, the technical risks of the applications, and the feasibility of decentralization. This is why Hyper is facing the decision with care, and this is why transparency on the specific choices will be important when they arrive.

⁂

13.7 — Questions and Answers: Clarifying the Chapter's Concepts

Question 1: Why does Hyper not simply choose the highest possible anchoring frequency to maximize security?

For the economic reason we described: every anchoring costs, and the costs are passed on to the users. **An excessively high frequency would make the rollup non-competitive from the cost point of view**, and potentially unsustainable in the initial phase when the transaction volume is still low. There is also a second reason: Bitcoin has limited total capacity, and every anchoring transaction competes with other Bitcoin transactions for the space in the blocks. **If many rollups anchored very frequently, we would saturate the space available on Bitcoin**, making fees rise for everyone, including the rollup itself. The optimal frequency is the one that uses Bitcoin efficiently, sufficient for security but not wasted. Concrete example: if Hyper anchored every minute, that would be 1,440 anchorings a day. At $5 each (under normal conditions), that would be $7,200 a day in fees alone. Over 100,000 rollup transactions a day, the cost per transaction would be 7 cents for the anchoring alone — high compared with the competing Ethereum Layer 2s, which are under a cent. The typical adaptive frequency of 20–30 minutes under normal conditions brings the cost per transaction well under a cent.

Question 2: If the frequency is adaptive, how do I as a user know when to expect a transaction's finality?

The system should expose this information through standard tools. **The rollup's explorer should show, for every transaction, the current status** ("executed on the rollup," "included in a batch," "anchored on Bitcoin," "finality reached") with specific timestamps. **Integrated wallets should show similar information**, perhaps with estimates of the finality time based on the current frequency. **For developers, the rollup's APIs should make it possible to query the finality status in real time.** Without these interfaces, adaptivity becomes opacity, and this is the main risk of the model. The Hyper team will have to invest significantly in observability tools to make adaptivity transparent. Concrete example: on the Ethereum blockchain, systems like Etherscan show for every transaction detailed information on how many confirmations it has received, when it was included in the block, and so on. For Hyper analogous functionality is expected, adapted to the rollup-Bitcoin context with the additional dimension of variable frequency.

Question 3: Does the adaptive model not risk being manipulated by the sequencer for its own purposes (extracting more MEV, censoring, and so on)?

It is a legitimate concern, and it requires specific safeguards. **The adaptive model must be governed by public, verifiable rules**, not by discretionary decisions of the sequencer. The rules specify under what conditions the frequency rises or falls, and any modification of the rules must pass through transparent governance mechanisms. **Moreover, the system should have minimum frequency limits** that the sequencer cannot violate even under stress conditions: for example, "anchor at least once every 2 hours regardless of conditions." This prevents scenarios where the sequencer slows the frequency indefinitely to extract more MEV. **Even with these safeguards, some margin of manipulation remains possible**, and this is one of the residual risks of rollups with a single sequencer. The progressive decentralization of the sequencer is also a response to this risk: with multiple sequencers, individual manipulation becomes more difficult. Concrete example: on Ethereum, there have been documented cases of block proposers who manipulated the inclusion of transactions to extract MEV. The decentralization of proposing is a structural response to this problem, and for Hyper a similar trajectory is expected.

Question 4: What are the typical finality times of the other rollups, for comparison?

On Ethereum, the times vary significantly by type of rollup. **Optimism and Arbitrum (Optimistic Rollups)** have instantaneous "soft" finality (transaction included in a batch within a few seconds) but "hard" finality of seven days (the challenge window). **zkSync and Starknet (ZK-Rollups)** have instantaneous "soft" finality and "hard" finality of a few hours (the time to produce and verify the proof). **For withdrawals toward Ethereum**, the Optimistic Rollups require the seven days, the ZK-Rollups the hours. **For Bitcoin Hyper**, the times will be structurally longer because of Bitcoin's slower finality. Instantaneous "soft" finality will be similar to that of the Ethereum rollups (transactions executed immediately on the rollup), but "hard" finality will be dominated by Bitcoin's confirmation hour plus the anchoring frequency. **The orders of magnitude are: 1–2 hours for most cases, with variations according to market conditions.** It is an acceptable level for most use cases, but significantly slower than the ZK rollups on Ethereum. Concrete example: for a moderate-value withdrawal from Optimism to Ethereum, there are fast-bridge services making it possible in a few minutes by paying a 0.1–0.3% fee. For Bitcoin Hyper, analogous services are expected that mitigate the wait for those needing speed.

Question 5: Does the adaptivity of the frequency mean the user experience will be inconsistent over time?

To a certain extent yes, but in a manageable way. **The experience for the transactions internal to the rollup does not change significantly**: users continue to do swaps, payments, interactions with applications in real time, regardless of the frequency. **What changes is the experience for the operations depending on finality**: withdrawals toward Bitcoin, high-value operations, certain cross-chain operations. Even for these, the variability is limited: we are talking about time differences on the order of tens of minutes, not hours. **For normal users, these differences are perceptible but not dramatic.** For sophisticated actors (traders, market makers, arbitrageurs), the differences can be significant but they are managed through specialized tools (fast bridges, dynamic pricing models). The inconsistency is there, but it is not chaotic: it is governed by predictable rules and adapted to market conditions. Concrete example: even today, the time to confirm a Bitcoin transaction varies significantly with market conditions. Users accept this variability as part of using Bitcoin. For Hyper, users are expected to accept a similar, perhaps more contained, variability.

Question 6: What happens if during an apnea the sequencer breaks down or misbehaves? Does the adaptive frequency not increase the apnea's duration?

It is a concern that deserves attention. **Under pathological conditions, the apnea's duration counts**: if the sequencer is dishonest, a longer window gives it more time to do potential damage. For this reason, even in the adaptive model, the frequency never falls below a preset minimum. **The system always maintains a "liveness guarantee"**: regardless of market conditions, anchoring at least with a certain minimum frequency. This limits the maximum risk. **Moreover, the rollups' security model is designed so that during the apnea the sequencer cannot steal the funds**: it can censor, it can delay, but it cannot unilaterally alter the state. **The more sophisticated defenses** — fraud proofs, validity proofs, forced inclusion — operate on the anchored commitment, not on the apnea's duration. Reducing the duration helps marginally but is not the main defense. For Hyper, the main defense comes from the rollup's overall architecture, not only from the anchoring frequency. Concrete example: if Optimism, in periods of stress, decided to anchor every 6 hours instead of every hour, it would not mean users lose their funds — it would only mean full finality is slower. Fundamental security is preserved by other mechanisms. For Hyper the same logic applies.

⁂

13.8 — WHAT TO TAKE AWAY FROM THIS CHAPTER

The anchoring frequency is a key parameter of the rollup's design, balancing three dimensions in tension with one another: finality for users, economic costs, technical security.

A universally optimal frequency does not exist. More frequent = rapid finality + better security + high costs. Less frequent = low costs + slow finality + a longer vulnerability window.

Bitcoin Hyper has chosen to treat the frequency as an adaptive parameter, regulated dynamically according to market conditions (Bitcoin fees, the rollup's volume, network stress). This choice was made explicit in the January 2026 research post.

Adaptivity has advantages over fixed frequencies: economic resilience under stress conditions, continuous optimization, the capacity to respond to long-term evolutions. It requires however greater implementation complexity and transparency in the rules.

Full finality is structurally tied to Bitcoin's times: the six-block confirmation hour is about an hour, regardless of the frequency chosen by the rollup. The frequency influences the users' average wait, not the minimum finality time.

For the everyday transactions on the rollup, the anchoring frequency is almost invisible. The user experiences instantaneous speed because they act on the current state. Bitcoin finality is a long-term guarantee not felt in immediate use.

For withdrawals toward original Bitcoin, the frequency translates into waiting time. Differences of 15–30 minutes between scenarios, acceptable for most users, mitigable through fast bridges for those needing speed.

Adaptivity requires observability infrastructure: explorers, wallets, APIs showing the current finality status for every transaction. Without these tools, adaptivity becomes opacity.

The adaptive frequency can be manipulated if not well designed: transparent governance of the rules, minimum frequency limits, and in the long term the decentralization of the sequencer to reduce the residual risks are needed.

For those evaluating the project, the clarity with which the team specifies the adaptivity rules is a thermometer of maturity. Publication of the specific parameters, simulations under different scenarios, audits of the adaptation mechanisms are the signals to look for before the mainnet launch.

Chapter 13 ends here. We have understood why the anchoring frequency is one of the most impactful parameters of the rollup's design, why Bitcoin Hyper has chosen to make it adaptive, and what the concrete implications are for users and developers. In ***Chapter 14 — Data Availability: the Problem Few Understand****, we will tackle the other great structural problem of rollups, the one I introduced in Chapter 4 and that now deserves an in-depth treatment: how does one guarantee that the raw transaction data remains available to anyone wanting to verify the rollup's state, even if the main team were to disappear? It is a chapter that will make you understand one of the subtlest and most important distinctions of the sector: the one between true rollups and validiums.*

NOTES

1 The six-confirmation rule derives from a probabilistic calculation in Satoshi's original whitepaper (section 11): the probability that an attacker with 10% of the computational power manages to reorganize the chain after six blocks

is below 0.1%.

The anchoring frequency: the rollup's *heartbeat*

The rhythm that balances **finality, costs, and operational security** on Bitcoin.

1 The beat that ties Hyper to Bitcoin

Between one anchoring and the next the rollup processes transactions at high speed. When it publishes a state root on Bitcoin, that state is **crystallized in the Layer 1**.

Every anchoring is a beat: *it synchronizes the fast rollup with slow, secure Bitcoin.*

Bitcoin Hyper L2
rapid transactions · batches · updated state

↓ state commitment · Merkle root ↓

₿ Bitcoin L1
checkpoints · finality · immutability

2 Three forces in tension

Raising the frequency improves finality and reduces the waiting window, **but raises the costs**. Lowering it brings costs down, **but lengthens settlement and finality**.

An optimal frequency for everything does not exist: **there is a balance to govern.**

3 More often or less often?

More frequent anchorings

- Faster finality.
- A shorter operational window.
- Better for withdrawals and delicate operations.
- Higher Bitcoin costs.

More spaced-out anchorings

- Lower costs.
- Wider batches.
- A more contained average cost per transaction.
- Slower finality.

More frequency = more rapidity, **but more cost**. *Less frequency = more efficiency,* **but more waiting**.

4 An adaptive frequency, not a rigid one

Bitcoin fees · L2 volume · finality demand · network stress → **Adapted anchoring frequency**

low fees + high volume → more frequent
high fees + low volume → more spaced out
network stress → closer together
high-value apps → more finality

Flexibility is useful only if the rules are **public, stable, and verifiable.**

5 Invisible every day, decisive in withdrawals

Everyday use

user → L2 app → balance updated at once

A rapid experience.

Withdrawal toward Bitcoin

request → batch → checkpoint → ₿ confirmations → BTC on L1

Here the frequency affects the times.

Hyper can optimize the moment of the anchoring, **but it cannot compress Bitcoin's finality time** *(~10 min/block, plus confirmations).*

THE KEY POINT

The anchoring frequency is the rollup's **economic and technical rhythm**. Anchoring often accelerates finality but costs more; anchoring less often reduces costs but increases the wait. Hyper's maturity will depend on the **transparency and verifiability** of the adaptive rules.

PART IV · THE SETTLEMENT LAYER

Chapter 14
Data Availability

The problem few understand

14.1 — The Photograph without the Negative

I want to begin this chapter with an image that explains perfectly why the theme of data availability is at once the most important and the least discussed of the rollups' problems. Imagine having a digital photograph signed by a notary, certified, perfectly authenticated. A photo worth millions of euros, because it certifies the owner of an important property. The photograph is kept in a safe, it is public, it is verifiable. **And yet, the photograph alone is not enough.** Without the original negative, without the raw data that generated the photograph, **you cannot demonstrate what really happened at the moment the photo was taken.** You can only say that the photograph exists, and that it is authentic as a document. But the specific content, the "what really happened," requires the negative.

This is exactly the problem of data availability in rollups. The state commitment anchored on Bitcoin is the notarized photograph: it is authentic, it is immutable, it is verifiable as a document. **But it is only a mathematical fingerprint, not the data that produced that fingerprint.** To reconstruct what actually happened in the rollup — who paid whom, which transactions were executed, what the detailed state of every account is — the raw data is needed. Without the raw data, the state commitment is an empty promise: it says "the state is this" without telling you which state.

FIGURE 14.1 **THE NOTARIZED PHOTOGRAPH AND THE NEGATIVE: WHY THE STATE COMMITMENT ALONE IS NOT ENOUGH.**

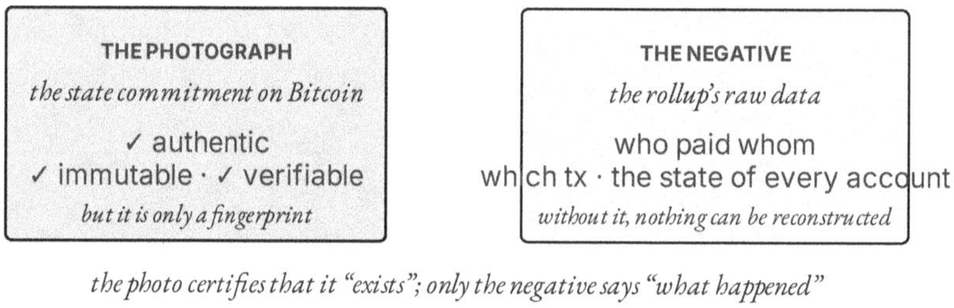

The state commitment anchored on Bitcoin is like a photograph signed by a notary: authentic, immutable, verifiable as a document. But it is only a mathematical fingerprint. To demonstrate "what really happened" in the rollup — which transactions, which balances, what state of every account — the negative is needed: the raw data that produced that fingerprint. Without the negative, the photograph certifies its own existence, not its own content.

And here lies the subtlety that many projects hide. **Without guaranteed data availability, independent verification of the rollup becomes impossible**, and the security model we have described in all the previous chapters turns into a rhetorical promise. **Without available data, fraud proofs cannot be produced. Without fraud proofs, the sequencer is not really bound to behave honestly. Without a bond to honesty, users must trust whoever runs the system. And a system where one trusts whoever runs it is not a rollup: it is a sidechain in disguise.** All the philosophical and technical difference we built in Chapter 6 plays out on this point.

FIGURE 14.2 **THE LOGICAL CHAIN THAT TIES DATA AVAILABILITY TO THE VERY NATURE OF THE ROLLUP.**

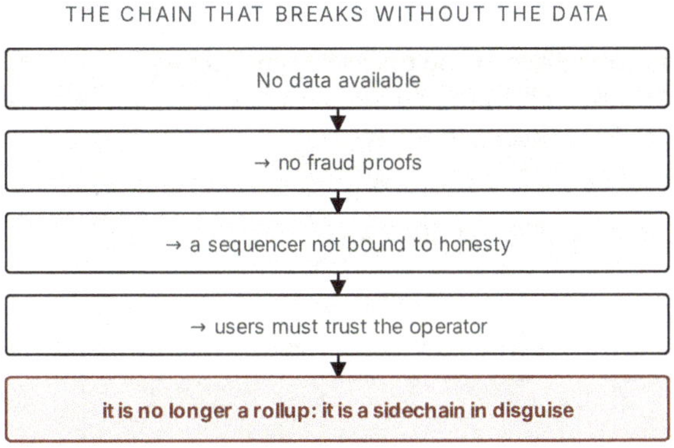

Without data availability, the state commitment is only a promise: a rollup's real security depends on the possibility of reconstructing and verifying the data that generated it. The chain is implacable: no data means no fraud proofs; no fraud proofs means a sequencer not bound to honesty; an unbound sequencer means users forced to trust the operator. And a system requiring trust in the operator is not a rollup — it is a sidechain in disguise. All the difference built in Chapter 6 plays out on this single link.

The Bitcoin Hyper team made the problem explicit in a specific research post in March 2026, recognizing it as "a first-order architectural challenge." It was a significant act of transparency, because many projects in the sector avoid speaking openly about the problem, preferring to take it as solved in vague ways. In this chapter I want to understand well what the problem is, why it is so important, what the roads to solve it are, and what Hyper is proposing. It is perhaps the most technically subtle chapter of Part IV, but it is also the one that will give you the sharpest lens for seriously judging any rollup project in the future.

⁂

14.2 — What "Data Availability" Concretely Means

Let us begin with a precise definition. **Data availability, in the context of rollups, is the guarantee that the raw transaction data is accessible to anyone, at any moment, in a verifiable way.** Let us see what it means to break this sentence down into its pieces.

"Raw transaction data" means the complete information of every transaction the rollup has processed: who the sender is, who the recipient is, which parameters were passed, which accounts were touched, which signatures were used, which logic was executed. They are the elementary bricks from which any observer can reconstruct the rollup's state by applying the transactions in sequence. **Without this raw data, the state is not reconstructible.**

"Accessible to anyone" means without permissions, without authorization, without having to trust anyone. It is not enough that the data exists somewhere: it must be publicly accessible, so that anyone in the world, equipped with time and technical skills, can download it and use it. If access to the data requires registering with a service, paying a subscription, asking the project team for permission, then the availability is not really "to anyone": it is "to whomever the team decides to let in." **This distinction is crucial for the permissionless verifiability that is one of the constitutive properties inherited from Bitcoin.**

"At any moment" means forever, persistently. It is not enough that the data is available today: it must be so also in five years, in ten years, in twenty. If the data of a certain period of the rollup is lost or deleted, the entire state of the rollup becomes potentially unverifiable from that point on. **Availability must be durable, not instantaneous.**

"In a verifiable way" means that whoever accesses the data must be able to verify that it is actually the right data, not manipulated or false versions. If someone provides me with "the rollup's transaction data" but I cannot be sure it is authentic, the value of the availability is zero. Verifiability is typically obtained through cryptographic commitments: the raw data is "committed" through hashes* that are published on-chain, and anyone can compare their own download with these hashes to verify authenticity.

Putting these four requirements together — raw, public, persistent, verifiable — the depth of the problem emerges. **It is not enough to say "the data is available": it must be guaranteed structurally, with mechanisms that work even when the project team no longer cooperates, even years later, even if nobody has a specific interest in keeping them alive.** It is a significant engineering challenge, and all the solutions that exist today have specific trade-offs.

FIGURE 14.3 **THE FOUR CONDITIONS THAT MUST HOLD SIMULTANEOUSLY FOR THE DATA TO BE TRULY AVAILABLE.**

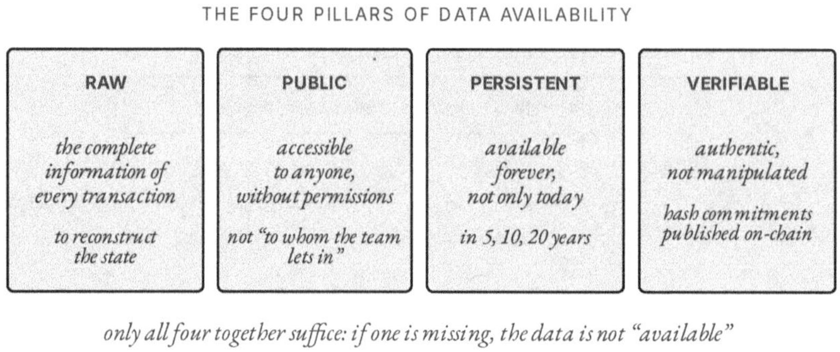

The data is not really available unless it is complete, public, persistent, and verifiable. It must be raw — the integral information of every transaction, from which to reconstruct the state; public — downloadable by anyone without permissions or dependencies on the team; persistent — retrievable not only today but years from now; verifiable — authenticatable through cryptographic commitments published on-chain. The four requirements hold only together: if one is missing, the guarantee of availability collapses and with it the permissionless verifiability inherited from Bitcoin.

---

* **Hash.** A short digital fingerprint, of fixed length, calculated from a piece of data of any size: the same information always produces the same hash, but from the hash one cannot go back to the original data. By publishing the hash on Bitcoin, anyone can then verify that the downloaded data corresponds exactly, without having been altered.

⁂

14.3 — Why Bitcoin Is Not Enough

An obvious question you might ask yourselves is: "Could Bitcoin itself not host the raw data[a] of the rollup's transactions? Bitcoin is already the most secure place in the world, why not use it also for data availability?" It is an intelligent question, and the answer is important because it shows why a separate solution is needed.

The problem is one of scale. Bitcoin has limited total capacity: in every block of about 4 megabytes,[b] it can host a few thousand standard Bitcoin transactions. The space for OP_RETURN[f] is even more limited (80 bytes per output), and even with Taproot[g] the usable structures are compact. **Compare this with the raw data that an active rollup can produce.** A rollup like Hyper, if it processes even just a few thousand transactions a minute, generates hundreds of megabytes of data every hour, gigabytes every day, terabytes a year. **These are orders of magnitude[c] beyond what Bitcoin can host.**

Trying to anchor all the raw data on Bitcoin would have two unacceptable consequences. **First consequence: the saturation of Bitcoin.** Bitcoin's space is a scarce resource contested among many users — native Bitcoin transactions, the Lightning Network,[d] applications like Ordinals,[e] other rollups. If Hyper occupied a large part of this space for its own raw data, Bitcoin fees would rise dramatically for everyone, and the system would not be sustainable. **Second consequence: prohibitive costs for Hyper.** Even assuming the space were available, paying Bitcoin fees to anchor gigabytes of data every day would make the rollup economically impracticable. The costs would end up on the users, and the rollup's fees would be so high as to make it non-competitive.

[a] **Raw data.** The complete, detailed set of all the transactions processed by the rollup, before being summarized in a fingerprint. It is enormously more voluminous than the state commitment: it is this bulk that could not be written in full on Bitcoin.

[b] **The block size.** Bitcoin deliberately limits the space of each block: the effective ceiling is about four million units of "weight," roughly equivalent to four megabytes. It is a deliberate constraint, which keeps the network light to verify for anyone, but makes space an intrinsically scarce resource.

[c] **Orders of magnitude.** An expression indicating enormous differences, measured in multiples of ten: saying that a quantity is "orders of magnitude" greater than another means it exceeds it by tens, hundreds, or thousands of times. Here it underlines how much a rollup's data exceeds the space available on Bitcoin.

[d] **Lightning Network.** Bitcoin's main second-layer network, designed for rapid, very low-cost payments off the chain. It is cited here as one of the uses competing for the scarce space of Bitcoin's blocks.

[e] **Ordinals.** A system, spreading since 2023, that makes it possible to "inscribe" content (images, texts, tokens) directly in individual satoshis, exploiting the space of Bitcoin's blocks. Cited here as an example of a further consumer of that already contested space, which contributes to driving its price up.

[f] **OP_RETURN.** A Bitcoin instruction that makes it possible to attach to a transaction a small amount of non-spendable data — at most 80 bytes. It is the simplest way to anchor a compact fingerprint on the chain, but the very reduced space makes it unsuitable for hosting a rollup's raw data.

[g] **Taproot.** A 2021 Bitcoin upgrade that makes it possible to anchor more articulated data structures than OP_RETURN. It nevertheless remains a technique designed for compact fingerprints and proofs, not for storing the volumes of data produced by a rollup.

FIGURE 14.4 **BITCOIN KEEPS THE SEAL, NOT THE ENTIRE WAREHOUSE.**

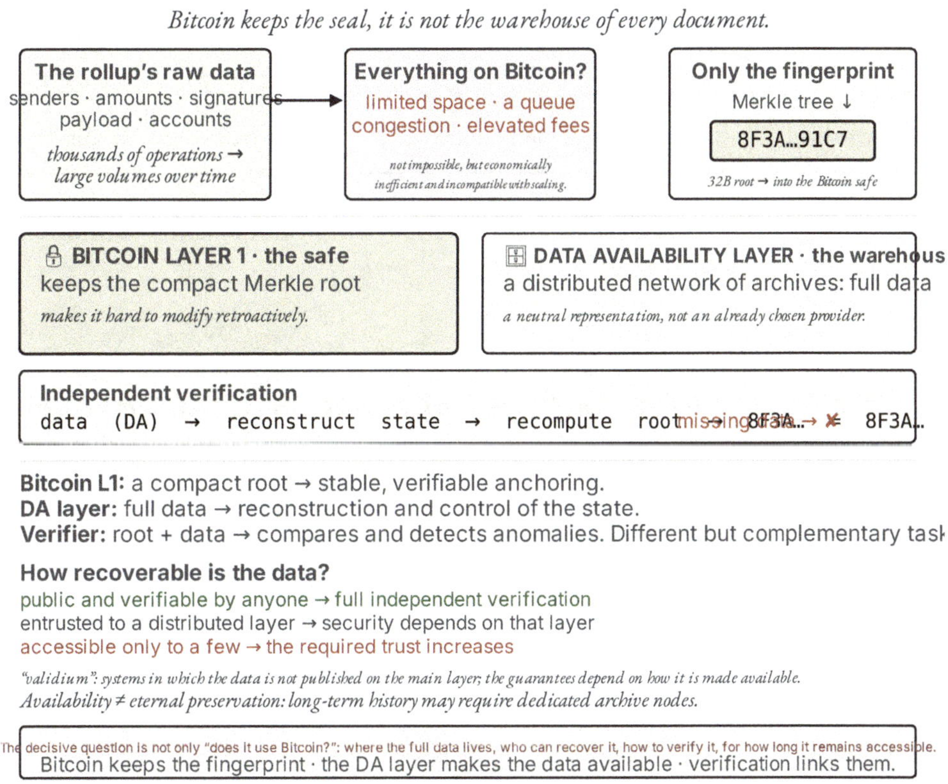

Bitcoin is suited to keeping a compact commitment, not the entire volume of the rollup's data: the Merkle root is anchored on Bitcoin, the full data remains available in a separate layer, and independent verification is born from the comparison between the two.

Bitcoin is designed to anchor compact commitments, not to host voluminous data. It is an architectural choice of Bitcoin itself, part of its philosophy of conservative minimalism that we explored in Chapter 1. The network is optimized to be a settlement layer, not a data availability layer. **For a rollup's data availability, a different solution is needed, built specifically for this purpose.**

There is a technical distinction worth introducing here, because it is the vocabulary the sector uses to discuss these alternatives. **A system where the raw data is publicly available is called a "true rollup."** A system where the raw data is kept private or accessible only to a restricted group is called a "validium." The difference between the two is precisely in the data availability model. **A true rollup inherits Bitcoin's security properties structurally; a validium makes similar promises but with a much weaker trust model.**

This distinction is important because many projects in the sector avoid clarifying where they stand. They present themselves as "rollups" without specifying whether they are true rollups or validiums, exploiting the ambiguity of the term. **For anyone seriously evaluating a project, the first question to ask is: "is the raw transaction data publicly available in a verifiable way? Where? How is persistence guaranteed?"** The answer to these questions says much more about the system's real security than any marketing slogan.

TABLE 14.1 **WHY BITCOIN ALONE IS NOT ENOUGH FOR THE RAW DATA.**

Dimension	What Bitcoin (L1) offers	What data availability requires
Capacity	A few megabytes per block, every ~10 minutes	Wide, continuous volumes of raw data
Cost	Elevated for every byte recorded	Sustainable over large quantities of data
Suitable function	Keeping the fingerprint (state commitment)	Preserving and making accessible the full data
Guarantee provided	Immutability of the anchored seal	Recoverability of the data by anyone

Bitcoin is optimized to keep the state's fingerprint immutably, not to store the raw data of millions of transactions. The Layer 1's capacity and costs make a dedicated data availability layer necessary, distinct from the anchoring of the commitment.

⁂

14.4 — The Possible Roads: Five Approaches to Data Availability

Having understood why Bitcoin alone is not enough, we can examine the possible roads for guaranteeing data availability. Hyper's March 2026 research post explores several strategies, and it is useful to review them systematically to understand the trade-offs of each.

TABLE 14.2 **FIVE APPROACHES TO DATA AVAILABILITY.**

Approach	In short	Trade-off
Distributed nodes	Multiple copies of the data in different places	Depends on the number of nodes
DA infrastructures	Dedicated networks (Celestia, EigenDA)*	External dependence
Redundant coding	Data reconstructible even if partial†	Greater complexity
Off-chain commitments	Fingerprint on-chain, data elsewhere‡	Risk if the data disappears

Economic incentives	Rewards those who preserve the data	A model to be designed

None of these approaches is resolutive on its own: data availability often comes from combining them. Some preserve and distribute, others add resilience, others strengthen the incentives to keep the data accessible over time.

* **DA (data availability) infrastructures.** Specialized networks — such as Celestia or EigenDA — whose only task is to preserve and make retrievable the raw data of other systems, guaranteeing its availability. Relying on one of them simplifies the project, but introduces a dependence on an external infrastructure, with its rules and its security.

† **Redundant coding (erasure coding).** A technique that adds to the data mathematically calculated redundancy information, so that it can be reconstructed in full even if a part is lost. It is the same principle used in reliable storage systems: more security against loss, at the price of greater complexity.

‡ **Off-chain commitments.** An approach in which only the fingerprint (hash) of the data is published on the main chain, while the real data remains off the chain. It minimizes the space occupied on Bitcoin, but if the external data disappears the fingerprint alone is not enough to reconstruct the state: it is the model called "validium."
lculated redundancy information, so that it can be reconstructed in full even if a part is lost. It is the same principle used in reliable storage systems: more security against loss, at the price of greater complexity.

FIGURE 14.5 **FIVE APPROACHES TO DATA AVAILABILITY, COMPARED.**

First road: distributed rollup nodes. The simplest model consists of making the rollup's nodes — the computers that run Hyper's software and maintain the state — preserve and distribute the raw data. The more independent nodes participate, the more robust the availability. When someone wants to verify the rollup's state, they download the data from any one of these nodes. **Advantages**: it is simple, it is well understood, it requires no external infrastructures. **Disadvantages**: the robustness depends entirely on the number and distribution of the nodes. If the nodes are few or concentrated in the hands of the project team, the availability is effectively centralized. If nobody has explicit economic incentives to operate long-term nodes, the persistence of the data over time is not guaranteed.

FIGURE 14.4·A **FIRST ROAD: DISTRIBUTED ROLLUP NODES, WHEN DATA AVAILABILITY DEPENDS ON THE NETWORK OF NODES.**

Rollup nodes: *computers that run the Layer 2 software, maintain the system's state, and can preserve and distribute the raw data needed for independent verification.*

Second road: specialized data availability blockchains. In recent years, blockchains designed specifically for data availability have emerged, the best known of which are Celestia and EigenDA. These blockchains do not execute complex smart contracts: their only purpose is to host the rollups' raw data, guaranteeing its verifiable availability through their own consensus mechanism. Hyper could publish its own raw data on one of these blockchains. **Advantages**: availability is guaranteed by the security model of the specialized blockchain, which is designed specifically for this. Costs are significantly lower than Bitcoin, because data availability blockchains are optimized for volume. **Disadvantages**: it introduces an external dependence that many Bitcoin-centric projects would prefer to avoid. If the data availability blockchain has problems (bugs, attacks, forks), Hyper suffers from it. The "everything on Bitcoin" philosophy gets diluted.

Third road: erasure coding and sharding. These are mathematical techniques that make it possible to "break" a large set of data into many fragments, in such a way that the original set can be reconstructed from a small percentage of the fragments. For example, with adequate erasure coding, a set of 100 fragments can be reconstructed from only 50 correctly preserved fragments. **This transforms the availability problem into a problem of distributed redundancy**: instead of needing every fragment to be preserved perfectly, it is enough that a sufficient percentage is available. **Advantages**: maximum resilience with minimum storage requirements for each participant. **Disadvantages**: it is technically complex, it requires sophisticated coordination, and the incentive model for participants must be designed with attention.

Fourth road: cryptographic commitments with off-chain data. A subtler variant consists of publishing on-chain (on Bitcoin or elsewhere) only "commitments" on the raw data — cryptographic hashes that demonstrate the existence of the data without publishing the data itself — while the actual data lives off-chain in some storage system. When someone wants to verify, they download the off-chain data and compare it with the on-chain commitments. **Advantages**: minimum use of on-chain space, maximum flexibility for off-chain preservation. **Disadvantages**: the availability of the off-chain data is not structurally guaranteed — it depends on who preserves it. If the off-chain system loses data, the on-chain commitments remain but become useless. This is the model of "validiums," and it has significant security trade-offs.

Fifth road: economic incentives for preservation. A strategy orthogonal to the others consists of building explicit economic incentives for third parties to preserve the data over the long term. Node operators could be paid proportionally to the data preserved, guarantee deposits could be required that are lost if the data disappears, rewards could be offered to those who demonstrate having certain data on demand. **Advantages**: it transforms data availability from "hoping someone preserves it" to "a verifiable economic commitment." **Disadvantages**: designing the economic mechanisms is difficult, it requires capital for the rewards, and it can be manipulated in non-obvious ways.

Hyper, according to the March 2026 post, is exploring combinations of these roads. **Probably the final solution will be hybrid**: distributed rollup nodes as the base, integrated with elements of erasure coding for resilience and of economic incentives for persistence. Publication on specialized blockchains like Celestia is a further possibility, but it would carry that external dependence that might not be desired.

⁂

14.5 — The Difference between a True Rollup and a Validium

Having described the roads, I would like to return with more precision to the distinction between a true rollup and a validium that I introduced in 14.3, because it is one of the questions where the sector's marketing tends to be most ambiguous and where the informed investor can easily get confused.

TABLE 14.3 **TRUE ROLLUP AND VALIDIUM: THE SAME FINGERPRINT, DIFFERENT GUARANTEES.**

Aspect	True rollup*	Validium†
Transaction data	Published on-chain	Preserved off-chain‡
Reconstruction of the state	Always possible	Depends on who preserves the data
Security	Inherited from the Layer 1	Weaker, conditional

The two models can publish the same fingerprint on Bitcoin, but they offer very different guarantees. The difference is not in the commitment, but in the availability of the raw data: without it, a validium cannot guarantee the autonomous reconstruction of the state.

TABLE 14.4 **WHAT CHANGES FOR THE USER: TRUE ROLLUP AND VALIDIUM COMPARED.**

Situation	True rollup	Validium
If the project team disappears	The state remains reconstructible and the funds recoverable	The data can become unreachable; funds at risk
Demonstrating one's own balance	Always possible, without permissions	Depends on the committee's cooperation
Who keeps the data	Anyone, publicly	A restricted group of operators
Cost of the system	Higher: more data published on-chain	Lower: data kept off the chain

The distinction is not theoretical: it affects what the user can do in critical moments. In a true rollup the ability to demonstrate one's own balance and withdraw the funds does not depend on the team's survival; in a validium that guarantee is conditional on who preserves the data.

[*] **True rollup.** A system in which the raw transaction data is published and accessible to anyone, so that anyone can reconstruct and verify the state autonomously. It is this that allows it to truly inherit the security of the Layer 1.

[†] **Validium.** A variant in which the raw data is kept off the main chain, entrusted to a restricted group. It is cheaper, but the possibility of reconstructing the state depends on the availability of that data: if it disappears, the guarantee fails.

[‡] **Off-chain.** Said of data or operations that take place outside the main blockchain. It reduces costs and occupied space, but shifts to other parties the guarantee that the data remains available and verifiable over time.

FIGURE 14.7 **THE SAME FINGERPRINT ON BITCOIN, VERY DIFFERENT GUARANTEES.**

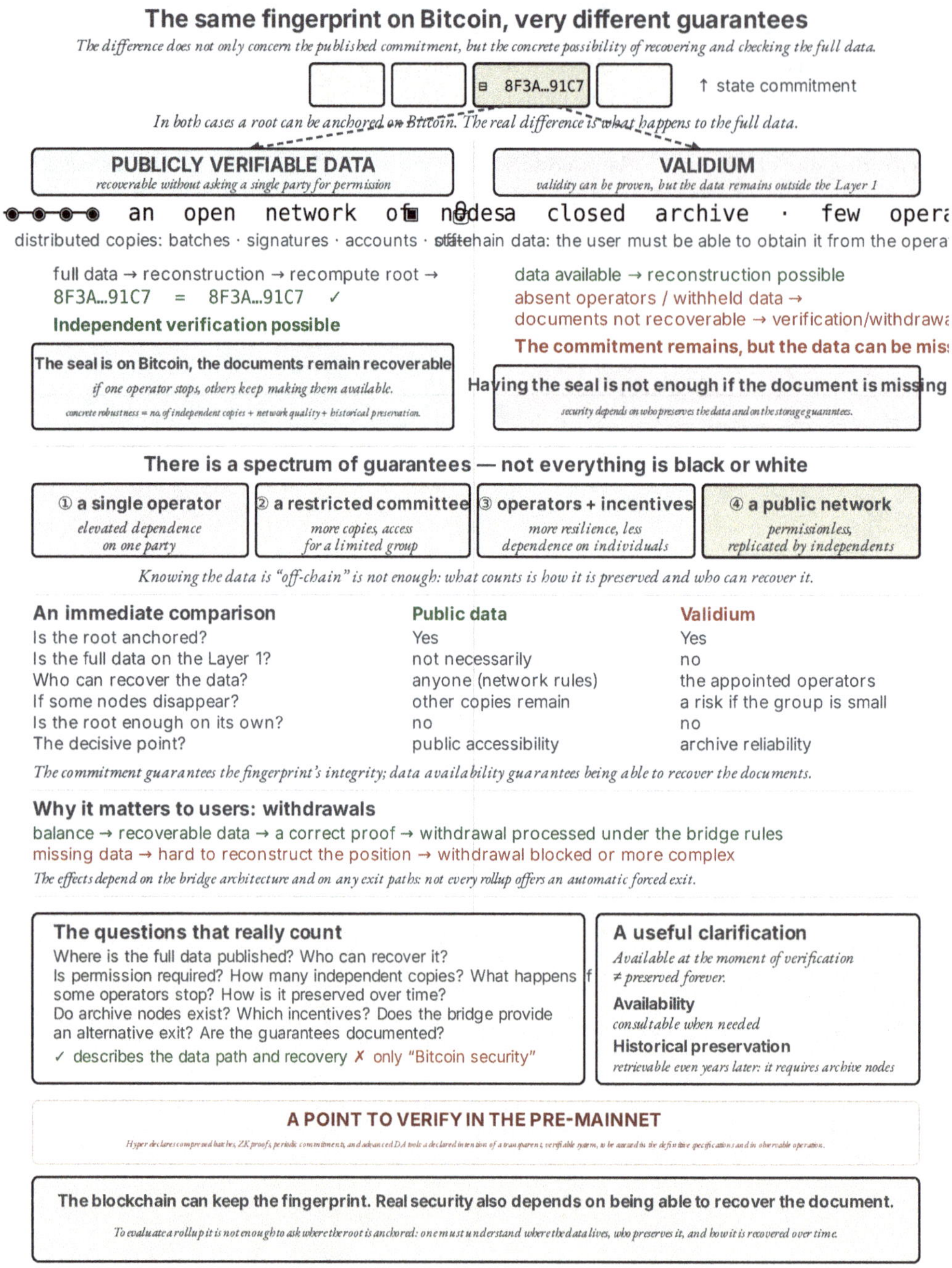

Two systems can anchor a Merkle root on the Layer 1 and offer very different guarantees. The decisive point is the concrete availability of the full data: if it can be recovered without permissions, independent verification remains possible; if it depends on few operators, the risk grows that the state becomes hard to reconstruct.

A **true rollup** is a system where the raw transaction data is publicly available in a verifiable way, accessible to anyone without permissions. The roads described in 14.4 — distributed nodes, specialized blockchains, erasure coding — are all possible ways to realize this property. **The key characteristic is permissionless verifiability**: anyone can, in principle, download the raw data and verify the rollup's state. Without having to ask anyone, without having to pay, without having to depend on a specific service.

A **validium** is a system where the raw transaction data is kept off-chain by a restricted group, typically a committee of operators or a specific service provider. The state commitments are still anchored on-chain (on Bitcoin or elsewhere), but to reconstruct what they represent, the data must be obtained from the group that holds it. **Verifiability is subordinate to the cooperation of the group keeping the data.** If the group decides not to provide the data, or if it disappears, the rollup's state becomes effectively inaccessible, even if the state commitments remain anchored.

The practical difference is enormous. **In a true rollup, the state is accessible forever, even if the project team disappears, even if every single operator leaves.** As long as someone in the world preserves the raw data (which is likely given that it is public and replicated), the state is reconstructible. **In a validium, the state depends on the continuous custody of the data by the specific group.** If that group fails, is attacked, decides to stop, the rollup's state becomes fragile.

The implications for the security of funds are concrete. **In a true rollup, users can always demonstrate their own balance and withdraw their own funds**, even if the project's main team no longer cooperates. An independent "forced exit" path exists. **In a validium, if the data disappears, users can no longer demonstrate their own balance**, and therefore can no longer withdraw the funds. The promise of "security inherited from Bitcoin" becomes empty: Bitcoin knows a state of the rollup existed, but nobody knows which one.

The projects' marketing tends to avoid this distinction. There is generic talk of "anchoring to Bitcoin," "Bitcoin-grade security," "decentralized verifiability," without clarifying whether it is a true rollup or a validium. **To understand the truth, specific questions must be asked**: where does the raw data live? Who preserves it? What guarantees do I have that it will be accessible in five years even if the project team no longer exists? Without clear answers to these questions, the project's status remains ambiguous.

For Bitcoin Hyper, the March 2026 post clearly indicates the intention of building a true rollup, not a validium. The roads explored — distributed nodes, erasure coding, verifiable cryptographic commitments — are all consistent with this objective. **But the intention is not the realization**: one must see how the final solution will be implemented, and to what extent it will really achieve decentralized data availability. It is one of the points where Hyper's pre-mainnet will be judged, and where the team's technical transparency will be crucial.

⁂

14.6 — The Long-Term Problem: Who Will Keep the Data in Ten Years?

There is a dimension of the data availability problem that deserves a dedicated section, because it is almost always underestimated: **the long term**. All the mechanisms we have described work if there are active operators maintaining the data. But what guarantees there will be active operators in ten years? In twenty years? **For a system that wants to be "Bitcoin-grade," the long term is not optional — it is the main term.**

Think of it in the comparison with Bitcoin itself. Bitcoin has existed for almost twenty years, and today's Bitcoin blockchain contains the complete history of all transactions since the 2009 genesis block. **This persistence is not due to Satoshi's original team**, but to an enormous ecosystem of independent nodes operated by thousands of people around the world, each with different incentives to maintain their own copy of the blockchain. Even if Satoshi disappeared tomorrow — indeed, he has de facto been gone for over ten years — Bitcoin would continue to exist, because its persistence is structurally decentralized.

For rollups, building this level of decentralized persistence is an enormous challenge. **Rollups are young**; even the most mature ones on Ethereum are only a few years old. They have not had the time to build ecosystems of independent operators comparable to Bitcoin's. **Moreover, the economic incentives for operating a rollup node are less clear** than those for mining Bitcoin: there is no substantial direct reward, and the motivation is typically altruistic or tied to specific commercial interests.

For a project like Hyper, which wants to build a system that survives its own team, the long-term problem requires architectural attention from the start. **If the system depends on operators the team pays directly, persistence is subordinate to the team's economic health.** If it depends on volunteers operating out of generic interest, persistence is subordinate to the project's appeal. **True decentralized persistence requires an incentive model that works even in the absence of the original team.**

The possible strategies are several. **One is economic**: token incentives rewarding those who operate nodes over the long term. Hyper could allocate a part of its own $HYPER token to operators, distributed gradually according to the data preserved. **Another is structural**: making data preservation a natural component of other ecosystem roles, so that whoever operates, for example, important DeFi applications must also preserve the data. **A third is collaborative**: integrations with public archives, digital libraries, preservation organizations that have a long-term institutional mandate.

Hyper has not published specific details on the long-term persistence strategy, and this is a point to monitor. **The March 2026 post mentions persistence as an objective but does not specify the mechanisms.** When the team releases more detailed documentation on the economic mechanisms and on the governance of the data availability layer, it will be one of the key moments for judging the project's maturity. **Without a clear model of long-term persistence, the promise of a "Bitcoin-grade" rollup remains partial**, because Bitcoin security is a security that works for decades, not for years.

⁂

14.7 — What Happens if Availability Breaks

I want to close the technical part of the chapter with a scenario few tackle: what concretely happens if a rollup's data availability breaks? It is an important exercise because it helps in understanding the gravity of the problem, and because the way a system handles this scenario is one of the most revealing tests of its robustness.

Let us imagine the worst scenario. Hyper has been launched, has grown to host billions of dollars in value, has millions of transactions in its own history. For some reason — a coordinated attack, an economic failure, a catastrophic event — the nodes that preserved the raw data begin to disappear. In a few weeks, many copies of the data start to vanish. Some historical archives become hard to recover; in an even graver scenario, recent data necessary to verify the current state could be missing too. What would happen?

Nota 1. The scenario described is deliberately extreme: it serves to isolate the data availability risk in its purest form. In practice, the total, simultaneous loss of all copies is improbable when the nodes are numerous and independent. It is precisely the degree of redundancy and independence that determines how remote this scenario is.

Nota 2. The loss of the historical archives must be distinguished from the loss of the recent data. The first compromises the reconstruction of the past; the second prevents verifying the current state and therefore operating safely. A rigorous due diligence evaluates the two eventualities separately, because they have different consequences and probabilities.

Nota 3. Long-term preservation is often entrusted to archive nodes: nodes that maintain the chain's entire history, not only the most recent state. It is they that make possible, even years later, the reconstruction and verification of the historical archives; their absence or concentration is one of the factors that make the scenario described concrete.

Nota 4. The gravity of such a scenario also depends on the value in custody at the moment of the failure: the higher the capital anchored to the rollup, the greater the consequences of a possible unavailability. It is one reason why the data availability layer's maturity should be evaluated before the deposited value grows, not after.

Nota 5. The case in which the data is temporarily unreachable must be kept distinct from the one in which it is definitively lost: in the first the funds remain recoverable once access is restored, in the second the reconstruction of the state can become impossible. The difference depends on the degree of redundancy with which the data is preserved.

Nota 6. A scenario of this type does not necessarily imply the loss of funds: if the state root remains anchored on Bitcoin and the data is recovered from even just one source, the state can be reconstructed. What is lost, in the absence of the data, is the possibility of verifying independently — and it is this, more than the nominal value, the property put at risk.

TABLE 14.5 **DATA LOSS: TWO SCENARIOS, DIFFERENT CONSEQUENCES.**

What is lost	Consequence	Gravity

Historical archives	The rollup's past history can no longer be reconstructed	Serious, but circumscribed
Recent data	The current state cannot be verified nor can one operate safely	Critical

Not all losses have the same weight: with the historical archives missing, the memory of the past is lost; with the recent data missing, the very possibility of using the system safely is blocked. It is the reason why the two eventualities must be evaluated separately.

FIGURE 14.8 **WHEN THE DATA DISAPPEARS: A ROLLUP'S SILENT CRISIS.**

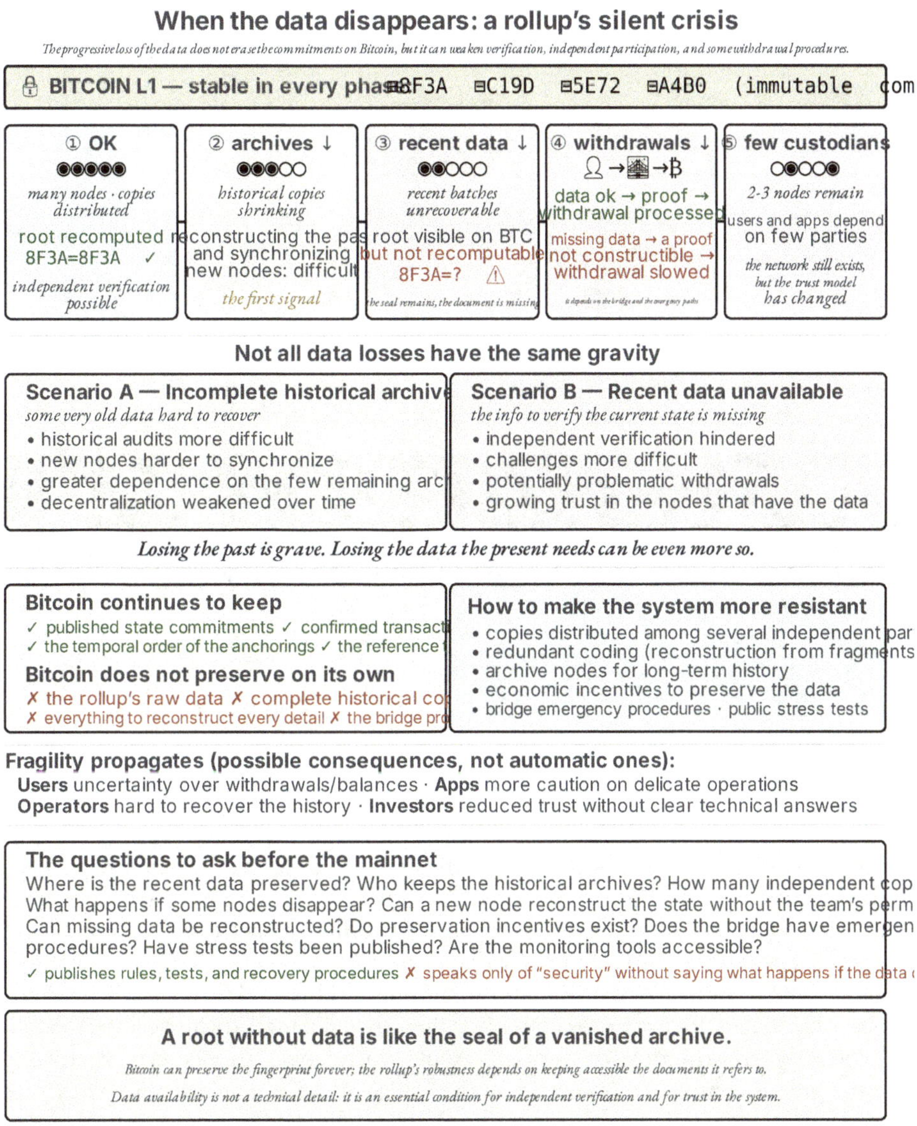

When the data becomes progressively less accessible, the commitments remain recorded on Bitcoin but independent verification can weaken. The loss of the historical archives makes it harder to reconstruct the past and start new nodes; the absence of the recent data needed for the current state can compromise checks, challenges, and some withdrawal procedures.

First effect: the commitments already published remain recorded on Bitcoin. Their mathematical fingerprint does not disappear merely because some of the rollup's archives become unreachable.

Bitcoin preserves the root, immutable, but it does not on its own guarantee the availability of the data to which it refers.

FIGURE 14.7 **A CONCEPTUAL STRESS TEST ON DATA AVAILABILITY: WHAT HAPPENS WHEN THE ROOT STAYS ANCHORED TO BITCOIN BUT THE RAW DATA IS NO LONGER INDEPENDENTLY VERIFIABLE.**

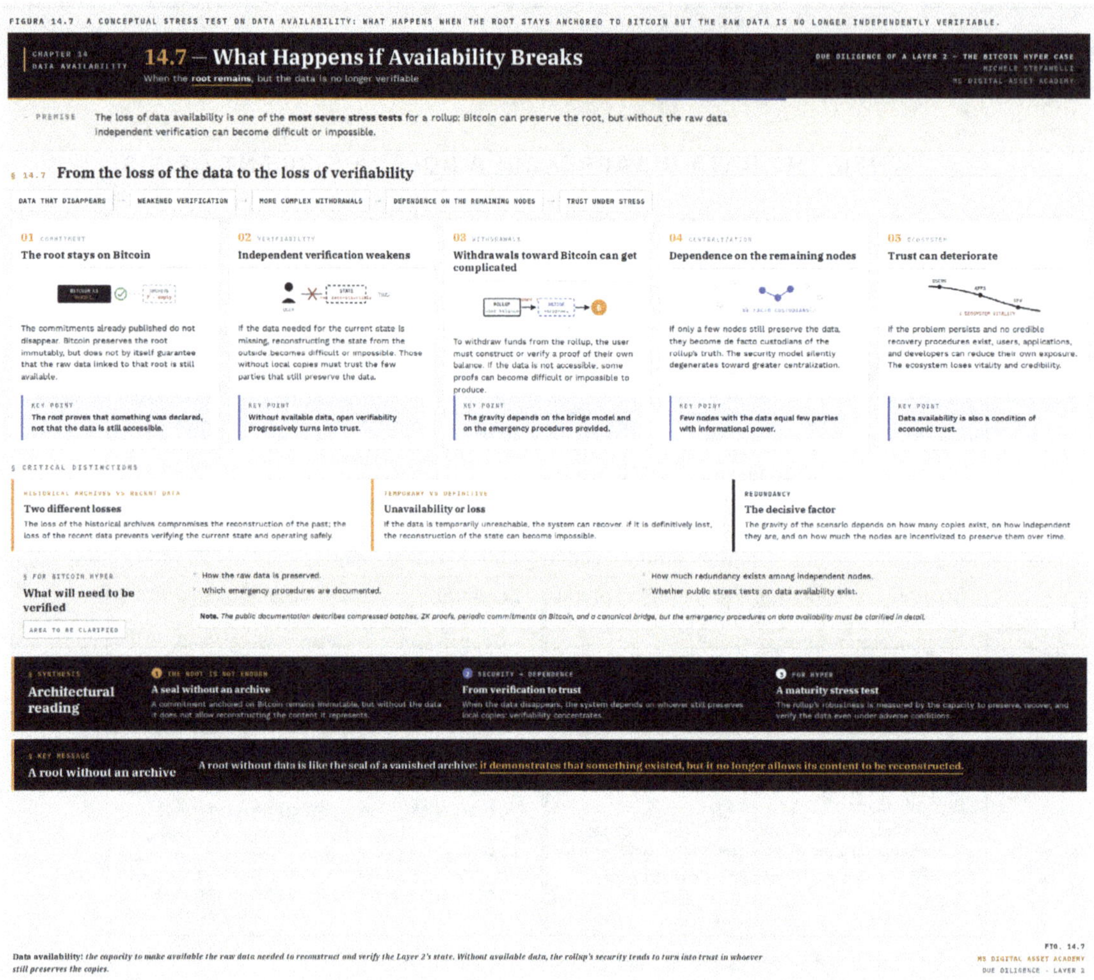

Second effect: independent verification weakens. If the data needed for the current state is missing, reconstructing it from the outside becomes difficult or impossible. The nodes that still possess local copies can continue to operate, but the other participants must trust those few parties more and more. The system loses an important part of its own open verifiability and approaches a model in which trust concentrates in the operators who still preserve the data.

Third effect: withdrawals toward Bitcoin can become problematic. To withdraw bitcoin from the rollup, the user must construct or verify a proof of their own balance. If the necessary data is no longer accessible, correctly constructing or verifying some withdrawal proofs can become difficult or impossible: the precise consequences depend on the bridge model and on any emergency procedures the protocol provides. In optimistic models the withholding of the data can prevent users from producing the necessary Merkle proofs; even in ZK models the unavailability of the data can make it hard to know the balances and update the state.

Fourth effect: dependence on the remaining nodes. If only few nodes still preserve the data, the system effectively depends on those few nodes. They become "de facto custodians" of the rollup's truth, with all the centralization implications this carries. The security model degenerates silently.

Fifth effect: the deterioration of the ecosystem. If the problem persists and no credible recovery procedures exist, trust in the ecosystem can deteriorate. Users can become more prudent, applications can reduce their own exposure, and new developers can hesitate before building on the rollup. These are possible consequences, not automatic effects identical in every architecture.

These are scenarios we hope never occur, but they show why the data availability problem is structural. **A well-designed rollup must resist these scenarios**, through mechanisms guaranteeing the persistence of the data even under adverse conditions. The design of these mechanisms is one of the most sophisticated aspects of rollup engineering, and it is where many projects in the sector are still weak.

For Bitcoin Hyper it will be important to understand how the architecture will react to stress scenarios: the loss of some nodes, the reduction of the available copies, difficulty recovering the historical archives, or the temporary unavailability of recent data. The public documentation describes the use of compressed batches, ZK proofs, periodic commitments on Bitcoin, and a canonical bridge for withdrawals, but it does not yet illustrate the emergency procedures in detail. Public stress tests and documented recovery mechanisms would therefore represent important signals of technical maturation. **A root without data is like the seal of a vanished archive: it demonstrates that something existed, but it no longer allows its content to be reconstructed.**

⁂

14.8 — Questions and Answers: Clarifying the Chapter's Concepts

Question 1: If the rollup's raw data is not anchored on Bitcoin, in what sense does the rollup "inherit Bitcoin's security"?

The inheritance is partial and must be understood precisely. Bitcoin guarantees **the immutability of the anchored state commitments**: once a commitment is recorded on Bitcoin, it is practically impossible to modify. Bitcoin does not directly guarantee the **availability of the raw data** that generated the commitment. That guarantee must come from separate mechanisms. **So the rollup inherits two of Bitcoin's three constitutive properties** (immutability and in large part permissionless verifiability, if availability is well designed) but must build its own mechanism to guarantee that the verifiability is actually actionable in practice. Concrete example: if you are handed a book with a notary's seal on the cover but the pages are blank, the seal is authentic but the book communicates nothing. The state commitment without data availability is exactly this: authentic but empty. Full Bitcoin security requires both the authenticity of the seal (which Bitcoin guarantees) and the availability of the content (which the data availability layer guarantees).

Question 2: If Hyper will use services like Celestia for data availability, is it not simply moving the problem to another blockchain?

To a certain extent yes, but with nuances. Celestia and the like are blockchains designed specifically to do data availability, with consensus models and incentives specifically optimized for this purpose. **They are significantly more robust than a cluster of nodes run by the Hyper team**, because they have their own community of independent operators, their own economic incentives, their own consensus mechanisms. **But certainly, depending on Celestia means that Hyper's security also depends on Celestia's security.** If Celestia has a problem, Hyper suffers from it. For projects that want to be "purely Bitcoin," this external dependence is a significant compromise. For others, it is an acceptable compromise in exchange for the robustness Celestia offers. Hyper's choice is not yet public, and it will probably be a compromise combining its own elements with external dependencies. Concrete example: today Optimism and Base use Ethereum itself for data availability, because Ethereum offers the "blob" space introduced with EIP-4844. For them, depending on Ethereum for availability is natural given that they already depend on Ethereum for settlement. For Hyper, depending on Bitcoin for settlement and on something else for availability creates two separate dependencies, each with its own security model.

Question 3: If the raw data is public, could any competitor not copy the rollup's applications and users?

The public transaction data reveals what happened, not the applications' internal mechanisms. **Smart contract code is public by nature on any transparent blockchain**, whether it is Ethereum, Solana, or a rollup like Hyper. Anyone wanting to copy an application can already do so today on any public chain. **The availability of the transaction data adds no new intellectual-property vulnerabilities**: it only reveals what was executed, similarly to how a look at Etherscan reveals all of Ethereum's transactions. **An application's value does not lie in the code (which is copyable) but in the community, in the integrations, in the brand, in the users' specific data.** All of these are hard to copy even with full data transparency. Concrete example: Uniswap is open source, its code is public, anyone could replicate it. But Uniswap remains the market leader because it has the liquidity, the users, the integrations. Transparency is not an enemy of valuable applications; it is a fundamental characteristic of theirs.

Question 4: How much of the difference between a true rollup and a validium is really important for normal users?

For normal users, under regular operating conditions, the difference is almost invisible. A validium and a true rollup can offer identical experiences from the point of view of everyday use: the same speed, the same costs, the same interface. **The difference manifests only in stress scenarios**: when the project team fails, when the system is attacked, when funds must be withdrawn under adverse conditions. **In those scenarios, the true rollup protects users, the validium exposes them.** For most users who never experience these scenarios, the detail is theoretical. For those putting significant capital at stake or thinking about the long term, the detail is crucial. **It is similar to insurance: in normal life it is invisible, but when it is needed, it makes the difference between a catastrophe and a managed inconvenience.** Concrete example: in 2022, some gaming sidechains had temporary problems where users could not access their own NFTs. They were protected by the settlement blockchain (they knew they existed), but they could not use them until the data was restored. For the users who were playing, it was a temporary inconvenience. For the users who had thousands of dollars invested, it was a traumatic experience.

Question 5: Could Hyper be a true rollup at the architecture level but become a validium de facto if in practice only the team preserves the data?

It is exactly the risk I mentioned in 14.6 about the long term. **Architecture and operational reality are different things, and the gap between the two is where many projects fail.** One can declare being a true rollup, one can put in place technical mechanisms for decentralized availability, but if in practice only the team pays the operators who preserve the data, the effect is that of a validium. **The distinguishing mark of a true rollup in practice is the presence of independent operators, with their own incentives, who do not depend on the project team's decisions to keep operating.** For Hyper, seeing how many independent operators emerge in the months and years after the mainnet launch will be one of the most important tests. If the operator ecosystem grows organically, the system is effectively decentralized. If it remains dominated by the team, the system remains effectively a validium in practical operation, even if a true rollup in design. Concrete example: Optimism had started with data availability managed entirely by the team. Over time, through various evolutions of the architecture and incentive mechanisms, it gradually decentralized this dimension too. For Hyper a similar trajectory is expected, but the speed and depth of the effective decentralization will be key factors.

Question 6: Do technical ways exist to demonstrate data availability without trusting the operators?

Yes, and it is one of the most innovative areas of current rollup research. The technique is called **"proof of data availability"** or **"data availability sampling,"** and it is at the base of blockchains like Celestia. The idea is elegant: instead of trusting that the operators preserve the data, users can randomly sample small fragments of the data and verify that they are actually available. Combined with erasure coding, it is enough for every user to verify a small number of fragments to give statistical guarantee that the entire data set is available. **It is a cryptographically solid mechanism that dramatically reduces the dependence on specific operators**, even if it requires sophisticated technical tools to be implemented correctly. Hyper could in the future adopt similar mechanisms, but they are technically complex and probably will not be present at the initial launch. Concrete example: Celestia's "data availability sampling" system allows a "light" node (even a phone) to verify with high probability that the data is available, without having to download the entire set. It is a remarkable property that demonstrates the level of sophistication reached in this research sector, and that could be adopted by rollups like Hyper in the medium term.

⁂

14.9 — WHAT TO TAKE AWAY FROM THIS CHAPTER

Data availability is the guarantee that the raw transaction data is accessible to anyone, at any moment, in a verifiable way. It is a structural property that requires specific mechanisms to be realized.

Without data availability, the state commitment anchored on Bitcoin becomes an empty promise. Authenticity is preserved but the content is inaccessible, making independent verification of the rollup's state impossible.

Bitcoin alone is not enough for data availability, for reasons of scale. Bitcoin space is scarce and costly, while the rollup's raw data is voluminous and growing. A separate availability layer is needed.

The distinction between a true rollup and a validium plays out on data availability. A true rollup has data publicly available in a verifiable way; a validium keeps it off-chain in a not publicly accessible way. The practical difference manifests in stress scenarios.

The possible strategies include distributed rollup nodes, specialized blockchains (Celestia, EigenDA), erasure coding, cryptographic commitments, economic incentives. Each strategy has specific trade-offs, and real solutions tend to be hybrid.

The long-term problem is central: it is necessary to guarantee that the data will be available in ten or twenty years, even in the absence of the original team. Without a clear model of decentralized persistence, the "Bitcoin-grade" promise remains partial.

Bitcoin Hyper publicly recognized the data availability problem in the March 2026 post. The intention of building a true rollup (not a validium) has been made explicit, but the specific technical solution is still in the research phase.

Architecture and operational reality are different things. A system can be designed as a true rollup but function de facto as a validium if independent operators do not emerge. The effective decentralization of data availability will be one of the project's crucial tests.

For normal users under regular conditions, the difference between a true rollup and a validium is almost invisible. It becomes crucial only in stress scenarios: the team's failure, attacks on the system, catastrophic long-term events.

For those evaluating the project, the clarity with which the team tackles data availability is one of the most revealing indicators of the project's technical maturity and seriousness. Detailed documentation, specific strategies, public incentive models are the signals to look for.

Chapter 14 ends here. We have tackled one of the subtlest and least discussed problems of rollups, understanding why data availability is a precondition of the entire security model, and how Bitcoin Hyper is facing the challenge. From here on, Part IV of the book (The Settlement Layer) closes. We are ready to enter Part V, dedicated to the sequencing layer and the consensus model.

*In **Chapter 15 — The Sequencer as a Technical and Governance Surface**, we will go down inside one of the rollup's components most charged with implications, understanding why whoever controls the order of transactions controls much more than it seems at first sight, and what Bitcoin Hyper's strategies are for managing this power in the short and long term.*

NOTES

1 The "data availability problem" is the question: "how can I be sure that a transaction's data is actually retrievable by all the network's nodes?" Without available data, it is not possible to challenge a fraudulent state. See Al-Bassam et al., *Fraud and Data Availability Proofs*.

Data availability: the *negative* that makes the rollup verifiable

Why the Merkle root on Bitcoin **is not enough** without the raw data that generated it.

1 The seal is not enough

The state commitment on Bitcoin is like a **notarized photograph**: authentic, immutable, and verifiable. But without the **negative** — the raw data — what happened cannot be reconstructed.

The root certifies that a state **existed**.
The data tells you **which state it was**.

Notarized photograph
the state commitment on Bitcoin
- ✓ immutable
- ✓ verifiable
- ✓ compact

Original negative
the rollup's raw data
`tx` `signatures` `accounts` `payload` `state`

2 When the data is truly available

Raw
The complete information of the transactions.

Public
Accessible to anyone, without permissions.

Persistent
Available over time, not only today.

Verifiable
Authenticatable via hash and commitment.

⚠ If **even one condition** is missing, **availability is not complete.**

3 Bitcoin keeps the seal, not the warehouse

Bitcoin is ideal for anchoring a **compact root**, not for preserving all the raw data of millions of transactions.

Bitcoin makes **the fingerprint immutable**.
The DA layer makes **the document recoverable**.

₿ Bitcoin L1 · `Merkle root 32B`
immutability · finality · **a public reference**

↓

Data Availability Layer
complete transactions, signatures, accounts, payload — **data recoverable for verification**

4 The possible roads

01 **Distributed nodes**
Multiple copies held by independent parties.

02 **DA infrastructures**
Dedicated networks: Celestia, EigenDA.

03 **Redundant coding**
Reconstructible even if fragments are missing.

04 **Off-chain commitments**
Hash on-chain, complete data elsewhere.

05 **Economic incentives**
Rewards for those who preserve the data over time.

No approach solves everything on its own: **robustness often comes from a combination.**

5 Same root, different guarantees

True rollup
- Data publicly available.
- Anyone can reconstruct the state.
- Independent verification possible.

Validium
- Data off-chain, in the hands of few operators.
- Verification subordinate to availability.
- Greater trust required.

The difference is not only where the root sits: **it is where the data lives and who can recover it.**

THE KEY POINT

A root without data is the seal of a **vanished archive**. **Bitcoin** keeps the fingerprint; the **Data Availability Layer** keeps the **possibility of verification**. Without available data, *trust minimization* becomes **trust in the operator**.

PART V

The Sequencing Layer

Who decides the order of transactions and why this is the hottest political point of the entire architecture.

PART V · THE SEQUENCING LAYER

Chapter 15
The Sequencer as a Technical and Governance Surface

Whoever orders decides, and whoever has power orders

⁂

15.1 — A Simple Question with Enormous Consequences

Let us begin this chapter with a question that seems trivial but that is one of the most implication-laden of all rollup design: **when ten transactions arrive at the same time, in what order do they get processed?** It seems a banal technical question, one of those decisions taken in a quarter of an hour and coded in a few lines. **In reality, it is one of the most deeply political questions of a blockchain system's entire architecture.**

Understanding why requires taking a step back. In a blockchain, the order of the transactions is not a formality: it is what determines who wins and who loses. If two people attempt to buy the same rare NFT at launch, whoever goes first takes the piece. If two traders notice an arbitrage[a] opportunity, whoever executes first captures the profit. If someone is about to be liquidated in a DeFi protocol, the order in which the transactions are processed determines whether the liquidator[b] takes the fees or whether the user manages to deposit additional collateral in time. **The order is not a detail: it is value. And whoever controls the order controls an enormous flow of value.**

---

[a] **Arbitrage.** The operation by which one exploits a price difference for the same good on different markets or at different moments, buying where it costs less and selling where it costs more. On blockchains these occasions last fractions of a second: arriving first is decisive, and it is one of the reasons why the order of transactions has value.

[b] **Liquidation and liquidator.** In decentralized lending protocols, whoever borrows funds deposits a guarantee (the collateral). If the value of that guarantee falls below a threshold, the position can be "liquidated": forcibly sold to repay the debt. The liquidator is whoever executes this operation, obtaining a fee in exchange. It is cited here to show how much the order of transactions counts: a few instants decide whether it is the liquidator who profits or whether the user makes it in time to save their own position by adding collateral.

TABLE 15.1 **WHY THE ORDER OF TRANSACTIONS IS VALUE.**

Situation	What the order decides
A rare NFT at launch	Whoever goes first secures the piece
An arbitrage opportunity	Whoever executes first captures the profit
A DeFi liquidation	Whoever precedes collects the fees or saves the position

In all these cases what changes is not what is executed, but in what order. This is why the power to order transactions translates directly into economic value — the theme that runs through the entire chapter on the sequencer and on MEV.

FIGURE 15.1 **WHO DECIDES WHICH TRANSACTION GOES FIRST.**

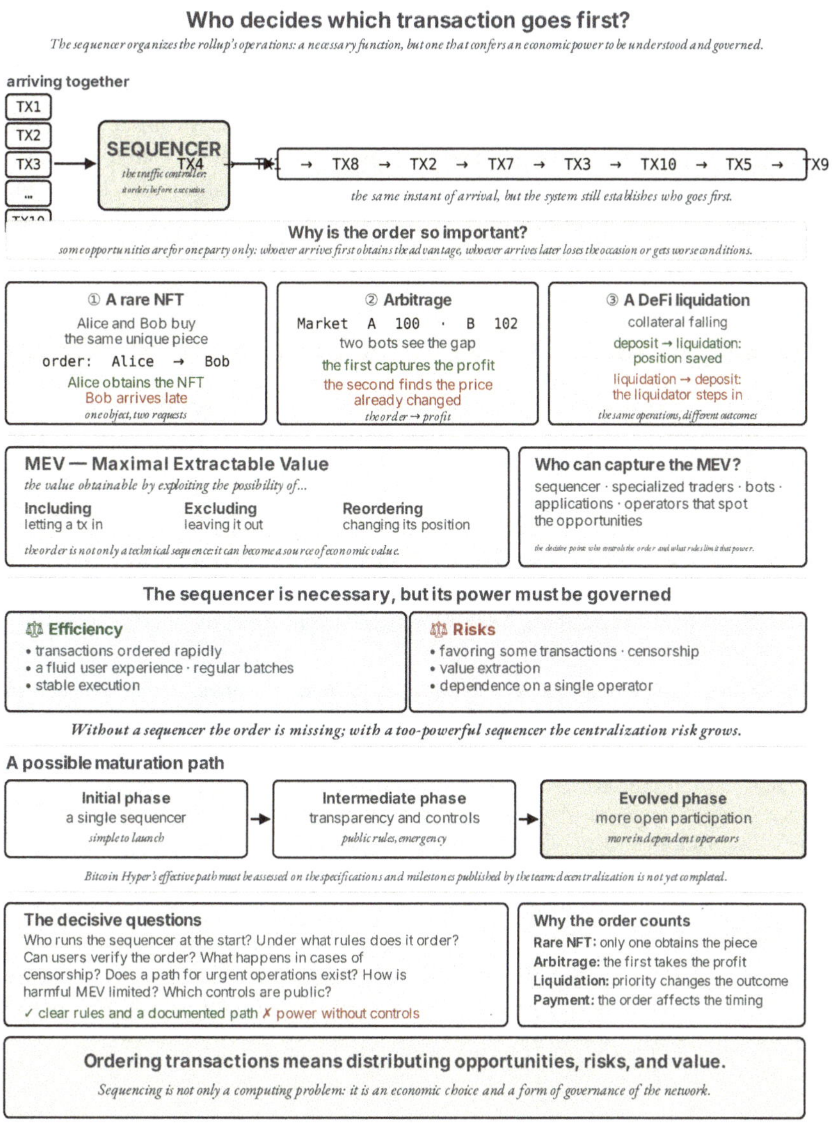

When several transactions arrive at the same time, the sequencer must establish an order. In many cases this choice is not neutral: it can determine who buys a rare NFT, who captures an arbitrage opportunity, or which operation is executed first in a DeFi position. Sequencing is therefore a technical function with significant economic consequences.

This is the first time in the book that we explicitly encounter the theme of **MEV**[1] — Maximal Extractable Value — which is one of the most important concepts for understanding modern on-chain finance. MEV is the economic value that can emerge from the possibility of including, excluding, or reordering certain transactions. Whoever controls the order occupies an important position, but specialized traders and bots capable of spotting opportunities and competing to exploit them can also intervene. On Ethereum, MEV has become a significant economic phenomenon, with specialized operators, sophisticated strategies, and tools built specifically to spot the opportunities. **The order is not a detail: it is value.**

For Bitcoin Hyper, as for every rollup, sequencing[a] is a strategic choice. Someone must order the transactions, because without a shared order[b] the system cannot function. But assigning this task to a single party also means concentrating a significant power in it. The question is not eliminating the sequencer, but understanding what rules, controls, and decentralization milestones can limit its risks. Bitcoin Hyper's public documentation dedicates specific attention to sequencing models and to the decentralization path, recognizing that establishing who orders the transactions is a central choice in the rollup's design: a **governance surface,**[c] not only a technical component. It is political in the most concrete sense of the term: it means deciding how a power is distributed and what rules prevent it from being used improperly.

In this chapter I want to do three things. First, concretely understand what a sequencer does and why its role is so sensitive. Second, describe MEV and its implications, because it is the connecting thread that ties everything together. Third, see how Hyper is tackling the problem, starting from a single sequencer[d] and designing a path of progressive decentralization.[e] It is a chapter that will make you understand an aspect of the blockchain world that marketing typically hides, but that is essential for judging any serious project in an informed way.

⁂

15.2 — The Sequencer: The Director of Transaction Ordering

Let us begin with the operational detail of what a sequencer does. We have already touched on it in various previous chapters, but now it is worth describing it with precision because many subtleties emerge from the details.

---

[a] **Sequencer / sequencing.** The sequencer is the component that receives the transactions and decides in what order to insert them before they are executed and anchored. Sequencing is this ordering activity. It seems a neutral task, but whoever performs it has the power to anticipate, delay, or exclude individual transactions: for this reason it is considered a sensitive point of the system.

[b] **Shared order.** The single sequence of transactions on which all the network's nodes agree. Without a shared order every node would see a different history and the system could not reach consensus: it is precisely to establish it that a sequencer is needed.

[c] **Governance surface.** An expression indicating a point of the system where one does not only decide "how the technology works," but "who is in charge" and under what rules. Defining who orders the transactions means distributing a power, and thus falls within the project's governance choices, not the purely engineering ones.

[d] **Single sequencer.** The configuration in which a single party — typically the project team — orders all the transactions. It is simple and quick to launch, but concentrates the power over ordering in a single entity: it is the starting point that progressive decentralization aims to overcome.

[e] **Progressive decentralization.** A strategy by which many projects start from a centralized, simple system — here a single sequencer run by the team — to then gradually distribute control to several independent parties. It allows launching sooner, but shifts into the future the proof that decentralization will really be realized.

FIGURE 15.2 **THE SEQUENCER: THE ROLLUP'S CONTROL TOWER.**

The sequencer does not sign in the users' place: it decides the order in which their transactions travel the network. In on-chain finance the order can modify timings, prices, and opportunities.

arrival → checks → queue → sequencing → execution+verification → checkpoint ₿

from the wallet to Bitcoin: a path of several components, not a single gatekeeper

1 · Arrival
wallets, DEXs, DeFi, games, bots, bridges →
RPC → the ordinary path toward the sequencer
RPC can be separate from the sequencer and have multiple endpoints

2 · Preliminary checks
signature · structure · accounts · fee payer ·
resources · freshness · duplicates
technical validity ≠ priority in the queue

3 · The queue — who goes first?
order of arrival (FIFO) · fee priority ·
a hybrid criterion · the protocol's rules
to be verified: which criterion and how much discretion
the criteria cannot yet be attributed with certainty to Hyper

4 · Ordering = power
include · delay · exclude · reorder
the order can shift economic value
swaps, liquidations, arbitrages, rare assets
changing the timing is enough, no need to forge a signature

5 · The SVM runtime executes
ordered batch → accounts → execution //
→ conflicts handled → new state
sequencing and execution are linked but distinct

6 · The proof (ZK)
state + batch → new root → validity proof
valid → accepted · invalid → rejected
the sequencer proposes, it does not make a false state true

7 · Data availability
batches → raw data → distributed archives
a root without data is a seal without a document

8 · Checkpoint on Bitcoin
state → compact commitment → anchoring ₿
Bitcoin receives a summary, not every operation

What can the sequencer do directly?

Yes · receive and order valid transactions (the central function)
Maybe · delay or exclude from the ordinary path → censorship must be countered
No · create the user's signature or modify a signed tx
It should not · make an incorrect root valid (proofs and verifiers prevent it)
Not automatically · open the bridge or change the protocol (administrative powers)

the sequencer controls the traffic; it should not control the system's truth on its own.

Do not confuse the roles — security is born from the separation of tasks
Sequencer orders and times · **Runtime** executes · **Proof** demonstrates correctness
Data availability makes the data recoverable · **Bridge** governs deposits/withdrawals · **Bitcoin L1** consolidates

A central function still to be defined in the details
Hyper declares SVM, aggregation/compression, ZK proofs, periodic commitments, and dedicates an update to sequencing models. To be clarified: RPC, mempool, priorities, batching, timing, censorship, powers, decentralization.
a warning signal: a single party that receives, orders, validates, publishes, and modifies the rules without controls

The sequencer does not possess the user's signature. It possesses the power to decide when it will enter the flow.
for this reason it must be observable, limited, and progressively less centralized.

The sequencer is the rollup's control tower: it receives the transactions through the ordinary path, applies preliminary checks, manages the queue, and builds ordered batches. Execution, cryptographic verification, data availability, and the periodic checkpoint on Bitcoin depend however on distinct components. The sequencer controls the transactions' traffic; it should not control the system's truth on its own.

The sequencer is the component that organizes the transactions' traffic in the rollup's ordinary path. **Users send operations through wallets and applications; the RPC infrastructure forwards them to the system; the sequencer collects the valid transactions, establishes an order, and builds batches destined for execution.**

The first activity is receiving the transactions. Every operation arrives digitally signed by its own sender and contains the instructions to execute, the accounts involved, and the information needed to pay the fees. In the SVM model, declaring the accounts touched is particularly important because it allows the runtime to distinguish independent transactions from those that come into conflict.

The second activity concerns the preliminary checks. Before execution, the system must verify that the signature is correct, that the transaction has a valid structure, that the requested accounts are indicated coherently, that the fee payer has the necessary resources, and that the operation respects the limits provided. **These checks should not depend on the sequencer's personal discretion: they must follow public, reproducible rules.**

A technically valid transaction, however, is not necessarily executed immediately. It can enter a queue together with many other operations. **And it is here that the most delicate part begins: the sequencer must establish which transactions go first, which are included in the subsequent batches, and which remain temporarily waiting.**

Several criteria are possible. A system can privilege the order of arrival, the fees offered, a hybrid criterion, or more articulated rules. **Bitcoin Hyper's public documentation does not yet clarify which policy will be definitively adopted.** It is an important choice, because the way transactions are ordered determines how much room exists for extracting economic value through timing and reordering.

After having defined the sequence, the sequencer builds ordered batches and passes them to the execution path. At this point different components come into play. **The SVM runtime applies the instructions and calculates the new state. The proof system must demonstrate the correctness of the transition. Data availability must make the data needed for verification recoverable.** The protocol finally publishes, at the intended frequency, a compact commitment of the state on Bitcoin.

It is important not to confuse these roles. **The sequencer decides the order of the traffic, but it should not be able to arbitrarily transform an incorrect state into a valid state.** It does not automatically possess the users' private keys and cannot create a valid signature in their place, nor freely modify an already signed transaction without invalidating it.

Its power nevertheless remains significant. It can attempt to delay a transaction, leave a valid operation in the queue, or place it in an unfavorable position relative to others. **In on-chain finance, a few seconds can affect the price obtained in a swap, the outcome of a liquidation, or the possibility of seizing an arbitrage.** The sequencer is therefore not the owner of the funds: it is the director of the order and of the timing. And it is precisely for this reason that it must be observable, limited by clear rules, and progressively less centralized.

⁂

15.3 — MEV: The Value Hidden in the Order

Now let us go inside MEV,[a] because it is the concept that gives substance to the whole discussion on the sensitivity of sequencing. **MEV is the acronym for Maximal Extractable Value**: it indicates the economic value that can emerge from the possibility of including, excluding, or modifying the order of the transactions.[b] Whoever controls the sequencing occupies an important position, but is not necessarily the only party capable of capturing this value. The term was born in the Ethereum[c] world in 2019. Originally it meant *Miner Extractable Value*,[d] because the power to order the transactions belonged to the miners[e]; the expression later became *Maximal Extractable Value*, a broader formula that also includes other parties.

Let us look at the main forms of MEV with concrete examples, because in the abstract it is hard to understand but with examples it becomes intuitive.

TABLE 15.2 **MEV: HOW THE ACRONYM'S MEANING HAS CHANGED.**

Reading	Origin	Who extracts the value
Miner Extractable Value	Ethereum, 2019	The miners who ordered the blocks
Maximal Extractable Value	The current meaning	Whoever controls the order: a sequencer too

Born to describe the value that Ethereum's miners could extract by reordering the transactions, the term then extended to any party that controls the order. In a rollup that party is the sequencer: this is why whoever orders the transactions occupies such a delicate position.

---

[a] **MEV.** It is the gain that whoever decides the order in which transactions are executed can extract. It does not come from a fee, but from the position of advantage of whoever sees the incoming operations and can arrange them in their own favor: for this reason it is considered a hidden cost and a source of power.

[b] **Including, excluding, reordering.** These are the three powers of whoever orders the transactions. They can insert their own operation at an advantageous point (for example just before someone else's), keep an unwelcome one out, or change the sequence to profit from it. It is from these three gestures that MEV is extracted.

[c] **Ethereum.** The second blockchain in importance after Bitcoin, born in 2015 and the first to make complex programs (the smart contracts) executed on the chain possible. It is on the Ethereum ecosystem that phenomena like MEV were first observed and studied.

[d] **Miner Extractable Value.** The acronym's original meaning: on Ethereum, in 2019, it was the miners who composed the blocks and thus decided the order of the transactions. When the power to order passed also to other parties — like the rollups' sequencers — the term was reinterpreted as Maximal Extractable Value.

[e] **Miner.** In proof-of-work-based blockchains, whoever makes computing power available to validate the transactions and produce new blocks, also deciding which transactions to include and in what order. On Ethereum, until 2022, it was the miners who controlled the ordering — whence the original name "Miner Extractable Value."

FIGURE 15.3 **THE MAIN FORMS OF MEV.**

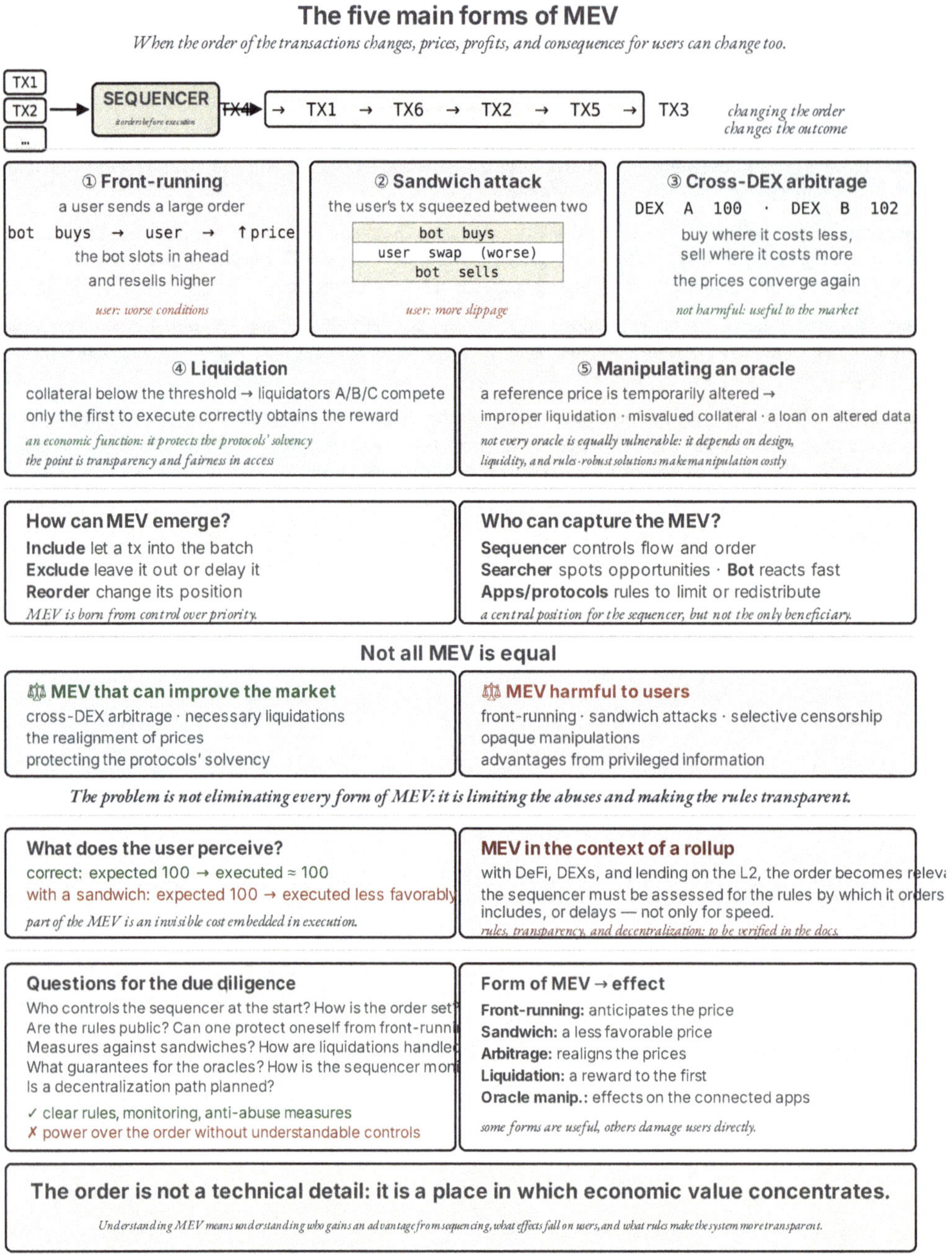

The possibility of including, excluding, or reordering transactions can generate different economic opportunities. Some, like arbitrage and liquidations, can contribute to the functioning of the markets; others, like front-running and sandwich attacks, can produce an invisible cost for users.

First form: front-running. Imagine a trader is about to place a large buy order for a token on a decentralized exchange, an order that will push the price up. Whoever sees the transaction in the queue before it gets executed can insert their own buy transaction **before** the trader's, buying at the low price, letting the trader's transaction push the price up, and then reselling at the higher price. Whoever has a privileged view of the pending transactions, or the ability to influence their order, can find themselves in a favorable position for anticipating a user's operation. **In a rollup, the sequencer's behavior and the rules of access to the transaction flow therefore become particularly important.**

Second form: the sandwich attack. It is a more sophisticated variant of front-running. Whoever controls the order inserts a buy transaction before the user's large order (the front-run), and then a sell transaction immediately after (the back-run), "sandwiching" the user. **On Ethereum, sandwich attacks have become one of the best-known forms of harmful MEV: the user receives a less favorable price and a part of the value is captured by whoever built the sandwich.**

Third form: cross-DEX arbitrage. When the same token shows different prices on different decentralized exchanges, an arbitrageur can buy on the cheaper market and sell on the more expensive one. This activity generates a profit, but it also performs a useful function: it contributes to realigning prices across different markets.

Fourth form: liquidation. In lending protocols, when a loan becomes under-collateralized, the position becomes liquidatable. **Several operators can compete to step in first and obtain the reward provided by the protocol.** Liquidations should not be described as necessarily predatory: they are also a useful tool for keeping lending protocols solvent. Here too, the transparency of the ordering rules is important.

Fifth form: manipulating the oracles. Some DeFi applications use prices drawn from decentralized markets. If an attacker manages to temporarily alter these prices, they can cause consequences for the protocols that use them: for example, an improper liquidation or an incorrect valuation of the collateral. The risk depends on how the oracle is built, on the liquidity available, and on the duration of the manipulation. **The more robust oracles use time-weighted averages (TWAP) and other devices to make the attack harder and more costly.**

All these forms of MEV exist in the Ethereum world and have developed into a sophisticated industry. **For a rollup like Hyper, the same dynamics will apply once the DeFi ecosystem is active**, because the mechanisms are fundamentally tied to the structure of decentralized finance, not to the specific blockchain.

One aspect must be emphasized for clarity. **Not all MEV is necessarily harmful.** Arbitrage helps realign prices across different markets; liquidations contribute to the stability of lending protocols. The problem arises when the order is exploited opaquely to the users' detriment, as happens in front-running and sandwich attacks. The decisive question is not only how much MEV exists, but who can capture it and what rules make this process transparent. **The problem is not MEV in itself, but who captures it and how.** Tools have been developed in the sector to make MEV management more orderly and competitive: *MEV-Boost*, for example, allows Ethereum validators to receive block proposals from a market of specialized builders; other mechanisms, like *MEV-Burn*, are still the object of research and aim to reduce or redistribute a part of the extracted value.

⁂

15.4 — The Sequencer as Gatekeeper: The Censorship Problem

Beyond MEV, there is another dimension of the sequencer's power that deserves separate attention: **the possibility of censoring**[a]. The sequencer, by deciding which transactions to include in the batches[b] and which not, can effectively block access to the rollup for specific users or specific operations.

Concretely, what does censorship mean in the context of a rollup? **In the context of a rollup, censoring means systematically refusing or delaying the inclusion of a valid transaction**[c]**.** The user respects the rules and pays the required fees, but their operation keeps staying out of the batches. Censorship can be targeted (against specific addresses), thematic (against certain types of transactions), or systemic (against entire categories of applications).

---

[a] **Censorship.** In a blockchain, the systematic refusal to include certain valid transactions. "Censorship resistance" is the property whereby no single party can prevent a user from operating: it is one of the fundamental values that a rollup should inherit from Bitcoin.

[b] **Batch (lot).** The group of transactions that the sequencer collects, orders, and processes together before anchoring them. Staying "out of the batch" means, for a transaction, not being processed.

[c] **Valid transaction.** A formally correct transaction — signed by the user and with the due fees — that the system should accept. Refusing or delaying it despite its being valid is precisely what censorship means.

Nota. The main defense against the sequencer's censorship is so-called forced inclusion: an alternative path that allows the user to impose the insertion of a transaction directly through the Layer 1, bypassing the sequencer. Its presence, timings, and activation costs are among the most important elements to verify in a rollup's definitive architecture: without a mechanism of this type, censorship resistance remains a declaration rather than a guarantee.

TABLE 15.3 **THE THREE FORMS OF SEQUENCER CENSORSHIP.**

Form	Target	Example
Targeted	Specific addresses	A single user or wallet kept out of the batches
Thematic	Certain transaction types	An entire category of operations systematically excluded
Systemic	Entire categories of applications	All the apps of a certain kind made unusable

Censorship is not always total: it can hit a single address, a type of operation, or an entire class of applications. In all cases the transaction is valid and the fees are paid; what is missing is the sequencer's willingness to include it.

FIGURE 15.4 **THE SEQUENCER AS GATEKEEPER.**

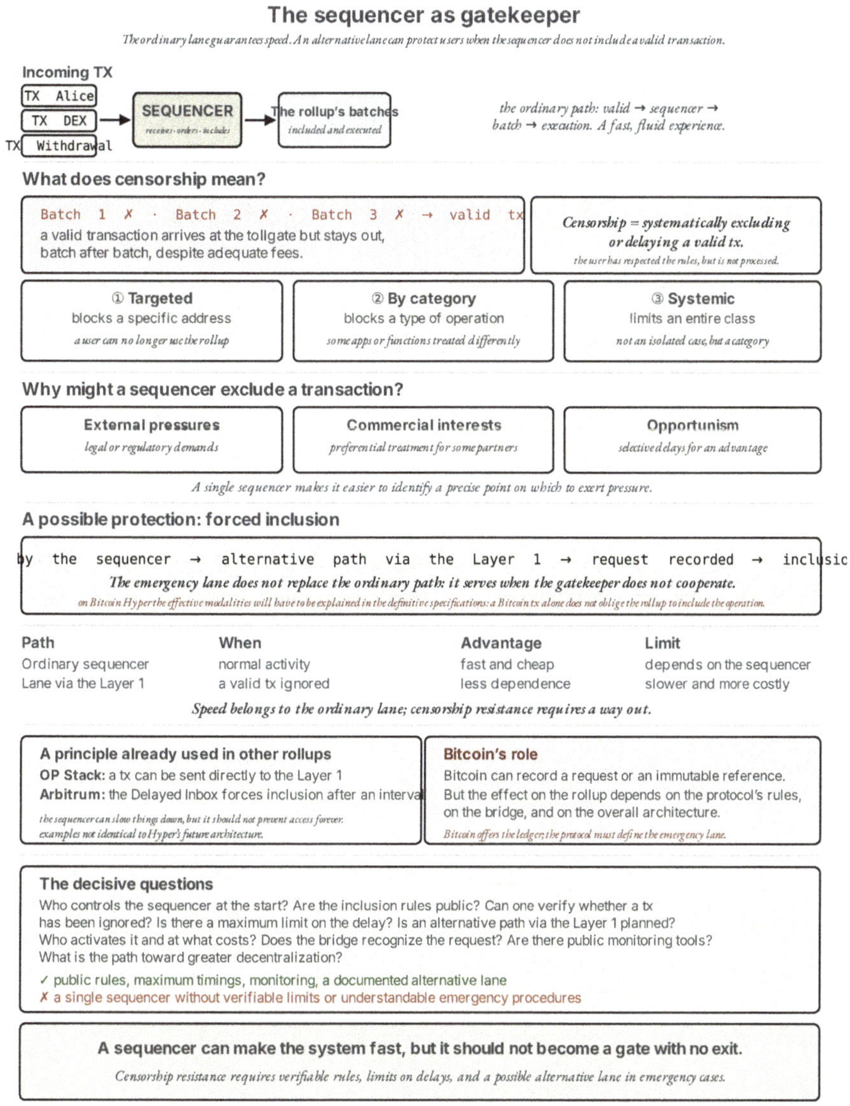

The sequencer performs a necessary function: it receives, orders, and inserts the transactions into the batches. If a valid operation is systematically excluded, a censorship risk emerges. Some rollups provide an alternative path through the Layer 1 to prevent the sequencer from being able to block access to the system indefinitely. The solution possibly adopted by Bitcoin Hyper will have to be described in the definitive technical specifications.

The reasons why a sequencer might censor are various. An operator can receive **external pressures**, can favor some applications over others out of **commercial interest**, or can selectively delay an operation out of **economic opportunism**. The point is not to claim this will necessarily happen, but to understand that a single sequencer concentrates a power that must be limited by transparent rules.

On Ethereum, the debate on sequencer censorship left the theoretical realm after the 2022 OFAC sanctions. Various validators and relayers began censoring transactions associated with sanctioned addresses, and this raised significant concerns about the network's censorship resistance. The theme emerged concretely after the sanctions introduced in the United States against Tornado Cash in 2022, subsequently removed in March 2025: the debate highlighted a general question, namely that when some operators of the blockchain supply chain apply filters to certain transactions it becomes important to understand whether the network offers alternative paths and maintains real censorship resistance. **Rollups with a single sequencer have this vulnerability in an amplified form**, because a single sequencer is easier to pressure than a thousand distributed validators.

One possible protection consists of providing an **alternative lane** (forced inclusion):* if the sequencer keeps ignoring a valid transaction, the user can record their own request on the Layer 1 under the rules established by the protocol. In this way, the system can prevent the sequencer from indefinitely blocking access to the rollup. The alternative path is normally slower and more costly, but it performs a last-resort function. In Ethereum rollups this logic is already used: in the OP Stack† transactions can be sent directly to the OptimismPortal contract on the Layer 1; on Arbitrum they can be recorded in the Delayed Inbox and forced after a defined interval if the sequencer keeps ignoring them.

For Bitcoin Hyper, this is a point to monitor with attention. The public documentation dedicates space to sequencing models and to the path toward greater decentralization, but it does not yet describe in detail a forced-inclusion procedure through Bitcoin Layer 1. **Before the mainnet it will be important to understand whether an alternative lane will exist, how it will work, and what timings and costs it will entail.** Without a procedure of this type, the promise of "censorship resistance" remains partial and users depend on the sequencer's good will, which is exactly the weak point the model should overcome. **The sequencer should not become a gate with no exit.**

⁂

15.5 — The Pragmatic Choice: A Single Sequencer at Launch

Having described the sequencer's powers and the problems it poses, we can now understand the choice Bitcoin Hyper has made explicit: **starting with a single sequencer run by the team, and designing a path of progressive decentralization over time**. It is a pragmatic choice that reflects a compromise between what is desirable in the long term and what is practicable at the start.

---

* **Forced inclusion.** It is the safeguard mechanism that allows a user to impose the insertion of their own transaction by going directly through the Layer 1, when the sequencer ignores it. It works like an emergency exit: slower and more costly than the normal way, but it guarantees that nobody can remain locked out of the rollup.

† **OP Stack and Arbitrum.** They are the two main families of rollups active on Ethereum: the first at the base of Optimism, the second eponymous. They are cited as concrete precedents because both already implement a form of forced inclusion — respectively the OptimismPortal contract and the Delayed Inbox — which serves as a reference model for what Bitcoin Hyper will have to provide.

FIGURE 15.5 **A SINGLE SEQUENCER CAN SIMPLIFY A ROLLUP'S INITIAL PHASE, OFFERING OPERATIONAL COORDINATION AND PREDICTABLE PERFORMANCE. ITS PRESENCE, HOWEVER, CONCENTRATES A SIGNIFICANT POWER. THE PROJECT'S QUALITY THEREFORE DEPENDS ON THE CONTROLS INTRODUCED AND ON THE CREDIBILITY OF THE PATH TOWARD PROGRESSIVELY MORE OPEN PARTICIPATION.**

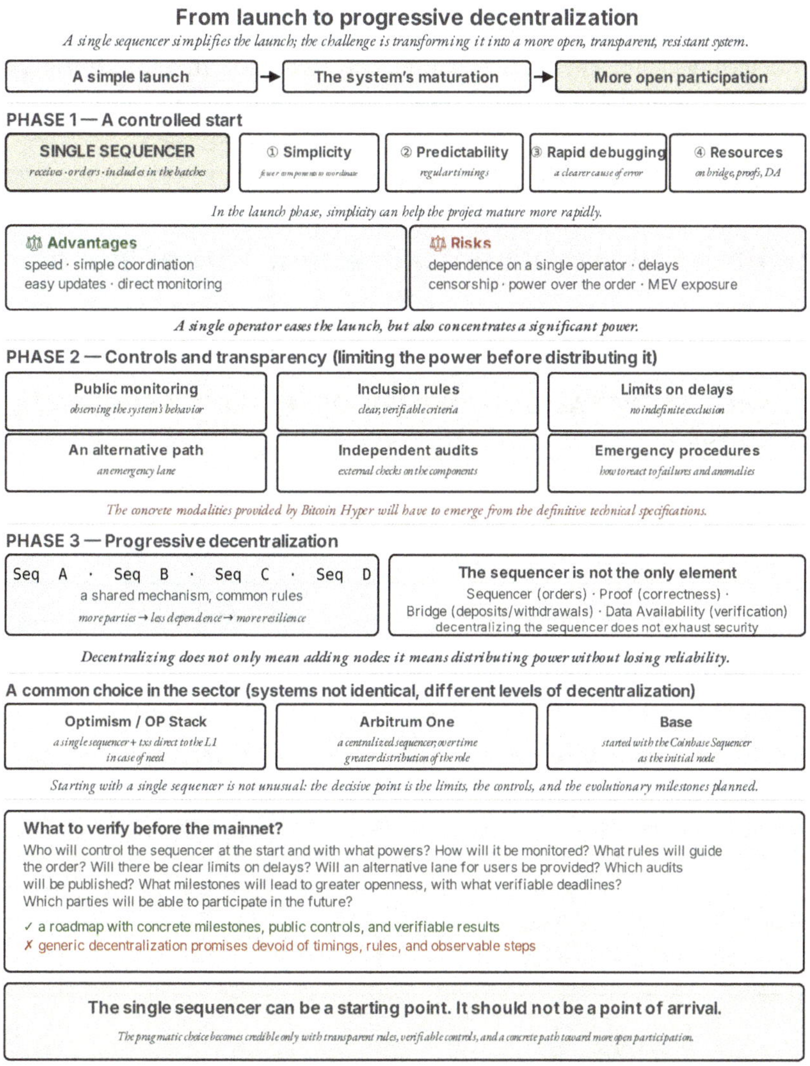

The reasons for starting with a single sequencer are concrete. **First reason: operational simplicity.** A single sequencer is infinitely simpler to manage than a distributed system of sequencers. One can iterate quickly, fix bugs rapidly, deploy updates without coordinating many actors. In the launch phase of a complex system, this agility is crucial.

Second reason: predictable performance. A single sequencer offers predictable latencies and throughput, because there is no distributed coordination introducing variance. For users, this translates into a fluid, predictable experience, important for building initial trust in the system.

Third reason: ease of analysis and debugging. When something goes wrong in a distributed system, understanding the problem is enormously harder than in a centralized system. For a young system where the bugs are still to be discovered, having a single observation point simplifies the analysis enormously.

Fourth reason: focusing the resources. Building a well-functioning distributed sequencer system requires significant engineering resources. In the initial phase, these resources are better spent on other components of the system (the Canonical Bridge, the proof model, data availability). Decentralizing the sequencer can wait until the other pieces are mature.

All these reasons are reasonable, and indeed the overwhelming majority of Ethereum's rollups started with single sequencers. Optimism, Arbitrum, Base still operate with single sequencers (with various nuances), despite years of operation. **Centralizing the sequencer at launch is not a Hyper-specific choice: it is the industry standard.**

The crucial point, however, is that the sequencer's centralization **not be presented as the system's final state.** If the Hyper team declared "we have a single sequencer and so it will remain," the security model would be that of a federated sidechain disguised as a rollup, and our whole discussion on the philosophical and technical difference of the rollup model would lose meaning. **Initial centralization is acceptable only if accompanied by a credible, timely path toward decentralization.**

Hyper has made this path explicit, and in the next section we will examine it in detail.

⁂

15.6 — The Path toward Decentralization: Three Phases

Hyper's January 2026 post on future sequencing models explicitly describes a path of progressive decentralization that unfolds in three phases, each with specific characteristics. Let us examine them.

FIGURE 15.7 **THE DECENTRALIZATION PATH OF HYPER'S SEQUENCER IN THREE PHASES.**

Phase	Operating model	Centralization and risk
1 · A controlled launch	A single sequencer run by the team.	High centralization, accepted as temporary; it depends on the team's integrity and on the transparency of the rules.
2 · Delegated participation	Third-party operators in rotation or shared signing[a] through committees.	Reduced but not eliminated; the team still controls the selection of the operators.
3 · Full decentralization	Auctions,[b] randomized leader election[c] or distributed committees with on-chain rules.[d]	No single operator holds significant control; the rules apply automatically.

Hyper's post does not commit to dates for each phase. It is precisely the concrete milestones — "Phase 2 within X months of the mainnet[e], Phase 3 within Y years" — that separate a credible roadmap from an "eternally promised" decentralization.

First phase: a controlled launch with a single sequencer. It is the initial phase, the one in which the system is starting. The sequencer is run by the main team, with full transparency on the operating rules but with centralized control over the decisions. In this phase the system still depends to a significant extent on the main team; for this reason the transparency of the rules and the possibility of monitoring the sequencer's behavior become particularly important. **This phase is the one most similar to a federated sidechain centralized on a single operator**[f], and it is important that it be explicitly temporary. The team has indicated that during this phase it will publish complete documentation on the sequencer's operation, so that the community can monitor the behavior and verify adherence to the public rules.

[a] **Shared signing (multisig).** A scheme in which an operation requires the signature of several parties instead of just one: nobody can act alone, the agreement of a minimum number of participants is needed. In sequencing committees it

distributes control over several operators.

[b] **Auctions (for sequencing).** A mechanism in which the right to order the transactions of a period is assigned to the highest bidder, instead of being reserved for a fixed party. It distributes the role in an open, competitive way, and can return to the network part of the value (the MEV) that would otherwise end up with the sequencer.

[c] **Randomized leader election.** A system that chooses by lot, at each turn, who will have the task of ordering the transactions. By drawing the "director" randomly and in rotation, one avoids the power stably concentrating on a single operator.

[d] **On-chain rules.** Rules written directly into programs on the chain, which apply by themselves without anyone needing to enforce them. Entrusting the selection of the sequencers to them means replacing trust in a person with an automatic procedure verifiable by anyone.

[e] **Mainnet.** A project's "main," definitive network, the one that manages real value, in contrast to the test networks (testnets) used for experimenting. The decentralization phases are measured in months or years from the mainnet's launch.

[f] **Federated sidechain.** A chain connected to Bitcoin whose operation is guaranteed by a restricted, predefined group of operators (a "federation"). Unlike a rollup, the security of the funds depends on the honesty of these operators, not on proofs verifiable on Bitcoin: this is why Hyper's first phase, with a single operator, resembles one.

Nota. The initial centralization of the sequencer is common to almost all rollups in production today, including Ethereum's main Layer 2s: it is not in itself a negative signal. The element that distinguishes a credible path from a vague promise is the presence of dated, verifiable milestones for the subsequent phases. A decentralization that is "planned" without concrete targets remains an intention; it becomes a commitment only when it is anchored to public, measurable milestones.

FIGURE 15.6 **THE PATH TOWARD THE DECENTRALIZATION OF SEQUENCING.**

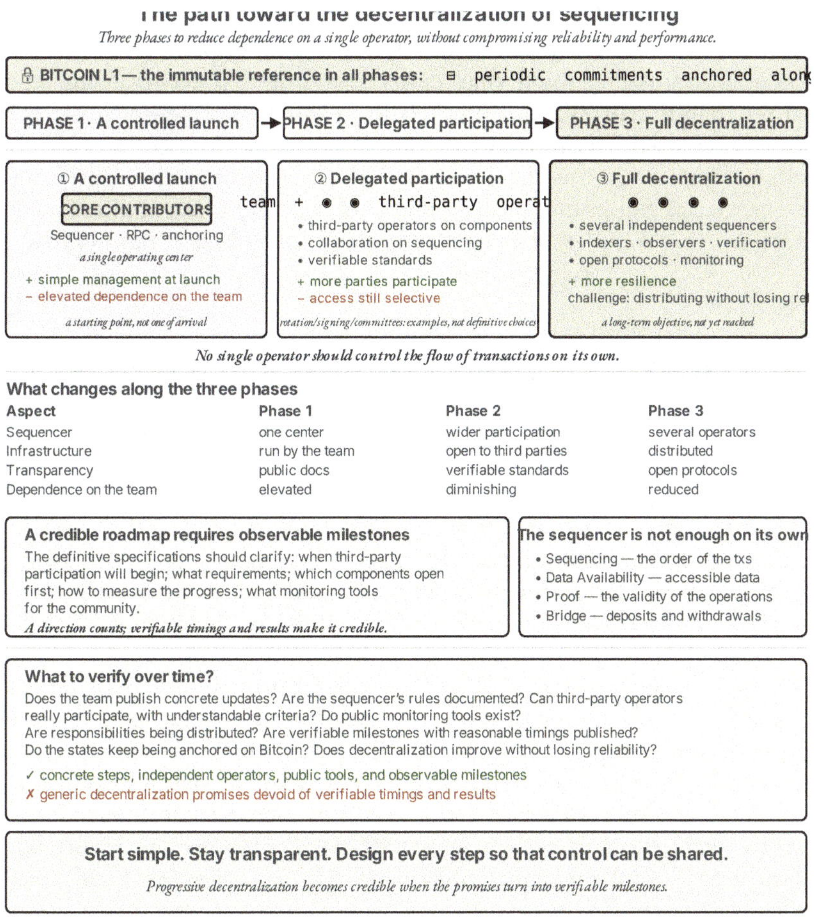

Bitcoin Hyper describes a roadmap in three phases: an initial controlled launch, a subsequent opening to third-party operators under verifiable standards, and, as a long-term objective, a more distributed infrastructure based on open protocols and states anchored on Bitcoin. Definitive timings and technical modalities will have to be verified in the project's subsequent updates.

Second phase: delegated participation. It is the intermediate phase, where independent third-party operators can begin participating in sequencing, but with defined access rules and operating standards. In this phase mechanisms like the rotation of the operators or forms of collaboration among several parties (for example, committees that sign the batches together) could be adopted; the concrete modalities will have to be defined in the technical specifications. **During this phase, centralization is reduced but does not disappear**: the team maintains significant control through the operator selection rules, and the participating operators must satisfy specific technical and operational requirements.

Third phase: complete decentralization. It is the long-term objective, where sequencing is really distributed without a central authority. Several models could be evaluated for reaching this objective: transparent auctions, periodic selection of the operators, or distributed committees with on-chain rules. **The essential point is not choosing a formula in advance, but preventing a single party from retaining significant control over the order of the transactions**, and ensuring the rules are applied automatically and verifiably.

The direction indicated is clear, but a roadmap becomes credible only when accompanied by observable milestones. It will therefore be important to verify when the first forms of external participation will be opened, what requirements will be demanded of the operators, and what tools will allow the community to measure the progress made. **Start simple, stay transparent, and design every step so that control can be shared.**

The post does not specify exact timings for completing the three phases, and this is a lack that deserves attention. **Without specific timings, "progressive decentralization" risks becoming "eternally promised decentralization."** A credible path should have concrete milestones: for example, "phase two within X months of the mainnet launch, phase three within Y years." Without these milestones, it is hard to assess the team's effective will to complete the path.

There is also a technical dimension that deserves attention. **Decentralizing the sequencer is enormously harder than decentralizing a blockchain's consensus.** Traditional blockchains have had decades to develop distributed consensus mechanisms (Proof of Work, Proof of Stake, BFT) that work robustly. For rollup sequencers, the mechanisms are still in the research phase. Optimism and Arbitrum, after years of existence, are still in intermediate phases of sequencer decentralization. **For Hyper, the realistic expectation is that complete decentralization will require years, not months.**

⁂

15.7 — What It Means for Users during the Initial Phase

Having understood the path, we can look at what it concretely means for users to operate on the rollup during the initial phase of a centralized sequencer. It is important to be clear about what is actually at stake, because marketing tends to minimize.

What is NOT at risk during the initial phase. Users do not risk losing their own funds because of the sequencer. The sequencer does not possess the private keys, cannot forge signatures, cannot invent transactions. **Even a completely dishonest sequencer could not empty the users' accounts.** The transactions executed and anchored on Bitcoin are in any case immutable. The rollup's state is reconstructible from the public data (assuming data availability is well managed).

What IS at risk during the initial phase. Users can suffer various forms of friction. **MEV extraction**: a dishonest sequencer can extract value through manipulated ordering, reducing the value of the users' transactions. **Selective censorship**: the sequencer might refuse to process certain transactions, forcing users to use forced-inclusion mechanisms (if available) or to wait. **Service availability**: if the sequencer goes offline, the rollup stops processing transactions until it comes back into operation. On Optimism, this has happened several times over the past years, with halts of hours or of an entire day. **Transaction privacy**: the sequencer sees all the transactions in the queue before they are processed, and this privileged visibility can be abused.

For most users doing everyday operations of moderate value, these risks are acceptable. **The sequencer can ruin the experience temporarily, but it cannot ruin the users' wallets.** For actors doing high-value or particularly MEV-sensitive operations, the risks can be significant and deserve attention.

There is a strategic consideration for the prudent investor or user: **monitoring the signals of good or bad management of the sequencer during the initial phase.** If the team communicates transparently, publishes operating metrics, responds rapidly to problems, correctly applies the public rules — these are all positive signals that the path of progressive decentralization will unfold as declared. If instead the team is opaque, the uptime is problematic, there are signals of selective censorship or of opportunistic MEV extraction — these are risk signals that must be taken seriously.

The sector's recent history gives us examples of both types. Optimism, after initial problems, developed transparency and responsiveness practices that built trust over time. Other, less-known projects managed sequencing opaquely and lost credibility. **For Hyper, the sequencer's initial phase will be one of the most visible tests of the team's maturity**, and the decisions the team will take will be important indicators for the project's future.

⁂

15.8 — Questions and Answers: Clarifying the Chapter's Concepts

Question 1: If Hyper's sequencer will initially be centralized, how is it different from a federated sidechain?

The difference is structural and must be understood precisely. **In a federated sidechain, the consortium of operators controls the funds**: it holds the multisig keys that keep the deposited bitcoin, and could theoretically collude to steal them. **In a rollup with a centralized sequencer, the sequencer controls the order of the transactions but not the funds**. The users' private keys remain with the users, and the bitcoin kept in the Canonical Bridge are protected by cryptographic mechanisms, not by the sequencer's honesty. **Even a completely dishonest sequencer cannot steal.** It can cause experience problems (MEV, censorship, availability), but it cannot take funds away. **This is the fundamental philosophical difference**, even if the two systems can look similar from the outside. Concrete example: if Liquid (a federated sidechain) decided tomorrow to disappear with the bitcoin, users would have no recourse. If Hyper's sequencer decided tomorrow to stop operating, users could (in theory, with the right mechanisms) withdraw their own bitcoin directly through the Canonical Bridge, without depending on the sequencer's cooperation. The difference is an abyss, even if in everyday use it might not be visible.

Question 2: Isn't MEV simply "the way markets work"? Why is it considered a problem?

MEV is a structural phenomenon that exists in any market system, and not all MEV is "bad." But the problem is that in the blockchain world, MEV has specific characteristics that make it more problematic than in other contexts. **First problem: it is opaque**. Users do not see that MEV is being extracted from their own transactions; they suffer it without knowing. **Second problem: it is asymmetric**. Only whoever controls the order can extract it, and this creates a concentration of value in few actors. **Third problem: it degrades the user experience**. Opportunistic MEV (sandwich attacks, front-running) translates into greater slippage and worse prices for users. **Fourth problem: it incentivizes centralization**. Whoever controls the sequencer has an enormous advantage, and this incentivizes the concentration of power. The modern research direction is to **make MEV transparent and redistributive**: mechanisms like MEV-Boost on Ethereum make it possible to capture MEV transparently and to redistribute it to the system's actors instead of leaving it in the hands of a single one. Hyper will have to develop similar mechanisms over time. Concrete example: Flashbots on Ethereum transformed MEV from an opaque, centralizing phenomenon into a transparent market, where MEV searchers compete openly and a part of the extracted value goes back to Ethereum's validators. It is an evolution that demonstrates how MEV can be governed instead of eliminated.

Question 3: If forced-inclusion mechanisms are important against censorship, why has Hyper not already implemented and documented them?

It is a legitimate question, and it must be addressed with honesty. Forced inclusion is technically complex to implement correctly because it requires integration between the sequencing layer and the settlement layer (Bitcoin in Hyper's case). The user must be able to demonstrate to the system, through a Bitcoin transaction, that they attempted to include a transaction the sequencer did not process, and the system must be able to force the inclusion automatically. **This requires specific Bitcoin primitives, specific rollup logic, and coordination with all the components of the system.** It is non-trivial work, and it is probably one of the areas where the Hyper team is investing resources in the months preceding the mainnet launch. **The fact that it is not yet documented does not mean it is not being worked on**, but it is fair to ask when specific documentation will arrive. **For prudent investors**, forced inclusion is one of the points to monitor in the coming months: without this mechanism, the promise of "censorship resistance" is incomplete. Concrete example: Optimism implemented forced-inclusion mechanisms only years after the initial launch. For Hyper, a similar trajectory is expected, though ideally a faster one given the sector's greater maturity.

Question 4: How do I know, as a user, whether the sequencer is extracting MEV from me or censoring my transactions?

For most users, recognizing MEV or censorship on individual transactions is difficult. **MEV manifests as greater-than-expected slippage** on exchange transactions, but understanding whether the slippage is due to MEV or to normal market liquidity requires sophisticated analysis. **Censorship manifests as transactions that are not included** within reasonable timings, but understanding whether it is censorship or congestion requires observing the system's behavior over time. **To recognize systemic problems, aggregate data is needed**: specialized analysts monitor the MEV extracted by the various sequencers, check transaction inclusion statistics, identify suspicious patterns. This data is published periodically by independent researchers, and it is the best way for normal users to assess whether a system is managing sequencing well or badly. **For Hyper, independent analysts are expected to emerge who will monitor the sequencer after the mainnet launch**, and their reports will be an important source of information. Concrete example: Flashbots, EigenPhi, MEV-Inspect, and other projects regularly publish data on the MEV extracted on Ethereum, allowing anyone to assess the behavior of the various sequencers and validators. For Hyper the development of analogous tools over time is expected.

Question 5: Is the sequencer's decentralization really reachable, or is it a promise that will always remain in the future?

It is a deep question that reflects a legitimate skepticism. On Ethereum, after five years of active rollups, the sequencer's decentralization is still largely to be realized. Optimism, Arbitrum, Base operate with largely centralized sequencers, though with forced-inclusion mechanisms that mitigate the worst risks. **Complete decentralization is technically hard, economically complex, and politically sensitive.** It is fair to be skeptical about decentralization promises, and it is fair to ask for concrete milestones instead of vague objectives. **That said, there are reasons to be moderately optimistic**: research on distributed sequencers is active, various projects are experimenting with different models (PBS, MEV-Burn, shared sequencers), and the industry is gradually maturing solutions that could be adopted at scale. **For Hyper, monitoring the concrete progress of the decentralization path will be more important than the declarations of intent.** If in the first years after the mainnet launch the team releases concrete milestones (the transition to phase two, the first independent operators, public operating statistics), it is a positive signal. If it stays stuck at the single sequencer, it is a signal of a problem. Concrete example: in 2024, Optimism released the "Superchain framework," which opens the way to a sequencer shared among several rollups. It is a concrete step toward decentralization, even if not a complete one. It is these types of concrete steps that must be monitored, not the generic promises.

Question 6: If Hyper's sequencer extracted too much MEV, users could turn to another rollup. Isn't there therefore an automatic brake on abusive behavior?

Yes, there is a market brake, but with important limits. **In principle, if users perceive that a rollup extracts too much MEV, they can migrate to a competitor rollup.** This is a real brake, and it explains why sequencers cannot abuse in a gross way: they risk losing the user base. **But the brake is limited for various reasons.** First: switching costs are significant. Migrating from one rollup to another requires transferring funds, rebuilding positions, reconfiguring wallets. It is not trivial. Second: MEV is opaque. Users often do not know how much MEV is extracted from their own transactions, so they cannot take informed migration decisions. Third: the network effect protects the dominant rollups. If a rollup already has most of the applications and the liquidity, users have reasons to stay there even with imperfect MEV. **For Hyper, in an initial phase where the ecosystem is still small, market pressure will be weak.** The sequencer could abuse significantly before users react. **In a mature phase, with a robust ecosystem and credible alternatives**, the pressure would be more effective. The trajectory over time is important: the more Hyper manages to decentralize the sequencer before it becomes large, the less market pressure will be needed as a brake. Concrete example: Arbitrum is more popular than Optimism in part because it extracted less MEV in an opaque way. Users, even without precise analyses, perceive over time which system is "fairer" and migrate accordingly. But the process is slow, and in the meantime a lot of MEV gets extracted.

⁂

15.9 — WHAT TO TAKE AWAY FROM THIS CHAPTER

The sequencer is the rollup's component that decides the order of the transactions, and this apparent technical formality is in reality a significant surface of power. Whoever controls the order controls important flows of value.

MEV (Maximal Extractable Value) is the value extractable by whoever controls the order, and it includes front-running, sandwich attacks, cross-DEX arbitrage, predatory liquidations, oracle manipulation. It is a billion-dollar industry in the Ethereum world.

Not all MEV is "bad": arbitrage and liquidations perform useful functions. The problem is who captures the MEV and how: opaque extraction by whoever controls the sequencer is a form of invisible taxation on users.

The sequencer also has a power of censorship: it can refuse to include certain transactions, blocking access to the rollup for specific users or operations. Forced inclusion is the technical mechanism for countering censorship, but it requires specific implementation.

Bitcoin Hyper starts with a single sequencer run by the team, a pragmatic choice reflecting the industry standard (Optimism, Arbitrum, Base did the same). Initial centralization is acceptable only if accompanied by a credible path of progressive decentralization.

The decentralization path unfolds in three phases: a controlled launch (the team's single sequencer), delegated participation (third-party operators with rules), complete decentralization (distributed sequencing without a central authority). Hyper has made the path explicit but not the specific timings.

The sequencer does not possess the users' private keys, so it cannot steal the funds. Its power is one of "ordering and timing," not of substitution. Even a dishonest sequencer can cause experience problems (MEV, censorship, availability) but not a loss of funds.

During the initial phase, users mainly risk frictions: MEV extraction, selective censorship, temporary service halts, a loss of transaction privacy. For most users these risks are acceptable; for actors sensitive to high value, they deserve attention.

To evaluate the project, monitoring the signals of good management of the sequencer during the initial phase is crucial. Transparency, responsiveness, respect for the public rules, concrete milestones of the decentralization path are the positive signals to look for.

Decentralizing the sequencer is technically hard and will probably require years. On Ethereum, after five years of active rollups, it is still largely to be realized. For Hyper, the realistic expectation is one of years, not months, but with concrete, measurable progress.

Chapter 15 ends here. We have understood why the sequencer is a governance surface and not only a technical component, why the initial centralization is pragmatic but temporary, and what the mechanisms are through which progressive decentralization can be realized. In ***Chapter 16 — A Single Sequencer at Launch: The Pragmatic Choice of the Start****, we will go down into the specific details of the initial phase, examining concretely what it means to operate with a single sequencer, what operating practices the Hyper team is announcing, and what metrics a prudent observer should monitor during this phase.*

NOTES

1 *Maximal Extractable Value*: the maximum value a sequencer can extract by reordering, including, or excluding transactions in the block. The term replaces the earlier "Miner Extractable Value" after Ethereum's transition to proof-of-stake.

The *sequencer*: whoever orders, decides

Why the order of transactions is a **technical, economic, and governance** surface.

1 The order is not neutral

When several transactions arrive together, someone decides which goes first. In DeFi, NFTs, and on-chain trading the order can determine **who gains, who loses, and who is left out**.

Ordering transactions means distributing opportunities, risks, and value.

TX1 TX2 TX3 TX4 TX5

▼ SEQUENCER · DECIDES THE ORDER ▼

TX4 → TX1 → TX3 → TX5 → TX2

EXAMPLES rare NFT: whoever goes first buys · arbitrage: whoever arrives first captures · liquidation: the order decides the outcome

2 The rollup's control tower

wallet · app · bot → RPC → sequencer → ordered batch → runtime SVM → proof → data avail. → checkpoint ₿

DOES orders · includes · delays · can exclude from the ordinary path

SHOULD NOT sign for users · modify signed txs · validate a false root · control bridge/proof/L1 on its own

The sequencer **controls the traffic**, *it should not control* **the system's truth**.

3 MEV: when the order becomes value

The **MEV** is the value that can emerge from the possibility of **including**, **excluding**, or **reordering** transactions.

LEVERS include: let a tx in · exclude / delay: leave it out or waiting · reorder: change its position

Front-running
A tx is anticipated to exploit its price effect.

Sandwich attack
The user is "squeezed" between two txs that worsen the price.

Arbitrage
Can realign prices across different markets.

Liquidations
They protect the protocols, but reward whoever arrives first.

Not all MEV is harmful: **the problem is who captures it, with what rules, and with how much transparency.**

4 The sequencer as gatekeeper

If a sequencer can ignore a valid transaction, it can turn into **a gate with no exit**. Censorship = the systematic exclusion or delay of a valid tx.

FORMS targeted (address) · thematic (operation type) · systemic (entire category)

Speed belongs to the ordinary lane. **Censorship resistance requires a way out.**

CENSORSHIP IN THE ORDINARY LANE

TX valid → Batch 1 ✗ · Batch 2 ✗ · Batch 3 ✗

WAY OUT · FORCED INCLUSION

user → Bitcoin L1 → request recorded →

inclusion under the protocol's rules

5 A starting point, not one of arrival

PHASE 1
Controlled launch
A single sequencer run by the team. Simple and fast, but centralized.

PHASE 2
Delegated participation
Third-party operators, rotation, shared signing. Reduced, not eliminated, centralization.

PHASE 3
Full decentralization
Several sequencers, on-chain rules, auctions or leader election. No single operator.

☑ A credible roadmap requires **verifiable milestones**, not generic promises.

THE KEY POINT

The **sequencer** is necessary to give the rollup order. But whoever orders can influence **value, priority, censorship, and MEV**. For this reason sequencing must be ***transparent, monitorable, limited by rules*** and **progressively decentralized**.

PART V · THE SEQUENCING LAYER

Chapter 16
A Single Sequencer at Launch

The pragmatic choice of the start

⁂

16.1 — Honesty about the Initial Phase

In the previous chapter we saw that Bitcoin Hyper, like most new-generation rollups, starts with a single sequencer run by the team. We also said that this is a pragmatic choice, acceptable if accompanied by a credible path toward decentralization. Now I want to go down into this initial phase with brutal honesty: **what exactly does it mean, in practice, to operate with a single team sequencer? What are the real trade-offs? What can go wrong? And how should the team's behavior be evaluated during this phase?**

This is one of those conversations the sector's marketing tends to avoid, because talking openly about the vulnerabilities of a centralized phase makes the project look less "decentralized" than it would like to seem. But it is precisely this honesty that separates serious analysis from propaganda. An informed investor must understand exactly what they are embarking on, must know what risks they are accepting in exchange for what potential rewards, and must have concrete tools for monitoring whether the project is keeping its promises. **All of this requires talking openly about the initial phase, without sweetening it.**

In this chapter I want to do four things. First, concretely describe what the team does during the initial phase: what decisions it takes, what infrastructure it manages, what responsibilities it has. Second, identify the specific risks of this phase, distinguishing between the inevitable ones and the mitigable ones. Third, explore the transparency and accountability practices that should accompany a single sequencer to make it acceptable. Fourth, provide a concrete checklist of metrics that a prudent observer should monitor during this phase. It is an operational chapter more than a theoretical one, and it will give you practical tools for evaluating Bitcoin Hyper in the months following the mainnet launch.

⁂

16.2 — What the Team Concretely Does during the Single-Sequencer Phase

Let us begin with the operational detail. When Bitcoin Hyper launches the mainnet with a single sequencer, the team will have specific operating responsibilities that must be articulated. It is not just "running a server." It is a complex set of functions that together keep the system standing.

FIGURE 16.1 **THE TEAM'S SIX OPERATING FUNCTIONS DURING THE SINGLE-SEQUENCER PHASE.**

#	Function	What it consists of
1	**The sequencer's infrastructure**	Running the servers 24/7: bandwidth, storage, backups, monitoring, scaling, incident management, deployments without interruptions.
2	**Ordering rules**	Defining and faithfully applying the public rules by which the sequencer orders the transactions and handles conflicts and duplicates.
3	**Updates and patches**	The software's life cycle: testing, gradual deployments, rollbacks. A wrong patch in production can compromise the service and the state's consistency.
4	**Communication and crisis management**	Timely response to halts, bugs, and attacks: explaining what happened, indicating actions and timelines, containing panic.

5	**Relations with regulators**	Interacting with the authorities: information requests, sanctions, compliance. In tension with the principles of decentralization (censorship risk).
6	**Economic management**	Keeping the balance between fees collected and anchoring costs on Bitcoin positive: pricing, anchoring frequency, operating costs.

Put together, these six functions reveal that whoever runs a single sequencer is in effect a blockchain financial services company with multiple, simultaneous responsibilities — not "a team of developers running a service." It is precisely this complexity that makes progressive decentralization important: distributing the responsibilities reduces the load and the points of failure.

First function: managing the sequencer's infrastructure. The sequencer is a software service that runs on real servers; it needs network bandwidth, storage, backups, continuous monitoring. The team must keep this infrastructure operational 24/7, manage scaling when the load increases, respond to incidents, deploy updates without interrupting the service. **It is heavy operational management work**, similar to what the large technology platforms do for their own mission-critical services.

Second function: defining and applying the ordering rules. The team must have written and published specific rules on how the sequencer orders the transactions: order of arrival, fee-based priority, conflict handling, treatment of duplicate or malformed transactions. These rules must be applied consistently in the software, and the team is responsible for their correct implementation. **The rules are public; the trust required is that they be applied faithfully.**

Third function: managing updates and patches. Like any complex software, the sequencer will have bugs, performance problems, optimization opportunities. The team must manage the software's life cycle: testing in a non-production environment, gradual deployments, handling possible rollbacks. **A wrong patch applied to the sequencer in production could have serious consequences**, from a temporary loss of service to state-consistency problems. The team has significant technical responsibility.

Fourth function: communicating with the community and managing crises. When something goes wrong — a service halt, a detected bug, an attack — the team must communicate promptly with users, explain what happened, declare what it is doing, give resolution timelines. **In the absence of timely communication, panic spreads and amplifies the problems.** Crisis management is a critical skill for any team that runs blockchain infrastructure.

Fifth function: relations with regulators and institutional bodies. In a regulatory landscape increasingly active in the crypto world, the team must manage interactions with the authorities: responding to information requests, handling possible sanctions or restrictions, maintaining compliance in different jurisdictions. **These interactions are delicate** because they can come into conflict with the ethics of decentralization: a team could be forced to censor certain transactions, and this creates tension with the project's principles.

Sixth function: the system's economic management. The sequencer receives fees from the transactions it processes, and pays others to anchor the state commitments on Bitcoin. The system's economic balance must be kept positive over time, otherwise the system becomes unsustainable. **The team must manage this economy**: adjusting the fees when necessary, optimizing the anchoring frequency, monitoring the operating costs. It is an activity that requires both technical and financial management skills.

Putting these six functions together, a picture emerges: **the team that runs a single sequencer is effectively a blockchain financial services company with multiple, simultaneous responsibilities.** It is very different from the simplified image of "a team of developers running a service." And this complexity is one reason why progressive decentralization is important: distributing these responsibilities among several independent actors reduces the operating load on any single team and decreases the points of failure.

⁂

16.3 — Structural Risks and Mitigable Risks

Let us now see what risks accompany the initial phase with a single sequencer. Some derive from the concentration of the role in a single operator; others depend above all on the way the team manages the system. Distinguishing the two categories — **structural**[a] risks and **mitigable**[b] risks — helps understand which limits require an evolution of the architecture and which problems can be reduced right away with greater discipline and transparency.

---

[a] **Structural risk.** It is a risk that depends on the system's architecture itself, not on the good or bad conduct of whoever manages it. As long as the sequencer is unique, for example, the possibility of censoring or of exploiting the order of transactions remains intrinsic: it is not eliminated with discipline, but only by changing the system's design — that is, by distributing the role among several operators. For this reason structural risks require an evolution of the architecture, not simple operational precautions.

[b] **Mitigable risk.** It is a risk that, though present, can be reduced right away with management choices: transparency, monitoring, timely communication of incidents, clear rules. It does not require redesigning the system, but discipline in running it. Distinguishing mitigable risks from structural ones is useful in a due diligence, because it clarifies what a project can improve today and what it will only be able to resolve by decentralizing over time.

TABLE 16.1 **RISKS OF THE SINGLE SEQUENCER: STRUCTURAL AND MITIGABLE.**

Structural risks[a]	Mitigable risks[b]
Service interruption[c]	Opacity of the decisions
Selective censorship[d]	A slow response to incidents
An advantage over the order (MEV)[e]	Inadequate communication
Dependence on the initial operator[f]	Postponed decentralization[g]

Structural risks are born from the concentration of the role and are reduced only by widening participation; mitigable ones depend on the quality of the execution and can be addressed right away with transparency, procedures, and observable milestones.

---

[a] **Structural risks.** They are the risks that descend from the system's very structure in this phase, that is, from having a single sequencer. They are not eliminated with good practices, but only by changing the architecture: distributing the role among several independent operators.

[b] **Mitigable risks.** They do not depend on the structure, but on how the team operates. They can be reduced right away with transparency, clear procedures, and rapid response times, without waiting for decentralization.

[c] **Service interruption.** It is the risk that the system temporarily stops accepting new operations if the only sequencer halts. It concerns the service's continuity (the so-called liveness), not the security of the funds, which remains guaranteed in any case.

[d] **Selective censorship.** The risk that the sequencer deliberately excludes or delays the transactions of certain users or applications, despite their being valid. It concerns not the security of the funds but the right to access the system freely.

[e] **An advantage over the order (MEV).** The risk that whoever orders the transactions exploits their own position to insert their own at the most profitable points, extracting value at the expense of the other users (the MEV already described in Chapter 15).

[f] **Dependence on the initial operator.** In the initial phase the system's reliability is tied to the health and correctness of the team that runs the only sequencer: if it fails, the whole service suffers until the role is distributed.

[g] **Postponed decentralization.** The risk that the distribution of control, announced as an objective, is continually postponed and in fact not realized. It is a risk mitigable only by dated, verifiable milestones.

First structural risk: service availability. If the single sequencer temporarily stops working — for maintenance, for an incident, for an attack — new operations can slow down or halt until the service is restored or any alternative paths provided by the protocol are activated. The states already anchored on Bitcoin remain valid and users do not lose funds, but for a certain time transactions cannot be made. It is a limit of the model: a single sequencer has a single point of failure. Internal redundancy can reduce downtime, but does not eliminate the risk. **Concrete example:** in the OP Stack the model with a single sequencer is described as more vulnerable to service halts; for this reason the possibility of sending transactions through Ethereum Layer 1 even during downtime is provided. For Hyper[2] similar episodes are expected, at least occasionally, during the initial phase.

Second structural risk: the capacity for selective censorship. A single sequencer technically possesses the capacity to delay or exclude some transactions. A possible alternative path through the Layer 1 can limit this power and prevent a valid operation from being blocked indefinitely. The team's transparency is important, but on its own it does not replace a technical protection. **Reference:** Arbitrum and the OP Stack document forced-inclusion or sequencer-bypass tools precisely to limit the effects of censorship and downtime.

FIGURE 16.2 **RISKS OF THE SINGLE SEQUENCER: STRUCTURAL AND MITIGABLE.**

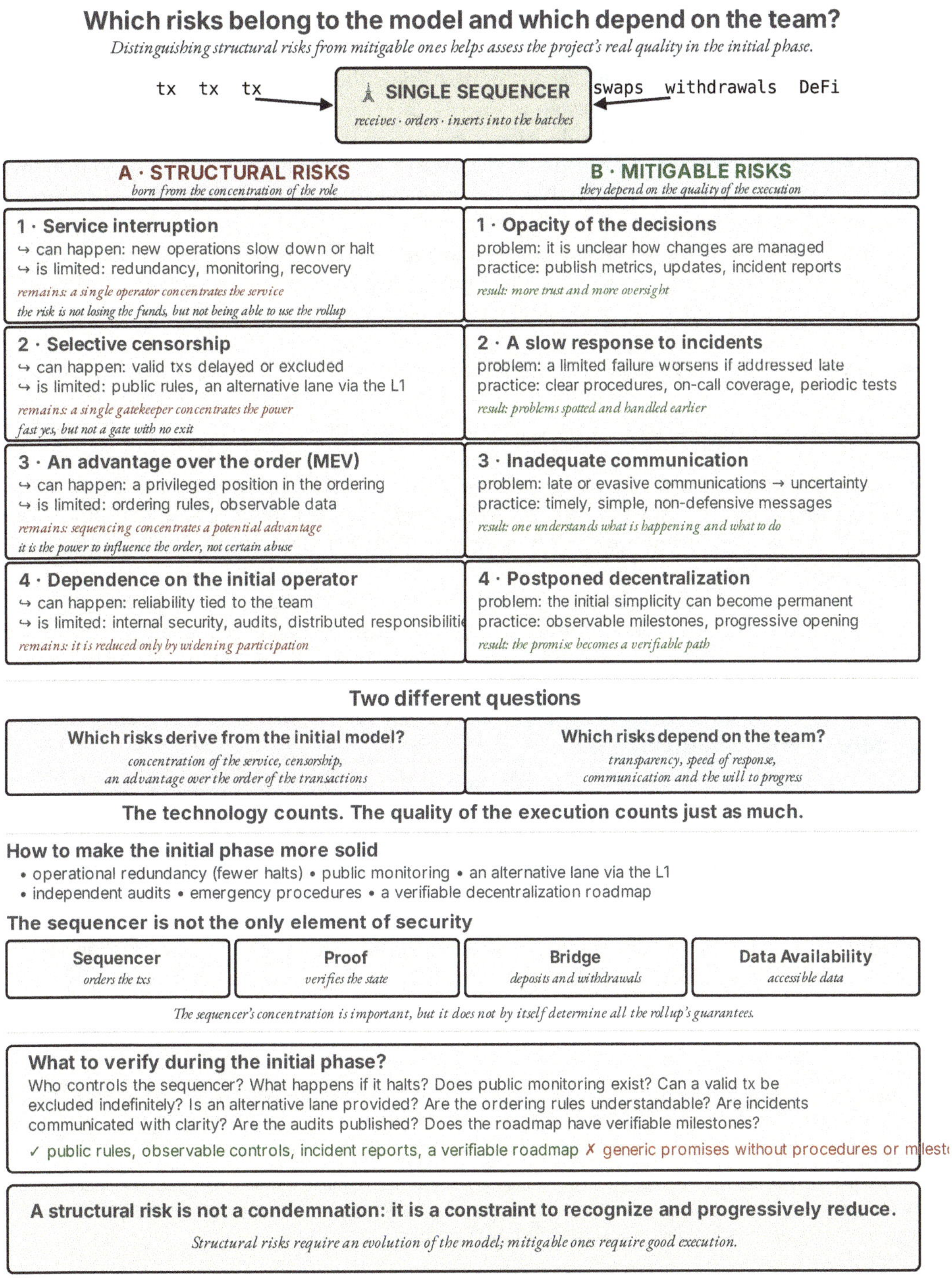

The risks of the single sequencer do not all have the same nature. Some are structural: they derive from the concentration of the service, of the power of inclusion, and of the ordering of the transactions, and they are truly reduced only with progressive decentralization. Others are mitigable and depend on the quality of the execution: transparency, response to incidents, communication, and concrete progress toward greater openness.

Third structural risk: a potential advantage in the ordering of the transactions. The sequencer occupies a privileged position because it receives and orders the transactions. This does not mean it will necessarily extract MEV to the users' detriment, but it makes the sequencing rules, transparency, and monitoring tools important.

Fourth structural risk: dependence on the initial operator. In the initial phase, the service's reliability and continuity still depend to a significant extent on the team that runs the sequencer. The proofs, the bridge, and data availability can limit some risks, but they do not eliminate the operational concentration. Bitcoin Hyper's public documentation[2] describes an initial model probably based on a single sequencer and a subsequent evolution toward a greater distribution of the role.

Mitigable risk one: opacity of the decisions. A scarcely transparent team can take questionable decisions without the community noticing. A transparent team regularly publishes operating metrics, incident logs, configuration changes. It is a choice of practice, not a structural constraint: largely mitigable by a team that wants to be transparent.

Mitigable risk two: slowness in responding to incidents. When something goes wrong, the team's response speed determines the severity of the impact. Teams with mature processes respond more rapidly; teams without processes respond late. Largely mitigable through mature operating procedures and periodic tests.

Mitigable risk three: inadequate communication. Even when the technical problems are handled well, communication with the community can amplify or reduce trust. Timely, clear, non-defensive communication builds trust; late, confused, evasive communication destroys it. Largely mitigable: it is a matter of internal culture.

Mitigable risk four: postponed decentralization. A team can remain comfortably in the single-sequencer phase because it is simpler, even when it could progress toward subsequent phases. A team with long vision invests in decentralization even when it is not strictly necessary. Largely mitigable: it is a strategic choice of the team.

The distinction between structural risks and mitigable risks guides the evaluation. The former require over time an evolution of the architecture: a greater distribution of sequencing, protection tools, and possible alternative paths for users. The latter depend above all on the quality of the execution: transparency, operating procedures, communication, and the capacity to transform the roadmap into observable progress. **A solid team does not eliminate every risk, but demonstrates that it recognizes it and addresses it with concrete tools.**

⁂

16.4 — The Practices That Make a Single Sequencer Acceptable

Having identified the mitigable risks, we can describe the specific practices that should accompany a single sequencer to make it an acceptable compromise for the initial phase. **They are practices that separate serious projects from improvised projects**, and that every informed user or investor should be able to observe before committing to the system.

Nota 1. "Acceptable" does not mean "ideal." A single sequencer remains a concentration of power; the practices described in this section do not eliminate the structural risk, but make it transparent and manageable during the initial phase. The distinction between a risk eliminated and a risk made observable is central to the whole due diligence.

Nota 2. These practices have a merit for the analyst: they are verifiable from the outside without accessing the code. Public documentation, incident reports, operating metrics, and timely communications can be observed by anyone, and their simple presence or absence is already a signal about the project's seriousness.

FIGURE 16.3 **THE TEN PRACTICES THAT MAKE A SINGLE SEQUENCER ACCEPTABLE IN THE INITIAL PHASE.**

Practice	What the team should do
1 · Transparency on the rules	Ordering rules, fee priority, conflict and queue handling documented; the sequencer's software ideally open source.

2 · Operating metrics	Public dashboards in near real time: processing times, inclusion rate, anchoring frequency, costs, halts, detectable MEV.
3 · Incident logs	Detailed, honest post-mortems on halts, bugs, and attacks: cause, intervention, prevention. A key indicator of maturity.
4 · A decentralization roadmap	Concrete, dated milestones for phases 2 and 3, with the technical prerequisites of each transition.
5 · Forced inclusion	An implemented, documented mechanism that allows the user to force the inclusion of their own transactions: the main technical defense against censorship.
6 · Separation of responsibilities	Multisignature for critical operations, keys distributed across different HSMs: no individual decides alone.
7 · Regular independent audits	Full reports (not summaries) on code, operating practices, key management, and emergency procedures.
8 · Compensation for damages	Predefined mechanisms (insurance, emergency funds) for damages from malfunctions. Rare in the sector, but a strong accountability signal.
9 · Independent observers	Encouraging external analysts and researchers with APIs and historical data: a critical feedback loop protecting users.
10 · Gradual governance	Technical forums, non-binding polls, proposal processes: prepares decentralization and creates a culture of participation.

Together, these ten practices define the level of accountability that makes a single sequencer acceptable for a well-managed initial phase. Bitcoin Hyper, on the basis of the available documentation, is working in this direction — but how much they will effectively be implemented will be judged by the facts, not by the promises, in the months following the mainnet launch.

Practice one: total transparency on the operating rules. The team should publish explicit, detailed, verifiable rules on how the sequencer operates. Not vaguely, but with technical specifications. What are the ordering criteria? What is the priority for the fees? What happens in the case of conflicting transactions? How is the queue handled when it exceeds certain limits? **All these rules should be documented publicly, and ideally the sequencer's software should be open source to allow verification.**

Practice two: regular publication of operating metrics. The team should publish public dashboards with key metrics: transaction processing times, inclusion rate, anchoring frequency, operating costs, any service halts, statistics on extracted MEV (if detectable). **These metrics should be updated in near real time**, so that anyone can monitor the system's operation.

Practice three: detailed incident logs. When problems occur — service halts, bugs, attacks — the team should publish detailed post-mortems explaining what happened, why, what was done to resolve it, what was done to prevent recurrences. **Honest post-mortems are one of the best indicators of a team's maturity.** Teams that hide or minimize problems typically have more systemic problems.

Practice four: a decentralization roadmap with milestones. As I said in the previous chapter, "progressive decentralization" without concrete milestones is only rhetoric. The team should publish a roadmap with specific timings: when will phase two with third-party operators start? When will phase three be reached? What are the technical prerequisites for each transition? **Without milestones, it is hard to assess whether the path is underway or has stalled.**

Practice five: forced-inclusion mechanisms implemented and documented. Even during the single-sequencer phase, users should be able to force the inclusion of their own transactions if the sequencer censors them. **This mechanism is the main technical protection against censorship.** If it is not implemented and well documented, the promise of "censorship resistance" is incomplete.

Practice six: separation of responsibilities inside the team. The team should have internal processes that prevent single individuals from taking unilateral decisions on the sequencer. Critical operations should require the multisignature of several team members. Sensitive cryptographic keys should be distributed across different hardware security modules. **These internal practices reduce the risk of a compromise of the single point of failure.**

Practice seven: regular independent audits. The team should undergo regular external security audits, publishing the full reports (not only summaries). The audits should cover not only the sequencer's code but also the operating practices, key management, emergency procedures. **Public, regular audits are the clearest signal of a team that wants to be accountable.**

Practice eight: compensation mechanisms in case of damages. Ideally, the team should have predefined mechanisms for compensating users in case of damages caused by a malfunction of the sequencer (for example, prolonged halts that caused financial losses). **These mechanisms are not common in the sector, but they represent an additional level of accountability.** They can be insurance, emergency funds, or other tools.

Practice nine: an active community of independent observers. The team should encourage the formation of a community of independent observers — analysts, researchers, crypto journalists — who monitor the system's operation and publish critical analyses. Ideally, providing them with specific tools to ease observation (APIs for metrics, access to historical data, and so on). **A community of observers is a critical feedback loop that protects users.**

Practice ten: gradual governance of the community. Even during the single-sequencer phase, the team can begin building governance mechanisms that involve the community. Structured forums for technical discussions, non-binding polls on important decisions, proposal processes that allow users to ask for changes. **This prepares the ground for the subsequent decentralization** and creates a culture of participation.

Together, these ten practices define a level of accountability that makes a single sequencer acceptable for a well-managed initial phase. **Bitcoin Hyper, on the basis of the available documentation, is working in this direction**, but how much these practices will effectively be implemented will be judged by the facts, not by the promises, in the months following the mainnet launch.

⁂

16.5 — What to Monitor during the Initial Phase: A Concrete Checklist

Having described what a responsible team should do, the practical question remains: how does an external observer verify whether those promises are actually being kept? An operational tool is needed, not a list of good intentions.

The checklist that follows answers this need. It is organized into **five evaluation dimensions** — technical, operational, economic, governance, and behavioral — and for each it proposes the concrete verification questions to ask oneself and the signal the answer carries with it. It is not a tool to use only once: its value emerges from repeated use over time, because many of the signals (cost stability, frequency of halts, respect of the milestones) can be read only by comparing successive observations.

FIGURE 16.4 **A MONITORING CHECKLIST FOR THE SINGLE-SEQUENCER PHASE: FIVE DIMENSIONS, VERIFICATION QUESTIONS, AND THEIR SIGNALS.**

Dimension	Verification question	Signal
Technical	Does a public dashboard with real-time operating metrics exist?	Absent = incomplete transparency.

	Are the ordering rules documented with technical detail?	Vague documentation = abuse possible.
	Is the sequencer's software open source and verifiable?	Closed code = obligatory trust.
	Is forced inclusion implemented, tested, documented?	Absent = censorship resistance only theoretical.
	Do independent explorers exist whose data matches the official one?	Agreement = a healthy system; discrepancies = problems.
	Are inclusion times stable and without suspicious patterns by address or type?	Suspicious patterns = possible selective censorship.
Operational	Are service halts communicated promptly with detailed post-mortems?	Frequency and handling reveal operational maturity.
	Does the team respond rapidly and with clarity to reported problems?	Response times = the real priority of accountability.
	Does the team communicate regularly even in the absence of problems?	Constant communication = maturity; silence = alarm.
	Are external security audits published, and by whom?	Public audits = the highest level of technical accountability.
Economic	Are transaction costs competitive and stable over time?	Erratic costs = problematic economic management.
	Does volume grow organically or driven by temporary incentives?	The growth pattern measures the real health.
	Are the applications diversified or concentrated on a few actors?	Diversity = a healthy ecosystem; concentration = fragility.
	Do independent quantitative analyses of the extracted MEV exist?	Public analyses = a mature sector; absence = opacity.
Governance	Does a decentralization roadmap with dated milestones exist?	Without milestones, the path is only theoretical.
	Does the team respect the milestones or postpone them regularly?	Frequent postponements = a loss of credibility.
	Do formal community proposal mechanisms exist, and are they used?	Formal governance = preparation for decentralization.
	Have independent operators declared interest and are they being involved?	Real operators = a transition effectively possible.

Behavioral	Does the team accept public criticism or does it tend to defend itself?	Openness = maturity; defensiveness = a cultural problem.
	Are proposed technical alternatives evaluated or dismissed out of hand?	Technical openness = a competent team.
	Is the team visible in conferences, research, and sector discussions?	Visibility in the ecosystem = the project's seriousness.
	How have any public conflicts been managed?	The handling of conflicts reveals the team's ethical quality.

How to use it. *The checklist is not exhaustive, but it covers the main dimensions on which to evaluate a project in the single-sequencer phase. Filling it in monthly for the first 12–24 months after the launch of Bitcoin Hyper's mainnet returns a well-founded picture of the project's trajectory, and makes it possible to distinguish in a specific — not impressionistic — way between "something is going well" and "something is going badly."*

⁂

16.6 — A Comparison with the Initial Phase of Other Rollups

To give context and calibrate expectations, it is useful to compare Bitcoin Hyper's initial phase with that of other well-known rollups. Seeing how they managed (or did not manage) the trade-offs of the single-sequencer phase helps understand what is realistic to expect.

Optimism, launched in 2021, operated for years with a single sequencer run by Optimism PBC (the foundation that develops the project). The management was generally transparent, with public post-mortems for the main service halts, but forced-inclusion mechanisms were implemented relatively late in the project's life cycle. The decentralization path was slow but steady, with the "Superchain" framework introduced in 2024 opening the way to sequencers shared among several rollups. **Lesson**: even a high-profile team needs years to progress significantly in decentralizing the sequencer.

FIGURE 16.6 **DECENTRALIZING THE SEQUENCER IS A PATH OF YEARS.**

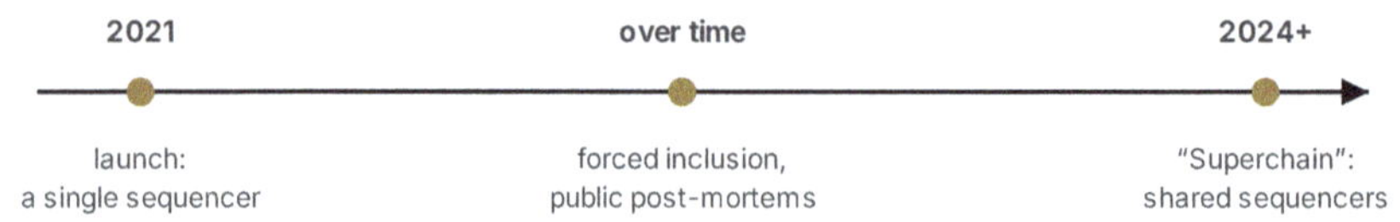

Years, not months: the Optimism case.

Optimism's path shows that decentralizing the sequencer is not a switch to flip at launch, but a slow progression that requires years even for a mature, well-funded project. It is a useful yardstick of realism for calibrating expectations about Bitcoin Hyper.

FIGURE 16.5 **THE SINGLE-SEQUENCER PHASE IN FIVE WELL-KNOWN ROLLUPS: MANAGEMENT, TRANSPARENCY, DECENTRALIZATION, AND THE MAIN LESSON.**

Rollup	Start	Operator	Transparency	Decentralization	Lesson

Optimism	2021	Optimism PBC	Good (public post-mortems)	Slow but steady; "Superchain" since 2024	Even a high-profile team takes years.
Arbitrum	2021	Offchain Labs / DAO	Average (a very stable sequencer)	Discussed in the DAO, limited concrete results	Stability and decentralization are different dimensions.
Base	2023	Coinbase	High by the sector's standards	Explicit centralization, no roadmap	Centralization can be a legitimate design choice.
zkSync	2023	Matter Labs	Good, but significant halts in 2024	Ambitious but still in an initial phase	High ambitions do not guarantee execution.
StarkNet	2022	StarkWare	Average; the sticking point: adoption	A difficult transition, the model revised several times	Distinctive technical choices have unexpected costs.

Four recurring patterns emerge from the five cases: the single-sequencer phase lasts years, not months; the quality of the execution varies enormously even with equal resources, and the team's maturity counts more than the technology; effective decentralization requires investments that manifest slowly; transparency is the main predictor of accountability over the long term.

Arbitrum, also launched in 2021, had a trajectory similar to Optimism's with some differences. The sequencer has historically been more stable (fewer documented halts), but operational transparency has been slightly lower. The sequencer's decentralization has been the object of various governance discussions through the Arbitrum DAO, but with limited concrete results. **Lesson**: operational stability and decentralization are different dimensions, and a team can excel in one without progressing in the other.

Base, launched in 2023 by Coinbase, has a particular model: it is explicitly run by a commercial company (Coinbase) that operates the sequencer. Transparency is high by the sector's standards, but the centralization is equally explicit: Coinbase has total control of the sequencer and has not published a detailed decentralization roadmap. **Lesson**: some rollups are explicitly "centralized" as a design choice, accepting this trade-off in exchange for other properties (operational efficiency, regulatory compliance). It is a legitimate choice for certain use cases, but different from the decentralized aspiration of projects like Hyper.

zkSync, by Matter Labs, had a more complicated path. Launched with great decentralization ambitions, it experienced significant service halts in 2024 that raised concerns about its operational maturity. Transparency has been generally good, but the sequencer's decentralization mechanisms are still in an initial phase. **Lesson**: high ambitions do not guarantee perfect execution, and the projects that promise the fastest decentralization do not always realize it.

StarkNet, by StarkWare, has distinctive technical characteristics (it is a ZK-rollup with the proprietary Cairo language). The initial phase was marked by adoption problems and by a difficult transition toward decentralization, with various adjustments of the sequencing model over time. **Lesson**: distinctive technical choices can have unexpected costs in the initial phase.

Putting these cases together, some patterns emerge. **First pattern: the single-sequencer phase typically lasts years**, not months. It is a reality of the sector that must be accepted. **Second pattern: the quality of the execution varies enormously** even among projects with similar resources. The team's maturity counts more than the technology. **Third pattern: effective decentralization requires significant investments** that manifest slowly. Projects that promise decentralization too rapidly typically under-execute. **Fourth pattern: transparency is the main predictor of accountability**[a] over the long term. Transparent teams tend to accumulate credibility that is reflected in correct behaviors.

---

[a] **Accountability.** It is the responsibility of accounting for one's own conduct: explaining the decisions taken, recognizing mistakes, and answering for them before the users. An "accountable" team is not one that never makes mistakes, but one that, when something goes wrong, communicates it with clarity and shows how it is being handled. This is why transparency is its main leading indicator: those who openly document halts and incidents tend, over time, to behave more correctly, because they have exposed themselves to public scrutiny.

For Bitcoin Hyper, these lessons suggest realistic expectations. **The single-sequencer phase will probably last at least 1–2 years after the mainnet launch.** During this phase, there will probably be service halts, bugs detected and fixed, periods of tension between the decentralization promises and the operational reality. **The project's quality will be measured not on the absence of problems (impossible) but on the handling of the problems** when they arise.

⁂

16.7 — Questions and Answers: Clarifying the Chapter's Concepts

Question 1: If the single sequencer is so full of risks, why not simply wait to have a decentralized system from the start?

For practical product-building reasons. **Building a system with a distributed sequencer from day one is enormously more complex than starting with a single sequencer and decentralizing progressively.** The problems are different: coordination among operators, consensus synchronization, conflict handling, stable performance under variable load. All these problems must be solved at the same time as the rest of the system (the Canonical Bridge, the proof model, data availability), creating massive engineering complexity. **Waiting to have everything perfect before launching means delaying even by years**, losing the market opportunity and the accumulated engineering energy. The "build, learn, decentralize" philosophy is today standard in the sector precisely because the alternative approaches have not worked well. Concrete example: various projects that attempted to launch with fully decentralized architectures from day one (some "alternative L1s" of 2021–2022) had enormous stability, security, and adoption problems, and many never reached maturity. The rollups that started centralized and decentralized progressively (Optimism, Arbitrum) are today the most established Layer 2 systems. The philosophy works, even if it requires patience.

Question 2: How do I, as a user, know whether the Hyper team is keeping its transparency promises during the initial phase?

There are several concrete indicators you can monitor. **First dimension: the presence of a public dashboard with operating metrics.** Visit the official site periodically and verify whether dashboards updated in real time exist. Compare what they show with what was announced. If the dashboard is missing, it is a negative signal. **Second dimension: the frequency and quality of the updates.** The Hyper team published regular posts up to the launch. After the mainnet launch, one would expect a continuation of this frequency, perhaps with monthly posts describing the system's operation, the metrics reached, the problems addressed. Prolonged silence is an alarm bell. **Third dimension: the existence of independent analysts.** Subscribe to crypto newsletters specialized in Bitcoin Layer 2s, follow independent researchers on X/Twitter. If nobody writes independent analyses on Bitcoin Hyper, it is a signal that the project is not attracting serious external attention. **Fourth dimension: comparison with other projects.** Compare Hyper's transparency with that of other Bitcoin rollups. If Hyper is less transparent than its competitors, it is a negative signal. If it is more transparent, it is a positive signal. Concrete example: today on Optimism you can find dashboards like [Optimism Status](https://status.optimism.io) and independent analyses on L2BEAT, DefiLlama, and specialized sites. For Hyper, the development of analogous tools over time is expected, and their presence or absence is an indicator of the ecosystem's health.

Question 3: If during the initial phase I suffer a damage (for example, sequencer halts make me lose a trading opportunity), do I have recourse? Can I obtain compensation?

In general no, and this is a real risk to be aware of. **The terms of service of most rollups are designed to limit the team's liability in case of malfunctions.** Users accept to use the system "as-is," recognizing that it is in an initial phase, that problems can occur, and that the team is not liable for indirect financial losses. **This is the reality of the sector, even for serious projects.** Some exceptions and mitigations exist. **First exception**: if the team commits gross errors or demonstrated negligence, in some jurisdictions legal recourse might exist, even if it is difficult and costly to pursue. **Second exception**: some projects have insurance or compensation funds for damages caused by specific bugs (not general incidents). Verify whether Hyper has such mechanisms. **Third mitigation**: for high-value operations, it is prudent not to concentrate on a single Layer 2 but to diversify. **Fourth mitigation**: monitor the system's status regularly and be prepared not to operate if you see signals of problems. Concrete example: during an Optimism halt in 2022, some users suffered losses (for example, liquidations of positions they could not manage because the system was down). Optimism PBC did not offer direct compensation, even though it published a detailed post-mortem. It is the sector's standard model, and one must be aware of it.

Question 4: How prudent is it to do high-value operations on Hyper during the single-sequencer phase?

It is an individual assessment that depends on many factors, but some general principles apply. **First principle: differentiate by type of operation.** Speculative operations (trading, yield farming, participating in airdrops) have different risk profiles from custody operations (long-term holding, a store of value). **For speculative operations**, the risk of the initial phase might be acceptable in exchange for the expected returns. **For long-term custody operations**, the risk is less justified during the initial phase. **Second principle: diversify.** Do not concentrate everything on a single Layer 2. Distribute among direct Bitcoin, the Lightning Network, various Layer 2s, in proportions that reflect your risk tolerance. **Third principle: monitor actively.** If you decide to operate on Hyper, do so with awareness of the risks and monitor the system's status regularly. Be ready to withdraw the funds if you see signals of problems. **Fourth principle: accept only risks you can afford.** Do not invest more than what you can afford to lose completely. This is true for any crypto, but it is particularly important for projects in an initial phase. **Fifth principle: time is your ally.** Waiting 6–12 months after the mainnet launch to see how the system behaves in real production is a prudent choice. The risks of the initial phase tend to manifest in the first months, and waiting for them to be resolved significantly reduces the exposure. Concrete example: in the first months after Optimism's launch in 2021, the system had various stability problems. Those who waited 12–18 months before committing significantly found a much more mature system, with significantly reduced risks. Patience is a legitimate strategy.

Question 5: If the Hyper team decentralizes the sequencer after a few years, how does it guarantee the transition without a loss of service?

The transition from a single sequencer to a distributed sequencer is one of the most delicate operations in a rollup's life, and it must be planned with care. **It typically happens in successive phases**, with a period of overlap. **Preparation phase**: the team identifies and onboards the independent operators, prepares the technical infrastructure, conducts tests in non-production environments, security audits specific to the new architecture. **Gradual transition phase**: the single sequencer continues to operate but independent operators begin participating with limited roles (for example, validating the decisions, but not proposing the batches). The system learns to manage the coordination. **Control handover phase**: control is gradually transferred to the independent operators, with the team reducing its own role. **Distributed operation phase**: the system operates with distributed sequencing, with the team in a support role rather than an operator role. **During all these phases, problems can occur**: bugs in the new architecture, conflicts among operators, attacks that exploit the transition. **Managing these risks is one of the project's most complex challenges**, and it is one of the reasons why the transition is slow. Concrete example: Optimism planned its own transition toward the "Superchain framework" for years, with various public research documents that allowed the community to participate in the design. For Hyper a similar process is expected, even if the specific timings will depend on the team.

Question 6: Is there a point at which I should stop using Hyper if I see negative signals during the initial phase?

Yes, and it is important to have specific criteria for deciding. **"Immediate exit" criteria**: these are serious signals that justify the complete withdrawal of the funds. Declarations by the team that it can no longer operate the system. Known security compromises that might have led to a loss of funds. A complete cessation of the team's communication for prolonged periods (weeks). Attempts by the team to unilaterally restrict the users' options without community consent. **"Gradual withdrawal" criteria**: signals that justify reducing the exposure without necessarily withdrawing everything immediately. Repeated patterns of badly managed service halts. Credible signals of selective censorship. Team communication that becomes defensive and less transparent over time. A decentralization roadmap that gets postponed repeatedly without convincing explanations. **"Increased monitoring" criteria**: signals that deserve attention but not immediate action. Bugs detected and handled correctly. Significant public criticism from the community. Growing competition from other projects that could reduce Hyper's relevance over the long term. **The important point is having pre-defined criteria**, because in moments of emotional stress it is hard to take rational decisions. Decide in advance what would trigger each response, and apply your criteria when they arise. Concrete example: in 2022, during the FTX collapse, some users applied pre-defined criteria and withdrew funds before the crash, avoiding losses. Others reacted emotionally too late and suffered losses. Having pre-defined criteria for any crypto system is a prudent practice.

⁂

16.8 — WHAT TO TAKE AWAY FROM THIS CHAPTER

The single-sequencer phase is a standard pragmatic choice in the rollup sector, adopted by Optimism, Arbitrum, Base, zkSync, and other major projects. Bitcoin Hyper is following the established model.

The team that runs a single sequencer is effectively a blockchain financial services company with multiple responsibilities: infrastructure, operating rules, updates, communication with the community, regulatory relations, economic management.

There are inevitable risks of this phase: dependence on the service's availability, the capacity for selective censorship, extraction of undistributed MEV, dependence on the team's integrity. They can be mitigated but not structurally eliminated.

There are mitigable risks: opacity of the decisions, slowness in responding to incidents, inadequate communication, scarce investment in progressive decentralization. They depend on the quality of the team's execution.

The practices that make a single sequencer acceptable include ten main dimensions: transparency on the operating rules, publication of metrics, detailed incident logs, a roadmap with milestones, forced inclusion implemented, separation of internal responsibilities, independent audits, compensation mechanisms, a community of observers, gradual governance.

A concrete checklist for monitoring the project includes technical, operational, economic, governance, and behavioral dimensions. Filling it in monthly for the first 12–24 months after the mainnet launch would give a clear picture of the project's health.

The comparison with other rollups shows useful patterns: the single-sequencer phase typically lasts years, the quality of the execution varies enormously even among projects with similar resources, transparency is the main predictor of accountability, effective decentralization requires significant investments that manifest slowly.

For users, prudence during the initial phase includes: differentiating by type of operation (speculative vs custody), diversifying among different systems, actively monitoring the status, accepting only sustainable financial risks, considering waiting 6–12 months before committing significantly.

Having pre-defined criteria for exiting or reducing the exposure is a prudent practice. Deciding in advance which signals would trigger which response protects from emotional decisions in moments of stress.

The project's quality will be measured not on the absence of problems (impossible) but on the handling of the problems when they arise. This is the real test of the Hyper team in the months following the mainnet launch.

Chapter 16 ends here. We have concretely examined what the single-sequencer phase means, what risks it entails, what practices make it acceptable, and how to monitor the team's execution. In ***Chapter 17 — Toward Distributed Sequencing: Rotation, Auctions, Leader Election****, we will go down into the technical details of the long-term strategies for taking control away from a single entity, examining the different architectures proposed in the research world and understanding which are the most promising for a Bitcoin rollup like Hyper.*

A single sequencer: a pragmatic *start*, not a point of arrival

When initial centralization is acceptable **only** with controls, transparency, and a verifiable roadmap.

1 A pragmatic launch choice

A single sequencer makes it simpler to **launch the rollup**, manage bugs, update the software, and guarantee predictable performance in the initial phase.

It is a good starting point only if it does not become the point of arrival.

Mainnet launch → single sequencer → monito-ring → matura-tion → progressive opening

ADVANTAGES a simpler launch · predictable timings · rapid debugging · less complexity · focus on bridge, proofs, and DA

2 Not just "running a server"

TEAM / SEQUENCER OPERATOR · A CRITICAL INFRASTRUCTURE OPERATOR

01	**Infrastructure**	servers, bandwidth, backups, uptime.
02	**Ordering rules**	priorities, queue, conflicts.
03	**Updates and patches**	deploys, rollbacks, tests.
04	**Crisis communication**	incident reports, notices.
05	**Regulatory relations**	requests, censorship risk.
06	**Economic management**	fees, anchoring costs.

3 Not all risks are equal

Structural risks · from the single role

- Service interruption.
- Selective censorship.
- An advantage over the order of the transactions.
- Potential MEV extraction.
- Dependence on the initial operator.

Mitigable risks · from the team's execution

- Opacity of the decisions.
- A slow response to incidents.
- Inadequate communication.
- Postponed decentralization.
- An absence of public metrics.

Structural *risks are reduced with the architecture's evolution;* **mitigable** *risks with discipline, transparency, and procedures.*

4 Transparency before decentralization

- ✓ Public operating rules
- ✓ A dashboard with real-time metrics
- ✓ Incident reports and post-mortems
- ✓ Documented forced inclusion
- ✓ Independent audits
- ✓ Separation of internal responsibilities
- ✓ APIs for independent observers
- ✓ A roadmap with dated milestones
- ✓ Gradual governance
- ✓ Emergency procedures

Trust must not be blind: **it must become verifiable.**

5 Due diligence continues after the launch

- **Technical** — uptime, inclusion, forced inclusion, explorer.
- **Operational** — halts, incident reports, response to bugs.
- **Economic** — tx costs, anchoring frequency, fees.
- **Governance** — milestones, opening to third parties, roadmap.
- **Behavioral** — transparency, response to criticism.

A mature team is not one that never makes mistakes: **it is one that recognizes, documents, and corrects its errors.**

THE KEY POINT

The **single sequencer** can be a pragmatic choice for starting, but it concentrates **service, order, timing, and operating power**. It becomes acceptable only if the team publishes **rules, metrics, audits, emergency procedures** and **verifiable milestones** toward decentralization.

PART V · THE SEQUENCING LAYER

Chapter 17
Toward Distributed Sequencing

Rotation, auctions, leader election

⁂

17.1 — The Hardest Problem of Modern Rollups

There is an emerging consensus in the rollup industry that is worth declaring openly at the start of this chapter: **decentralizing the sequencer is one of the hardest technical challenges that Layer 2 projects are facing today**. Not because it is theoretically impossible, not because ideas are lacking, but because all the proposed models have significant trade-offs, and none has yet clearly demonstrated that it works in production at scale. As I write, even Ethereum's most mature rollups — Optimism, Arbitrum, Base, zkSync — are still largely in a centralized-sequencer phase, with various decentralization experiments still to be consolidated.

TABLE 17.1 **DISTRIBUTED SEQUENCING MODELS**

Model	Advantages	Disadvantages	Examples in the sector
Fixed rotation	Simple, fair, predictable	Not very resilient to MEV; a compromised sequencer blocks the turn	Optimism (roadmap), Arbitrum (proposal)
Competitive auctions	Maximum monetization of the role	Pay-to-play: it excludes small operators	Espresso Systems, Suave
Leader election (PoS)	Rapid finality, low latency	A possible concentration of power on a few validators	Astria, Polygon CDK
A shared sequencer	Liquidity and interop among rollups	Dependence on an external layer	Espresso, Astria (shared)

Hyper's position: *the public roadmap indicates a transition from a single sequencer to rotation, with the possibility of evolving toward auction-based models depending on the ecosystem's maturity. No choice is definitive at the mainnet launch.*

For Bitcoin Hyper, which launches in 2026 in a sector where the sequencer's decentralization is still the object of active research, the problem is even more acute. **The team cannot simply "copy" an established solution, because no established solution exists.** It must do its own research, experiment with models, adapt them to the specific context of a rollup anchored to Bitcoin, and do so while the system is in production and manages real value. It is engineering work done while the plane is in flight, and it requires skills, patience, and humility.

Hyper's January 2026 research post on future sequencing models explores the main possible strategies without committing to a specific choice. This is technical honesty: the team recognizes that it does not yet know what the final solution will be, and is exploring the possibilities in public. **In this chapter I want to go down into these possibilities**, understand how they work conceptually, what trade-offs they entail, and which are best suited to Hyper's context. It will be a chapter technically denser than others, but it will give you concrete tools for judging the choices the team will announce in the coming years.

I begin with an observation that synthesizes the problem. **In traditional systems, decentralization is achieved through distributed consensus**: many participants contribute to deciding together what is valid. Bitcoin does it with Proof of Work, Ethereum with Proof of Stake. **For rollups, however, "consensus" is not the main challenge**: consensus is already guaranteed by the anchoring on the main blockchain. The challenge is a different one: **who proposes, in real time, the sequences of transactions**

that will then be anchored? This is an ordering function, not a consensus one, and it requires different mechanisms. This is exactly the theme of the chapter.

⁂

17.2 — What "Decentralizing the Sequencer" Means: Three Dimensions of the Problem

Before exploring the specific strategies, it is useful to define with precision what "decentralizing the sequencer" means. The term is often used vaguely, referring to something generically "distributed," but in reality there are at least three distinct dimensions that can be decentralized, and understanding which ones is important for evaluating the proposals.

First dimension: who can propose the batches. In the centralized model, there is a single operator (the team) that proposes all the batches.

Nota 1. "Decentralizing the sequencer" is an expression that summarizes distinct problems: who can propose the batches, who verifies their validity, and who guarantees that nobody can censor. Treating them as a single item is one of the most frequent mistakes in reading roadmaps: a project can decentralize one dimension and leave the others centralized.

Nota 2. The sequencer's decentralization is today an open frontier for the entire rollup sector, not only for Hyper: even Ethereum's main Layer 2s are working on it progressively. For this reason it must be evaluated as a path with verifiable milestones, not as a switch turned on or off.

TABLE 17.2 **DECENTRALIZING: A TRADITIONAL BLOCKCHAIN AND A ROLLUP COMPARED.**

Aspect	Traditional blockchain	Anchored rollup
What must be decentralized	The consensus on the state	The proposal and ordering of the batches
Where the truth comes from	From the vote of many nodes	From the anchoring on Bitcoin, already guaranteed
The challenge that stays open	Reaching the agreement	Who proposes the transactions and in what order

In a traditional blockchain, decentralization serves to produce the truth; in a rollup that truth is already guaranteed by the anchoring, and the stakes shift to who orders the transactions. It is this difference that makes the sequencer problem specific to Layer 2s.

FIGURE 17.2 **DECENTRALIZING THE SEQUENCER: THREE DIMENSIONS TO DISTINGUISH.**

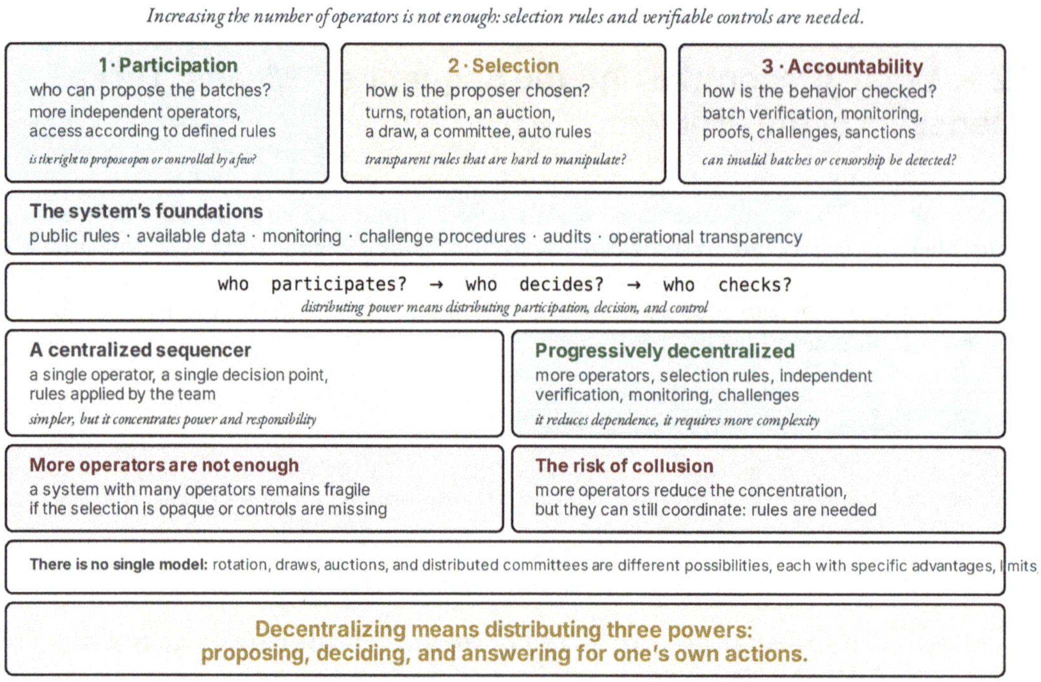

The sequencer's decentralization must be evaluated along three distinct dimensions. The first concerns who can propose the batches. The second concerns the rules by which the proposer is chosen at a given moment. The third concerns the mechanisms that make it possible to verify the operators' behavior and to intervene in case of abuse. The presence of several parties is important, but not sufficient.

In the decentralized model, **several independent operators have the right to propose batches**, according to pre-defined rules. This is the most visible dimension and the one most people associate with "decentralizing the sequencer." But on its own it is not enough: having many operators who can propose does not guarantee that the system is fair or resistant to collusion.

Second dimension: how it is decided who proposes at a given moment. Even with many potential operators, at every moment someone must propose. The selection rules determine the system's dynamics: random rotation, competitive auctions, reputation criteria, internal consensus among operators. **Different rules produce very different behaviors,** even with the same pool of operators.

Third dimension: how it is verified that whoever proposes behaves correctly. Even with multiple operators and selection rules, a mechanism is needed to guarantee that every proposal is valid and that any incorrect behaviors (censorship, abusive MEV, invalid batches) are detected and punished. **Without accountability mechanisms, decentralization is only apparent**: many actors who can behave badly potentially have greater power than a single one who knows it is being observed.

The specific strategies we will see in the next sections address these three dimensions in different ways. Some are strong on one dimension and weak on another. Some are complete but complex to implement. **Understanding the three dimensions separately allows you to evaluate every proposal in a structured way,** instead of stopping at generic slogans.

TABLE 17.3 **THE THREE DIMENSIONS OF THE SEQUENCER'S DECENTRALIZATION.**

Dimension	Essential question	Centralized model	Objective	What to verify

Participation	who can propose a batch?	a single operator (the team) produces all the batches	more independent operators according to rules	number, independence, requirements, access
Selection	how is the active operator chosen?	not needed: there is a single sequencer	a transparent rule for choosing the proposer	rotation, draws, auctions, duration, manipulation
Verification of behavior	how is compliance with the rules checked?	it depends on the team's integrity	independent verification, detection, and challenges	batch validity, data, monitoring, MEV, sanctions
Resistance to collusion	can several operators coordinate?	the power is already concentrated	reducing the stable control of a few	distribution of power, incentives, relationships
Evolution over time	is it already operational or only declared?	management in the team's hands	concrete, documented, verifiable steps	roadmap, milestones, public tests, results

The sequencer's decentralization cannot be evaluated with a single question. Increasing the number of operators is useful, but not sufficient. One must also analyze the rules by which the proposer is selected, the verification mechanisms, the resistance to collusion, and the concrete implementation path.

⁂

17.3 — Strategy One: Random Rotation

Let us begin with the conceptually simplest strategy. **Random rotation** provides for a fixed pool of sequencer operators, with a cryptographic mechanism that randomly selects one for each batch (or group of batches). The selected one proposes, the others verify. When the next batch arrives, another random operator is selected from the pool.

Let us see how it works concretely. **The operators' pool**: a certain number of entities, perhaps dozens or hundreds, have deposited collateral and qualified as operators. The exact number depends on design choices, but it is typically in the order of dozens or a few hundreds. **The selection mechanism**: a deterministic cryptographic function, based on a verifiable random seed (for example, the hash of a recent Bitcoin block), selects one of the operators. **The service period**: the selected operator proposes batches for a certain period (for example, until the next anchoring), then another is selected. **The accountability mechanism**: if the selected operator behaves badly or does not respond, slashing mechanisms exist that reduce its collateral, and replacement mechanisms that allow others to take over.

The **advantages of random rotation** are significant. **Fairness**: every qualified operator has the same probability of being selected, avoiding a concentration of power. **Resistance to collusion**[a]: to control the system persistently, an attacker would have to control the majority of the pool's operators, something costly and visible. **Conceptual simplicity**: the model is easy to explain and to understand, reducing the system's opacity. **Censorship resistance**: even if a specific operator wants to censor certain transactions, it will have to wait its own turn, and in the meantime other operators could process the censored transactions.

The **disadvantages** are just as important. **Variable performance**: different operators can have different technical capacities, and therefore processing times can vary unpredictably. **Inefficiency in extracting legitimate MEV**[b]: the system makes it harder to extract MEV in a coordinated way (a good thing for users) but also for legitimate actors like the arbitrageurs who keep the markets efficient. **Onboarding complexity**[c]: to participate as an operator, significant technical infrastructure, capital for the collateral, and 24/7 operating capacity are needed. This limits the pool of real participants. **Vulnerability to large operators**: if a few large operators have most of the collateral, they can dominate the pool even with random selection.

---

[a] **Collusion.** The secret agreement among several operators to coordinate to the detriment of the system or of the users — for example by manipulating the order of the transactions. Random rotation makes it difficult: to control the system stably one would have to agree with the majority of the pool, something costly and hard to hide.

[b] **Legitimate MEV.** Not all the value extracted from the order of the transactions is harmful: arbitrage, which realigns prices across different markets, is a useful activity that keeps the markets efficient. A system that hinders every form of MEV ends up penalizing these legitimate actors too, not only the predatory ones.

[c] **Onboarding.** The process by which a new participant becomes part of the system as an operator: it requires technical infrastructure, capital to lock up as collateral, and the capacity to operate without interruptions. The more complex and costly this process is, the fewer operators manage to really participate — and the lower, in fact, is the decentralization achieved.

Random rotation is a conceptually solid strategy but with non-trivial implementation. It has been proposed in various research models, and some projects are experimenting with it, but in production at scale it is still in an initial phase. **For Hyper, it would be a sensible choice for the "delegated participation" phase** — the intermediate phase between a single sequencer and a completely distributed one — because it balances decentralization and manageability.

⁂

FIGURE 17.3 **STRATEGY ONE: THE SEQUENCER'S RANDOM ROTATION, FROM THE QUALIFIED POOL TO SLASHING.**

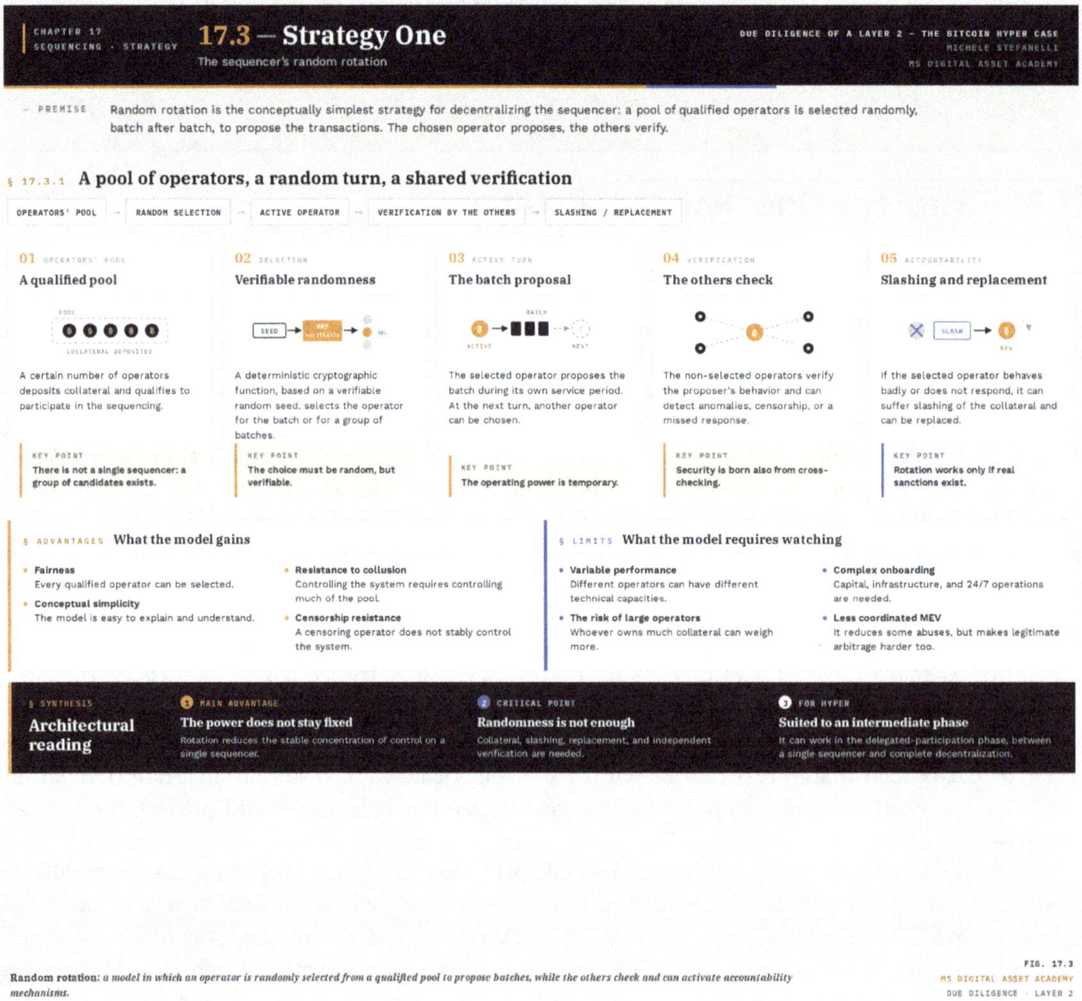

17.4 — Strategy Two: Auction-Based Sequencing

The second strategy is conceptually different and adopts a market approach. **Auction-based sequencing** provides that the rights to propose batches are sold at auction among the interested operators. Whoever offers the most, wins. The value paid at the auction is typically redistributed (to the project's treasury, to the other operators, to the users), creating an explicit economic mechanism.

Let us see the nuances. **The type of auction**: there are many possible models (English, sealed-bid, Vickrey, first-price auctions), each with different economic properties. The choice of the model significantly influences the participants' behavior. **The auction's frequency**: one can hold an auction for each batch, per time epoch, per block. The more frequent the auctions, the more granular the control, but the greater the overhead. **The beneficiaries**: the value paid at the auction can go in different directions: the project's treasury, redistribution to the non-winning operators, a discount on the users' fees, a burn (destruction) to reduce the token's inflation.

The **advantages of auction-based sequencing** are notable. **Explicit capture of the MEV**: whoever wins the auction obtains the right to extract MEV from the transactions, and pays in exchange. The MEV becomes transparent and redistributed instead of opaque and concentrated. **Efficient selection**: whoever offers the most is typically whoever can extract the most value, and is therefore incentivized to operate efficiently. **Self-financing of the system**: the auctions' payments contribute to financing the operations, reducing or eliminating the need for other financing mechanisms. **Resistance to capture**: to control the system, an attacker must continually win auctions with high bids, a cost that grows over time.

FIGURE 17.4 **STRATEGY TWO: AUCTION-BASED SEQUENCING, WHEN THE RIGHT TO PROPOSE BATCHES BECOMES A MARKET.**

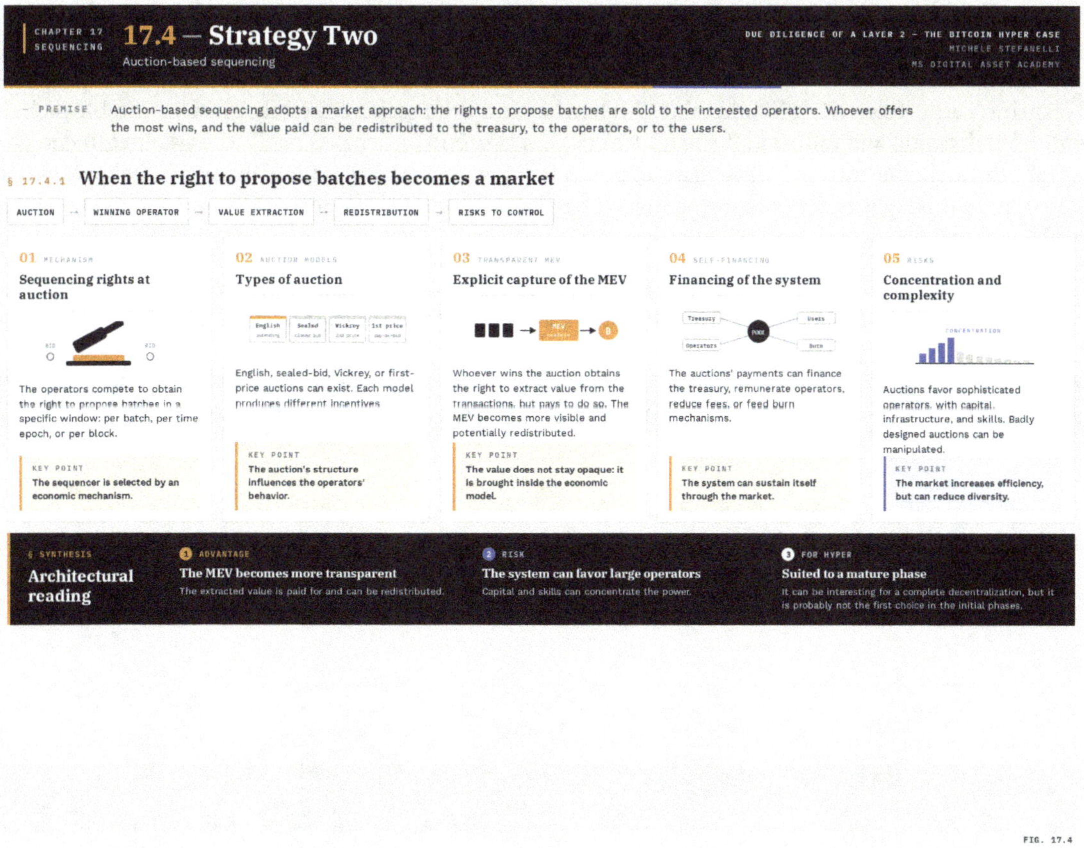

Auction-based sequencing: *a model in which the right to propose batches is assigned through economic competition among qualified operators.*

The **disadvantages** are significant and deserve attention. **Concentration on sophisticated actors**: winning auctions requires capital, infrastructure, and sophisticated skills. The system tends to favor large specialized operators at the expense of smaller participants, paradoxically reducing the pool's diversity. **Pressure on the margins for users**: whoever wins auctions must recover the investment by extracting value, and this value typically comes from the users' transactions. Even if the MEV is redistributed, users might pay more compared to systems with minimized MEV. **The mechanism's complexity**: designing auctions robust against various forms of manipulation is remarkably complex. There are many ways in which a badly designed auction can be abused. **Performance volatility**: whoever wins has incentives to maximize value extraction during their own time, and this can create behaviors that are not optimal for users.

Auction-based sequencing is particularly interesting because it has found concrete application in the Ethereum world through mechanisms like MEV-Boost and PBS (Proposer-Builder Separation). They are sophisticated models that separate the role of "proposing" (who decides to propose) from that of "building" (who builds the optimal batch), creating competitive markets for each level.

For Hyper, auction-based sequencing could be an interesting choice for the complete-decentralization phase, because it creates market mechanisms that work autonomously without requiring central governance. But it also requires the maturity of the system and of the ecosystem, and it will probably not be the first choice in the initial phases.

⁂

17.5 — Strategy Three: Leader Election with Internal Consensus

The third strategy is the most complex conceptually, but in some respects the most complete. **Leader election with internal consensus** provides for a set of operators that operate their own internal consensus system to select, batch after batch, the leader who will propose the next one. The leader changes frequently according to rules shared among the operators.

Let us see how it works. **The operators' set**: similar to random rotation, there is a pool of qualified operators. **The leader-selection mechanism**: instead of random selection or an auction, the operators use an internal consensus protocol to choose the next leader. Possible models include PBFT (Practical Byzantine Fault Tolerance), Tendermint, Avalanche, and other schemes established in the blockchain world. **Verification and fallback**: if the leader does not respond or behaves badly, the system can detect it rapidly through the internal consensus and select a new leader. **Punishing incorrect behaviors**: the operators that behave badly (proposing invalid batches, going offline repeatedly, censoring in an evident way) lose collateral.

FIGURE 17.5 **STRATEGY THREE: LEADER ELECTION WITH INTERNAL CONSENSUS, WHEN THE SEQUENCER BECOMES A COORDINATED SYSTEM.**

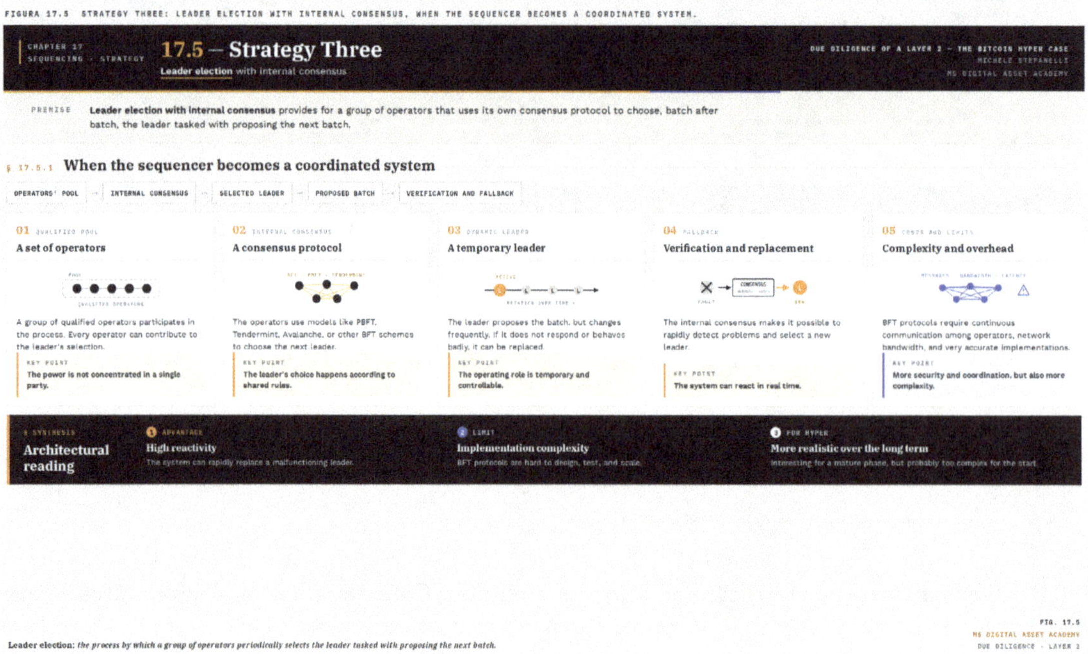

The **advantages of leader election with internal consensus** are distinctive. **Reactivity**: the internal consensus makes it possible to detect and respond rapidly to problems, replacing malfunctioning leaders in real time. **Fault resistance**: the system keeps working even if a significant percentage of the operators goes offline or behaves badly, up to a threshold (typically a third for classic BFT). **Fairness**: with appropriate design, every qualified operator has a chance of being leader, avoiding a concentration of power. **Coordination among operators**: the internal consensus eases coordination for managing complex decisions (for example, parameter changes, emergency management).

The **disadvantages** are notable. **Implementation complexity**: BFT consensus protocols are notoriously hard to implement correctly. The sector's history is full of subtle bugs in BFT implementations that have had serious consequences. **Communication overhead**: the operators must exchange messages continuously to maintain the consensus. This requires significant network bandwidth and introduces latencies. **Vulnerability under attack**: BFT protocols work well up to a certain threshold of malicious operators, but fail in a potentially catastrophic way beyond that threshold. **Scaling difficulty**: adding many operators to the pool enormously increases the communication overhead. There is a practical limit to the number of operators (typically dozens, not thousands).

Leader election with internal consensus is the conceptually most sophisticated model, and it is the one on which the main modern BFT blockchains are based (Cosmos, Solana, Sui, Aptos). **For rollups, it is an interesting direction but still in a research phase**: no main rollup has yet implemented a complete leader-election system in production.

For Hyper, this strategy could be interesting over the long term, perhaps adapted to the rollup's specific context. But it is probably too complex for the initial phases, where simpler models like random rotation or auctions are more realistic.

⁂

17.6 — Hybrid Models: Combining the Strategies

In practice, real systems tend to combine elements of several strategies, not to use one pure. **Hybrid models can capture the advantages of different approaches while mitigating their disadvantages**, and they are probably the most realistic direction for Hyper over the medium-long term.

Let us see some interesting combinations.

Random rotation with auction elements. The system uses random rotation as the default, but allows the operators to "buy" additional service turns through auctions. This combines basic fairness (random rotation) with market flexibility (auctions for those who want more capacity). The auctions' proceeds can be redistributed among all the operators, compensating those who give up their own turns.

Leader election for the coordination, an auction for the building. A version of Ethereum's PBS model: the internal consensus selects the "proposer" who decides to propose, and then a market of "builders" (batch builders) competes to provide the optimal batch. This separates the responsibility of proposing (who decides) from that of building (who optimizes), creating competitive markets at different levels.

Random rotation with governance for the parameters. The operational functioning is based on random rotation, but the structural decisions (who can join the pool, what the slashing rules are, and so on) are taken through governance mechanisms that involve the wider community, not only the operators.

A multi-level model. The system has several levels of operators with different responsibilities: a "high" level of a few operators with internal consensus for strategic decisions, an "operational" level of more operators with random rotation for the daily sequencing, a "verifier" level of independent observers that monitor the behavior. Each level has its own selection and accountability model.

For Hyper, the final choice will probably be a hybrid model adapted to the specific context. **The January 2026 post explicitly mentions "a network of participants" with "gradually expandable sequencing responsibility,"** suggesting a modular architecture where different models can coexist and evolve over time.

⁂

FIGURE 17.6 **HYBRID MODELS: COMBINING THE DECENTRALIZATION STRATEGIES TOWARD MODULAR ARCHITECTURES.**

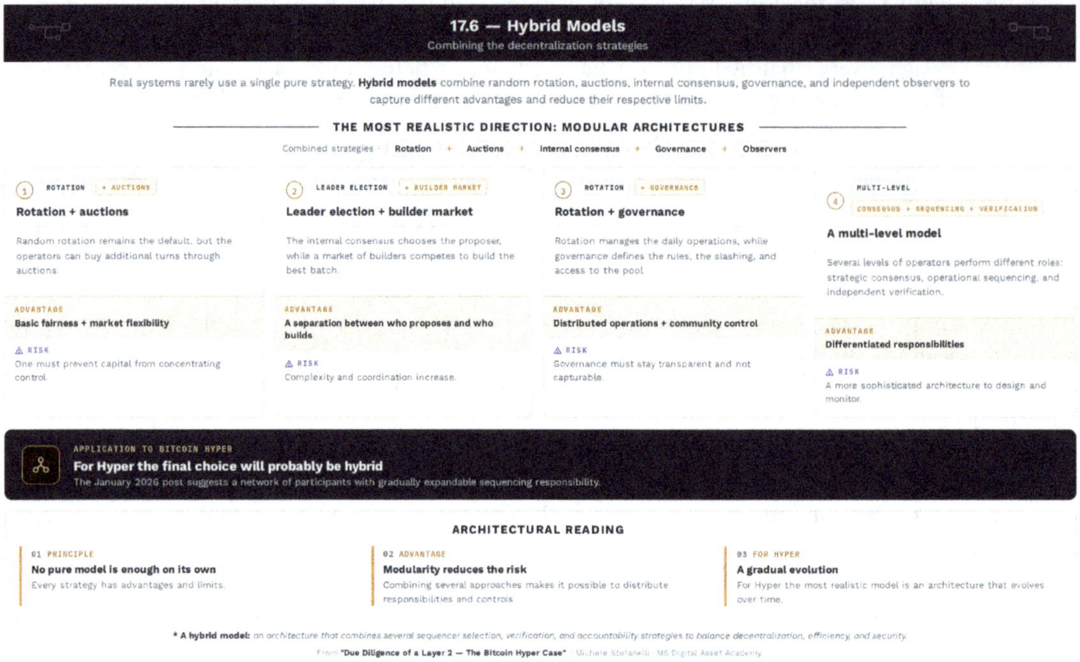

17.7 — The Specific Challenges of the Bitcoin Context

Now let us see how the general strategies adapt to the specific context of a rollup anchored to Bitcoin, because there are distinctive challenges that make the problem different from that of Ethereum's rollups.

First challenge: Bitcoin's timing. Bitcoin produces blocks every ten minutes. Any internal consensus mechanism for Hyper's sequencer must operate at higher speeds, but not so rapid that it cannot synchronize with the anchoring times. This creates a specific constraint: the internal consensus among operators must be fast (seconds or tens of seconds), but the "structural" decisions must align with Bitcoin's blocks.

FIGURE 17.7 **THE SPECIFIC CHALLENGES OF THE BITCOIN CONTEXT: THE FIVE CONSTRAINTS TO DESIGN AROUND BITCOIN.**

Second challenge: verification on Bitcoin is limited. Unlike Ethereum, where smart contracts can verify complex logic, Bitcoin only allows limited verification of states. This means that many accountability mechanisms that work on Ethereum (automatic slashing, complex verification of proofs, on-chain dispute management) are not directly available on Bitcoin. Hyper will have to implement most of the accountability logic off-chain, with a limited anchoring of cryptographic proofs on Bitcoin.

Third challenge: the ecosystem of operators. To build a pool of independent operators for Hyper, one must attract participants with capital, technical skills, and the willingness to operate over the long term. **Bitcoin has a tradition of dedicated operators (the miners), but that infrastructure is specialized for proof-of-work, not for rollup sequencing.** Hyper must build a new category of operators, and this is ecosystem work that requires years.

Fourth challenge: the economic incentives. On Ethereum, rollup operators can be incentivized through various mechanisms denominated in ETH, and the economic model is well defined. For Hyper, where the native token is $HYPER but the main asset is bitcoin, the economic structure is more complex. One must decide in what currency to pay the operators, how to manage the fees, how to structure the collateral and the slashing.

Fifth challenge: conformity with the Bitcoin philosophy. The Bitcoin ecosystem tends to be more conservative than the Ethereum ecosystem, with greater emphasis on simplicity, robustness, censorship resistance. Very sophisticated sequencing models could be perceived as "not Bitcoin" by the more rigorist part of the community, even if technically solid. Hyper must balance technical innovation and community acceptance.

All these challenges do not make the sequencer's decentralization impossible for Hyper, but they make it **context-specific**. The solutions that work for Ethereum are not directly transferable, and Hyper will have to do its own research to adapt them. **This is one of the reasons why the Hyper team is exploring the options in public**: it wants to build community consensus on the specific choices, and to do so transparently.

⁂

17.8 — The Realistic Trajectory over Time

I want to close the technical part of the chapter with a realistic look at the temporal trajectory. **In how many years could Hyper realistically reach the sequencer's complete decentralization?** It is a speculative question, but a useful one for calibrating expectations.

FIGURE 17.8 **THE REALISTIC TRAJECTORY OVER TIME: A POSSIBLE ROADMAP OF THE SEQUENCER'S DECENTRALIZATION.**

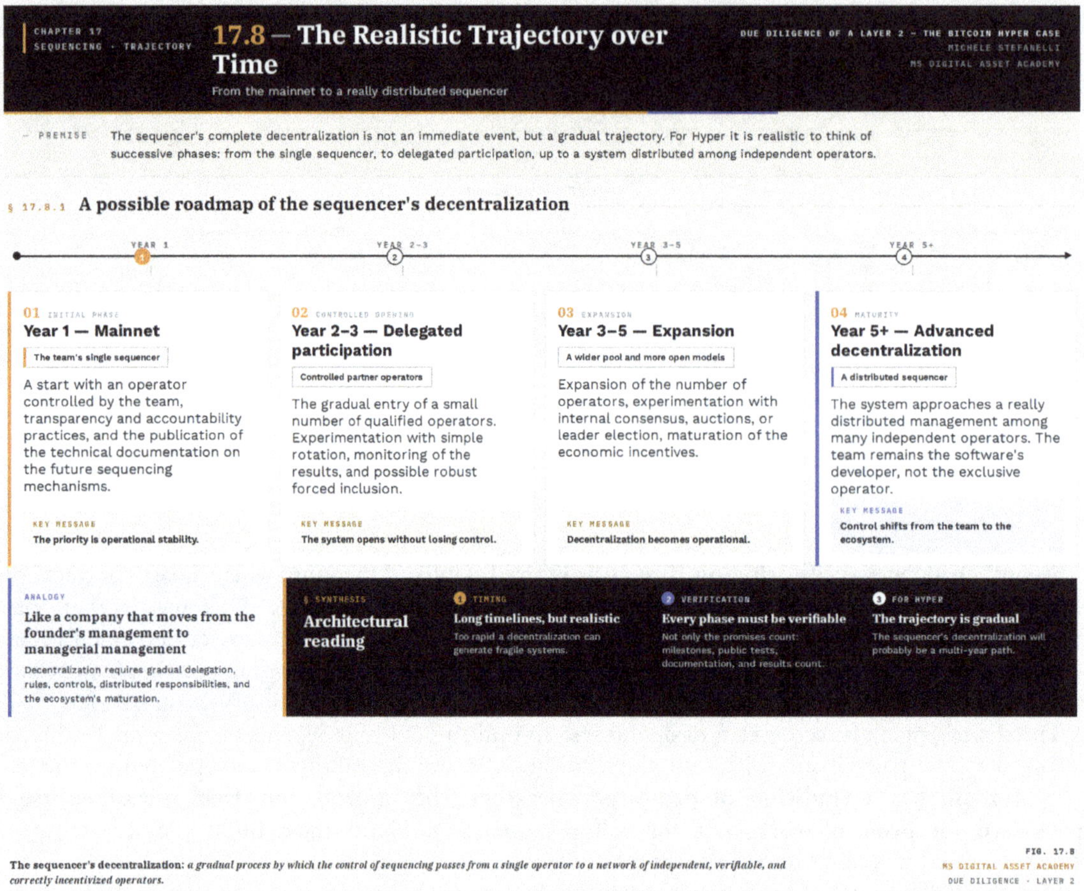

On the basis of the other rollups' experience and of the problem's intrinsic complexity, we can sketch a realistic scenario. **Year 1 (the mainnet launch)**: the team's single sequencer, with transparency and accountability practices like those described in the previous chapter. The start of the publication of detailed technical documentation on the future sequencing mechanisms. **Year 2–3**: the first phase of "delegated participation," probably with a small number of partner operators added to the system in a controlled way. Experimentation with simple rotation models, monitoring of the results. A possible initial implementation of robust forced inclusion. **Year 3–5**: expansion of the operators' pool, perhaps through more open mechanisms. Implementation of internal consensus among operators, experimentation with auctions or leader election. Maturation of the economic model, with the incentives fully operational. **Year 5+**: an approach to complete decentralization, with the sequencer really distributed among many independent operators. The Hyper team moves to a role of developer of the software but not exclusive operator of the system.

These are long timelines, and they might seem disappointing compared with the expectations of those who would like immediate decentralization. But they are aligned with what we have seen in the Ethereum world, and they reflect the problem's real complexity. **Faster timelines are possible only by accepting compromises on quality or on robustness**, and these compromises can produce fragile systems that fail under stress.

There is an analogy that can help. **The sequencer's decentralization is like a company's transition from founder management to managerial management.** Companies typically go through this transition in 5–10 years, with various phases: first the founder controls everything, then gradually delegates to managers, then creates formal processes, then finally withdraws gradually leaving the company to the structured management. The process takes time because skills, trust, processes, culture must be built. The same holds for rollups: decentralization requires building an ecosystem of operators, developing technical mechanisms, consolidating governance, building community culture.

For Hyper's investors and users, accepting these timelines is part of the judgment on the project. Those who expect complete decentralization within 2–3 years of the launch will probably be disappointed. Those who expect a well-managed multi-year path can be satisfied, even if the progress will be gradual rather than dramatic.

⁂

17.9 — Questions and Answers: Clarifying the Chapter's Concepts

Question 1: If the sequencer's decentralization is so difficult, why do all rollups promise it?

Because it is a marketing standard of the sector, and not promising progressive decentralization would be interpreted as admitting a wish to stay centralized. **The reality is that many projects promise more than they can realistically realize**, at least in the timelines they often suggest. For investors, it is important to distinguish between generic promises of "progressive decentralization" and specific commitments with milestones, technical prerequisites, and regular updates. The first type is marketing; the second is a project. **For Hyper, it will be important to monitor whether the promises turn into concrete actions in the months following the mainnet launch.** If you see publications of detailed technical documents, experiments with partner operators, milestones reached as announced, it is a positive signal. If you see only generic declarations without concrete actions, it is a signal of a problem. Concrete example: in the Ethereum world, various projects have promised the "imminent" decentralization of the sequencer for years, without realizing it. Others (like Optimism with the Superchain framework) have made concrete, measurable progress. The difference is visible over time, not in the words.

Question 2: Which of these strategies seems to you the most probable that Hyper will adopt?

I cannot predict with certainty, but I can make some informed observations. **The probable model: an evolutionary hybrid.** Hyper will start with a single sequencer, will gradually evolve toward a model with a small number of partner operators (probably 5–15 entities) with simple rotation, and will then expand progressively toward more sophisticated models. **Random rotation is probably better suited to the initial phases** because it is simple and manageable, even if it has limitations. **Auctions could be introduced subsequently** to manage the MEV transparently, once the ecosystem is mature. **Leader election with internal consensus is probably too complex for Hyper in the coming years**, even if it could be considered over the long term. **For the readers who want to evaluate the real progress**, the important thing is following the team's research posts and announcements, where the specific choices will emerge gradually. Concrete example: Optimism developed its own "fault proof system" through various public research documents (the "Kona" model, various successive proposals) before implementing it in production. For Hyper a similar trajectory is expected on the sequencing models.

Question 3: If the sequencer's decentralization is so complex, isn't it better to accept that the system will stay semi-centralized and protect it with other mechanisms?

It is a legitimate position that some experts of the sector defend. The argument is: **if the sequencer's centralization does not allow the funds to be stolen (because the security properties come from the anchoring on Bitcoin and from data availability), then perhaps decentralizing it is not a priority, at**

least not at the cost of the technical complexity. One could instead concentrate the resources on other dimensions: robust forced-inclusion mechanisms, regular audits, transparent communication, the legal accountability of the operating team. **There is something true in this position, and it is one of the arguments of the "centralized by choice" model that projects like Base have adopted.** The other side of the coin is that centralization, even if it does not allow direct thefts, creates other risks: selective censorship, concentrated MEV, dependence on regulatory decisions about single actors, systemic fragility. **Progressive decentralization is not a dogma, but it is a useful direction for reducing these risks.** For Hyper, which has aspirations of being "Bitcoin extended" more than "yet another blockchain," decentralization is probably a strategic value worth pursuing even if it costs time. Concrete example: the success of Bitcoin itself is largely due to its radical decentralization. Federated sidechains like Liquid have found their own market niche, but they have not become what Bitcoin is. For Hyper, choosing the decentralized model (even if difficult) has long-term positioning implications.

Question 4: The January 2026 post explores these strategies but does not commit to any. Is this normal, or is it worrying?

It is normal for a project in a pre-mainnet phase, and it is also a sign of technical honesty. **The Hyper team is recognizing that it does not yet know what solution it will finally adopt, and is exploring the options in public.** This is better than alternatives like committing prematurely to a choice that then proves problematic, or generically promising "decentralization" without specifics. **It becomes worrying if the pattern persists beyond certain timelines.** If in the months following the mainnet launch the team keeps exploring options without concrete choices, then there is a problem. **For those who monitor the project, the important thing is seeing progress in the decisions**: first the exploration of options (the current phase), then the experimentation with prototypes, then the implementation of concrete solutions, then progressive expansion. If this progress manifests in the next 12–24 months, it is a positive signal. If it stays stuck at the exploration, it is a signal of a problem. Concrete example: Optimism published its own first document on fault proofs in 2020. It went through various intermediate models over time. It implemented an initial version in production in 2024, after four years of progressive evolution. For Hyper a similar trajectory is expected on the sequencing models, with constant even if not dramatic progress.

Question 5: If I am interested in participating as a Hyper operator in the future, when should I start preparing?

It is a long-term investment that requires planning. **First dimension: technical skills.** Operating a rollup node requires skills in distributed systems, networking, security, operational management. If you do not have these skills, start building them now through experience with other blockchain systems (running Bitcoin and Ethereum nodes, proof-of-stake validators). **Second dimension: capital.** Most distributed sequencing models require significant collateral from the operators. Start estimating how much capital might be required and plan accordingly. The typical figures for other projects are in the order of hundreds of thousands or millions of dollars. **Third dimension: relationships with the project.** Start participating in the project's community, contributing to technical discussions, building a reputation. When the Hyper team begins selecting partner operators, it will want actors with a history of constructive contribution. **Fourth dimension: monitoring the progress.** Follow the research posts and the announcements. The technical specifications for the operators will become clearer over time, and you will have to adapt your preparation accordingly. **In terms of realistic timelines**, participating as a second-phase operator could become possible 18–24 months after the mainnet launch. Starting to prepare 6–12 months earlier is reasonable. Concrete example: if Hyper launches the mainnet in early 2027, the operators' pool could open partially toward the end of 2028 or the beginning of 2029. Starting to build technical skills and relationships in 2027–2028 is reasonable for those who are seriously interested.

Question 6: Are there sequencing models that could rapidly become obsolete because of new cryptographic techniques?

Yes, and this is one of the most interesting aspects of the sector. **Cryptographic research is producing new techniques that could radically change how rollups are made.** Three directions in particular are worth mentioning. **First direction: native zk-proofs on Bitcoin.** If in the future Bitcoin introduced opcodes that allow zk-proofs to be verified directly (through proposals like OP_CAT or variants), the sequencing model could simplify enormously. Even more: the direct verification of the proofs would reduce the dependence on social accountability mechanisms. **Second direction: encrypted mempools.** Techniques like threshold encryption make it possible to build transaction pools where the sequencer's operators cannot see the content of the transactions in real time. This would eliminate much of the opaque MEV, because the operators could not extract it without having privileged information. **Third direction: shared sequencing.** The idea that several rollups share the same sequencer, instead of each having its own, is emerging as an interesting paradigm. It reduces the ecosystem's fragmentation and allows economies of scale. **For Hyper, these evolutions could make certain sequencing models obsolete over the medium term**, and the team will have to stay flexible. The March 2026 post on "multi-decade scalability" explicitly emphasizes the importance of a modular architecture that can integrate future innovations. This is one of the most important aspects of the design, and it must be monitored. Concrete example: Ethereum's PBS model became the standard only in 2022–2023, while before completely different models were used. The sector's speed of evolution is high, and projects that do not adapt risk becoming technologically obsolete.

⁂

17.10 — WHAT TO TAKE AWAY FROM THIS CHAPTER

The sequencer's decentralization is one of the hardest technical challenges of modern rollups, and no main rollup has yet demonstrated a complete solution in production at scale.

There are three distinct dimensions of decentralization: who can propose, how it is decided who proposes at a given moment, how correct behavior is verified. A complete solution must address all three.

Three main strategies emerge from the research: random rotation (simple but with a vulnerability to large operators), auctions (efficient for the MEV but complex to design), leader election with internal consensus (sophisticated but with high overhead).

Hybrid models that combine elements of these strategies are probably the most realistic direction. Every pure model has significant trade-offs that can be mitigated by combining elements of them.

The Bitcoin context poses specific challenges that differentiate Hyper from Ethereum's rollups: Bitcoin's longer timing, limited verification on the main blockchain, an ecosystem of operators to build from scratch, a more complex economic structure, conformity with the Bitcoin philosophy.

The realistic trajectory for complete decentralization is one of years, not months: 1 year of a single sequencer, 2–3 years of delegated participation, 5+ years for complete decentralization. Faster timelines require compromises on quality.

Bitcoin Hyper is exploring the options in public in the January 2026 post, recognizing that the final choice will require experimentation and maturation. This is technical honesty, but the concrete progress must manifest in the coming months/years.

The sequencer's decentralization is not a dogma, but it is a strategic direction for reducing risks that otherwise stay open: selective censorship, concentrated MEV, regulatory dependence, systemic fragility.

The future evolutions of cryptography (native zk-proofs on Bitcoin, encrypted mempools, shared sequencing) could radically change the scenario in the coming years. Hyper must stay flexible to integrate them.

For those who evaluate the project, monitoring the concrete progress on the sequencing models is one of the most important indicators of the technical maturity and of the seriousness of the decentralization promises.

Chapter 17 ends here. We have understood the possible strategies for the sequencer's decentralization, the specific challenges of the Bitcoin context, and the realistic trajectory over time. From here on, Part V of the book (The Sequencing Layer) closes. We are ready to enter Part VI, dedicated to the security model and to the system's defensive architecture.

*In **Chapter 18 — Security by Design, Not by Audit: The Constitutional Principle**, we will examine the philosophy with which Bitcoin Hyper is addressing security, going beyond the sector's standard approach (periodic audits after development) toward a structural approach (security integrated into the design decisions from the start). It is a paradigm shift that the team made explicit in the February 2026 post, and that deserves attention because it reflects the project's engineering maturity.*

Toward the *distributed* sequencer

Rotation, auctions, and leader election: three roads for taking control away from **a single operator**.

1 Decentralizing the order

In a rollup the final truth is anchored on Bitcoin, but someone must still **propose and order the batches** in real time.

THE CRITICAL KNOT who proposes? · who decides the order? · who checks the behavior?

users' transactions → ordered batch → state root → anchoring ₿

The problem is not only having more operators: *it is distributing the power to propose, choose, and check.*

2 Three decisive questions

Participation
Who can propose the batches? A single team or several independent operators?

Selection
How is the proposer chosen? Turns, a draw, an auction, a committee, or on-chain rules.

Accountability
How is it checked? Monitoring, proofs, challenges, sanctions, and verifiable data.

ⓘ More operators **are not enough** if the selection is opaque or controls are missing.

3 Rotation, auctions, leader election

1 Random rotation
PRO simple, understandable, fairer.
LIMITS variable performance, dominant operators, a complex pool.

2 Competitive auctions
PRO more transparent MEV, explicit monetization, a market.
LIMITS it favors capital, pay-to-play, economic complexity.

3 Leader election
PRO reactive, fault-resistant, coordinated.
LIMITS complex, communication overhead, hard to scale.

Every model distributes the power differently, **but introduces new trade-offs.**

4 Not a one-shot choice, but a path

PHASE 1
A single sequencer
An operating team. Simple and fast, but centralized.

→ PHASE 2
Delegated participation
Partner operators. Rotation or limited committees.

→ PHASE 3
Distributed sequencing
More operators. Verifiable auctions, draws, or internal consensus.

→ PHASE 4
A mature model
Public accountability, monitoring, sanctions, governance.

The sequencer's decentralization is a **trajectory of years**, *not a switch to flip at launch.*

5 The Bitcoin context changes the problem

Bitcoin's timing
~10 min/block: fast but synchronized with the settlement.

Limited on-chain verification
Bitcoin does not execute complex smart contracts.

An ecosystem of operators
A new category of sequencers must be built.

Economic incentives
Balancing $HYPER, BTC, fees, collateral, slashing.

The Bitcoin philosophy
Innovating without betraying simplicity and robustness.

Hyper's solution will have to be **technically solid and culturally compatible with Bitcoin**.

THE KEY POINT

Decentralizing the sequencer means distributing three powers: **proposing, choosing, and checking**. **Rotation, auctions, and leader election** are possible roads, but **none eliminates all the trade-offs**. Hyper's credibility will depend on **verifiable milestones, independent operators, public rules** and real accountability.

PART VI

Security

Security by design, two-level security, graceful degradation, defenses against a malicious sequencer. The choices that separate a serious rollup from a disguised sidechain.

PART VI · SECURITY

Chapter 18
Security by Design, Not by Audit

The constitutional principle

⁂

18.1 — Two Philosophies Compared

I want to begin this chapter with a distinction that is never explained clearly enough in the crypto world, but which is the heart of how a serious project differentiates itself from an improvised one. **There are two radically different philosophies of doing security in a complex software system, and understanding the difference changes the way you evaluate any blockchain project.**

First philosophy: security as an additional layer. The system is built, made to work, the desired functionalities are reached, and then — at the end, before the launch or right after — an audit firm is called in to "check the security." The firm examines the code, identifies vulnerabilities, writes a report, the developers apply patches where possible. The system is certified as "audited" and goes into production. **This is the dominant approach in the crypto sector**, and it is what most investors associate with "security": a stamp on a document saying that someone has checked.

Second philosophy: security as a structural principle. The project begins by asking not "how do I make this thing work" but "how do I design this thing to be structurally hard to attack." Every architecture decision is taken considering the security implications. Every component is designed by minimizing the attack surface*. Every interaction among components is made as transparent and verifiable as possible. **The audit, in this philosophy, becomes an external confirmation of an attention that has already been constant**, not a final check that substitutes for the lack of previous attention.

The Bitcoin Hyper team made its adherence to the second philosophy explicit in a research post published in February 2026, significantly titled "Security by Architecture." It was an act of strategic positioning, because few companies in the sector are willing to openly declare their own security philosophy so explicitly. **In this chapter I want to understand what this philosophy concretely means, see how it applies in Hyper's choices, and give you the tools for judging whether the team's declarations are matched by the facts.**

There is an important aspect to clarify from the start. **These two philosophies are not mutually exclusive**: even a project that adopts "security by design" still does audits, even a project that only does audits has some design-conscious practice. The difference is one of **emphasis and priority**. A "security by design" project considers the audit a confirmation check; a "security by audit" project considers the audit the main (or only) guarantee. The practical consequences are enormous, and we see them in this chapter.

---

* **Attack surface.** The set of all the points where a system can be hit: interfaces, components, data entry points. Reducing it — that is, having fewer exposed and simpler parts — means offering fewer footholds to a potential attacker. It is one of the cardinal principles of "security by design": less exposed surface, fewer things that can break or be exploited.

⁂

18.2 — Why Security by Audit Is Not Enough

Let us begin with an honest critique of the dominant approach, because understanding its limits is the prerequisite for appreciating the alternative. **Security by audit, on its own, has failed systematically in the crypto world**, and the numbers are unequivocal.

In recent years, the crypto sector has experienced catastrophic exploits worth billions of dollars, and the overwhelming majority of these exploits hit systems that had been audited. Wormhole, which lost 320 million dollars in 2022 after publishing audits. Ronin Bridge, which lost 625 million dollars in 2022. Nomad, which lost 190 million in 2022. Multichain, which lost over 100 million in 2023. **All these systems had public audit reports at the moment of the attack.** And yet they were proven vulnerable.

FIGURE 18.1 **CATASTROPHIC EXPLOITS ON AUDITED SYSTEMS AND THE FIVE STRUCTURAL LIMITS OF THE AUDIT AS THE ONLY SECURITY STRATEGY.**

System	Year	Loss	Audit status
Ronin Bridge	2022	625 M $	Audited
Wormhole	2022	320 M $	Audit published
Nomad	2022	190 M $	Audited
Multichain	2023	>100 M $	Audited

Structural limit of the audit	Consequence
1. Limited in time	Weeks to examine months or years of development: certain corners stay unexplored.
2. Limited in scope	It examines the smart contracts, not infrastructure, key management, emergency procedures.
3. Limited to the knowledge of the moment	A 2024 audit ignores the attacks discovered in 2025; yesterday's secure is vulnerable today.
4. Few observation points	One or two firms: if both fail to see the problem, the problem survives.
5. Commercial, not technical	The auditor is paid by the project: cautious language, nuanced judgments, few critical reports.

Billions of dollars lost on systems that were all audited demonstrate that the audit is necessary but insufficient. The five limits are not solved with "better" audits: they are structural. Hence the chapter's thesis — security must be designed from the start as an architectural principle, not added as a final certification.

Why do audits fail so often? For structural reasons that cannot be solved simply by doing "better" audits.

First reason: audits are limited in time. An audit firm typically has a few weeks to examine a system that has been developed for months or years. Even with excellent teams, it is impossible to cover all the code in depth in such short times. Inevitably, certain corners stay unexplored.

Second reason: audits are limited in scope. An audit typically examines the code of the specified smart contracts. It does not examine the operating infrastructure, the key-management practices, the emergency procedures, the interactions with external services. Many historical exploits have happened in these areas outside the scope.

Third reason: audits are limited to the knowledge of the moment. An audit done in 2024 knows nothing of the attacks that will be discovered in 2025. The sector evolves constantly, new attack techniques emerge, and systems that were secure by yesterday's standard can become vulnerable today.

Fourth reason: audits are very few observation points. Typically a system is audited by one or two firms. If both fail to see the same problem, the problem survives. The model depends on the idea that someone else has seen, and this is not always true.

Fifth reason: audits are often commercial, not technical. Audit firms are paid by the project they audit. They do not want to produce overly critical reports that damage their clients. They tend to issue nuanced judgments, to use cautious language, to avoid "killing" projects. **The result is that many audits are fundamentally certifications of mediocre quality, not guarantees of robustness.**

Putting these reasons together, it emerges that security by audit is a **necessary but insufficient** approach. Audits serve and contribute, but on their own they are not enough to guarantee a robust system. To obtain real robustness, a different approach is needed from the start.

Bitcoin Hyper, in the February 2026 post, explicitly recognized these limits: "Security in a rollup environment is not something that gets added at a later stage. It is architectural. Every design choice widens or reduces the attack surface. Bitcoin Hyper considers security a structural principle and not only an auditing milestone." It is a declaration that reflects maturity, but it must be supported by concrete choices, and in the next sections we see which.

⁂

18.3 — The Principles of Security by Design

Having understood the limits of the audit-only approach, let us see what doing "security by design" concretely means. There are established guiding principles in the world of critical software engineering (aviation, medicine, defense systems) that apply directly to the blockchain context.

First principle: minimization of the attack surface. Every component of a system is a potential attack surface. More components, more points where something can go wrong. Security by design begins by asking: is this functionality really necessary? If yes, can it be implemented with the minimum possible code? Can it be isolated from the rest of the system so that any problems are contained? **Bitcoin itself is the highest example of this principle**: its Script virtual machine is deliberately limited to reduce the attack surface. Hyper, in its choices, should apply the same principle where possible.

Second principle: separation of responsibilities. Different components of the system should have clearly separated responsibilities, with well-defined interfaces. A failure in one component should not propagate to the whole system. **In the February 2026 post, Hyper makes this principle explicit**: "An important aspect is the sequencer risk. If a sequencer halts, censors, or proposes invalid state transitions, the system must be resilient. This is why the separation between execution and settlement is important." The structural separation among levels (execution, sequencing, settlement, data availability) is exactly this principle.

Third principle: graceful degradation. When something goes wrong — because something will always go wrong in complex systems — the system should slow down in a controlled way, not collapse unpredictably. Hyper's post says exactly this: "It is about graceful degradation. If a component encounters problems, the network should slow down safely rather than collapse unpredictably." It is a philosophy borrowed directly from Bitcoin, which is designed to "fail safe" rather than "fail dangerous."

Fourth principle: transparency and verifiability. Everything the system does should be observable and verifiable by independent third parties. One cannot defend what one cannot observe, and one cannot trust what one cannot verify. **The publication of open-source code, of operating metrics, of historical data are practical elements of this principle.**

Fifth principle: a presumption of hostility. Security systems must be designed assuming that someone will try to attack them. Not "if" attacked, but "when." This changes the way of thinking: instead of asking "is this enough for normal use," one asks "does this hold up against a motivated, well-funded attacker looking for weak points." It is a more paranoid mindset, but it is what separates projects that survive over time from those that fail.

Sixth principle: defense in depth. A single protection layer is fragile; an attacker who overcomes it has complete access. Several overlapping layers make the attack enormously harder, because each must be overcome independently. **For rollups, defense in depth translates into: anchoring on Bitcoin (immutability) + data availability (verifiability) + proof mechanisms (validity) + forced-exit mechanisms (resistance to capture) + community monitoring (accountability). Every layer serves, and together they are much more robust than each separately.**

Seventh principle: minimizing trust. Every time a system "requires trusting" an actor, it has introduced a point of vulnerability. Security by design constantly works to reduce these points, replacing them with cryptographic verifications or structural guarantees. **In the rollup, trust in the sequencer is the main residual point to minimize**, and it is the reason why progressive decentralization is strategically important.

Eighth principle: security for the worst case, not the average one. One designs for catastrophic scenarios, not for normal conditions. What happens if the project's team disappears? What happens if

Bitcoin has a controversial fork? What happens if Bitcoin's fees explode? **A robust system has answers to these questions, it does not assume they never occur.**

These eight principles are the vocabulary of security by design. **Now let us see how they apply concretely in Bitcoin Hyper's choices**, going on to examine the architecture through these lenses.

⁂

18.4 — How the Principles Translate into Hyper's Choices

Let us now put the principles just described into practice, seeing how they manifest (or should manifest) in Bitcoin Hyper's specific choices. This exercise is useful because it transforms the philosophical declarations into concrete decisions that we can evaluate.

A modular architecture. The organization of the system into separate levels (SVM execution, sequencing, settlement on Bitcoin, data availability) implements the principle of the separation of responsibilities. A problem in one level is contained and does not immediately propagate to the others. **This is a security-by-design choice**, even if it is also presented as a flexibility choice for future evolutions.

SVM execution with tight constraints. The choice of SVM with the declared-accounts model implements the principle of minimizing the attack surface. Every transaction explicitly declares what it will touch, reducing the possibilities of unexpected interactions. **The perfect determinism required by parallel execution** — which we addressed in Chapter 10 — is another example: the system imposes rigid constraints that eliminate sources of non-determinism, reducing the attack surfaces.

Anchoring on Bitcoin. The anchoring of the state commitments on Bitcoin implements the principle of defense in depth. Even if all the rest of the system is compromised, the anchored states remain immutable, and this is a protection layer that resists almost any type of attack internal to the rollup.

Public availability of the data. The commitment to a true rollup model (with public, verifiable data) instead of a validium (with private data) implements the principle of transparency and verifiability. Anyone can verify what happened, reducing the dependence on trust in the operators.

Forced-inclusion mechanisms (in development). The intention to implement mechanisms that allow users to force the inclusion of transactions, even if the sequencer censors them, implements the principle of minimizing trust. Even with a centralized sequencer, the user does not depend completely on the sequencer's good will.

A single sequencer at launch with a decentralization path. This choice is more nuanced. The single sequencer somewhat violates the principle of minimizing trust (it requires trust in the team), but the progressive decentralization path is a long-term mitigation. **It is a pragmatic compromise**, acceptable if the decentralization path is effectively realized within the announced timelines.

Exploration of multiple consensus models. The fact that the team is exploring various models (random rotation, auctions, leader election) instead of committing prematurely to a single one reflects the principle of security for the worst case. **By exploring multiple options, the team can choose the most robust one after comparing them seriously**, instead of adopting the first one that seems to work.

Transparency in the research posts. The publication of regular technical research documents (on data availability, on the sequencing models, on determinism, on long-term scalability) implements the principle of transparency. It shows that the team is thinking about the issues openly, and allows the community to participate in the evaluation process.

A "future-proof" architecture. The intention to design the system so that it can evolve over time, integrating future innovations (new Bitcoin opcodes, new cryptographic techniques, new consensus models), implements the principle of security for the worst case. **One assumes that the technological landscape will change, and designs to adapt**, instead of committing to a static solution.

Putting these elements together, it emerges that Hyper's choices seem in line with the principles of security by design. **This is a positive signal for the project's technical evaluation.** However, declarations and intentions are not enough on their own: one must see how these choices translate into practice in the months and years after the mainnet launch.

⁂

18.5 — What the Hyper Team Has Not Yet Demonstrated

To be honest in the evaluation, we must also identify what has not yet been demonstrated of Hyper's security model. The philosophical declarations are important, but they are only the starting point. The real verification comes from practice.

A robust implementation of the Canonical Bridge. The bridge between Bitcoin and Hyper is the most critical component for the security of the users' funds, and the February 2026 post addresses it only generically. **The specific implementation, the key-management procedures, the emergency mechanisms have not yet been publicly documented in detail.** This is one of the most important points to monitor before the mainnet launch.

A complete proof model (fraud or validity). The proof system that makes it possible to detect and challenge incorrect behaviors of the sequencer is essential for the security model, but the team has not yet committed to a specific model. **Random rotation, auctions, or leader election are possible, but which will be adopted and how it will be implemented is not yet clear.**

Implemented forced-inclusion mechanisms. The intention is there, the specific technical documentation is not. **Without robust forced inclusion, the promise of "censorship resistance" is incomplete.** Seeing a concrete implementation will be an important test.

Complete, public independent audits. The team has mentioned the intention to undergo audits, but the reports have not yet been published. **Quality public audits, from several independent firms, are a standard the project will have to reach before the launch.**

Stress tests and attack simulations. A system can be designed well but behave badly under real pressures. Stress tests, attack simulations, systematic fuzzing are practices that produce concrete evidence of robustness. **We do not yet know how much Hyper has invested in these tests or what results it has produced.**

Active bug bounty programs. Paying external researchers to find bugs is one of the most effective ways of discovering problems before the attackers do. **The Hyper team has mentioned the intention to have a program, but the details (amounts, scope, process) are not yet publicly known.**

An operational track record. One thing is declaring security principles, another is applying them under real operational pressure. **Hyper's track record will be built only after the mainnet launch**, through how the team will manage incidents, detected vulnerabilities, attempted attacks. There is no shortcut for this experience.

Demonstrated resistance to various classes of attacks. There are dozens of attack classes documented in the blockchain world (reentrancy, integer overflow, MEV abuse, oracle manipulation, governance attacks, and so on). **Seeing how Hyper concretely behaves when exposed to real attempts of these categories will be the definitive test.**

These elements are not criticisms of the project: they are simply things that cannot yet be judged because the system is not yet in production. **For those who evaluate the project, monitoring these elements in the months following the launch will be essential.** The philosophical declarations of Chapter 18 will be verified or disproven by the facts.

⁂

18.6 — A Comparison with Other Projects: Who Really Does Security by Design

To give context, it is useful to compare Hyper's approach with that of other projects in the sector. **Which projects really do security by design, which do only security by audit, and where does Hyper sit?**

The original Bitcoin is the reference. It was designed from scratch with the principle of maximum security, with deliberate conservative choices (a limited Script, slow blocks, consensus conservatism). Every modification to the protocol is examined for years before being implemented. **It is the supreme example of security by design**, and all the other projects are judged with this as the implicit benchmark.

Ethereum shows a mixed approach. On one hand, the original design had compromises (a serial EVM, inefficient gas, various weaknesses). On the other, the subsequent evolutions (proof-of-stake with the merge, new opcodes, EIP-4844) were designed with greater attention to security. **Ethereum has improved significantly over time**, even if it does not reach Bitcoin's rigor.

Optimism and Arbitrum have taken different roads. Optimism invested in fault proofs from the start (even if the implementation was gradual), showing attention to security by design. Arbitrum has a well-designed architecture but perhaps less public emphasis on the security philosophy. **Both have had minor incidents that they managed reasonably well**, but neither has yet been seriously put to the test by major attacks.

Solana has different priorities. It concentrated on performance more than on pure security by design, and experienced various stability problems in the early years. It has improved significantly over time, but its approach to security is more "pragmatic" than "principled." **For Hyper, inheriting SVM also means inheriting some of Solana's design choices, and it is important that the team has added its own security constraints.**

Solana Labs and other SVM teams have become more attentive to security over time, and today their approach is more mature than at the origins. The SVM community has developed specific security practices that Hyper can inherit.

Cosmos and other BFT blockchains have traditionally emphasized the technical robustness of the consensus, but have had various incidents relating to smart contracts or cross-chain interconnections. **They show that security by design of the consensus is not enough**: security by design of the whole architecture is needed.

Federated sidechains like Liquid show the opposite approach. They chose explicit centralization as an acceptable trade-off for certain properties (efficiency, compliance). **They are neither security by design nor security by audit**: they are security by delegated trust. It is legitimate for certain use cases, but it is a very different model from the one Hyper is attempting.

Putting these comparison points together, it emerges that **Hyper positions itself with explicit declarations of "security by design,"** but the context is competitive: other projects that are part of Bitcoin Layer 2s or of Ethereum's rollups have different backgrounds and different priorities. **Hyper's competitive advantage on the security axis will depend on how the declared principles translate into concrete implementation**, and on whether this implementation holds up to the test of production.

For those who evaluate the project, a useful test is comparing the quantity and quality of technical documentation published by Hyper with that of other projects. **The more the documentation is specific, detailed, and addresses adverse scenarios, the more one can believe that security has been thought through in depth.** Vague, generic documentation, focused only on the happy paths, is instead a signal of limits in the approach to security.

⁂

18.7 — The Team's Culture as a Security Factor

An often undervalued dimension of security by design is the **team's internal culture**, because many of the principles described depend on how decisions are taken daily. **A team with a security culture takes defensive decisions even when nobody is watching**; a team without this culture takes decisions that optimize for other objectives and then tries to "patch" security afterwards.

Let us see the main elements of a security culture.

The practice of rigorous code review. Every code change is examined by at least one other expert developer, who has the power to ask for modifications or to reject the change. Code reviews are not formalities: they are real opportunities to find problems. **Teams with a security culture invest significant time in thorough code reviews.**

Systematic threat modeling.[*] Before designing a component, the team asks itself: "how could this be attacked? Who would have an interest in attacking it? What could they obtain?". Threat modeling guides the design decisions, identifying risks before the code is written.

Tests as a first-class citizen. Unit tests, integration tests, stress tests, property-based tests are a normal part of development, not a final addition. **Teams with a security culture write tests that actively try to break the system, not only to confirm its normal functioning.**

Tolerance for those who raise concerns. When a team member raises their hand to say "I have a doubt about this choice," the team takes the doubt seriously instead of dismissing it. This requires a culture of openness and technical humility, and it is one of the main factors that separate excellent teams from mediocre ones.

Learning from others' mistakes. The team studies the incidents that have hit other projects, understands how they happened, and adapts its own practices. **Every big exploit in the sector is a learning opportunity**, and teams with a security culture exploit this opportunity.

Investment in operational security. The people who manage the cryptographic keys, the production deployments, the responses to incidents are carefully selected, trained, and supported. The operating procedures are documented and rigorously followed. **Operational security is often more important than code security**: many historical exploits have exploited operations problems, not bugs in the code.

Internal transparency about the limits. The team members are honest with one another about what they know and what they do not know, about what has been tested and what has not, about which are the risk areas. This internal honesty prevents decisions based on wrong assumptions.

For Bitcoin Hyper, **we cannot directly observe the team's internal culture from the outside**, but we can deduce it from indirect signals. The quality of the published research posts. The precision of the technical language used. The team's response to public criticism. The frequency and quality of the updates. **These signals, monitored over time, give a reasonable idea of the team's culture**, even if they are not definitive proof.

On the basis of what is publicly available up to the first quarter of 2026, **the Hyper team seems to have a serious technical culture**: the research posts are well written, openly address the challenges, recognize the limits, and show technical sophistication in the discussion of the alternatives. They are all positive signals. But the definitive proof will come from practice, after the mainnet launch.

---

* **Threat modeling.** It is the systematic exercise of imagining in advance how a system could be attacked: one lists the possible aggressors, the objectives they might pursue, and the attack paths, in order to design the adequate defenses from the start. It does not correct problems after they have emerged, but tries to foresee them before the code is written.

⁂

18.8 — Questions and Answers: Clarifying the Chapter's Concepts

Question 1: If security by design is better than security by audit, why do many projects limit themselves to audits?

For economic and cultural reasons. **Doing security by design is significantly more expensive than doing audits**: it requires additional development time, specialized skills, more rigorous processes, and the acceptance of longer timelines before the launch. In a sector where market pressure pushes for fast launches, many teams choose the quicker path. **Moreover, security by audit is "sellable"**: it produces a document, a certification, a marketing claim ("audited by X"). Security by design is hard to communicate to the public — how does one demonstrate that one has designed well? **For projects that have marketing priorities over technical priorities, security by audit is enough.** For projects that want to build something robust over the long term, security by design is necessary. Concrete example: between 2020 and 2022, dozens of DeFi protocols did audits and were hacked anyway. The sector's explosive growth created pressure for fast launches, and many teams chose superficial audits instead of rigorous design. The result was the great wave of hacks of 2022, which destroyed billions of dollars of users' value.

Question 2: How do I, as a user, evaluate whether a project really does security by design?

There are concrete indicators you can observe. **First indicator: the depth of the technical posts.** A team that does security by design publishes technical documents that address adverse scenarios, discuss trade-offs, recognize limits. A team that does only security by audit publishes only promotional material. **Second indicator: openness to criticism.** When external researchers raise technical concerns, the team responds with technical arguments, not with defensiveness or dismissal. **Third indicator: transparency about incidents.** When something goes wrong (and something always goes wrong), the team publishes detailed post-mortems instead of minimizing or hiding. **Fourth indicator: investment in tests and simulations.** The team publishes results of tests, fuzzing, attack simulations, demonstrating that it has actively looked for the problems. **Fifth indicator: a serious bug bounty program.** Significant bounty amounts (tens or hundreds of thousands of dollars) and a transparent process for the management. **Sixth indicator: operational history.** For mature projects, how they managed past incidents. For new projects like Hyper, this indicator is not yet available, but it will become crucial after the launch. Concrete example: Compound Finance developed its own security-by-design reputation through years of rigorous technical documentation, the transparent management of various minor incidents, and an established bug bounty program. For new projects, it is reasonable to expect 12–24 months of operations to build a comparable reputation.

Question 3: If Hyper is still in a pre-mainnet phase, is it too early to judge the security?

Yes and no. **It is too early to judge the operational security**, which is built only through experience in production. But **it is not too early to judge the philosophical and design orientation**, which manifests in the design choices and in the published documentation. On the basis of the research posts published up to the first quarter of 2026, it is possible to make an initial evaluation that seems positive: the team shows a principled approach, serious technical documentation, a recognition of the limits, an open exploration of alternatives. **This initial evaluation can be confirmed or disproven in the months following the mainnet launch**, through how the system behaves in production. **For prudent investors, the sensible approach is**: giving credit to the current positive indications, but waiting for concrete evidence before committing heavily. **Not jumping to definitive judgments, neither positive nor negative, before the facts.** Concrete example: in 2020, before the mainnet launch, various Ethereum L2 projects showed promising philosophical indications. Some kept their promises (Optimism, Arbitrum), others never really took off. The evaluation phase was resolved only after 12–18 months of production. For Hyper a similar trajectory is expected.

Question 4: Doesn't the principle of a "presumption of hostility" lead to excessive paranoia and to developments that are too slow?

It is a delicate balance. **An excess of paranoia produces systems that are too complex and never get completed**; an excess of lightness produces systems that get attacked. **The right balance depends on the context and on the value at stake.** For a system that manages billions of dollars, as Hyper could become if it succeeds, significant paranoia is justified. For an experimental prototype, excessive paranoia would be inappropriate. **The mature practice of critical software engineering** has developed ways of managing this balance: focusing the paranoia on the most critical components (key management, the anchoring of the funds, validity proofs), and accepting greater pragmatism in the less critical components (user interfaces, development tools, documentation). Hyper must make similar choices, and part of the team's maturity is in knowing how to balance these aspects. Concrete example: aviation software systems (DO-178C) impose different levels of rigor depending on the component's criticality. Code that manages the flight is audited in an extreme way; code that manages the passengers' entertainment has more relaxed standards. Contextualized security by design is more effective than uniform paranoia.

Question 5: If a project does security by design but launches with bugs anyway, what value did the approach have?

The approach does not guarantee an absence of bugs, it guarantees a lower frequency and severity. **Even projects that do security by design will have bugs**, because any complex software has them. The difference is in how quickly the bugs are detected, how well they are managed, and how rarely they become exploitable vulnerabilities. **A project with security by design will typically have**: minor bugs discovered in the development phase instead of in production, vulnerabilities identified in the audits instead of by the attackers, minor incidents without catastrophic consequences, rapid recovery when the problems manifest. **A project with only security by audit will more frequently have**: critical bugs discovered in production, vulnerabilities exploited by attackers before being identified, major incidents with significant losses, slow and painful recovery. **Security by design does not promise perfection, it promises robustness.** Concrete example: in 2024, both Optimism and Polygon had significant bugs detected. Optimism, with a more mature security culture, managed the problem rapidly with minimal user impact. Polygon had more disruptive incidents. Both had bugs; the quality of the management was different, and this difference reflects the different security cultures.

Question 6: Are there projects that have done security by design well and that can serve as a model for Hyper?

Yes, some examples are particularly instructive. **Bitcoin itself, as I said, is the supreme reference.** Its conservative philosophy, its minimalist choices, its conservatism about changes are models to emulate. **MakerDAO has developed a notable security culture over time**, with rigorous audit and governance processes before every parameter change. It has had incidents (the "Black Thursday" of 2020), but it managed recovery and adaptation in an exemplary way. **Liquity has similar priorities**: few changes, minimized code, extensive audits. **For Layer 2s, Optimism invested significantly in fault proofs from the start**, even if the complete implementation arrived only after years. **StarkWare has a very rigorous approach to the security of zk systems**, with public technical research of high quality. **For Bitcoin Hyper, studying these examples** and adapting them to its own context would be a wise choice. The Bitcoin community has traditionally high security standards, and projects that present themselves as an "extension of Bitcoin" must reach those standards to be credible in the community. Concrete example: Hyper could publish a formal "security policy," similar to MakerDAO's or Compound's, that explicitly declares the principles adopted, the processes followed, the emergency procedures. This would give the community a concrete reference point for evaluating the seriousness of the security-by-design declarations.

⁂

18.9 — WHAT TO TAKE AWAY FROM THIS CHAPTER

There are two radically different philosophies of security: security by audit (a final check of a system developed without a specific emphasis on security) and security by design (security as a structural principle in the architecture decisions).

Security by audit is insufficient on its own. Audits limited in time, in scope, in the available knowledge, and often commercial rather than technical. Many catastrophic exploits in the sector have hit audited systems.

Security by design follows established principles: minimization of the attack surface, separation of responsibilities, graceful degradation, transparency, a presumption of hostility, defense in depth, minimization of trust, security for the worst case.

Bitcoin Hyper made its adherence to security by design explicit in the February 2026 post. The modular architecture, the SVM execution with constraints, the anchoring on Bitcoin, the transparency mechanisms reflect the principles.

Several elements have not yet been demonstrated: the implementation of the Canonical Bridge, a complete proof model, forced inclusion, public audits, stress tests, an operational track record. These are the points to monitor.

The team's internal culture is a critical factor: code review, threat modeling, systematic tests, tolerance for those who raise concerns, learning from others' mistakes, operational security, internal transparency. It is deduced from external signals.

Bitcoin Hyper faces a competitive landscape: the original Bitcoin as the reference, Optimism and Arbitrum as the benchmarks of Ethereum's rollups, Solana as the source of SVM but with a different security tradition, federated sidechains as alternatives with the opposite approach.

For users, evaluating security by design means observing concrete signals: the depth of the technical posts, openness to criticism, transparency about incidents, investment in tests, a bug bounty program, operational history.

Security by design does not guarantee an absence of bugs, but it guarantees a lower frequency and severity. Bugs detected in development instead of in production, vulnerabilities identified in the audits instead of by the attackers, incidents managed rapidly.

The real verification of security by design happens only in production, and for Hyper it will manifest in the months and years following the mainnet launch. The current philosophical declarations are positive signals but not definitive proofs.

Chapter 18 ends here. We have understood the security-by-design philosophy that Hyper declares it adopts, we have examined the principles that guide it, we have seen how they apply in the project's specific choices, and we have identified what has not yet been demonstrated. In ***Chapter 19 — Two-Level Security: Execution Integrity and Settlement Integrity****, we will go down into the detail of the two main levels of the security model, seeing how the first level protects the "how" of the transactions and the second protects the "final ledger," and how Hyper is designing both.*

NOTE

1 The expression recalls the formula *security by design* of the Anglo-Saxon engineering literature, in opposition to *security by obscurity* and to *security by audit*: security is a property that is designed into the system, not added at the review stage.

18.6 — The Audits Published at the Time of the Pre-Sale: What They Cover and What They Do Not Cover

At this point of the chapter, and before closing it, I want to address a question that the project's marketing presents compactly — "Bitcoin Hyper is audited" — and that deserves a more precise examination. At the time of writing this first edition (July 2026), Bitcoin Hyper presents **two published security audits**: one by Coinsult and one by SpyWolf[1]. The question is not whether the audits exist. The question is: **what exactly do they cover?**

Both audits have as their object **exclusively the pre-sale ERC-20 contract**, deployed on Ethereum mainnet in May 2025, with a pre-minted supply of 21 billion tokens. The verifications performed are the typical ones of a standard checklist for ERC-20 tokens: the absence of hidden *mint* functions, the absence of a *blacklist*, the absence of a *honeypot*, the absence of high sell fees, the absence of arbitrary trading pauses, the absence of upgradable proxies, the absence of ownership backdoors. Coinsult summarizes it thus: "owner cannot mint, no honeypot options, trading is enabled, no high sell fees, zero high-risk or medium-risk issues found". SpyWolf performs a parallel checklist with a "Passed" outcome.

They are useful verifications. They reduce the risk of a direct *rug pull* from the contract itself and of some well-known categories of SWC vulnerabilities. But it is essential that the reader understand **what these audits do not cover**:

- They do not cover the **Canonical Bridge** — the component that will have to mediate the BTC flows between Bitcoin L1 and Hyper's Layer 2, and that historically is the most vulnerable point of any rollup.

- They do not cover the **sequencer** — the component that orders the rollup's transactions and that concentrates technical and political surface (Ch. 15).
- They do not cover the **Bitcoin Relay Program SVM** — the on-chain program that will have to verify Bitcoin's states inside the SVM.
- They do not cover the **generation and verification of the ZK proofs** — the cryptographic heart of the rollup model declared by the whitepaper.
- They do not cover the **Data Availability** model — the guarantee that the data is effectively retrievable to allow challenges (Ch. 14).
- They do not cover the **staking contract** and the reward-distribution mechanisms (Volume II, Ch. 30).

The editorial implication is precise: the marketing statement "Bitcoin Hyper is audited" is **technically correct on the ERC-20 perimeter** and **materially partial on the declared Layer 2**. For a retail investor reading the project's home page, the distinction can appear pedantic. For a prudent investor who is evaluating a position on a pre-mainnet asset, it is instead the heart of the question: **the Layer 2 system — the effective object of the investment thesis — at the time of the pre-sale is not audited by any external firm**, because the Layer 2 system does not yet exist in a stable form to audit. The published audits concern the ERC-20 that represents a *promise* of access to the Layer 2, not the Layer 2 itself.

The operational consequence for the reader: in the due diligence framework of Volume II (Appendix E, §E.2 Questions on the technology, and §E.7 Questions on the risks), the question "how many independent audits have been completed?" must always be integrated with "**on what perimeter?**". An audit is not a generic stamp of approval: it is a stress exercise on a specified perimeter, which produces a report. Extending the audit's probative value beyond its own perimeter is the first methodological mistake of those who evaluate a project on the basis of the marketing declarations.

Security by *design*, not only by audit

Why a secure rollup is born from the architecture, not from a final stamp. Audits are **necessary but not enough**: what always counts is the verified **perimeter** and the separation of duties among the levels.

1 A final audit or structural security?

Security by audit · a final check

- Development first, checks later.
- Corrective patches on an already built system.
- The audit is treated as a stamp.
- Security is a delegated guarantee.

Security by design · a structural principle

- Security is in the project from the start.
- A modular architecture with separate levels.
- Trust minimized with rules and proofs.
- The audit is an external confirmation.

The audit verifies. The design prevents. *They are not alternatives: a robust system requires both.*

2 Audited does not mean invulnerable

Many crypto systems hit by exploits worth hundreds of millions were **already audited**. An audit always has limits of **time, scope, knowledge, and perimeter**: they are structural, and are not solved with "better" audits.

AUDIT PASSED — a stamp on a perimeter

01 **Limited time** — A few weeks for months or years of code.

02 **Limited scope** — Often only specific smart contracts.

03 **Knowledge of the moment** — New attacks emerge after the audit.

04 **Few observers** — If the auditors do not see it, the problem remains.

05 **A commercial constraint** — Prudent, non-definitive language.

An audit is necessary, but it is not an absolute guarantee.

3 The constitutional principles of security

1. **A minimal surface** — Fewer components, fewer attack points.
2. **Separate responsibilities** — Every level has a precise duty.
3. **Graceful degradation** — It slows down instead of collapsing.
4. **Transparency** — What happens is observable.
5. **Verifiability** — Anyone checks data, proofs, and states.
6. **A presumption of hostility** — Designing assuming motivated attackers.
7. **Defense in depth** — Several levels, not a single barrier.
8. **Minimized trust** — Rules and proofs in place of trust.

Security is not a module: it is a property of the entire architecture.

4 From the philosophy to the architecture

Level	Role
SVM execution	Declared accounts, determinism, clear constraints.
Sequencing	Tx order, MEV/censorship risk, progressive decentralization.
Proof system	Verification of the correctness of the state transitions.
Data Availability	Raw data accessible and verifiable by third parties.
Canonical Bridge CRITICAL	BTC deposits and withdrawals: the most critical component to audit.
Bitcoin L1	State commitments, immutability, final settlement.

Every level must limit the others' risk: *security is born from the separation of duties.*

5 The right question: an audit of what?

Already audited · the pre-sale ERC-20 contract

- No hidden mint
- No blacklist
- No honeypot
- No high sell fees
- No upgradable proxy
- No evident backdoors

To audit / verify · the Layer 2 system

- Canonical Bridge
- Sequencer
- Bitcoin Relay Program SVM
- ZK proofs
- Data availability
- Staking and rewards
- Emergency procedures
- Key management

"Audited" is not an absolute word. *What always counts is the* perimeter *of the audit.*

THE KEY POINT

Real security is not born from a **final stamp**. It is born from an architecture that **reduces trust**, separates the responsibilities, makes the data verifiable, and degrades in a controlled way. Audits are needed, but they must cover

PART VI · SECURITY

Chapter 19
Two-Level Security

Execution integrity and settlement integrity

⁂

19.1 — Two Questions, Two Answers

When one talks about the security of a rollup, there is a frequent simplification worth dismantling right away: one tends to talk about "security" as if it were a single, monolithic property. **In reality, in a serious rollup, there are at least two well distinct security dimensions, each with its own mechanisms, its own threats, its own solutions.** Confusing them is one of the most common mistakes of those who evaluate projects in the sector, and marketing gladly takes advantage of this confusion to be vague.

FIGURE 19.1 **TWO-LEVEL SECURITY: EXECUTION AND SETTLEMENT**

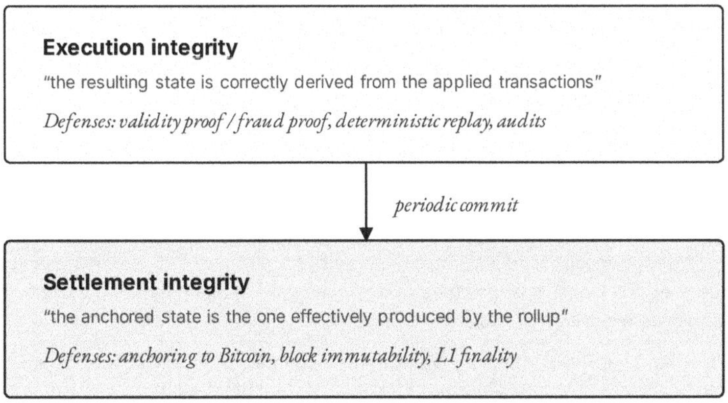

Two distinct questions: *"is the state right?" is an execution question; "is the right state really anchored?" is a settlement question. A serious rollup answers both — a system that answers only one of the two is just a disguised sidechain.*

The two dimensions are born from two different questions that every user of the system should ask themselves.

First question: when the system executes my transactions, does it do so correctly? This is the question of **execution integrity**. I am asking Hyper to apply my transaction, and I want a guarantee that the system interprets my request in the right way, applies the correct logic, modifies the states in the expected way. If I do a swap[a], I want to be sure that the price applied is the correct one according to the protocol's[b] rules, not a manipulated price. If I sign a transfer transaction, I want to be sure that the system transfers exactly the amount I specified, not more, not less, not to a different recipient.

Second question: can the historical ledger of the transactions be modified after being crystallized? This is the question of **settlement integrity**.[c] I am asking whether, once the system has recorded one of my transactions as definitive, someone can go back and modify that record. If I receive a payment of 10 BTC today, I want to be sure that in a year those 10 BTC are still mine in the ledger, and that nobody — neither the project's team, nor external actors, nor system errors — can delete them or modify them retroactively.

They are two really different questions. The first concerns **how** the system processes the transactions; the second concerns **whether what the system has processed stays stable**. A system could be perfect on the first dimension and fragile on the second, or vice versa. **To be really secure, it must be robust on both simultaneously**, and the mechanisms that guarantee each are different.

Hyper's research post on the security principles, published in October 2025, makes this distinction explicit in a notable way. It states: "Bitcoin Hyper's security model is composed of two levels.[d] The first is execution integrity, which guarantees that SVM programs are executed deterministically[f] and cannot be altered by sequencers or off-chain actors. The second is settlement integrity, which guarantees that every rollup state is correctly anchored to Bitcoin and can be verified independently."

In this chapter I want to go down into both levels, understand the specific mechanisms that protect each, and see where Hyper is in its own implementation path. It is a chapter that will make you understand a fundamental thing: **security is not a binary state, it is a layered structure, and every layer has specific technical characteristics that deserve separate attention.**

⁂

19.2 — The First Level: Execution Integrity

Let us begin with the first level, because it is the one that most directly impacts the daily user experience. **Execution integrity[e] is the guarantee that, given an input, the system produces exactly the correct output according to the protocol's rules.** Not an output that resembles the right one, not an output that is "close enough," but exactly the right one.

---

[a] **Swap.** The exchange of one crypto-asset for another inside a decentralized application, at a price determined by the protocol's rules. It is one of the most common operations in decentralized finance (DeFi).

[b] **Protocol.** The set of automatic rules that govern an application or a blockchain system, written in the code and the same for everyone. "According to the protocol's rules" means: according to what the system provides, without discretionary exceptions.

[c] **Settlement integrity.** It is the guarantee that, once recorded as definitive, a transaction can no longer be modified or deleted by anyone. It does not concern the computation of the result, but its stability over time: it derives from the anchoring to Bitcoin, which makes the past immutable.

[d] **The two-level model.** Hyper distinguishes two separate guarantees: that the system computes the right result (execution) and that that result, once fixed, no longer changes (settlement). They are independent — a system can be solid on one and fragile on the other — and to be secure it must be so on both.

[e] **Execution integrity.** It is the guarantee that the system always computes the correct result, and not one that is merely plausible. On a blockchain there are no approximations: a balance, a transfer, the outcome of an application must be exactly the ones provided by the rules, because the users' funds are founded on those numbers. It is the first of the two security levels treated in the chapter.

[f] **Deterministic.** It is said of a computation that, starting from the same starting point, always produces the same identical result, with no margins of randomness. It is the property that allows every node of the network to obtain the same outcome and therefore to agree: without determinism, different nodes could arrive at different balances, and the system could not reach a shared agreement.

FIGURE 19.2 **EXECUTION INTEGRITY AND ITS THREATS.**

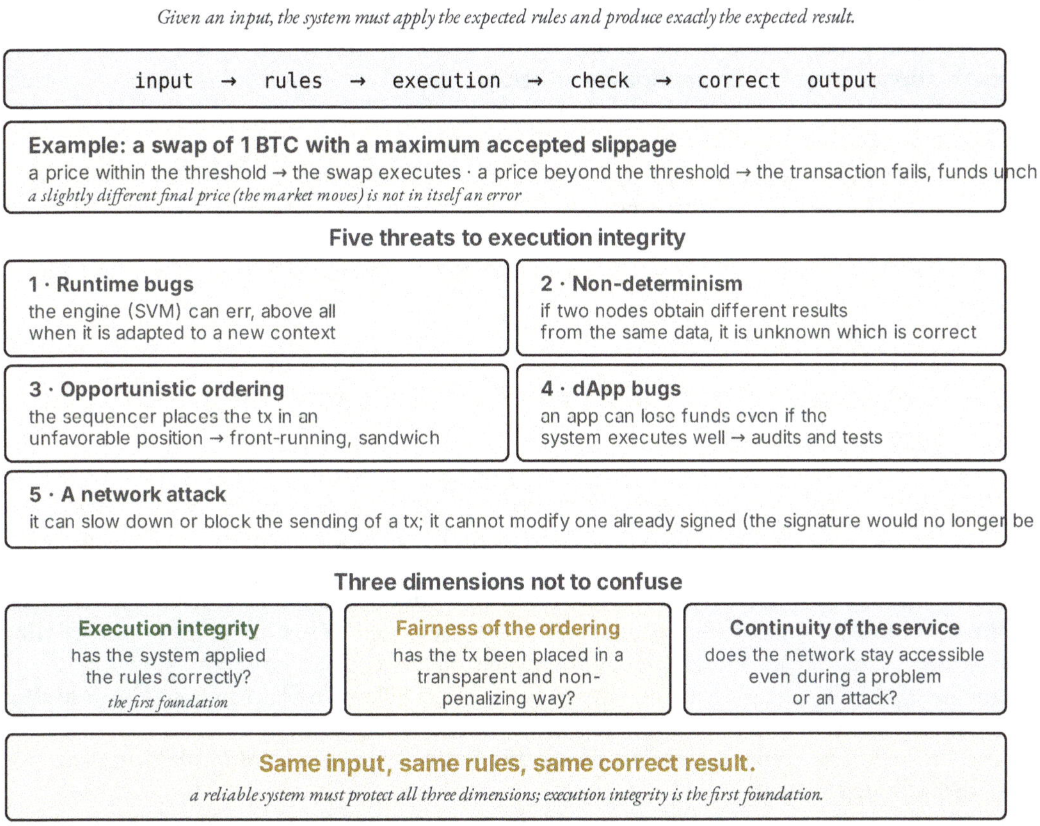

Execution integrity guarantees that, given an input, the system correctly applies the rules and produces the expected result. The threats can arise from runtime bugs, non-determinism, opportunistic ordering of the transactions, errors in the single applications, or attacks on the network infrastructure. It must be distinguished from the fairness of the ordering and from the continuity of the service: a reliable system must protect all three dimensions.

To understand why this is important, let us think about what could go wrong if execution integrity were compromised. Imagine wanting to exchange 1 BTC for a certain quantity of another token on a decentralized exchange running on Hyper. The protocol's rules, based on the pool's liquidity and on other parameters, should produce a certain specific price. You expect that price, or a very close one, accepting a small variation (slippage) for the natural movements of the market.

What would happen if the system, because of a bug or a manipulation, executed your swap at a significantly worse price? You would lose value, the protocol would betray its promise, the market would become unreliable. If this happened occasionally, the system would be unusable for serious applications. If it happened systematically in a predictable way, someone could exploit it to extract value from the honest participants. **Execution integrity is the foundation on which any serious financial application is built.**

Let us see concretely what threatens execution integrity and which mechanisms protect it.

First threat: bugs in the virtual machine. If SVM has bugs — perhaps subtle ones, activated only in particular cases — some transactions could produce results different from those specified by the program's logic. For Hyper, inheriting SVM also means inheriting the risk of virtual-machine bugs, even if SVM's maturity on Solana significantly reduces this risk.

Second threat: non-determinism of the execution. As we saw in Chapter 10, if the execution is not perfectly deterministic, different nodes can obtain different final states starting from the same transactions. This is an extreme form of integrity violation: the "correct result" becomes ambiguous because different nodes compute different results.

Third threat: manipulation by the sequencer. Even if the virtual machine is perfect and the execution is deterministic, the sequencer has the power of ordering the transactions. By manipulating the order, it can create situations where the "correct result" becomes significantly worse for some users, even if technically compliant with the rules.

Fourth threat: bugs in the application programs. Even if the underlying system is perfect, the specific programs (smart contracts) can have their own bugs. A bug in the code of a DeFi protocol can cause wrong behaviors, a loss of funds, exploitable vulnerabilities.

Fifth threat: network attacks. Even with all the rest perfect, network attacks (DDoS, censorship, interception) can compromise the execution of the transactions, delaying them, modifying them, blocking them.

For each of these threats, Hyper's security model must have specific answers. Let us see them.

⁂

19.3 — Defenses of the First Level: How Execution Integrity Is Protected

Now let us enter the details of the specific mechanisms that Hyper is designing to protect execution integrity. They are several and reinforce one another, applying the defense-in-depth principle we saw in the previous chapter.

Defense one: SVM's maturity. SVM has been in production on Solana for years, has processed billions of transactions, has been examined by many researchers. **This maturity is one of the main security assets that Hyper inherits from the choice of SVM.** The most serious bugs of the virtual machine have probably already been discovered and fixed on Solana itself. **However, this inheritance is not total**: Hyper is adapting SVM to the rollup-Bitcoin context, and these modifications can introduce new, specific bugs. **The Hyper team must do specific audits of its own SVM implementation**, not only rely on the inherited maturity.

Defense two: rigorous determinism constraints. As we saw in Chapter 10, Hyper is actively working to guarantee that the SVM operates in a perfectly deterministic way in the rollup context. Rigid constraints on the execution order, on account access, on the visibility at execution time are all mechanisms that protect from non-determinism. **Every detail of the runtime must be bit-for-bit deterministic**, and this is significant engineering work.

Defense three: the transparency of the sequencer's ordering. To limit the sequencer's capacity to manipulate the transactions, Hyper is developing public ordering rules that the sequencer must follow. The more specific and verifiable these rules are, the less discretion the sequencer has. Combined with the sequencer's progressive decentralization (which we will see realized over time), this significantly reduces the threat of manipulation.

Defense four: forced-inclusion mechanisms. Even if the sequencer tries to censor or delay certain transactions, users should be able to force their inclusion through direct Bitcoin transactions. This is a structural protection against the sequencer's abuse. **Hyper has mentioned the intention to implement forced inclusion, but the specific details are still in development.**

Defense five: development standards for the applications. To limit the threat of bugs in the application programs, the ecosystem must develop best practices and well-audited standard libraries. The Anchor framework, which Hyper inherits from Solana, is already an example of this: it provides standard patterns that reduce the possibility of common bugs. **Moreover, bug bounty programs incentivize the discovery of vulnerabilities before their exploitation.**

Defense six: infrastructural redundancy. To protect from network instability, the rollup's infrastructure must be geographically distributed, with redundant fallbacks, with recovery mechanisms. A single data center going offline should not stop the system. This is an operational dimension more than a design one, but it is just as important.

Defense seven: monitoring and anomaly detection. Real-time monitoring systems that detect anomalous behaviors — spikes of errors, suspicious transaction patterns, deviations from the normal metrics — make it possible to respond rapidly to problems before they propagate. **Hyper's February 2026 post on the monitoring-first architecture makes this priority explicit.**

Putting these seven defenses together, execution integrity is protected by many overlapping layers. **Even if one fails, the others keep operating.** It is exactly the defense-in-depth principle in action.

⁂

19.4 — The Second Level: Settlement Integrity

Let us now move to the second security level, the one that protects the historical ledger once the transactions have been processed. **Settlement integrity is the guarantee that, once a rollup state has been crystallized, that state can no longer be modified.**

To understand why this is important, think about what the historical ledger of a financial system represents. It is the ultimate truth about who owns what, about who paid whom, about which contracts have been entered into. If this ledger can be modified retroactively, **all the trust in the system collapses**: nobody can build durable applications, nobody can rely on past transactions, nobody can really own digital assets in a definitive way.

The original Bitcoin has settlement integrity as its fundamental property. Once a Bitcoin transaction has sufficient confirmations, modifying it would require redoing all the proof-of-work accumulated after it, an economically prohibitive operation. **This is the reason why Bitcoin is "digital currency" and not a company's database**: nobody can unilaterally modify the historical ledger.

For a rollup, settlement integrity is more complex to guarantee because the rollup's state lives on a system different from Bitcoin (the rollup itself) but must somehow inherit Bitcoin's immutability properties. And it is here that the whole mechanism of anchoring the state commitments that we saw in the settlement chapters comes into play.

Let us see concretely what threatens settlement integrity and which mechanisms protect it.

First threat: the sequencer publishes wrong state commitments. If the sequencer publishes on Bitcoin a state commitment that does not correspond to the effective result of the execution of the transactions, the rollup's declared state diverges from the real state. Without corrective mechanisms, users could find themselves with balances different from the effective ones.

Second threat: the raw data of the transactions disappears. Even if the state commitments are correct, if the raw data of the transactions is lost, the state is no longer verifiable. As we saw in Chapter 14, this transforms the rollup into a system effectively dependent on trust, even if the state commitments remain anchored on Bitcoin.

Third threat: Bitcoin itself is unstable. Even if the rollup does everything correctly, if Bitcoin suffers a major attack or a controversial fork, the anchored state commitments could be called into question. This is a remote but not impossible scenario, and it must be considered.

Fourth threat: the loss of the cryptographic keys. If the keys that allow the rollup's state to be updated are lost or compromised, the system could enter a blocked or vulnerable state. This is an operational dimension, but with consequences for the integrity.

Fifth threat: errors in the bridge's code. The Canonical Bridge is the point where real value (bitcoin) is held in custody and where the rights are modified. Bugs in the bridge's code can entail a loss of funds or the creation of illegitimate tokens.

For each of these threats, Hyper must have specific answers.

⁂

19.5 — Defenses of the Second Level: How Settlement Integrity Is Protected

Let us see the mechanisms that protect the second security level. They are largely the ones we have already examined in previous chapters, but it is useful to put them together in the specific perspective of security.

Defense one: robust anchoring on Bitcoin. The state commitment anchored on Bitcoin becomes practically immutable after the standard confirmations. To modify the state, it would take an attack on Bitcoin itself, which is economically prohibitive. **This is the basis of the whole settlement model.** The technical choices about the anchoring (OP_RETURN, Taproot, timelocks, as we saw in Chapter 12) influence the efficiency, but in all cases the anchoring provides Bitcoin-grade immutability.

Defense two: the proof model (fraud proofs or validity proofs). This is the mechanism that protects against wrong state commitments published by the sequencer. With a fraud proof, anyone can publish a proof that demonstrates the error, and the system rejects the wrong state commitment. With a validity proof (zk-SNARK), the correctness is demonstrated mathematically before the state commitment is accepted. **Hyper is exploring a hybrid model**, and the specific details will be crucial for the level of security obtained.

Defense three: public availability of the data. Without data availability, fraud proofs become impossible to build (the data to verify the state is missing), and therefore the entire security model collapses. **Hyper's commitment to a true rollup model (with public data) is therefore a crucial defense of the second level, as well as of the first.**

Defense four: forced-exit mechanisms. Even if all the other mechanisms fail, users should be able to withdraw their own funds through forced-exit procedures that operate directly on the Bitcoin blockchain, without depending on the collaboration of the sequencer or of other operators of the system. **These mechanisms are in development for Hyper**, and their robustness will be one of the project's fundamental tests.

Defense five: robust management of the bridge's keys. The Canonical Bridge holds the users' real bitcoin in custody, and its security depends critically on the management of the cryptographic keys. Multisignature, hardware security modules, the separation of responsibilities are standard practices, but their specific implementation for Hyper will be the object of scrutiny.

Defense six: independent audits of the bridge's code. The Canonical Bridge's code is one of the most critical components of the project, and it must be audited in depth by several independent firms. **Hyper has mentioned the intention to undergo audits, but the specific reports are not yet published.** When they arrive, they will be among the most important documents for evaluating the project.

Defense seven: emergency plans for extreme scenarios. What happens if Bitcoin has a 51% attack? What happens if a critical vulnerability is discovered in the rollup's software? What happens if the project's team is forced to stop operating? **A robust system has specific plans for these scenarios**, even if hopefully they will never occur. Preparation is part of security.

Putting these seven defenses together, settlement integrity is protected by multiple, overlapping mechanisms. **Even in adverse scenarios, the user has various roads for recovering their own funds and for verifying the system's state.**

⁂

19.6 — The Interaction between the Two Levels

An important thing to understand is that the two security levels are not independent: they reinforce each other and together produce a protection superior to the sum of the parts. Let us see how.

Execution integrity is a precondition of useful settlement integrity. Even if the state commitments are perfectly anchored on Bitcoin, if the execution that produced them is wrong, the system crystallizes errors instead of truth. Bitcoin would guarantee the immutability of wrong states, which has no value. **Therefore execution integrity must be guaranteed before talking about settlement integrity.**

Settlement integrity makes it possible to verify execution integrity retrospectively. If I have doubts about the execution of a past transaction, I can take the raw data (data availability guaranteed), re-execute it on my own copy of the system (deterministic execution), and verify whether the result corresponds to the state commitments anchored on Bitcoin. **This retroactive verification mechanism is what gives practical meaning to the minimization of trust.**

The proof mechanisms connect the two levels. Fraud proofs or validity proofs verify that the performed execution produces the declared state commitment. If the execution is wrong, the proofs reveal it; if the execution is correct, the proofs confirm it. **They are the technical bridge between the two levels.**

The complete security model emerges from the integration. No single mechanism is sufficient on its own. Anchoring without correct execution is useless. Correct execution without anchoring is temporary. Data availability without proof mechanisms is incomplete. Forced exit without data availability is impossible. **All the pieces must work together**, and the system's design is the choreography that puts them together.

For Hyper, this means that the evaluation of the security cannot limit itself to examining a single component. **One must examine the whole system, see how the pieces connect, evaluate whether there are weak points in the interfaces between components.** A system can have individually strong components but fail in the integration, and this is one of the most common types of vulnerability in distributed systems.

Hyper's October 2025 post explicitly emphasizes this integrated vision: "The guiding idea is simplicity. Bitcoin does not execute complex logic on-chain; it provides finality. Bitcoin Hyper's role is to extend it without overcomplicating it. The security layer acts as a trust bridge: fast execution upstream, immutable settlement downstream." **This sentence encapsulates the idea that the two levels must work together, each doing its own part.**

⁂

19.7 — The Proof Model: Fraud Proofs vs Validity Proofs

Now let us address a specific aspect that deserves separate attention, because it is the technical heart of the rollups' security model: the choice between **fraud proofs** and **validity proofs**. The two models represent different philosophies of how to guarantee the correctness of the state commitments, and Hyper has indicated that it wants to explore a hybrid model.

The fraud proofs model (Optimistic). The state commitment is published without immediate cryptographic proofs of correctness. The system "optimistically" accepts the state commitment as valid, but gives anyone a time window (typically seven days) to publish a fraud proof that demonstrates the error. If a valid proof is published, the state commitment is rejected, the operator that proposed it is punished (slashing), and the system proceeds with the correct state.

Advantages of the optimistic model. A reduced computational cost: producing a state commitment is fast, because it does not require building complex cryptographic proofs. Compatibility with existing virtual machines: SVM or EVM can be used almost without modifications. Maturity: the model is well understood, implemented by Optimism and Arbitrum on Ethereum, tested in production for years.

Disadvantages of the optimistic model. A long challenge window: complete finality for the operations requires waiting for the window (seven days on Optimism). For withdrawals toward the main blockchain, this wait is significant. The need for active "watchers": the system works only if someone effectively verifies the state commitments and publishes fraud proofs if necessary. If nobody verifies, errors could pass unnoticed. A vulnerability to censorship of the window: if the sequencer manages to censor the fraud proofs during the window, the wrong state commitment passes.

The validity proofs model (ZK-rollup). Together with the state commitment, a mathematical proof (a zk-SNARK or zk-STARK)* is published that demonstrates that the state commitment is the correct result of the execution of the transactions. The proof is verifiable in constant time, independently of the computation's complexity.

Advantages of the validity model. Immediate finality: once the proof is verified, the state commitment is definitive. No challenge windows. Mathematically robust security: it does not depend on active watchers; the mathematics guarantees the correctness. Rapid withdrawals: for withdrawals toward the main blockchain, there is no wait.

Disadvantages of the validity model. Enormous computational complexity: producing zk proofs for complex executions is computationally very costly, and requires specialized hardware. Limited maturity: zk systems are evolving rapidly, but they are still in an initial phase compared with optimistic rollups. High operating costs: all the infrastructure for generating proofs has significant costs that are reflected on the fees.

The hybrid model. Hyper has indicated that it wants to combine elements of both models. We do not yet know the specific details, but there are several possible combinations. One possibility is using optimistic as the base model, with the possibility of "accelerating" finality via zk proofs for specific cases (for example, for large withdrawals). Another possibility is using zk proofs only for certain types of critical operations, keeping the optimistic model for the rest.

For the Bitcoin community, there is an additional consideration. **Bitcoin does not natively support the verification of complex zk proofs**, while Ethereum does. This means that, on Ethereum, validity proofs can be verified directly on the main blockchain; on Bitcoin, the verification would have to be done off-chain or through more sophisticated mechanisms. This technical limitation of Bitcoin significantly influences which model is realistically implementable.

For Hyper, monitoring the final choice and its implementation will be one of the most important points of the technical evaluation. The chosen model influences everything: finality times, costs, robustness, implementation complexity.

---

* **Zero-knowledge proofs (zk-SNARKs and zk-STARKs).** Cryptographic techniques that make it possible to demonstrate mathematically that a computation has been executed correctly, without having to redo it and without revealing the data it operates on. Applied to a rollup, they allow Bitcoin to ascertain the validity of a state by trusting the proof instead of a time window for challenges. SNARK and STARK are two families of these proofs, with different compromises among size, speed, and security requirements.

⁂

19.8 — Questions and Answers: Clarifying the Chapter's Concepts

Question 1: If security is on two levels, is it possible for one to work perfectly and the other not?

In theory yes, and this is the reason why the distinction is important. **In practice, however, the two levels are interconnected**: problems in one often manifest in the other too. A wrong execution that produces a wrong state commitment is a failure of the first level, but it also becomes a problem of the second level when the state commitment is anchored. A loss of data availability is a problem of the second level that prevents the verification of the first. **Systems with vulnerabilities in one of the two levels tend to have visible problems in both**, and this makes the distinction useful for the diagnosis rather than for an absolute separation. For users, what counts is the system's overall robustness. For engineers, understanding which level is responsible for which type of problem helps build the right defenses. Concrete example: if a system produces inconsistent states across different nodes, the problem is probably in the first level (non-deterministic execution). If a system has consistent states but users cannot verify them independently, the problem is in the second level (data availability). An accurate diagnosis points toward the correct solutions.

Question 2: Is the hybrid proof model Hyper is exploring really the best, or is it a political compromise?

It is legitimate to ask. **On one hand**, hybrids can capture different advantages at the cost of greater complexity. One could use optimistic for the standard operations (low cost, acceptable finality) and validity proofs for critical operations (high cost, immediate finality). This balances costs and benefits intelligently. **On the other**, hybrids are more complex to implement, to audit, to understand. They increase the attack surface and introduce possible non-intuitive interactions between the two models. The history of software engineering suggests that simplicity is a virtue, and hybrids must justify themselves significantly. **For Hyper, the choice will depend on specific factors**: Bitcoin's technical capacities (limited for validity proofs), the maturity of zk technologies for SVM (evolving), the trade-offs acceptable to the community. Probably there is no "best" answer in absolute terms, but a "best given the circumstances." Concrete example: Optimism chose pure optimistic for years, and only in 2024 did it begin exploring complementary validity proofs. Polygon instead chose validity proofs as its main direction from the start. Both are serious projects, and the different choice reflects different priorities and capacities; it is not that one is "right" and the other "wrong."

Question 3: If data availability is a precondition of fraud proofs, and Hyper does not yet have a complete solution for data availability, will fraud proofs be effectively usable at the launch?

It is a key question that deserves careful reflection. **In theoretical terms, fraud proofs require data availability to work**: without the data, nobody can build the fraud proof. If Hyper launches with data availability managed primarily by the team, and fraud proofs are part of the security model, then effectively the robustness of the security model depends on the quality of the team's management. **This is a real compromise** that cannot be ignored. **In practice, however, there are nuances.** Ethereum's rollups all started with some degree of centralization in data availability, and gradually decentralized. The initial phase of compromise is accepted if accompanied by a credible path toward decentralization. **For Hyper, the key is transparency about this compromise**: the team must be clear that full security still requires work, and that users during the initial phase partially depend on the quality of the team's management. **Without this transparency, the system would be in a gray zone similar to a federated sidechain**, even if architecturally it is set up as a rollup. Concrete example: Optimism, during the first years, had a "theoretical" fault proof not yet completely implemented. Users operated substantially with trust in the team, even if the conceptual model was trustless. Only in 2024 were the fault proofs completely implemented. For Hyper, a similar trajectory is expected: an initial period of admitted compromises, followed by progressive maturation.

Question 4: What would happen if Bitcoin itself had a major attack or a controversial fork? Would Hyper's settlement integrity collapse?

It is a remote but not impossible scenario, and it deserves to be considered. **In the case of a 51% attack on Bitcoin** that allowed recent blocks to be rewritten, Hyper's state commitments anchored in those blocks could also be called into question. However, 51% attacks on Bitcoin are economically prohibitive (they would require billions of dollars of hardware), and therefore represent an extreme scenario. **In the case of a controversial Bitcoin fork** (like the 2017 situation with Bitcoin Cash), Hyper would have to choose which branch of the blockchain to consider canonical. This decision would have implications for the anchored states, and could be the object of dispute in the community. **For scenarios of this type, Hyper should have contingency plans**: how to choose the canonical branch, how to communicate with the community, how to manage any state commitments that might have been anchored on branches that become "losers." **The management of these extreme scenarios is one of the most sophisticated aspects of a rollup's design**, and it is rarely discussed publicly. For Hyper, seeing whether the team addresses these questions in future documentation will be an indicator of engineering maturity. Concrete example: during the Ethereum fork of 2016 (the DAO hard fork), many projects had to choose which chain to consider canonical. Some chose Ethereum (the hard fork), others Ethereum Classic (the original chain). The consequences for users depended on the choices made. For Ethereum's rollups today, the position is clear (they follow Ethereum), but it is because the fork has been resolved. In new situations, the decisions would be there to take.

Question 5: How realistic are the forced-exit mechanisms, given that they do not yet exist in a complete implementation for Hyper?

Forced-exit mechanisms are conceptually clear but technically complex to implement correctly. **On the conceptual side**: the user builds a proof of their own state (balance, position) based on the available raw data, and uses this proof to build a Bitcoin transaction that asks the Canonical Bridge to release the corresponding funds. The bridge verifies the proof against the anchored state commitments and, if valid, releases the funds without requiring the sequencer's collaboration. **On the implementation side**: every detail requires attention. How are the proofs built? How big are they? How are they verified? How are edge cases managed (a user with complex positions, multiple simultaneous withdrawals, race conditions)? **Hyper must specify and implement all this**, and so far the public documentation is generic. **For users**, monitoring the publication of specific technical documentation on forced exits will be important. Without these mechanisms implemented and audited, the promise of "Bitcoin-grade security" remains partial, because in adverse scenarios users might have no way of recovering their own funds independently of the team. Concrete example: Optimism implemented forced-inclusion mechanisms (a simplified version of forced exit) gradually over time. Initially, these mechanisms had significant limitations (high costs, long waits, unhandled edge cases). They refined over time. For Hyper a similar trajectory is expected.

Question 6: If I have funds on Hyper, what should I monitor to be sure that both security levels are working?

There are concrete indicators you can monitor regularly. **For the first level (execution integrity)**: verifying whether there have been incidents of non-deterministic execution (nodes producing different states), monitoring the transactions' processing times (slowdowns can indicate problems), following announcements of bugs detected in the SVM-Hyper, checking whether the explorers independent of the team show states coherent with the official ones. **For the second level (settlement integrity)**: regularly verifying that the state commitments are anchored on Bitcoin within the expected times, checking the state of the Canonical Bridge (how many bitcoin it holds in custody, are they coherent with the state commitments), monitoring the availability of the raw data (do third parties exist that preserve it and make it accessible), following announcements of fraud proofs or controversies about the state commitments. **For both**: reading the post-mortems of any incidents, evaluating the transparency and rapidity of the team's responses, monitoring the community of independent observers to see whether they report problems. **Practical tools**: the project's public dashboards, multiple explorers, specialized social accounts that monitor L2s, possibly private monitoring services if you manage significant value. **For high-value funds**, it is prudent not to concentrate everything in a single system, independently of how secure it seems. Diversification among direct Bitcoin, Lightning, and various Layer 2s is a protection against systemic vulnerabilities specific to a single system. Concrete example: today on Optimism there are dashboards like l2beat.com that monitor various security indicators (fault proofs, the sequencer's multisig, the quality of the audits, and so on). For Hyper the development of analogous tools over time is expected, and their availability will be a signal of the ecosystem's maturity.

⁂

19.9 — WHAT TO TAKE AWAY FROM THIS CHAPTER

A rollup's security has two distinct dimensions: execution integrity (the transactions are processed correctly) and settlement integrity (the historical ledger cannot be modified after the fact). Confusing them is a common mistake that marketing exploits.

Execution integrity is protected by multiple mechanisms: SVM's maturity, rigorous determinism constraints, the transparency of the sequencer's ordering, forced inclusion, development standards for the applications, infrastructural redundancy, real-time monitoring.

Settlement integrity is protected by other mechanisms: robust anchoring on Bitcoin, the proof model (fraud or validity), public availability of the data, forced exit, the management of the bridge's keys, audits of the code, emergency plans.

The two levels are interconnected: correct execution is a precondition of useful settlement, settlement allows the retroactive verification of the execution, the proof mechanisms connect the two levels. The complete security model emerges from the integration, not from the sum.

There are two main proof models: fraud proofs (optimistic, with a challenge window) and validity proofs (zk, with immediate finality). Both have significant trade-offs. Hyper is exploring a hybrid model.

Bitcoin does not natively support the verification of complex validity proofs, and this influences the realistic choices for Hyper. Bitcoin's technical limitations are effective constraints, not just preferences.

Hyper will launch with various security elements still to mature: complete forced exits, public audits, a specific proof model, the decentralization of data availability. The maturation path will be an important part of the project's evaluation.

Security is not a binary state, it is a layered structure with overlapping mechanisms. Even if one layer fails, the others keep operating. Defense in depth is the guiding principle.

For users, monitoring both security levels requires different tools and attention to specific indicators. The ecosystem of observers and monitoring tools will develop over time after the mainnet launch.

Hyper's complete security will manifest only in the months and years following the launch. The current philosophical and architectural declarations are positive signals, but the real proof comes from operational practice under stress.

Chapter 19 ends here. We have understood the two security levels that protect a rollup, the specific mechanisms of each, and how they reinforce each other. In ***Chapter 20 — Graceful Degradation: How to Design a System That Does Not Collapse****, we will go down into another fundamental principle of security design, the one that Bitcoin Hyper made explicit in the February 2026 post: a system's capacity to slow down in a controlled way under stress instead of collapsing unpredictably, a philosophy borrowed directly from Bitcoin.*

Security on two *levels*

Correct execution above, immutable settlement below. **No single mechanism is enough on its own**: security is born from the integration among a deterministic SVM, a controllable sequencer, proofs, available data, the bridge, and the anchoring on Bitcoin.

1 Security is not a single thing

UPPER LEVEL
Execution integrity
Are the transactions executed correctly?
transactions → SVM → new state

↓

LOWER LEVEL
Settlement integrity
Is the correct state anchored immutably?
state root → commitment → Bitcoin L1

The state must first be **correct***, then made* **immutable***. Two distinct but interdependent guarantees.*

2 The system computes the right result

Execution integrity: given an input, the rollup produces exactly the output provided by the protocol's rules — not one that is "close enough."

user input → SVM rules → deterministic execution → correct output ✓

THREATS runtime bugs · non-determinism · opportunistic ordering · dApp bugs · network attacks

DEFENSES SVM maturity · rigorous determinism · declared accounts · public sequencer rules · forced inclusion · audits · anomaly monitoring

Same input, same rules, same correct result.

3 The correct result becomes immutable

Settlement integrity: the rollup's state, once consolidated, can no longer be modified retroactively.

new state → Merkle root → state commitment → anchoring ₿ · L1 finality

THREATS a wrong commitment · unavailable raw data · bridge bugs · compromised keys · extreme Bitcoin instability

DEFENSES anchoring on Bitcoin · fraud / validity proofs · public data availability · forced exit · key management · Canonical Bridge audits · emergency plans

Bitcoin makes the commitment immutable, **but the rollup must demonstrate that that commitment is correct.**

4 The bridge between the two levels: the proofs

Fraud proof · Optimistic
It temporarily accepts the state, but opens a window to challenge it.
PRO simpler, less costly, compatible with complex VMs.
LIMITS it requires active watchers, a challenge window, available data.

Validity proof · ZK
It publishes a mathematical proof that demonstrates the state's correctness.
PRO immediate finality, a cryptographic proof, fewer challenges.
LIMITS more complex, costly, hard to verify on Bitcoin.

Hyper will have to **clarify the final model** *— optimistic, validity, or hybrid: the choice affects costs, finality, and robustness.*

5 No layer is enough on its own

A deterministic SVM — computes the correct state → **Sequencer** — orders under observable rules → **Data Availability** — makes the raw data available → **Proof system** — demonstrates or challenges → **Canonical Bridge** — BTC deposits and withdrawals (CRITICAL) → **Bitcoin L1** — anchors and makes immutable

ⓘ **Correct execution without settlement is temporary.** Immutable settlement without correct execution crystallizes errors.

THE KEY POINT

Bitcoin Hyper's security must protect **two levels**: the execution, so that every transaction produces the correct result; the settlement, so that that correct state becomes **immutable on Bitcoin**. Real security is born from the **connection** among the SVM, the proofs, the available data, the bridge, and the L1 anchoring.

PART VI · SECURITY

Chapter 20
Graceful Degradation

How to design a system that does not collapse

⁂

20.1 — A Philosophy That Comes from Far Away

There is a principle of critical systems[a] engineering that deserves to enter the vocabulary of anyone who seriously wants to understand how reliable software is built, and that is particularly relevant for Bitcoin Hyper. The principle is called **graceful degradation**[b], an expression we can render as **controlled degradation**. It indicates the capacity of a system to keep performing at least the essential functions when stress[c] increases or when one of its components encounters a problem: the system can slow down or temporarily limit some services, but it avoids collapsing unpredictably. It is a design philosophy that runs through decades of engineering, from telecommunications networks to airplanes, from medical systems to the data centers of the big technology companies, and it deserves to be understood because it is one of the most undervalued aspects of a blockchain system's robustness.

---

[a] **Critical systems.** Systems in which a failure can have serious consequences — for people's safety, health, or money — and which for this reason are designed with reliability standards much higher than ordinary software. Airplanes, medical equipment, and financial infrastructures are examples: it is from this tradition that the principle of controlled degradation comes.

[b] **Graceful degradation** (controlled degradation). It is the capacity of a system to react to an overload or a failure by continuing to perform at least the essential functions, instead of halting completely. An elevator that, in a fault, stops safely at the nearest floor rather than plummeting is an effective image of it. Applied to a blockchain, it means that in the face of a problem the system can slow down or suspend some secondary services, but it protects what really counts — the users' funds — avoiding an unpredictable collapse.

[c] **Stress (system stress).** Any condition that puts the system under pressure beyond its normal functioning: a surge of requests, the failure of a component, an attack. It is in stress situations that one sees the difference between a system that degrades in a controlled way and one that collapses.

TABLE 20.1 **CONTROLLED DEGRADATION AND COLLAPSE: TWO RESPONSES TO STRESS.**

Under stress	A fragile system	Controlled degradation
Behavior	Sudden collapse	Gradual slowdown
Essential functions	They stop	They stay available
Predictability	Unpredictable outcome	Controlled outcome

The difference does not lie in avoiding every problem — impossible in any system — but in the way the system reacts when the problem presents itself. A well-designed infrastructure slows down or limits some services without ever compromising the essential functions.

FIGURE 20.1 **CONTROLLED DEGRADATION: SLOWING DOWN WITHOUT COLLAPSING.**

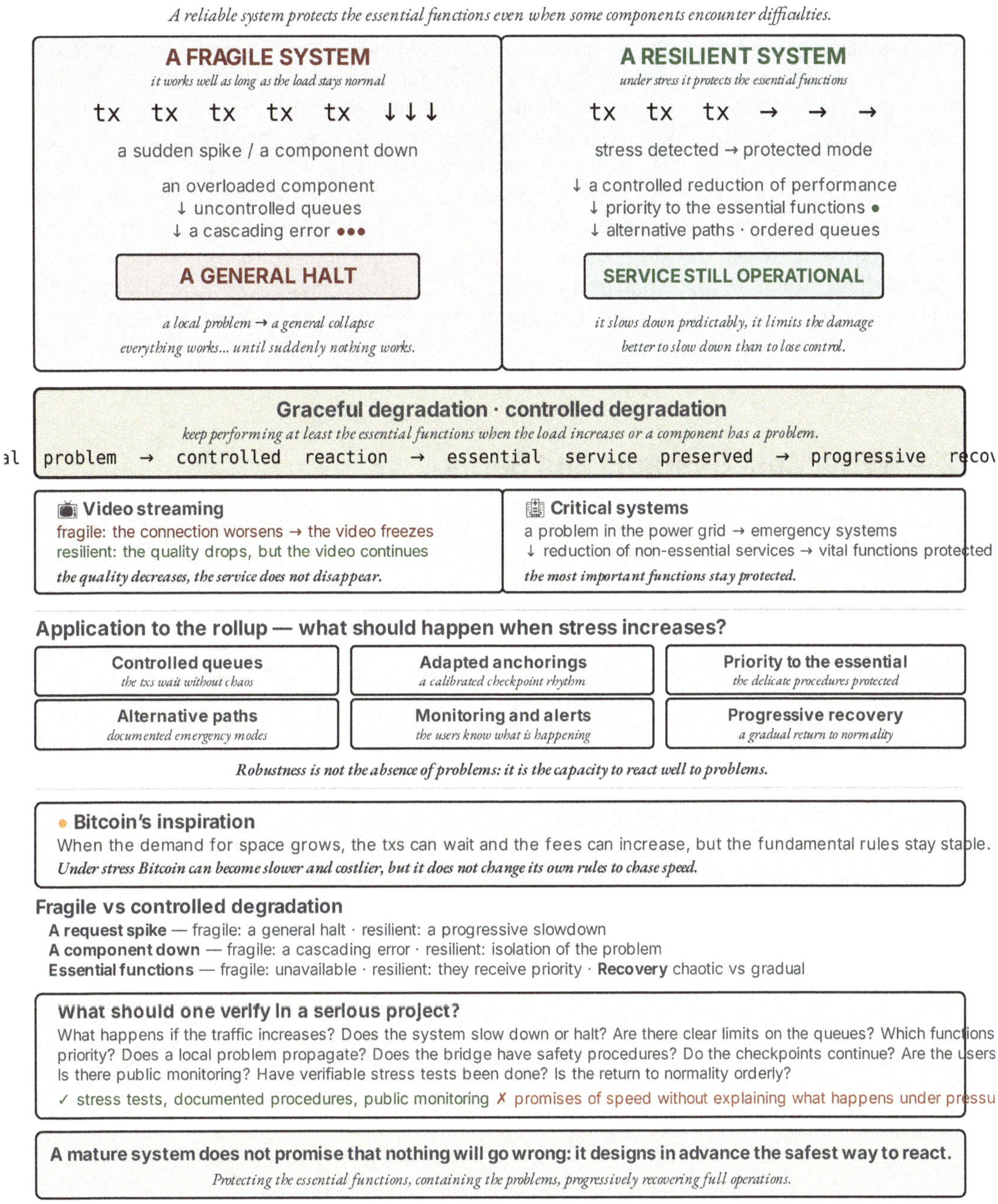

Controlled degradation is the capacity of a system to react in an orderly way when stress increases or when a component encounters difficulties. A fragile system can collapse suddenly; a resilient system temporarily reduces some performance, protects the essential functions, and progressively returns to full operations. Bitcoin Hyper[2] explicitly recalls this principle: the real quality will emerge from the technical specifications, the stress tests, and the network's observable behavior.

To understand intuitively what it means, think of two streaming services. The first works perfectly when the connection is stable, but freezes completely as soon as the network quality worsens. The second reacts differently: it temporarily reduces the definition of the image, limits some secondary functions, and keeps transmitting the content. The quality decreases, but the essential service stays available. **The first system is "fragile"; the second applies a "controlled degradation."** A reference to the elevator also holds, with a safer formula: a well-designed elevator, when it detects an overload, does not start and warns the users — it does not try to keep functioning unpredictably.

In the post dedicated to security by architecture (February 2026), the team recalls the principle of controlled degradation:* **if a component encounters difficulties, the system should slow down safely instead of collapsing unpredictably**, a trait that Bitcoin Hyper² declares it wants to inherit from its own base, Bitcoin. It is an important philosophical declaration, because it positions the project in a serious engineering tradition, and because it implicitly challenges the approach of many crypto projects that emphasize peak performance without thinking about what happens when the peak is exceeded.

In this chapter I want to do four things. First, understand why some systems react badly to the unexpected and how a local problem can turn into a general halt. Second, observe how Bitcoin offers a useful example of robustness under stress: when the demand for space in the blocks increases, the transactions can wait longer and the fees can rise, but the network's fundamental rules stay stable. Third, apply these principles to the different components of Bitcoin Hyper². Fourth, understand which concrete signals help distinguish a really resilient project from a project optimized only for normal conditions.

⁂

20.2 — Why Most Systems Fail Badly

Let us begin with an apparently strange but fundamental question: **why do many software systems, when subjected to unexpected stress †, risk collapsing suddenly instead of slowing down in an orderly way?** Understanding this natural tendency is the prerequisite for understanding why graceful degradation is an active design choice, not the default state.

The answer lies in a series of patterns that emerge naturally in software development, above all when the team concentrates on the functionalities without thinking about the edge cases.‡

---

* **Controlled degradation (graceful degradation).** It is the property by which, under strain, a system gradually reduces its performance instead of stopping completely: it slows down predictably while keeping the essential functions. It is not a spontaneous behavior, but a deliberate design choice.

† **Unexpected stress.** A strain the system had not been prepared to face: a sudden surge of requests, the failure of a component, an attack. It is in unexpected conditions, more than in normal ones, that a system's real robustness reveals itself.

‡ **A cascading collapse.** It is the opposite behavior: a problem that arises at a single point, instead of staying contained, propagates rapidly and halts the entire system. It is the typical outcome of systems not designed for the edge cases, in which a small failure triggers a general standstill.

FIGURE 20.2 **HOW A CASCADING COLLAPSE IS BORN.**

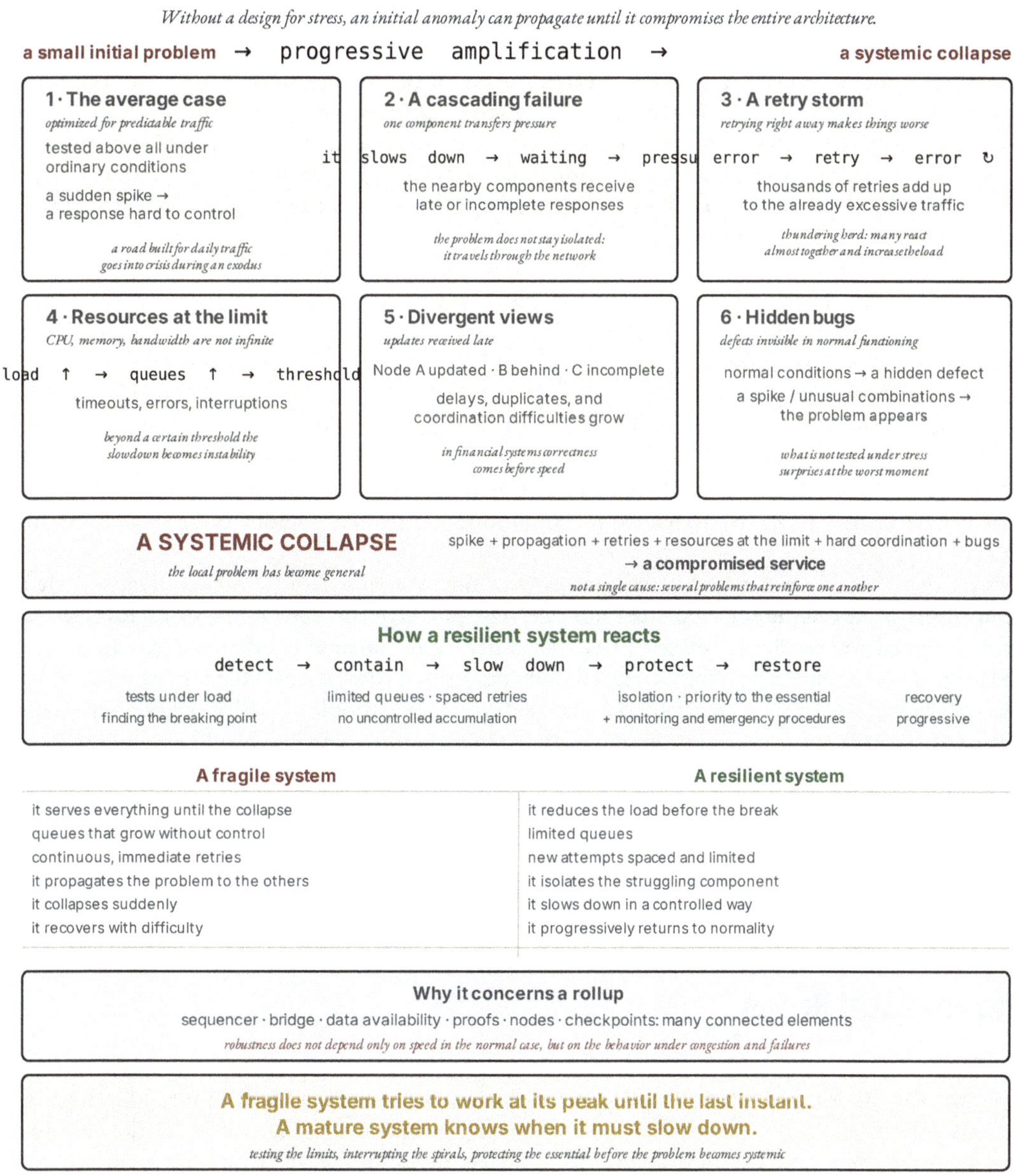

A cascading collapse is often born from the progressive amplification of a small initial problem. A component slows down, the requests accumulate, the retries increase the load, and the resources reach the limit. A resilient system interrupts this spiral through stress tests, limits on the queues, controlled retries, isolation of the problems, and a temporary reduction of performance.

First pattern: optimization for the average case. Development teams test the software with normal loads, realistic traffic, standard conditions. The whole design is thought out to do well under these conditions. **When the system encounters conditions outside the "tested average case," the behavior becomes unpredictable**, because nobody has thought about how it should behave. A sudden traffic spike? Underestimated resources. An unusual transaction pattern? Untested logic. An unstable network connection? Non-robust code.

Second pattern: the cascading failure. Modern systems are composed of many elements connected to one another. If one slows down, it can transfer the problem to the others: the requests stay waiting, the queues increase, and the nearby components receive a greater load. **A small local malfunction can thus turn into a general problem.** This dynamic is particularly insidious because it is hard to predict: it manifests only under real stress, not in laboratory tests.

Third pattern: the retry storm. When an operation fails, the most intuitive reaction is to retry immediately. But if thousands of users or automatic services do the same thing at the same moment, the new requests further increase the traffic and prevent the system from recovering. **Thus a "retry storm" is born: a storm of retries that feeds the problem instead of solving it.** To avoid this spiral, resilient architectures apply a maximum number of attempts and progressively longer waits between one retry and the next, often with a small random element to prevent everyone from retrying simultaneously.

Fourth pattern: the exhaustion of resources. When the load exceeds certain thresholds, the system's computational resources (memory, bandwidth, computing capacity) run out. **When memory, bandwidth, or computing capacity reach the limit, queues, timeouts, and errors increase.** The system can become unstable, and recovery can take time.

Fifth pattern: inconsistent states. Under stress, some components can receive the updates late or temporarily have an incomplete view of the situation. **In financial and blockchain systems, the rules must be designed precisely to prevent these operational difficulties from compromising the correctness of the shared state.** The correctness and coherence of the state cannot be sacrificed simply to obtain greater availability or speed.

Sixth pattern: hidden bugs. Some defects stay invisible during ordinary functioning and appear only when the system reaches unusual conditions. **They can stay hidden for years**, manifesting only when the system reaches unexpected conditions. This is why the most useful tests do not verify only the normal behavior: they push the system to the limit and observe what happens beyond the saturation point.

Putting these six patterns together, it emerges why most systems fail in a non-gradual way: **it is the natural result of development that does not actively consider the edge cases, of architectures that are not designed for resilience, of tests that concentrate on normal conditions.** To obtain graceful degradation, active engineering effort is needed that goes against these natural tendencies.

The blockchain world is particularly exposed to these problems. **Blockchains are complex distributed systems, with real value at stake, that operate under adverse conditions (attacks, traffic spikes, network congestion).** These risks therefore deserve particular attention: it is not enough to measure the speed reached under ideal conditions, one must understand how the system reacts when something goes wrong.

⁂

20.3 — How Bitcoin Manages Stress without Changing the Fundamental Rules

To understand what Bitcoin Hyper can inherit in terms of graceful degradation, we must look at how the original Bitcoin implemented this principle. Bitcoin has operated since 2009 and has gone through numerous periods of congestion, variations of computing power, and changes of network conditions. Its experience therefore offers useful examples for understanding how a distributed system can react to stress without continuously modifying its own fundamental rules.

TABLE 20.2 **THE MECHANISMS WITH WHICH BITCOIN ABSORBS STRESS.**

Mechanism	Stress it absorbs
The difficulty adjustment[a]	Variations of the computing power
The mempool (queue)[b]	Transaction spikes
Variable fees[c]	Demand above the available space
Tolerant propagation[d]	Network delays among the nodes

Temporary forks[e]	Two valid blocks almost simultaneous

None of these mechanisms eliminates slowdowns completely: Bitcoin does not increase its own capacity under pressure, but distributes the load over time while preserving the coherence of the fundamental rules. It is exactly the logic of controlled degradation applied to a distributed network.

[a] **The difficulty adjustment.** Bitcoin periodically recalibrates how "difficult" it is to produce a block, so that one comes out roughly every ten minutes, whatever the computing power connected to the network. If the miners increase, the difficulty rises; if they decrease, it falls. It is the mechanism that keeps the chain's rhythm stable.

[b] **The mempool.** It is the transactions' "waiting room": the set of those already sent but not yet included in a block. When more transactions arrive than a block can contain, the mempool grows longer and acts as a buffer, absorbing the spikes without anything being lost.

[c] **Variable fees.** The fees of Bitcoin transactions are not fixed: they rise when the demand for space in the blocks exceeds the supply and fall when it drops. This market regulates access to a scarce space, giving priority to those who pay more without blocking the network.

[d] **Tolerant propagation.** Information travels among the nodes with small delays and in a non-guaranteed order. Bitcoin is designed to work anyway: the nodes realign as they receive the data, without requiring everyone to see everything at the same instant.

[e] **Temporary forks.** It can happen that two miners find a valid block almost simultaneously, creating two versions of the chain. The network resolves the divergence on its own by adopting the one that first receives the next block; the other is abandoned. It is a momentary misalignment, not a break.

FIGURE 20.3 **HOW BITCOIN ABSORBS STRESS.**

If traffic, computing power, or network conditions change, Bitcoin reacts with several complementary mechanisms.

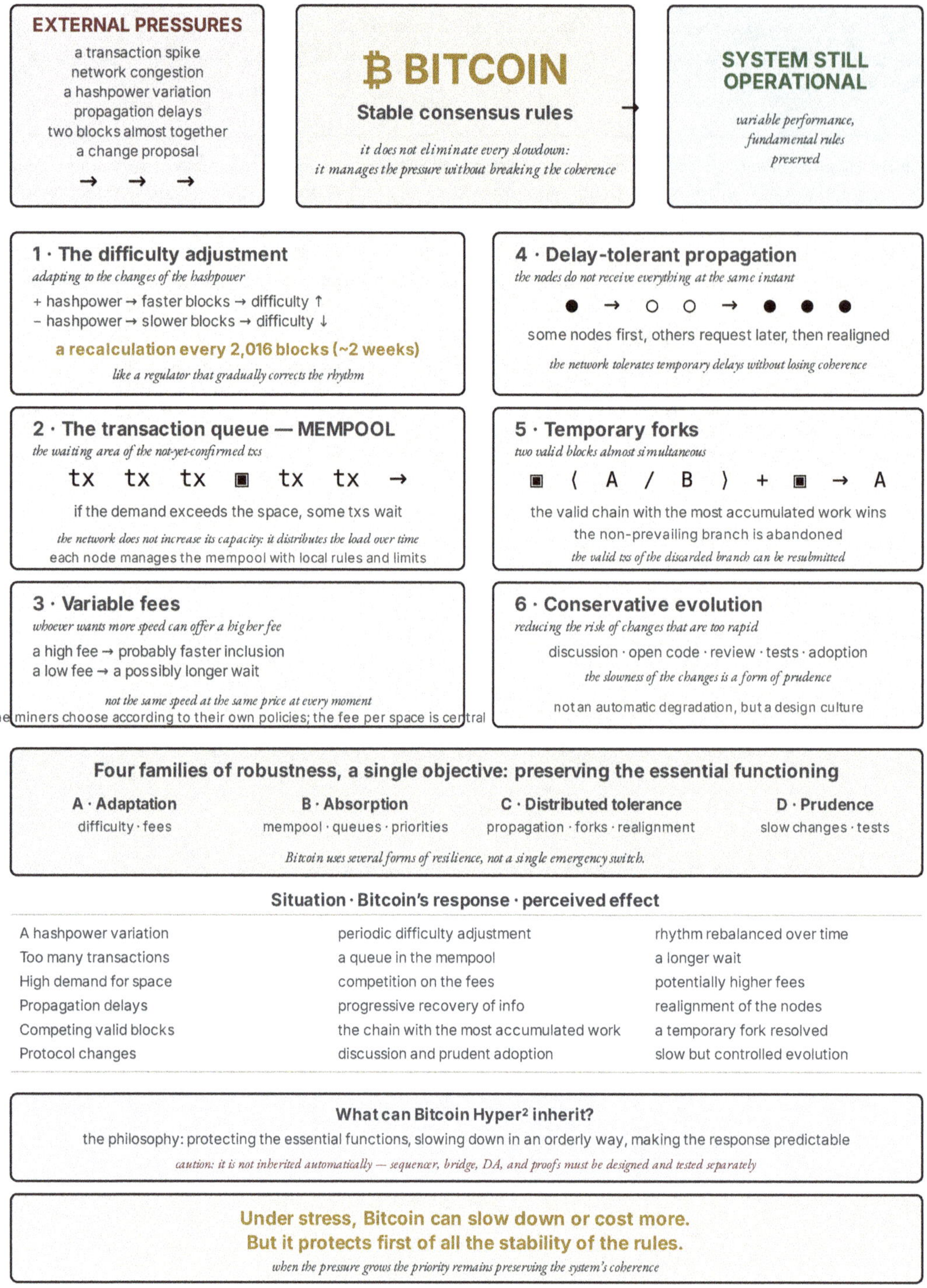

Bitcoin uses several tools to react to variable conditions without sacrificing the stability of the rules. The periodic difficulty adjustment rebalances the rhythm of the blocks; the mempool and the fees absorb the congestion; the peer-to-peer network tolerates temporary delays; competing valid forks are resolved by following the chain with the most accumulated work. Prudence in the upgrades completes this philosophy of robustness.

First mechanism: the difficulty adjustment. Bitcoin produces blocks every ten minutes on average. This is not a constant: it is the result of a dynamic mechanism that adjusts the difficulty of the proof-of-work every 2,016 blocks, using as a reference an ideal interval of about two weeks. **When the network's total computational power increases, the difficulty increases to bring the block time back toward equilibrium.** When it decreases, the difficulty decreases. This mechanism helps the system rebalance the rhythm of the blocks over time. The adaptation is not immediate: if the computing power changes abruptly, the blocks can temporarily arrive more slowly or more rapidly, until the next recalculation of the difficulty.

Think of it as a change of dynamic equilibrium. Even after very wide variations of the available computing power, the block times have remained roughly constant over time. **This is graceful degradation in action**: the system adapts progressively, without collapsing and without accelerating uncontrollably.

Second mechanism: the transaction queue (mempool). When more transactions arrive than can quickly enter the blocks, Bitcoin does not collapse: many stay temporarily waiting in the nodes' mempools. **The miners choose which ones to include according to their own policies; in practice, the fee offered for the space occupied is a central criterion.** The system does not stop: it redistributes the load over time. The mempools, however, are not infinite: when they reach the configured limit, some nodes can remove the least competitive transactions to protect their own resources.

Third mechanism: the fee market. When many people wish to enter the blocks quickly, the competition for the available space increases. **Whoever has greater urgency can offer a higher fee; whoever can wait can choose a lower fee.** The fees are not set by a central algorithm: they emerge from the demand for space in the blocks and from the decisions of users and miners. It is not a perfect or painless system, but it allows the network to distribute the load over time without uncontrollably increasing its own capacity.

Fourth mechanism: delay-tolerant propagation. Bitcoin does not require every node to receive every piece of information at the same instant. **Messages travel through a global network under a best-effort model, and some can arrive late.** If a node realizes it has missed a block, it can request it later and realign. This tolerance is crucial for robustness under variable network conditions, where perfect, instantaneous propagation is impossible.

Fifth mechanism: the management of forks. Occasionally, two miners find valid blocks almost simultaneously, creating a temporary fork. **Bitcoin manages this situation with elegance**: the nodes temporarily follow the branch they see first, and when one of the valid branches accumulates more work, they converge toward that chain and abandon the non-prevailing branch. The transactions of the abandoned branch can be resubmitted and included later, as long as they remain valid and have not already been confirmed in the prevailing chain. **The system manages a temporary divergence without manual intervention.**

Sixth mechanism: prudence in the changes. Bitcoin evolves slowly. The most important modifications require discussion, code review, tests, and a wide confrontation among independent parties. **It is not an automatic mechanism of controlled degradation, but a design culture**: reducing the risk that an overly rapid upgrade introduces new fragilities. The evolution is slow but robust.

Putting these six mechanisms together, Bitcoin has built a system that adapts to an extremely wide variety of conditions without collapsing. **Traffic spikes? The fees rise and the waiting times lengthen, but the system continues.** A sudden reduction of the hash rate? **The difficulty rebalances at the next recalculation and the system carries on.** Delays, congestion, and temporary divergences are not eliminated completely, but they are managed through known rules and mechanisms that allow the network to realign.

This is the lesson Bitcoin Hyper can gather. It is not enough to promise speed under ideal conditions. **A mature system must explain what happens when the traffic increases, when a component slows down, or when the network encounters unexpected conditions.** The anchoring on Bitcoin offers an important base, but the Layer 2's resilience is not born automatically: it must be designed, tested, and demonstrated in the individual components.

⁂

20.4 — How Hyper Can Apply Controlled Degradation

Let us now see how the principle of controlled degradation could translate into the different components of Bitcoin Hyper. For each there is a simple question: what should happen when the load increases or when a part of the system encounters difficulties? A fragile architecture reacts unpredictably; a resilient architecture slows down, limits the damage, and protects the essential functions.

TABLE 20.3 **HYPER'S SEVEN COMPONENTS AND THEIR CONTROLLED DEGRADATION.**

Component	Under stress	Resilient response
Sequencer	A transaction spike	A queue with limits and priorities: longer waits, service operational
Anchoring	High Bitcoin fees	More spaced checkpoints: lower costs, slower finality
Data availability	Nodes offline	More copies and redundant fragments: verification still possible
SVM execution	A transaction too heavy	A compute limit per transaction: only that one fails
RPC nodes	Too many requests	Balancing and limits: a clear error rather than a blackout
Canonical bridge	Simultaneous withdrawals	An ordered queue and estimates: correctness first, then speed
Peer-to-peer network	Reduced connectivity	Progressive resynchronization: coherence is not sacrificed

For every component the same principle holds: recognizing the stress, temporarily reducing the performance, and protecting the essential, instead of forcing the system beyond the limit until the collapse. It is the concrete translation of controlled degradation into Hyper's architecture.

FIGURE 20.4 **SEVEN COMPONENTS, SEVEN RESPONSES TO STRESS.**

A mature rollup does not promise that nothing will ever go wrong: it designs in advance how to prevent a local problem from becoming general.

BITCOIN HYPER²
the operating center of the Layer 2 · ₿ periodic checkpoints on Bitcoin

detect → contain → slow down → protect → restore

1 · Sequencer — a transaction spike
fragile: an uncontrolled queue → timeouts → unstable
resilient: a controlled queue, clear limits and priorities
longer waits but the service still operational; distributing the load over time instead of pretending to clear it

2 · Anchoring — high Bitcoin fees
fragile: the same rhythm at any cost
resilient: more spaced checkpoints, larger batches
a visible trade-off: lower costs now, slower finality until conditions improve

3 · Data Availability — nodes offline
fragile: few concentrated copies → weakened verification
resilient: more copies and redundant fragments
recovery from the remaining nodes, reconstruction, independent verification still possible

4 · SVM execution — a tx too heavy
fragile: one operation absorbs all the resources
resilient: a compute budget for every transaction
it exceeds the limit → its tx fails, the rest of the system stays protected · isolating the problem

5 · RPC nodes — too many requests
fragile: everything is accepted until saturation
resilient: more endpoints, load balancing, cache, rate limits
better a declared wait or a clear error than a completely unreachable service

6 · Canonical Bridge — simultaneous withdrawals
fragile: opaque queues, unpredictable times
resilient: an ordered queue, proof verification, time estimates
privileging correctness and transparency over absolute speed

7 · Peer-to-peer network — reduced connectivity
fragile: the nodes rapidly lose a common view
resilient: synchronization and progressive realignment
the speed can decrease; coherence must not be sacrificed

A principle common to all the components
not forcing beyond the limit · recognizing the stress · reducing temporarily · protecting the essential · returning gradually
every component requires a different response, but the philosophy stays the same

Component · possible stress · controlled response

Component	Possible stress	Controlled response
Sequencer	too many transactions	an ordered queue and clear limits
Anchoring	high fees	a calibrated frequency, larger batches
Data Availability	some nodes offline	distributed copies and reconstruction
SVM execution	a tx too heavy	a compute limit, an isolated error
RPC	too many requests	load balancing and temporary limits
Canonical Bridge	many withdrawals together	a transparent queue, predictable times
The node network	reduced connectivity	synchronization and realignment

OBSERVABILITY — one does not react to what one does not see
component health · queues · resources · anchoring status · data availability · bridge status · network delays · incidents
monitoring is not an accessory: it is the nervous system of resilience

A design scenario — to be demonstrated in practice
Hyper² recalls this philosophy; the real quality will emerge from specifications, stress tests, and the network's observable behavior. A design declaration is not an already demonstrated guarantee.

The system can become slower. It should not become uncontrollable.
resilience is not a single feature: it is a discipline applied to every component

Controlled degradation must be designed component by component. The sequencer, the anchorings, data availability, the SVM runtime, the RPC nodes, the canonical bridge, and the peer-to-peer network can react to stress in different ways. The common principle is preventing a local problem from causing a general collapse: slowing down in an orderly way, protecting the essential functions, and progressively recovering full operations.

Component one: the sequencer. If more transactions arrive than can be processed rapidly, the system should prevent the queue from growing without control. **A possible solution consists in keeping an ordered queue, establishing clear limits, and communicating understandable waiting times to the**

users. Some operations could be processed more slowly or temporarily rejected, but the service should stay stable.

Component two: the anchoring on Bitcoin. If the Layer 1 fees increase, always keeping the same rhythm can become expensive. **A flexible system can consider more spaced checkpoints and larger batches.** The price to pay is a longer wait before the next consolidation: it is a compromise between economic sustainability and speed, which we already encountered in Chapter 13.

Component three: data availability. If some nodes stop working, the data necessary for the verification should not disappear immediately. **Resilience can be strengthened by distributing more copies and by using techniques that make it possible to reconstruct the information even when some fragments are missing.** The concrete solution will however have to be verified in the definitive specifications: erasure coding and sharding today belong to the project's research space, not to an already implemented configuration.

Component four: the execution of the transactions. A single program should not be able to consume resources without limits and slow down the entire system. **In the SVM environment, every transaction has a maximum compute budget (compute units): if it exceeds the expected limit, it fails without compromising the other operations.** Moreover, if one of a transaction's instructions fails, all its modifications to the state are rolled back. The principle is simple: isolating the error before it propagates.

Component five: the RPC nodes, that is, the access points used by wallets and applications to dialogue with the network. If too many users send requests at the same moment, the service can slow down. **A good architecture distributes the load, temporarily limits the requests, and clearly communicates any waits.** The objective is not guaranteeing the same speed at every instant, but avoiding a general halt.

Component six: the Canonical Bridge. If many users simultaneously ask to withdraw BTC, the system should process the requests in an orderly, transparent way. **The times could lengthen, but the users should be able to understand the state of their own operation and receive reliable indications.** The concrete procedures will have to be evaluated when the definitive specifications are published: the general flow described by the project provides for a withdrawal request on the Layer 2, the generation of a proof, validation through the canonical bridge, and the release of the BTC on the Layer 1.

Component seven: the peer-to-peer network[a]. What happens if the connectivity among the rollup's nodes worsens? **The protocol should tolerate temporary delays in the propagation and allow the nodes to realign progressively when the connectivity improves.** The speed can decrease, but the correctness of the shared state must not be sacrificed.

For each of these components, controlled degradation does not arise spontaneously. **It requires limits, ordered queues, monitoring, emergency procedures, and stress tests.** Bitcoin Hyper's public documentation shows that the theme has been recognized. The architecture's concrete quality, however, will emerge only when it will be possible to observe the system's behavior under pressure, after the mainnet launch.

---

[a] **Peer-to-peer network.** It is a network in which the participants — the "nodes" — communicate directly with one another, peer to peer, without a central server acting as an intermediary. Every node receives and retransmits the information to the others, so that the data propagates through the entire network. It is the architecture on which Bitcoin and the other blockchain systems are founded, because it eliminates a single point of control; the flip side is that, if the connectivity among the nodes degrades, the propagation slows down and the system must know how to react without halting.

⁂

20.5 — Monitoring as a Precondition of Controlled Degradation

There is an aspect of controlled degradation that deserves a dedicated section: **one cannot manage what one cannot observe.** To react well under stress, one must know what is happening in the system, which components are slowing down, and where the pressure points are forming. Monitoring[a] collects known signals: response times, errors, queues, resource usage. Observability[b] takes a further step: it helps understand even unexpected problems, following the system's behavior through metrics, logs, and traces[c].

Bitcoin Hyper's public documentation dedicates a specific update to the monitoring-first architecture[d] and presents the system's visibility as a principle to incorporate from the start. **The message is clear: monitoring should not be added only after the launch, when the first problems emerge.** Observability is connected to transparency and to trust in the rollup.

---

[a] **Monitoring.** The continuous collection of already-expected signals about a system's functioning — response times, errors, queues, resource usage — to notice promptly when something departs from the norm. It answers known questions: "is it working as it should?".

[b] **Observability.** The capacity to understand a system's internal state from what it produces toward the outside, to the point of being able to investigate even problems not foreseen in advance. It is a step beyond monitoring: not only "is it working?", but "why is it behaving this way?".

[c] **Metrics, logs, and traces.** The three types of data on which observability is founded: metrics are numerical measures over time (for example the transactions per second); logs are textual records of events; traces follow the path of a single operation through the system's various components.

[d] **Monitoring-first architecture.** A design approach in which the capacity to observe the system is provided from the start, as a basic requirement, and not added at a later stage. It means building the system already predisposed to be measured, inspected, and diagnosed.

FIGURE 20.5 **THE ROLLUP'S CONTROL TOWER.**

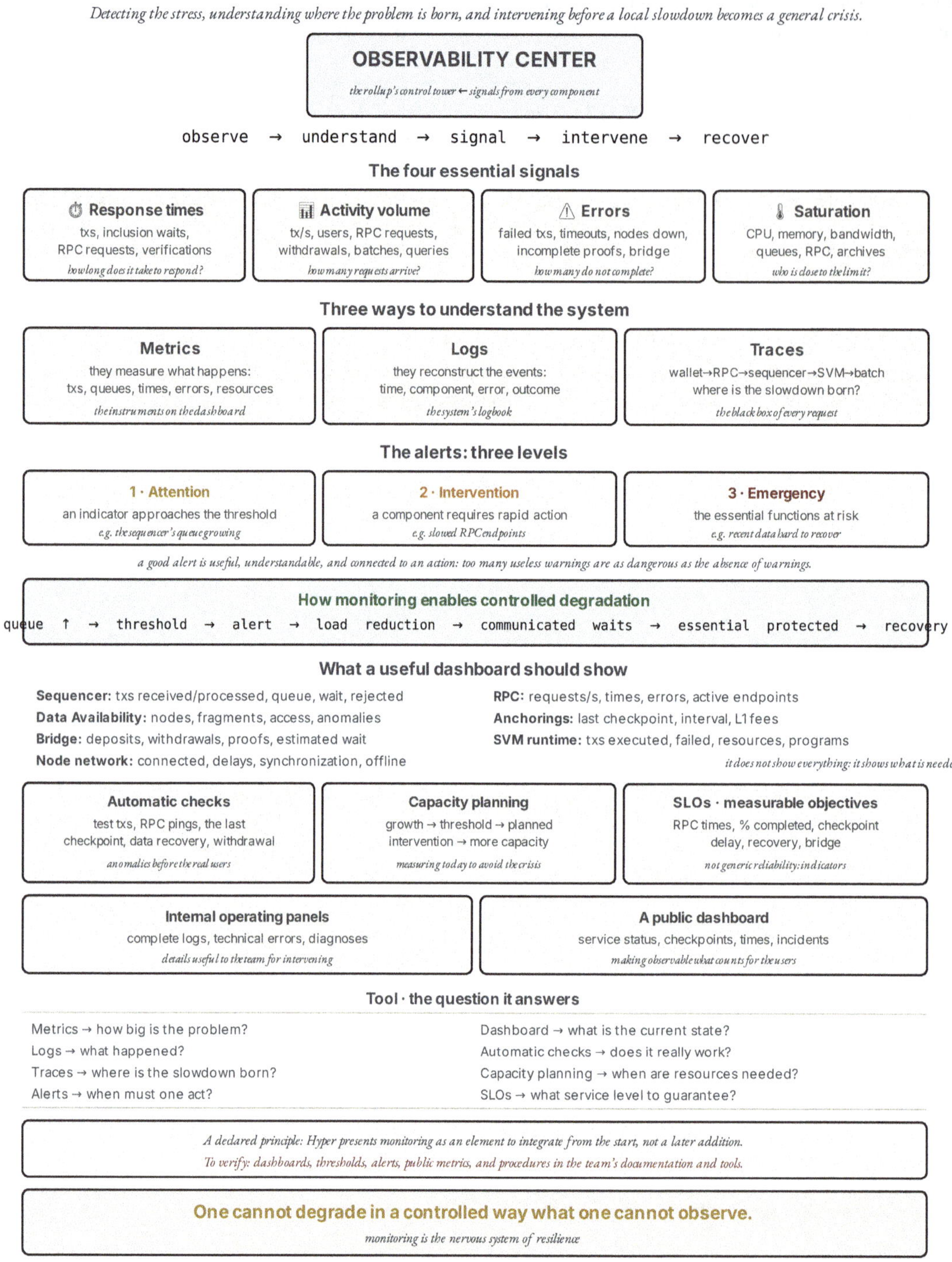

Controlled degradation requires observability. Metrics, logs, traces, alerts, and dashboards make it possible to detect the stress, understand where a problem is born, and intervene before a local anomaly propagates. The quality of Bitcoin Hyper's monitoring-first architecture will have to be evaluated through public tools, understandable metrics, documented procedures, and the network's observable behavior.

Let us see concretely what monitoring-first means for Hyper.

First element: instrumentation. Every component should produce useful information about its own functioning: processing times, queues, errors, and resource usage. **These signals make it possible to**

quickly recognize when a part of the system is approaching the limit.

Second element: the logs. The most important events should be recorded in an orderly way, with date, time, and enough context to reconstruct what happened. **When a problem emerges, the logs are the logbook that helps understand its origin.**

Public metrics. For the users and for the community it would be important to be able to consult a public dashboard with the essential indicators: service status, anchorings, response times, any incidents, and the progress of the recovery. **The effective presence of these tools will have to be verified after the launch.**

Alerts. Alerts serve to warn the team when a problem requires an intervention. **They must be selected with care: too many useless warnings can confuse the operators, while a good alert signals a concrete problem and suggests an action.** An excess of notifications produces habituation and can slow down the response to real incidents.

Traces. Another important function consists in following the journey of a request through the different components. **If a transaction slows down, one must understand where it stopped: in the RPC node, in the sequencer, in the execution, or in a subsequent step.** Traces help pinpoint the exact spot where the problem is born.

Continuous automatic checks. Even when the system seems to work normally, small automatic checks can verify that the essential operations keep behaving as expected. **These checks must be designed with prudence, to prevent the test itself from introducing new problems.**

Capacity planning. The historical metrics also serve to predict when the system might reach its own limits. **If a queue grows progressively or the RPCs approach saturation, the team can intervene before the problem becomes urgent.** Capacity planning transforms a late reaction into an anticipated decision.

All these practices are standard in the high-reliability software industry (cloud providers, financial services, telecommunications), but they are not always applied rigorously in the crypto world. **Hyper makes explicit that it wants to adopt the monitoring-first architecture**, and this is a choice that, if implemented seriously, would distinguish the project from most competitors.

For the users, the monitoring-first architecture translates into concrete advantages. **Greater transparency**: one can observe in real time how the system is performing. **A faster diagnosis of the problems**: when something goes wrong, one quickly understands what and why. **More timely communication**: the team can communicate promptly when there are problems, basing itself on concrete data. **Greater reliability over time**: continuous monitoring makes it possible to prevent problems before they manifest.

For those who evaluate the project, the monitoring-first architecture should not remain an abstract declaration. **After the launch it will be important to verify the presence of public dashboards, readable metrics, timely communications about the incidents, and measurable service objectives.** Monitoring really becomes part of security only when it allows the operators to intervene rapidly and the users to understand what is happening.

⁂

20.6 — What Controlled Degradation Could Mean for Users

All this technical discussion has concrete implications for the user experience[a], and it deserves to be translated into practical scenarios. **In a system designed for controlled degradation, users should experience understandable, progressive slowdowns, not sudden, unpredictable collapses.**

TABLE 20.4 **CONTROLLED DEGRADATION: WHAT CHANGES FOR THE USER.**

Under heavy load[b]	A fragile system[c]	Controlled degradation
Confirmation of the transactions[d]	It halts	It slows down predictably

Fees[e]	Unpredictable	They increase gradually
Messages to the user[f]	Opaque errors	A clear, understandable state

For the user the difference is tangible: a fragile system stops working without explanations, while a system designed for controlled degradation stays usable, communicates what is happening, and allows one to decide whether to wait or to pay more for priority.

[a] **User experience.** The concrete way in which a person perceives and uses the system: how clear, predictable, and reliable it is in daily use. Controlled degradation is measured precisely here: not in the abstract, but in what the user sees and endures when something goes wrong.

[b] **Heavy load.** The condition in which the requests directed at the system exceed its ordinary capacity — for example a sudden surge of transactions. It is the testing ground that distinguishes a fragile system from one designed to degrade in a controlled way.

[c] **A fragile system.** A system that, once its threshold is exceeded, stops working at once and without warning, instead of slowing down in an orderly way. It is the opposite of controlled degradation: the small overload turns into a total halt.

[d] **Confirmation of the transactions.** It is the moment when an operation is accepted and included by the system. Under high load a fragile system stops confirming and halts; one designed for degradation slows down predictably, staying operational nonetheless.

[e] **Fees and priority.** When the requests exceed the available space, the fees rise because the users compete to be served first. In a well-designed system the increase is gradual and the user can choose whether to pay more for priority or to wait for better conditions.

[f] **Messages to the user (observability).** It is the system's capacity to communicate clearly what is happening. An "opaque" error leaves the user without explanations; a "clear" state tells them whether to wait, retry, or pay more, transforming a disruption into a manageable wait.

FIGURE 20.6 **WHAT THE USER SEES WHEN THE SYSTEM IS UNDER PRESSURE.**

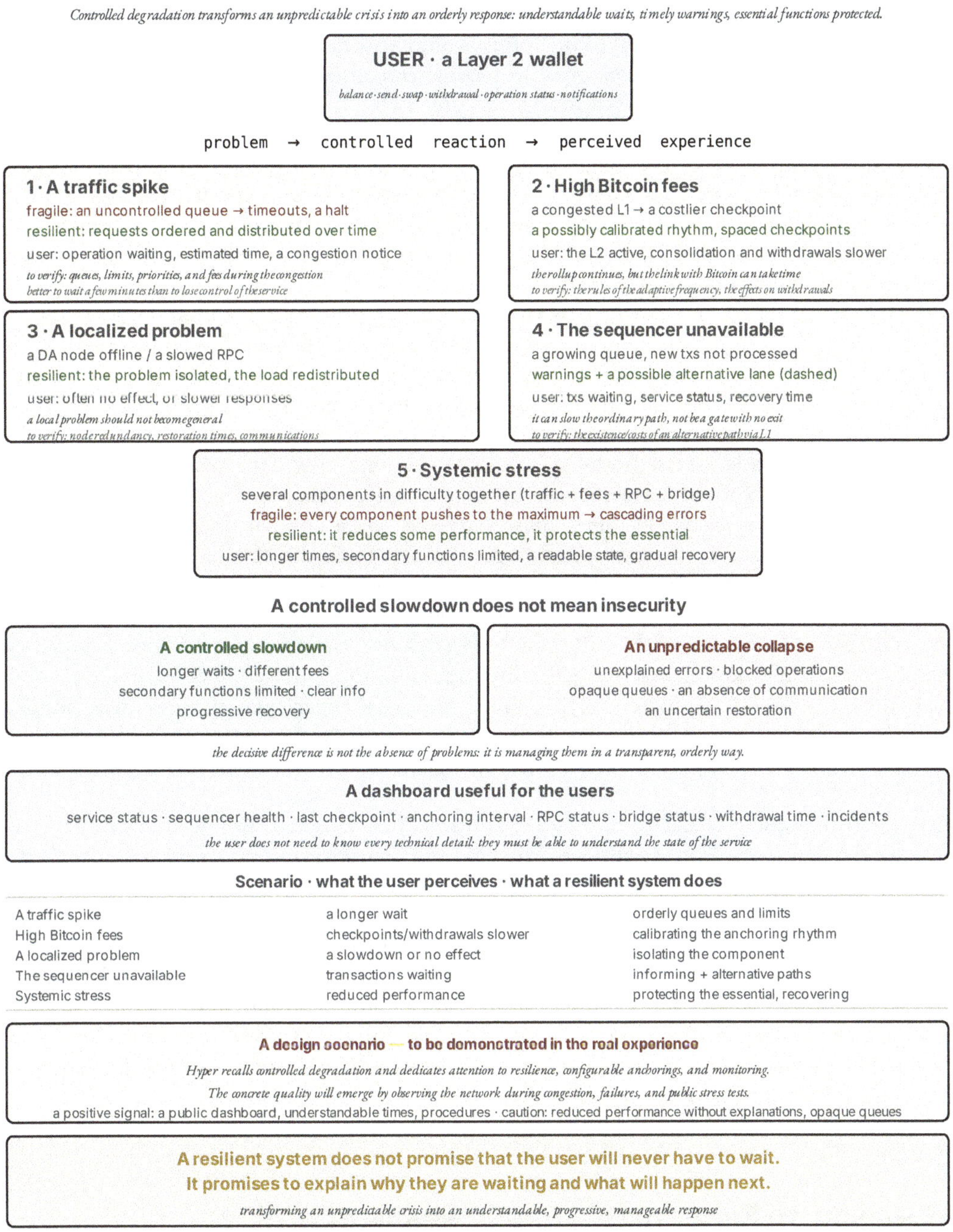

Controlled degradation seen by the users. During a stress phase, the rollup can become temporarily slower or less convenient to use. The difference from an unpredictable collapse consists in the capacity to manage queues, delays, and limitations in a transparent way, protecting the essential functions and clearly communicating the state of the service.

Scenario one: a traffic spike. When many more transactions arrive than normal (for example during a significant market event), the waiting times can lengthen. Some operations could be processed more slowly or temporarily rejected to prevent the queue from growing without control. **The users should receive clear information about the state of the service and be able to decide whether to wait or retry later.** The precise priority rules will have to be documented by the protocol. In the meantime the applications keep working, the funds stay safe, and the state of the system stays consistent.

Scenario two: high Bitcoin congestion. When Bitcoin's fees are high, the rollup could calibrate the rhythm of the anchorings, publishing more spaced checkpoints and aggregating larger batches. **The price to pay would be a longer wait before the next consolidation and, potentially, longer times for some withdrawals.** The operations internal to the rollup would instead continue normally. The frequency of the anchorings is presented as a configurable parameter connected to costs, security, finality, and recovery; a definitive algorithm is not yet publicly documented.

Scenario three: a problem in one component. If a component of the rollup has problems (for example a data availability node goes offline), and the architecture has sufficient redundancy, **a problem limited to a single component could have reduced effects on the user's experience.** In the most serious cases, the service could slow down and the team should clearly communicate what is happening. Data availability, redundant encoding, and node diversity are design themes recalled by the project, but the definitive configuration will have to be verified.

Scenario four: an attack or censorship by the sequencer. A robust rollup should provide a procedure of last resort to prevent a problem or an incorrect behavior of the sequencer from indefinitely blocking a valid transaction. **In some Ethereum rollups there are forced inclusion mechanisms through the Layer 1.** For Bitcoin Hyper it will be necessary to verify whether an analogous solution will be adopted and how it will concretely work on Bitcoin.

Scenario five: systemic stress. If the system enters a state of generalized stress, the users see **a progressive degradation of the performance** but not a complete collapse. The system could **slow down the new transactions, temporarily limit some requests, space out the anchoring frequency**. In a scenario of generalized stress, the system should protect first of all the correctness of the state and the essential functions. **It will be important to verify which emergency procedures will be provided for the bridge and which tools will allow the users to recover control of their own assets in the most serious cases:** the ordinary flow of the withdrawals through proof and canonical bridge is described, but a complete forced exit procedure for emergency situations is not yet publicly documented.

In all these scenarios, the pattern is the same: **the user experience changes in a predictable, controlled way, it does not collapse.** The users can adapt, and the ecosystem keeps functioning. **It is exactly what one would expect from a system designed according to the principle of controlled degradation.**

There is an important aspect to underline. Controlled degradation does not mean an absence of inconveniences. **It means that slowdowns, queues, and temporary limitations are managed in an understandable way and communicated clearly.** No system can guarantee perfect performance under every condition. A mature system demonstrates its own quality precisely in the difficult moments: it recognizes the problem, protects the essential functions, and progressively returns to normality.

For those who operate on the rollup, understanding the philosophy of graceful degradation helps set realistic expectations. **Do not expect perfect performance under all conditions**: no system can provide it. Expect excellent performance under normal conditions, and controlled degradation under adverse conditions. **When the system slows down, it is not necessarily a sign of a problem**: it could be the system protecting itself from worse problems.

⁂

20.7 — How to Recognize a Really Resilient Project

Having understood what controlled degradation means, let us see how to distinguish projects that really implement it from projects that limit themselves to declaring it. **There are concrete indicators you can observe to evaluate a project's maturity on this dimension.**

TABLE 20.5 **DECLARED RESILIENCE AND REAL RESILIENCE: HOW TO TELL THEM APART.**

Indicator	Only declared	Really implemented
Incident management[a]	No public report	Detailed post-mortems[b]

Behavior under load[c]	Only assertions	Documented stress tests[d]
Transparency	Generic communications	Public metrics and dashboards[e]

Resilience is not evaluated from the declarations, but from the observable evidence: incident reports, tests under load, and operational transparency distinguish a project that has really designed controlled degradation from one that limits itself to citing it.

---

[a] **Incident management.** The way a project faces malfunctions: whether it recognizes, documents, and corrects them transparently, or minimizes and silences them. It is one of the most honest signals of a system's real maturity.

[b] **A post-mortem.** It is the public account that, after a failure, reconstructs its causes, effects, and the corrections adopted. Publishing it is a sign of a mature technical culture: it demonstrates that the team faces errors openly, instead of hiding them.

[c] **Behavior under load.** How the system reacts when the requests grow until they put it under pressure. Asserting it in words is worth little: what counts is having verified it with concrete tests and having made the results public.

[d] **Stress tests.** Trials conducted by deliberately subjecting the system to extreme conditions — many more transactions than normal, simulated failures — to observe how it reacts before it really happens. They are what transforms resilience from a promise into a verified property.

[e] **Public metrics and dashboards.** They are the dashboards that show the state of the system in real time — confirmation times, queues, fees, availability. Making them public allows anyone to verify autonomously whether the system works as declared, without having to take it on trust.

FIGURE 20.7 **TEN SIGNALS OF A REAL RESILIENCE.**

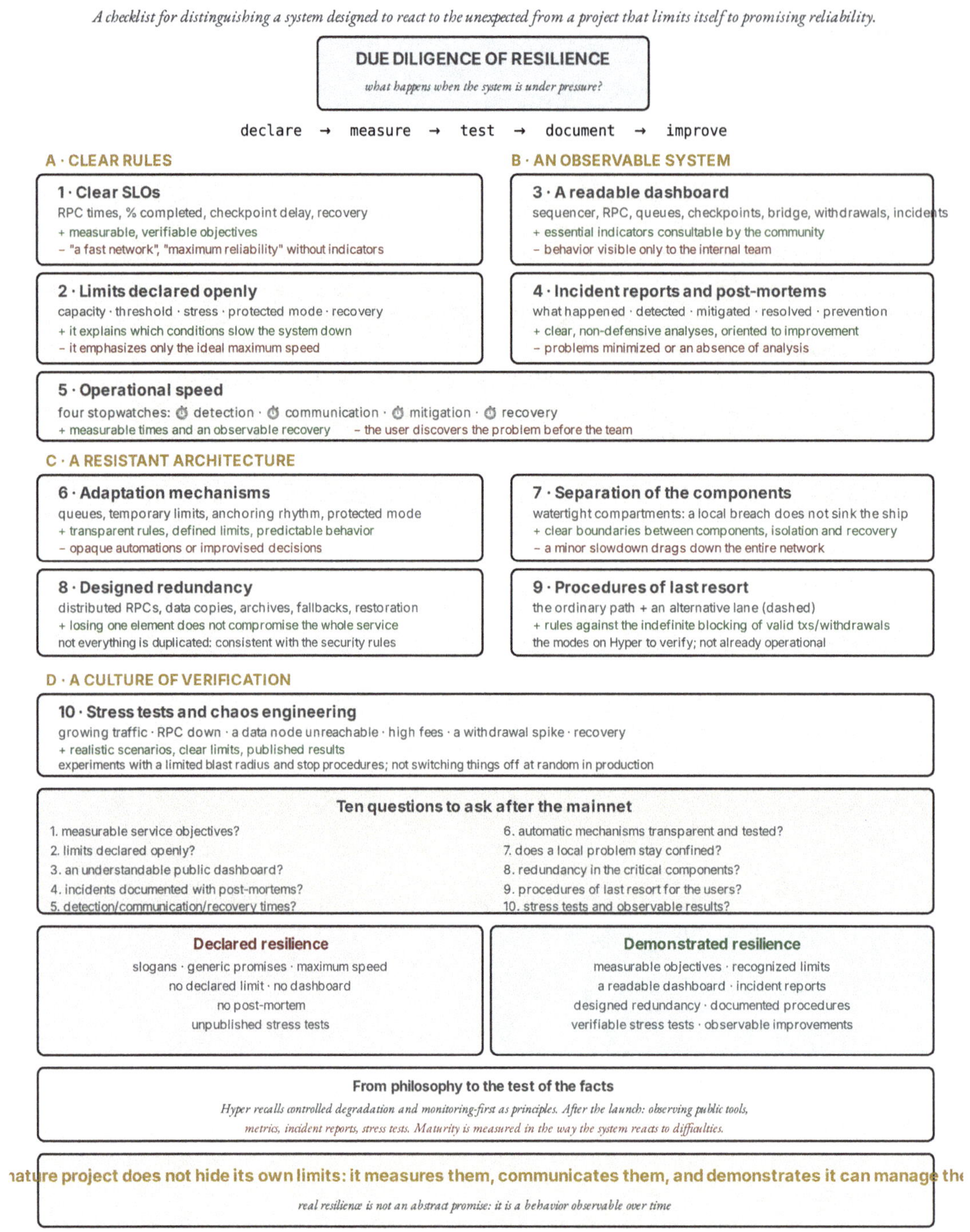

Ten signals for evaluating a project's real resilience. Measurable objectives, public dashboards, incident reports, controlled adaptation, isolation of the problems, designed redundancy, procedures of last resort, and observable stress tests make it possible to distinguish a declared philosophy from an architecture really capable of reacting to the unexpected.

First indicator: measurable service objectives and documented behaviors under stress. A mature project should explain what happens when the traffic increases, when a component slows down, or when an emergency procedure needs to be activated. **SLOs make it possible to transform generic words like "fast" or "reliable" into verifiable objectives**: the SLI is the quantitative measure of the service level, the SLO the target value, the SLA an agreement that provides explicit consequences in case of non-compliance.

Second indicator: an understandable public dashboard. The users do not need to see every technical detail, but they should be able to check the general state of the service, the last checkpoint, the health of the RPCs, any queues, and the state of the bridge. **A public dashboard makes it possible to verify whether the real behavior corresponds to the project's declarations.** Latency, traffic, errors, and saturation are the four fundamental signals to monitor in a service intended for users.

Third indicator: an incident-management track record. When problems occur, how are they managed? Does the team communicate rapidly? Does it publish an analysis of the causes? Does it indicate which interventions will be adopted to prevent the incident from repeating? **A post-mortem is the written account of the incident, of its impact, of the actions taken, of the causes, and of the interventions necessary to reduce the probability or the impact of analogous events**, and it is one of the best indicators of how the system will behave in the future.

Fourth indicator: automatic adaptation mechanisms. Does the system have a configurable anchoring frequency? Do the queues and the limits adapt to the load? **Automatic mechanisms can be useful, but they are not positive in themselves: they must have understandable rules, clear limits, monitoring tools, and stop procedures.** An opaque or untested automation can amplify the problem instead of solving it.

Fifth indicator: isolation of the problems. A resilient architecture is designed so that the malfunction of one component stays confined as much as possible. **The objective is preventing a local slowdown from dragging down the entire system**, confining the impact of a problem within a defined perimeter and leaving the components outside that perimeter operational.

Sixth indicator: redundancy in the critical components. Do the most delicate components have designed alternatives? Are there several RPC endpoints? Is the data replicated? Are the restoration procedures documented? **Redundancy does not consist simply in duplicating every element: it must be consistent with the protocol's security.**

Seventh indicator: procedures of last resort for the users. A mature project should explain what the user can do if the ordinary path stops working. **Any mechanisms of forced inclusion, emergency exit, or alternative recovery are important because they reduce the dependence on the cooperation of a single operator.** For Bitcoin Hyper it will be necessary to verify which procedures will actually be implemented.

Eighth indicator: a culture of stress tests and chaos engineering. Does the team carry out controlled experiments to understand how the system reacts to the unexpected? Does it simulate traffic spikes, RPC slowdowns, the temporary loss of some nodes, or an increase of the Bitcoin fees? **The most delicate experiments must begin in safe environments, have a limited blast radius, and provide rapid stop modes.** It is a discipline of experimentation aimed at verifying the reliability of complex distributed systems, still rarely adopted in the crypto world.

Ninth indicator: measurable response times. When a problem emerges, one must distinguish four phases: detection, communication, mitigation, and recovery. **A mature operating team does not limit itself to solving the problem: it makes understandable the path followed to bring the system back to normality.**

Tenth indicator: transparency about the limits. No system offers perfect performance under every condition. **A serious team explains openly what the network's limits are, which events can cause slowdowns, and which procedures are activated in the difficult moments.** Absolute promises are less credible than an honest description of the trade-offs.

For Bitcoin Hyper, these ten indicators constitute a concrete checklist to use after the mainnet launch. **The monitoring-first architecture and the reference to controlled degradation represent an interesting starting point.** The real evaluation, however, will depend on what it will be possible to observe: dashboards, metrics, stress tests, emergency procedures, incident reports, and progressive improvements. Resilience is not an initial declaration: it is a behavior demonstrated over time.

⁂

20.8 — Questions and Answers: Clarifying the Chapter's Concepts

Question 1: If graceful degradation is so important, why is it not emphasized more in the marketing of crypto projects?

For marketing reasons, ironically. **Graceful degradation is a concept difficult to communicate to the general public.** Saying "our system can reach 100,000 transactions per second" is clear and attractive. Saying "our system slows down in a controlled way under stress instead of collapsing" is more nuanced and less exciting. **Moreover, speaking of degradation implies admitting that there will be moments of stress**, and this goes against the "our system is always perfect" message that many projects want to communicate. **The result is that the projects that do graceful degradation best often hide it in their own marketing**, while projects that optimize for the peaks without thinking about the edge cases emphasize it (because they can show impressive numbers). **For informed investors, recognizing this bias is useful**: looking for evidence of long-term thinking and of robustness under stress, not only peak numbers. A concrete example: in 2021–2022, various L1 projects (Solana, Avalanche, various others) competed on TPS numbers. Solana, which had higher peaks, also had more stability incidents. Avalanche, with more conservative numbers, was more stable. The marketing emphasized the peaks, but the robustness over time was different.

Question 2: How can I know whether Hyper is implementing graceful degradation, given that the system is not yet in production?

Before the mainnet launch, you can observe indirect signals. **First signal: the quality of the technical documentation.** Do Hyper's research posts explicitly mention principles like graceful degradation, monitoring-first, separation of the components? Are they developed in detail or only hinted at? **Second signal: the team's language.** Does the team speak openly of adverse scenarios, of trade-offs, of limits? Or only of successes and optimizations? **Third signal: the presence of public tests.** Are there public testnets where the community can experience the system's behavior under stress? Are the results of load tests published? **Fourth signal: the admission of not knowing yet.** A mature team admits which aspects are still in the research and experimentation phase, instead of declaring everything solved. Hyper has shown this honesty in various posts (on data availability, on the sequencing models, on determinism). **After the mainnet launch**, the indicators become more concrete: public dashboards, the management of incidents, behavior under real loads. The evaluation refines over time. A concrete example: before Optimism's launch, it was difficult to evaluate the system's robustness. The first months after the launch revealed both strengths (rapid recovery from minor incidents) and weaknesses (some prolonged halts). The complete evaluation emerged only after 12–18 months of operations.

Question 3: Graceful degradation requires significant investments. Does it not slow down the development of the product?

Yes, and this is a real trade-off that deserves to be recognized honestly. **Implementing graceful degradation requires additional time**: thinking about the edge cases, building adaptation mechanisms, doing stress tests, designing monitoring. All this adds months or years to the development cycle. **For projects that compete on launch speed**, this investment can seem an unjustifiable luxury. **For projects that aim at long-term robustness**, it is a necessary investment. **Hyper has chosen the second road**, and it is consistent with the project's general "Bitcoin-grade" philosophy. If Hyper had wanted only to launch quickly to seize market opportunities, it would probably have skipped much of the graceful degradation. **The fact that the team emphasizes these principles indicates long-term priorities, not short-term opportunism.** For the users, this means they can expect a slower launch but a more robust system. For investors, it means that the project's evaluation must consider multi-year horizons, not immediate results. A concrete example: Bitcoin itself grew much more slowly than other projects of its early years (Ripple, Litecoin, various altcoins). But it survived and prospered precisely because of its robustness, while many competitors that were growing more rapidly have disappeared.

Question 4: Are there crypto systems that have implemented graceful degradation particularly well, besides Bitcoin?

Yes, some examples are particularly instructive. **Lightning Network has implemented well-designed graceful degradation**: when the payment channels are congested, the transactions slow down in a controlled way, with possible reroutes through alternative channels. The system does not collapse even when some nodes go offline. **MakerDAO showed notable robustness during the "Black Thursday" of March 2020**, when the price crash caused massive liquidations. The system had problems (the famous "0 DAI bid" that allowed acquiring collateral without paying), but it did not collapse, and the governance was able to respond and adapt. **Uniswap V3 has managed multiple traffic spikes over the years** without significant incidents, demonstrating a robust architecture. **Among Ethereum's Layer 2s, Optimism and Arbitrum have both managed various incidents reasonably**, even if not perfectly. **Solana, by contrast, has had various network halts that showed weaknesses in graceful degradation**, even if it is improving over time. The pattern is that projects that emphasize peak performance without sufficient investment in robustness tend to have more catastrophic incidents. For Hyper, inheriting the SVM, the team must have done specific work to improve graceful degradation compared to the Solana baseline. It will be important to see whether this investment translates into superior stability in production.

Question 5: Can graceful degradation be maintained even during a progressive decentralization of the sequencer?

It is an important question because it touches a real trade-off. **When the sequencer is centralized, it is relatively easy to implement graceful degradation**: a single operator with a complete view of the system can make coordinated decisions. **When the sequencer is distributed, coordination becomes more complex**, and maintaining gradual behaviors under stress requires sophisticated mechanisms of consensus and coordination among operators. **Historical examples suggest that the transition can introduce temporary instabilities**: during architecture changes, incidents tend to increase before stabilizing at lower levels. **For Hyper, this means that the sequencer's transition will require particular attention**: graceful degradation properties will have to be maintained even during and after the transition, and this adds complexity to the design. **On the other hand, once stabilized, a distributed system can have graceful degradation superior to a centralized one**, because many independent operators can compensate for local problems. The long-term stability can therefore be better, even if the short-term stability during the transition is worse. It is an acceptable trade-off for most serious projects. A concrete example: Ethereum's transition from proof-of-work to proof-of-stake (the Merge) in 2022 was managed with care precisely to minimize the instabilities during the transition. It worked better than expected, but it was the result of years of active preparation.

Question 6: If the system keeps working even under significant stress, how can I know when there are real problems?

It is a perceptive question, because graceful degradation can indeed hide problems if there is no adequate transparency. **The answer is precisely the monitoring-first architecture we have discussed.** Without transparent monitoring, the users might not notice that the system is operating in degraded mode. **With transparent monitoring**, the users see in real time: the current processing times compared to the normal ones, the fees required compared to the baseline, the state of the various components, any active warnings. If the system is operating in degraded mode for some reason, the users can know it and adapt their own behavior. **The Hyper team has the responsibility of making this visibility real**, through public dashboards, regular communications, proactive alerts on known problems. **For the users, developing the habit of checking the state of the system before important operations is a prudent practice.** It does not replace general trust in the system, but it protects from specific inconveniences during periods of stress. A concrete example: today on Ethereum, before doing high-value operations, it is prudent to check the gas tracker to see the state of the fees and the network activity. This practice will apply just as well on Hyper, and the tools for doing it will be part of the ecosystem that will develop around the rollup.

20.9 — WHAT TO TAKE AWAY FROM THIS CHAPTER

Graceful degradation is the capacity of a system to slow down in a controlled way under stress instead of collapsing unpredictably. It is a principle of critical systems engineering applied to the blockchain context.

Most software systems fail in a non-gradual way for structural reasons: optimization for the average case, cascading failures, positive feedback loops, the exhaustion of resources, inconsistent states, hidden bugs.

The original Bitcoin implemented graceful degradation through specific mechanisms: the difficulty adjustment, a mempool with priorities, the adjustment of the fees, delay-tolerant propagation, the management of forks, the conservatism of the changes.

Hyper can apply graceful degradation to all its components: the sequencer (with a transaction queue), the anchoring (an adaptive frequency), data availability (replication and encoding), the execution (resource limits), the RPC nodes (rate limiting), the Canonical Bridge, the peer-to-peer network.

Monitoring is a precondition of graceful degradation. One cannot degrade gradually what one cannot observe. The monitoring-first architecture is a structural component, not a cosmetic addition.

For the users, graceful degradation translates into predictable changes under stress: longer waiting times, higher fees, slower finality, but the system keeps working and the funds stay safe.

There are ten concrete indicators for evaluating whether a project really does graceful degradation: SLA documentation, public dashboards, an incident-management track record, automatic adaptation mechanisms, separation of the components, redundancy, forced action, chaos engineering, response times, transparency about the limits.

Crypto marketing tends not to emphasize graceful degradation because it is difficult to communicate and implies admitting moments of stress. Projects that do graceful degradation best often hide it in their marketing.

Implementing graceful degradation requires significant investments that slow down development. It is an acceptable trade-off for projects that aim at long-term robustness, not for those that compete on launch speed.

Bitcoin Hyper made its adherence to the principle explicit in the February 2026 post, but the true verification comes from the observation of concrete indicators after the mainnet launch. Philosophical declarations are a starting point, not a guarantee.

---

*Chapter 20 closes here. We have understood a fundamental security principle that is often ignored in crypto marketing, and is instead central to the long-term robustness of any blockchain system. In **Chapter 21 — Defenses against a Malicious Sequencer: The Challenge Architecture**, we will go into the detail of a specific aspect of the security model that we have touched upon in various previous chapters, seeing concretely how the system can protect the users even against an actively malicious sequencer, through forced inclusion mechanisms, forced exit, and proof systems that allow the community to challenge incorrect behaviors.*

Controlled degradation: slowing down without *collapsing*

How a mature rollup protects the essential functions when stress increases. It is not about **avoiding every problem** — impossible — but about reacting in an orderly way instead of collapsing all of a sudden.

1 Not everything must work at its peak, always

A fragile system · it crashes at once

- Uncontrolled queues
- Cascading errors
- Chaotic recovery
- Timeouts
- A general halt

A resilient system · it slows down, it does not collapse

- Ordered queues
- Priority to the essential
- Progressive recovery
- Clear limits
- Alternative paths

Better to slow down predictably than to lose control of the system.

2 Collapse is born from small, amplified problems

a small problem → a growing queue → a retry storm → resources at the limit → inconsistent states → a general halt

1. **The average case** — tested only under normal conditions.
2. **A cascade** — one component transfers pressure.
3. **A retry storm** — thousands of retries worsen the load.
4. **Saturation** — CPU, memory, bandwidth, queues at the limit.
5. **Divergent states** — nodes with incomplete or delayed data.
6. **Hidden bugs** — defects that emerge only under stress.

A mature system knows when it must slow down before breaking.

3 Bitcoin absorbs stress without changing the rules

external stress (spikes, fees, hashpower) → **₿ Bitcoin** (stable consensus rules) → **system still operational** (slower or costlier, not inconsistent)

- **Difficulty adjustment** — rebalances the rhythm of the blocks.
- **Mempool** — absorbs the waiting transactions.
- **Variable fees** — distribute the priority.
- **Tolerant propagation** — the nodes realign over time.
- **Temporary forks** — the chain with the most work wins.
- **Prudent upgrades** — slow but robust evolution.

Bitcoin can slow down, **but it does not sacrifice the coherence of its own fundamental rules.**

4 Seven components, seven responses to stress

COMPONENT	UNDER STRESS	RESILIENT RESPONSE
Sequencer	a transaction spike	a queue with limits and priorities; communicated times
Anchoring on Bitcoin	high Bitcoin fees	more spaced checkpoints, larger batches
Data Availability	some nodes offline	redundant copies, reconstructible data
SVM execution	a transaction too heavy	compute budget: only that tx fails
RPC nodes	too many requests	load balancing, rate limits, clear errors
Canonical Bridge	many simultaneous withdrawals	an ordered queue, verified proofs, estimates
Peer-to-peer network	reduced connectivity	synchronization and progressive realignment

The system can become slower. **It should not become uncontrollable.**

5 Monitoring-first: observing in order to react

One cannot protect what one cannot see. Controlled degradation requires **observability**: four essential signals to follow in real time, with the tools to intervene before the collapse.

- **Response times** — *how long does it take to respond?*
- **Activity volume** — *how many requests arrive?*
- **Errors** — *how many do not complete?*
- **Resource saturation** — *who is close to the limit?*

metrics · logs · tracing · alerts · a public dashboard · automatic checks · capacity planning · measurable SLOs

THE KEY POINT

A mature rollup does not promise that nothing will go wrong. It designs in advance **how to react**: detecting the stress, containing it, slowing down, protecting the essential, and recovering progressively. Bitcoin Hyper's real resilience will have to be **demonstrated** by dashboards, stress tests, incident reports, and the network's observable behavior after the mainnet.

PART VI · SECURITY

Chapter 21
Defenses against a Malicious Sequencer

The challenge architecture

⁂

21.1 — The Principle of Operational Distrust

I want to begin this chapter with a statement that may seem paradoxical but is one of the most solid principles of security engineering: **to build systems that require minimal trust, one must design them starting from the assumption that anyone could become malicious.** Not because one thinks they will become malicious, but because the possibility must be considered, and the system must keep working even in that case.

FIGURE 21.1 **THE SEQUENCER'S CHALLENGE ARCHITECTURE**

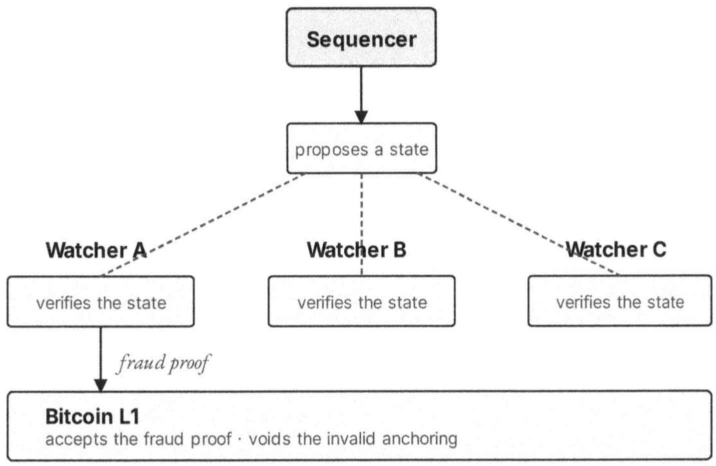

Reading: *anyone can act as a watcher. If the sequencer tries to anchor an invalid state, a single honest watcher presenting a fraud proof to Bitcoin is enough to void it. The system is secure as long as at least one honest watcher exists — it does not require a majority.*

For Bitcoin Hyper, this principle applies with particular force to the sequencer. In the previous chapters we saw that the sequencer has significant power: it orders the transactions, controls inclusion, can extract MEV, can censor. We also saw that, during the initial phase, it will be run by the team with all the transparency and accountability practices we described. **But what happens if, despite everything, the sequencer begins to misbehave?** The team gets compromised by an attack. The cryptographic keys are stolen. The team unilaterally decides to censor certain transactions. Regulatory pressures force the team into incorrect behaviors. **All these scenarios are possible, and a robust system must have concrete answers for each of them.**

The challenge architecture is precisely this set of answers. **It is the mechanisms that allow the users to operate even when the sequencer is malicious or compromised**, recovering control of their own assets through paths that do not depend on the cooperation of the sequencer itself. They are the "last" level of defense, the one that activates when the previous levels have failed, and for this reason it deserves a dedicated chapter.

I want to do four things in this chapter. First, describe concretely the malicious behaviors a sequencer can adopt, because without a clear picture of the threats it is difficult to understand the defenses. Second, examine the specific forced inclusion mechanisms that allow the users to force the processing of their own transactions even against the sequencer's will. Third, look at the forced exit, the definitive mechanism that makes it possible to withdraw one's bitcoin directly from the Canonical Bridge without depending on the sequencer. Fourth, understand how these mechanisms integrate with the proof model (fraud proof or validity proof)* to form the complete system of defenses. It is a technical but fundamental chapter, because the existence and quality of these defenses is what separates a serious rollup from a disguised federated sidechain.

⁂

21.2 — The Threat Map around the Sequencer

Let us begin with a map of the threats around the sequencer. The exercise is important because different risks require different defenses. Some behaviors depend directly on the power to order the transactions; others involve proofs, data availability, the bridge, or administrative keys. Before speaking of the defenses, one must understand precisely which power we are trying to limit.

Nota 1. Mapping the threats before evaluating the defenses is the standard method of threat modeling, the discipline with which a system's security is analyzed starting from "who could do what, and how". Applying it to the sequencer means not settling for the question "is it secure?", but asking which specific behaviors are possible and which countermeasures make them improbable or costly.

Nota 2. Not all the sequencer's threats have the same origin: some derive from the sole power of ordering the transactions, others involve proofs, data availability, the bridge, or administrative keys. Keeping them distinct is essential, because an effective defense against one category can leave another completely uncovered.

Nota 3. Forced inclusion is the mechanism that allows a user to impose the processing of their own transaction even if the sequencer refuses to accept it, asserting it directly through Bitcoin. It is the defense against censorship: it guarantees that nobody can be excluded from the system indefinitely.

Nota 4. Forced exit is the ultimate guarantee: it allows the user to recover their own bitcoin directly from the bridge on Bitcoin even if the sequencer stops working or becomes hostile. It is what distinguishes a rollup, where the custody of the funds does not depend on the operator, from a federated sidechain.

Nota 5. The Canonical Bridge is the official bridge connecting Bitcoin and the rollup, holding the deposited bitcoin and regulating deposits and withdrawals according to verifiable rules. It is the point through which the forced exit passes, and for this reason one of the most sensitive components of the entire architecture.

* **Fraud proof and validity proof.** They are the two ways a rollup demonstrates that its own state is correct. The fraud proof is used by "optimistic" rollups: the state is accepted unless someone, within a time window, demonstrates its incorrectness. The validity proof is used by "zero-knowledge" rollups: every state is accompanied by a mathematical proof that immediately certifies its correctness. They are the technical framework on which all the defenses described in the chapter rest.

FIGURE 21.2 **TEN THREATS TO DISTINGUISH WITH PRECISION.**

Censorship, delays, MEV, data unavailability, and abuse of the administrative powers are not the same problem: every risk requires a specific defense.

⚡ Liveness · ⚖ Fairness

SEQUENCER
it receives, orders, and inserts the transactions into the batches

🛡 Safety · 🏛 Governance

four different properties → four families of defenses

A · POWERS PROPER TO SEQUENCING — what the sequencer can do directly

1 · Selective censorship
a valid TX always stays out of the batches
addresses, categories, apps
defense: monitoring, limits on the delays, a possible alternative lane via L1

2 · Strategic delay
a TX held back → the price changes → worse conditions for the user
defense: metrics on the inclusion times and understandable rules

3 · Manipulation of the order
A B C → C A B
front-running · back-running · sandwich
defense: observable rules, MEV analysis, distribution of the sequencing

4 · Collusion
a preferential lane for market makers, bots, selected funds
defense: public rules, a verifiable order, independent analysis

5 · Privileged information
seeing the flow before the others → a possible market advantage
defense: rules on access to the flow, separation of the roles, transparency

6 · A service halt
sequencer offline → the queue stalled
liveness ≠ correctness of the state
defense: redundancy, restoration, alternative paths

B · THREATS INVOLVING OTHER COMPONENTS — the sequencer should not be able to realize them alone

7 · An incorrect state root
expected root 8F3A...91C7 ≠ proposed 4D9B...72E1
VALIDITY PROOF → an invalid proof → the proposal rejected
the sequencer can propose, not make true what is false
to verify: the proof system, the verifiers, audits, the bridge rules

8 · Unavailable data
the root on Bitcoin + missing data → independent verification compromised
the seal stays visible, but without the document it is not enough
defense: verifiable DA, distributed copies, recoverability

C · GOVERNANCE AND ADMINISTRATIVE POWERS — they do not automatically belong to the sequencer

9 · A unilateral change of the rules
whoever holds the keys can change fees, priorities, limits, the bridge parameters, upgrades
directing the traffic ≠ rewriting the rules of the road
defense: transparent governance, audits, limits on the powers

10 · Abuse of the emergency procedures
protected mode: correct vs improper use
limiting damage / blocking or extorting
an emergency brake is useful, but with clear rules
defense: circumscribed powers, public logs, time limits

For every risk always ask
1. who concretely holds the power? · 2. which property is threatened? · 3. which control limits the risk?
different threats require different defenses

Threat · origin · property at risk · defense to verify

Selective censorship · sequencer · access · limits on the delays, an alternative lane
Strategic delay · sequencer · fairness · metrics on the inclusion times
Opportunistic reordering · sequencer · MEV · rules and monitoring
Collusion · sequencer + privileged parties · fairness · transparency and independent analysis
Privileged information · pre-inclusion access · fairness · separation of the roles
A service halt · sequencer · liveness · redundancy and alternative procedures
An incorrect root · state publication · safety · validity proofs and verifiers
Unavailable data · data availability · verifiability · distributed copies, recoverability
A change of the rules · governance and keys · predictability · limits on the powers and audits
Abuse of the emergencies · governance · continuity and trust · circumscribed powers, public logs

an effective defense begins with the correct attribution of the powers: the sequencer is a gatekeeper, but security depends on the entire architecture.

A declared direction, to be verified in the details
Hyper indicates that the sequencing power should become replaceable: if the sequencer misbehaves, halts, or censors, the network should be able to work around the problem. The actual procedures must be verified in the technical specifications.

The sequencer can control the traffic.
It should not control the system's truth on its own.
whoever orders the transactions should not be able to arbitrarily validate the state, hide the data, or change the rules

The threats around the sequencer belong to different categories. Censorship, delay, opportunistic reordering, and a service halt depend directly on the sequencing power. The publication of an incorrect state root and the unavailability of the data must be countered through proofs, validation rules, and data availability. Unilateral changes and the abuse of the emergency procedures depend instead on the administrative powers assigned to the team. Distinguishing the roles is the first step in designing effective defenses.

Threat one: selective censorship. Censorship can hit specific addresses, categories of transactions, or interactions with certain applications. The theme became particularly visible in the sector after the sanctions introduced in the United States against Tornado Cash in 2022, subsequently lifted in March 2025. **The technical point remains general: when there is a single party that controls access to the rollup, it becomes important to understand whether the users have an alternative path.**

Threat two: strategic delay. The sequencer does not openly block the transaction, but leaves it waiting long enough to change its economic outcome. **In a DeFi environment even a few seconds can affect the price obtained, a liquidation, or an arbitrage opportunity.**

Threat three: manipulation of the order. The sequencer can arrange the transactions in a sequence favorable to itself or to privileged parties. **Front-running, back-running, and sandwich attacks are examples of how the ordering can turn into economic value.**

Threat four: the publication of an incorrect state root. A sequencer or another operator in charge of the publication can try to propose an incorrect state root. **In an architecture based on validity proofs, the cryptographic proof should prevent an invalid transition from being accepted.** This is why one must evaluate the proof system, the bridge rules, and the audits, not only the sequencer's behavior.

Threat five: the unavailability of the data. The system publishes a root, but the data necessary to reconstruct its meaning is not recoverable. The problem can depend on the sequencer, on the data availability operators, or on the overall structure of the protocol. **Without accessible data, independent verification weakens**: even in ZK rollups the user may not know their own balance or may fail to interact with the most recent state when the data is withheld.

Threat six: a service halt. If the sequencer stops working, the new transactions can stay waiting. The cause can be deliberate, but also operational: an attack, a failure, or an error. **It is important to distinguish the availability of the service from the correctness of the state: a standstill can temporarily prevent the normal use of the rollup without automatically changing the users' balances.** As a general reference, some Ethereum rollups make it possible to bypass the sequencer through a queue on the parent chain, forcing the inclusion of a transaction after the expected period.

Threat seven: a unilateral change of the rules. This risk does not derive automatically from sequencing. **It emerges when the team or the same operator also controls the administrative keys, the protocol parameters, or the upgrade procedures.** One must therefore verify who can change fees, priorities, limits, and the bridge rules.

Threat eight: collusion with privileged parties. The sequencer could use its own ordering power to favor selected operators (for example market makers, MEV bots, funds). The risk depends on the mempool model, on access to the pre-inclusion data, and on the actual rules of the protocol.

Threat nine: abuse of the pending information. Even without directly changing the order, early access to the flow of the transactions can offer an economic advantage. **Like collusion, this risk depends on the mempool model, on access to the pre-inclusion data, and on the separation of the roles provided by the protocol.**

Threat ten: abuse of the emergency procedures. A system can provide a protected mode or pause powers to limit damage during an incident. **These tools can be useful, but they become delicate if they are too broad or controlled by a single party.** One must understand who can activate them, within which limits, and with which forms of transparency.

The threat map is therefore more articulated than it may seem. **Some risks concern the sequencer directly: censorship, delay, reordering, and a service halt. Others must be contained by independent controls: validity proofs, data availability, and the bridge rules. Still others depend on the governance and the administrative powers assigned to the team.** The system's robustness is born from the separation of the roles: whoever orders the transactions should not be able to control the state's truth on their own, hide the data, or change the rules.

The official page dedicated to the future sequencing models states that the sequencer's power should become replaceable: if the sequencer misbehaves, halts, or attempts censorship, the network must be able to work around the problem. **The direction is significant; the actual procedures will however have to be verified in the technical specifications.** Let us see in the next sections which specific mechanisms Hyper is designing for each family of risks.

⁂

21.3 — Forced Inclusion: An Emergency Lane against Censorship

Let us begin with the mechanism that defends against the first three malicious behaviors (censorship, delay, manipulation of the order). **Forced inclusion is the mechanism that allows the users to force the**

inclusion of their own transactions in the rollup, even if the sequencer does not want to process them.

Forced inclusion is an emergency lane conceived above all to counter prolonged censorship and the sequencer's unavailability. **The idea is simple: if a valid transaction keeps being ignored by the ordinary path, the user should be able to register their own request through an alternative channel recognized by the protocol.** From that moment the sequencer should not be able to leave it out indefinitely. This protection can also limit an indefinite delay, but it does not automatically eliminate MEV nor prevent every manipulation of the order.

The principle is already used in some rollups built on Ethereum. **In Arbitrum, for example, the user can send a transaction to the Delayed Inbox on the parent chain.** If the sequencer does not process it within the expected window — ordinarily 24 hours — the forced inclusion function can be called. In the OP Stack there is an analogous logic: the user can send a transaction through the OptimismPortal contract on the Layer 1, reducing the dependence on the sequencer during a period of downtime or in case of censorship. The time windows and the concrete rules differ between the two architectures.

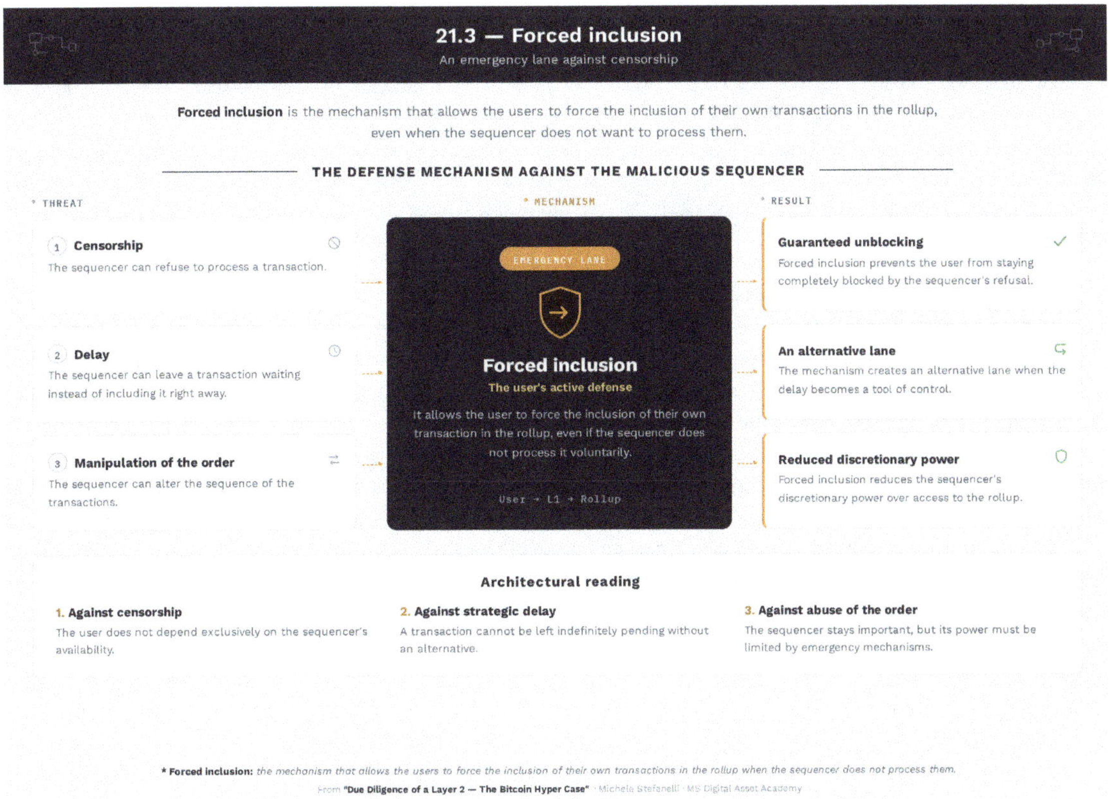

On Bitcoin, the design requires specific steps. **Bitcoin can record a message, a reference, or a commitment immutably, but it does not autonomously interpret the rollup's logic.** The Layer 2 protocol must therefore establish how to recognize the request, verify its validity, and give it a binding effect after a defined interval. Publishing a piece of data on Bitcoin is not enough: a binding derivation rule for the Layer 2 is needed.

Forced inclusion does not guarantee speed and does not eliminate every form of MEV. **It is a safeguard against indefinite exclusion, not a tool for obtaining immediate execution.** A transaction inserted through the emergency lane could arrive too late for a DeFi operation sensitive to seconds, and it does not necessarily prevent other transactions from being ordered before or after. It does not replace the validity proofs, data availability, or the bridge's security rules. The procedure, moreover, can be more expensive than the ordinary path, because it requires the use of the Layer 1 and additional steps: the precise structure of the costs however depends on the protocol adopted.

For Bitcoin Hyper, the presence of a lane alternative to the sequencer is a point to monitor with attention before the mainnet. **The consultable public materials describe the canonical bridge for deposits and withdrawals, the Bitcoin Relay Program for the verification of Bitcoin headers and**

proofs, the ZK proofs, and the periodic anchorings on Bitcoin, but they do not yet document a forced inclusion procedure in detail. It remains to be clarified whether a possible procedure will use the bridge, a dedicated module, or another rule of the protocol, in which form, with which costs, and after which time threshold.

⁂

21.4 — Forced Exit: A Way Out When the Ordinary Path Halts

Let us now move to the mechanism that defends against the most extreme threats: a service halt[a], the publication of incorrect state commitments, the refusal to publish data. **The forced exit[b] is the mechanism that allows the users to withdraw their own bitcoin directly from the Canonical Bridge, without depending on the cooperation of the sequencer or of any other operator of the system.**

---

[a] **A service halt.** It is the situation in which the operator that runs the rollup — in particular the sequencer — stops processing the transactions, because of a failure, a deliberate choice, or a blockage. In a centralized system the user would remain a hostage: they could neither operate nor recover their own funds. It is precisely the scenario that the emergency exit mechanisms, like the forced exit, must neutralize.

[b] **Forced exit.** It is the guarantee that the user can recover their own bitcoin by turning directly to the anchoring mechanism on Bitcoin, even when the sequencer does not cooperate. It is the difference between a system from which one can always take back what is one's own and one in which, if the operator halts, the funds stay trapped. Its effective presence and robustness is one of the most important elements to verify in a Layer 2: without it, every promise of "security" remains conditional on the good will of those who run the network.

One of the most important protections to evaluate is the possible presence of a forced exit procedure: an emergency door conceived to allow the users to recover their own BTC when the rollup's ordinary path does not work. **The objective is reducing the dependence on the sequencer and on the other operators.** For Bitcoin Hyper, however, the concrete modes of this procedure do not yet appear described in the consultable public details.

The official documentation illustrates the ordinary withdrawal in a simple way. **The user starts a request on the Layer 2; the system verifies the state and generates a proof for the canonical bridge; after the validation, the BTC are released toward the user's Bitcoin address.** This is the path used when the system works normally. The forced exit would instead be a different path: a procedure of last resort to use when the normal flow is not available or cannot be considered reliable.

FIGURE 21.4 **FORCED EXIT: A WAY OUT WHEN THE ORDINARY PATH HALTS.**

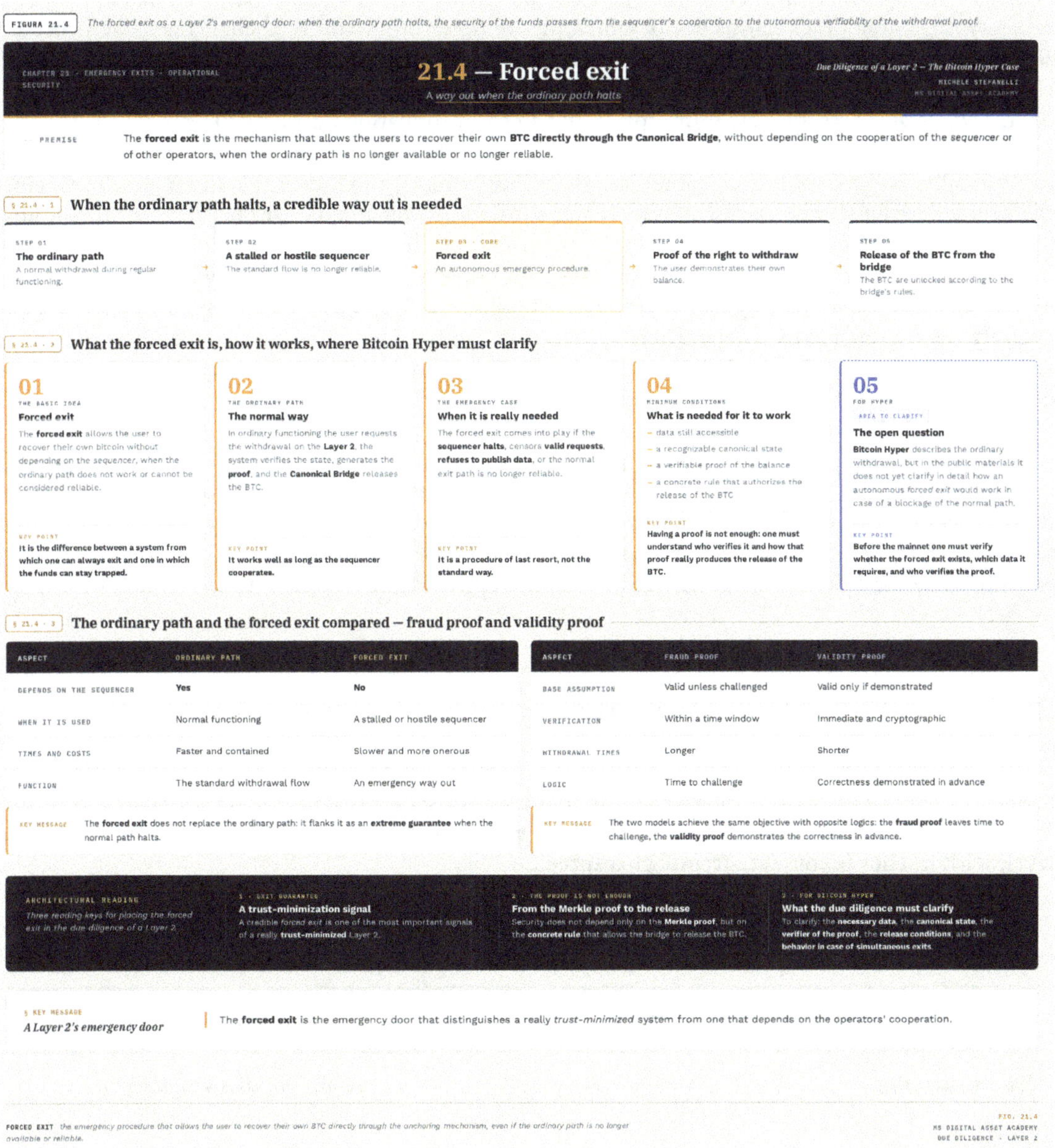

The most difficult question concerns the exceptional cases. What happens if the sequencer stops working? What can the user do if a valid request is censored? Is there an autonomous procedure if the team or other operators are not available?

In general terms, a credible forced exit requires at least four conditions. **First: the necessary data must stay accessible,** otherwise the user cannot reconstruct their own balance. **Second: one must know which state of the rollup is recognized as canonical. Third: the user must be able to build a verifiable proof of their own right to the withdrawal. Fourth: the proof must produce a concrete effect on the BTC locked in the bridge.**

This last point is particularly important. On Ethereum, a contract on the Layer 1 can verify a proof and directly apply the exit rules. **On Bitcoin, instead, the outputs can be spent only by respecting the conditions provided by the relevant script or through the operational mechanism established by the bridge.** It is therefore not enough to generically present a Merkle proof: a Merkle proof can demonstrate that a balance belongs to a state represented by a certain root, but one must understand who verifies it, which state is recognized as canonical, and how a valid proof actually authorizes the release of the BTC. *The heart of the security is not only the proof: it is the rule that opens the vault.*

The procedure's times depend on the validation model. In optimistic systems a window may be necessary during which an incorrect request can be challenged; in systems based on validity proofs, a valid cryptographic proof can reduce or eliminate the need for a traditional challenge. **The procedure also depends on data availability: if the data necessary to reconstruct the balance is not recoverable, the user may fail to build the proof.** The anchoring of the root on Bitcoin does not solve the problem on its own: it preserves the state's fingerprint, not all the information necessary to reconstruct it.

The forced exit does not represent a universal guarantee against any risk. It does not solve data unavailability on its own, it does not replace the validity proofs, and it does not automatically eliminate the bridge's administrative risks. It can moreover turn out slower and more expensive than the ordinary path, to a degree depending on the format of the proof, on the data published on Bitcoin, and on the technical structure chosen by the protocol. **The presence of a credible emergency door is however one of the elements that distinguish a really trust-minimized system from a system that depends entirely on the operators' cooperation.** It is not the only criterion — data availability, proofs, the bridge's conditions, and the administrative powers also count — but it is one of the most revealing questions of the entire due diligence.

For Bitcoin Hyper, the question remains open and deserves the utmost attention. The official site describes the ordinary withdrawal through state verification, the generation of a proof, and validation by the canonical bridge. **It does not yet clarify, however, how a user can autonomously recover their own BTC if the ordinary path stops working.** Before the mainnet it will be necessary to understand whether a forced exit will exist, which data it will require, who will verify the proof, which conditions will authorize the release of the funds, and what will happen if many users try to exit simultaneously.

⁂

21.5 — The Proof System: The Backbone of Correctness

I have mentioned the "proof model" at various points without going into it specifically. Now is the moment to do so, because it is the mechanism that gives substance to all the defenses we have described. **Without a well-designed proof model, forced inclusion and the forced exit work only at a superficial level; with it, they become structural guarantees.**

TABLE 21.2 **FRAUD PROOF AND VALIDITY PROOF: TWO PROOF MODELS.**

Aspect	Fraud proof*	Validity proof†
Base assumption	Valid unless challenged	Valid only if demonstrated
Verification	Within a time window‡	Immediate and cryptographic
Withdrawal times	Longer	Shorter

The two models achieve the same objective — guaranteeing the correctness of the state — with opposite logics: the fraud proof presumes validity and leaves an interval to challenge it; the validity proof demonstrates it in advance. The choice affects costs, finality times, and the user experience.

* **Fraud proof.** A model in which the proposed state is taken as valid unless proven otherwise: anyone, within a time window, can demonstrate that it is wrong and have it rejected. It is cheaper, but it forces one to wait for the end of the window before a withdrawal becomes definitive.

† **Validity proof.** The opposite model: every update is accompanied by a cryptographic proof that attests its correctness in advance. There is no need to wait for challenges — the verification is immediate — but the proof is more complex to generate.

‡ **Time window (challenge window).** It is the interval within which, in a fraud proof system, an observer can flag an incorrect state. As long as the window is open the result is not definitive: it is the reason why withdrawals turn out slower.

FIGURE 21.5 **THE PROOF SYSTEM: THE BACKBONE OF CORRECTNESS.**

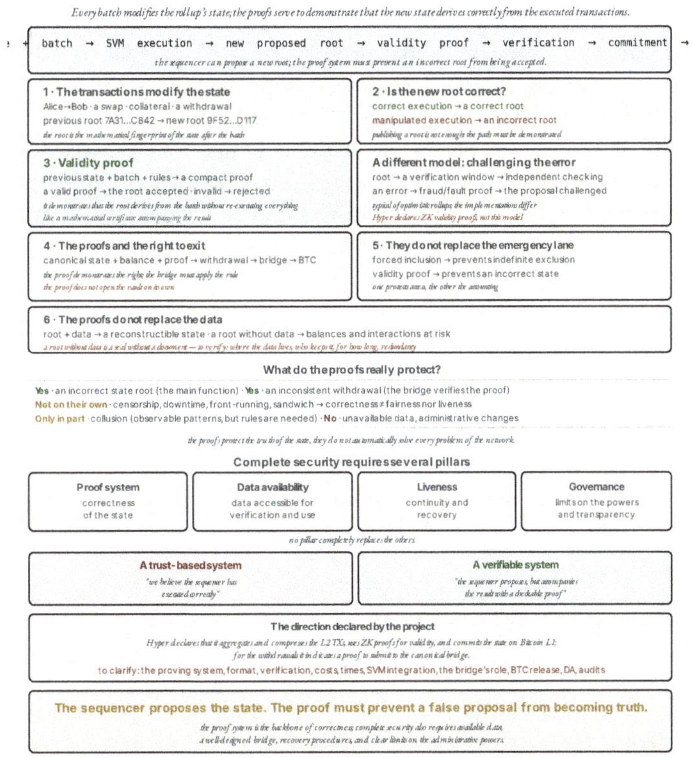

The proof system is the backbone of the rollup's correctness. A validity proof serves to demonstrate that the new state root derives correctly from the execution of the batch and prevents an invalid transition from being recognized as canonical. The proofs, however, do not automatically solve censorship, MEV, downtime, data unavailability, or governance risks: complete security requires several complementary pillars.

The proof system is one of the main pillars of the rollup's security, because it makes it possible to verify the correctness of the state commitments. **It does not solve every incorrect behavior of the sequencer on its own, but it prevents an invalid state transition from being accepted as true.** Its role becomes particularly important in the withdrawals, where a proof must demonstrate that the request is consistent with the state recognized by the protocol.

In the sector there are two big families of models. **In optimistic rollups, a transition can be challenged through a fraud proof or a fault proof.** In ZK rollups, a validity proof demonstrates the transition's correctness before the new state is recognized. Bitcoin Hyper's public documentation indicates the use of ZK proofs to guarantee the validity of the transactions; the definitive technical specifications will have to clarify the concrete implementation.

First defense: preventing the acceptance of an incorrect state. The sequencer can propose a new state root, but in a model based on validity proofs that root should not become canonical if the associated proof does not pass the verification. The proof therefore transforms a declaration of the sequencer into a checkable result.

Forced inclusion addresses a different problem: preventing a valid transaction from being excluded indefinitely. The validity proof protects the correctness of the accounting; forced inclusion protects access to the system. The two defenses can cooperate, but they are not the same thing.

The link with the forced exit is instead closer. **To withdraw BTC in an emergency situation, the user should be able to demonstrate their own right using a state recognized by the protocol.** The proof is necessary, but not sufficient: one must also clarify how the canonical bridge verifies the request and which rule concretely authorizes the release of the funds.

Data availability remains an essential prerequisite, above all in the models based on challenges: without data, the independent observers cannot reconstruct the execution and demonstrate the error.

Even in ZK models, the state data remains important because the users must be able to know their own balances and carry out new operations.

The proof system does not automatically eliminate collusion or MEV. A sequence of transactions can be mathematically valid and yet favor a privileged party. For these risks, ordering rules, transparency, monitoring, and a progressive reduction of the sequencer's power are needed.

The proof system transforms an essential part of the trust into a verifiable rule. **The sequencer proposes the result, but it should not be able to arbitrarily make an incorrect state valid.** Complete security however requires more elements: available data, a well-designed bridge, emergency procedures, and limits on the administrative powers. For Bitcoin Hyper, the declared direction is the recourse to ZK proofs; the real quality of the model will emerge from the technical specifications, the audits, and the tests published before the mainnet.

⁂

21.6 — The Watcher Network: The Rollup's Sentinels

There is an aspect of the defenses against a malicious sequencer that is often overlooked but is in fact essential: **the community of independent watchers[a] who monitor the system and activate the challenge mechanisms[b] when necessary.** Without this active community, even the best technical mechanisms become theoretical.

---

[a] **Independent watchers.** They are parties external to the team — developers, analysts, other operators — who autonomously check the network's behavior, recalculating its state and comparing it with what is published. They do not need permissions: the data made available is enough for them. Their presence is what transforms the guarantees "on paper" into real guarantees, because a challenge mechanism really exists only if someone is able, and has an interest, to activate it.

[b] **Challenge mechanisms.** They are the procedures that make it possible to flag and reject an invalid state proposed by the sequencer: for example a fraud proof, with which one demonstrates that a result violates the protocol's rules. They work like a right of appeal: they make the operator non-arbitrary, because any incorrectness of theirs can be proven and voided. They remain however potential tools until there is a community capable of using them: this is why the watcher network and the challenge mechanisms are two faces of the same defense.

TABLE 21.3 **WHY THE INDEPENDENT WATCHERS ARE ESSENTIAL.**

Technical mechanism	Requires that someone...
Fraud proof	detects the incorrect state and challenges it in time
Forced inclusion	notices the censorship and activates the procedure
Forced exit	recognizes the blockage and starts the exit

21.6 — The watcher network

The rollup's sentinels

The technical mechanisms against a malicious sequencer become really effective only if there is a **network of independent watchers** capable of monitoring the system, verifying the data, and activating the challenges when necessary.

From the theoretical guarantee to the real guarantee

• **Watchers** → • **Verification** → • **Challenge** → • **Transparency**

KEY COMPONENT

Independent watchers

The community that checks the rollup

Developers, analysts, operators, reviewers, researchers, and monitoring services autonomously check the network's behavior, recalculate the state, and compare the results with what is published.

KEY MESSAGE

No permissions are needed: what is needed is available data, open tools, and technical skills.

1 Challenge mechanisms

Procedures that make it possible to flag and reject an invalid state.

They work like a right of appeal: if the sequencer proposes an incorrect state, someone must be able to prove it and void it through fraud proofs, fault proofs, or analogous procedures.

KEY MESSAGE

A challenge really exists only if someone can and wants to activate it.

2 Optimistic rollups

Security depends on active challengers.

If an incorrect state root is published, at least one honest watcher must detect it and challenge it within the expected window.

KEY MESSAGE

In optimistic models, active watchers and available data are a direct part of the security model.

3 ZK rollups

The state's validity is verified cryptographically.

An invalid root should be rejected by the cryptographic verifier, without depending on the hope that someone manually spots the error.

KEY MESSAGE

The watchers nevertheless remain necessary for censorship, delays, ordering, upgrades, the bridge, and data availability.

4 Data and verifiability

Without accessible data there is no independent checking.

The watchers must be able to access the data necessary to reconstruct the state, verify the anchorings, analyze incidents, and check the system's behavior.

KEY MESSAGE

Distinguishing between data availability at the relevant moment and historical recoverability over time.

5 Tools and incentives

Monitoring requires infrastructure, time, and skills.

Open source software, independent nodes, public APIs, archive nodes, readable dashboards, bug bounties, grants, research, and rewards connected to correct challenges are needed.

KEY MESSAGE

The incentives must be calibrated with prudence to avoid opportunistic behaviors.

EXPERIENCES TO OBSERVE **References in the Layer 2 landscape**

L2BEAT

Independent analysis of the risks of Layer 2s: the sequencer, state validation, data availability, and the possibility of exit.

OP Stack

It documents the role of the challenger and of the infrastructures necessary to contest invalid claims.

Arbitrum BoLD

It introduces watchtower validators, bonding pools, and challenge procedures to sustain the challenge system.

Architectural reading

1. **The guarantees must be activated**
A challenge mechanism is not enough if nobody is able to use it.

2. **Transparency requires tools**
Nodes, APIs, dashboards, archive nodes, and open source software transform the checking into a real practice.

3. **The community does not replace the protocol**
The watchers are not the protocol, but they prevent the protocol from becoming a black box.

* **Independent watchers:** *parties external to the team who autonomously check the network's behavior, verify the published data, and can activate or support challenge mechanisms.*

From **"Due Diligence of a Layer 2 — The Bitcoin Hyper Case"** · Michele Stefanelli · MS Digital Asset Academy

The distinction between optimistic models and ZK models is essential. **In optimistic rollups, if an incorrect state root is published, a challenger must detect the problem and present a fault proof or a fraud proof within the expected window.** In this case, the presence of at least one honest, active watcher becomes a direct part of the security model, and it requires the data to be available for independent verification. In ZK rollups, instead, an invalid root should be rejected by the cryptographic verifier: the correctness of the state should not depend on the hope that someone manually spots the error.

This does not make the independent watchers superfluous. Numerous aspects remain that a validity proof cannot control on its own. **The sequencer could censor some transactions, delay them, or order them in a way economically unfavorable to certain users.** If the sequencer censors a transaction, the affected user or a support service should be able to detect the problem and use the possible alternative lane provided by the protocol: the community can make systematic censorship patterns visible, but the individual user's right should not depend on public mobilization. The data, moreover, must stay available and recoverable, and every relevant upgrade introduces administrative powers to keep watch over.

The watchers can be independent node operators, security reviewers, researchers, developers, on-chain analysts, data archivists, monitoring services, and specialized journalists. Different roles respond to different risks. To do this work, concrete tools are needed: open source software, independent nodes, public APIs, archive nodes, readable dashboards, and enough data to reconstruct the state.

The watchers must be able to access the data necessary to verify the state and analyze the incidents. **It is useful to distinguish data availability — the possibility of verifying a block at the relevant moment — from historical recoverability, that is, the capacity to find that data again in the future,** which can be supported by archive nodes or by external storage systems.

Continuous monitoring requires time, infrastructure, and skills. **This is why a mature ecosystem can provide incentives: bug bounties, grants for open source tools, research funding, or rewards connected to correct challenges.** The economic design must however be prudent, because badly calibrated incentives can generate new opportunistic behaviors. Arbitrum BoLD offers a concrete example: the nodes can operate as watchtower validators and the participants can use bonding pools to sustain a challenge, with a limited reward for those who correctly defend the system.

In the Ethereum ecosystem, independent analysis and transparency tools dedicated to Layer 2s have emerged. **L2BEAT, for example, offers in-depth comparisons among protocols and highlights risks concerning the sequencer, state validation, data availability, and the possibility of exit.** The best practices can be studied by observing more mature ecosystems: the OP Stack documents the role of the challenger and of the infrastructures necessary to contest invalid claims; Arbitrum describes watchtower validators, bonding pools, and challenge procedures. Bitcoin Hyper will be able to use these experiences as a reference, but it will have to adapt them to Bitcoin's specific characteristics and to its own ZK model.

For those who evaluate Bitcoin Hyper, the presence of independent watchers will be an important indicator after the mainnet launch. **One will have to verify whether anyone will be able to run a node, recover the data, analyze the anchorings, check the inclusion times, and understand the bridge's behavior.** Independent dashboards, public audits, open source tools, and a culture capable of welcoming technical criticism will also be relevant. The community does not replace the protocol: it prevents it from becoming a black box.

⁂

21.7 — Layered Defenses: From the Foundations to the Emergency Door

Putting together everything we have seen, a hierarchy of defenses[*] emerges that protects the users against various forms of malicious behavior of the sequencer. **Understanding this hierarchy helps to see the complete system, not only the individual pieces.**

TABLE 21.4 **THE LAYERED DEFENSES AGAINST AN INCORRECT SEQUENCER.**

Defense layer	Protects from...
The proof system	False or invalid states proposed by the sequencer
Forced inclusion	Censorship of valid transactions
Forced exit	A service blockage or a refusal to cooperate
Independent watchers[†]	Abuses that nobody detects and challenges

The defenses are not alternatives but complementary: each covers a different form of malicious behavior. It is their combination — not a single mechanism — that determines how really resistant a rollup is to an incorrect sequencer.[‡]

[*] **Layered defenses (defense in depth).** The principle by which security does not rely on a single protection, but on several independent levels: if one gives way, another keeps protecting. No layer alone is sufficient; it is their combination that makes the system robust.

[†] **Independent watchers.** Parties external to the team — anyone who runs a node or analyzes the public data — who verify the system's behavior and can raise the alarm. Their existence prevents the protocol from becoming a "black box" controllable only from the inside.

[‡] **An incorrect sequencer.** A sequencer that abuses its own role: it censors transactions, reorders them to its own advantage, or proposes false states. It is the adversary against which all the defenses described in this chapter are conceived.

FIGURE 21.7 **LAYERED DEFENSES: HOW TO PROTECT THE USERS FROM AN INCORRECT SEQUENCER.**

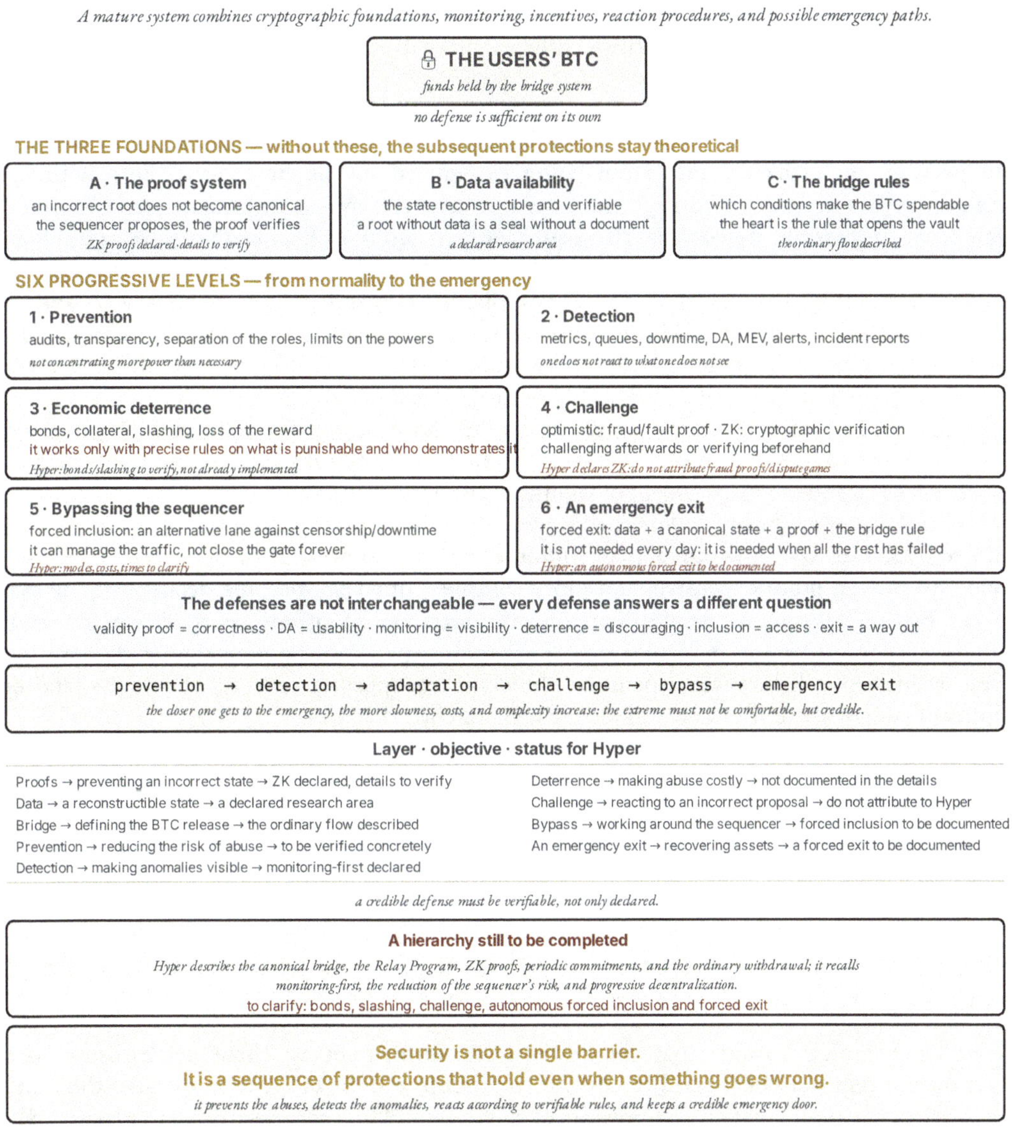

The rollup's security is born from overlapping defenses. The proof system, data availability, and the bridge rules constitute the foundations. Prevention, detection, possible economic deterrence, challenge procedures, a possible bypass of the sequencer, and an emergency exit add progressive levels of protection. The most extreme defenses are slower and more expensive, but they serve to prevent the user from depending completely on the cooperation of a single operator.

Before describing the operational levels, one must distinguish the foundations on which the entire architecture rests: **the proof system, data availability, and the rules of the canonical bridge.** The proof system must prevent an incorrect state from being recognized as valid. Data availability must make the data necessary to reconstruct the state recoverable. The bridge must establish in a verifiable way how the deposited BTC can be released. Without these conditions, the subsequent defenses risk remaining only theoretical.

First level: prevention. Audits, transparency, monitoring, separation of the roles, and limits on the administrative powers reduce the probability that the sequencer or other operators abuse their own position. The best defense is limiting the power before it has to be countered.

Second level: detection. Dashboards, metrics, alerts, and independent watchers serve to make censorship, downtime, anomalous delays, problems in data availability, and suspicious behaviors in the ordering of the transactions visible. A sanction is useless if the problem stays invisible.

Third level: economic deterrence. Some protocols require bonds or collateral and provide sanctions when an incorrect behavior is demonstrated according to precise rules. **The loss of reputation can add further pressure, but it is not equivalent to a slashing applied automatically by the protocol.** For Bitcoin Hyper it will be necessary to verify whether bonds will exist, which conducts will be punishable, and who will be able to demonstrate them.

Fourth level: challenge and escalation. In optimistic rollups, an independent observer can challenge an invalid transition through a fraud proof or a fault proof. **In ZK models, instead, the validity proof should prevent an incorrect state from being recognized in the first place.** Formal procedures nevertheless remain necessary to manage incidents, operational disputes, and anomalous behaviors.

Fifth level: a possible bypass of the sequencer. An alternative lane serves to prevent a valid transaction from being excluded indefinitely. In the rollups built on Ethereum there are forced transaction mechanisms through the Layer 1. **For Bitcoin Hyper it will be necessary to understand whether an analogous solution will be introduced, with which rules, costs, and time thresholds.**

Sixth level: a possible emergency exit. In the most serious cases, the user should have a credible procedure available to recover their own BTC without depending entirely on the cooperation of the ordinary path. **For Bitcoin Hyper, this protection will have to be documented with precision:** the necessary data, the usable state root, the format of the proof, the bridge rules, the conditions for the release of the BTC, and the management of simultaneous withdrawals.

The rollup's security therefore does not depend on a single protection, but on the overlapping of several defenses. **The first ones operate continuously and try to prevent or detect the problems; the last ones are slower, more expensive, and more complex, but they become decisive in the extreme cases.** For Bitcoin Hyper, the design direction is interesting: ZK proofs, periodic commitments on Bitcoin, the canonical bridge, the monitoring-first architecture, and the path toward decentralization. The real evaluation will however depend on the definitive specifications, on the audits, and on the possibility of concretely verifying every level of the hierarchy.

⁂

21.8 — Questions and Answers: Clarifying the Chapter's Concepts

Question 1: If the forced inclusion and forced exit mechanisms are so important, why are they not already implemented and well documented?

For concrete technical reasons that deserve honesty. **Implementing these mechanisms correctly requires deep integration between Bitcoin and the rollup**, and the integration through the Canonical Bridge is one of the most complex components of the system. While the execution layer (native SVM) is relatively simpler to implement by inheriting from Solana, the bridge is specific to the Bitcoin-Hyper context and must be built from scratch. **Bugs in the bridge are potentially catastrophic**: they could allow malicious actors to steal the held bitcoin, or block the users' funds. For this reason, the bridge requires extensive audits, tests under stress, attack simulations before going into production. **Hyper is probably investing significantly in this work in the pre-mainnet months**, and the complete documentation will arrive when the design is stabilized. **For prudent investors**, monitoring the publication of specific technical documentation on the bridge and on the forced action mechanisms will be one of the most important criteria before the launch. **Without these mechanisms implemented and**

audited, the promise of a "true rollup" remains partial. A concrete example: Optimism implemented forced action mechanisms gradually over time, with various iterations of the design. The complete version arrived years after the initial launch. For Hyper a similar trajectory is expected, even if ideally faster given the maturity of the sector.

Question 2: The forced exit seems very complex to use. Could a normal user really activate it if necessary?

In practice, most users will not build forced exits manually. **They will lean on specialized tools and services** that simplify the process. Integrated wallets could offer "forced exit" as a button, handling all the underlying complexity. Third-party services could offer forced exit as a paid service. The community of independent watchers could publish standardized tools. **The forced exit is therefore more accessible than it may seem from the technical description**, even if it remains a "last resort" operation that most users will never have to use. **That said**, the complexity remains real for pathological situations where all the standard services are compromised or offline. In those scenarios, the users might have to resort to more direct tools, and this would require significant technical skills or specialized assistance. **To minimize these edge cases**, it is important that the community develops diversified, redundant tools, so that if one is offline, others are available. A concrete example: today on Optimism there are various tools to facilitate withdrawals toward Ethereum. Most users do not directly use the bridge's "raw" interface but services that simplify the process. For Hyper the development of a similar ecosystem of tools is expected.

Question 3: What would happen if the Canonical Bridge itself were compromised or had bugs? Would the forced exits still work?

It is the most catastrophic scenario, and it must be faced honestly. **If the Canonical Bridge is compromised, the forced exit mechanisms might not work**, because they depend on the logic of the bridge itself to validate the proofs and release the funds. **In this extreme case**, the users might have no way to recover their own bitcoin. For this reason, the security of the Canonical Bridge is the most critical point of Hyper's entire architecture. **The defenses against this scenario are multiple.** Extensive and repeated audits of the bridge code. Multisignature for the bridge's critical operations, so that no single actor can authorize unilateral actions. Hardware security modules for the cryptographic keys. Significant bug bounties to discover vulnerabilities before the attacks. Emergency procedures for temporary pauses of the bridge in case of detected problems. **Even with all these defenses, the bridge risk is not zero**, and it is one of the reasons why prudent investors diversify among different systems and do not concentrate everything on a single Layer 2. A concrete example: in 2022, various cross-chain bridges had catastrophic exploits (Wormhole, Ronin, Nomad). They are cases that remind one how critical the security of bridges is, and that serve as a warning for Hyper. The team will have to invest significantly to avoid similar fates.

Question 4: If the community is so important for the defenses, how does one build it before the mainnet launch?

It is an important question because it touches the "chicken-and-egg" problem: a community is needed to validate the system, but it is difficult to build a community around a system that does not yet exist. **The possible strategies are several.** Pre-mainnet, the team can attract watchers through high-quality technical research posts, early access programs for developers, technical events, bounties for those who contribute to the analysis of the system. **During and after the launch**, the community grows naturally if the system attracts real usage. The more value operates on the rollup, the more the independent watchers have reasons to take an interest in it. **Investments in open tools** (open source, documentation, public APIs) facilitate the creation of an ecosystem of analysts. **Collaborations with academic institutions and think tanks** can produce quality independent analyses that attract attention. **For Hyper specifically**, inheriting part of the SVM community from Solana is an advantage: researchers who already work on the SVM can extend their own attention to Hyper. **On the other hand**, attracting the more rigorist Bitcoin community, which tends to be skeptical toward sophisticated Layer 2s, will be a specific challenge. The quality of the technical communication and the demonstration of fidelity to Bitcoin's principles will be crucial. A concrete example: Optimism's ecosystem of watchers developed gradually over the course of 2–3 years after the launch. Initially there were few dedicated analysts, today it is a significant industry with dozens of entities. For Hyper a similar trajectory is expected, and the first 12–18 months will be particularly important for establishing the foundations.

Question 5: The defense mechanisms you describe are powerful, but they slow the system down. Is that not a problem for applications that require speed?

It is a real trade-off that deserves recognition. **The most robust security mechanisms tend to require time**: challenge windows, multiple verifications, Bitcoin confirmations. All this adds time compared to a system that simply "trusts" the sequencer. **For applications that require extreme speed**, these times can be problematic. **The answer lies in the distinction between "soft finality" and "hard finality" that we have seen in various chapters.** For the daily operations on the rollup (swaps, payments, interactions with dApps), the users operate with the sequencer's soft finality, which is almost instantaneous. Hard finality (Bitcoin-grade) is reached in longer times (hours or days), but it is important only for certain categories of operations: withdrawals toward native Bitcoin, operations of very high value, long-term custody withdrawals. **Most users, most of the time, do not experience the delays of maximum security**, because they operate inside the soft finality. **The defense mechanisms serve for when things go wrong**, not for the normal functioning. Think of them like insurance: it is not needed for daily driving, but it is essential for when an accident occurs. A concrete example: for a swap on Hyper, the user sees the result in a few seconds (the sequencer's soft finality). If they then want to withdraw the tokens toward native Bitcoin, they will have to wait for hard finality (perhaps a few hours), but for most internal operations this is not necessary.

Question 6: Are there projects that have implemented all these defense mechanisms well, or are they still theoretical?

A combination of the two things, and it is important to be honest about the current state of the art. **The original Bitcoin implemented all its defense mechanisms in an exemplary way**, but its model is simple (native Bitcoin transactions, no complex smart contracts). For rollups, the situation is more complex. **Optimism and Arbitrum on Ethereum have fraud proofs in production**, even if the complete version arrived only recently. Forced inclusions are implemented with various limitations. Forced exit works but with significant times and costs. **zkSync and Era have validity proofs in production**, avoiding some problems of the optimistic rollups but introducing others (the complexity of the zk system). **For Bitcoin rollups, the state of the art is still evolving.** The Bitcoin context poses specific constraints (the lack of complex smart contracts, limited verification capacity) that make certain mechanisms more difficult to implement. **Hyper finds itself in an interesting position**: it can learn from the experience of other rollups, but it must adapt the solutions to the Bitcoin context. **The innovation Hyper must do** is significant, and the quality of this innovation will show only over time. For prudent investors, the realistic expectation is that Hyper will launch with partial defense mechanisms and perfect them over time, similarly to what the Ethereum rollups did in their own first years. A concrete example: Optimism launched the mainnet in 2021 with incomplete security mechanisms, and perfected them over the course of 3–4 years. The complete fault proofs arrived only in 2024. For Hyper a similar trajectory is expected, even if ideally faster.

⁂

21.9 — WHAT TO TAKE AWAY FROM THIS CHAPTER

To build systems that require minimal trust, one must design them starting from the assumption that anyone could become malicious, including the sequencer. The challenge architecture is the set of mechanisms that protects the users in this scenario.

There are at least ten malicious behaviors a sequencer can adopt: selective censorship, strategic delay, manipulation of the order, incorrect state commitments, a refusal to publish data, a service halt, a unilateral change of the rules, collusion, abuse of privileged information, extortion through the emergency mechanisms.

Forced inclusion is the mechanism that allows the users to force the inclusion of their own transactions in the rollup, even if the sequencer does not want to process them. It works through specific Bitcoin transactions that include the rollup's transaction as data.

The forced exit is the mechanism that makes it possible to withdraw bitcoin directly from the Canonical Bridge, without depending on the sequencer's cooperation. It is the definitive mechanism for recovering control of one's own assets in catastrophic scenarios.

The proof model (fraud proof or validity proof) is the backbone of the defenses, translating technical trust into verifiable trust. The proofs make it possible to detect and challenge incorrect behaviors.

The community of independent watchers is an essential component of the defenses. Without an active community, even the best technical mechanisms become theoretical. Data availability, analysis tools, economic incentives, transparency in the disputes are all elements that facilitate the creation of this community.

The defenses form a hierarchy with six levels: prevention, economic deterrence, detection, challenge, bypass, forced exit. Every level has different characteristics, and the system works best when all are well implemented.

For Hyper, the forced inclusion and forced exit mechanisms are still in development. The intention is clearly expressed in the research posts, but the specific implementation details are not yet public. They will be among the most important mechanisms to monitor before the mainnet launch.

The security of the Canonical Bridge is the most critical point of Hyper's entire architecture. Extensive audits, multisignature, hardware security modules, significant bug bounties are all necessary defenses for protecting this component.

The state of the art of the defense mechanisms is still evolving, even for the most mature rollups on Ethereum. For Hyper, the realistic expectation is to launch with partial defenses and perfect them over time, similarly to the trajectory of Optimism and Arbitrum.

Chapter 21 closes here. We have examined in detail the defenses that protect the users against a malicious sequencer, seeing concretely how forced inclusion, the forced exit, the proof model, and the community of watchers combine to form a complete system of protection. From here on, Part VI of the book (Security) closes. We are ready to enter Part VII, dedicated to the developers' experience and to the application ecosystem.

In ***Chapter 22 — The Developer Experience: Inheriting the Solana Ecosystem****, we will see how Bitcoin Hyper, through the choice of the native SVM, inherits an already consolidated ecosystem of tools, libraries, frameworks, and skills. We will examine concretely what it means for a Solana developer to work on Hyper, and how this inheritance can accelerate the creation of applications in the project's first months.*

Defenses against a *malicious* sequencer

How to prevent whoever orders the transactions from also controlling the system's truth. A serious rollup **does not trust the sequencer**: it assumes it can censor, halt, or propose false states, and limits it with **layered defenses**.

1 Not trusting the sequencer: limiting it

Sequencer receives → orders → proposes batches

Proof system verifies the correctness of the state.

Data Availability makes the raw data available.

Bitcoin L1 / Bridge anchors and regulates the settlement.

The sequencer can manage the traffic. **It must not control the system's truth on its own.**

2 Ten risks to distinguish

A · DIRECT POWERS OF SEQUENCING
1 Selective censorship
2 Strategic delay
3 Manipulation of the order
4 Collusion with privileged parties
5 Pre-inclusion info
6 A service halt

B · THEY INVOLVE OTHER COMPONENTS
7 An incorrect state root
8 Unavailable data

C · GOVERNANCE / ADMIN POWERS
9 A unilateral change of the rules
10 Abuse of the emergency procedures

Different threats require different defenses: *censorship, MEV, missing data, and the bridge are not the same problem.*

3 Forced inclusion: the lane against censorship

ORDINARY PATH — fast · cheap · everyday

user → wallet → RPC → sequencer → batch → L2

EMERGENCY LANE · TO CLARIFY FOR HYPER — slower · more expensive · for exceptional cases

user → a request on Bitcoin L1 → the L2 protocol recognizes it → mandatory inclusion

PROTECTS prolonged censorship · sequencer downtime · an indefinite delay

NOT ON ITS OWN front-running · sandwich · an incorrect state root · unavailable data · bridge bugs

4 Forced exit: the bridge's emergency door

🔒 BTC locked in the Canonical Bridge — recoverable without the sequencer's cooperation

ORDINARY WITHDRAWAL

an L2 request → a proof → bridge → BTC on Bitcoin

1 **Available data** reconstructing one's own balance.

2 **A canonical state** which commitment to use.

3 **A verifiable proof** balance, account, Merkle path, root.

4 **A release rule** when the proof opens the vault.

The proof is not enough: **a concrete rule is needed that makes the BTC held by the bridge spendable.**

5 Layered defenses and independent sentinels

- **Proof system** prevents invalid states · ZK declared.
- **Data Availability** makes the state reconstructible.
- **The bridge rules** when the BTC can exit.

1 **Prevention** audits, separated roles
2 **Detection** dashboards, alerts
3 **Deterrence** bonds/slashing · to verify
4 **Challenge** ZK validity proofs
5 **Bypass** forced inclusion
6 **Emergency exit** forced exit

node operators · data archivists · auditors · researchers · MEV analysts · public dashboards

The community does not replace the protocol: *it prevents it from becoming a black box.*

THE KEY POINT

A sequencer can order the transactions, but it must not be able to **block the users indefinitely**, impose false states, or close the exit door. The defense is born from several levels: proofs, available data, a verifiable bridge, independent watchers, forced inclusion and forced exit. For Bitcoin Hyper the direction is clear; the **credibility** will depend on the technical specifications, the audits, and the public tests.

PART VII

Developer Experience and the Ecosystem

Inheriting the Solana ecosystem means precise practical consequences for those who will build on top of Hyper. Tools, observability, infrastructure.

PART VII · DEVELOPER EXPERIENCE AND THE ECOSYSTEM

Chapter 22
The Developer Experience

Inheriting the Solana ecosystem

22.1 — The Decisive Factor Many Underestimate

If you ask an average crypto investor what makes a Layer 2 successful, they will probably speak of security, low costs, speed, tokenomics[a]. All correct. But if you ask an experienced technology entrepreneur, or an engineer who has seen many projects be born and die, they will give you a different answer: **the most underestimated factor in the success of a blockchain platform is the quality of the developer experience[b].** Not the elegance of the whitepaper[c], not the sophistication of the consensus[d], not the marketing numbers. It is the ease with which a developer can build something real, test it, deploy it, and make it work well for the users.

---

[a] **Tokenomics.** The set of economic rules of a crypto project: how many tokens exist, how they are distributed, at what rate they enter circulation, and which incentives they create. It is often at the center of marketing, but on its own it says nothing about the technical solidity or the actual usefulness of the system.

[b] **Developer experience.** It is the overall ease with which a programmer manages to build, test, and put an application into operation on a platform: it depends on the quality of the tools, of the documentation, of the examples, and of the support. It is a factor often invisible to end users but decisive, because a network attracts applications — and therefore value — only if building on top of it is simple and reliable. Ethereum and Solana owe a large part of their success precisely to an excellent developer experience.

[c] **Whitepaper.** It is the document with which a project presents its own vision, architecture, and objectives. It serves to communicate the idea, but it describes intentions, not results: an elegant whitepaper does not guarantee that the system works or gets adopted. For this reason, in a due diligence, it should be read as a starting point to verify — comparing it with code, tools, and real applications — not as proof of what the project is already able to do.

[d] **Consensus.** The mechanism with which the nodes of a network agree on a single shared version of the transactions. It can be technically sophisticated, but on its own it does not determine the success of a platform: what counts more is how easy and reliable it is to build on top of it.

TABLE 22.1 **WHAT MAKES A LAYER 2 SUCCESSFUL: PERCEPTION AND REALITY.**

What gets noticed first	What really decides
Security and speed	The ease of building applications
Low costs	The quality of the development tools
Tokenomics and marketing	Developers who stay over time

The most visible elements of a Layer 2 are not the ones that determine its success. An infrastructure prospers when developers manage to build, test, and distribute applications with ease: it is the development experience, more than the technology itself, that transforms a project into a living ecosystem.

FIGURE 22.1 **FROM THE INFRASTRUCTURE TO THE APPLICATIONS: THE DECISIVE ROLE OF THE DEVELOPERS.**

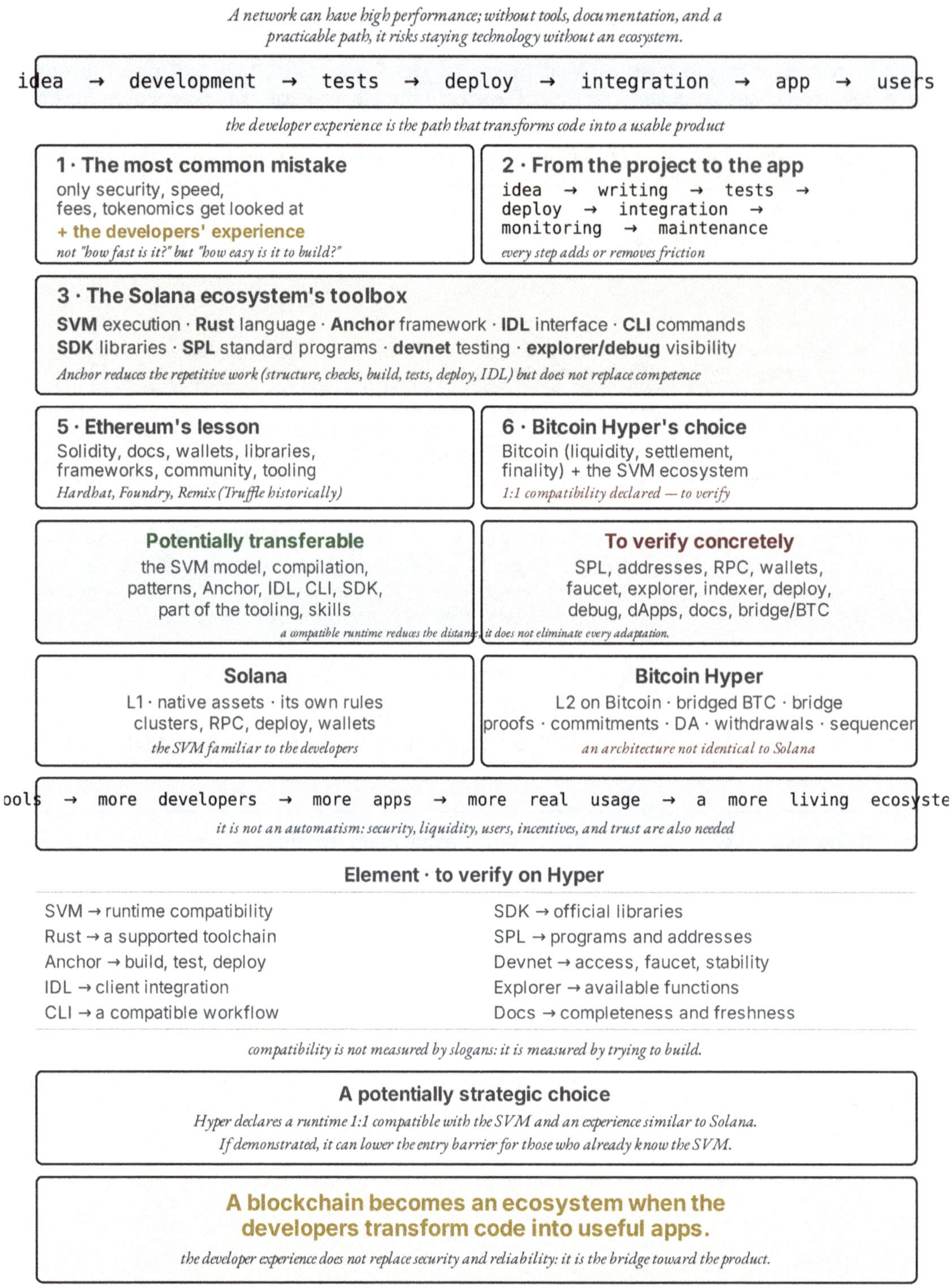

The developer experience is the bridge between infrastructure and applications. A compatible SVM runtime can allow the developers to find familiar concepts, tools, and workflows again. The compatibility declared by Bitcoin Hyper will have to be verified through a public devnet, technical documentation, standard programs, RPC endpoints, deployment tools, and reproducible examples.

The expression developer experience does not mean only the ease of programming. **It means the entire environment in which the developer works: languages, frameworks, libraries,**

documentation, testing tools, RPC endpoints, test environments, explorers, debugging, and the community's support. Every step — writing the code, testing it, spotting the errors, distributing it, connecting it to wallets and interfaces, monitoring it, and updating it — can make the path simpler or more difficult.

Ethereum's history offers a useful lesson. **Ethereum did not establish itself because it was technically perfect.** Its growth depended on several factors, but one of the most important was the progressive development of an environment in which building turned out possible: Solidity, documentation, wallets, libraries, frameworks, and an ever wider community. Over time different tools emerged: Truffle and Ganache played a relevant role in the first phase; today the landscape includes environments like Hardhat, Foundry, and Remix.

Solana too invested in a recognizable development experience. **Anchor has become one of the main frameworks for building Solana programs and it simplifies writing, testing, deployment, and interaction with the on-chain programs.** Around the SVM there are moreover command-line tools, SDKs, standardized programs, test environments, and development patterns by now known to an international community.

For Bitcoin Hyper, the choice of a runtime declared compatible with the SVM therefore represents a strategic possibility. **The official site states that the runtime is 1:1 compatible with the SVM and that, from the developer's point of view, the devnet uses the same commands and a behavior analogous to Solana.** If this compatibility gets demonstrated concretely, the developers already used to the SVM environment will be able to find familiar concepts, tools, and workflows again.

Compatibility however does not mean complete identity. **Hyper is not Solana: it is a Layer 2 connected to Bitcoin, with a canonical bridge, cryptographic proofs, periodic state commitments, data availability, and withdrawal procedures toward the Layer 1.** It will therefore be necessary to understand which tools can be reused without changes, which standard programs are really available, and which adaptations are required by the new context.

The decisive question is not only whether Hyper uses the SVM. **The question is how faithfully it manages to transfer the developer's path: installation, build, tests, deployment, RPC, explorer, debugging, libraries, and documentation.** A compatible runtime is an important starting point; to become a competitive advantage it must transform itself into a really usable development experience.

In this chapter I want to do four things. First, what inheriting an SVM environment means from the developer's point of view. Second, which tools can be reused and which must be adapted. Third, which differences derive from the fact that Hyper is not Solana, but a Layer 2 connected to Bitcoin. Fourth, which concrete signals will make it possible to understand whether the declared compatibility will really translate into an application ecosystem.

⁂

22.2 — What Inheriting a Development Ecosystem Really Means

Before descending into the specific details, it is worth making conceptual clarity on what "inheriting a development ecosystem[a]" means. It is not an abstraction: it is a concrete set of resources that required years and millions of dollars to be built, and that become available to Hyper without a specific development cost.

TABLE 22.2 **WHAT INHERITING A DEVELOPMENT ECOSYSTEM MEANS.**

Inherited resource	Why it counts
Language and framework[b]	Rust[c] and Anchor[d] already known to SVM developers
Libraries and tools[e]	Reusable code without rewriting it
Widespread skills[f]	An already formed community of developers

Inheriting an ecosystem is not an abstraction: it means making immediately available resources — languages, tools, skills — that required years and substantial investments to be built. It is the most concrete potential advantage of the choice of the SVM, to verify however in the real portability[g].

---

[a] **Development ecosystem.** The set of languages, tools, libraries, documentation, and competent people that revolve around a technology. Inheriting it means starting with all of this already ready, instead of having to build it from zero — an enormous saving of time and resources.

[b] **Language and framework.** The programming language (Rust) and the basic tools (like Anchor) with which the programs get written. By inheriting them from Solana, Hyper allows the developers already expert in the SVM to work without having to learn anything new.

[c] **Rust.** A modern programming language, known for speed and safety, adopted by Solana and by the SVM for writing the on-chain programs. Being already widespread means that many developers know how to use it without having to start over from scratch.

[d] **Anchor.** The most used framework for developing programs on the SVM: it provides ready structures and automatisms that simplify the work and make it safer, reducing the code to write by hand.

[e] **Libraries and tools.** Collections of code already ready and tested — for example for managing tokens or exchanges — that the developers reuse instead of rewriting everything from zero. They reduce times, costs, and errors.

[f] **Widespread skills.** The set of developers who already know the SVM environment. It is a "network effect" advantage: the more people master a technology, the easier it is to find talents, examples, and support.

[g] **Portability.** The ease with which a program written for one platform (here Solana) can be transferred to and work on another (Hyper) without substantial changes. It is the real testing ground of the declared inheritance: it must be verified, not taken for granted.

FIGURE 22.2 **THE SVM COMPATIBILITY BRIDGE.**

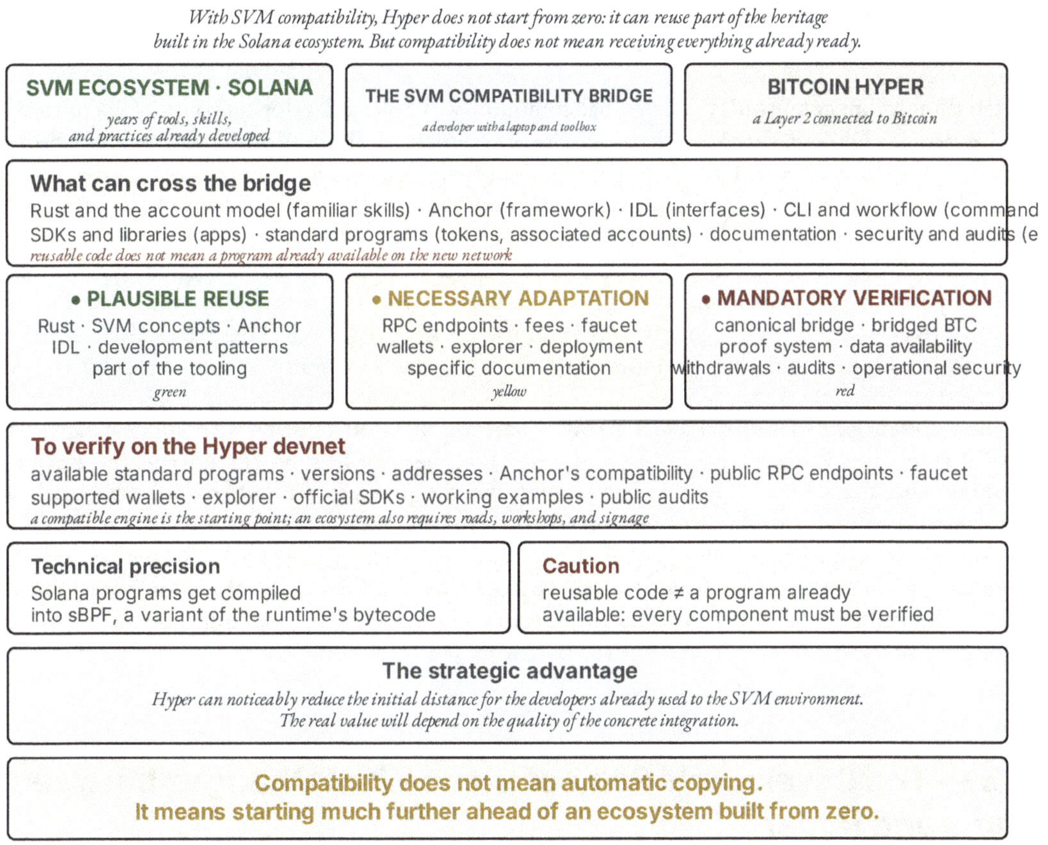

SVM compatibility can allow Bitcoin Hyper to reuse skills, development models, and part of the tooling matured in the Solana ecosystem. The advantage is not automatic: standard programs, versions, addresses, RPC, wallets, explorer, deployment procedures, and audits must be verified in the specific context of the rollup connected to Bitcoin.

First dimension: language and runtime. Solana uses Rust as the main language for the programs (smart contracts), compiled into eBPF (extended Berkeley Packet Filter) as executable bytecode. **For Bitcoin Hyper, this means that the developers write in Rust exactly as they would for Solana**, and the produced bytecode runs natively on Hyper. There is no new language to learn, no new syntax to adapt to, no new execution paradigm to understand.

Second dimension: development framework. Anchor is the standard framework for building Solana programs, and it has revolutionized the SVM developer experience since its launch. Anchor provides decorators and macros that enormously simplify development: automatic management of serialization, validation of the accounts, generation of the IDL (Interface Definition Language), integrated tests. **For Hyper, Anchor works practically without changes.** A developer who has experience with Anchor can build programs for Hyper with the same productivity they would have on Solana.

Third dimension: standard libraries. SPL (Solana Program Library) contains standard implementations of many common patterns: tokens (the equivalent of Ethereum's ERC-20), NFTs (the equivalent of ERC-721/1155), governance, vesting, staking. **These libraries have been tested for years in production on Solana**, they have passed extensive audits, they have been used to manage billions of dollars of value. Hyper inherits them for free, and the developers can build complex applications leaning on already consolidated components.

Fourth dimension: tooling. Solana has developed an ecosystem rich in tools: the Solana CLI for interacting with the blockchain, the Solana Test Validator for local testing, the Solana Explorer for visualizing transactions, various debuggers and profilers. **For Hyper, these tools work by changing only the network endpoint**, as we saw in Chapter 9. The learning curve for starting to develop on Hyper is practically zero for those coming from Solana.

Fifth dimension: documentation and tutorials. The Solana ecosystem has produced enormous quantities of documentation: official guides, tutorials, code examples, videos, courses. **All this material is in large part directly applicable to Hyper**, even if produced for Solana. A developer who wants to learn SVM development finds abundant resources, and can apply what they learn both on Solana and on Hyper.

Sixth dimension: community. The global community of Solana developers counts tens of thousands of active people: Discord, forums, Twitter/X, Stack Overflow, GitHub. **Technical questions find rapid answers**, common problems have documented solutions, experts are available for consultations. For Hyper, this community is in large part accessible, even if initially it will be necessary to build specific communities for Hyper's unique themes (the Canonical Bridge, settlement on Bitcoin, and so on).

Seventh dimension: security practices. The Solana ecosystem has developed specific security practices: patterns for correctly managing the accounts, standard signature checks, protections against common attacks (reentrancy, signature malleability, integer overflow). **These practices are directly applicable to Hyper**, and the developers benefit from the experience accumulated by the Solana community.

Eighth dimension: specialized audit firms. There are many audit firms with specific experience in the SVM (OtterSec, Halborn, Neodyme, and others). **Hyper can lean on these firms for audits of its own smart contracts**, benefiting from their consolidated expertise. Without this inheritance, it would be necessary to wait years for firms to develop specific expertise on a new runtime.

Putting these eight dimensions together, what emerges is that inheriting the Solana ecosystem is an enormous competitive asset. **It is equivalent to receiving for free years of accumulated work and hundreds of millions of dollars of the ecosystem's investments.** Hyper must do its own work to integrate the specific Bitcoin context, but the base work is already done.

⁂

22.3 — The Developer's Point of View: What Changes between Solana and Hyper

To give concreteness, let us describe the practical experience of a developer who wants to port an application from Solana to Hyper, or build a new one specific to Hyper. Let us see what changes and what stays identical, because this detail determines the speed with which the application ecosystem can grow.

FIGURE 22.3 **FROM SOLANA TO HYPER: WHAT STAYS IDENTICAL, WHAT CHANGES.**

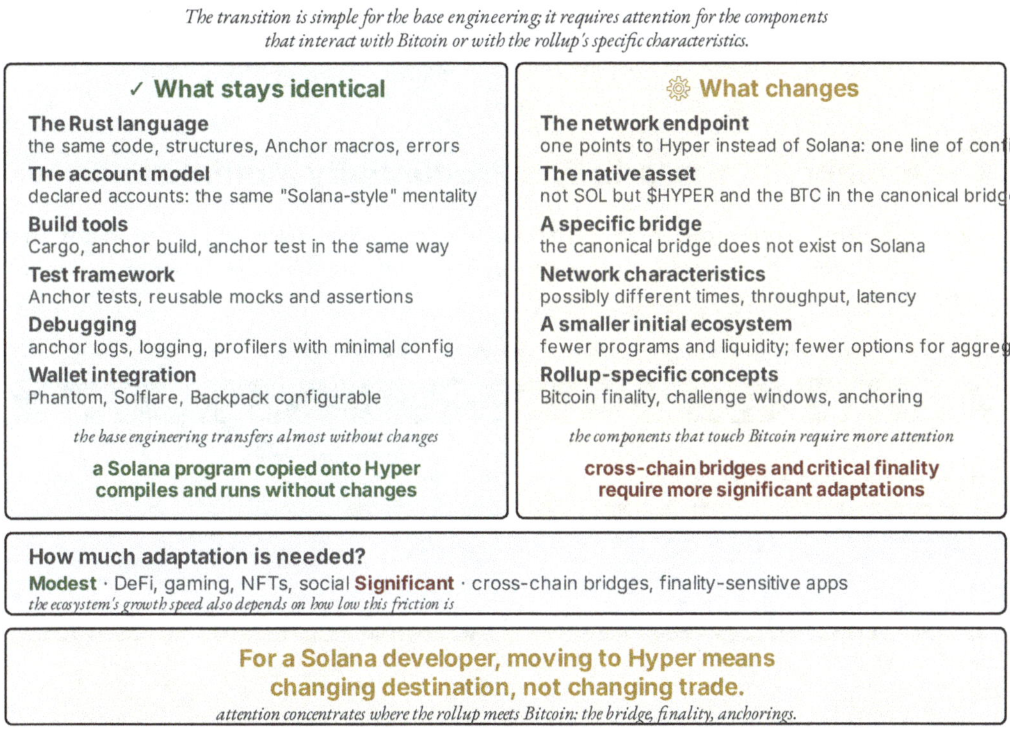

The transition from Solana to Hyper is relatively simple for the base engineering — language, account model, build, tests, debugging, and wallet integration stay almost identical — but it requires specific attention for the components that interact with Bitcoin or with the rollup's characteristics: the native asset, the canonical bridge, finality, challenge windows, and anchoring. For DeFi, gaming, NFTs, and social the adaptations are modest; for cross-chain applications or ones sensitive to finality times they are more significant.

The first part of the path should turn out familiar. **Bitcoin Hyper declares a 1:1 compatibility with the SVM and states that it natively executes Solana programs on its own rollup architecture.** If this compatibility gets fully confirmed by the devnet, a developer will be able to keep using Rust, the account model typical of the SVM, and many of the already known patterns.

Anchor too could represent an important point of continuity. The framework is used in the Solana ecosystem for writing, testing, distributing, and connecting the programs to the applications. The workflow includes tools like `anchor build` and `anchor test`, while the RPC endpoints establish to which network the operations get sent.

This however does not mean that a dApp can be copied from Solana to Hyper by pressing a single button. **Some elements will have to be configured or verified: RPC endpoints, fees, deployment, SDKs, wallets, explorer, standard programs, and debugging tools.** A compatible runtime reduces the distance, but an application ecosystem also requires working infrastructures around the runtime.

There are moreover characteristics specific to the new context. On Solana the native asset used for the fees is SOL. **Bitcoin Hyper's official documentation instead indicates HYPER as the network's native token, destined for transactions, staking, and governance.** The project also describes a canonical bridge for the deposit and withdrawal of the BTC, a Bitcoin Relay Program, ZK proofs, and periodic commitments of the state on Bitcoin Layer 1.

For a developer, these differences become relevant above all when the application interacts directly with Bitcoin or with the rollup's infrastructure. **A simple application built around SVM logic might require contained adaptations; a service that manages deposits, withdrawals, finality, or assets coming from the bridge instead requires a deeper understanding of Hyper's specific architecture.**

The initial ecosystem too will inevitably be different. Solana already has wallets, programs, liquidity, protocols, and integrations developed over time. Hyper will have to demonstrate which components are actually available on its own devnet and which external services really support the new network.

The concluding point is simple. SVM compatibility can noticeably reduce the learning curve; it does not however eliminate the need to verify the concrete integration. **The decisive question is not only whether a program can be compiled, but whether it can be distributed, tested, and used reliably by the users.** The engine can be familiar; the road is not exactly the same.

⁂

22.4 — Anchor Framework: The Productivity Multiplier

It is worth dedicating a specific section to the Anchor framework, because it is probably the most impactful tool of the SVM developer experience, and understanding its characteristics helps to understand why the Solana ecosystem grew so rapidly.

FIGURA 22.4 **ANCHOR: THE PRODUCTIVITY MULTIPLIER, FROM CODE TO DAPP.**

FIGURE 22.5 **FROM THE SVM HERITAGE TO THE HYPER ECOSYSTEM.**

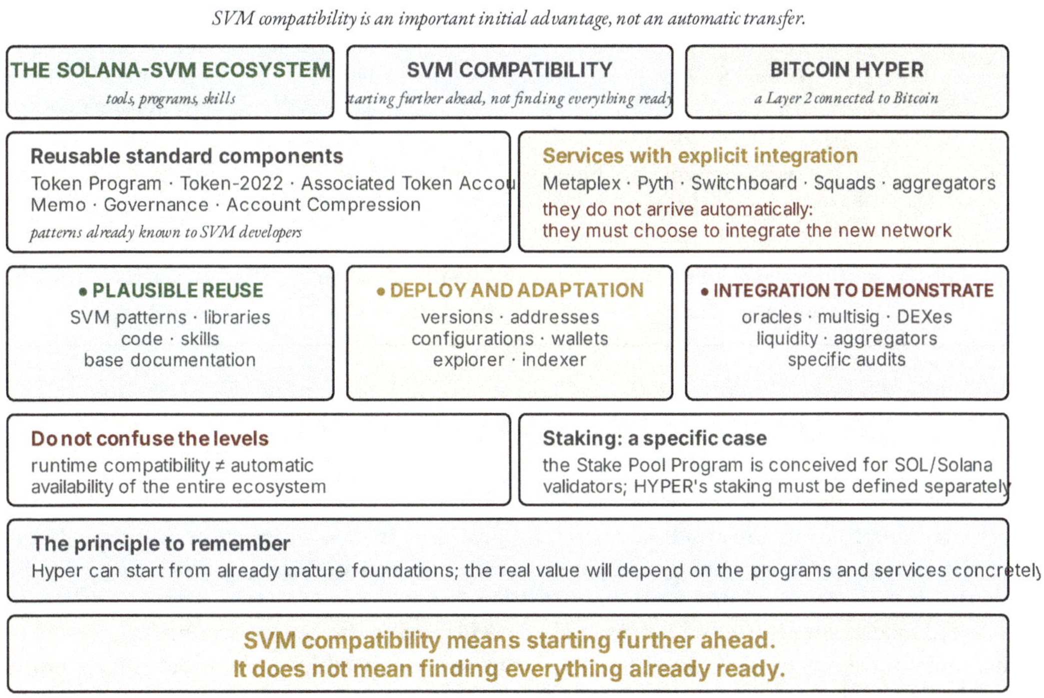

SVM compatibility can allow Bitcoin Hyper to reuse code, skills, and programs matured in the Solana ecosystem. The actual availability is however not automatic: standard programs, versions, addresses, wallets, explorer, and external services must be distributed, integrated, and verified in the new context.

TABLE 22.4 **WHICH COMPONENTS OF THE SOLANA ECOSYSTEM COULD BE REUSED?**

Component	What is it for?	Possible value for Hyper	What to verify?
Token Program	creating, transferring, minting, and burning tokens	models already known to SVM developers	deployment, address, wallets, explorer
Token-2022	tokens with additional functionality	more sophisticated applications	supported extensions, compatibility, audits
Associated Token Account	a standard account for every wallet and token	simpler integration	availability and address of the program
Memo Program	annotations associated with the transactions	payments and classification	support and explorer
Governance	on-chain proposals and votes	building DAOs	version, deployment, integration
Account Compression	managing large quantities of data or assets	apps with many users or digital objects	indexer, data recoverability, audits

Metaplex	digital assets, collections, and metadata	NFTs and gaming	supported standards and integrations
Oracles	verifiable external data	DeFi applications	integration of Pyth, Switchboard, or others
Multisig	shared management of funds and authorizations	teams and DAOs	Squads or equivalent tools
Aggregators	searching for the best exchange routes	a more efficient user experience	active DEXes, liquidity, integrations

SVM compatibility reduces the initial work, but it does not automatically make every component available. To become usable, each program or service must be distributed, configured, integrated, and verified in the new environment.

Beyond Anchor, the Solana ecosystem makes available numerous standard programs, libraries, and services that simplify the construction of the applications. **It is an important heritage, because it spares the developers from having to recreate every component starting from zero.** For Bitcoin Hyper, the declared compatibility with the SVM therefore represents a potential advantage: a part of the code and models already used on Solana could be readapted to the new environment.

One must however avoid a simplification: **runtime compatibility does not mean automatic availability of the entire ecosystem.** Every program must be distributed on the new network, configured correctly, and integrated with wallets, explorer, and applications.

Among the most relevant standard components are the **Token Program**, which manages the creation, transfer, minting, and burning of the tokens, and its evolution **Token-2022**, which adds advanced optional functionality like fees on the transfers or delegations. The **Associated Token Account** provides an easily findable standard account for every wallet and token, simplifying the integration of the applications. The **Memo Program** makes it possible to add short annotations to the transactions, useful for payments and the classification of the operations.

For the more complex applications there are the **Governance** program, which manages on-chain proposals and votes for the construction of DAOs[a], and **Account Compression**, which reduces the cost of managing large quantities of accounts or assets and can favor applications with many users or digital objects. On the digital-asset front, **Metaplex** manages collections, metadata, and royalties and is the base of the NFT and gaming ecosystem.

An important part of the ecosystem, however, is not made up of simple libraries, but of **external services that must choose to integrate the new network.** Oracles[b] like **Pyth** and **Switchboard** bring verifiable external data necessary to the DeFi protocols; multisignature tools like **Squads** allow teams and DAOs to manage funds and authorizations in a shared way; the **aggregators** search for the most convenient exchange routes among the different DEXes[c], improving the users' experience. These services do not arrive automatically: their presence will depend on the integrations actually realized.

A particular case concerns **staking.** Solana's Stake Pool Program is designed for SOL and for the Solana validators; HYPER's staking model will therefore have to be defined separately and cannot be taken for granted as a simple inheritance.

The overall picture is therefore twofold. On one hand, Hyper can start from already mature foundations, avoiding reinventing consolidated components. **On the other, the speed with which the application ecosystem will develop will depend on which programs and services get concretely distributed, integrated, and verified in the new environment.** How many projects will decide to port their own applications or build new ones specifically for Hyper is the next theme to face.

⁂

22.6 — Strategies for Attracting Developers and Applications

Even with the best developer experience in the world, a Layer 2 needs real developers and applications to be successful. **Inheriting the Solana ecosystem is a great advantage, but it requires active strategies to translate itself into effective adoption.** Let us see the main strategies that Hyper can use and that we already see mentioned in the project's posts.

---

[a] **DAO (decentralized autonomous organization).** A form of organization whose operating rules and whose decisions are managed collectively by the participants through votes recorded on the chain, without a central authority. The governance programs serve precisely to build and manage them.

[b] **Oracles.** Services that bring onto the blockchain data coming from the external world — for example market prices — in verifiable form. They are indispensable to the financial applications (DeFi), which without a reliable price could not operate correctly.

[c] **DEX (decentralized exchange).** A crypto-asset exchange platform that operates through programs on the chain, without an intermediary that has custody of the funds. The aggregators compare several DEXes to find the most convenient exchange route for the user.

Strategy one: direct economic incentives. Grant programs offer financing to developers who build applications on the rollup. **The grants can go from a few thousand to hundreds of thousands of dollars**, depending on the scale of the project. Hyper can use part of its own token treasury to finance a robust grant program, attracting developers who otherwise might not consider the project. Historical examples of effective programs include the grants of Optimism, Arbitrum, and Base, which have catalyzed the development of hundreds of applications.

Strategy two: liquidity mining and incentives for the users. To attract real users to the applications built on Hyper, incentives can be needed: rewards in tokens for those who provide liquidity, airdrops for those who use specific applications, prizes for those who reach certain milestones. **These incentives create the initial network effects necessary** for an application to be able to take off. Without users, the applications die; without applications, the users do not come.

FIGURE 22.6 **FROM THE TECHNOLOGY TO THE ECOSYSTEM: THE VIRTUOUS CIRCLE OF ADOPTION.**

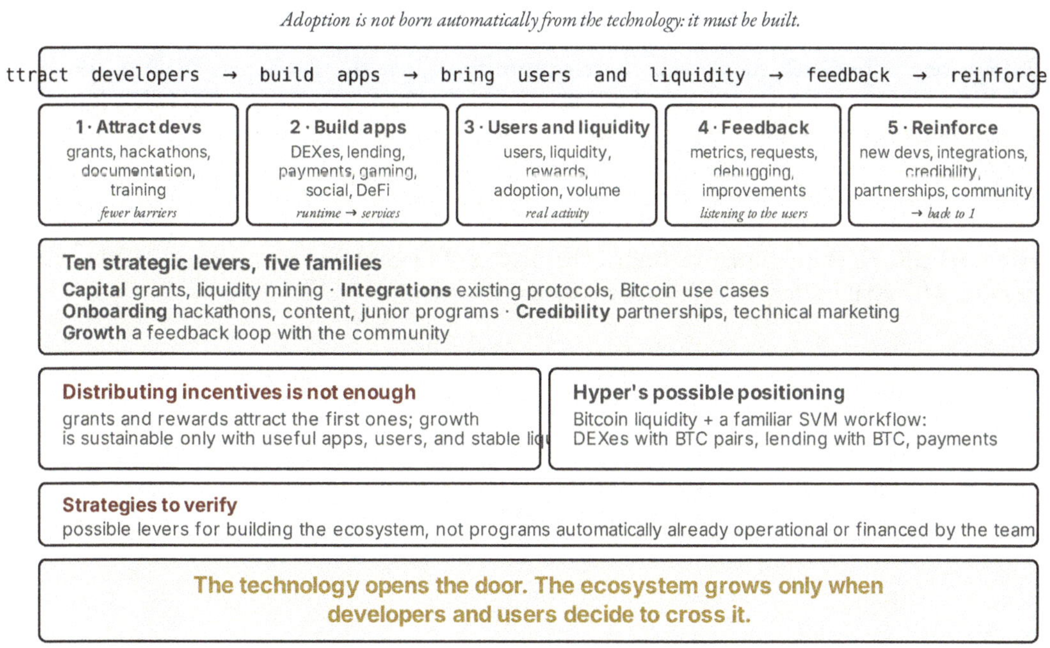

The growth of a blockchain ecosystem requires a virtuous circle: tools and incentives attract developers, the developers build applications, the applications bring users and liquidity, the feedback improves the infrastructure, and the greater credibility attracts new projects. SVM compatibility can offer Bitcoin Hyper an initial advantage, but adoption must be built over time.

Strategy three: integrations with existing protocols. Convincing already established Solana protocols to deploy also on Hyper enormously accelerates the maturation of the ecosystem. If Jupiter, Marinade, Drift, or other Solana leaders decide to support Hyper, the ecosystem starts already with competitive levels of liquidity and functionality. **Hyper can facilitate these integrations** by offering technical support, favorable economic conditions, joint marketing.

Strategy four: a focus on specific use cases. Instead of competing with Solana or Ethereum on all fronts, Hyper can position itself on specific use cases where it has distinctive advantages. The main one is clear: **applications that want to access native Bitcoin liquidity through a Solana-grade developer experience.** This includes DEXes that support BTC pairs, lending protocols with BTC as collateral, derivatives tied to BTC, payment applications. **Specializing in this niche can attract developers who have no comparable alternatives elsewhere.**

Strategy five: hackathons and events. Hackathons offer developers opportunities to explore the system, build prototypes, receive mentoring. **Solana has had enormous successes with its own hackathons** (Solana Breakpoint, Solana Hyperdrive), which have generated dozens of successful projects. Hyper can do the same, possibly collaborating with Solana for joint events.

Strategy six: educational content. Tutorials, documentation, videos, courses specific to Hyper help to lower the entry barrier. **Some of the greatest successes in attracting developers have come from free educational content of high quality,** like that produced by the Solana Foundation and by organizations of the community. Hyper must invest in the production of content specific to the project's unique themes (the Canonical Bridge, the integration with Bitcoin, the proof model).

Strategy seven: partnerships with academia and institutions. Collaborations with universities for research, academic workshops, technical conferences help to build technical credibility and to attract high-level talent. **The original Bitcoin benefited significantly from academic studies**, and Hyper can do the same with its own specific innovations.

Strategy eight: programs for junior developers. While attracting senior developers is important, building a pipeline of junior developers who learn on Hyper is a long-term investment. **Training programs, bootcamps, internships, scholarships can create the next generations of Hyper developers.**

Strategy nine: developer-focused marketing. Differently from marketing for users, marketing for developers requires specific approaches: presence at technical conferences, contributions to technical discussions, technical blog posts of high quality, sponsorship of relevant open source projects. **Building a technical reputation in the developer community is the work of years**, but it is essential for long-term success.

Strategy ten: a feedback loop with the community. When the developers use the system and identify limits or feature requests, the project's team must listen and respond. **A team that ignores the developer community rapidly loses credibility**, while a team that incorporates the feedback builds long-term loyalty.

For Hyper, the execution of these strategies will be one of the main factors in the success or failure of the project. **The technology inherits a lot from Solana, but the community and the application ecosystem specific to Hyper must be built.** The first 12–18 months after the launch of the mainnet will be crucial for establishing the foundations of this ecosystem.

FIGURE 22.7 **WHAT HYPER INHERITS AND WHAT IT MUST STILL BUILD.**

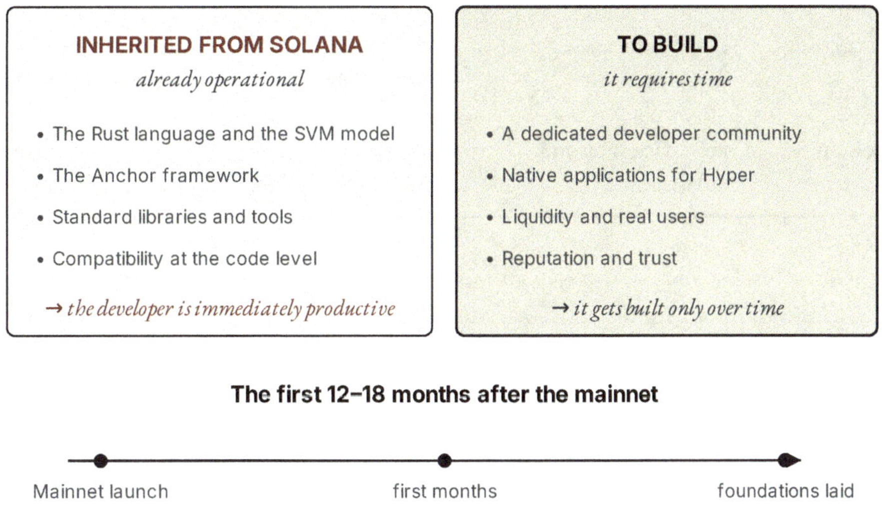

The technology is inherited; the community and the ecosystem are the real challenge.

Compatibility with Solana zeroes the learning curve and makes a developer immediately productive, but it does not automatically transfer community, applications, and liquidity: these must be built from zero. It is in the first twelve to eighteen months after the launch of the mainnet that it will become clear whether the foundations of Hyper's specific ecosystem manage to consolidate.

TABLE 22.5 **TEN STRATEGIES FOR BUILDING THE APPLICATION ECOSYSTEM.**

Strategy	Objective	Potential advantage	What to verify?
Grants for the developers	financing new applications	reducing the projects' initial cost	budget, criteria, transparency, results
Liquidity mining	bringing users and liquidity	initial activity and network effects	duration, sustainability, quality of the users
Integration with protocols	bringing already known services	accelerating the maturation	real agreements, deployment, security, liquidity
A focus on use cases	positioning where there is an advantage	avoiding generic competition	real demand, differentiation, usefulness
Hackathons and events	prototypes and meetings between teams	letting projects and talents emerge	participants, quality, continuity
Documentation and content	reducing the learning curve	building more rapidly	updated guides, examples, tutorials, support
Partnerships with universities	technical credibility and research	attracting skills and talents	concrete collaborations, workshops, projects

Programs for juniors	a pipeline of new skills	strengthening the ecosystem over time	bootcamps, scholarships, internships, continuity
Technical marketing	a reputation among the developers	reaching teams and open source projects	quality of the content, credibility of the team
A feedback loop	improving tools and infrastructure	transforming the problems into updates	public channels, response speed, roadmap

The strategies do not all have the same effect and must not be considered automatically already operational. Sustainable growth is born from the combination of initial incentives, useful applications, real liquidity, effective documentation, and continuous listening to the developers.

⁂

22.7 — Risks and Limits of the SVM Inheritance

To be honest in the evaluation, we must also face the risks and the limits of inheriting the Solana ecosystem. Not everything is positive, and ignoring the weak points would be dishonest.

FIGURE 22.7·A **RISKS AND LIMITS OF THE SVM INHERITANCE — FIRST PART: THE FOUR INITIAL RISKS (TECHNICAL, STRUCTURAL, CULTURAL, OF ECOSYSTEM).**

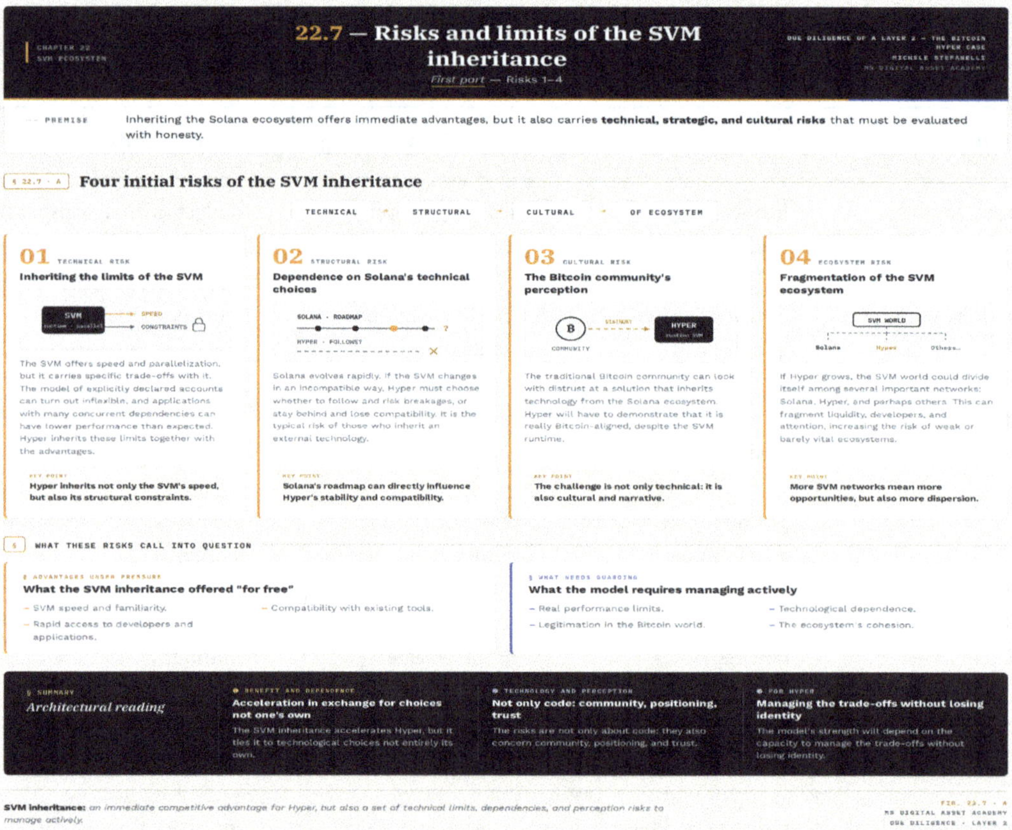

First risk: inheriting the limits of the SVM. The SVM has made specific design choices that have trade-offs. **The model of explicitly declared accounts, for example, is fast but inflexible**: certain patterns that are simple on Ethereum require workarounds on the SVM. **Parallel execution requires**

attention to the dependencies, and applications that have many accounts in concurrent reading/writing can have worse performance than expected. **For Hyper, these limits apply in the same way as on Solana**, and the developers must understand them.

Second risk: dependence on Solana's technical choices. Solana evolves continuously, and the decisions of the Solana team influence what is possible on Hyper. If Solana introduces breaking changes in the SVM, Hyper must decide whether to follow (risking breaking existing applications) or to stay behind (risking losing compatibility). **This is a structural risk of any project that inherits a third-party technology.**

Third risk: the Bitcoin community's perception. The traditional Bitcoin ecosystem tends to be skeptical toward technologies associated with other ecosystems. **Hyper, being based on the SVM, could be perceived as "less Bitcoin" compared to alternatives that use more Bitcoin-native languages (like Stacks with Clarity, or BitVM).** Convincing the Bitcoin community that Hyper is genuinely Bitcoin-aligned, despite the different technological inheritance, will be a cultural challenge.

Fourth risk: fragmentation of the SVM ecosystem. If Hyper is successful, there will be at least two major SVM networks (Solana and Hyper), plus potentially others. **This fragmentation divides the community, divides the liquidity, divides the developers.** Every network must justify its own existence, and there is a risk that some become "dead ecosystems" if they do not manage to attract sufficient activity.

FIGURE 22.7·B **RISKS AND LIMITS OF THE SVM INHERITANCE — SECOND PART: THE FOUR SUBSEQUENT RISKS (DEPENDENCE, GROWTH, OPERATIONAL, PERCEPTION).**

Fifth risk: dependence on Anchor. Anchor is an essential tool, but it is maintained by a specific entity (Coral Network, part of the Backpack ecosystem). If Anchor stops being actively maintained, or if it has problems, Hyper suffers. **This is a risk of dependence on a single critical component**, mitigated by the availability of the open source code but not eliminated completely.

Sixth risk: Solana-ported vs Hyper-native applications. Applications simply "ported" from Solana to Hyper might not fully exploit Hyper's distinctive characteristics (the integration with Bitcoin, the specific finality, and so on). **To grow truly, Hyper needs not only porting but native applications** that are built specifically for its context. Building these applications requires developers who understand both the SVM and Bitcoin deeply.

Seventh risk: subtle differences that cause bugs. Even if Hyper inherits largely from the SVM, there are differences (the Bitcoin finality, the Canonical Bridge, possible performance differences). **Applications that assume certain characteristics of Solana could behave unexpectedly on Hyper**. Identifying and managing these differences is continuous work.

Eighth risk: the perception of "copying" instead of innovating. Some voices in the community could criticize Hyper for "not innovating enough" and for "sticking the SVM onto Bitcoin". **Defending**

the choice of the SVM as a strategically solid decision requires clear communication: Hyper's innovation is not in the runtime, but in the integration of the SVM with Bitcoin through the Canonical Bridge and in the settlement mechanisms.

Putting these risks together, what emerges is that inheriting the Solana ecosystem is an enormous competitive asset, but it is not free of trade-offs. **For the investors and the developers who evaluate Hyper, considering both the benefits and the risks of the inheritance is important.** The benefits are significant and immediate; the risks manifest themselves over time and require active management.

⁂

22.8 — Questions and Answers: Clarifying the Chapter's Concepts

Question 1: If it is so easy to port applications from Solana to Hyper, why should developers choose Hyper instead of Solana?

The question is central, and the answer depends on the specific context of the application. **For applications that have no need to interact with Bitcoin, Solana is probably the better choice**: a more mature ecosystem, higher liquidity, a bigger community, more numerous complementary applications. **For applications that derive value from the integration with Bitcoin, Hyper becomes attractive**: access to native bitcoin, security anchored to Bitcoin, a "Bitcoin rollup" narrative that has strong appeal in certain segments of the market. Examples of ideal applications for Hyper: DEXes that want native BTC liquidity, lending protocols where BTC is collateral, derivatives on BTC, payment applications that want Bitcoin-grade settlement. **In summary, Hyper does not replace Solana; the two networks have different value propositions.** A concrete example: a protocol like MakerDAO, which wants to broaden its own collateral base beyond Ethereum, could find Hyper attractive for offering CDPs backed by native BTC. On Solana, this would not be possible with the same elegance, because Solana has no native integration with Bitcoin.

Question 2: Is the Anchor framework really so revolutionary? It does not seem like it does anything particularly special.

Anchor's impact is easy to underestimate if one has never written Solana programs in pure Rust. **Try for a moment to think about how much repetitive code is needed to manage serialization, deserialization, validation of accounts, error handling manually.** For real applications, this repetitive code can represent 70–80% of the total. **Anchor automates practically all of this**, leaving the developers only the 20–30% of actual application logic. **The impact on productivity is enormous**, and on the quality of the code too: less manual code means fewer bugs, fewer attack surfaces, fewer vulnerabilities. For an executive who must decide whether to build on Solana/Hyper or on Ethereum, the difference between "20–30% of application code with a modern framework" and "10–15% of application code with an equivalent EVM framework" is significant in development times. A concrete example: a team that wants to build a simple DEX might take 2–3 months on Ethereum with modern tooling, and 1–1.5 months on Solana with Anchor. The difference multiplies for more complex projects.

Question 3: How expensive will it be for Hyper to attract developers? Is it a sustainable investment?

The costs are significant but proportionate to the long-term benefits. **Typical grant programs for Layer 2s have budgets on the order of tens or hundreds of millions of dollars**, distributed over periods of 2–5 years. Optimism has distributed grants for over 100 million dollars, Arbitrum has similar programs. **For Hyper, reaching the same level would require a similar investment**, possibly through its own token treasury. **Sustainability depends on the ratio between the value created and the costs incurred.** If a grant of one million dollars attracts an application that generates ten million dollars of value (fees, economic activity) on the rollup in the first years, it is clearly positive. If the application generates much less, the investment does not pay itself back. **The art is evaluating the projects correctly to allocate the**

grants to the applications with potential. A concrete example: some of Optimism's most successful grants went to Velodrome (DEX), Synthetix (derivatives), Lido (staking). Together, these applications contributed to bringing billions of dollars of value onto Optimism, amply justifying the initial investment. For Hyper, identifying the equivalent applications specific to its own context will be the key to the success of the grant programs.

Question 4: How realistic is it to think that highly successful Solana applications will decide to port themselves also onto Hyper?

It is variable, and it depends on the specific cases. **For applications that serve blockchain-agnostic users (for example, NFT marketplaces, social applications), porting onto Hyper can seem low priority** compared to other investments. **For applications that serve users specifically interested in Bitcoin (BTC-centric DEXes, BTC lending protocols), Hyper could be strategically important. The porting decisions will depend on multiple factors**: opportunities to access new categories of users, costs of adapting to the Hyper context, support available from the Hyper team, economic conditions of the incentive programs. **Historically**, most successful applications concentrate initially on a single blockchain before considering multi-chain deployment. **For Hyper, attracting the porting of Solana applications will probably happen in phases**: first some "scout" applications that test the system, then, if Hyper proves promising, more mainstream applications. A concrete example: Uniswap, after being on Ethereum for years, extended to Optimism, Arbitrum, Polygon, and others. The process is gradual, and every new chain must demonstrate value before attracting first-tier protocols. For Hyper a similar process is expected.

Question 5: For a developer who wants to start with Hyper today, what would the practical steps be?

Before the launch of the mainnet, the options are limited but existing. **First step**: learn Solana and the Anchor framework, because everything you learn is directly applicable to Hyper. There are many free courses, tutorials, code examples. **Second step**: follow Hyper's official channels (the website, Twitter/X, Telegram, possible Discords) for updates on the devnet/testnet and on early access programs for developers. **Third step**: if interested in participating in the devnet, contact the Hyper team through the official channels (the email contact@bitcoinhyper.com has been mentioned in various posts). The team has indicated a willingness to grant selective access to serious developers. **Fourth step**: start thinking about which applications could specifically exploit the Hyper context (the Bitcoin integration, the specific settlement) instead of being simple ports. **Fifth step**: after the launch of the mainnet, participate in the grant and incentive programs that the team will announce. A concrete example: for a DeFi application that wants to be among the first on Hyper, preparing technically before the launch of the mainnet (developing on Solana and adapting) can make it possible to launch within the first weeks of the mainnet, benefiting from the early-mover incentives. Strategic timing is important.

Question 6: If Hyper does not manage to attract developers, does it have a chance of surviving?

In a limited way, but with reduced growth prospects. **Without a robust application ecosystem, a Layer 2 becomes mainly a custody tool** (people keep bitcoin in custody on the rollup but do not use them actively). **This model can survive**, but it generates much less value (through fees, economic activity, network effects) compared to Layer 2s with vibrant ecosystems. **The main risk is that Hyper becomes "yet another dead Layer 2"**: technically working but irrelevant in the market. The sector has seen various projects follow this trajectory. **To avoid this fate, attracting developers is critical**, and the first 12–18 months after the launch of the mainnet will be determining. **Positive signals would include**: dozens or hundreds of applications deployed in the first months, millions of dollars of value in DeFi protocols, partnerships with first-tier Solana protocols, successful hackathons. **Negative signals would include**: few protocols beyond the team itself, low and static locked value, a lack of partnerships, a decline of interest from the developer community. A concrete example: various Layer 2s launched in 2022–2023 with great promises (some "Bitcoin Layer 2s", some new Ethereum rollups) became irrelevant after the first 12 months because they did not manage to attract developers and applications.

Hyper must avoid this trajectory, and the inheritance of the Solana ecosystem is a great help, but on its own it is not sufficient.

⁂

22.9 — WHAT TO TAKE AWAY FROM THIS CHAPTER

The developer experience is one of the most underestimated factors in the success of a blockchain platform. Ethereum and Solana won in large part thanks to the quality of their own developer experience, not only to their technical characteristics.

Bitcoin Hyper, through the choice of a native SVM, inherits for free the entire Solana development ecosystem, accumulated in years of work and hundreds of millions of dollars of investments.

The inheritance covers eight main dimensions: the Rust language, the Anchor framework, the SPL libraries, tooling, documentation, community, security practices, specialized audit firms. For each one, Hyper finds itself with mature resources from day one.

For a Solana developer, the transition to Hyper requires few adaptations. The code runs practically identical, the tools work by changing only the endpoint, the experience is familiar. The learning curve is almost zero.

The Anchor framework is the most important productivity multiplier. It automates serialization, validation, the generation of the IDL, the test framework, error handling. It reduces the repetitive code by 70–80%, allowing the developers to concentrate on the application logic.

The SPL libraries provide standard implementations of common patterns: tokens, NFTs, governance, staking, account compression, and others. They have been tested in production on Solana for years and are available for free for Hyper.

Active strategies are necessary to translate the inheritance into effective adoption: economic incentives, integrations with existing protocols, a focus on specific use cases, hackathons, educational content, partnerships.

Real risks exist: inheriting the limits of the SVM, dependence on Solana's technical choices, a critical perception from the Bitcoin community, fragmentation of the ecosystem, dependence on Anchor.

For applications that want Bitcoin integration, Hyper offers a distinctive value proposition compared to Solana or to other alternatives. For Bitcoin-agnostic applications, Solana probably remains the better choice.

The success of the application ecosystem will be measured in the first 12–18 months after the launch of the mainnet. The number of applications deployed, the locked value, partnerships with major protocols, the developer community's activity are the metrics to monitor.

Chapter 22 closes here. We have understood why the developer experience is critical for the success of a Layer 2, how Hyper inherits the Solana ecosystem, which specific tools are available, and which strategies are necessary for attracting developers and applications. In ***Chapter 23 — Observability and Infrastructure****, we will examine the tools that allow developers, users, and observers to see what is happening in the system in real time, and why a robust observability infrastructure is an essential component of any serious blockchain ecosystem.*

NOTES

1 Anchor is the dominant framework for writing Solana programs in Rust. Developed by Coral, it reduces the boilerplate of the account model and provides automatic serialization. Repository: github.com/coral-xyz/anchor.

Developer Experience: the bridge toward the *ecosystem*

How Bitcoin Hyper can inherit tools, skills, and workflows from the Solana-SVM environment. **Compatibility is not automatic copying**: it means starting further ahead, not with an already complete system.

1 A fast network is not enough: developers are needed

idea → code → tests → deploy → wallet → app → users

less friction = more applications = more users = more ecosystem

What gets noticed right away	What decides over time
speed · low fees · security · tokenomics	tooling · documentation · examples · SDK · support · community

The developer experience is the bridge between infrastructure and a real product.

2 The SVM compatibility bridge: Hyper does not start from zero

The Solana-SVM ecosystem
Rust, Anchor, IDL, CLI, SDK, SPL, devnet, documentation, community

⟶ SVM COMPATIBILITY BRIDGE

Bitcoin Hyper
Layer 2 on Bitcoin: bridge, proofs, DA, settlement, L1 finality

Plausible reuse	Necessary adaptation	Mandatory verification
Rust · account model / SVM · Anchor · IDL · patterns · part of the tooling	RPC · wallet · explorer · faucet · deploy · fees · docs	Canonical Bridge · bridged BTC · proof system · DA · withdrawals · audits · Bitcoin finality

Compatibility does not mean automatic copying: **it means starting much further ahead** *of an ecosystem built from zero.*

3 Familiar tools for those who know Solana

- **Rust** the language of SVM programs.
- **Anchor** build, tests, deploy, accounts, IDL.
- **IDL** the program ↔ client interface.
- **CLI** commands on the network, accounts, programs.
- **SDK** libraries for apps and wallets.
- **SPL / standard** token, ATA, memo, governance.
- **Devnet** the pre-mainnet test environment.
- **Explorer / debug** tx, logs, errors, state.

For a Solana developer, moving to Hyper means **changing destination, not changing trade** *— provided the tooling and the services are actually deployed.*

4 Anchor reduces the repetitive work

Manual development	Development with Anchor
account management · signature checks · serialization · errors · tests · client integration	macros · constraints on the accounts · a generated IDL · build/test commands · structured errors · an ordered workspace

less repetitive code → less friction → more time on the application logic

ⓘ **Anchor helps, but it does not replace audits, independent tests, and technical competence —** *it is not a security guarantee.*

5 Inheriting is not enough: the ecosystem must be built

tools → developers → applications → users / liquidity → feedback ↺ IMPROVES

LEVERS: grants · hackathons · documentation · junior dev · integrations · liquidity mining · partnerships · public feedback

BTC-NATIVE USE CASES: DEXes with BTC pairs · lending with BTC collateral · payments · derivatives on BTC

The technology can be ***inherited***. **The community, the applications, and the liquidity must be won.**

THE KEY POINT

Bitcoin Hyper can start with an advantage: the **familiarity of the Solana-SVM ecosystem** — Rust, Anchor, IDL, SDK, CLI, and already known patterns reduce the friction. But the compatibility must be **demonstrated in the field**: devnet, RPC, wallets, explorer, standard programs, **bridge**, documentation, audits, and real applications.

Chapter 23
Observability and Infrastructure

Seeing what is happening

⁂

23.1 — A Network Is as Alive as It Is Observable

There is a concept that distributed-systems engineers know well but that rarely enters the discussions about the crypto world: **a system practically exists only to the extent that it can be observed.** Put like that it sounds like a philosophical phrase, but it has very concrete technical consequences. A system that works perfectly but whose state nobody can see is, from the point of view of the users and the operators, indistinguishable from a broken system. If I cannot see my balance, I cannot trust that it exists. If I cannot see whether my transaction has been processed, I cannot be sure of having sent it. If I cannot see the state of the network, I cannot decide whether it is the right moment to operate.

For Bitcoin Hyper, this principle translates into a practical need: **it is not enough to build a technically excellent rollup; one needs to build the infrastructure that allows everyone — users, developers, operators, researchers — to see what the rollup is doing in real time.** Without this infrastructure, the rollup exists as a technical object but not as a living ecosystem.

Hyper's research post of October 2025, dedicated explicitly to observability and to the infrastructural services, states an important thing: **"A network is as alive as it is observable."** It is not just rhetoric. It is a recognition that observability is not an accessory of the system but a structural component of it, on a par with execution, settlement, and data availability. A rollup without adequate observability is like a bank without account statements: technically it works, but nobody can trust it.

In this chapter I want to do four things. First, describe concretely what "observability" means in a blockchain system, and which different levels deserve to be considered. Second, examine the specific tools of the observability infrastructure: explorers, RPC, indexers, dashboards, alerting. Third, understand how these tools must integrate Hyper's specificities compared to Solana, in particular the interaction with Bitcoin and the settlement mechanisms. Fourth, evaluate the current state of Hyper's observability infrastructure and what to monitor in the months following the launch of the mainnet. It is a chapter that will make you see an aspect of the system that often goes unnoticed but that concretely determines the experience of all the actors in the ecosystem.

⁂

23.2 — The Levels of Observability

Let us begin with a conceptual distinction. **The observability of a blockchain system is not a single property but a set of overlapping levels**, each with different characteristics and uses. Understanding the levels helps to see which tools are needed and whom they serve.

First level: observability of the transactions. It is the most visible and familiar level for normal users. When I make a transaction, I want to see whether it has been transmitted to the network, whether it has been included in a batch, whether it has been anchored on Bitcoin, whether it has reached complete finality. I also want to see the technical detail: how much fee I paid, which accounts were touched, which state was modified. **Explorers like the Solana Explorer (for Solana) or Etherscan (for Ethereum) serve exactly this level.** For Hyper, an equivalent explorer is needed, adapted to the rollup's specificities.

Second level: observability of the state. More sophisticated than the transactional level. I want to query the current state of the system: what is the balance of a certain account, which tokens it owns, which programs are deployed at a certain address, what is the state of a certain application program. **For complex applications, programmatic access to the state is essential.** Wallets, dApps, trading bots, analysts, all need to query the state in different ways.

FIGURE 23.2A **FROM THE SINGLE TRANSACTION TO THE UPDATED STATE.**

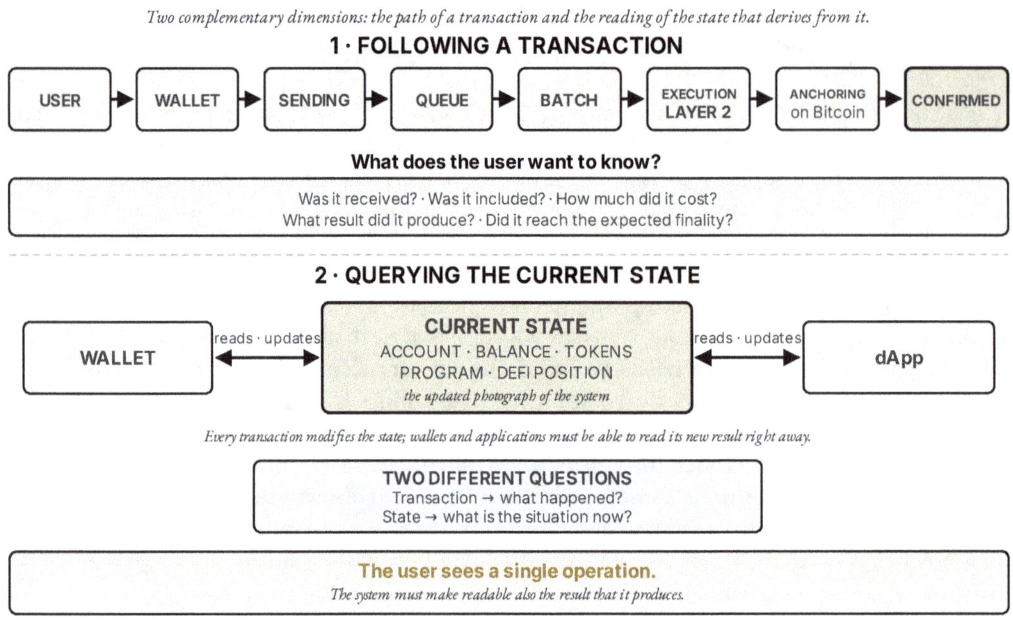

The first level of observability follows the path of the single transaction: sending, inclusion, execution, and finality. The second level makes it possible to query the updated state of the system: balances, tokens, programs, and application positions. The two dimensions are connected: every transaction modifies a state that wallets and dApps must be able to read.

Third level: historical observability. I want to see not only the current state but also the history. All the transactions of a certain account in the last six months. The evolution of the price of a certain token over time. The interactions with a certain application program. **Historical observability requires indexing infrastructure that archives and organizes the historical data** in ways that allow efficient queries. Without this infrastructure, obtaining simple answers like "how much did I spend in fees in the last month?" becomes practically impossible.

Fourth level: observability of the network metrics. I want to understand the general health of the system: how many transactions per second it is processing, how congested the mempool is, what the current anchoring frequency is, how many independent operators are active. **These aggregated metrics make it possible to evaluate the state of the system** independently of a specific transaction or account.

FIGURE 23.2B **LOOKING BACK AND OBSERVING THE NETWORK'S HEALTH.**

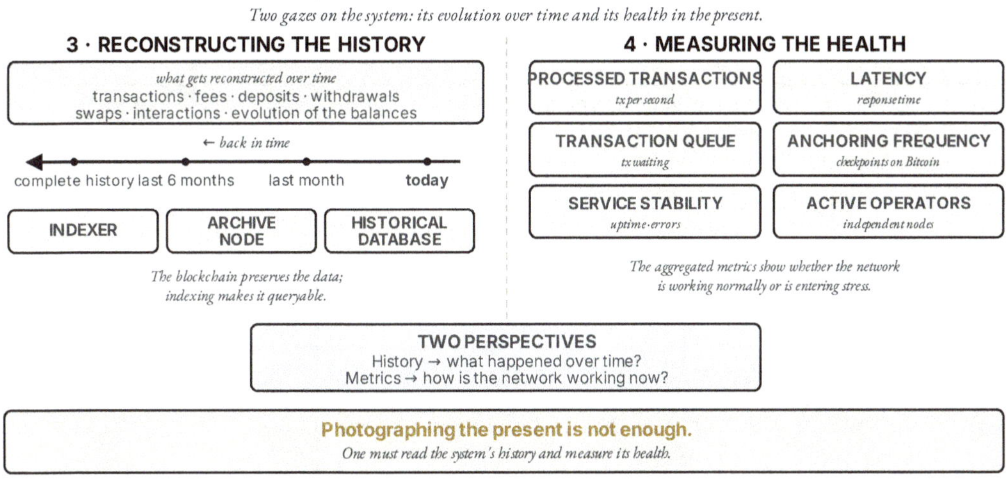

Historical observability makes it possible to reconstruct transactions, balances, and fees over time thanks to indexers, archive nodes, and specialized databases. The aggregated metrics show instead the general health of the network: volume of the operations, latency, congestion, frequency of the anchorings, and stability of the services.

Fifth level: observability of the cross-chain interactions[b]. Specific to Hyper, I want to see how the rollup is interacting with Bitcoin: how many state commitments have been anchored, how many bitcoin are held in the Canonical Bridge[a], how many forced inclusion requests are active, which transactions are crossing the bridge in both directions. **This level is specific to cross-chain systems** like Hyper, and it requires specialized infrastructure.

---

[a] **Canonical Bridge.** It is the official bridge through which the bitcoin enter and exit the rollup: when a user deposits BTC, these stay locked on Bitcoin and a corresponding quantity becomes usable on Hyper; at withdrawal the reverse happens. Observing it means being able to verify at any moment that the bitcoin in custody correspond to those represented on the Layer 2 — an essential check, because it is precisely on the bridge that a large part of the risk of a cross-chain system concentrates.

[b] **Cross-chain.** It indicates everything that happens between two distinct blockchains — here Bitcoin and the Layer 2 Hyper — rather than within a single one. The cross-chain interactions (deposits, withdrawals, anchorings) are the most delicate to observe and to secure, because they involve two systems with different rules and times that must stay coherent with each other. For this reason a Layer 2 anchored to Bitcoin requires specialized monitoring tools, capable of following an operation on both sides of the bridge.

FIGURE 23.2C **MAKING THE CONNECTION BETWEEN HYPER AND BITCOIN VISIBLE.**

The connection with Bitcoin must not only be declared: it must be observable.

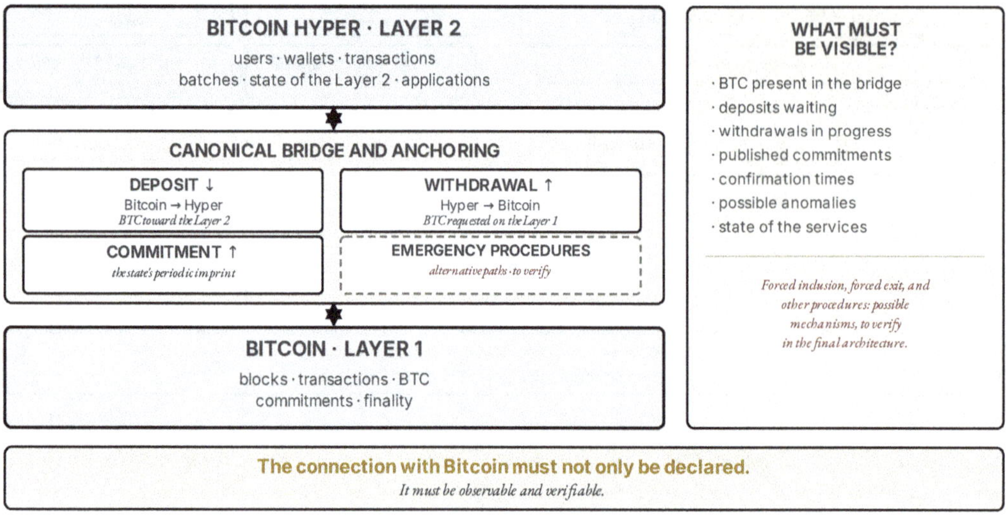

A Layer 2 connected to Bitcoin requires specific tools for making visible deposits, withdrawals, the BTC present in the bridge, and the commitments published on the Layer 1. Cross-chain observability makes it possible to verify the concrete working of the connection between the two environments and to spot possible waiting operations or anomalies.

Sixth level: observability of the security mechanisms. I want to see whether the proof model is working correctly: are there active fraud proofs[a], are there disputes in progress, the state of the emergency mechanisms[b], possible alerts on detected anomalies. **This level is critical for the long-term trust in the system**, and it is particularly important for sophisticated actors who must do in-depth due diligence.

---

[a] **Active fraud proofs.** In an optimistic rollup every published state is presumed correct until proven otherwise. Seeing "active" fraud proofs means observing the defense mechanism at work: someone has contested a state deemed wrong and the network is verifying it. Their presence is not in itself a negative signal — on the contrary, it demonstrates that the control system works; the total absence of any contestation, conversely, can simply indicate that nobody is keeping watch.

[b] **Emergency mechanisms.** They are the procedures foreseen for the edge cases — for example the sequencer that stops operating or refuses to include transactions. Typically they allow the user to withdraw their own funds directly through Bitcoin, without depending on the rollup's cooperation. Observing their state means verifying that this "escape route" is really available and not only declared on paper.

FIGURE 23.2D **OBSERVING SECURITY: NOT ONLY WHEN EVERYTHING WORKS.**

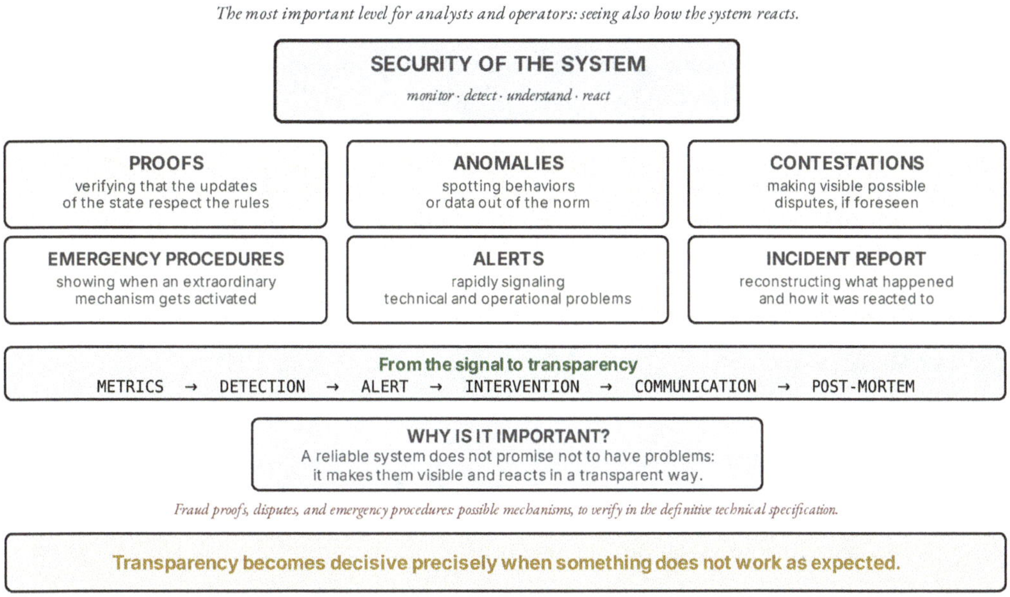

The observability of security makes it possible to monitor proofs, anomalies, alerts, possible contestations, and emergency procedures. It is the most important level for analysts, developers, and professional operators, because it shows not only the ordinary working of the network, but also the capacity to detect and manage the incidents.

Putting these six levels together, what emerges is that complete observability is a significant infrastructure, not a single tool. For Hyper, building this infrastructure — or facilitating its construction by the community — is one of the ecosystem's tasks. Let us see in the next paragraphs the specific tools.

⁂

23.3 — The Block Explorer: The Primary Access Point

Let us begin with the most visible tool: the **block explorer**. It is a web interface, consultable also from a smartphone, that transforms the data recorded by the network into information readable by a person. In simple terms, it performs for a blockchain a function similar to that of a search engine: it makes it possible to enter an address, the identifier of a transaction, or the reference to a block and to reconstruct what happened.

For most users, the block explorer represents the main point of contact with the Layer 2 after the wallet. The wallet makes it possible to carry out an operation; the explorer makes it possible to verify it. It does not have custody of the funds and it cannot modify or cancel a transaction. It shows what the network has recorded and, when it is designed correctly, it makes it possible to understand with which level of consolidation the operation has been acquired by the system.

In a rollup anchored to Bitcoin, this function becomes even more important. It is not enough to know that a transaction has been received by the Layer 2. One must be able to follow its path: from the initial sending to the inclusion in a batch, from the generation of the commitment to the publication of the reference on Bitcoin.

Following the path of a transaction

The first task of an explorer is showing in a clear way the life of every transaction.

When a user carries out an operation, the system assigns it a **hash**, that is, a unique cryptographic identifier. We can imagine it as the transaction's fingerprint: a sequence of characters that makes it possible to find it again and to distinguish it from all the others.

The page dedicated to the transaction should show at least the moment in which it was received, its current state, the fees paid, and the accounts involved. In an SVM environment, it is not always correct to speak only of sender and recipient. A single operation can involve several accounts and activate one or more **instructions**, that is, commands addressed to the network's programs.

To make the reading accessible also to those who have no technical skills, the explorer should place next to the raw data an understandable summary. The user should be able to understand immediately whether they made a transfer, used a decentralized application, interacted with the bridge, or received an error.

In a Layer 2 like Hyper, the transaction's page should distinguish with precision different levels of progress. For example:

- received by the system;
- processed by the sequencer;
- included in a batch;
- connected to a commitment of the state;
- anchored to a Bitcoin transaction;
- progressively consolidated on the Bitcoin network.

The **sequencer** is the component that receives the transactions, establishes their order, and groups them for processing. A **batch** is a set of aggregated operations. The **state commitment** is instead a synthetic cryptographic imprint of the updated state of the Layer 2: it makes it possible to bind the system to a determined result without publishing every single operation in full on the Bitcoin blockchain.

The concrete terminology will have to depend on Hyper's definitive architecture. In particular, the explorer should not use in a generic way the word "finalized" without explaining which level of certainty has been reached. The confirmation internal to the Layer 2, the inclusion in a batch, the anchoring on Bitcoin, and the number of confirmations obtained on the main blockchain are distinct steps.

FIGURE 23.3A **THE BLOCK EXPLORER: READING A TRANSACTION STEP BY STEP.**

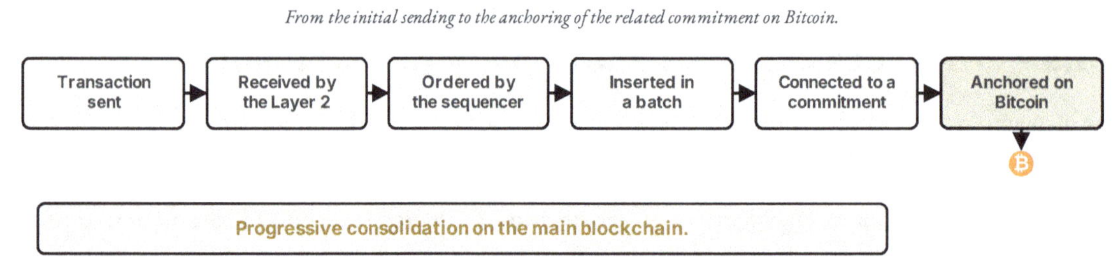

The block explorer must make it possible to follow the transaction's path: from the initial sending to the anchoring of the related commitment on Bitcoin.

Observing accounts, tokens, and programs

The second task of the explorer is showing the current state of the system.

In an SVM environment, an **account**[a] does not represent only a user's wallet. It is the fundamental unit through which the network preserves information. Some accounts contain balances; others store data; still others host executable programs. This distinction is important because it makes it possible to understand which components were actually involved in a transaction.

An account's page should show the available balance, the tokens[b] held, the history of the operations, and the possible programs with which the account has interacted. For a non-technical reader it is useful that the explorer clearly separates the essential information from the more specialist details.

The programs too should have a dedicated page. A **program**[c] is a set of executable instructions used by the decentralized applications. Its card should indicate at least the program's address, the recent transactions, the associated accounts and, when possible, the verified code or a public reference to its documentation.

The verification of the code is a particularly important element. Knowing that a determined program has been used is not enough. For a serious due diligence one must understand whether the code distributed on the network corresponds to the publicly examinable one and whether independent audits are available.

---

[a] **Account.** In the SVM model it is the basic unit with which the network preserves information: not only a user's wallet, but any "box" that can contain a balance, data, or a program. Every transaction declares in advance which accounts it intends to read or modify.

[b] **Token.** A unit of digital value recorded on the blockchain: it can represent a currency, a share, a right, or a good. An account can hold several tokens of different types, which the explorer lists on its card.

[c] **Program.** It is the equivalent, in the SVM world, of what elsewhere is called a smart contract: a set of executable instructions, published on the chain, that the decentralized applications call upon to operate. Being able to verify its code is essential in a due diligence.

FIGURE 23.3B **FROM THE SINGLE ACCOUNT TO THE PROGRAMS.**

Not only wallets and balances: also state accounts, programs, and interactions.

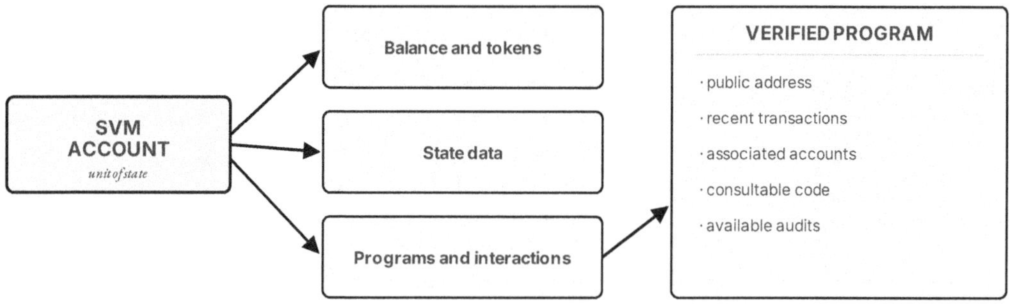

In an SVM environment, the explorer does not show only wallets and balances. It must make readable also the state accounts, the programs involved, and the interactions between the applications.

Making the connection with Bitcoin visible

An explorer designed for Hyper should go beyond the functions common to traditional explorers. Its quality will depend above all on the capacity to make readable the relationship between the Layer 2 and Bitcoin.

For every transaction it should be possible to reconstruct at least four steps:

1. in which batch it was inserted;
2. to which commitment of the state it is connected;
3. when the commitment was published or anchored on Bitcoin;
4. which level of consolidation it has reached on the main blockchain.

This path should be presented through navigable links. From the page of the single transaction, the user should be able to open the corresponding batch; from the batch they should be able to reach the commitment; from the commitment they should be able to consult the reference to the transaction recorded on Bitcoin.

The objective is to avoid the anchoring remaining an abstract formula. A really observable system must allow an independent party to follow the path of the data and verify the relationship between what happens on the Layer 2 and what gets published on the main blockchain.

The Canonical Bridge dashboard

A specific section of the explorer should be dedicated to the **Canonical Bridge**. The bridge is the mechanism that makes it possible to transfer BTC between Bitcoin and the Layer 2. The term "canonical" indicates that it is the bridge recognized by the protocol's official architecture, not an external application added afterwards.

The dashboard should show the incoming deposits, the requested withdrawals, the completed operations, the average processing times, and the overall amount of the BTC managed by the system. For each operation it would be useful to visualize the connection between the original Bitcoin transaction, the proof verified by the Bitcoin Relay Program, and the corresponding movement on the Layer 2.

For the withdrawals, the user should be able to understand in which phase the request is: received, verified, authorized, or completed on the Bitcoin network. In this case too, the definitive terminology will have to faithfully reflect the actual working of the protocol.

The bridge dashboard does not represent only a convenience tool. It is an essential component of the risk evaluation. If the bridge constitutes the crossing point of the BTC, its transparency makes it possible to observe possible slowdowns, anomalies, operational concentrations, or differences between deposited funds and activity recorded on the Layer 2.

FIGURE 23.3C **FROM THE LAYER 2 TO BITCOIN: BATCHES, COMMITMENTS, AND THE BRIDGE.**

Two distinct paths: the BTC through the bridge and the data through the commitments.

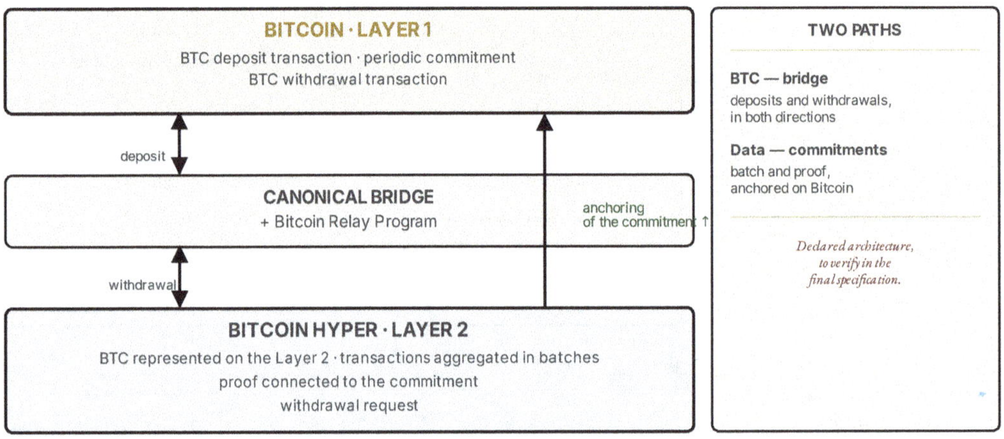

An explorer specific to Hyper should show separately the path of the BTC through the bridge and the path of the data through batches and periodic commitments.

Making the anomalous situations observable too

A mature explorer must not show only what works regularly. It must help to understand also what happens when the ordinary flow meets a problem.

Hyper's definitive architecture will have to clarify which tools are foreseen in the case in which the sequencer does not include a transaction, a withdrawal suffers a delay, or a contestation emerges on the validity of the state. If mechanisms of **forced inclusion**, **forced exit**, or dispute management get introduced, the explorer will have to make them visible through dedicated sections.

The *forced inclusion* is a procedure that makes it possible to request the insertion of a transaction even when the normal path through the sequencer does not work correctly. The *forced exit* is an emergency exit procedure. A *dispute* is instead a contestation relating to the state or to the validity of a determined operation.

These functionalities must not be considered already operational just because they are useful in the abstract. It will be necessary to verify whether they will actually be foreseen, how they will work, which times they will require, and which information they will make publicly consultable.

Advanced search and reading of the data

As the network's activity increases, the simple search by hash or address is no longer sufficient. A quality explorer must make it possible to filter and aggregate the information.

The user should be able to search for a transaction, an account, a block, a batch, a commitment, or a program. They should moreover be able to select a time interval, distinguish the different categories of operations, and consult aggregated data: number of transactions, transferred volumes, fees paid, activity of the bridge, and frequency of the anchorings on Bitcoin.

The charts too perform an important function, provided they stay readable. An essential dashboard could show the network's activity over time, the number of processed transactions, the average cost of the operations, the size of the batches, the frequency of the commitments, and the state of the deposits and the withdrawals.

These data do not serve only the investors or the analysts. They help the users to understand whether the network is congested, they allow the developers to spot anomalies, and they make it possible for independent researchers to evaluate the operational quality of the system.

Tools for developers

Behind a well-designed explorer there is a broader infrastructure. The data must be collected, ordered, and made queryable. The **indexer*** is the component that reads the network's information and organizes it so as to allow rapid searches. Without an efficient indexer, even a fast network can turn out difficult to consult.

---

* **Indexer.** The service that collects the blockchain's raw data and reorganizes it in an easily queryable form — a bit like a book's analytical index, which makes it possible to find right away what is needed without leafing through all the pages. Without an efficient indexer, obtaining a piece of information from the chain would require retracing its entire history.

The developers moreover need **APIs**, that is, interfaces that allow an application to automatically query the network's data. An application could use an API to check the state of a deposit, verify whether a transaction has been confirmed, or reconstruct an account's history.

Next to the APIs, **webhooks** can be useful. A webhook automatically sends a notification when a specific event occurs. For example, an application could receive an alert when a deposit on the bridge gets recognized, when a withdrawal gets completed, or when a determined account receives a token.

A mature ecosystem should offer clear technical documentation, code examples, test environments, and simple procedures for integrating these tools into the applications. The explorer visible to the user represents only the surface of a more articulated system, composed of RPC, indexers, APIs, data flows, and monitoring services.

FIGURE 23.3D **AN EXPLORER USEFUL TO DEVELOPERS TOO.**

The visible surface of a broader data infrastructure.

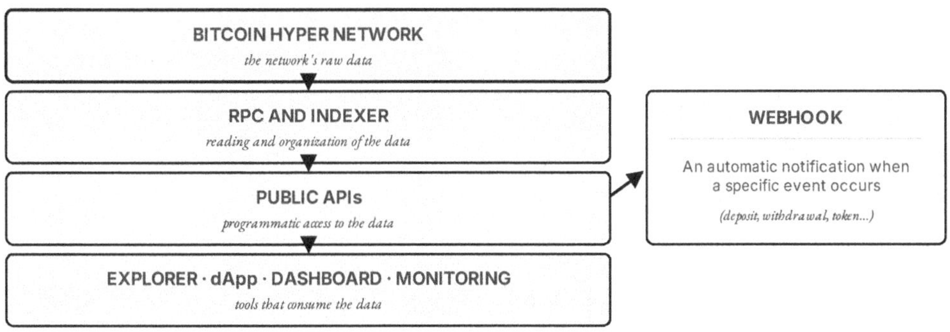

The explorer is the visible surface of a broader infrastructure. RPC, indexers, APIs, and webhooks allow the applications to read the data and react to the network's events.

User experience and accessibility

The explorer's quality also depends on its simplicity of use.

The pages must load rapidly, even when the network produces a high quantity of data. Consultation from a smartphone must be easy. The essential information must be visible immediately, while the more technical details can be organized in expandable sections.

It is useful to foresee a multilingual interface, a structure accessible also to users with disabilities, and a system of understandable labels. An error should not be shown only through a technical code: when possible, the explorer should explain in a synthetic way what happened.

A good explorer must manage to speak simultaneously to three different audiences: the user who wants to verify a payment, the developer who must analyze a complex transaction, and the analyst who wants to observe the overall health of the network.

Why several independent explorers are needed

The existence of an official explorer represents a first step, but it is not sufficient. A healthy ecosystem should favor also the birth of independent explorers and infrastructural services managed by different parties.

The reason is simple. If a single explorer exists and that service becomes unavailable, a relevant part of the users temporarily loses the capacity to observe the network. If several tools query verifiable data through different infrastructures, it is possible to compare the information and more easily spot errors, delays, or incomplete representations.

The plurality of the explorers, however, does not automatically guarantee decentralization. Two graphically different interfaces could depend on the same indexer or on the same RPC. The due diligence must therefore push beyond the number of available sites and ask which data sources they use, who manages the underlying infrastructure, and whether an independent party can reconstruct the information starting from the public data.

The Solana ecosystem offers a useful example. Next to the Solana Explorer, independent tools like Solscan and specialized infrastructural providers are available. Hyper should aim at an analogous evolution, adapted to the specific needs of a Layer 2 anchored to Bitcoin.

FIGURE 23.3E **WHY SEVERAL INDEPENDENT EXPLORERS ARE NEEDED.**

Plurality is useful only if the underlying infrastructures are really distinct.

FRAGILE SCENARIO	MORE ROBUST SCENARIO
A single explorer	Several independent explorers
A single indexer	Differentiated infrastructures
A single RPC	Alternative RPCs
No comparison possible	Comparable data
Visibility interrupted in case of failure	Greater continuity of observation
a single source = a single point of fragility	*Verify the underlying dependencies too.*

The presence of several interfaces is useful only if the services do not all depend on the same infrastructure. The decentralization of observability requires comparable data sources.

To evaluate Hyper after the launch of the mainnet, the explorer's quality will be one of the first indicators to observe. A fast but superficial explorer is not enough. A really useful explorer must make visible the transactions, the accounts, the programs, the bridge, the batches, the commitments, and the connection with Bitcoin.

Observability is not an accessory of the Layer 2: it is what makes it publicly verifiable.

⁂

23.4 — RPC: The Infrastructure for the Applications

In the previous paragraph we observed the block explorer: the tool that allows a person to search for a transaction, check a balance, or verify the connection between the Layer 2 and Bitcoin. The applications need to access the same data, but they cannot do it by manually consulting a web page. They must query the network automatically.

It is here that the **RPC** infrastructure comes into play.

The acronym means *Remote Procedure Call*. In simple terms, an application sends a request to a service connected to the blockchain and receives a structured answer.

A wallet can ask what the balance of an account is. A dApp can check whether a transaction has been confirmed. An explorer can retrieve the history of the operations. A bot can continuously monitor a decentralized application. A payment system can verify whether a deposit has arrived correctly.

The RPC is therefore the informational bridge between the network and the software that uses it.

FIGURE 23.4A **RPC: THE INVISIBLE BRIDGE BETWEEN APPLICATIONS AND THE NETWORK.**

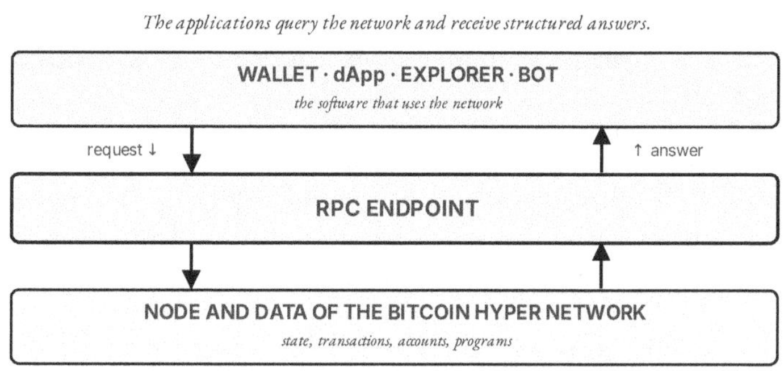

The RPC endpoint allows the applications to query the network and receive structured answers without manually consulting a block explorer.

In an SVM ecosystem, the requests are normally addressed to an **endpoint**, that is, a network address to which the application can connect. The service receives the question, consults the node or its own data infrastructure, and returns an answer readable by the program.

The working generally stays invisible to the end user, but it deeply influences the experience of use. When a wallet rapidly shows the updated balance, when a dApp loads the data without slowdowns, or when an explorer reconstructs a complex transaction, behind the interface RPC, nodes, indexers, and monitoring systems operate.

From the request to the answer

The essential mechanism is linear.

The application formulates a question: for example, "what is the balance of this account?" or "has this transaction been confirmed?". The request gets sent to the RPC endpoint. The infrastructure consults the available state and returns the answer.

In an SVM environment, the requests can perform different functions:

- reading the balance of an account;
- retrieving the data associated with a program;
- checking the state of a transaction;
- sending a new operation to the network;
- simulating the execution before the sending;
- verifying the node's health;
- receiving notifications when an event occurs.

The **simulation** is particularly useful. It makes it possible to evaluate the probable behavior of a transaction without recording it on the blockchain. An application can thus spot an error, estimate the consumption of resources, or avoid sending an operation destined to fail.

It is important to understand one point: the RPC does not coincide with the blockchain and does not modify the rules of the consensus. It is an access door to the data and to the functions of the system. If this door is slow, unstable, or excessively centralized, even a technically efficient network can offer a disappointing experience.

Public endpoints and private endpoints

Not all endpoints perform the same function.

The **public endpoints** are normally accessible without a commercial contract. They serve for starting to develop, carrying out tests, making occasional queries, and allowing the users to interact with the network without immediately purchasing a dedicated service.

This openness carries a limit. The resources are shared among numerous users. To avoid overloads, the public endpoints generally apply a **rate limit**, that is, a maximum number of requests allowed in a determined interval of time. When the limit gets exceeded, the infrastructure can slow down or temporarily refuse the requests.

The **private or dedicated endpoints** answer a different need. They are aimed at production applications: wallets, exchanges, decentralized protocols, payment systems, professional explorers, and automated services. They can offer greater capacity, technical assistance, higher limits, geographic distribution, and contractual availability levels. The term **SLA**, or *Service Level Agreement*, indicates precisely the commitment assumed by the provider with respect to the quality and the continuity of the service.

For Hyper it will be necessary to have both categories. The public endpoints will have to reduce the entry barrier for the developers. The private endpoints will have to sustain real applications even when the traffic will increase.

FIGURE 23.4B **PUBLIC AND PRIVATE ENDPOINTS: TWO DIFFERENT FUNCTIONS.**

Two complementary tools, with different purposes and guarantees.

PUBLIC ENDPOINT	PRIVATE OR DEDICATED ENDPOINT
Tests and initial development	Production applications
Shared access	Dedicated resources
Rate limit	Higher capacity
No strong guarantee	Possible SLA
Facilitated onboarding	Operational continuity

Both are necessary for a healthy ecosystem.

The public endpoints reduce the entry barrier. The private endpoints sustain applications that require greater reliability and operational capacity.

Compatibility with the SVM ecosystem: from the promise to the verification

Bitcoin Hyper declares that it wants to use a runtime compatible with the Solana Virtual Machine. The **runtime** is the software environment that executes the programs distributed on the network.

If this compatibility gets implemented in a sufficiently complete way, the developers will be able to reuse a part of the skills, of the libraries, and of the tools already employed in the Solana ecosystem.

The potential advantage does not concern only the possibility of programming in Rust or of using the Anchor framework. It also concerns the way in which wallets, dApps, explorers, and automated services dialogue with the network.

The verification, however, will have to be concrete. It will not be enough to state that Hyper uses an SVM environment. It will be necessary to check which RPC methods are really supported, whether they produce coherent results, how the errors get managed, which libraries work without changes, and which adaptations are necessary.

A developer should be able to connect their own software, query an account, distribute a program, simulate a transaction, send it, follow its state, and receive notifications in real time.

The concept of confirmation too will require particular attention. In a Layer 2 anchored to Bitcoin it will be necessary to distinguish at least four moments:

1. the reception of the transaction;
2. the processing internal to the Layer 2;
3. the inclusion in the batch and the connection with the state commitment;
4. the periodic anchoring of the commitment on Bitcoin.

Compatibility with an already known paradigm can reduce the learning curve. It must not however become a shortcut in the due diligence. An SVM runtime does not automatically make Hyper equivalent to Solana in every operational detail.

FIGURE 23.4C **SVM COMPATIBILITY: A SEQUENCE OF VERIFICATIONS.**

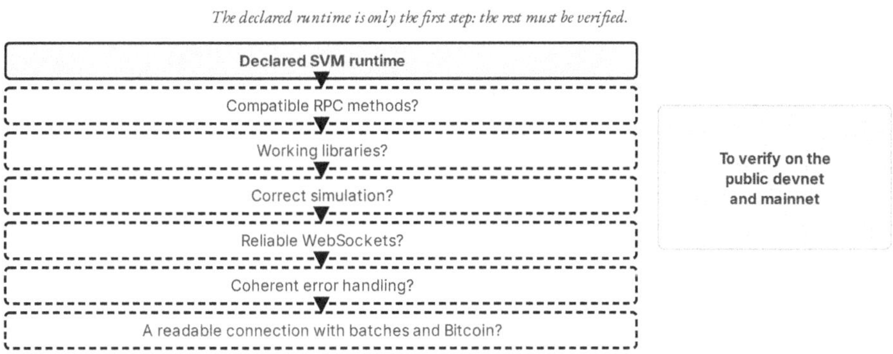

Compatibility with the SVM cannot be deduced from the runtime alone. It must be verified through the entire path used by the applications.

HTTP, WebSocket, and streaming: three different modes

Not all applications need the same type of access to the data.

For checking a balance or retrieving a transaction, an ordinary request via HTTP is often sufficient. The application formulates a question and receives an answer.

Some services must instead react immediately to the events. A wallet may want to show the arrival of a payment. An explorer must update the state of a transaction. A dApp may need to know when the balance of an account changes.

WebSocket connections keep open a persistent channel between the application and the RPC infrastructure. Instead of continuously repeating the question "has anything changed?", the software receives a notification when the event it subscribed to occurs.

For applications that must process a very high quantity of data, even more advanced **streaming** tools can be needed. Streaming transfers continuous flows of information and can turn out useful for professional bots, monitoring systems, indexers, and financial applications with high operational intensity.

It is appropriate to keep the levels distinct:

- HTTP for the punctual queries;
- WebSocket for the real-time updates;
- advanced streaming for the most intensive data flows.

For Hyper, the presence of reliable HTTP and WebSocket endpoints will represent an essential requirement. The possible availability of more sophisticated streaming tools will constitute a further indicator of the ecosystem's maturity.

FIGURE 23.4D **HTTP, WEBSOCKET, AND STREAMING: THREE LEVELS OF ACCESS.**

Growing timeliness and complexity, for different needs.

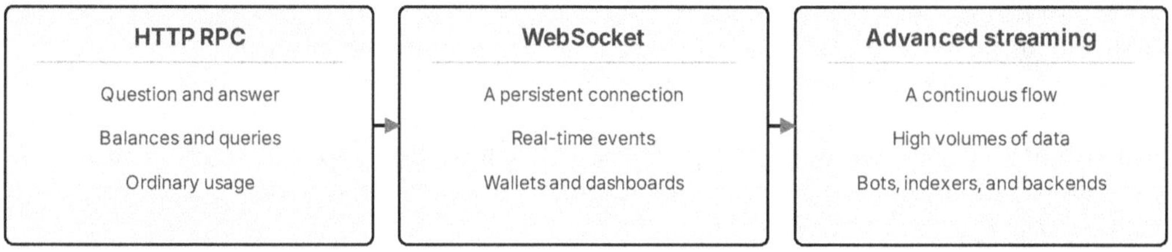

HTTP requests are suited to punctual queries. WebSocket and streaming make it possible to react to the events with growing levels of timeliness and complexity.

Current state, history, and indexers

An application does not always need only the latest available information.

A wallet must show the previous transactions. An explorer must reconstruct an account's chronology. An analyst may want to compare different periods. An auditor must be able to examine an anomaly that happened weeks before.

Historical queries require infrastructures capable of preserving and organizing the data over time.

Not all nodes necessarily maintain the entire chronology of the network. Some can progressively eliminate a part of the older data to reduce the archiving costs. To obtain a complete view, archive nodes and dedicated indexers can therefore be needed.

An **indexer** is a service that collects the data produced by the network, orders it, and makes it rapidly queryable. It performs a function similar to that of a book's analytical index: it does not create the content, but it makes it possible to find it again without having to reread every page.

For Hyper, the historical archive should also include data specific to the rollup:

- previous batches;
- state commitments;
- references to the anchorings on Bitcoin;
- deposits and withdrawals through the Canonical Bridge;
- possible errors or anomalous procedures.

FIGURE 23.4E **CURRENT STATE AND HISTORICAL ARCHIVE.**

Two paths: the snapshot of the present and the reconstruction of the past.

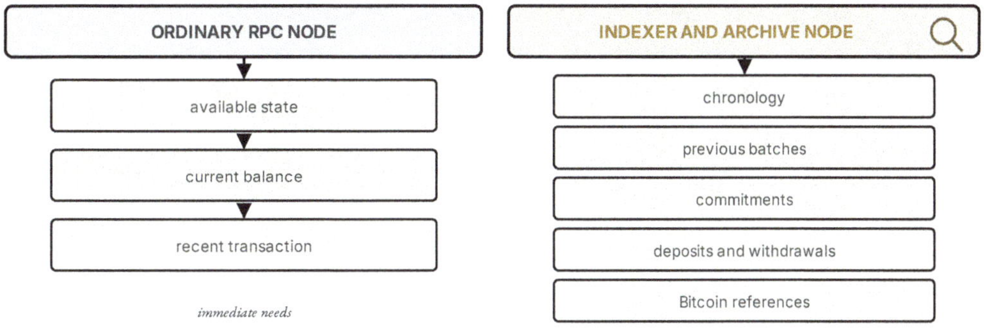

The ordinary RPC answers the immediate needs. The indexers and the historical archives make it possible to reconstruct the network's evolution over time.

A really verifiable system cannot limit itself to showing what happens in the present. It must make it possible to reconstruct what happened in the past.

Efficiency of the requests

When an application must retrieve a lot of information, sending a separate request for every datum can turn out inefficient.

Batch requests make it possible to aggregate several queries into a single sending. This reduces the **overhead**, that is, the additional cost produced by the management of numerous separate requests.

The compression of the answers too can contribute to reducing the quantity of transferred data. This optimization must not however be considered a uniform characteristic of every endpoint. It depends on the transport level, on the implementation, and on the provider used.

The objective is not to accumulate the largest possible number of functions. It is to build a coherent, documented, and predictable infrastructure.

Performance and reliability

The quality of an RPC infrastructure is measured through verifiable parameters.

The first is the **latency**: the time necessary to receive an answer after having sent a request. A contained latency makes wallets, explorers, and dApps more reactive.

There is however no single value valid for every operation. The check of a balance is generally less demanding than a complex historical search. The performance can moreover change based on the geographic distance, on the congestion, on the provider's load, and on the quantity of data requested.

The second parameter is the **uptime**: the percentage of time during which the service stays available. For a professional application even brief interruptions can produce relevant effects.

One must then observe:

- average times and response percentiles;
- stability during the traffic peaks;
- propagation speed of the updates;
- correctness of the returned data;
- capacity to recover after an interruption;
- clarity of the technical documentation.

For Hyper, thresholds like a latency below 100 milliseconds for the standard queries or an uptime above 99.9% can be used as orientational objectives. They will however have to be verified through public measurements, tests under load, and continuous monitoring.

FIGURE 23.4F **MEASURING THE QUALITY OF THE SERVICE.**

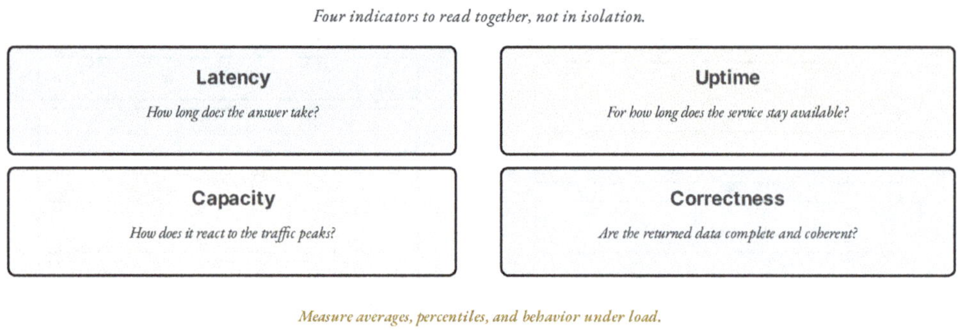

The quality of an endpoint is not measured through a single number. One must observe speed, continuity, capacity, and correctness of the answers.

Geographic distribution

Even in digital systems, physical distance continues to matter.

If an endpoint is very far from the user, every request takes more time to reach the service and come back. To reduce the latency, professional providers distribute their own infrastructure in several geographic areas.

For an international ecosystem, the presence of access points in Europe, North America, and Asia represents a reasonable evaluation criterion.

The geographic distribution, however, does not automatically coincide with decentralization. A single provider can control many servers scattered around the world and still remain a single point of commercial and operational dependence.

Diversity of the providers and continuity of the service

A healthy ecosystem should not depend on a single endpoint nor on a single operator.

If the main provider suffers an interruption, applies more restrictive limits, raises the prices, or blocks determined requests, numerous applications can stop working simultaneously.

To reduce this risk, wallets and dApps should adopt **fallback** strategies. The term indicates the automatic switch to an alternative endpoint when the main one does not respond correctly.

Resilience requires several levels:

- public endpoints managed by the project;
- independent professional services;
- the possibility of configuring alternative providers;
- accessible node software;
- documentation for the operators;
- monitoring tools;
- automatic fallback systems.

The Solana ecosystem represents a useful term of comparison. Specialized providers like Helius, QuickNode, Alchemy, and Triton One offer different combinations of RPC, WebSocket, APIs, webhooks, streaming, and access to the historical data.

For Hyper, the entry of independent operators would constitute a positive signal, but it must not be taken for granted. It will depend on the technical compatibility, on the market demand, on the quality of the documentation, and on the simplicity with which new parties will be able to start and maintain the service.

FIGURE 23.4G **RPC RESILIENCE: AVOIDING A SINGLE POINT OF DEPENDENCE.**

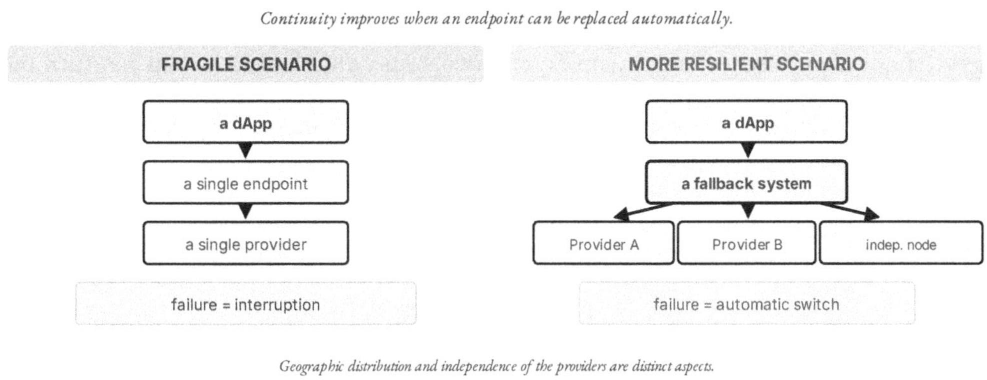

The continuity of the service improves when the applications can automatically replace an unavailable endpoint with an alternative infrastructure.

Centralization of the access and decentralization of the network

The RPC infrastructure introduces an often neglected risk.

A blockchain can be decentralized at the consensus level and stay fragile on the plane of the access. If most users use applications dependent on the same few endpoints, a failure or a commercial decision can temporarily compromise a relevant part of the ecosystem.

The decentralization of the access does not replace the decentralization of the consensus, but it completes it.

To evaluate Hyper after the launch of the mainnet, verifying the existence of a working endpoint will not be enough. It will be necessary to ask:

- how many providers are available;
- how independent they are;
- which RPC methods they support;
- which historical data they preserve;
- where they are distributed geographically;
- how they react to the traffic peaks;
- how simple it is to replace them;
- whether an independent operator can start an alternative service.

An application can be built on top of a blockchain. But the quality of the experience also depends on the invisible infrastructure that allows the software to dialogue with the network.

The decentralization of the consensus is not enough: access to the data too must avoid excessive dependencies.

⁂

23.5 — Indexers: Organizing the History

In the previous paragraph we saw that the RPC infrastructure allows the applications to dialogue with the network. A wallet can query the balance of an account. A dApp can check the state of a transaction. An explorer can retrieve recent information.

This direct access is indispensable, but not always sufficient.

When the questions become more complex, repeatedly querying the blockchain can turn out slow and inefficient. To reconstruct an account's chronology, calculate the fees paid during a determined period, or analyze the overall activity of a program, one must acquire numerous data, interpret them, and order them.

It is here that the **indexer** comes into play.

An indexer is a system that reads the data produced by the network, organizes it in a queryable structure, and makes it easily accessible to the applications. In simple terms, it performs a function similar to that of a book's analytical index: it does not create the content and does not modify what has been written, but it makes it possible to rapidly find the information again without having to reread every page.

The comparison with a traditional archive helps to understand the difference. The RPC resembles the direct consultation of the original documents. The indexer resembles instead an ordered, updated catalog equipped with search tools. Both are necessary. The first makes it possible to verify the source. The second makes it possible to use the data in an efficient way.

FIGURE 23.5A **RPC AND INDEXER: TWO COMPLEMENTARY FUNCTIONS.**

A direct source and an organized archive: different roles, both necessary.

RPC	INDEXER
Queries the network	Organizes the history
Reads the available state	Builds a searchable archive
Sends transactions	Interprets the events
Answers punctual requests	Answers complex questions

A direct source and an organized archive: both are necessary.

The RPC makes it possible to consult the network directly. The indexer organizes the data over time and makes the complex queries efficient.

A simple question that can become complex

Let us consider an apparently elementary request:

> How many transactions has a determined account carried out in the last three months and what overall amount has it paid in fees?

Without an indexer, the application would have to identify the correct time interval, retrieve the relevant blocks or transactions, filter the operations connected to the account, and sum the fees. The problem becomes even more demanding when the question concerns thousands of accounts, an entire protocol, or a long historical series.

With an indexer, the information has already been acquired and ordered. The same question can transform itself into a query on a structured database. The result no longer depends on the repeated scanning of the blockchain, but on the capacity of the indexed archive to rapidly retrieve the pertinent records.

It does not mean that every query gets resolved instantly. The actual speed depends on the structure of the database, on the quantity of the data, and on the load of the system. The fundamental difference is another: the heavy work gets carried out progressively during the indexing, not repeated in full every time a user formulates a question.

FIGURE 23.5B **ONE QUESTION, TWO PATHS.**

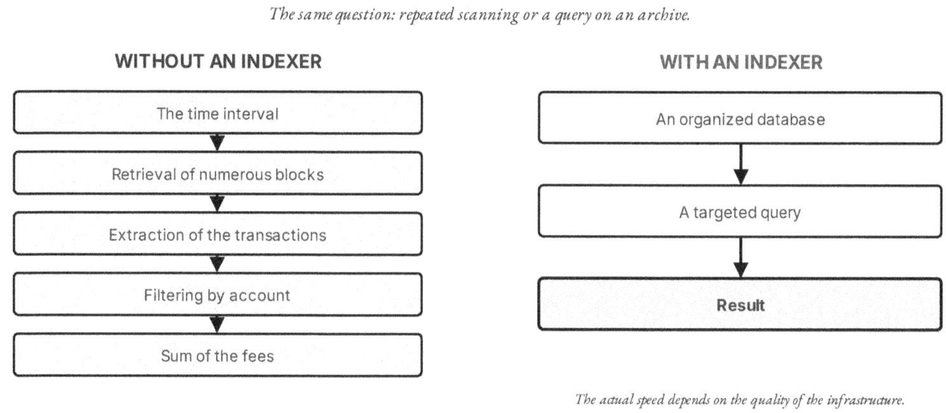

The indexer avoids repeating the entire scanning of the blockchain every time. The work gets carried out progressively during the acquisition of the data.

From the raw datum to the readable information

Indexing does not consist only in copying data from a node to a database.

The transactions produced by an SVM environment can contain coded instructions, references to multiple accounts, and interactions with different programs. For an application it is not enough to know that a transaction exists. One must understand what it represents.

An indexer must therefore go through several steps:

1. acquiring the raw datum;
2. identifying the accounts and the programs involved;
3. interpreting the instructions;
4. classifying the event;
5. saving the result in a queryable structure.

A sequence of bytes can thus become an understandable entry: a token transfer, a deposit on the bridge, a withdrawal request, an interaction with a decentralized exchange, or a modification of a program's state.

This process is often called **parsing**. The term indicates the transformation of a raw technical datum into an ordered structure usable by the software. The quality of the parsing is essential. If a complex transaction gets interpreted in an incomplete way, the subsequent statistics too can turn out wrong.

FIGURE 23.5C **FROM THE RAW DATUM TO THE READABLE INFORMATION.**

Parsing transforms a technical sequence into an understandable event.

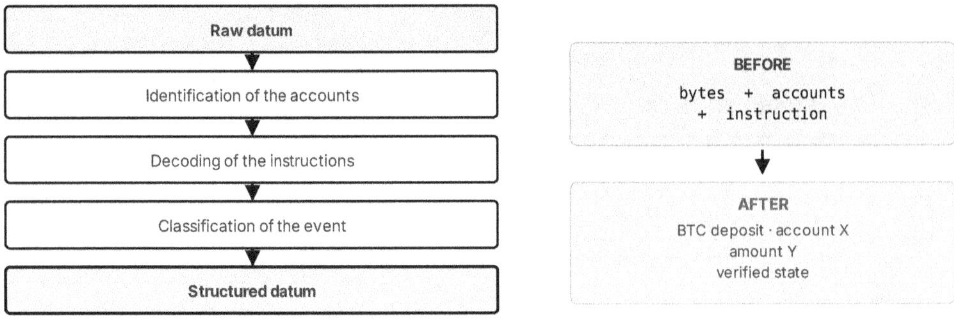

Indexing does not consist only in copying data. Parsing transforms technical instructions into information usable by the applications.

General-purpose indexers and specialized indexers

Not all indexers must carry out the same work.

A general-purpose indexer tries to cover a very broad part of the network's activity. It can feed an explorer, an analytics platform, or a data service destined for many different applications.

An application indexer selects instead only what a specific dApp needs. A decentralized exchange protocol may want to monitor swaps, liquidity, and fees. A payment system can concentrate on credits and confirmations. Tax software can reconstruct transfers, costs, and movements between wallets.

For Hyper, the indexer of the Canonical Bridge will also be particularly important. It will have to connect the Bitcoin deposits, the verification of the proofs, the representation of the BTC on the Layer 2, the withdrawal requests, and the corresponding transactions on the main blockchain.

A security indexer will instead be able to monitor anomalous events: delays of the sequencer, incongruences between batches and commitments, processing errors, or differences between the internal state of the Layer 2 and the data progressively anchored on Bitcoin.

Completeness does not necessarily consist in concentrating every piece of information in a single database. It consists in making possible a reliable, documented, and verifiable reconstruction.

FIGURE 23.5D **SEVERAL INDEXERS FOR DIFFERENT NEEDS.**

Every application selects and organizes the data it needs.

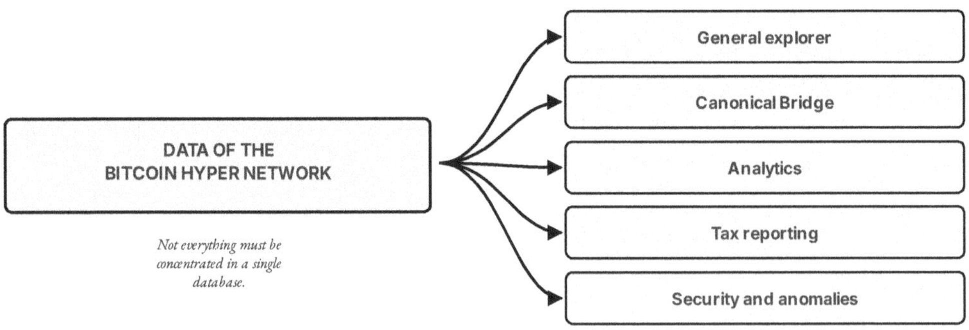

The indexers can be general-purpose or specialized. Every application selects and organizes the data necessary to its own working.

Organizing the data through a schema

After the acquisition and the parsing, the data must be ordered.

A **relational database** organizes the information through tables connected to one another. One table can contain the transactions. Another the accounts. Yet another the programs, the batches, or the commitments.

The relations make it possible to pass from one element to the other. From a transaction's page one can go back to the account involved. From the account one can reconstruct the chronology. From the batch one can reach the commitment. From the commitment one can locate the reference published on Bitcoin.

In other cases NoSQL databases, column stores, engines dedicated to time series, or combinations of different technologies can be more suitable.

The technical choice depends on the purpose. An explorer requires rapid searches and intuitive navigation. An analytics dashboard must calculate historical series and aggregations. An algorithmic trading system privileges speed and continuous updating. Tax software must guarantee completeness, traceability, and export of the data.

There is no single schema valid for every use. There is however a common requirement: the data must be coherent, understandable, and traceable to the original source.

Making the data accessible to the applications

Once organized, the data must be exposed through interfaces usable by the developers.

REST APIs normally make it possible to call predefined resources: a transaction, an account, a list of events, or a historical series.

GraphQL APIs adopt a different approach. They allow the application to ask exactly for the necessary fields, building more flexible queries.

These are not the only possibilities. Some applications can use controlled SQL queries, specialist endpoints, webhooks, or streaming flows.

For Hyper, the quality of the infrastructure will not depend on the mandatory adoption of a specific standard. It will depend on the capacity to offer documented, stable tools suited to different needs.

A good indexer must make simple what would otherwise be complex: retrieving an account's history, analyzing a program's activity, following the bridge, comparing time intervals, and building reliable dashboards.

FIGURE 23.5E **FROM THE NETWORK TO THE APIS.**

Acquiring, interpreting, and organizing before exposing the data.

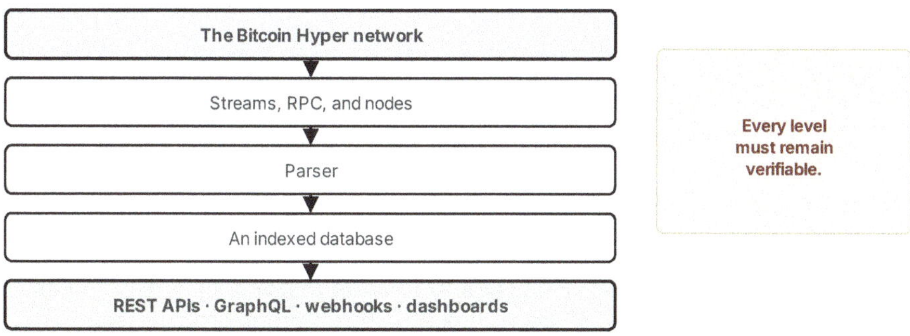

The indexer acquires, interprets, and organizes the data before making it available to the developers through dedicated interfaces.

Precalculated aggregations

Many questions recur frequently.

How many transactions have been processed today? What is the overall transferred volume? How much has been paid in fees? Which programs turn out most used? How many BTC have entered or exited through the bridge?

Calculating these values every time starting from the single transactions would be inefficient. For this reason an indexer can maintain **precalculated aggregations**. They are progressively updated results: daily volume, average fees, number of active accounts, average size of the batches, frequency of the commitments, aggregated deposits and withdrawals.

The usefulness is similar to that of an already prepared instrument panel. The system does not have to redo the entire calculation every time; it updates the value when new data arrives.

The aggregations must however remain verifiable. A dashboard should not show only the final number. It should make it possible, when necessary, to go back to the elementary data used to calculate it.

Real-time updating and recovery of the history

An indexer cannot limit itself to building an archive of the past. It must remain synchronized with the network.

Every new transaction must be acquired, interpreted, and saved. The temporal distance between the on-chain event and its availability in the database is called **indexing lag**.

For some applications, a delay of a few seconds can be acceptable. For others, like payment systems or monitoring tools, it can be necessary to reduce it further.

Speed is however not the only criterion. If the indexer temporarily loses the connection or suffers an interruption, it must be able to resume the work without leaving gaps. For this reason **checkpoints** are useful, control points that indicate up to where the data has been processed correctly.

The **backfill** makes it possible instead to retroactively recover the missing events. A reliable indexer must know how to work in both directions: following the present in real time and reconstructing the past when necessary.

FIGURE 23.5F **REAL TIME, CHECKPOINTS, AND BACKFILL.**

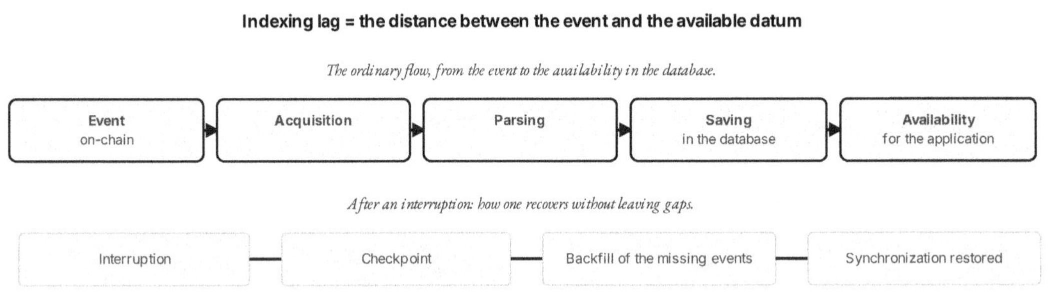

A mature indexer must follow the present and recover the past. Checkpoints and backfill avoid gaps after an interruption.

Provisional states, consolidation, and rollback

Blockchains do not always produce immediately irreversible data.

Some information can be available very rapidly but still preserve a provisional character. If the chain considered valid changes or if a block gets excluded, the indexer must correct its own database.

This operation is called **rollback**: the cancellation of the changes connected to the data that no longer belongs to the canonical history of the system.

In Hyper the question will require particular attention. The indexer will have to distinguish several levels:

1. transaction received by the Layer 2;
2. transaction processed by the sequencer;
3. inclusion in the batch;
4. generation of the state commitment;
5. publication of the commitment on Bitcoin;
6. progressive consolidation of the anchoring on the main blockchain.

The definitive technical documentation will have to clarify which states can still be modified, which become stable, and which procedures must be applied in case of rollback, reorganization, or anomaly. The indexer must not hide this complexity. It must make it readable.

FIGURE 23.5G **FROM THE LAYER 2 TO THE BITCOIN ANCHORING.**

Dashed = a still provisional state. Solid line = consolidation on Bitcoin.

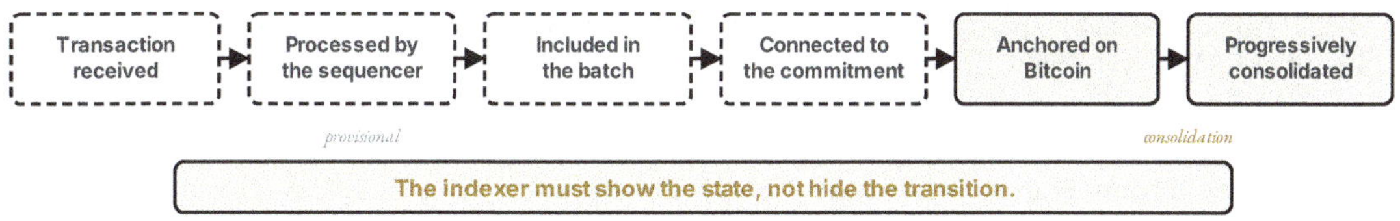

For Hyper, the indexer should clearly distinguish the different levels of acquisition and consolidation of the transaction.

Verifiability and independent reconstruction

An indexer can enormously simplify access to the data, but it also introduces a new dependence.

If an application uses a single centralized database and cannot verify the provenance of the information, the risk is evident: a parsing error, an incomplete update, or an operational problem can produce inexact results.

To reduce this fragility, several levels of control are needed:

- a connection between the indexed datum and the original transaction;
- the possibility of reconstructing the database starting from the public data;
- documentation of the schemas;
- versioning of the parsers;
- monitoring of the indexing lag;
- backfill procedures;
- comparisons between independent indexers.

In this case too, plurality does not automatically mean decentralization. Two different services can depend on the same data source, on the same parsers, or on the same underlying infrastructure.

The due diligence must therefore ask not only how many indexers exist, but also how independent they are and how simple it is to verify their results.

FIGURE 23.5H **AVOIDING A NEW CENTRALIZED DEPENDENCE.**

The indexer must not become a black box.

FRAGILE SCENARIO	VERIFIABLE SCENARIO
A single indexer	Several independent indexers
An undocumented parser	Versioned parsers
A non-reconstructible database	Backfill from the public data
No comparison	Comparable results
An error difficult to spot	More visible anomalies

The indexer simplifies access to the data, but it must not become a black box. The quality increases when the results can be reconstructed and compared.

The Solana ecosystem as a term of comparison

The Solana ecosystem offers several useful examples.

The official documentation distinguishes ordinary RPC access from the indexing and streaming solutions necessary for professional uses. Tools based on Geyser and Yellowstone gRPC make it possible to receive updates relating to accounts, transactions, blocks, and slots directly through high-performance data flows.

The Graph supports Solana through Substreams destined for real-time indexing and historical access. Helius offers APIs, webhooks, and transactions interpreted in more readable formats. Other providers make available streaming services and specialized infrastructures.

Solana Beach belongs to a partially different category: it is above all a network monitor, a validator explorer, and an account search tool. It stays useful for observability, but it must not be confused with a general-purpose indexer.

For Hyper, an analogous ecosystem could emerge progressively. It must not however be taken for granted. Technical documentation, accessible nodes, reliable data flows, parsing tools, stable APIs, and independent operators will be needed.

Why the indexers are indispensable

For some applications, the indexer represents an improvement. For others, it represents a necessary condition.

An aggregator of decentralized exchanges must compare numerous data. An analytics dashboard must reconstruct the activity over time. Tax software must classify movements and costs. A reporting system must produce coherent results. An algorithmic trading application must rapidly process large quantities of information.

Without mature indexers, all these activities become slow, fragile, or economically inefficient.

To evaluate Hyper after the opening of the mainnet, verifying that the transactions get processed will not be enough. It will be necessary to observe whether their history can be acquired, interpreted, queried, and reconstructed by independent parties.

The RPC shows what the network knows at this moment. The indexer makes it possible to reconstruct how the system got here.

The blockchain produces the data. The indexer transforms it into usable knowledge.

⁂

23.6 — Dashboards and Aggregated Metrics

In the previous paragraphs we followed a progressive path.

The block explorer allows a person to analyze a transaction, an account, or a program. The RPC infrastructure allows the applications to query the network automatically. The indexers collect the historical data, interpret it, and organize it in searchable archives.

There remains however another need.

Not all users want to examine thousands of transactions or build complex queries. Whoever evaluates the overall health of a Layer 2 needs a synthetic view: a few clear indicators, readable historical series, and signals capable of rapidly highlighting possible anomalies.

It is here that the **dashboards** come into play.

A dashboard is a digital instrument panel. It transforms large quantities of data into charts, counters, tables, and indicators. The principle is similar to that of a car's instrument panel: the driver does not directly observe the working of every component of the engine, but checks speed, fuel, temperature, and warning signals.

A good blockchain dashboard performs an analogous function. It does not replace the elementary data and does not eliminate the need to verify the sources. It offers however a first immediate reading of the system.

FIGURE 23.6A **GRANULAR DATA AND A SYNTHETIC VIEW.**

The summary at the top stays useful only if connected to the data that generates it.

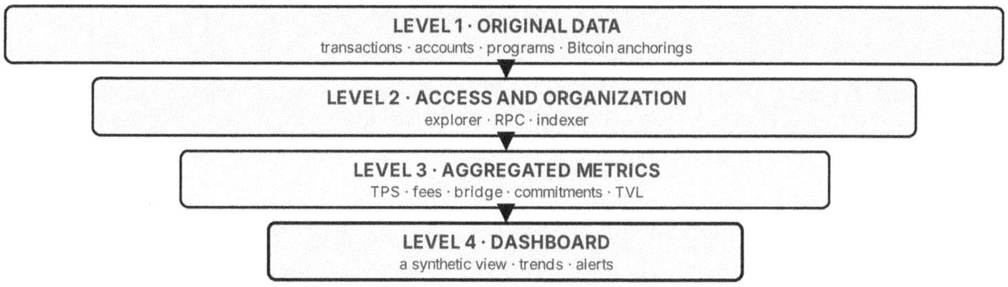

The dashboards represent the synthetic level of observability. They must remain connected to the granular data from which they derive.

For Hyper, the dashboards should make it possible to answer five fundamental questions:

1. Is the network working regularly?
2. Is the connection with Bitcoin being updated with the expected frequency?
3. Is the Canonical Bridge operating correctly?
4. Does the application ecosystem show real usage?
5. Can the published metrics be verified by independent parties?

Network health dashboards

The first category concerns the operational state of the Layer 2.

A network health dashboard should show how many transactions get processed, how long they take to be processed, which fees the users pay, and whether anomalous queues exist.

The number of **transactions per second**, abbreviated as TPS, represents a first indicator. It measures how many operations get processed in a determined interval of time. This value is useful, but it must not be interpreted in isolation.

A network can show a high number of transactions even when a relevant part of the activity depends on bots, internal operations, or repetitive transfers of minimal value. To evaluate the real usage one must observe several data together:

- overall transactions;
- operations attributable to the users;
- transferred economic volume;
- average fees;
- average inclusion time;
- share of the failed operations;
- distribution of the activity among the accounts.

FIGURE 23.6B **THE NETWORK'S HEALTH IS NOT MEASURED WITH A SINGLE NUMBER.**

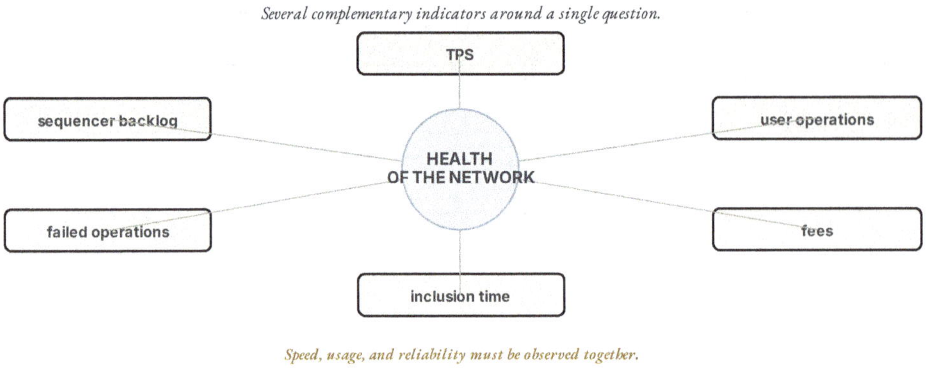

The number of transactions per second is useful, but it is not enough. A correct evaluation requires several complementary indicators.

In a sequencer-based system, it can be useful to monitor also the transaction queue. The **sequencer** is the component that receives the operations, establishes their order, and groups them for processing.

It is not appropriate to speak automatically of a mempool until the definitive architecture has clarified the working of the system. The dashboard should show what really happens: received transactions, waiting operations, delays, backlog, and possibly rejected requests.

The **TVL**, or *Total Value Locked*, too can be visualized in the general dashboard, but it must be defined with precision. The TVL indicates the value of the assets locked in the protocols. It does not necessarily coincide with the BTC transferred in the bridge, with the staking of the native token, or with the entire value exposed to the risks of the Layer 2.

FIGURE 23.6C **A HIGH TPS DOES NOT AUTOMATICALLY MEAN ADOPTION.**

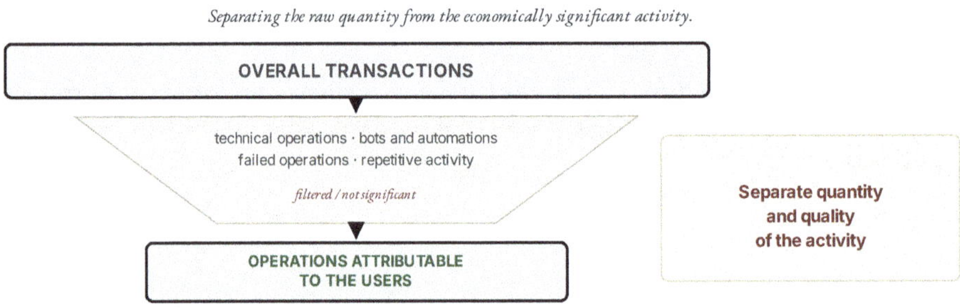

A network can process numerous transactions without automatically generating a significant economic usage. The dashboard must help to distinguish the different components of the activity.

Anchoring and liveness dashboards

For a Layer 2 connected to Bitcoin it is not enough to know how many transactions have been processed. One must understand whether the system is regularly publishing the expected references on the main blockchain.

Liveness measures the infrastructure's capacity to keep operating and updating the state over time. In simple terms, it answers the question: is the system continuing to live or has it stopped?

Hyper declares that it wants to aggregate and compress the transactions, produce ZK proofs, and periodically publish commitments of the state on Bitcoin.

The **state commitment** is a synthetic cryptographic imprint of the updated state of the Layer 2. It makes it possible to bind the system to a determined result without recording every single operation in full on the main blockchain.

A dedicated dashboard should show:

- overall number of the commitments;
- average frequency of the anchorings;
- date and time of the last update;
- interval elapsed since the last commitment;
- average size of the batches;
- number of transactions per batch;
- possible delays with respect to the expected frequency;
- a navigable link to the corresponding Bitcoin transaction.

These data make it possible to distinguish a simply fast network from a network capable of regularly maintaining its own connection with Bitcoin.

FIGURE 23.6D **FROM THE TRANSACTION TO THE ANCHORING ON BITCOIN.**

The regularity with which the Layer 2 updates the connection with Bitcoin.

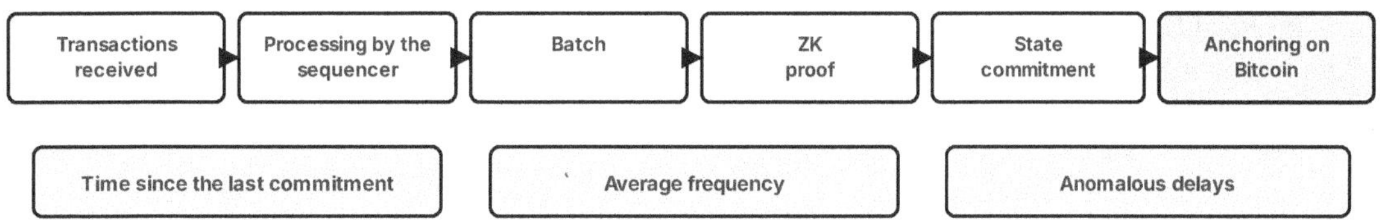

The liveness dashboard must show with what regularity the Layer 2 updates its own connection with Bitcoin.

Security dashboards

The third category concerns the security mechanisms.

A security dashboard should not limit itself to showing a reassuring green signal. It should make readable the processes through which the system verifies the state, detects the anomalies, and manages the possible malfunctions.

Since Hyper declares the use of zero-knowledge proofs, the dashboard should show at least:

- generated proofs;
- waiting proofs;
- verified proofs;
- rejected proofs;
- average generation time;
- average verification time;
- possible errors;
- delays above the norm.

ZK proofs, or *zero-knowledge proofs*, are cryptographic tools used to attest the correctness of a processing without publishing all the underlying data in full.

One must not automatically attribute to Hyper systems of disputes, fraud proofs, forced inclusion, or forced exit. If such mechanisms are foreseen in the definitive architecture, the dashboard will have to make them visible through dedicated sections. Until that moment they must remain elements to verify.

The security dashboard should also show the past incidents, the updates of the protocol, and the possible periods of inactivity. Transparency does not consist only in communicating when everything works correctly. It consists also in making the anomalies observable.

FIGURE 23.6E **THE SECURITY DASHBOARD MUST SHOW THE ANOMALIES TOO.**

Not only the green signals: also what requires attention.

ORDINARY WORKING	ANOMALOUS SITUATIONS
Generated proofs	Delayed proofs
Verified proofs	Rejected proofs
Published commitments	Missing anchorings
Regular frequency	Out-of-threshold intervals
Coherent state	Verification errors

Transparency does not consist only in showing the green signals.

A really useful security dashboard makes observable both the regular working and the events that require attention.

The Canonical Bridge dashboard

The Canonical Bridge deserves an autonomous instrument panel.

The bridge is the mechanism that connects Bitcoin and the Layer 2. It receives the deposits, verifies the necessary information, represents the BTC inside the new environment, and subsequently manages the withdrawals toward the main blockchain.

The dashboard should show at least:

- BTC overall deposited;
- BTC represented on the Layer 2;
- number and value of the deposits;
- number and value of the withdrawals;
- waiting operations;
- average recognition times;
- average exit times;
- possible failed transactions;
- temporal distribution of the flows;
- links to the original Bitcoin transactions.

One distinction is particularly important. The BTC held or managed by the bridge do not automatically coincide with the TVL of the DeFi protocols. A user can transfer BTC onto the Layer 2 and keep them in their own wallet without depositing them in any protocol. Likewise, the value locked in a decentralized application can include assets different from the BTC transferred through the official bridge.

The dashboard should therefore clearly separate:

1. value transferred by the canonical bridge;
2. value present in the protocols;
3. assets introduced through possible third-party bridges;
4. tokens used for the staking;
5. value overall exposed to the dependencies of the architecture.

FIGURE 23.6F **BRIDGE, TVL, AND EXPOSED VALUE: THREE DIFFERENT CONCEPTS.**

Three distinct magnitudes, not to be confused nor summed lightly.

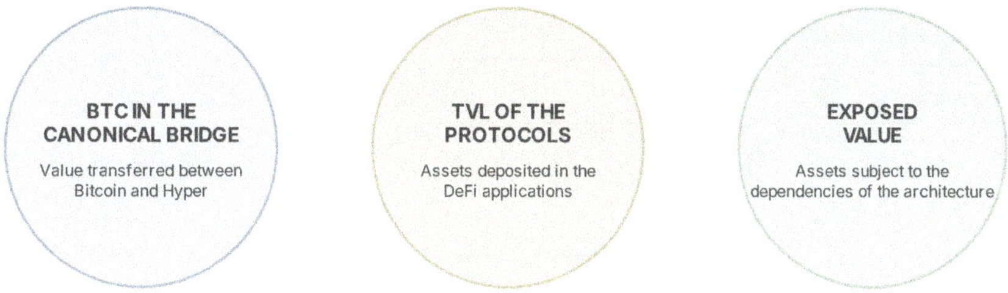

Measure separately before aggregating.

The BTC transferred through the bridge, the TVL of the applications, and the value overall exposed to the risks of the system are not synonyms.

The application ecosystem dashboard

A programmable network does not live only on transactions. It lives also on the applications built on top of it.

An ecosystem dashboard should show which protocols are actually used, which volumes they generate, and how much value gets deposited in the different services.

For a Hyper environment, the following could be useful:

- decentralized exchanges ordered by volume;
- DeFi protocols ordered by TVL[a];
- fees generated by the applications;
- number of active wallets;
- new wallets;
- recurring users;
- most used stablecoins and assets;
- distribution of the activity among the applications;
- possible digital collections or non-financial applications.

In this case too, the numbers require interpretation. A wallet does not necessarily equal a person. A user can control numerous addresses. A bot can generate thousands of operations. A promotional campaign can produce a temporary increase of the activity without creating a lasting usage.

To understand the quality of the traction[b] one must place next to the daily data a temporal perspective: weekly and monthly activity, retention of the users, share of recurring wallets, and concentration of the operations.

Retention measures how many users come back to use the system after the first access. It is a useful indicator to distinguish momentary curiosity from progressive adoption.

---

[a] **TVL** (Total Value Locked). It is the overall value of the funds deposited by the users in the decentralized finance protocols of an ecosystem — in lending, exchanges, liquidity pools. It is often used as a synthetic measure of the activity and of the trust, but it must be read with caution: it can inflate as an effect of temporary incentives or of the revaluation of the deposited tokens, and it does not necessarily reflect a real and lasting adoption.

[b] **Traction** (trazione). It is the measure in which a project is actually attracting and retaining users, developers, and real activity. An isolated peak is not enough: real traction is recognized over time, observing whether the people come back to

use the system (the retention) rather than trying it once and abandoning it. It is one of the most honest indicators of a network's state of health, because it is harder to inflate artificially than a single daily number.

FIGURE 23.6G **ACTIVE WALLETS DOES NOT EQUAL UNIQUE USERS.**

The same count of wallets can hide very different realities.

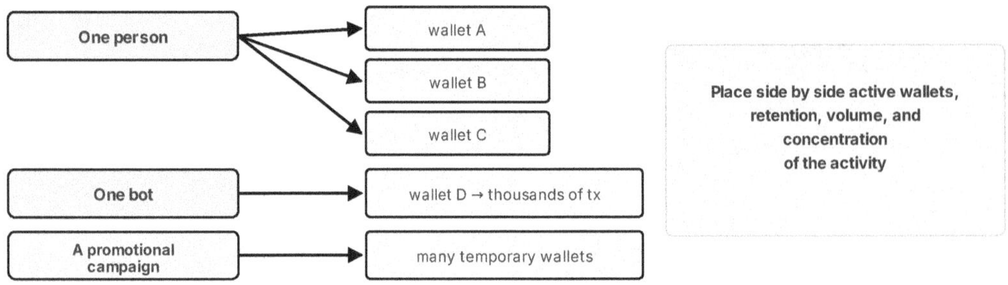

The number of active wallets is useful but it does not automatically coincide with the number of real users. It must be interpreted together with other indicators.

Analytics dashboards and historical comparisons

The most advanced dashboards do not limit themselves to describing the present. They make it possible to observe the evolution over time.

An analytics dashboard could show:

- trend of the fees;
- trend of the number of transactions;
- growth of the bridge;
- frequency of the anchorings;
- average processing time;
- activity by hour of the day;
- distribution of the wallets;
- concentration of the TVL;
- usage of the applications;
- comparisons with other Layer 2s.

These tools are useful for researchers, analysts, and investors, but they must avoid superficial comparisons. Comparing two networks on the basis of the TPS alone can be misleading. A payment network, a decentralized exchange, and a platform for general-purpose applications can generate very different activity.

The TVL too requires caution. A high value can depend on a few depositors, on temporary incentives, or on the revaluation of the underlying assets. To understand the real dynamics one must distinguish new deposits, withdrawals, price variations, and concentration of the liquidity.

Readable metrics and verifiable metrics

A well-designed dashboard must not only be nice to look at. It must make it possible to understand where the numbers come from.

Every indicator should be accompanied by:

- a definition;

- the source of the data;
- the update frequency;
- the time interval;
- the calculation methodology;
- possible exclusions;
- a link to the granular data;
- the possibility of export.

For example, the item "daily active wallets" should clarify whether it counts every address that signs at least one transaction, only the accounts that produce economic activity, or also the addresses involved passively.

The item "TVL" should specify whether it includes tokens in staking, assets transferred from the bridge, stablecoins, native tokens, and liquidity deposited in the protocols.

The item "transactions per second" should clarify whether it includes internal operations, failed transactions, or only actually completed operations.

The difference between an informative dashboard and a promotional dashboard emerges precisely from these details.

Official sources and independent dashboards

A project's team can offer an official dashboard. It is useful, because it makes it possible to know the indicators considered priorities by the developers.

It is however not sufficient.

A mature ecosystem should favor also independent dashboards, built by third parties through public and reconstructible data. The possibility of obtaining coherent results from different sources increases the trust in the infrastructure.

In the world of the Ethereum Layer 2s, L2BEAT offers an interesting model: it does not show only value and activity, but it analyzes risks, sequencer failure, proposer failure, data availability, costs, and frequency of the updates.

DefiLlama performs a different function: it aggregates metrics relating to decentralized finance, like TVL, volumes, fees, and revenues.

Dune finally allows the analysts to directly query the on-chain data, build personalized charts, and publish dashboards open to the community.

For Hyper, the progressive presence of analogous tools would represent a positive signal. Not only because it would make it simpler to consult the data, but because it would make it possible to compare different interpretations.

FIGURE 23.6H **AN OFFICIAL DASHBOARD AND INDEPENDENT VERIFICATION.**

The metrics acquire value when they can be compared.

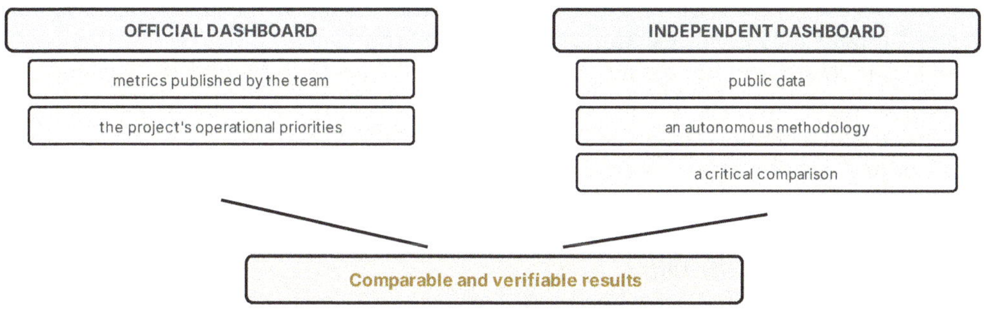

An official dashboard is useful, but observability becomes more robust when independent parties can reconstruct and compare the metrics.

A culture of observability

The dashboards do not constitute a graphic ornament added at the end of the project. They are part of the culture of observability.

A mature Layer 2 must make visible what happens when everything works regularly and what happens when delays, errors, or anomalies emerge.

An official dashboard rich in data can be useful. An independent dashboard can add a critical perspective. An explorer makes it possible to go down to the single transaction. The APIs allow the analysts to autonomously reconstruct the results. These levels must remain connected.

To evaluate Hyper after the launch of the mainnet, observing a colorful chart or a high number of transactions will not be enough. It will be necessary to ask:

- how the metrics were calculated;
- from which data they derive;
- with what frequency they get updated;
- which elements are excluded;
- whether they are exportable;
- whether independent parties can reconstruct them;
- whether the anomalies get shown with the same clarity as the favorable results.

The quality of a dashboard does not depend on the number of the charts. It depends on the possibility of transforming the summary into verification.

⁂

23.7 — Alerting and Proactive Monitoring

In the previous paragraphs we progressively built the observability system.

The block explorer allows a person to consult a transaction, an account, or a program. The RPCs allow the applications to query the network automatically. The indexers organize the historical data. The dashboards transform large quantities of information into synthetic indicators.

These tools make the system readable. It is not always sufficient, however, to be able to search for a datum when a doubt emerges.

Some problems require immediate attention. If the sequencer stops processing transactions, if the anchorings on Bitcoin accumulate delay, if the bridge does not complete the withdrawals, or if a program records an anomalous behavior, the system must not wait for someone to manually open a dashboard. It must detect the event and promptly alert the interested parties.

It is here that **proactive monitoring** and **alerting** come into play. Monitoring is the continuous process through which the infrastructure collects and evaluates operational signals. Alerting intervenes when a rule detects a significant condition and generates a notification.

The difference is simple. The dashboard shows what is happening. Monitoring continuously checks what is happening. Alerting signals when something requires attention.

From the data to the signals

A distributed system produces numerous signals.

The **metrics** are numerical measurements: latency, number of transactions, error rate, size of the batches, frequency of the anchorings, processing time of the proofs.

The **logs** are punctual recordings of events: a received request, a rejected transaction, a bridge error, a restart of the node.

The **traces** reconstruct the path followed by a request through several components. They can help to understand, for example, whether a delay originated in the wallet, in the RPC endpoint, in the sequencer, in the indexer, or in the bridge.

The **on-chain events** are finally happenings directly connected to the network: the variation of an account, the confirmation of a transaction, the modification of a program's state, the publication of a commitment.

Proactive monitoring collects these signals, puts them in relation, and compares them with rules defined in advance.

How an alert is born

An alert should not be generated by just any variation. One must establish a significant condition.

A rule can be very simple:

> Send a warning if the time elapsed since the last commitment exceeds the expected threshold.

Or more articulated:

> Generate a critical alert if the number of waiting withdrawals grows beyond a determined threshold, the average exit time increases, and the bridge has not completed operations for several consecutive intervals.

Every alert should contain at least:

- date and time;
- the component concerned;
- severity;
- the metric or event that activated the rule;
- the observed value;
- the expected threshold;
- the duration of the anomaly;
- a link to the granular data;
- the operational person in charge;
- the recommended procedure.

A good notification must not limit itself to saying that a problem exists. It must help the recipient to understand where to look and which action to take.

Three levels of severity

Not all events deserve the same attention. An effective system should distinguish at least three levels.

The **informational** level records a useful but not urgent event: a completed transaction, a scheduled update, the regular publication of a commitment.

The **warning** level signals a condition to observe: latency above the norm, a contained delay of the sequencer, an increase of the failed transactions, growth of the withdrawal queue.

The **critical** level requires immediate intervention: prolonged unavailability of the RPCs, a block of the bridge, missed publication of the commitments, repeated errors in the generation or verification of the proofs, anomalous behavior of a critical program.

The thresholds must be calibrated with attention. If every minimal variation produces an alarm, the system generates noise. If the thresholds are too permissive, the problem gets detected too late.

Alerts for the users

The users need simple and understandable notifications.
A wallet or an application should be able to signal:

- transaction received;
- transaction processed;
- inclusion in the batch;
- the connected anchoring published on Bitcoin;
- deposit recognized by the bridge;
- withdrawal started;
- withdrawal completed;
- failed operation;
- temporary slowdown of the service;
- scheduled update.

The terminology must avoid ambiguity. Saying that a transaction is "confirmed" may not be enough. In a Layer 2 anchored to Bitcoin one must distinguish the internal confirmation, the inclusion in the batch, the connection with the commitment, and the subsequent consolidation on the main blockchain.
For the non-technical user, the notification should be synthetic. For those who want to go deeper, it should offer a link to the explorer and to the details of the operation.

Alerts for developers

The developers must observe the behavior of their own applications.
A program distributed on the network can keep working without interrupting itself completely, but start showing signals of degradation:

- an increase of the errors;
- latency above the norm;
- anomalous consumption of resources;
- failed transactions;
- unexpected modifications of the state;
- differences with respect to the expected behavior;
- dependence on unavailable RPCs;
- delay of the indexers;
- loss of WebSocket events.

For financial applications, even a partial degradation can have relevant consequences. A mature system should therefore allow the developers to set personalized rules, receive webhooks, correlate logs and metrics, and connect every alert to the original transactions.

Alerts for infrastructure operators

The operators must monitor the working of the fundamental components.
For Hyper, a proactive infrastructure should observe at least:

- availability of the nodes;
- latency of the RPCs;
- error rate;
- load of the sequencer;
- number of waiting transactions;
- size of the batches;
- frequency of the commitments;
- state of the ZK proofs;
- delay of the indexers;
- synchronization with Bitcoin;
- activity of the Bitcoin Relay Program;
- working of the Canonical Bridge;
- waiting deposits and withdrawals.

These signals must be correlated. If the explorer slows down, the problem could depend on the indexer. If a dApp does not update the balances, the cause could be found in the RPCs or in the WebSocket connections. If the waiting withdrawals increase, one must understand whether the delay derives from the bridge, from the relay, from the generation of the proofs, or from the Bitcoin blockchain.

The objective of monitoring is not producing more numbers. It is reducing the time necessary to spot the cause.

Alerts for security

Security requires an autonomous category.

Since Hyper declares that it wants to use ZK proofs and periodic commitments on Bitcoin, the system should signal:

- missed generation of a proof;
- delay above the threshold;
- a rejected proof;
- a commitment not published;
- a Bitcoin anchoring not recognized;
- a difference between the expected state and the observed state;
- anomalous behavior of the bridge;
- a divergence between deposits and represented BTC;
- unusual activity of the privileged accounts;
- an unforeseen modification of a critical component.

If the definitive architecture introduces emergency procedures, disputes, forced inclusion, or forced exit, these events too will have to be monitored and made publicly readable.

The security alerts should not stay confined to the internal operators alone. The most relevant events must be communicated to the community through official channels and a consultable history.

Alerts for analysts and risk managers

The economic metrics too can generate useful signals.

An alert can highlight:

- a sudden reduction of the TVL;
- relevant withdrawals from the Canonical Bridge;
- an anomalous increase of the deposits;
- a growing concentration of the liquidity;
- a significant variation of the volumes;
- an increase of the fees;
- growth of the failed transactions;
- anomalous activity of a few wallets;
- a slowdown of the anchorings;
- a modification of the protocol's parameters.

These signals must be interpreted with caution. An increase of the deposits does not automatically represent good news. A reduction of the TVL does not necessarily imply a structural problem. A peak of transactions can depend on bots or promotional campaigns.

The alert does not replace the due diligence. It only indicates that an event deserves a deeper look.

WebSocket, webhooks, and notifications

The alerting infrastructure can use different tools.

WebSocket connections keep open a persistent channel between the application and the service. They are useful when a wallet, an explorer, or a dApp must receive continuous updates in real time.

The **webhooks** follow a different model. When an event occurs, the system automatically sends a message toward an address configured by the developer. This mechanism makes it possible to activate external procedures: sending a notification, updating a database, opening a ticket, or starting an automatic check.

The notifications destined for the people can travel through:

- wallets;
- mobile applications;
- email;
- SMS;
- Slack;
- Discord;
- Telegram;
- incident management platforms;
- operational dashboards.

The diversification of the channels must be proportionate to the severity. An informational event can appear only in the wallet. A critical problem must rapidly reach those who have the responsibility of intervening.

Avoiding the noise

A mature alerting must not only detect problems. It must avoid submerging the operators with useless notifications.

Three functions are particularly important.

Deduplication avoids sending the same alarm several times.

Grouping joins connected events. If a single failure produces one hundred secondary errors, the recipient must receive an understandable notification, not one hundred separate messages.

Inhibition prevents the sending of secondary alerts when a main problem has already been spotted. If an RPC node is offline, it can be useless to separately notify every error generated by the applications that depend on that node.

Silences are moreover necessary, that is, temporary suspensions of the notifications during planned maintenance or situations already taken in charge.

The objective is not reducing transparency. It is making the alarm useful.

From the alert to the incident

An alert does not automatically coincide with an incident. The alert signals an anomalous condition. The incident is born when that condition requires operational management.

For the most important events there should be a clear procedure:

1. detection;
2. classification of the severity;
3. notification;
4. taking charge;
5. diagnosis;
6. containment;
7. restoration;
8. public communication;
9. subsequent analysis;
10. updating of the procedures.

The final phase is essential. After a relevant problem, the team should publish a **post-mortem**, that is, a report that describes what happened, which components were involved, how the problem was resolved, and which changes were introduced to avoid the repetition of the event.

Transparency does not consist in stating that the system will never have problems. It consists in making them visible, addressing them, and learning from them.

Official alerts and independent services

Hyper's team will be able to offer official alerts for the main events. This will be useful, but not sufficient.

A mature ecosystem should favor also independent services:

- public bots;
- third-party dashboards;
- bridge monitors;
- anchoring verifiers;
- alert systems for developers;
- economic analysis services;
- independent status pages;
- community observers.

The plurality of the services reduces the risk that all observability depends on a single party. In this case too, the number of the tools is not enough. One must understand which data they use, how rapidly they react, whether they can be verified, and whether they depend on the same underlying infrastructure.

A culture of timely reaction

Alerting is not an accessory added after the launch. It is part of the design of reliability.

To evaluate Hyper after the opening of the mainnet, asking whether dashboards and explorers exist will not be enough. It will be necessary to verify:

- which events get monitored;
- which thresholds activate an alert;
- how rapidly the notifications arrive;
- which channels are available;
- how deduplication and escalation get managed;
- whether a history of the incidents exists;
- whether the errors get communicated publicly;
- whether independent parties can build alternative services.

A transparent system does not show only what has already happened. It alerts promptly when something requires attention.

⁂

23.8 — What Makes Hyper's Observability Distinctive

In the previous paragraphs we analyzed the fundamental tools of observability: block explorer, RPC, indexers, dashboards, and alerting systems.

Many of these components by now belong to the ordinary infrastructure of a programmable blockchain. A wallet must be able to query the balance of an account. A dApp must send transactions and receive updates. An explorer must make programs and operations readable. An indexer must organize the chronology. A dashboard must summarize the state of the network.

For Hyper, however, this level is not enough.

The project declares that it wants to use an SVM environment to execute programmable applications and, at the same time, to periodically anchor the state of the Layer 2 to the Bitcoin blockchain.

This double nature introduces a further necessity. The infrastructure must show what happens inside the Layer 2, but also make readable the relationship between the Layer 2 and Bitcoin. It must make it possible to follow the BTC transferred through the bridge, observe the batches, verify the commitments, understand the state of the proofs, and distinguish the internal rapidity from the finality deriving from the main blockchain.

Hyper's observability should therefore not limit itself to imitating Solana's. It should extend it with tools specific to an SVM environment anchored to Bitcoin.

FIGURE 23.8A **TWO LEVELS OF OBSERVABILITY.**

The ordinary tools of an SVM environment, plus a level specific to Bitcoin.

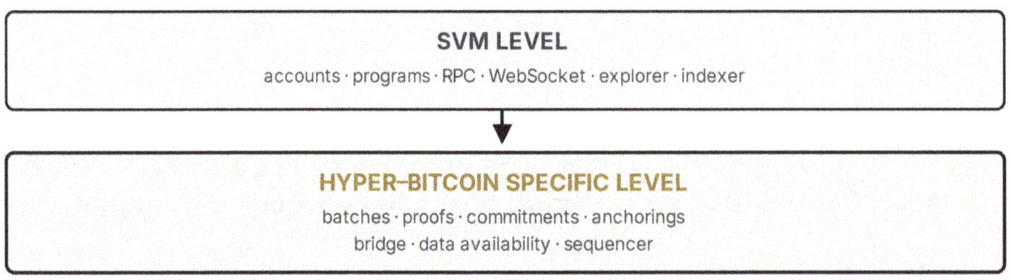

Hyper requires the ordinary tools of an SVM environment and an additional level destined to make the connection with Bitcoin readable.

From the single transaction to the anchoring on Bitcoin

The first distinctive element concerns the transaction's path.

In an ordinary blockchain, the user wants to know whether an operation has been received, processed, and confirmed. In a Layer 2 anchored to Bitcoin, the answer requires several levels.

A transaction can be:

1. received by the Layer 2;
2. ordered by the sequencer;
3. processed;
4. included in a batch;
5. associated with a proof;
6. connected to a state commitment;
7. anchored to a Bitcoin transaction;
8. progressively consolidated on the main blockchain.

The **batch** is a set of aggregated transactions. The **state commitment** is a synthetic cryptographic imprint of the updated state of the Layer 2. The anchoring consists in the publication of a reference on the Bitcoin blockchain.

These steps must be navigable. From the page of the single transaction, the user should be able to reach the batch. From the batch they should be able to open the proof. From the proof they should be able to go back to the commitment. From the commitment they should be able to consult the Bitcoin transaction, the block that included it, and the number of confirmations obtained.

Finality must not be represented through a simple green label. The explorer should clearly distinguish:

- the confirmation internal to the Layer 2;
- the inclusion in the batch;
- the publication of the commitment;
- the inclusion in the Bitcoin blockchain;
- the number of Bitcoin confirmations;
- the level of consolidation reached.

FIGURE 23.8B **FROM THE TRANSACTION TO THE BITCOIN CONSOLIDATION.**

Different phases: internal state, cryptographic connection, Bitcoin consolidation.

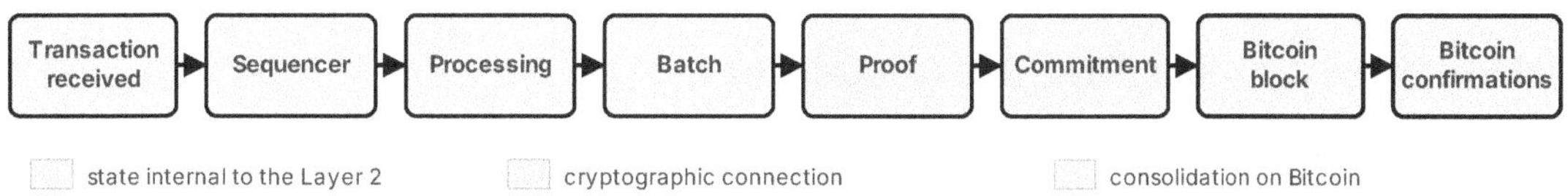

The confirmation internal to the Layer 2, the inclusion in the batch, and the consolidation on Bitcoin are different phases. The explorer must make them navigable.

The frequency of the anchorings as an operational metric

The anchoring* must not be observed only at the level of the single transaction. It must be analyzed also as a continuous process.

The dashboard† should show:

- the expected frequency of the commitments;
- the actual frequency;

- the time elapsed since the last anchoring;
- the average interval;
- the maximum interval;
- out-of-threshold delays;
- the average cost of the publication on Bitcoin;
- the size of the batches;
- the number of aggregated transactions;
- the variations over time.

These data help to understand whether the relationship between Hyper and Bitcoin stays regular even when the traffic increases or when the fees of the main blockchain become higher.

A commitment published occasionally is not enough to demonstrate the quality of the system. The due diligence must observe the continuity.

---

[*] **Anchoring.** The act with which the rollup publishes on Bitcoin the imprint of its own state, giving it a certain date and order. Observing its frequency over time — not only the single publication — is what reveals whether the bond between Hyper and Bitcoin stays regular even under load or with high fees.

[†] **Dashboard.** An instrument panel that collects and shows in real time the key metrics of a system, making its state visible at a glance. Here it is the tool that allows an independent observer to verify the regularity of the anchorings without having to trust the team's declarations alone.

FIGURE 23.8C **MEASURING THE REGULARITY OF THE ANCHORINGS.**

Continuity counts as much as the single publication.

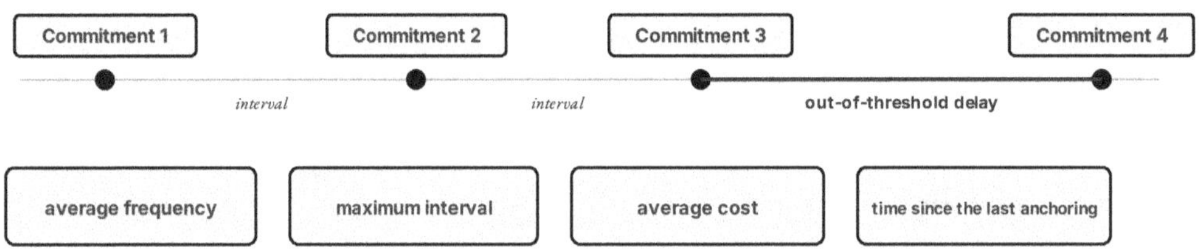

The quality of the anchoring also depends on the continuity. A dashboard must highlight delays, variations, and costs over time.

Making the Canonical Bridge transparent

The second distinctive element concerns the Canonical Bridge.

The bridge[*] is the mechanism that makes it possible to transfer BTC between Bitcoin and Hyper. The term "canonical" indicates the bridge recognized by the protocol's official architecture.

According to the model declared by the project, the user sends BTC toward a Bitcoin address monitored by the bridge. The Bitcoin Relay Program[†] verifies the headers of the blocks and the proofs of the transactions. After the verification, an equivalent quantity of BTC gets represented on the Layer 2. During the reverse path, a withdrawal request and a proof allow the release of the BTC toward the main blockchain.

A dedicated dashboard should make every step readable:

- deposit sent on Bitcoin;
- transaction detected;
- proof verified by the relay;
- BTC represented on the Layer 2;

- possible usage in the applications;
- withdrawal request;
- verification of the state;
- release on Bitcoin;
- final confirmations.

---

[*] **Canonical Bridge.** The official bridge that connects Bitcoin and the rollup, holding the deposited bitcoin in custody and regulating deposits and withdrawals according to verifiable rules. It is "canonical" because it is recognized by the protocol's architecture, and for this reason one of the most sensitive components: it is there that the funds pass between the two levels.

[†] **Bitcoin Relay Program.** The component that allows the Layer 2 to "read" Bitcoin in a verifiable way: it checks the headers of the blocks and the proofs of the transactions, so as to ascertain that a deposit has really happened on the base chain before representing it on the rollup.

FIGURE 23.8D **CANONICAL BRIDGE: DEPOSIT AND WITHDRAWAL.**

Two opposing flows between Bitcoin and the Layer 2

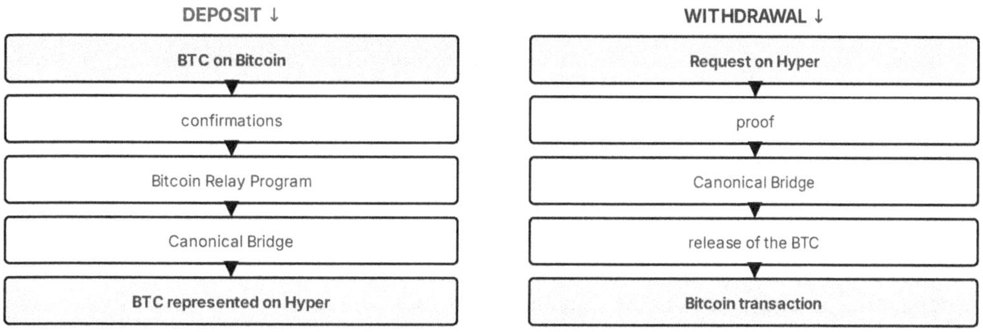

The bridge connects two different environments. Every step must be visible and connected to the original transactions.

The bridge must moreover be reconcilable[a]. The dashboard should compare:

- BTC overall deposited;
- BTC recognized by the relay[b];
- BTC represented on the Layer 2;
- BTC waiting for withdrawal[c];
- BTC already released;
- pending operations;
- possible differences to explain.

Trust does not derive only from the overall number visualized. It derives from the possibility of verifying the coherence between the different steps.

---

[a] **Reconcilable.** A system is reconcilable when its numbers can be compared and made to square with one another. For the bridge it means being able to verify, at any moment, that the bitcoin deposited and locked on Bitcoin correspond exactly to those represented on the Layer 2, net of withdrawals and operations in progress. It is the same logic with which one checks an account statement: if the accounts do not square, there is a problem to explain. The possibility of reconciling in a public and independent way is what transforms trust into verification.

[b] **Relay.** The component that transmits to the Layer 2 the verifiable information coming from Bitcoin — the headers of the blocks and the proofs of the transactions — so that the rollup can ascertain autonomously which deposits have really

happened on the base chain. It is the eye with which the bridge "looks at" Bitcoin without having to trust third parties.

[c] **Withdrawal (from the Layer 2).** The operation with which the user brings their own BTC back from the rollup to the Bitcoin chain: they send a request, the system verifies its validity, and the bridge releases the funds. Monitoring the BTC "waiting for withdrawal" serves to check that the exits get fulfilled in the expected times.

FIGURE 23.8E **RECONCILING THE BRIDGE.**

Comparing deposits, representation, withdrawals, and actual release.

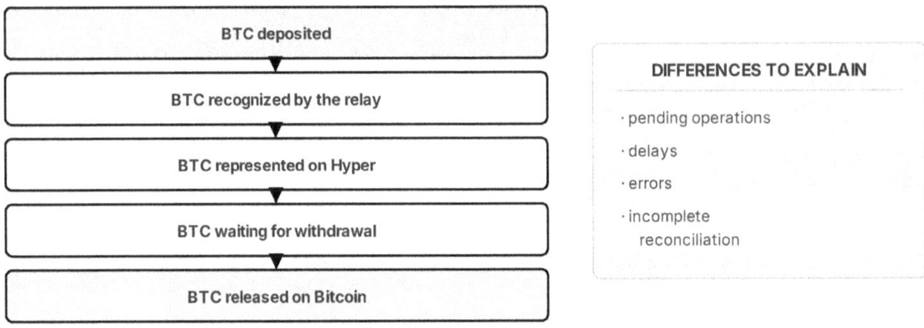

The bridge dashboard must make it possible to compare deposits, representation on the Layer 2, withdrawals, and the actual release of the BTC.

Making the proof pipeline visible

The third distinctive element concerns the security model.

Hyper declares that it wants to use ZK proofs. These proofs should attest the correctness of the processing without publishing every detail in full on the main blockchain.

For a common user a summary can be enough. For an auditor, a developer, or an analyst, more precise information is needed. The dashboard should show:

- the identifier of the proof;
- the connected batch;
- the time interval covered;
- the number of transactions involved;
- the state of the generation;
- the state of the verification;
- the time needed;
- possible errors;
- the associated commitment;
- the connected Bitcoin anchoring.

It is important to avoid generic formulations. A generated proof does not equal a verified proof. A verified proof does not automatically equal a commitment already included in a Bitcoin block. An included commitment does not equal an anchoring already consolidated through several confirmations.

The dashboard must keep these phases separate. If the definitive architecture introduces also disputes, challenges, or fraud proofs, it will have to make them visible through specific sections. Until complete technical specifications are published, these functionalities must remain hypotheses to verify.

FIGURE 23.8F **THE PROOF PIPELINE.**

Generated, verified, anchored: distinct phases not to be confused.

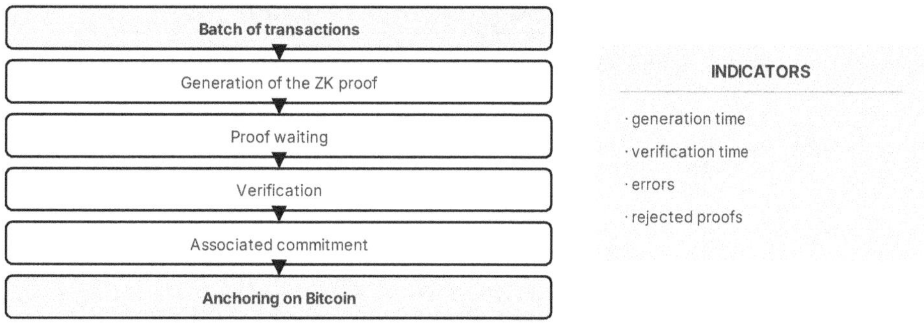

A generated proof, a verified proof, and a commitment anchored on Bitcoin represent different phases of the pipeline.

Data availability: being able to reconstruct, not only observe

A commitment and a proof do not exhaust the theme of transparency.

To really verify a Layer 2 one must understand where the data necessary to reconstruct the state is available.

Data availability answers this question:

> If an operator stopped cooperating, could an independent party recover the information necessary to reconstruct the state of the system?

The dashboard should indicate:

- which data gets published;
- where it is preserved;
- with what frequency it gets updated;
- which commitments identify it;
- which historical period is available;
- whether independent copies exist;
- which procedures allow the recovery;
- whether delays or gaps are present;
- whether an external node can reconstruct the state.

Data availability must not remain a technical formula hidden in the documentation. It is a component of the operational security. An observable network does not show only the final result. It also makes it possible to reconstruct the path that produced it.

FIGURE 23.8G **DATA AVAILABILITY: CAN THE STATE BE RECONSTRUCTED?**

Can an independent party reconstruct the state?

FRAGILE SCENARIO	VERIFIABLE SCENARIO
Incomplete data	Recoverable data
A single source	Independent copies
No backfill	Recovery procedures
An opaque commitment	A connection between data and commitments
A non-reconstructible state	A testable reconstruction

A commitment is not enough. Data availability determines whether the state can be reconstructed even without the cooperation of the main operator.

Sequencer: observing who orders the transactions

The sequencer is the component that receives the transactions, determines their order, and groups them for processing.

This function produces efficiency, but it also introduces a dependence. If a single operator controls the sequencer, one must understand what can happen in case of malfunction, censorship, or opportunistic use of the position.

A dedicated dashboard should show:

- the number of active operators;
- identities or public addresses;
- participation criteria;
- the share of batches produced by each party;
- periods of inactivity;
- rotation;
- geographic distribution;
- concentration;
- latency;
- anomalous events;
- replacement procedures;
- the progress of the decentralization path.

If the sequencer stays centralized during an initial phase, the dashboard should communicate it with clarity. Decentralization must not be represented as a switch turned on or off. It is a path composed of verifiable stages.

FIGURE 23.8H **SEQUENCER: MEASURING THE DECENTRALIZATION PATH.**

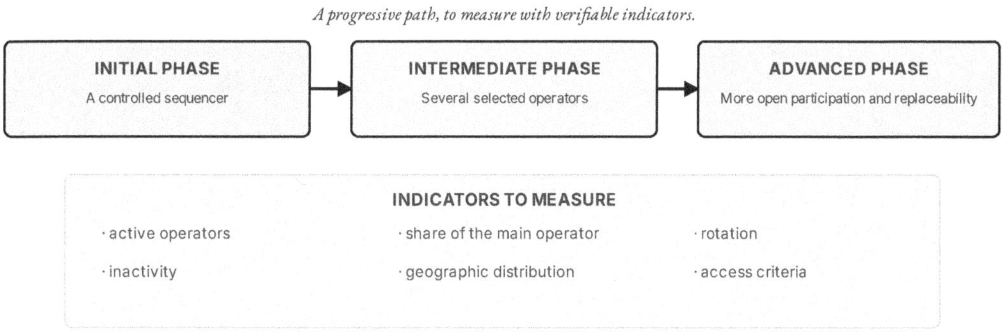

The decentralization of the sequencer is not an abstract statement. It must be measured through progressive and verifiable indicators.

Forced inclusion, forced exit, and emergency procedures

A mature Layer 2 must explain what happens when the ordinary path stops working.

If the sequencer does not include a transaction, does the user have an alternative procedure? If a withdrawal stays blocked, is it possible to exit the system without the operator's cooperation? Which times are foreseen? Which costs? Which proofs must be presented?

In some Layer 2s there are mechanisms of **forced inclusion** and **forced exit**. The forced inclusion makes it possible to request the insertion of a transaction through an alternative path. The forced exit, sometimes called an *escape hatch*, makes it possible to withdraw the funds when the ordinary path is not available.

For Hyper one must not presume that these tools are already operational. One must wait for the definitive technical documentation. If they get introduced, they will have to be fully observable:

- the request presented;
- date and time;
- the account concerned;
- the amount;
- the reason;
- the deadline;
- the state of the procedure;
- the cost;
- the outcome;
- the possible delay;
- links to the Bitcoin transactions.

The emergency procedure is useful only when it can be understood and used in the moment of need.

FIGURE 23.81 **THE ORDINARY PATH AND THE EMERGENCY EXIT.**

An ordinary path and a possible alternative exit route.

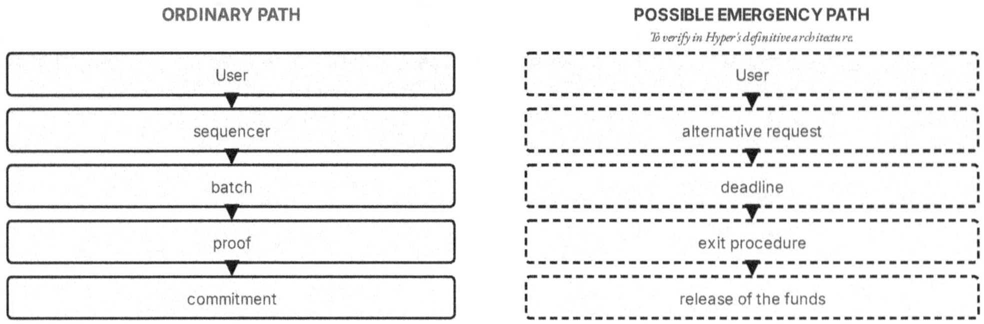

The emergency procedures must be documented and observable. For Hyper, their possible existence still has to be verified.

Unified views between Bitcoin and Hyper

Hyper's observability should moreover connect two different environments.

On one side there is the Bitcoin blockchain, with its own blocks, transactions, fees, and confirmations. On the other there is the Layer 2, with accounts, programs, batches, proofs, and commitments.

For the end user, the path must turn out readable without becoming opaque. A cross-chain view should make it possible to follow, for the **deposit**: Bitcoin transaction → inclusion in the block → number of confirmations → verification of the relay → recognition of the bridge → BTC represented on Hyper. And for the **withdrawal**: request on Hyper → verification of the state → proof → authorization of the bridge → Bitcoin transaction → confirmations on the main blockchain.

The simplicity of the interface must not erase the technical complexity. It must make it understandable.

Official tools and independent observers

The project's team will be able to offer official explorers and dashboards. They will be useful for understanding which metrics it considers priorities.

They will however not be sufficient. A really verifiable ecosystem should also allow the birth of:

- independent explorers;
- anchoring monitors;
- bridge dashboards;
- proof verifiers;
- data availability services;
- sequencer monitors;
- independent alerts;
- analytics tools;
- reconciliation software;
- community observers.

The plurality of the tools reduces the risk that the entire representation of the system depends on a single party. In this case too, the number of the interfaces is not enough. Two different dashboards can use the same indexer, the same RPC, or the same data processed by a single provider. The due diligence must verify the underlying dependencies.

FIGURE 23.8L **OFFICIAL VIEWS AND INDEPENDENT OBSERVERS.**

The official information acquires value if comparable with independent sources.

OFFICIAL TOOLS	INDEPENDENT OBSERVERS
The project's explorer	Alternative explorers
Bridge dashboard	Reconciliation monitors
State of the proofs	External verifiers
Sequencer metrics	Concentration analysis
Official communications	Independent alerts

A comparable and verifiable system

Observability becomes more robust when the official information can be compared with independent reconstructions.

A more articulated observability

Putting these elements together, a conclusion emerges.

Hyper requires a level of observability potentially more articulated than the one normally necessary for an SVM blockchain, because it must make readable also the anchoring to Bitcoin, the Canonical Bridge, the proof model, the data availability, and the decentralization path of the sequencer.

The difference is not only quantitative. It is qualitative: a Layer 2 anchored to Bitcoin introduces new steps, new dependencies, and new risks to make observable. It is not enough to visualize transactions, accounts, and programs. One must make readable:

- batches;
- proofs;
- commitments;
- Bitcoin anchorings;
- confirmations;
- data availability;
- deposits;
- withdrawals;
- reconciliation of the bridge;
- the sequencer;
- the decentralization path;
- possible emergency procedures.

This extension represents a technical challenge, but also an evaluation criterion. To analyze Hyper after the launch of the mainnet, asking whether the network is fast will not be enough. It will be necessary to verify whether every relevant step can be observed, connected to the original data, and reconstructed by independent parties.

The most important observability is not the one that shows many numbers.
It is the one that makes the system's dependencies visible.

⁂

23.9 — The State of the Art of Hyper's Observability and What to Monitor

Let us conclude with a realistic evaluation of the current state of Hyper's observability, on the basis of what is publicly available up to the first quarter of 2026, and with concrete indications of what to monitor in the months following the launch of the mainnet.

Current state (pre-mainnet). The devnet is operational and accessible, with basic tools for experimentation: an internal explorer, a public RPC, technical documentation. **The level of observability is adequate for developers who test applications**, but not for production use. This is expected for the pre-mainnet phase.

What to monitor after the launch of the mainnet.

Month 1–3: basic infrastructure. Verify that the official explorer is operational, well working, accessible. Check the availability of the public RPCs. Note the quality of the available technical documentation. See whether public dashboards with updated operational metrics exist. **In these first months, observability will probably be limited** but it must exist at a basic level.

Month 3–6: emergence of the services ecosystem. See whether other RPC providers start supporting Hyper. Note whether alternative explorers developed by third parties emerge. Check whether indexing services (like The Graph or equivalents) are indexing Hyper. **In this phase, a healthy diversification of services indicates a growing ecosystem.**

Month 6–12: maturation of the analytics tools. See whether analytics dashboards dedicated to Hyper appear (equivalents of L2BEAT, DefiLlama). Note whether independent researchers publish technical and economic analyses of the rollup. Check whether the traditional analysis companies (Glassnode, Messari, and so on) start covering Hyper. **This is a phase of consolidation of the professional observability.**

Year 2+: mature observability. Expect a complete observability ecosystem, similar to that of mature Layer 2s: multiple explorers with different characteristics, competitive RPCs among providers, mature indexers, rich analytics dashboards, consolidated alert services, regular academic and market research. **If observability does not reach this level within 18–24 months, it is a signal that the ecosystem is struggling to grow.**

Indicators of problems.

Only the team's tools. If after 12 months the only observability tools are the official ones of the Hyper team, it means that the independent community has not formed. This is a signal of centralization of the ecosystem.

Slowness of the updates. If the data in the official explorers is frequently updated with delay, or if the RPCs are often slow, it indicates underlying infrastructural problems.

Lack of analytical coverage. If independent researchers and analysts do not regularly produce content on Hyper, it means that the ecosystem is not attracting professional attention.

Difficulty of access to the historical data. If it is difficult or expensive to obtain historical data for advanced analyses, it indicates that the indexing infrastructure is not mature.

For investors and users, monitoring these aspects of observability in the months following the launch is useful for evaluating the health of the ecosystem. **A healthy ecosystem grows in observability over time; an ecosystem in difficulty stays stagnant or degrades.**

⁂

23.10 — Questions and Answers: Clarifying the Chapter's Concepts

Question 1: If observability is so important, why do many crypto projects neglect it?

For economic and priority reasons. **Building quality observability infrastructure requires significant investments** that do not directly produce measurable economic value. The team that builds explorers and dashboards does not generate fees like the team that builds a DEX or a lending protocol. For projects with limited resources, observability tends to be considered a "nice-to-have" instead of a "must-have". **Moreover, observability tends to be a public good**: once it exists, it benefits everyone, but it is difficult to capture value from its usage. This creates a classic problem of under-investment in public goods. **For Hyper, the challenge is balancing the investment in observability with other necessary investments**, and probably the team will have to bear a significant part of the initial cost, hoping that the independent ecosystem grows over time to reduce the dependence on the team. Concrete example: Solana has invested significantly in the official Solana Explorer, and the Solana Foundation has funded various third-party observability projects. For Hyper a similar trajectory is expected, even if the available funds are probably more limited.

Question 2: Can I build an application on Hyper without worrying about observability?

For initial development, yes; for production, absolutely not. **During the initial development of an application**, the basic tools (public RPCs, a basic explorer) are sufficient for testing and debugging. One can experiment, deploy prototypes, do demos without sophisticated observability infrastructure. **For production applications that manage real value, observability becomes critical.** Without proactive monitoring, one cannot detect problems before they become serious. Without historical analysis, one cannot optimize performance or understand usage patterns. Without alerting, one reacts to the problems only when the users complain. **The good practice is**: integrating observability tools from the initial phases of the project, even if at a basic level, and refining over time. This makes it possible to capture significant metrics from day one and to build baselines for future comparisons. Concrete example: serious DeFi protocols monitor in real time variables like trading volume, slippage, liquidity, possible anomalous transactions, and have alerts configured to intervene rapidly. Without these tools, even a technically perfect protocol risks having serious problems when motivated attackers emerge.

Question 3: How do I verify whether the observability of a Layer 2 is up to standard?

There are concrete indicators that you can verify. **First indicator: the presence of multiple independent explorers.** A system with a single explorer (usually the official one) is less robust than one with 3–5 alternative explorers managed by third parties. **Second indicator: the quality of the RPC documentation.** Verify that the documentation is complete, updated, with practical examples. Badly documented RPCs suggest underlying infrastructural problems. **Third indicator: the presence of public indexers.** Services like The Graph provide access to the historical data. The presence of active subgraphs for the system is an indicator of maturity. **Fourth indicator: updated public dashboards.** Verify that the dashboards get updated in real time, not with data weeks old. **Fifth indicator: media and analytical coverage.** Do services like L2BEAT, DefiLlama, Messari, Glassnode cover the system with regularity? Do they publish detailed reports and security indicators? **Sixth indicator: an active research community.** Are there blogs, papers, independent analyses that deepen technical aspects of the system? **For Hyper specifically**, these indicators should be monitored in the 12–24 months after the launch of the mainnet. The growth trajectory is more important than the instantaneous state. Concrete example: Optimism has progressively built a rich observability ecosystem that today rivals that of the Ethereum mainnet. Initially it was limited; over time it grew. For Hyper a similar trajectory is expected, and the speed of this growth will be one of the main health indicators.

Question 4: Aren't observability and privacy in tension with each other?

Yes, and it is a trade-off that every blockchain system faces. **The tension is structural**: greater observability means more information publicly accessible, and this reduces the privacy of the users. A transaction that is completely transparent on the blockchain is also completely exposed to the observers. **Original Bitcoin has this characteristic**: all the transactions are publicly verifiable, and this is considered a desirable property for the security of the system, but it compromises individual privacy. **For the users who want privacy**, various strategies exist: using new addresses for every transaction, mixing services (inadvisable in many contexts for regulatory reasons), technologies like zk-SNARKs that allow cryptographic privacy. **For Hyper**, privacy is not an emphasized aspect of the value proposition. The system inherits Solana's transparency, and the users who want greater privacy should use specific solutions. **The right balance** depends on the use case: for regulated financial applications, transparency is value; for privacy-critical applications, it is a limit. Concrete example: tokens like Monero or Zcash offer structural privacy, but at the cost of reduced observability. Bitcoin and Ethereum offer maximum observability but limited privacy. For Hyper applications, the developers can use privacy techniques at the application layer (like stealth addresses) if the use case requires it.

Question 5: The Hyper team could be tempted to limit observability to hide problems of the system. How does one protect oneself from this?

It is a legitimate concern, and the main defense is the decentralization of observability. **If observability depends only on the team's tools**, the team can control it, limit it, manipulate it. **If many independent tools managed by third parties exist**, the team's control diminishes dramatically. The community can independently verify the state of the system, identify problems, publish analyses. **The Hyper team has mixed incentives with respect to observability.** On the one hand, it wants the system to be transparent and well monitored to build trust. On the other, in moments of stress it could be tempted to reduce the visibility on specific problems. **The structural answer is**: guaranteeing that the raw data is always publicly accessible, even if the official explorers do not show it completely. This allows third parties to build their own tools, independent from the team. **For the users**, the way to protect oneself is not depending exclusively on official tools but also on independent sources. When there are discrepancies between official and independent tools, the latter tend to be more reliable (fewer incentives to manipulate). Concrete example: during crises of Ethereum Layer 2s, the official explorers at times showed incomplete or delayed data, while independent tools like L2BEAT maintained accurate data. Relying on multiple sources is prudent practice.

Question 6: How long will it take for Hyper's observability ecosystem to reach maturity?

It depends on the success of the adoption, but a realistic estimate is 18–36 months after the launch of the mainnet. **Let us compare with other projects.** Optimism was launched in 2021. **The observability ecosystem grew progressively**: in the first 6 months it was limited, in the first 12 months it was beginning to mature, in the first 24 months it was robust. Today, after 4–5 years, it is equivalent to that of Ethereum itself. **For Hyper, a similar but perhaps faster trajectory is expected** thanks to the inheritance from Solana: some tools can adapt more rapidly, benefiting from the accumulated experience. **Factors that accelerate the maturation**: high initial adoption of developers and users, significant investments of the team in official observability, active support to developers of third-party tools, partnerships with existing providers (like Helius, Solana Beach). **Factors that slow down**: low initial adoption, lack of dedicated investments, a closed ecosystem, lack of adequate documentation. **For investors and users**, the realistic expectation is to see basic infrastructure in the first 6 months, progressive maturation in the following 12–18 months, and mature infrastructure within 24–36 months. **This is the natural timeline for a project of this complexity**, and expecting faster times could be unrealistic.

⁂

23.11 — WHAT TO TAKE AWAY FROM THIS CHAPTER

A network is as alive as it is observable. Observability is not an accessory of the system but a structural component of it, on a par with execution, settlement, and data availability.

Observability has six overlapping levels: transactions, state, history, network metrics, cross-chain interactions, security mechanisms. Every level requires specific tools and serves different actors.

Block explorers are the primary access point for most users. For Hyper, high-quality explorers are needed with functionalities specific to the rollup-Bitcoin context. The diversity of explorers (official and third-party) is important for the decentralization of observability.

RPC is the infrastructure for the applications. The Solana inheritance means compatibility with the existing APIs, which is a great advantage. The diversity of RPC providers is important for the resilience of the ecosystem.

Indexers organize the history in ways that allow efficient complex queries. For advanced applications (aggregators, analytics dashboards, tax reporting), the indexer is not an addition but a necessity.

Dashboards and aggregated metrics offer synthetic views of the state of the system. They are useful for various actors: users, developers, operators, investors, researchers.

Alerting and proactive monitoring notify important events in real time. For production applications, they are a fundamental part of the operations.

Hyper's observability has distinctive aspects compared to Solana: tracking of the Bitcoin anchoring, the state of the Canonical Bridge, visibility of the proof model, forced inclusion and forced exit, decentralization metrics of the sequencer. These aspects require specific infrastructure.

To evaluate Hyper's observability after the launch of the mainnet, monitor progressively: basic infrastructure in the first 3 months, emergence of the services ecosystem at 6 months, maturation of the analytics tools at 12 months, mature observability at 24–36 months.

The decentralization of observability is the defense against attempts by the team to hide problems. Independent tools, accessibility of the raw data, independent media coverage are essential protections for the users.

---

*Chapter 23 closes here. We have understood why observability is a structural component of a Layer 2, which tools are necessary, how they apply specifically to Hyper, and how to monitor the growth of the observability infrastructure in the months following the launch. In **Chapter 24 — Infrastructural Services and Operational Workflows**, we will examine the other support services that are part of a mature blockchain ecosystem: key management, custody, oracles, security solutions, integration with traditional systems, and how Hyper can develop this level of services over time.*

Observability: seeing what is *happening*

Explorers, RPC, indexers, and dashboards to transform a technical rollup into a verifiable ecosystem. **Without observability**, even a working system remains a black box.

1 Without visibility there is no trust

Opaque network · *black box*	**Observable network** · *verifiable*
non-verifiable balance · unreadable bridge · trust in the team · non-traceable transaction · invisible network state	visible balance · monitorable bridge · independent verification · traceable transaction · public metrics

A rollup must not only work. **It must make its own working visible.**

2 The six levels of observability

1. **Transactions** — sending, inclusion in the batch, cost, outcome, finality.
2. **State** — accounts, balances, tokens, programs, positions.
3. **History** — past tx, fees, activity, time series.
4. **Network metrics** — TPS, latency, queues, errors, uptime, anchorings.
5. **Cross-chain ₿ / Hyper** — deposits, withdrawals, BTC in the bridge, commitments, confirmations.
6. **Security** — proofs, anomalies, alerts, incident reports, disputes.

Complete observability is not a single tool: **it is a layered structure.**

3 The tools: explorer, RPC, and indexer

Block Explorer	**RPC**	**Indexer**
a readable interface for users and analysts	*the invisible bridge between network and applications*	*the organized archive of the history*
transactions · accounts · programs · batches · Bitcoin commitments	reading balances · sending tx · simulating operations · querying programs · real-time events	reconstructing chronologies · searching events · feeding dashboards · analyzing bridge, volumes, anomalies

The explorer shows. The RPC connects. The indexer organizes the history.

4 The critical point: observing the bridge with Bitcoin

BITCOIN HYPER L2	transactions → batches → state → commitments
CONNECTION	Canonical Bridge · Bitcoin Relay Program · proofs · deposits / withdrawals · state commitments
BITCOIN L1	BTC transactions · anchorings · confirmations · finality

TO MAKE VISIBLE: BTC in the bridge · waiting deposits · withdrawals in progress · published commitments · Bitcoin confirmations · average times · anomalies

The connection with Bitcoin must not only be declared: **it must be observable and verifiable.**

5 From declared observability to mature observability

PRE-MAINNET	MONTHS 1-3	MONTHS 3-6	MONTHS 6-12	YEAR 2+
Basic tools	**Official explorer**	**External providers**	**Analytics**	**Mature ecosystem**
devnet, internal explorer, RPC, docs.	public RPCs, dashboards, metrics.	independent RPCs, alt explorers, indexers.	dashboards, DeFi, bridge metrics, research.	multiple explorers, alerts, observers.

RISK SIGNALS: only official tools · slow or unstable RPCs · a superficial explorer · delayed data · a poorly readable bridge · no independent coverage

The maturity of the ecosystem is measured **also by who can observe it without depending on the team.**

THE KEY POINT

Observability transforms Bitcoin Hyper from **technical infrastructure** into a **verifiable ecosystem**. Explorers, RPC, indexers, dashboards, metrics, and alerts must make visible transactions, state, **bridge, commitments, and Bitcoin anchorings**. Without observability the rollup remains a black box; with observability — and **independent** tools, not only official ones — it becomes a system that users, developers, and researchers can check.

PART VII · DEVELOPER EXPERIENCE AND THE ECOSYSTEM

Chapter 24
Infrastructural Services and Operational Workflows

The ecosystem of supporting services

⁂

24.1 — The invisible plumbing of the digital economy

There is a fact that is little discussed but fundamental for anyone who wants to understand how a mature blockchain ecosystem really works: **a significant part of the economic value of a mature ecosystem arises from the services that develop around the base infrastructure.** This sentence sounds counterintuitive, but it becomes obvious if you think about it in the traditional world. Banks alone are not worth much; the network of services that rests on banks (POS, payment gateways, custodians, brokers, advisors, audits, and so on) generates most of the economic value. **The same holds for blockchain systems.** The Bitcoin Hyper rollup, on its own, is not enough. It needs custodians[a] who can manage bitcoin for institutions. It needs oracles[b] that bring external data on-chain[c]. It needs reliable providers of cryptographic keys. It needs integrations with traditional financial systems. It needs compliance tools[d] for institutional use. It needs insurance solutions. **This level of services is one of the main enablers of adoption**, and its development or absence largely determines the success or failure of a project.

Think of it as the «invisible plumbing» of a city. The visible streets are important, but beneath them exist systems of water, gas, electricity, telecommunications that make urban life possible. A city that has only streets but no plumbing does not work; a city with mature plumbing works naturally. **For Bitcoin Hyper, the rollup is the visible «street»; the infrastructural services are the «plumbing» that makes it actually usable.**

Hyper's research post of October 2025 on infrastructural services makes this vision explicit. **The team acknowledges that good execution capacity, on its own, is not enough to create a genuinely usable network: infrastructural services capable of sustaining developers, applications, and users are needed.** It is a mature acknowledgment that many crypto projects avoid because they prefer to concentrate on the narrative of their own main product. Hyper, by acknowledging this dimension, shows a strategically healthy perspective.

---

[a] **Custodians (custody).** Professional operators who hold and manage bitcoin on behalf of third parties — banks, funds, businesses — with key protection, controls, and regulatory compliance. They are the entry door of large capital, which rarely can or wants to hold assets on its own.

[b] **Oracles.** A blockchain is a closed system: it knows only what is written inside it and cannot «see» on its own data from the outside world, such as the price of bitcoin or the outcome of an event. Oracles are the services that fill this gap, bringing external information on-chain in a form usable by smart contracts. They are an infrastructure as necessary as it is delicate: an unreliable or manipulable oracle becomes a weak point, because many financial applications depend on the data it provides.

[c] **On-chain.** Said of a piece of data or an operation recorded directly on the blockchain, and therefore public, permanent, and verifiable by anyone. «Bringing data on-chain» means making it available to the system in reliable form: it is exactly the task of oracles.

[d] **Compliance tools.** Tools that help operators meet regulatory obligations — anti-money laundering, customer identification, reporting to the authorities. For an institutional investor they are not optional: without them, it cannot operate, however sound the underlying technology may be.

FIGURE 24.1 **THE INVISIBLE PLUMBING OF THE DIGITAL ECONOMY.**

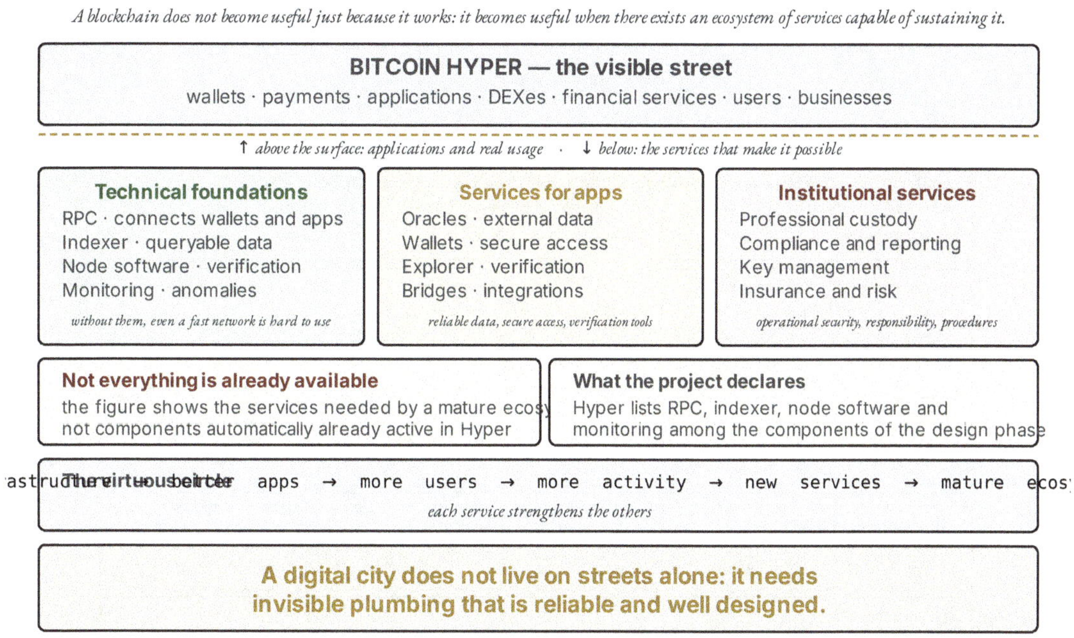

The rollup represents the visible part of the ecosystem. Below the surface operate technical, application, and institutional services: RPC, indexers, node software, monitoring, oracles, wallets, bridges, custody, key management, and compliance tools. The real maturity oj the network depends on the quality of this invisible infrastructure.

In this chapter I want to do four things. First, map the main types of infrastructural services needed for a mature Layer 2, distinguishing between the essential ones and the accessory ones. Second, examine in detail the services most critical for Bitcoin Hyper: institutional custody, oracles, key providers, compliance solutions. Third, understand the operational workflows that integrate these services into the daily functioning of the system. Fourth, assess the current state of Hyper's infrastructural services and what to monitor in the months following the mainnet launch. It is a chapter that will show you a level of the system that marketing typically neglects but which is where much of the real success is played out.

⁂

24.2 — The map of infrastructural services

Let us begin with a conceptual mapping of the infrastructural services that a mature Layer 2 needs. For each category, we look briefly at the function and the relative importance.

Category one: custody. The services that hold crypto assets on behalf of others. They range from self-custody wallets (the user keeps the keys) to enterprise custody (a professional service keeps the keys for institutions). **For Hyper, custody is particularly critical because the system handles real bitcoin**, and the quality of the custody solutions determines the trust of institutional investors.

Category two: key management. The services that generate, store, rotate cryptographic keys securely. They range from personal hardware wallets to enterprise hardware security modules (HSM). **For applications that handle significant value, professional key management solutions are essential.**

FIGURE 24.2 **THE MAP OF THE INFRASTRUCTURAL SERVICES OF A MATURE LAYER 2.**

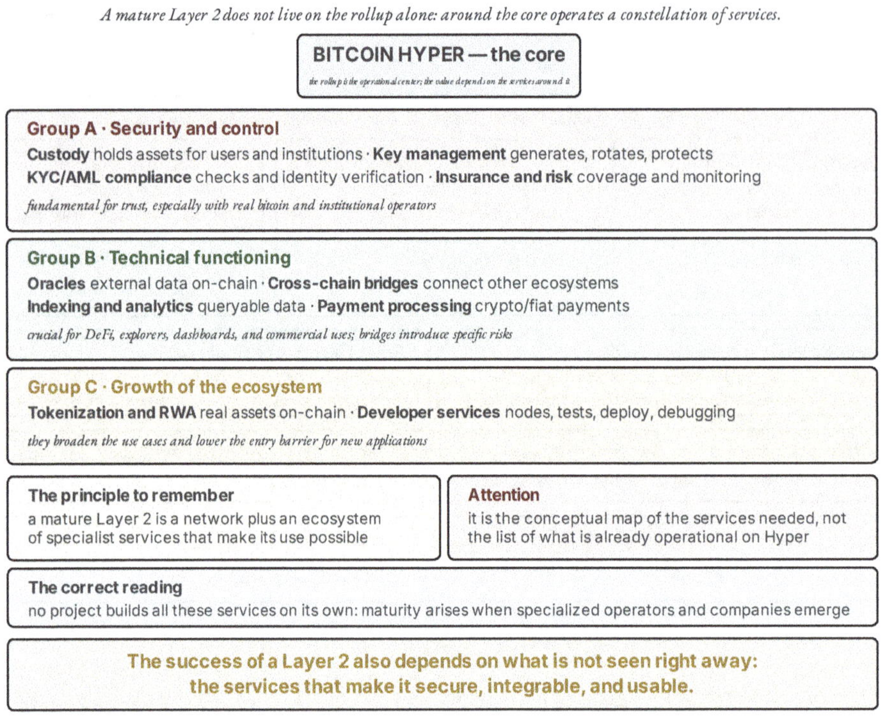

A mature Layer 2 ecosystem requires much more than the rollup alone. Around the operational core develops a constellation of infrastructural services: custody, key management, oracles, bridges, analytics, compliance, risk coverage, payments, tokenization, and developer tools. The quality and presence of these services directly influence the real adoption of the system.

Category three: oracles. The services that bring data from the outside world on-chain in a verifiable way. Asset prices, sporting events, weather data, election results. **For serious DeFi applications, reliable oracles are practically requirements**: without accurate price data, lending protocols fail, derivatives break, stablecoins lose their pegging.

Category four: cross-chain bridges. While the Canonical Bridge handles the Bitcoin-Hyper integration, applications might need integrations with other chains (Ethereum, Solana, Cosmos). **Cross-chain bridges enable this connectivity**, even though they introduce specific risks.

Category five: indexing and analytics. Already discussed in Chapter 23, it is the level that organizes data for complex queries and advanced analyses.

Category six: compliance and KYC/AML[a]. For applications that serve institutional or regulated users, services are needed that verify identities, monitor suspicious transactions, generate reports for authorities. **Without these services, institutional adoption is limited.**

Category seven: insurance and risk management. Solutions that protect against incidents: insurance policies for smart contracts, emergency funds, risk monitoring systems. **For applications that handle significant value, these solutions reduce the final risk of users.**

Category eight: payment processing. Services that facilitate payments, typically between crypto and fiat or between different cryptocurrencies. **For payment applications, these services are essential for practical utility.**

Category nine: tokenization and RWA. Services that make it possible to represent real assets (real-world assets) on the blockchain: real estate, commodities, debt, equity. **It is a growing sector** that could significantly expand the use of Hyper if well developed.

Category ten: developer services. Services specific to developers: node hosting, deployment automation, testing infrastructure, debugging tools. These accelerate the development of applications and lower the entry barrier for new projects.

Putting these ten categories together, it emerges that a mature ecosystem requires a vast range of specialist services. **No project can build them all internally**: they depend on the emergence of specialized companies and teams that fill the various niches. **For Hyper, attracting and supporting these services will be a crucial part of the ecosystem's growth strategy.**

---

[a] **KYC/AML.** These are two regulatory obligations typical of the financial world. KYC (Know Your Customer) requires verifying the identity of whoever uses a service; AML (Anti-Money Laundering) requires monitoring transactions to identify and report suspicious flows. They are the point of contact between the open and pseudonymous nature of a blockchain and the rules to which banks and regulated operators must submit: without them, the access of institutional actors remains effectively precluded.

TABLE 24.2 **THE TEN CATEGORIES OF INFRASTRUCTURAL SERVICES.**

Category	Function	Why it matters	Relevance for Hyper
Custody	holding assets for users, businesses, and institutions	trust also depends on the quality of custody	very high: the system revolves around real bitcoin
Key management	protection, rotation, and administration of keys	without it, theoretical security weakens	very high, for professional and institutional operators
Oracles	provision of reliable external data on-chain	many DeFi dApps do not work without accurate data	very high if DeFi is to grow seriously
Cross-chain bridges	connection with other blockchain ecosystems	increases interoperability, liquidity, and use cases	high, with strong attention to security risks
Indexing and analytics	organization of data for queries and dashboards	makes the system readable and monitorable	high: improves usability and transparency
Compliance and KYC/AML	support for regulatory requirements and identity	without it, institutional adoption remains limited	high, in an enterprise and financial perspective
Insurance and risk management	protection from incidents, vulnerabilities, and losses	reduces perceived and actual risk	medium-high, for high-value services
Payment processing	payments and flows between crypto and other instruments	turns the network into a practical instrument	high, if the project aims at operational use
Tokenization and RWA	bringing real-world assets on-chain	expands the economy beyond crypto-native use	potentially very high in the medium-long term
Developer services	operational tools for developers	lowers friction and accelerates new applications	extremely high: the ecosystem depends on the ease of building

Infrastructural services can be distinguished by function, but they operate interdependently. Some strengthen security, others improve technical functioning, still others make institutional adoption possible or accelerate the growth of the ecosystem. The maturity of

Bitcoin Hyper will also depend on the ability to attract and coordinate these levels of service.

⁂

24.3 — Institutional custody: the key to the adoption of large capital

Let us begin with custody, because it is the most critical infrastructural service for attracting significant capital. **For many institutional operators, the availability of professional custody solutions or of enterprise infrastructures for key management represents an essential condition for operating on Hyper.** Its absence limits the potential base of users and of value.

Let us see why institutional custody is so important and what requirements it must meet.

Why institutions need specific custody[a]. A bank, an investment fund, a family office cannot simply hold bitcoin in a personal wallet. **They have regulatory requirements** that impose asset segregation, audit trails, compliance procedures. **They have security requirements** that call for multisignature, granular controls, recovery procedures. **They have operational requirements** that call for integration with existing systems, standardized reporting, 24/7 support. All these requirements are met by specialized custodians, not by self-custody[b] solutions.

---

[a] **Custody.** It is the service of holding digital assets on behalf of third parties: a specialized operator stores and protects the cryptographic keys that control the funds, offering guarantees of security, controls, and regulatory compliance. For a private individual custody is a choice; for banks, funds, and family offices it is often an obligation, because they cannot hold bitcoin with the same instruments as a single user. The quality of the available custody is therefore a condition for the entry of large capital into an ecosystem.

[b] **Self-custody.** It is the opposite situation: the user keeps their own keys, without entrusting them to anyone. The advantage is total control — «not your keys, not your coins» — and the absence of intermediaries; the disadvantage is full responsibility, because losing the keys means losing the funds, with no one to turn to. It is the model preferred by the most rigorous bitcoiners, but hardly compatible with the operational and regulatory constraints of an institutional investor.

FIGURE 24.3 **INSTITUTIONAL CUSTODY: THE KEY TO THE ADOPTION OF LARGE CAPITAL.**

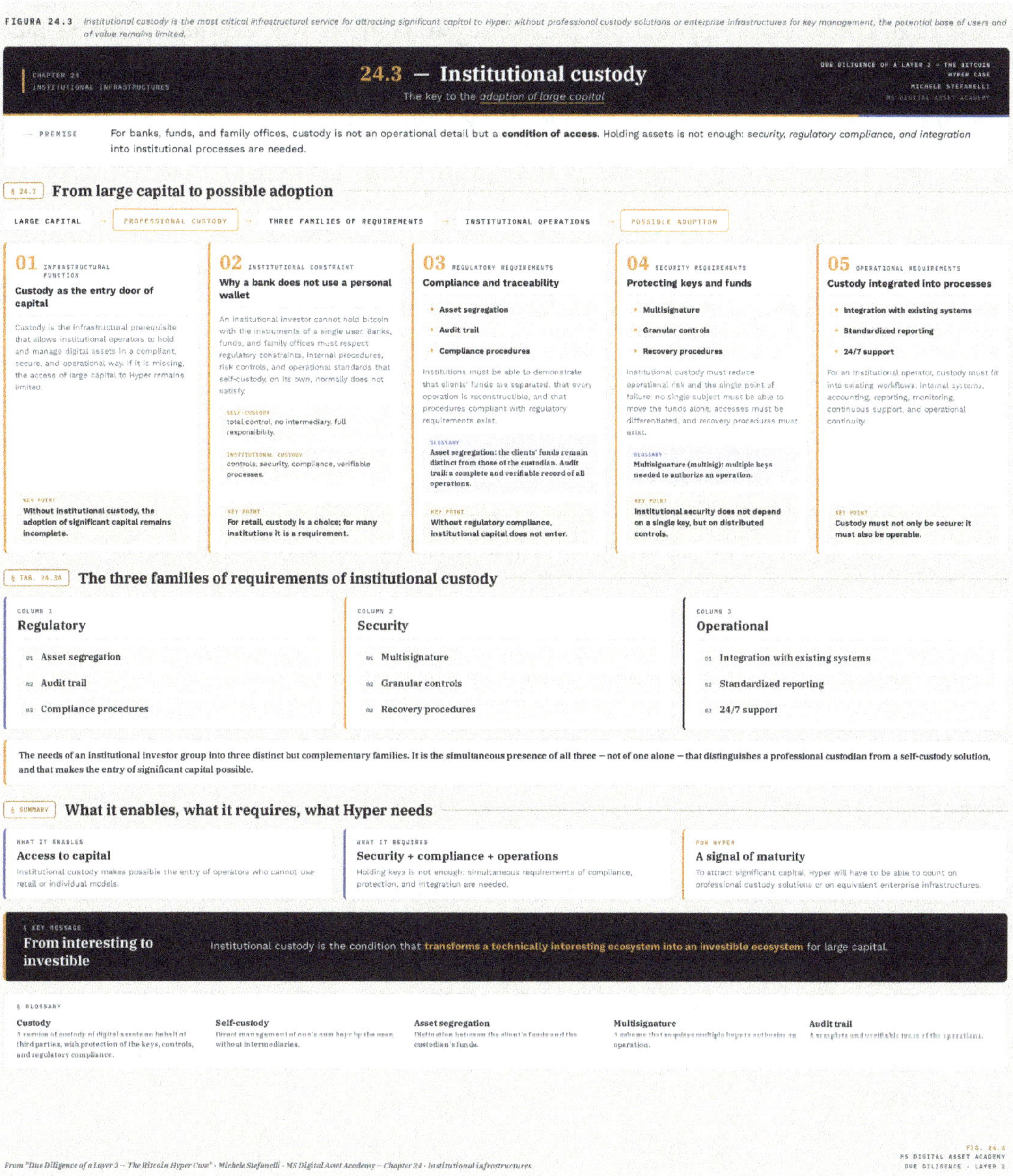

Characteristics of an enterprise-grade custodian.

Physical and logical security. Tools adequate to the risk profile, such as HSM, MPC, secure hardware, or cold storage, accompanied by organizational controls and independent verifications; datacenters with controlled physical access, network segregation, 24/7 monitoring, geographic redundancy.

Multisignature and governance. Critical operations require multiple signatures, with configurable thresholds (for example, 3 of 5, or 4 of 7). The keys are distributed across different locations, with well-documented emergency procedures.

Compliance and reporting. Conformity with applicable regulations (SOC 2, ISO 27001, possibly specific insurance), detailed reports for audits, integration with the client's compliance systems.

Insurance. Insurance coverage for catastrophic losses, typically for significant amounts (tens or hundreds of millions of dollars).

Track record. A multi-year operational history, demonstration of handling significant volumes without incidents, periodic external certifications.

For Hyper, the enterprise custody ecosystem will have to develop over time. Custodians established in the Bitcoin world (BitGo, Anchorage Digital, Coinbase Custody, Fireblocks, Copper) will be able to extend their services to the rollup, but this will require time for technical developments and for the custodians' internal approval processes. **Integration times will depend on the technical maturity of the network, on actual demand, on audits, and on the providers' internal processes.**

There is an interesting point regarding Hyper specifically. **Since the system handles native bitcoin**, custodians that already support Bitcoin can potentially extend to Hyper more easily than they can for other Layer 2s. **Continuity with their own existing Bitcoin infrastructures is an advantage.** For Ethereum L2s, custodians must adapt different infrastructures; for Hyper, they can largely reuse those they already have for Bitcoin.

For anyone assessing Hyper, the emergence of partnerships with first-tier enterprise custodians will be one of the most important indicators of institutional adoption. **Announcements of integration with BitGo, Anchorage, or equivalents, are signals of real traction**, independent of the token's price movement or the volume of transactions.

TABLE 24.3B **THE ENTERPRISE CUSTODIANS CITED AND THEIR PROFILE.**

Custodian	Profile
BitGo	Among the pioneers of qualified multi-asset custody for institutions
Anchorage Digital	First crypto bank to obtain a federal charter in the United States
Coinbase Custody	Institutional custody arm of the Coinbase group
Fireblocks	Custody and transfer infrastructure based on MPC technology
Copper	Custody and settlement aimed at institutional investors and operators

These are operators already established in the custody of Bitcoin. Since Hyper handles native bitcoin, these custodians could extend their services to it more easily than to other Layer 2s; any integration, however, must be verified in fact and not taken for granted.

⁂

24.4 — Oracles: the bridge between the real world and the blockchain

Let us move on to oracles, which deserve a dedicated section because they are often the weak point of DeFi applications and merit specific attention for Hyper.

What oracles are and why they are needed. Blockchains are closed systems: they know what has happened on-chain but have no direct knowledge of the outside world. For many use cases, however, it is necessary to bring data from the outside world on-chain. **The price of Bitcoin in dollars, the result of a football match, the temperature in a city, the outcome of an election**: all these data are useful for on-chain applications (price-based payments, sports betting, climate derivatives, prediction markets), but the blockchain itself does not know them.

Oracles solve this problem. **They are systems that observe the outside world, collect data from reliable sources, and bring it on-chain in a verifiable way.** Applications can then read this data and use it in their own logic.

FIGURE 24.4A **THE BASIC IDEA: THE ORACLE AS A BRIDGE TO THE OUTSIDE.**

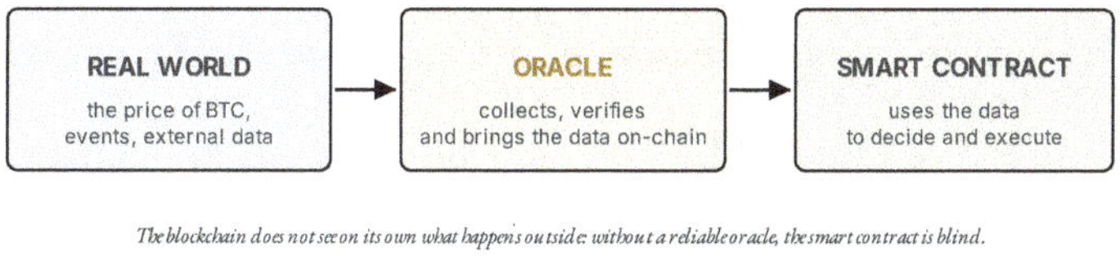

A blockchain knows only the data written inside it. The oracle is the service that bridges this distance, bringing on-chain information from the outside world in a form usable by smart contracts. It is a link as necessary as it is delicate: if the data provided is wrong or not up to date, the application that relies on it decides badly, while functioning in a technically correct way.

FIGURE 24.4 **ORACLES: THE BRIDGE BETWEEN THE REAL WORLD AND BLOCKCHAIN APPLICATIONS.**

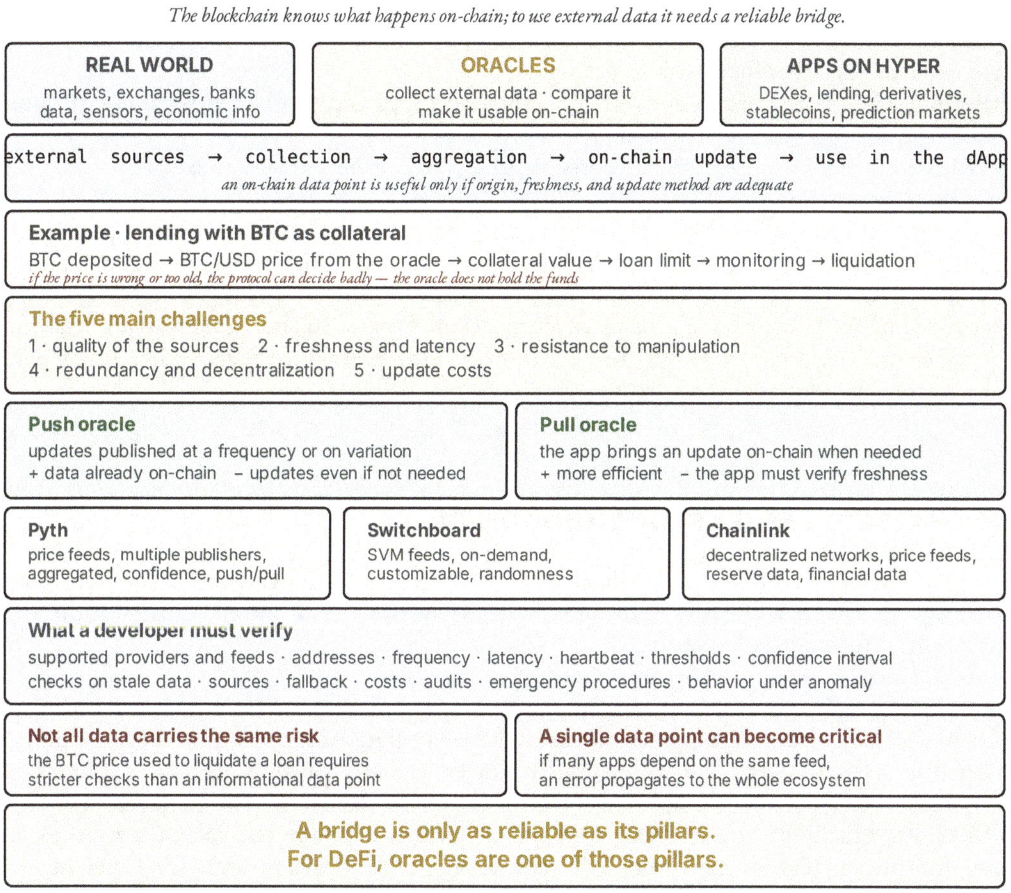

Smart contracts do not autonomously know the outside world. Oracles collect data from external sources, aggregate it, and make it usable on-chain. For financial applications such as lending and derivatives, security depends on the quality of the sources, the freshness of the updates, the resistance to manipulation, the redundancy, and the operating costs.

Technical challenges of oracles.

Reliability of the source. On-chain data is only as reliable as the source it comes from. If an oracle reports the BTC price of a manipulated exchange, the users of the applications that rely on that oracle suffer the consequences.

Latency. Between the moment an event happens in the real world and the moment it is available on-chain, there is a delay. For time-sensitive applications (trading, liquidations), latency can make a significant difference.

Resistance to manipulation. Attackers can attempt to manipulate oracles for profit. Recent history has seen famous attacks where the manipulation of oracles caused significant losses (example: various flash loan attacks on DeFi protocols).

Decentralization. An oracle managed by a single entity is a single point of failure. **The use of multiple sources and independent operators can reduce the risk of depending on a single point of failure. Overall robustness, however, also depends on the quality of the data, on the aggregation rules, and on the emergency procedures.**

Cost. Calling an oracle on-chain costs fees, and more sophisticated oracles cost more. For applications that use oracles intensively, the costs can be significant.

Existing solutions that could extend to Hyper.

Pyth Network. Already mentioned, it is probably the most important oracle for the SVM ecosystem. **Pyth aggregates data coming from numerous publishers and returns prices accompanied by a confidence interval. It supports pull and push update models, to be used according to the application's needs.** It has a strong Solana presence and could extend rapidly to the rollup.

Switchboard. Another Solana oracle with characteristics complementary to Pyth. Good for customized data that Pyth does not cover, and for applications that require pull-based oracles (oracles updated on demand) rather than push-based ones.

Chainlink. The market leader in oracles on Ethereum. Expansion to Hyper would be possible and beneficial, but requires specific developments.

Specialized oracles. For specific data (sports, weather, etc.), dedicated oracles exist that could support Hyper if there were demand.

For Hyper, the availability of reliable oracles is a precondition for serious DeFi applications. **The availability of reliable integrations with providers such as Pyth, Switchboard, Chainlink, or equivalent services will be one of the elements to monitor in order to assess the maturity of Hyper's DeFi ecosystem.** Without oracles, lending protocols cannot value collateral, derivatives cannot settle, stablecoins cannot maintain their pegging. Attracting Pyth, Switchboard, and other major oracles is therefore a strategic priority of the project.

⁂

24.5 — Wallets and key management

While enterprise custody serves institutions, most users operate through personal wallets. **The user experience with wallets is the first point of contact with the system**, and the quality of the available wallets significantly influences adoption.

Let us see the main types of wallet and what Hyper can expect.

Hot wallets.[a] Software wallets that keep the private keys accessible (in the device's memory, not physically isolated). Advantages: easy to use, they integrate with dApps, they support many functionalities. Disadvantages: more vulnerable to attacks (malware, phishing, browser exploits).

For Solana, the popular hot wallets are Phantom, Solflare, Backpack. **The declared compatibility with SVM could facilitate the integration of wallets already active in the Solana ecosystem. Actual support for Bitcoin Hyper, however, will require a specific decision and development by each provider.**
patibility with SVM makes this extension relatively simple. The speed with which the major wallets add Hyper will be one of the indicators of initial interest.

Hardware wallets.[b] Dedicated physical devices that keep the private keys isolated. **Examples of multichain hardware wallets are Ledger and Trezor. Coldcard**[c] **represents instead a specialized solution for the custody of Bitcoin on Layer 1.** Advantages: maximum security, the keys never leave the device. Disadvantages: less convenient, they require physical operations, they cost money.

For Hyper, integration with Ledger and Trezor is important for users who want to hold significant value. **Ledger and Trezor already support Solana, but the integration with Bitcoin Hyper will have to be verified specifically for signatures, assets, software wallets, and bridge flows.**

[a] **Hot wallet.** A wallet whose private keys remain accessible on the device — computer or phone — and therefore always connected. It is convenient and immediate for operating, but more exposed: if the device is compromised by malware or by a phishing attack, the keys can be stolen.

[b] **Hardware wallet ("cold" wallet).** A dedicated physical device that stores the private keys isolating them from the computer: operations must be confirmed on the device itself, so that the keys never leave it. It offers much higher security, at the price of less convenience and a purchase cost.

[c] **Coldcard.** A hardware wallet specialized exclusively in the custody of Bitcoin on Layer 1, designed for maximum security. Unlike Ledger and Trezor, which support many networks, it relies on the simplicity of a single goal: protecting bitcoin.

FIGURE 24.5 **WALLETS AND KEY MANAGEMENT: THE ACCESS DOORS TO THE ECOSYSTEM.**

There is no perfect wallet for every need: each solution balances simplicity, security, and control.

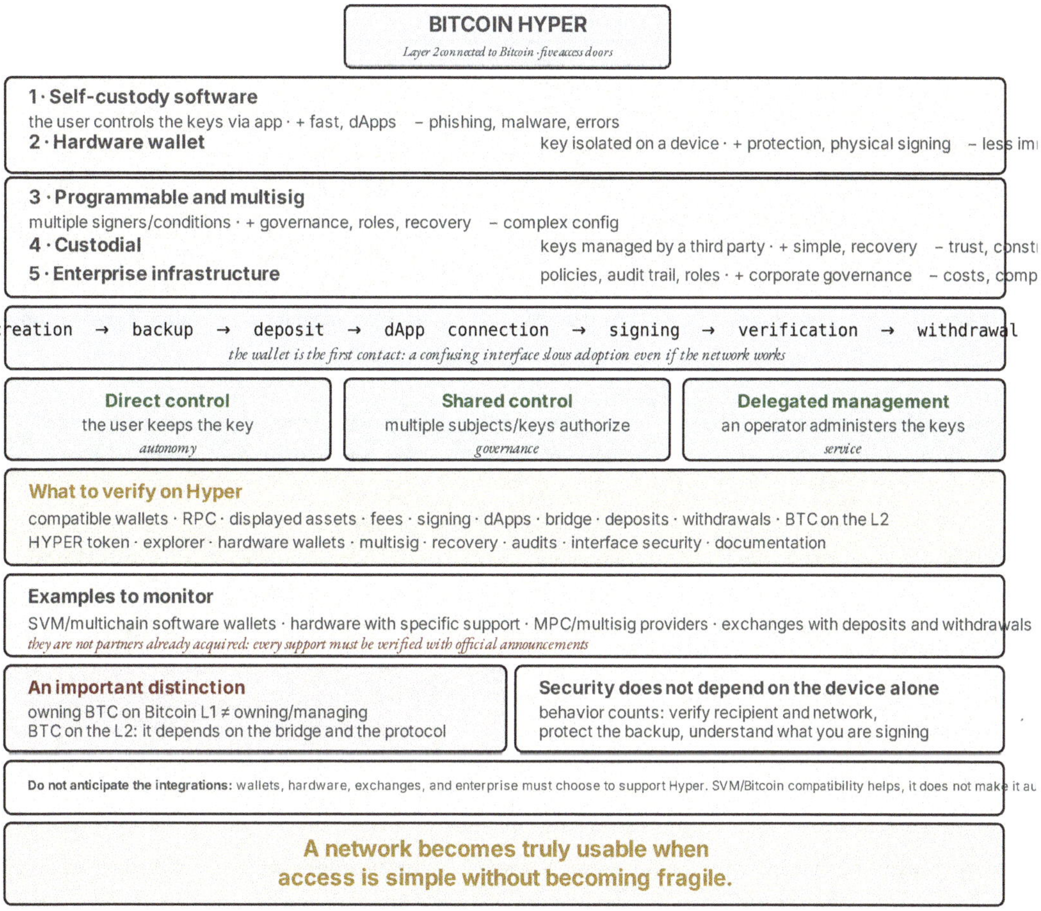

Wallets represent the first access door to the ecosystem. Self-custody software wallets, hardware wallets, programmable solutions, custodial services, and enterprise infrastructures respond to different needs. SVM compatibility can facilitate integration with existing tools, but actual support for Bitcoin Hyper must be verified for each provider, asset, and operational path.

Programmable wallets and multisig solutions. Wallets implemented as on-chain smart contracts, with advanced functionalities: multisignature, daily limits, social recovery, account abstraction. Advantages: sophisticated functionalities, more flexible recovery. Disadvantages: more expensive (initial deploy + gas for every operation), dependence on the quality of the contract's code.

For Solana, account abstraction is handled differently than for Ethereum (thanks to the specific architecture of SVM), but analogous concepts exist. **For Hyper, the evolution of these patterns will follow what happens on Solana,** with possible adaptations for the Bitcoin integration.

Custodial wallets. Wallets managed by third parties (exchanges, custodians) where the user has logical control but the keys are kept by the custodian. Advantages: easy to use, simplified management.

Disadvantages: they require trust in the custodian, they are subject to regulation.

For Hyper, integration with major exchanges is important to facilitate capital inflows and outflows. **Exchanges such as Coinbase, Kraken, Binance will have to add support** for the rollup, and this requires development time and internal compliance processes.

Enterprise wallets. Dedicated solutions for corporate use, with multisignature, configurable governance, audit trail, integration with enterprise systems. Examples: Fireblocks, BitGo, Anchorage. **For B2B applications on Hyper**, these solutions are probably necessary.

Putting these types together, it emerges that the wallet ecosystem for Hyper will develop gradually. **The wallet ecosystem will develop progressively. The signals to monitor will be the actual support of software wallets, the integration with hardware wallets, the availability of multisig and enterprise solutions, and the opening of deposits and withdrawals by the exchanges.**

TABLE 24.5 **TYPES OF WALLET AND KEY MANAGEMENT.**

Type	Who is it for?	Strength	Main limit	Verify on Hyper
Self-custody software	frequent users of dApps and payments	simple and fast access to apps	exposure to phishing, malware, errors	compatible wallets, interface, signing, RPC, backup
Hardware wallet	those protecting significant amounts	greater isolation of the keys	less immediate, specific integration	supported devices, apps, signing, bridge, withdrawals
Programmable and multisig	teams, DAOs, families	thresholds, roles, recovery procedures	complex config, depends on the software	programs, audits, compatibility, recovery, dApps
Custodial	those who prefer to delegate management	simplified experience, support	dependence on the intermediary, less control	operators, deposits, withdrawals, times, segregation
Enterprise infrastructure	businesses, funds, B2B applications	policies, audit trail, roles, monitoring	costs, complexity, onboarding	providers, MPC/multisig, reporting, bridge, incidents
Exchange wallet	those who buy, sell, or transfer on a platform	simple access to liquidity and conversions	the user does not control the keys, operational limits	exchanges supporting the network, deposits, withdrawals, fees

The different types of wallet are not perfectly interchangeable alternatives. They respond to different needs: ease of use, direct control, protection of savings, shared governance, or corporate operations. The maturity of the ecosystem will depend on the availability of multiple reliable and genuinely integrated solutions.

⁂

24.6 — Compliance and KYC/AML: the price of mainstream adoption

Let us now tackle a topic that many in the crypto community would prefer to ignore but which is fundamental for mainstream adoption: **compliance services**[*]. They are the services that allow applications to operate in conformity with applicable regulations. **For many regulated services and for a significant part of institutional adoption, adequate compliance tools represent an essential condition.** Not all decentralized applications, however, must identify every user[†]: the obligations depend on the nature of the service, on the operator involved, and on the applicable jurisdiction.

What these services include.

---

[*] **Compliance.** It is the set of procedures and services that allow an application to operate in compliance with applicable laws and regulations. In the crypto world it concerns above all the points of contact with the traditional financial system, not necessarily the base protocol.

[†] **User identification (KYC/AML).** For some regulated services the obligation kicks in to verify the identity of clients (KYC, «Know Your Customer») and to monitor flows to prevent money laundering (AML, anti-money laundering). It is not the blockchain that imposes it: the obligation falls on the operator of the service, depending on the jurisdiction.

FIGURE 24.6 **COMPLIANCE AND KYC/AML: TWO LEVELS NOT TO BE CONFUSED.**

The base protocol and compliance services must not be confused: each control intervenes where needed.

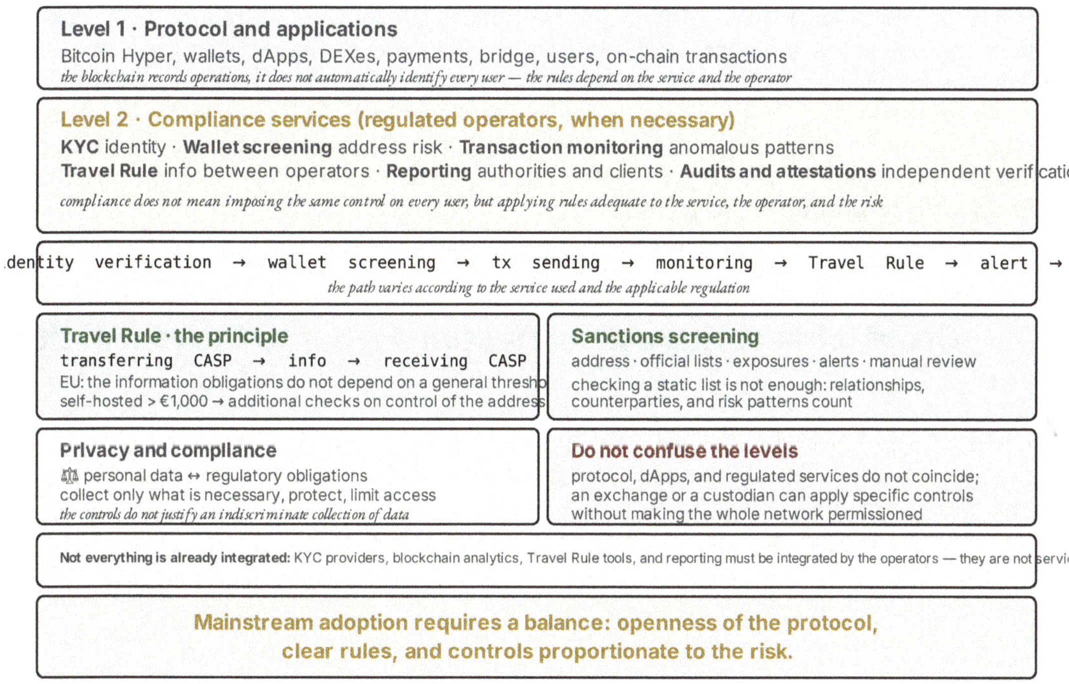

The base protocol and compliance services must not be confused. Wallet screening, transaction monitoring, KYC, Travel Rule, reporting, and audits intervene at the points of the ecosystem where they are necessary according to the service offered, the operator involved, and the applicable regulation. The maturity of the system depends on the ability to integrate these controls without introducing excessive simplifications.

KYC (Know Your Customer). Verification of the users' identity: identity documents, proof of address, possibly video verification. Necessary for regulated applications.

AML (Anti-Money Laundering). Monitoring of transactions to identify suspicious patterns, screening of addresses against sanctions lists (OFAC SDN, UN, EU), reports to competent authorities when necessary.

Travel Rule compliance. The Travel Rule requires regulated operators to collect and transmit information on the transferor and the transferee according to the rules applicable in the relevant jurisdiction. **In the European Union, the information obligations on transfers of crypto-assets involving a CASP do not depend on a general minimum threshold;** for transfers above 1,000 euros to or from self-hosted addresses, additional checks on the control of the address are envisaged. For crypto, the implementation of these obligations is a specific challenge.

Tax reporting. Generation of tax reports for users and for authorities. Necessary for many users who must declare crypto gains/losses.

Audits and attestations. Audits of smart contracts to certify security, reserve attestations for stablecoins, operational audits for services.

Well-known providers in the sector.

Chainalysis and **Elliptic** are the leaders in the analytics and compliance market. They provide tools to identify risky addresses, trace flows of funds, generate reports for authorities. **For Hyper, integration with these providers will be important** for applications that want to operate in a regulated manner.

TRM Labs offers similar services with a focus on real-time monitoring.

Sumsub and **Jumio** are KYC/AML providers that facilitate the compliant onboarding of users.

For Hyper, these services will raise philosophical tensions with the more privacy-oriented Bitcoin community. **The argument «Bitcoin is private money» is in tension with «Hyper supports regulatory compliance».** The balancing will be delicate: to attract mainstream and institutional adoption, Hyper will have to support compliance; to keep the faith of the Bitcoin community, it will have to preserve privacy options for those who choose them.

The probable answer is a two-level model. The base rollup supports all the functionalities and the native transparency of SVM, similarly to Solana. Specific applications can implement KYC/AML on top, for their own institutional users, without imposing it on all users of the rollup. **This separation preserves freedom at the base level while allowing regulation at the application level**, and it is the model that most Ethereum Layer 2s have adopted.

For anyone assessing Hyper, the emergence of regulated applications (DEXes with KYC, compliant stablecoins, institutional lending services) will be one of the indicators of mainstream adoption. **Without this level of services, Hyper would remain a system interesting for crypto-natives but marginal for the broader financial system.**

⁂

24.7 — Cross-chain bridges: connecting Hyper to the rest of the world

While the Canonical Bridge handles the Bitcoin-Hyper integration, applications might need integrations with other chains. **Cross-chain bridges enable this connectivity but introduce specific risks** that deserve attention.

Types of cross-chain bridge.

FIGURE 24.7 **CROSS-CHAIN BRIDGES: USEFUL CONNECTIONS, RISKS TO ISOLATE.**

Bridges connect Hyper to the rest of the world, but every connection introduces its own risk model.

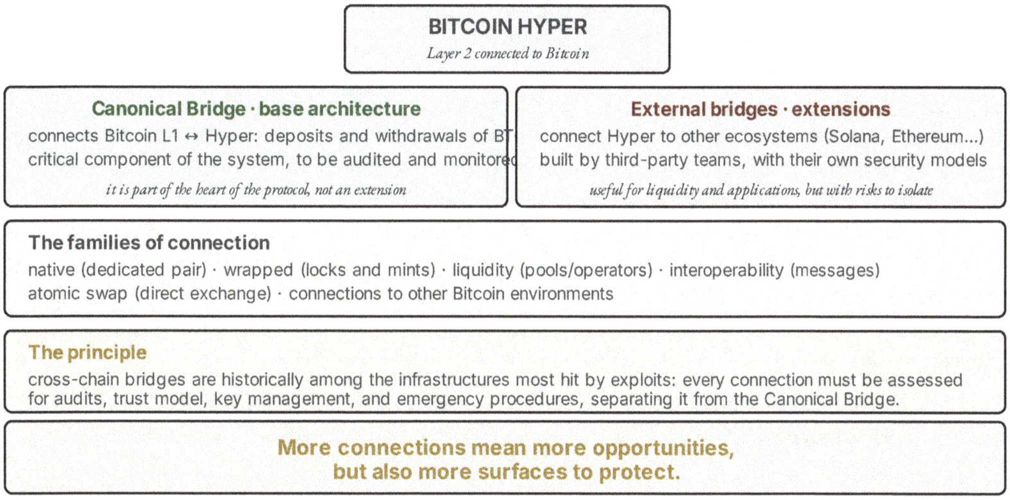

Bridges connect Bitcoin Hyper to other ecosystems and broaden its use cases, but every connection introduces its own risk model. The Canonical Bridge belongs to the base architecture of the rollup; bridges to other networks are extensions built by external parties, to be assessed separately for audits, trust model, and emergency procedures.

Native bridges. Specific to particular pairs of chains, built by the teams of the chains themselves. **Hyper's Canonical Bridge is an example** for the Bitcoin-Hyper pair.

Multichain interoperability protocols. They make it possible to transfer assets or messages between different blockchains. Wormhole, LayerZero, and other specialized protocols fall into this category, but they can adopt very different architectures and security models.

Native bridges for specific assets. Focused on a specific asset (for example, Wrapped BTC) across various chains.

Atomic swap bridges. They allow direct exchanges between chains without a centralized bridge. **They can reduce some trust dependencies, but they require technical compatibility between the chains, adequate liquidity, and a more complex user experience.**

Specific risks of bridges. Cross-chain bridges have been the target of some of the biggest exploits in crypto history. **Wormhole lost about 320 million dollars in 2022; Ronin lost over 600 million after the compromise of the keys needed for withdrawals; Nomad lost about 190 million after an update that made artfully constructed transactions processable.** These incidents had different causes: errors in cryptographic verification, key compromise, configuration problems, or vulnerabilities introduced during an update. The risk does not arise from a single weak point, but from the entire architecture of the bridge.

The reasons for the risks are structural. **Bridges hold significant value** to facilitate cross-chain exchanges. **They are attractive targets for attackers. The technical complexity is high**, because correctly handling the coordination between different chains requires sophistication that facilitates errors.

For Hyper specifically.

The **Canonical Bridge** (Bitcoin-Hyper) is the most critical bridge, built directly by the Hyper team. Its security is a precondition of the whole system.

The **bridges from/to other Bitcoin Layer 2s** (Stacks, Rootstock, Lightning) could emerge for cross-Layer 2 applications.

The **bridges from/to non-Bitcoin ecosystems** (Solana, Ethereum, Cosmos) would be useful for accessing existing liquidity and applications, but they introduce risks that users must understand.

Hyper's strategy. The team will probably focus initially on the Canonical Bridge, perfecting it and auditing it intensively. **Bridges to other ecosystems will emerge gradually over time**, built by specialized external teams rather than by the Hyper team itself. This separation of responsibilities is sensible: the core team focuses on the core components, while the ecosystem builds the extensions.

The declared positioning (June 2026). In a communication published on the official channels on June 26, 2026, the team describes cross-chain access not as a separate function, but as part of the user's overall journey: the declared goal is to reduce the barriers between different networks, starting from the premise that the future of the sector will hardly exist on a single chain. It is a positioning communication, not a technical document: it does not indicate which families of connection will be adopted, with which protocols or parties, nor with which trust model. The declared direction — a unified experience, sustained by an infrastructure that «should not make itself noticed» — therefore remains to be documented and verified according to the criteria set out in this section: audits, trust model, key management, and emergency procedures for each connection.

For users, the availability of multiple cross-chain connections can increase choice and access to liquidity. **It does not automatically guarantee greater resilience: every new bridge adds dependencies, attack surfaces, and possible different versions of the same asset.** Using well-audited bridges with a solid track record is essential; the attraction of promotional rates from lesser-known bridges is not worth the associated risks.

TABLE 24.7 **TYPES OF CROSS-CHAIN CONNECTION AND ASSESSMENT CRITERIA.**

Type	How does it work?	Advantage	Main risk	Verify on Hyper
Canonical Bridge Bitcoin–Hyper	handles deposits and withdrawals between Bitcoin L1 and the L2	using BTC in the Hyper ecosystem	critical component of the whole system	architecture, proofs, audits, times, limits, release rules
Native bridge between two networks	connects a specific pair with dedicated rules	targeted integration	depends on the security model adopted	team, contracts, audits, keys, upgrades, emergencies
Bridge for wrapped assets	locks/holds an asset and mints a representation	portability of the assets	depends on the bridge and the underlying assets	custody, reserves, redemption, audits, liquidity, versions
Liquidity-based bridge	pools/operators advance assets on the destination	faster transfers	insufficient liquidity, slippage, operators	pools, depth, fees, limits, times, risk model
Interoperability protocol	transmits messages between contracts on different networks	complex multichain applications	verifiers, configurations, external dependencies	protocol, verification model, audits, relayers, fallback
Atomic swap	direct exchange between users with cryptographic conditions	reduces some dependencies on intermediaries	compatibility, liquidity, ease of use	assets, times, liquidity, failure to complete, usability
To other Bitcoin environments	integrates Hyper with networks/services	broadens the use cases in the	each environment has different rules	compatibility, assets, trust model,

	around Bitcoin	Bitcoin ecosystem	and security	audits, documentation

Cross-chain connections are not all equivalent. Some transfer assets, others transmit messages, others use liquidity or atomic exchanges. The assessment must consider separately the Canonical Bridge, which belongs to the base architecture, and the extensions built by external parties.

⁂

24.8 — Insurance and risk management

We conclude the map of infrastructural services with one that is often neglected but increasingly important: **crypto insurance**[a]. It is the set of solutions that can transfer or attenuate a part of the economic risk arising from specifically envisaged events: exploits[b], custody problems, depegs, operational incidents, or other circumstances defined in the coverage conditions.

Types of insurance and risk coverage available. In the crypto world the term «*insurance*» is used in a broad sense, but not all solutions are insurance policies in the legal sense: some mutuals expressly state that their coverage is not an insurance contract, but rather a form of discretionary protection with assessment of claims according to pre-established rules; other models combine audits, contests, and bug bounties with an optional financial coverage, often structured in favor of the protocols' teams rather than of end users.

[a] **Crypto insurance.** The set of mechanisms which, in the world of cryptocurrencies, offer economic coverage against losses due to failures, attacks, or malfunctions. Only in part are they true insurance policies in the legal sense: often they are mutual funds or forms of discretionary protection, with their own rules and limits to be read carefully.

[b] **Exploit.** The exploitation of a flaw or an error in the code of a system to gain an undue advantage from it — typically stealing funds. It is one of the most feared events in the crypto world, and it is among the main risks that insurance coverage seeks to indemnify.

FIGURE 24.8 **RISK PROTECTION: FOUR OVERLAPPING LEVELS.**

Insurance does not replace security: it intervenes when the other levels have not been enough.

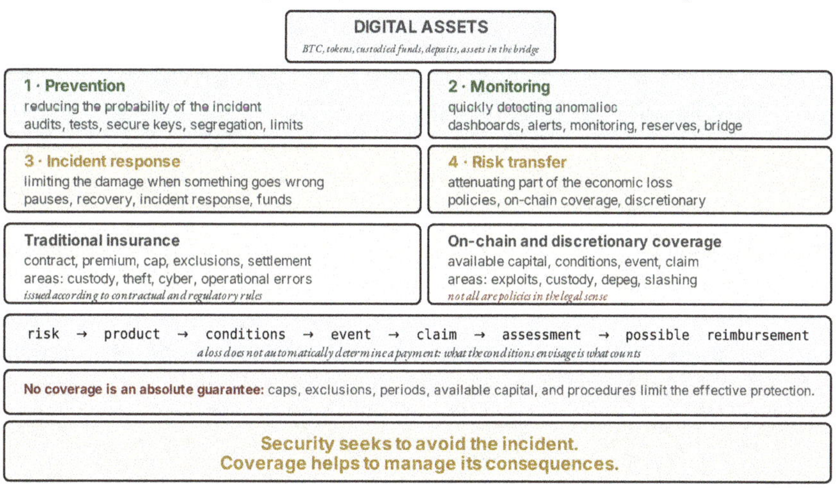

Risk management requires several overlapping levels: prevention, monitoring, incident response, and transfer of the economic risk. Traditional insurance, on-chain coverage, and discretionary solutions can attenuate some losses, but they do not replace audits, good engineering, operational procedures, and continuous controls.

Smart contract cover. Policies that pay if a specific smart contract is exploited. Examples of providers: Nexus Mutual, InsurAce, Sherlock.

Custodial cover. Policies on the risk of loss for custodians. Typically purchased by enterprise custodians to offer protection to their own clients.

Stablecoin cover. Policies on the risk of de-pegging[a] of stablecoins.

Bridge cover. Policies specific to the risks of cross-chain bridges.

Operational cover. Policies for operational risks of crypto companies: employee errors, DDoS attacks[b], system failures.

---

[a] **De-pegging.** It is the loss of a stablecoin's anchoring to the value it is supposed to maintain — usually a dollar. When a stablecoin «breaks the peg», that is, stops being worth exactly the unit it is anchored to, a flight can be triggered that worsens its detachment. It is one of the most feared risks in decentralized finance, because many applications take for granted that that value remains stable: if it fails, the effect propagates to everything that rests on it.

[b] **DDoS** (Distributed Denial of Service). It is an attack that aims to make a service unreachable by flooding it with requests from very many sources simultaneously, until its resources are saturated. It does not aim to steal funds, but to paralyze the system: in the context of a Layer 2 it can, for example, congest the nodes that users use to interact with the network. It is an operational risk, distinct from code vulnerabilities, which requires dedicated infrastructural defenses.

State of the crypto insurance market.

The market still remains in evolution. **The available capacity is uneven and varies considerably according to the risk, the provider, the asset, the protocol, and the contractual conditions.** The fact that a loss occurs does not automatically imply a reimbursement: conditions, limits, exclusions, coverage periods, and claim assessment procedures count.

For Hyper. For Bitcoin Hyper, the availability of coverage will develop progressively only if genuinely used applications, public audits, an operational track record, and sufficient economic demand emerge. **The presence of specific products will therefore be an indicator of the ecosystem's maturation, not an automatic result of the mainnet launch.** Coverage, moreover, does not eliminate the need for audits, bug bounties, monitoring, asset segregation, emergency procedures, incident response, operational limits, and diversification.

For institutional investors, the availability of insurance is a critical factor. **Without insurance, certain types of capital cannot operate** even if the technology is solid. The emergence of insurance solutions is therefore an important indicator of possible mainstream adoption.

TABLE 24.8 **TYPES OF INSURANCE AND RISK COVERAGE IN THE CRYPTO SECTOR.**

Type	What does it protect?	Strength	Main limit	Verify for Hyper
Protocols and smart contracts	losses from exploits or envisaged technical events	attenuates the economic risk	does not cover every vulnerability or loss	protocols included, events, exclusions, caps, audits
Custody coverage	losses or unavailability of custodied assets	relevant for exchanges, custodians, investors	variable scope and covered parties	custodians, assets, segregation, caps, reimbursement
Depeg coverage	loss of value of anchored assets beyond thresholds	mitigates a specific and measurable risk	threshold, duration, and calculation method are decisive	stablecoins, price feeds, thresholds, periods, liquidity

Bridge coverage	risks of bridges and cross-chain transfers	addresses a very sensitive surface	not all bridges included, different architectures	Canonical Bridge, external bridges, audits, conditions
Slashing coverage	losses from penalties in staking	useful for validators and staking providers	depends on the network's rules and the causes	staking model, operators, events, calculation
Commercial insurance	theft, cyber, errors, operational damage	supports professional adoption	coverage and exclusions depend on the policy	operators, scope, assets, jurisdiction, caps
Emergency fund	part of the losses according to established rules	rapid first response during an incident	limited capital and discretionary rules	amount, governance, activation, transparency
Security program	risks within a program with audits and bug bounties	integrates prevention and consequence management	may cover the team, not every end user	beneficiary, terms, limits, audits, reimbursement

Risk coverages are not all equivalent. Traditional insurance, on-chain mutuals, discretionary coverage, emergency funds, and security programs with optional protection adopt different rules. Before assessing the effective protection, one must verify covered events, exclusions, beneficiaries, caps, available capital, and reimbursement procedures.

⁂

24.9 — Operational workflows: how everything integrates

After mapping the services, let us see how they integrate into real operational workflows. Let us examine a few examples to make things concrete.

Workflow one: retail user making a swap on a Hyper DEX.

FIGURE 24.9 **THREE OPERATIONAL WORKFLOWS: FROM THE SIMPLE SWAP TO INSTITUTIONAL MANAGEMENT.**

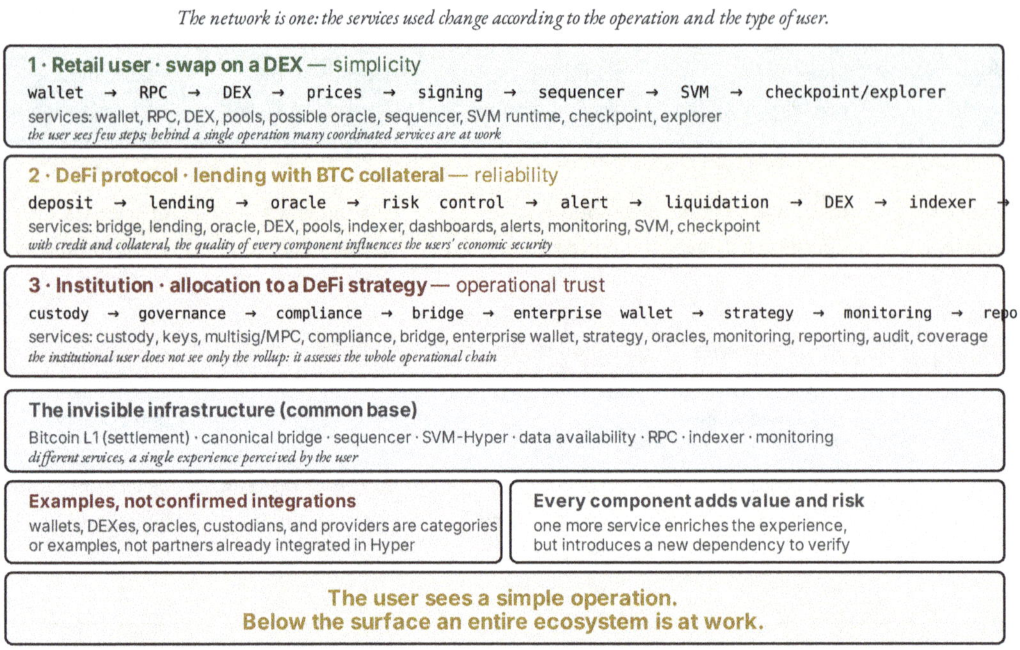

Infrastructural services combine in different ways according to the type of operation. A retail swap requires wallet, RPC, liquidity, sequencer, and explorer. A lending protocol adds oracles, risk controls, indexer, and monitoring. An institutional workflow additionally requires custody, governance, compliance, reporting, audit trail, and possible coverage. The quality of the experience depends on the integration of the whole stack.

The user opens their wallet (Phantom, Solflare). The wallet is connected to a public Hyper RPC. **The user selects a DEX available on the network. If a compatible aggregator exists, the system can compare multiple pools to identify the most convenient exchange path.** When the application's logic requires it, the protocol consults a compatible oracle to obtain up-to-date price data. The user signs the transaction. The transaction is sent to the rollup's sequencer. The sequencer includes it in a batch. The batch is executed on the SVM-Hyper. The resulting state commitment is anchored on Bitcoin. The user sees the confirmation in real time through the explorer.

In this apparently simple workflow, the following are involved: wallet, RPC, oracle, DEX, aggregator, sequencer, Bitcoin blockchain, explorer. **Each one is an infrastructural service that must work correctly** for the user to have a smooth experience.

Workflow two: DeFi protocol managing lending positions.

A user deposits BTC as collateral to borrow stablecoins. The protocol must constantly monitor the BTC price (oracle). If the price falls below critical thresholds, the protocol must liquidate the position (interacting with DEXes for rapid exchanges). The positions' data is indexed for analyses and dashboards. Important events (liquidations, large deposits) generate alerts. The periodic reconciliations with the custodian (for custodied BTC) require integration with enterprise systems.

In this more complex workflow: oracles, DEXes, indexers, alert systems, custodians, enterprise systems. **The quality of every component influences the security of the users' funds.**

Workflow three: institution allocating capital to a DeFi strategy on Hyper.

The institution deposits BTC with an enterprise custodian (BitGo). **The custodian, if it supports the network, transfers the BTC onto the rollup through the Canonical Bridge.** The institution approves the allocation through internal multisignature processes. A management smart contract (governed by the institution) deploys the funds to a specific DeFi strategy. The system monitors performance in real time, generating reports for management. KYC/AML compliance is verified at all relevant points. A complete audit trail is available for regulatory inspections. **Possible risk coverage can**

attenuate some losses arising from incidents of the smart contracts, according to pre-established conditions, limits, and exclusions.

This institutional workflow involves practically every infrastructural service: custody, bridge, governance, monitoring, compliance, audit, insurance. **Every component must be enterprise-grade** for the institution to be able to operate.

Putting these examples together, it emerges that **the experience of different users depends on different subsets of the infrastructural services.** The retail user sees only wallet, DEX, explorer; the institutional user sees the whole stack. **To attract the diversity of users, Hyper must have adequate infrastructure for every level**, and this requires the development of the whole ecosystem, not only of the base rollup.

TABLE 24.9 **THREE OPERATIONAL WORKFLOWS COMPARED.**

Workflow	Goal	Main services	What must work?	Verify on Hyper
Retail · swap on a DEX	exchanging an asset with a simple experience	wallet, RPC, DEX, pools, oracle, sequencer, SVM, explorer	interface, signing, quotation, liquidity, latency, confirmation	wallets, RPC, DEXes, real liquidity, oracles, fees, times, explorer
DeFi · lending with BTC	using BTC as collateral to obtain liquidity	bridge, lending, oracle, DEX, pools, indexer, dashboards, alerts, monitoring	updated prices, thresholds, liquidations, data, monitoring	assets, feeds, latency, fallback, liquidity, audits, rules, emergencies
Institution · DeFi strategy	operating with controlled and accountable processes	custody, keys, multisig/MPC, compliance, bridge, enterprise wallet, strategy, monitoring, reporting, audit, coverage	governance, authorizations, segregation, deposits/withdrawals, reports, continuity	integrated providers, audits, procedures, bridge, reporting, compliance, incidents, coverage

The same network can offer very different experiences. The retail user perceives above all simplicity and speed. A DeFi protocol requires reliable data, liquidity, and continuous controls. An institutional investor instead assesses the whole operational stack: custody, authorizations, compliance, reporting, audit, and risk management.

⁂

24.10 — Current state and what to monitor

We conclude with a prudent assessment of the current state of Bitcoin Hyper's infrastructural services, on the basis of the information publicly available as of this edition, and with some concrete indications on what it will be useful to monitor in the subsequent phases.

Current state (pre-mainnet).

The project has announced the launch of a first version of the devnet[a]. **The public materials moreover describe development activities dedicated to wallets, bridge, explorer, RPC[b], indexer, node software, and monitoring.** The concrete availability of the individual tools and their level of openness to the community must be verified progressively. **The developers who work with Hyper rely mainly on the Solana ecosystem**, exploiting the SVM compatibility. For the services specific to the

Bitcoin context (custody, bridge, oracles with BTC prices), they rely on the existing infrastructures of the Bitcoin world.

---

[a] **Devnet (development network).** A preliminary version of the network, reserved for developers and tests, where functions and tools are tried out before the public launch. It does not handle real value: it serves to test the system. It is the stage Bitcoin Hyper is at before the mainnet, the definitive network.

[b] **RPC.** It is the technical channel through which applications and wallets communicate with the network: they send transactions and read the state of the chain. A public and reliable RPC is an indispensable base infrastructure: without it, wallets and explorers could not work.

FIGURE 24.10 **FROM THE DEVNET TO A MATURE ECOSYSTEM: THE FOUR PHASES TO MONITOR.**

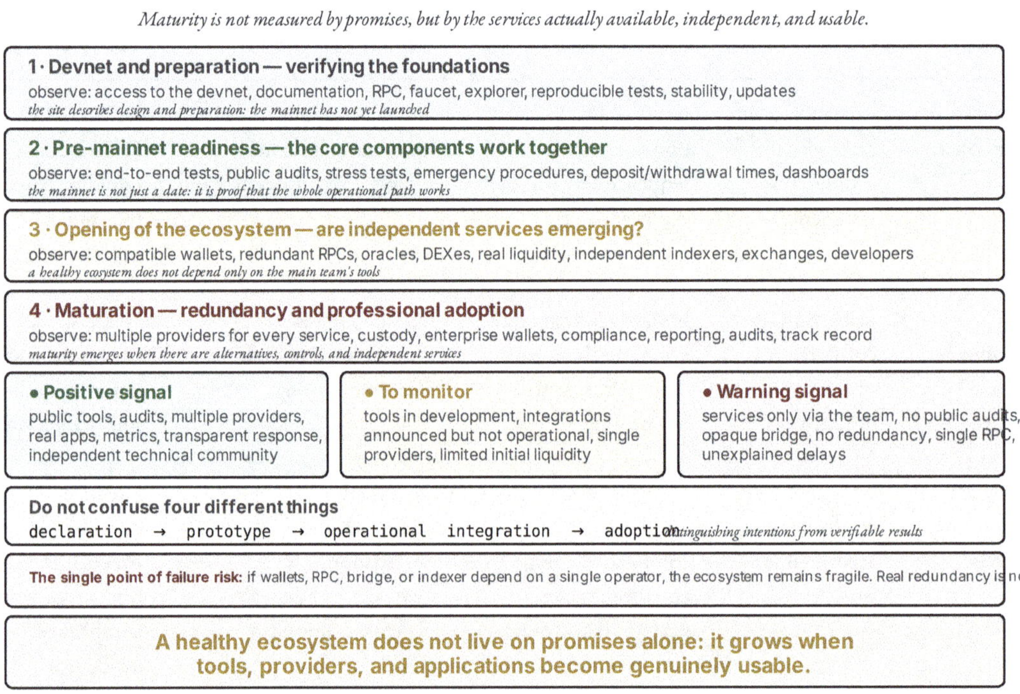

The maturity of a Layer 2 is not measured only by the completion of the protocol. Four steps must be observed: availability of the devnet, readiness before the mainnet, opening of the ecosystem to independent services, and progressive maturation toward redundancy and professional adoption. Wallets, RPC, explorers, bridges, oracles, exchanges, custody, and applications must be assessed through genuinely operational integrations.

What to monitor in the subsequent phases.

Devnet and technical preparation. Verify public access to the devnet, the documentation, the RPC endpoints, the faucet, the explorer, the reproducible tests, and the regularity of updates. It is the phase in which the technical foundations are assessed before any application promise.

Readiness before the mainnet. Observe the end-to-end tests, the public audits, the stress tests, the emergency procedures, the deposit and withdrawal times, the stability of the bridge, and the presence of dashboards and operational documentation. The mainnet is not just a date: it is the demonstration that the whole operational path works.

First post-mainnet phase and opening to independent providers. Verify whether genuinely compatible wallets, redundant public RPCs, integrated oracles, usable DEXes, real liquidity, independent indexers, support from hardware wallets and exchanges, and a community of external developers emerge. A healthy ecosystem does not depend only on the tools developed by the main team.

Maturation, redundancy, and professional adoption. In this phase maturity emerges from the availability of multiple alternatives for every critical service, from the reduction of single points of failure, from the presence of professional custody, enterprise wallet infrastructure, reporting, compliance, updated audits, incident management, and applications with real users. Maturity emerges when the ecosystem has alternatives, controls, and independent services.

Indicators of problems.

Lack of integrations with major services. If after 12 months the major wallets, the RPC providers, the oracles have not integrated Hyper, it is a signal of little interest from the ecosystem.

Services only from the team. If the only services available are those of the Hyper team, it indicates that the independent ecosystem is not forming.

Slowness in institutional partnerships. If partnerships with enterprise custodians, major exchanges, or compliance services do not emerge, institutional adoption remains limited.

Concentration on a few critical services. If the availability of a single service (example: a single RPC, a single bridge) creates a single point of failure for the ecosystem, it is a systemic vulnerability.

For investors and users, monitoring these aspects of the infrastructure in the months following the launch is useful for assessing the health of the ecosystem and the potential for long-term adoption. **A healthy ecosystem sees continuous growth of infrastructural services; an ecosystem in difficulty remains stagnant or contracts.**

TABLE 24.10 **CHECKLIST FOR MONITORING THE INFRASTRUCTURAL MATURITY OF BITCOIN HYPER.**

Area	What to observe?	Positive signal	Warning signal
Devnet and mainnet	accessibility, stability, documentation, end-to-end tests, launch	public devnet, reproducible tests, mainnet with metrics	inaccessible environment, launch without public tools
Wallets	compatibility, assets, signing, connection to dApps	multiple independent wallets with documented support	a single wallet from the team or merely declared compatibility
RPC	public endpoints, latency, stability, redundancy	multiple endpoints and providers with measurable performance	dependence on a single endpoint, frequent interruptions
Explorer and indexer	transactions, state, historical data, analyses	clear explorer, independent indexers, updated data	limited visibility or data only via the team
Canonical Bridge	deposits, withdrawals, proofs, times, audits, emergencies	tested flows, audits, public dashboards	opaque architecture, absent audits, problems kept quiet
Oracles	feeds, sources, updates, latency, fallback	reliable providers, updated data, fallback	a single feed, obsolete prices, no fallback
Exchanges	deposits, withdrawals, assets, fees, times	multiple platforms with operational flows	listing without deposits/withdrawals of the Layer 2

Custody and enterprise wallets	providers, keys, governance, segregation, reporting	independent solutions with verifiable audits	no provider or dependence on a single operator
Compliance and reporting	analytics, reporting, tools for regulated entities	complete data, professional integrations	difficulty reconstructing operations, no tools
Applications and liquidity	dApps, protocols, developers, users, liquidity	diversified growth not only from incentives	demo apps, fragile liquidity, few services
Redundancy	alternatives for the critical services	multiple wallets, RPCs, indexers, independent providers	single point of failure in essential components
Operational transparency	metrics, incident reports, roadmap, post-mortems	timely communication, verifiable data	silence during problems, vague announcements

Infrastructural maturity does not depend on a single announcement. It must be assessed over time through accessible tools, audits, operational integrations, independent providers, redundancy, and real usage. A healthy network progressively reduces its dependence on the main team and makes the functioning of the most critical services verifiable.

⁂

24.11 — Questions and answers: clarifying the chapter's concepts

Question 1: If infrastructural services are so important, why does the marketing of crypto projects concentrate almost exclusively on the core technology?

For reasons of communication and competitive positioning. **The core technology is the sellable product**: specific claims can be made (TPS, costs, security), comparisons with competitors can be drawn, narratives can be created. **Infrastructural services are more diffuse and less «ownable»**: no project can boast a monopoly on oracles or custodians, because these services are naturally provided by third parties. **For sophisticated investors, remembering that the real value comes from the complete ecosystem, not only from the core**, is an important corrective to the marketing narrative. Concrete example: the success of Ethereum does not come so much from the EVM itself (which is technically less sophisticated than SVM) but from the enormous ecosystem of services that has been built around it: oracles, exchanges, custodians, developers, applications. When investors understand this dynamic, they assess projects more realistically.

Question 2: Can we actually predict which infrastructural services will develop for Hyper, or is it speculation?

We can make informed predictions based on patterns observed in other Layer 2s. **Pattern one: fundamental services (wallets, RPC, oracles) tend to extend rapidly** from mature systems to new systems when technical compatibility exists. Hyper's SVM compatibility makes rapid extension from Solana likely. **Pattern two: enterprise services (custody, compliance) tend to require more time** for integrations because they involve the providers' internal processes. Expect 6–18 months for them to emerge. **Pattern three: niche services emerge in proportion to the volume** of the system. Without significant adoption, specialized services have no market. **Pattern four: some services win through network effects.** Once an oracle or a wallet becomes dominant, it is difficult to compete with them. For Hyper, attracting the major players early is strategically important. **Specific predictions are inevitably speculative**, but the general trajectory is predictable based on historical patterns. Concrete example: in the first 12 months of Optimism, the infrastructural ecosystem followed exactly this trajectory: basic wallets and RPCs within 3 months, enterprise custody between 6–12 months, mature ecosystem at 18–24 months. For Hyper a similar trajectory is expected, possibly slightly accelerated thanks to the Solana inheritance.

Question 3: If Hyper is based on Bitcoin, why is specific insurance needed? Isn't Bitcoin itself already sufficient «insurance»?

Bitcoin offers insurance for certain categories of risk but not for others. **Bitcoin guarantees the immutability of the anchored states**, but it does not guarantee the absence of bugs in Hyper's smart contracts, it does not guarantee the security of third-party custodians, it does not guarantee the absence of operational errors. **For example**: if a DeFi protocol on Hyper has a bug and loses users' funds, Bitcoin does not help. The rollup's state will include the loss, and the states anchored on Bitcoin will confirm the loss immutably. **Insurance protects against these specific risks**: contract bugs, operational errors, exploits. It is a protection complementary to that offered by Bitcoin, not a substitute. **For applications that handle significant value**, having multiple levels of protection is prudent: well-audited code + insurance + diversification + proactive monitoring. Each covers different risks. Concrete example: Nexus Mutual's policies paid out various claims when DeFi protocols were exploited. Without those policies, the users of those protocols would have suffered total losses. For Hyper the development of similar insurance is expected over time.

Question 4: Don't compliance and KYC/AML go against the principles of crypto?

It is a real philosophical tension that deserves honest acknowledgment. **The original crypto movement**, from the creation of Bitcoin onward, has emphasized pseudonymity, privacy, censorship resistance, financial freedom. **Compliance and KYC/AML are in tension with these values. But the real world is pluralistic.** Different users have different priorities, and different applications serve different use cases. For applications that serve informal retail users, heavy compliance is excessive and undesirable. For applications that serve institutions or regulated users, compliance is a precondition. **The pragmatic answer is to allow both models**, letting users choose. Hyper at the base level preserves the open nature of SVM. Applications built on top can implement KYC/AML if they serve users who require it. **This two-level model satisfies both constituencies**: crypto purists can use base applications, the regulated can use compliant applications. The philosophical tension remains, but it is managed practically. Concrete example: Ethereum supports both completely decentralized DEXes like Uniswap and regulated exchanges like Coinbase. Both operate on the same blockchain, serving different constituencies. For Hyper the same pattern is expected.

Question 5: What would happen if a critical infrastructural service (for example, a large oracle) had a major failure?

The consequences depend on the concentration and the diversification of the system. **In a well-diversified system**, where multiple oracles compete and protocols use combinations of oracles, the failure of a single one causes temporary inconvenience but not systemic collapses. **In a concentrated system**, where one oracle dominates and protocols depend on it critically, the failure can be catastrophic. **Recent history offers examples.** In 2020, Chainlink had a period of malfunction that caused problems for various DeFi protocols. The protocols that had implemented fallbacks to alternative sources survived without significant damage; those that depended exclusively on Chainlink had problems. **For Hyper specifically**, promoting diversity of oracles, of RPC providers, of other services is strategically important. **The centralization of infrastructural services is a systemic risk** that manifests itself in adverse scenarios. Concrete example: during the collapse of Terra/Luna in 2022, various oracles gave different readings of the price of UST while the pegging was breaking. The protocols that had robust logic against inconsistent readings defended themselves better than those that blindly trusted a single source. The lesson is general: robustness comes from diversification.

Question 6: For a team that wants to build an application on Hyper, what is more important: the quality of the rollup or the quality of the infrastructural ecosystem?

Both, but in different proportions depending on the application. **For simple applications** (tokens, NFTs, basic DeFi), the quality of the rollup is probably more important. If the rollup works well, the application can work even with basic infrastructural services. **For complex applications** (advanced DeFi, institutional applications, integration with traditional systems), the quality of the infrastructural ecosystem becomes crucial. Without reliable oracles, enterprise custodians, compliance, complex applications cannot work. **In practice**, teams should assess the quality of the complete ecosystem, not only the core technology. **Useful questions to ask include**: does the ecosystem have all the services my application needs? Is the quality of the available services adequate? Are there multiple providers for every critical service (for redundancy)? Is the ecosystem growing or stagnating? For Hyper specifically, some teams might find it advantageous to wait 6–12 months after the mainnet launch to see how the ecosystem develops, before committing fully. Concrete example: a team that wants to build a BTC derivatives protocol might find Hyper attractive for the Bitcoin narrative, but if the BTC oracles are not yet reliable on the rollup, the protocol cannot work well. The assessment requires detail on the specific services available at the time.

⁂

24.12 — WHAT TO TAKE HOME FROM THIS CHAPTER

Most of the value of a blockchain system comes from the supporting services, not from the system itself. Think of them as «invisible plumbing» that makes the use of the rollup possible.

The infrastructural services for a mature Layer 2 include ten main categories: custody, key management, oracles, cross-chain bridges, indexing and analytics, KYC/AML compliance, insurance and risk management, payment processing, tokenization and RWA, developer services.

Institutional custody is the most critical service for attracting significant capital. Without enterprise-grade custody solutions, financial institutions cannot operate on Hyper.

Oracles are bridges between the real world and the blockchain. For serious DeFi applications, reliable oracles are practically requirements. Pyth Network, already present on Solana, is the most likely candidate to extend rapidly to Hyper.

Personal wallets are the first point of contact with the system. The SVM inheritance means that Phantom, Solflare, Backpack can extend to Hyper relatively easily. Hardware wallets (Ledger, Trezor) require more time.

Compliance and KYC/AML are in tension with crypto principles, but necessary for mainstream adoption. The two-level model (open rollup + compliant applications) satisfies both constituencies.

Cross-chain bridges enable connectivity but introduce risks. The Canonical Bridge is Hyper's critical bridge; bridges to other ecosystems will emerge gradually from specialized external teams.

Crypto insurance is still nascent but increasingly important. For applications that handle significant value, multiple levels of protection (well-audited code + insurance + diversification + monitoring) are prudent.

Real operational workflows integrate many infrastructural services simultaneously. The experience of different users depends on different subsets of services: retail users see only wallet, DEX, explorer; institutional users see the whole stack.

To assess Hyper's infrastructural ecosystem after the mainnet launch, monitor progressively: basic integrations in the first 3 months, emergence of specialized services at 6 months, maturation of the ecosystem at 12 months, mature ecosystem at 24+ months.

Chapter 24 closes here, and with it Part VII (Developer Experience and the Ecosystem) and the entire arc of Volume I. We have understood the infrastructural services needed for a mature Layer 2, how they apply to Hyper specifically, and how to monitor the growth of the ecosystem in the months following the launch.

From here onward opens ***Volume II****, dedicated to competitive analysis, tokenomics, and systematic due diligence. Before leaving Volume I, however, it is worth pausing to gather what we have built: that is what the conclusion that follows does.*

The invisible plumbing of the *Hyper* ecosystem

Why a mature Layer 2 needs services, workflows, and specialized operators. The map shows the services **needed** by a mature ecosystem — not components already active on Hyper.

1 The rollup is the street, the services are the plumbing

ABOVE THE SURFACE: wallets · DEX · payments · applications · users · businesses

BELOW THE SURFACE: RPC · indexer · nodes · monitoring · custody · keys · oracles · compliance · insurance

A digital city does not live on streets alone: **it needs invisible plumbing that is reliable and well designed.**

2 Ten services that make the ecosystem mature

A · SECURITY AND CONTROL

Custody
holds assets for users and institutions.

Key management
generates, protects, rotates, governs the keys.

KYC/AML compliance
regulatory obligations for regulated operators.

Insurance & risk
attenuates losses, manages operational risk.

B · TECHNICAL FUNCTIONING

Oracles
external data on-chain: prices, events, feeds.

Cross-chain bridges
to other ecosystems, beyond the Canonical.

Indexing & analytics
queryable data, history, and metrics.

Payment processing
flows between crypto, fiat, and commercial services.

C · ECOSYSTEM GROWTH

Tokenization & RWA
real-world assets on-chain.

Developer services
nodes, tests, deploy, debug, automation.

A mature Layer 2 is **a network plus an ecosystem of specialist services.**

3 The four pillars of real adoption

Institutional custody

a personal wallet is not enough: segregation, audit trail, governance, recovery, reporting.

TO VERIFY
integrated custodians, supported bridge, procedures, audits.

Oracles

DeFi does not work without reliable external data: prices, liquidations, derivatives.

TO VERIFY
providers, feeds, latency, sources, fallback, costs, audits.

Wallets and keys

the first access door: software, hardware, multisig, custodial, enterprise.

TO VERIFY
compatible wallets, signing, HYPER, BTC on the L2, recovery.

Compliance

the protocol stays open; apps integrate regulatory controls when needed.

TO VERIFY
KYC, screening, monitoring, Travel Rule, reporting.

Mainstream adoption requires **openness of the protocol** *and specialized services at the edges of the ecosystem.*

4 More connections, more responsibility

Canonical Bridge
connects Bitcoin L1 and Hyper · a critical part of the base architecture.

External bridges
to other ecosystems · useful for liquidity, to be assessed separately.

Insurance / risk cover
can attenuate some losses, within limits · it does not replace security.

Risk management
audits, bug bounty, operational limits, emergency funds, incident response.

ⓘ One more service can enrich the experience, but **it introduces a new dependency to verify.**

Security seeks to avoid the incident. **Coverage helps to manage its consequences** — *it does not eliminate it.*

5 Operational workflows: what the user does not see

1 Retail · swap on a DEX

wallet → RPC → DEX → prices → signing → sequencer → SVM → explorer

Goal: a simple, fast, readable experience.

2 DeFi protocol · BTC lending

BTC deposit → bridge → lending → oracle → risk → alert → liquidation → indexer

Goal: correct prices, orderly liquidations.

3 Institution · DeFi strategy

custody → governance → compliance → bridge → enterprise wallet → monitoring → reporting → audit

Goal: control, reporting, continuity.

The user sees a simple operation. **Below the surface an entire ecosystem is at work.**

THE KEY POINT

Bitcoin Hyper will not be judged by the rollup alone, but by the **ecosystem** that will manage to grow around it: custody, keys, wallets, oracles, **bridge**, compliance, analytics, insurance, payments, and developer services — the invisible plumbing of real adoption. Maturity will be measured **after the mainnet**: actual integrations, independent providers, audits, and working workflows.

END OF VOLUME I

Conclusion of Volume I

From the technical machine to the market judgment

At the end of a journey twenty-four chapters and seven parts long, the reader possesses something they did not have at the beginning: a working map of how Bitcoin Hyper declares that it operates. The verb is chosen with care. This volume has not established whether the project will keep its promises, and that was not its task. It has done something different, and in some ways more lasting: it has built, piece by piece, the language needed to understand what those promises really mean, what technical conditions must come true for them to stop being promises, and at which points of the architecture the questions concentrate that no promotional material can close on the reader's behalf.

The journey has not been a sum of topics, but a chain of necessities, in which each chapter was born from a question left open by the previous one. We started from Bitcoin's deliberate limit and from the problem of extending it without touching it; that problem led us to the map of the possible solutions and, within that map, to the rollup model; the rollup forced us to dismantle its anatomy into its four components; execution brought us to the Solana Virtual Machine and to the discipline it requires; settlement obliged us to understand how a complex state can speak to Bitcoin through compressed commitments; the commitments revealed to us their dependence on data availability; the data brought us back to the figure that orders the transactions, the sequencer, and to the power that ordering entails; that power imposed on us the theme of defenses and of security understood as architecture; and security, in turn, showed us that none of this lives without tools, observers, and an ecosystem that makes it practicable.

Before leaving the volume, it is worth rereading this chain in its entirety. Not to repeat what has been said, but to finally see the machine assembled, with the gears in their place and the joints in plain sight. Only then will it become clear why the next step can no longer be technical, and why Volume II will have to change nature, questions, and tools.

A system strong because limited

The book's starting point is an observation that, outside the Bitcoin world, still sounds paradoxical: Bitcoin's strength coincides with its limits. A network that has been running uninterruptedly for seventeen years, that adds a block every ten minutes, that processes a few transactions per second and whose internal language can do, on purpose, very few things. Seen through the eyes of those who design applications, these are flaws. Seen through the eyes of those who safeguard value, they are exactly the properties that make Bitcoin credible as a definitive ledger: the predictability of the rules, the possibility of verifying them with modest hardware, the resistance to capture, the neutrality with respect to whoever uses it. Every characteristic that makes Bitcoin «backward» as a platform is the same one that makes it solid as a foundation.

From here the volume's first focusing: Bitcoin was not born to execute complex applications, and treating it as an incomplete application platform means misunderstanding it. Bitcoin is, before anything else, a settlement layer. Its trade is to give finality, security, and irreversibility to what is recorded on it. Its limitation is not an accident along the way that some future update will correct: it is an architectural choice, defended over time by a community that considers conservatism a security value, not a laziness.

Once this premise is accepted, the consequence arrives on its own. Whoever desires programmability, speed, and modern applications must not ask Bitcoin to change, because a Bitcoin that changed to please the applications would lose precisely the qualities that the applications would want to inherit. They must build on top of Bitcoin, not inside Bitcoin. And it is here that the problem shifts plane: once it is understood that the base is not to be touched, everything that matters happens at the upper level. If execution takes place off the chain, it becomes decisive to understand who orders it, how it is verified, and in what way its result comes back to speak with Bitcoin. The entire volume has been, at bottom, the orderly unfolding of this single sentence.

The tension that defines the project

Bitcoin Hyper is born inside this conceptual torsion, and the most honest way of describing it is as the attempt to hold together two needs that pull in opposite directions: keeping Bitcoin intact as a settlement base, and bringing on top of Bitcoin an execution level that is fast, programmable*, and familiar to today's developers. The book's introduction had condensed this tension into two images: on one side the perfect vault, secure and deliberately incapable of doing almost anything; on the other a rapid, cheap, and lively network, with a different security model† and an operational history not free of shadows. The project is the attempt to make the solidity of the first image coexist with the speed of the second, without the one corrupting the other.

The architecture that follows from it is the three-layer one‡ that we have traversed throughout the volume: at the bottom Bitcoin, untouched, which continues to do its trade at its usual rhythm; in the middle the rollup, where transactions are collected, ordered, and executed at high speed; at the top the applications, the layer that the user sees and touches. The design is elegant, and precisely for this reason it must be handled with caution: its elegance is also its wager. The fast layer does not inherit the finality of the slow layer merely by declaring itself connected to it; it can inherit it only by construction, through precise mechanisms, and under the conditions that this volume has reviewed one by one. The progression that leads up to here — from Bitcoin's deliberate limit to Hyper's architectural wager — can be condensed into a single logical movement.

---

* **Programmability.** The capacity of a platform to execute programs (the so-called smart contracts) that define complex operations automatically. Bitcoin limits it on purpose; it is precisely what a Layer 2 like Hyper aims to add, without however touching the base chain.

† **Security model.** The set of assumptions and mechanisms on which the protection of a system depends: who must behave honestly, which guarantees are verifiable and which instead require trust. Bitcoin and a rollup have different security models, and it is their compatibility — not speed alone — that determines how much the connection is worth.

‡ **Three-layer architecture.** The structure on which the entire volume rests: Bitcoin as the settlement base; above it the rollup, which collects and executes transactions at high speed; on top the applications the user uses. Each layer depends on the one below, and the solidity of the base rises upward only if the connection is built with the right mechanisms.

FIGURE C.1 **FROM THE PROBLEM TO THE SOLUTION: WHY A LAYER 2 IS NEEDED.**

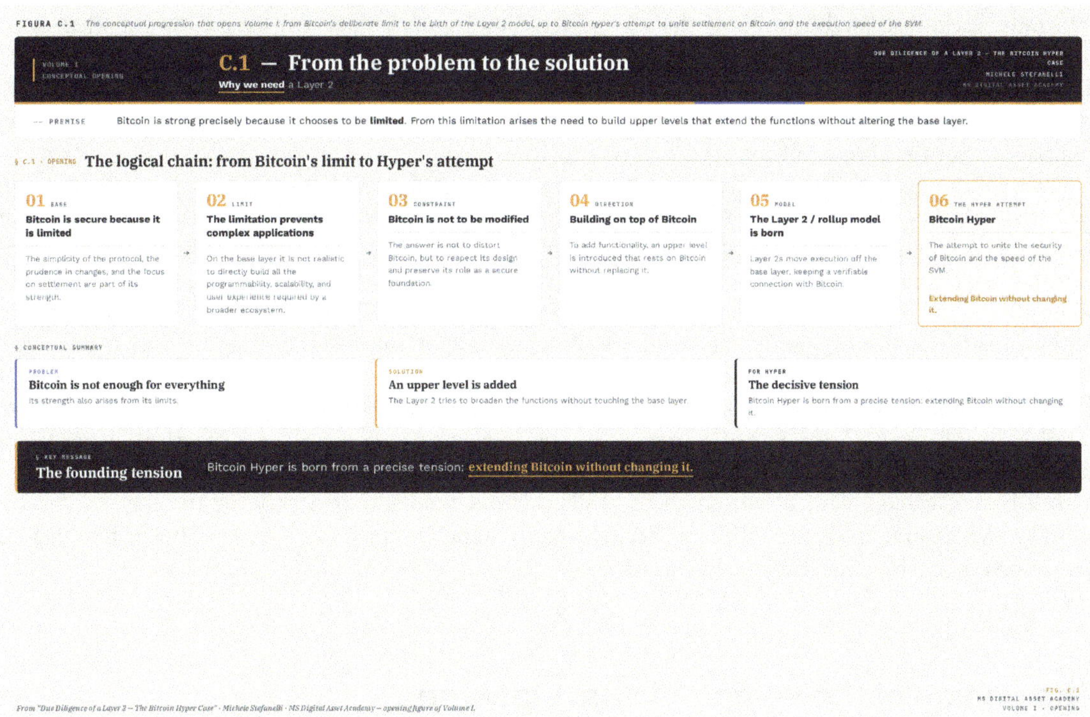

For this reason, asking only whether Bitcoin Hyper is fast means asking the wrong question. Any system that renounces the guarantees of the base chain is fast: speed, on its own, does not distinguish a serious architecture from a shortcut. The right question concerns the connection: whether a level that is by construction faster and less guaranteed manages to hook onto a slower and more solid level in such a way that the solidity truly rises upward, in what forms, with what timing, and under what conditions. It is the yardstick with which the volume has measured every component, and it is the yardstick that the reader should carry with them well beyond the specific case of Hyper.

⁂

The rollup as an architecture of separation

The map of the possible solutions — forks, sidechains, rollups — showed us why the rollup represents today the most serious architectural compromise for extending Bitcoin. A sidechain lives on its own security: it has its validators, its rules, its perimeter of trust, and with Bitcoin it maintains an essentially reputational relationship. A rollup, if complete, does something different: it publishes what anyone needs to reconstruct and verify what has happened above, and entrusts to the base chain the finality of its own states. The difference is not one of nuance but of category, because it determines who must be believed on their word and who, instead, can be checked.

The volume has also shown a second reason, less cited but no less important, why the rollup model is the road most coherent with Bitcoin's nature: the question of fragmentation. A sidechain, to function, must give life to a parallel representation of bitcoin, which lives inside a separate perimeter of trust and is worth as much as the federation or the mechanism that holds it in custody; multiplying the sidechains multiplies the «twins» of the asset, each with its own, non-equivalent guarantees. A well-built rollup aims at something different: keeping the value circulating on the upper floor hooked to the base chain through a canonical channel, so that the unit of account remains one and its redeemability depends on verifiable rules rather than on the reputation of an intermediary. It is a difference the user perceives little on quiet days and very much on difficult days; and naturally the concrete quality of this property depends on the design of the bridge that realizes it — a theme we will return to, because it is there that the greatest risk concentrates.

The anatomy of the model gave us the four names that have accompanied the whole book: execution, sequencing, settlement, and data availability. Four components, four distinct problems, four families of solutions. Execution establishes how the new state is computed; sequencing establishes in what order the world enters the system; settlement establishes how the state reaches Bitcoin and consolidates there; data availability establishes whether someone, other than whoever runs the system, will ever be able to verify that all this has happened according to the rules. None of the four is optional, and none can compensate for the absence of the others.

From this anatomy follows a distinction that the volume has repeated until making it a reflex: what is executed, what is published, and what is definitively settled are three different planes, with different timings, different guarantees, and different parties responsible. In the user's daily experience the three planes blur together, because the interface shows an operation «concluded» in a few instants. In technical reality, between the sequencer's word and finality on Bitcoin runs a distance made of batches, commitments, anchorings, and time windows. A large part of the misunderstandings that surround Layer 2s arises from collapsing these three planes into a single one.

For the same reason, «rollup» is not a magic word but a set of technical conditions. When some conditions are missing — data not retrievable, commitments not verifiable, no practicable avenue of contestation — the word remains, but the substance thins out, and what is left resembles a sidechain with a better lexicon. This attention to vocabulary is not academic pedantry: in the Layer 2 market words move capital, and due diligence begins exactly here, in translating every label into a list of conditions that can be checked one by one.

⁂

The choice of the Solana Virtual Machine

On the execution component, Bitcoin Hyper has made its most recognizable and, in some ways, most courageous choice: adopting the Solana Virtual Machine, going against the current of a sector that, when it extends Bitcoin, tends to look at compatibility with the Ethereum ecosystem. It is a decision that carries with it an entire world, for better and for constraint.

For better, the SVM offers what has made it known: a parallel execution model founded on accounts, in which every transaction declares in advance which portions of state it intends to touch, allowing everything that does not conflict to run simultaneously. From this derive high throughput, low latencies, and minimal costs, but above all a patrimony that no virtual machine born from scratch could offer at its debut: consolidated languages, frameworks like Anchor, wallets, libraries, development tools, and the habits of thousands of developers who could, in principle, bring to Hyper what they already know how to do.

For constraint, the same choice imposes its discipline. Determinism, which the volume has defined as the invisible constraint of speed, is not a detail for specialists: the SVM's rapidity arises from rigid rules on how programs must be written, on how dependencies must be declared, on how much computation a single transaction can consume. Whoever develops on Hyper inherits from Solana not only the advantages, but also the account model with its rough edges, the operational limits, and the learning curve. Hyper imports an entire execution culture into Bitcoin's perimeter, and the graft between two communities with such different philosophies is an experiment as interesting as it is not a given.

There is finally an aspect of determinism that deserves to be underlined in this venue, because it ties the execution level to everything that came after: a rigidly deterministic execution is not only the condition of speed, it is also the condition of verifiability. If the same ordered set of transactions produces, by construction, the same identical state on any machine that re-executes it, then independent verification becomes conceptually possible: anyone with the data can redo the computation and compare the result with what has been declared and anchored. Determinism, which to the developer presents itself as a constraint, is for the observer the premise of every check. But it is a premise, precisely: it turns into effective checking only if the data is available and if someone has the tools and incentives to re-execute it — and it is exactly the thread that led the volume from the execution level to those of settlement and data availability.

The volume has moreover fixed two cautions worth restating in closing. The first: compatibility is an accelerator, not a guarantee. It makes the migration of tools and applications possible; it does not assure it, because developers and capital move for incentives, not for technical affinity. The second: the performance the SVM expresses on Solana does not transfer automatically to a rollup anchored to Bitcoin, where data management, the cadence of settlement, and the surrounding infrastructure change. What the volume was able to record is a promise turned demonstration — SVM programs in native execution in a test environment — not yet a performance measured under mainnet conditions, under real load and with real adversaries. The distinction between demo and production will run through the whole judgment that remains to be built.

⁂

Speaking to Bitcoin: state commitments and anchoring

If Bitcoin does not execute Hyper — and it must not — a language is needed with which Hyper can speak to it. That language, which the volume has examined up close, is state commitments: compact cryptographic fingerprints, typically Merkle roots, capable of condensing into a few dozen bytes a state composed of millions of accounts, balances, and transactions. Their precious property is selective verifiability: whoever possesses the underlying data can prove that a specific detail belongs to the committed state, without having to republish the entire state. It is the mechanism that allows a system minuscule in capacity, like Bitcoin, to act as guarantor for a system enormously larger in activity.

Anchoring a commitment on Bitcoin, therefore, does not mean publishing Hyper on Bitcoin: it means delivering to the base chain a seal, not the content. The technical roads to do so exist and differ from one another. OP_RETURN is the simple and explicit way: readable by anyone, sustained by a consolidated standard, but limited in space. Constructions based on Taproot offer more capacity and flexibility, at the price of less immediate readability. Structures with timelocks become relevant when the anchoring must incorporate time constraints, contestation windows, or exit paths. No road is free of charge; each one trades something — space, clarity, complexity, cost — and the choice says a lot about the priorities of whoever makes it.

Alongside the «how», the volume has insisted on the «how often». The anchoring frequency is the heartbeat of the relationship between Hyper and Bitcoin: dense anchorings entail higher costs but shorten the window of exposure and bring finality closer; sparse anchorings save money but lengthen the time in which the rollup's state lives on the sole word of whoever runs it. On this rhythm depends the distance between the two finalities that the book has distinguished with care: the soft finality, almost instantaneous, that the sequencer offers for daily operations, and the hard finality, of Bitcoin grade, which is reached over longer times and truly counts when the value at stake is high or when returning toward the base chain.

Above everything, a point that the volume has restated until making it unequivocal: an anchored commitment proves that a certain state was declared by a certain date, and in a certain order with respect to others. It gives a certain date. It does not prove, on its own, that that state is correct. Settlement without available data and without verification tools is notarization, not security. How much Bitcoin Hyper can legitimately call itself «anchored to Bitcoin» is therefore not decided with a slogan, but with the concrete quality of this relationship: what is anchored, with what frequency, with what verifiability, and with what real possibilities of contestation.

⁂

Data availability: where the promise meets its limit

And here we are at the point that the volume has presented as the problem that few understand and on which, more than on any other, the seriousness of the entire model depends. A state commitment without the data that sustains it is a seal on a box that no one can open: it guarantees that the content has not been altered, but it does not make it possible to know what it contains, nor whether the content respects the rules. Without available data there is no independent verification; without independent verification, all the properties that make a rollup interesting go back to resting on trust toward whoever runs it.

The problem does not admit the most obvious solution, because Bitcoin cannot host the volumes produced by a level that executes thousands of operations per second: publishing everything on the base chain is materially impossible, besides being contrary to its nature as a settlement layer. The practicable roads, which the volume has reviewed, are others: distributed nodes that replicate and serve the data; infrastructures dedicated to availability; redundancy codes that make it possible to reconstruct the whole starting from fragments; commitments published on-chain with data held elsewhere and verified by sampling; economic incentives so that storing and serving the data pays off over time. None of these roads, on its own, is free of weak points. Credible architectures, here more than elsewhere, arise from the combination of several mechanisms, each covering the limits of the others.

Data availability is the point where the rollup's promise meets its practical limit. It is here that it is decided whether verifiability is an exercisable right — data retrievable, from independent sources, at any moment it is needed — or a declaration of principle. And it is also, historically, the chapter on which projects' documentation tends to be less explicit. For Bitcoin Hyper, the definitive design of data availability is among the things that the technical documents will have to make explicit, complete, and checkable; not by chance, it will be one of the first benches on which Volume II will measure the distance between what the communication promises and what the specifications actually say.

⁂

Order as a form of power

Climbing back up the stack, the volume encountered a figure that the technical lexicon tends to present as a simple component and which is, in reality, a center of power: the sequencer. Ordering transactions is not a neutral service. Whoever decides which operations enter the system, in what position and with what timing, exercises a power of measurable economic value: they can anticipate, delay, exclude; they can extract value from the ordering itself. For this reason the sequencer is not only a technical surface but a governance surface, and the formula the book has used remains the most honest synthesis: whoever orders decides, and whoever has power orders.

Starting with a single sequencer, run by the team, is the pragmatic choice with which almost all rollups have debuted: it simplifies the engineering, maximizes performance, reduces coordination problems in the most fragile phase of the system's life. The volume has not treated it as a fault, but as a condition acceptable only on two requirements. The first is a credible trajectory toward the distribution of ordering: sequencer rotation, auctions for the right to order, leader election mechanisms, hybrid models — strategies that the book has examined each with its own costs, its own complexities, and its own attack surfaces. The second is the existence of operational counterweights* during the centralized phase: first among them a forced inclusion lane, which allows a valid transaction to enter the system even against the will of whoever orders. In rollups built on Ethereum this lane passes through Layer 1; for Bitcoin Hyper, the form, rules, costs, and timing of an analogous mechanism remain to be clarified, and the volume has indicated them among the points to watch with the greatest attention in the months preceding the mainnet. The entire arc — from the pragmatism of the start to the counterweights of the centralized phase, up to the promised distribution — can be fixed in an overall trajectory.

---

* **Operational counterweights.** Mechanisms that limit the power of whoever orders the transactions, guaranteeing users a protection even when the system is still centralized in a single operator. The main one is forced inclusion, which allows a valid transaction to enter the system even against the sequencer's will. They are the equivalent, in a technical architecture, of the checks and balances that in institutions prevent a single power from acting without limits.

FIGURE C.2 **THE SEQUENCER: FROM TECHNICAL COMPONENT TO SURFACE OF POWER.**

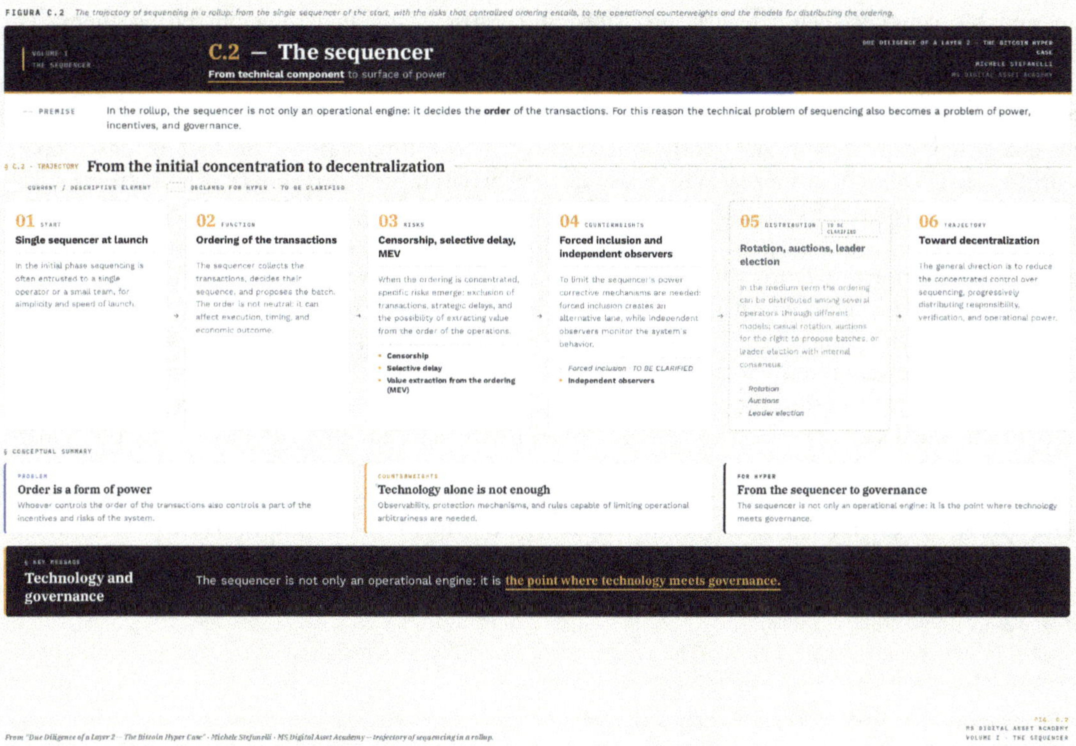

The lesson of this part of the book goes beyond the specific case: it is not enough to ask who executes the transactions; one must understand who decides in what order they enter the system, and what the user can do on the day that order is denied to them.

⁂

Security as architecture, not as promise

The part dedicated to security opens with what the volume has called the constitutional principle: security by design, not by audit. An audit photographs a code at an instant; a system lives in motion, under adversaries endowed with incentives, and its resilience depends on how it is built, not on how many times it has been inspected. Audits are necessary, and Volume II will read them attentively for what they cover and for what they cannot cover; but no quantity of audits can replace mechanisms designed to resist, detect, and react.

Inside this principle, the volume has distinguished two integrities that it is a category error to confuse: execution integrity, that is, the guarantee that the rules have been applied correctly to the transactions, and settlement integrity, that is, the guarantee that what reaches Bitcoin truly corresponds to what has happened above. They can fail separately, for different causes, and they require different defenses. A system can execute perfectly and settle badly; it can punctually settle states computed incorrectly. Only by keeping the two planes distinct does one understand where to look when something does not add up.

The third pillar is graceful degradation. A mature system is not judged by how it works on good days, but by how it behaves on bad days: it must not collapse at the first failure, it must lose functions in a predictable order, remain observable while doing so, and preserve ways out for those who have deposited value in it. The difference between an incident and a catastrophe, the volume has shown, often lies in the design of the degradation more than in the probability of the failure.

Finally, the architecture of contestation: the hierarchy of overlapping defenses that separates a defensible system from one that asks for trust. At the base, prevention — limits to administrative powers, transparency, separation of roles — and detection — metrics, dashboards, independent observers that make censorship, delays, and anomalies visible. Then economic deterrence, where bonds exist, sanctionable conducts defined with precision, and parties capable of demonstrating them. Then contestation proper: in optimistic rollups, the possibility of challenging an invalid transition by means of fraud proof or fault proof[*]; in zero-knowledge models, the validity proof[†] that aims to prevent from the start the recognition of an erroneous state. Finally, the extreme defenses: the sequencer bypass and the emergency exit [‡], slow and costly, but decisive in the limit cases. The first defenses operate continuously; the last ones are hoped to be useless, and precisely for this reason they must truly exist.

For Bitcoin Hyper, the declared direction looks to zero-knowledge proofs, to periodic commitments on Bitcoin, and to a gradual path of decentralization, with the Canonical Bridge[§] as the most critical point of the entire architecture: the place where errors would be gravest and where audits, redundancies, and emergency procedures will have to be most solid. Which proofs will be concretely available, with what properties and from when; in what form forced inclusion and emergency exit will exist; how the team's residual powers and the incident procedures will be documented: all this belongs to verification, not to the premise. And the conceptual closing of Part VI holds as a permanent criterion: the security described in the documents becomes real only when its mechanisms are implemented, usable, and used — when an independent observer can exercise them with tools within their reach, and not merely read of their existence. The thread that has run through the central parts of the volume can be represented, at this point, as a single chain of verifiability, in which every link is a condition and no link is optional.

---

[*] **Fraud proof / fault proof.** In «optimistic» rollups, the mechanism by which anyone can demonstrate that a published state transition is erroneous, having it annulled. The system takes as valid what is proposed, but leaves a window of time to contest it with a proof: it is on this possibility that its security rests.

[†] **Validity proof.** In «zero-knowledge» models, a cryptographic proof published together with the state that demonstrates its correctness in advance. Unlike the fraud proof, it does not require a contestation window: an erroneous state is not recognized from the start, because without a valid proof it is not accepted.

[‡] **Emergency exit.** The route that allows the user to recover their funds directly from Bitcoin when the system becomes unusable or hostile — for example if the sequencer stops working. It is slow and costly, but it is the ultimate guarantee that the custody of the funds does not depend on the operator's good will.

[§] **Canonical Bridge.** The official bridge that connects Bitcoin and the rollup, holding the deposited bitcoin in custody and regulating deposits and withdrawals according to verifiable rules. It is the point through which the emergency exit passes and, for this reason, the most sensitive component of the entire architecture: it is there that errors would be gravest.

FIGURE C.3 **THE CHAIN OF VERIFIABILITY.**

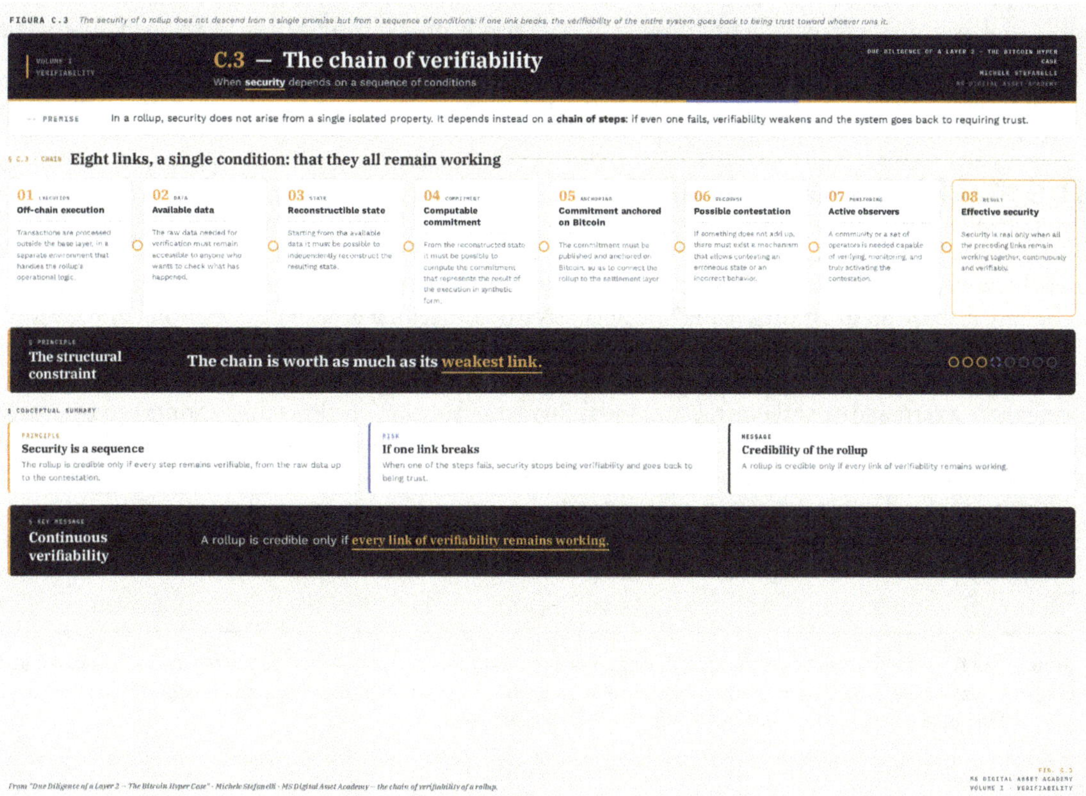

⁂

From the protocol to the ecosystem

The last part of the volume shifted its gaze from the protocol to what surrounds it, starting from an observation that technical enthusiasm tends to forget: a technology does not become an ecosystem merely by being technically possible. Between a rollup that works and a rollup that is used runs the same distance that separates a paved road from a city. It takes wallets that people can really use, explorers that make what happens readable, reliable and redundant RPC endpoints, indexers that transform raw data into queryable information, dashboards, bridges, development kits, well-kept documentation, support for those who build. And higher up, for the adoption that counts economically, institutional custody services, reliable oracles, compliance tools, payment infrastructures.

On this terrain the SVM inheritance is Hyper's most concrete potential shortcut: Anchor and Solana's toolbox can drastically reduce the initial friction, and existing wallets, libraries, and services could extend to the rollup at contained costs. But the volume has fixed here too the distinction that counts: compatibility is an invitation, not a migration. It is measured after the fact, in applications actually released, liquidity present, active developers, infrastructure operated by parties independent of the team. A declared ecosystem is a list of logos; a working ecosystem is a set of services that answer when they are called.

The volume has left, on this terrain, also a methodological indication that will prove useful in what follows: an ecosystem is not judged in an instant, but along a progression. In the first months after a possible launch it is reasonable to expect the basic integrations — wallets, explorers, reliable endpoints; then, if the system attracts real activity, the emergence of specialized services; over longer horizons, the maturation of custody, oracles, and institutional-grade tools. Observing the order and the timing of this progression says more about the health of a Layer 2 than any announcement: living ecosystems grow in recognizable layers, merely declared ones remain lists.

Within this picture, observability deserves a separate mention, because it welds the last part of the book to all the preceding ones. Seeing what is happening — with public explorers, accessible metrics, exportable data — is not a luxury for enthusiasts: it is the material condition for the right of verification and contestation, built by the chapters on security, to be practicable by someone who is not the team itself. A Layer 2 is not only a protocol: it is a network of tools, operators, developers, users, and incentives. Its vitality is measured in observable activity, not in pages of documentation.

⁂

The machine seen as a whole

If one wanted to compress the entire volume into a single movement, the machine would appear like this. Bitcoin settles, and nothing else is asked of it: it safeguards finality and history. Hyper executes, and to be fast it must do so off the chain. The Solana Virtual Machine accelerates execution and gives it a shape familiar to those who already build in its ecosystem. State commitments[*] compress what happens above into minuscule, verifiable fingerprints. Anchorings[†] carry those fingerprints into Bitcoin's history, giving them a certain date and order. Data availability[‡] decides whether those fingerprints can be opened and checked by anyone, or will remain seals on closed boxes. The sequencer establishes the order in which the world enters the system. The defenses — forced inclusion[§], proofs, ways out — limit the arbitrariness of whoever administers that order. Independent observers transform the right to contest from a written clause into a possible fact. And the tools, lastly, transform the protocol into an inhabitable place. We can then recompose the machine into a single image.

---

[*] **State commitments.** Compact cryptographic fingerprints — typically Merkle roots — that condense the rollup's entire state into a few dozen bytes. They allow Bitcoin, minuscule in capacity, to act as guarantor for a much larger system: whoever possesses the data can prove that a detail belongs to the committed state.

[†] **Anchoring.** The act of writing on Bitcoin the fingerprint of the rollup's state, not its content. It gives the fingerprint a «certain date» and an order with respect to the others: it proves that a certain state was declared by a certain moment, without however demonstrating its correctness on its own.

[‡] **Data availability.** The condition whereby the raw data behind a fingerprint remains retrievable from independent sources. Without it the fingerprint is a seal on a box that no one can open: it guarantees that the content has not been altered, but does not make it possible to verify it.

[§] **Forced inclusion.** The mechanism that allows a valid transaction to enter the system even if the sequencer refuses to process it. It is the defense against censorship: it guarantees that no one can be excluded indefinitely from the rollup.

FIGURE C.4 **THE TECHNICAL MACHINE OF BITCOIN HYPER.**

Read in sequence, this recomposition restores the elegance of the design. Read with the eye of due diligence, it restores something more useful: every link of this chain has a failure mode of its own and a verification question of its own, and the chain, as a whole, is worth as much as its weakest verifiable link. An impeccable execution does not compensate for unavailable data; a frequent anchoring does not compensate for the absence of avenues of contestation; a brilliant ecosystem does not compensate for a fragile bridge. Solidity, in architectures so stratified, does not add up: it is inherited from the worst point.

There is then a final warning, which the volume has held firm since the first chapter and which is worth carrying beyond its last page. The parts of this machine do not all live on the same plane of reality: some are implemented and have been shown in operation, others are specified in the documents, still others are declared directions. The book has kept these planes distinct with deliberate insistence, because confusing them is exactly the error that a due diligence exists to prevent — and it is also the error that promotional communication, by its nature, tends to favor. Always knowing on which plane each statement rests is, perhaps, the single most precious competence this volume leaves as an inheritance.

⁂

What technology cannot decide

Having arrived at this point, the reader has a technical understanding that few popular materials make it possible to reach. And yet precisely this understanding, brought to completion, reveals its own boundary. Knowing how Bitcoin Hyper should work does not yet say whether it is working, to what extent, and under what economic, documentary, and market conditions. The architecture defines what is possible; it is the incentives, the capital, the documents, and the competition that decide what becomes real. The question, from here onward, changes nature: no longer the project as it should be, but the project as it is, today, measured against its own declarations and against the alternatives.

It is the work of Volume II, and its agenda descends point by point from what the first volume has built. Hyper will have to be placed in its competitive landscape — Lightning Network, Stacks, Rootstock, Mintlayer, and the new generation of Layer 2s on Bitcoin — because no project is judged in a vacuum, and every alternative solves a different problem at a different price. The tokenomics of $HYPER will have to be examined — supply, distribution, unlock schedules, alignment between those who build and those who finance — and the pre-sale, with the expectations and implicit obligations that an early raise generates. The audits will have to be read for what they cover and, with equal attention, for what they cannot cover. The actual state of the devnet and of the ecosystem at the moment of the analysis will have to be measured, and the documentary gaps catalogued: the distance, point by point, between what the marketing promises and what the technical documents actually specify. And all this will have to be translated into operational tools: the signals to monitor over time, of confirmation and of alarm; the minimum conditions for a mainnet to be able to call itself credible; the regulatory, documentary, and execution risks; and finally an orderly and replicable due diligence method, applicable to any project in the pre-mainnet phase, not only to this one.

There is, in this passage, also a change of posture that it is good to declare. On a project in the pre-mainnet phase, the honest judgment cannot take the form of a definitive yes or no: it takes the form of conditions, thresholds, and scenarios. What the first volume has made possible is precisely this type of judgment: transforming every architectural promise into an observable condition — a document that must appear, a mechanism that must work, a metric that must move — and tying trust to their coming true, not to their announcement. Volume II will order these conditions into an explicit evaluation path, distinguishing what will have to be true before the mainnet from what may reasonably mature afterward.

The passage from the first to the second volume is therefore not a change of subject, but a logical necessity. The first volume has established what must be verified; the second verifies. Neither of the two suffices on its own: without the technical grammar, the market judgment slides into mood and narratives; without the market judgment, the grammar remains an elegant and inoffensive exercise. And it is worth keeping in mind, entering the second half of the journey, two asymmetries that the history of this sector has shown more than once: an elegant architecture can fail for economic, documentary, or execution reasons; an imperfect architecture can survive and prosper through the strength of its ecosystem. The judgment will therefore have to broaden well beyond the technical, without however ever losing the rigor that the technical has taught. This handover lends itself to being summarized in a two-column scheme: together, the index of the journey completed and the map of the one that begins.

FIGURE C.5 **FROM VOLUME I TO VOLUME II: FROM FUNCTIONING TO JUDGMENT.**

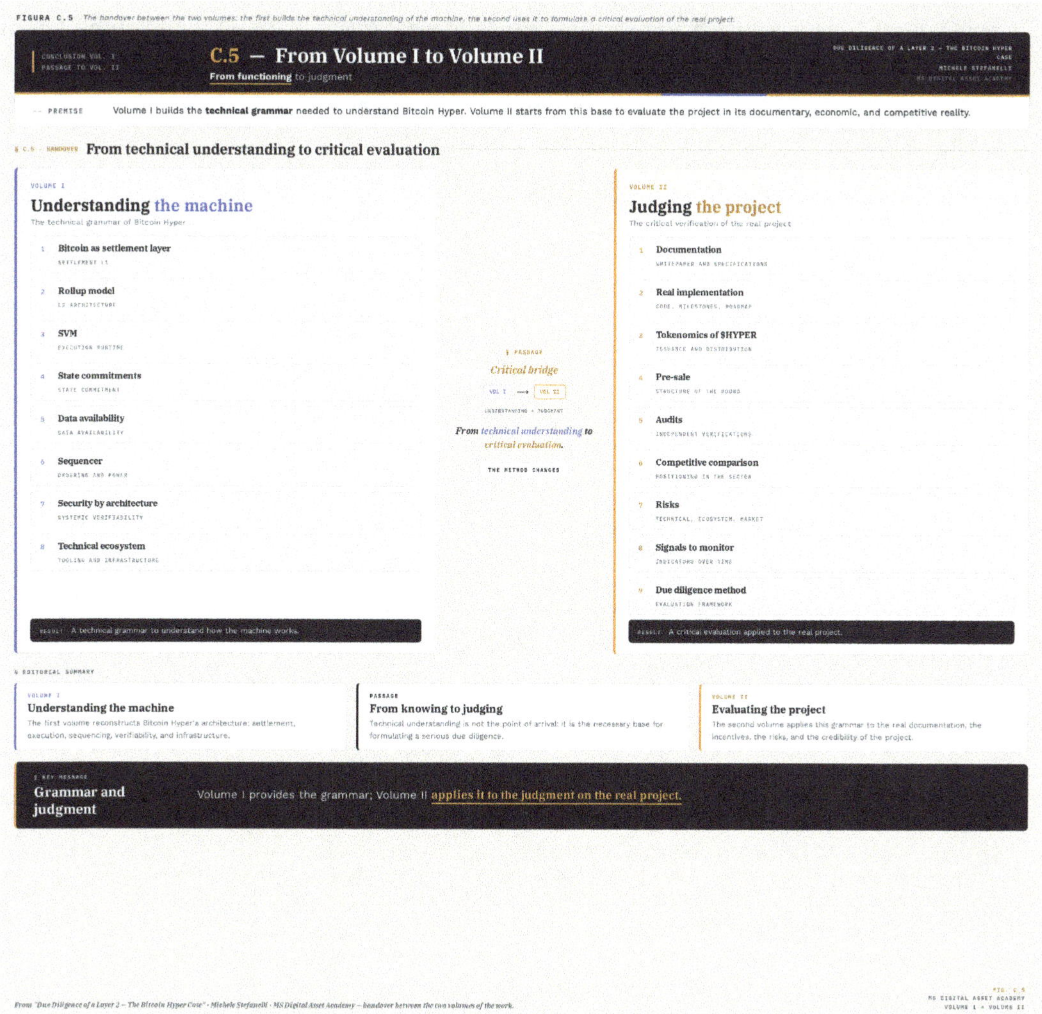

⁂

A grammar, not a verdict

This volume does not deliver a verdict on Bitcoin Hyper. It delivers a grammar for judging it. It is an outcome less noisy than a sentence, but more honest and more lasting: no sentence on a project in the pre-mainnet phase can be solid if one does not first know what to look at, where to look at it, and how to recognize an answer that is not enough.

The verdict, when it comes, will not be able to arise from the enthusiasm of those who want to believe in it, nor from the distrust of those who have already decided. It will be able to arise only from the capacity to distinguish: the promise from the implementation; the architecture from the marketing; compatibility from security; anchoring from real settlement; speed from verifiability; the declared ecosystem from the working ecosystem. These are the six distinctions that this volume has built chapter after chapter, and which on their own are worth more than any opinion, because they remain valid even when opinions change.

The first volume closes here, at the exact point where the technical machine has been dismantled down to the last gear and reassembled before the reader's eyes. Now we know where the security passes and where the risk accumulates; we know which guarantees are written into the architecture and which remain entrusted to documents yet to be published; we know what to ask, whom to ask it of, and how to recognize an insufficient answer. The second volume begins from this threshold: no longer from the question of how Bitcoin Hyper should work, but from the verification of how much of this architecture is already documented, implemented, sustainable, and credible in the real market.

There is a distance between what a project promises and what it actually does. This volume has built the instrument to measure it. The next one begins to measure.

⁂

APPENDIX A

Technical Glossary

The fundamental terms for understanding Bitcoin Hyper and the Layer 2 sector

⁂

Preamble: how to use this glossary

I want to spend a few words on how this glossary is structured, because it is different from traditional technical glossaries. **Traditional glossaries are organized alphabetically**, with brief, isolated definitions. They are useful as quick-reference tools, but they do not help in understanding how the concepts connect to one another. **This glossary is organized conceptually**: the terms are grouped by thematic area, and each definition tries to show the connections with other related terms.

The objective is twofold. **On one hand**, to provide clear and accurate definitions of technical terms that recur in the book and in Bitcoin Hyper's documentation. **On the other**, to build a conceptual map that allows the reader to navigate the sector's vocabulary with greater awareness, seeing how each concept fits into a broader picture.

An important note: some terms have slightly different meanings depending on the specific context. As far as possible, the definitions presented here reflect the usage made of them by Bitcoin Hyper and the Bitcoin Layer 2 sector in general. For usage in other contexts (Ethereum Layer 2, Cosmos, etc.), some nuances may differ.

⁂

Section 1: The fundamentals of Bitcoin

Bitcoin (BTC). The original cryptocurrency, created by Satoshi Nakamoto and launched in January 2009. It is the reference decentralized digital money system, with a market capitalization on the order of trillions of dollars. **For Bitcoin Hyper, BTC is the main asset held on the rollup through the Canonical Bridge.** Everything the rollup does, ultimately, revolves around enabling programmable applications that operate with BTC.

Bitcoin blockchain. The distributed ledger that tracks all Bitcoin transactions since genesis. Composed of chronologically ordered blocks, each block containing a set of transactions. **For Bitcoin Hyper, the Bitcoin blockchain performs the role of settlement level**: the rollup's periodic states are anchored to the Bitcoin blockchain to inherit its immutability.

Block. A unit of the Bitcoin blockchain, containing a set of transactions and a reference to the previous block. **Bitcoin produces a block every 10 minutes** on average, with a maximum size of 1 megabyte (excluding witness data, up to 4 MB with SegWit). **For Bitcoin Hyper, every Bitcoin block represents an anchoring opportunity**: the sequencer can include state commitments of the rollup in the Bitcoin transactions of a new block.

Mining. The process through which the nodes of the Bitcoin network compete to produce new blocks, solving cryptographic problems (proof-of-work) and receiving as a reward new bitcoin plus the fees of the included transactions. **For Bitcoin Hyper, mining is not directly involved**: the rollup has its own sequencing system separate from Bitcoin's mining, but it uses the Bitcoin blocks produced by the miners as the basis for anchoring.

Confirmations. The number of blocks that have been added to the blockchain after a transaction was included. The more confirmations there are, the more secure the transaction is considered. **Industry standard**: 1 confirmation for small amounts, 6 confirmations for standard amounts, 100+ confirmations for large amounts (mining reward). **For Bitcoin Hyper**, confirmations determine the finality of the anchored states: after 6 Bitcoin confirmations on the anchoring, the state is considered Bitcoin-grade finalized.

UTXO (Unspent Transaction Output). Bitcoin's fundamental model for tracking value: instead of «balances» as in bank accounts, Bitcoin keeps track of «unspent outputs» of previous transactions. **For Bitcoin Hyper, UTXO is native Bitcoin's model, but the rollup adopts the SVM account model**: this difference is one of the technical complexities to manage in the integration between the two chains.

Bitcoin Script. Bitcoin's limited scripting language, deliberately not Turing-complete for security reasons. It allows simple operations (multisignature, timelocks, hash-based conditions) but does not support complex logic. **For Bitcoin Hyper, the limitations of Bitcoin Script are the fundamental reason why a Layer 2 exists**: complex programmable applications cannot be built directly on Bitcoin.

Taproot. The Bitcoin upgrade activated in 2021 (BIP 340–342) that improves the privacy and flexibility of scripts. It introduces Schnorr signatures and a more efficient structure for complex scripts. **For Bitcoin Hyper, Taproot enables more efficient anchoring mechanisms** and potentially more sophisticated forms of interaction with the rollup.

OP_RETURN. A special Bitcoin Script operation that allows including up to 80 bytes of arbitrary data in a transaction, marking the output as unspendable. **For Bitcoin Hyper, OP_RETURN is a possible mechanism for including state commitments in Bitcoin transactions**: small overhead, publicly verifiable data.

⁂

Section 2: Layer 2 and scaling architectures

Layer 1 (L1). The main blockchain, secure and immutable, but typically with scalability limitations. Bitcoin and Ethereum are the most important Layer 1s of the crypto sector. **For Bitcoin Hyper, Bitcoin is the reference Layer 1**: everything the rollup does is ultimately secured by the Bitcoin Layer 1.

Layer 2 (L2). A scalability solution built on top of a Layer 1, which inherits the security of the Layer 1 while adding scaling capacity. **Bitcoin Hyper is a Layer 2 of Bitcoin**, similarly to how Optimism and Arbitrum are Layer 2s of Ethereum.

Rollup. A specific Layer 2 architecture that executes transactions off-chain but publishes the results on-chain in compressed form. **Technical definition**: a rollup has four integrated components: off-chain execution, on-chain settlement, data availability, and a proof model. **For Bitcoin Hyper, «rollup» is the reference architectural category**, even though the complete implementation of all the components takes time to mature.

Sidechain. Another Layer 2 architecture that operates as a separate blockchain with its own nodes and its own consensus, connected to the Layer 1 through a bridge. **Key difference from the rollup**: the sidechain has its own independent consensus; the rollup inherits the security of the Layer 1. **Rootstock is a federated sidechain of Bitcoin**, while Bitcoin Hyper is designed as a rollup.

Validium. A variant of the rollup where transaction data is not published on the Layer 1. **Trade-off**: greater scalability and lower costs, but inferior security (data availability depends on a restricted set of validators). **For Bitcoin Hyper, the choice between «true rollup» and «validium» is still in the final definition phase**, with significant implications for the effective security of the system.

Optimistic rollup. A type of rollup that assumes the validity of transactions by default, with a contestation period (typically 7 days) during which anyone can contest with a fraud proof. **Examples**: Optimism, Arbitrum. **Advantages**: simpler implementation. **Disadvantages**: long withdrawal times (days).

ZK rollup (zero-knowledge rollup). A type of rollup that uses cryptographic validity proofs (typically zk-SNARKs or zk-STARKs) to mathematically demonstrate the correctness of transactions. **Examples**: zkSync, StarkNet, Polygon zkEVM. **Advantages**: fast withdrawals (hours instead of days). **Disadvantages**: more complex implementation, higher computational costs for generating the proofs.

Hybrid rollup. An approach that combines elements of optimistic and ZK rollups. **For Bitcoin Hyper, the proposed architecture is hybrid**: initially optimistic with an evolution path toward ZK proofs.

⁂

Section 3: Specific components of a rollup

Sequencer. The rollup component that orders transactions into batches, executes the logic off-chain, and produces the new states. **For Bitcoin Hyper, the sequencer at mainnet launch will be centralized, run by the team**, with a path of progressive decentralization over time.

Centralized sequencer. The typical initial mode of rollups, where a single operator (typically the project's team) runs the sequencing. **Advantages**: simpler implementation, quality control in the first months. **Disadvantages**: central point of trust, theoretical possibility of censorship, vulnerability to problems of the single operator.

Decentralized sequencer. The long-term objective: sequencing distributed among several independent operators, through mechanisms such as rotation, auctions, or leader election. **For Bitcoin Hyper, the decentralization of the sequencer is a long-term objective** but will probably not be completed in the first 2–3 years after the mainnet.

State commitment. A compressed representation of the current state of the rollup, typically through a Merkle root or equivalent. **For Bitcoin Hyper, state commitments are periodically anchored to the Bitcoin blockchain** to inherit its immutability.

Merkle tree. A cryptographic data structure that allows representing a large set of data through a single root hash (Merkle root), with the possibility of proving the inclusion of specific elements via compact proof paths. **For Bitcoin Hyper, Merkle trees are used for state commitments**: the entire state of the rollup is compactly represented in a Merkle root published on Bitcoin.

Anchoring. The process of publishing rollup information (typically state commitments) on the Bitcoin blockchain. **It typically happens periodically**: every X minutes or every Y batches, through Bitcoin transactions that include the data via mechanisms such as OP_RETURN or Taproot outputs.

Anchoring frequency. The frequency with which the rollup publishes state commitments on Bitcoin. **Trade-off**: more frequent anchoring means better finality but higher costs (each anchoring requires a Bitcoin transaction); less frequent means savings but greater latency for Bitcoin-grade finality. **For Bitcoin Hyper, the anchoring frequency will be adaptive**: more frequent under high load, less frequent in periods of low activity.

Data availability (DA). The property that the rollup's transaction data is publicly accessible so that anyone can reconstruct the state. **Critical for the «true rollup» vs «validium» classification**: true rollups publish the data on-chain or on a verifiable DA layer.

Data availability layer. Specialized systems that provide data availability guarantees at lower costs than publishing everything on the Layer 1. **Examples**: Celestia, EigenDA, Avail. **For Bitcoin Hyper, the choice of the DA layer (direct Bitcoin, separate layer, hybrid) is still being defined.**

Fraud proof. A cryptographic proof that demonstrates that a specific rollup transaction was executed incorrectly. **Used in optimistic rollups**: during the contestation period, anyone can submit a fraud proof to overturn an invalid state. **For Bitcoin Hyper, fraud proofs are part of the security model under development.**

Validity proof. A cryptographic proof (typically zk-SNARK or zk-STARK) that demonstrates that every rollup transaction was executed correctly. **Used in ZK rollups**: the proof is verified immediately, with no contestation period. **For Bitcoin Hyper, validity proofs are a long-term objective.**

Forced inclusion. A mechanism that allows users to force the inclusion of a transaction in the rollup through an operation directly on Layer 1. **Important**: it protects against sequencer censorship. **For Bitcoin Hyper, forced inclusion is a critical mechanism under development.**

Forced exit. A mechanism that allows users to withdraw their funds from the rollup even without the sequencer's cooperation, typically through operations directly on Layer 1. **Important**: it protects against catastrophic scenarios (compromised sequencer, team that disappears). **For Bitcoin Hyper, forced exit is one of the most critical mechanisms for the robustness of the system.**

⁂

Section 4: The Solana Virtual Machine and the SVM model

Solana Virtual Machine (SVM). The virtual machine that executes programs on Solana. **Distinctive characteristics**: massive parallelization through the declared account model, throughput on the order of thousands of TPS, sub-second latencies. **For Bitcoin Hyper, the adoption of the SVM is the fundamental architectural decision**: all the technical inheritance and the developer experience derive from this choice.

Sealevel. Solana's parallelization runtime, which allows concurrent execution of transactions that do not overlap on the same accounts. **For Bitcoin Hyper, Sealevel is the mechanism that makes the high throughput possible** through efficient parallelization.

Account model. The state model of the SVM (and Ethereum), where each account has persistent state identified by a public key. **Difference from Bitcoin's UTXO model**: instead of tracking unspent outputs, it tracks account states that are modified by transactions.

SVM program. The equivalent of a «smart contract» in the SVM. Typically compiled in BPF (Berkeley Packet Filter) format, it can be deployed and invoked by transactions. **For Bitcoin Hyper, existing SVM programs can be deployed with minimal adaptations**, benefiting from the Solana inheritance.

Anchor framework. The most popular development framework for the SVM, which provides abstractions and tooling for writing programs more ergonomically than raw SVM code. **For Bitcoin Hyper, Anchor is the main supported development framework**.

SPL (Solana Program Library). The standard library of SVM programs, the equivalent of OpenZeppelin for Ethereum. It includes standard implementations of tokens (SPL Token), governance, multisig, and other common patterns. **For Bitcoin Hyper, SPL libraries work natively**: Solana patterns are directly transferable.

Determinism. The property that every execution of the same transactions in the same order produces the same final state, regardless of the executor. **Critical for rollups**: without determinism, different nodes could produce different states from the same transactions, breaking the consistency guarantee. **For Bitcoin Hyper, the SVM's determinism is an invisible but fundamental constraint**.

RPC (Remote Procedure Call). The standard protocol through which applications interact with a blockchain node. **For Bitcoin Hyper, the RPCs are SVM-compatible**: existing libraries (Solana Web3.js, Anchor SDK) work with minimal adaptations.

⁂

Section 5: Bridges and custody

Cross-chain bridge. A mechanism that allows moving assets between different blockchains. **For Bitcoin Hyper, the central bridge is the Canonical Bridge** which manages the transfer of bitcoin between native Bitcoin and the rollup.

Canonical Bridge. Bitcoin Hyper's official bridge between native Bitcoin and the rollup. **How it works**: users deposit bitcoin to an address controlled by the bridge, receiving corresponding BTC on the rollup; to withdraw, the process is reversed. **Security characteristics**: they depend on the specific implementation (initial custody model, decentralization path).

Wrapped BTC (WBTC). A token on other blockchains (typically Ethereum) that represents bitcoin held by specific custodians. **Difference from Hyper**: WBTC is held by a specific custodian (BitGo for WBTC); Hyper's Canonical Bridge is designed to evolve toward a more decentralized model.

Centralized custody. A custody model where a single operator (or a restricted entity) holds the cryptographic keys that control the funds. **Advantages**: simple implementation. **Disadvantages**: central point of trust, vulnerability to problems of the custodian.

Federated custody. A custody model where a consortium of operators (federation) collectively holds the keys through multisignature. **Example**: Rootstock's Powpeg. **Advantages**: no single point of failure. **Disadvantages**: dependence on the integrity of the federation.

Multisignature (multisig). A cryptographic mechanism where multiple signatures are needed (e.g.: 3 of 5, 4 of 7) to authorize an operation. **For Bitcoin Hyper, multisignature is at the base of the initial custody models**.

Decentralized custody. The long-term objective: custody where the keys are distributed among many independent operators, with no central points of trust. **For Bitcoin Hyper, decentralized custody is the objective of the Canonical Bridge's evolution path**.

Enterprise custody. Professional crypto custody services for institutions. **Examples**: BitGo, Anchorage Digital, Coinbase Custody, Fireblocks, Copper. **Important for Bitcoin Hyper**: institutional adoption depends on the availability of enterprise custody integrated with the system.

HSM (Hardware Security Module). Specialized hardware devices for holding cryptographic keys securely. **Industry standard**: FIPS 140–2 Level 3 certification or higher for enterprise use. **For Bitcoin Hyper, HSMs are part of the custody infrastructure of enterprise custodians**.

⁂

Section 6: Security and threat models

Threat model. The formal description of who the possible attackers are, what capabilities they have, and what objectives they may pursue. **For Bitcoin Hyper, the threat model includes**: malicious users, a compromised sequencer, a compromised bridge custodian, systemic attacks (DDoS, denial-of-service), hostile governments.

Censorship. An attempt by an actor (typically the sequencer) to refuse specific transactions. **Mitigation on Bitcoin Hyper**: forced inclusion makes it possible to bypass the sequencer's censorship.

Double-spending. An attempt to spend the same bitcoin twice. **In native Bitcoin, prevented by PoW consensus. For Bitcoin Hyper, prevented by a combination of sequencer integrity and Bitcoin anchoring**.

Sybil attack. An attack where a single attacker creates many false identities to influence the system. **Mitigation**: staking mechanisms, collateral requirements, proof-of-work.

51% attack. An attack where a group controls more than 50% of the system's consensus power, being able to rewrite recent history. **In native Bitcoin, extremely costly. For Bitcoin Hyper, the security inherited from Bitcoin protects against this at the settlement level, but the sequencer has its own separate vulnerabilities.**

Reentrancy. A smart contract vulnerability where a contract calls another that re-enters the original contract before the first invocation is completed. **Famous exploit**: the DAO attack on Ethereum. **In the SVM, structurally prevented** by the declared account model.

Security audit. A formal examination of a system's code and architecture by specialized firms. **Reputable firms in the sector**: Trail of Bits, OtterSec, Halborn, Quantstamp, Kudelski. **For Bitcoin Hyper, audits published before the mainnet launch are critical for trust**.

Bug bounty. A program that pays rewards to those who identify and report vulnerabilities responsibly. **Significant bounties**: $10K for minor bugs, $100K-$1M for critical vulnerabilities. **For Bitcoin Hyper, a robust bug bounty program is an essential component of the security strategy**.

⁂

Section 7: Tokenomics and governance

Native token. The cryptocurrency token used by the system for various functions (fees, staking, governance). **For Bitcoin Hyper, $HYPER is the native token.**

$HYPER. Bitcoin Hyper's native token. **Probable roles**: fee payment, incentives for operators, governance, collateral, access to specific functionalities, value-capture of the system's success.

Tokenomics. The economic structure of the token: distribution, vesting, supply, value-capture mechanisms. **Key components**: allocation among team/investors/treasury/ecosystem, vesting schedule, issuance model, burning mechanisms.

Vesting. The schedule through which tokens are progressively unlocked to recipients. **Typical pattern**: a 12-month cliff (no unlock), then linear vesting over the following 24–36 months.

Cliff. The initial period of a vesting during which no token is unlocked. **Function**: to discourage immediate exits by contributors, aligning long-term incentives.

Total supply. The maximum quantity of tokens that will ever exist, or the current circulating quantity. **Important distinction**: circulating total supply vs maximum total supply.

Staking. Locking tokens as collateral to participate in the system (e.g.: validating blocks, voting in governance) and receive rewards. **For Bitcoin Hyper, staking will be part of the mechanism of progressive decentralization of the sequencer**.

Liquid staking. A variant where users who stake receive a representative token (e.g.: stHYPER) that they can use in other DeFi protocols. **Advantage**: it combines staking yield with capital flexibility.

On-chain governance. A system where decisions on the protocol are made through votes of the token holders, with results implemented automatically through smart contracts. **Pros**: transparent, democratic, automatic. **Cons**: risk of plutocracy, technical complexity, slowness.

Off-chain governance. A system where decisions are made through public debate and then implemented manually by the developers. **Pros**: flexibility, quality of decisions. **Cons**: less transparent, depends on specific figures.

Treasury. Funds controlled by the protocol (typically in the native token + other assets) used to finance development, partnerships, marketing, grants. **For Bitcoin Hyper, the allocation and management of the treasury is an important part of the tokenomics.**

Buyback-and-burn. A mechanism where part of the protocol's fees is used to buy tokens on the market and then destroy them, reducing the supply over time. **Effect**: deflationary pressure on the token's price.

⁂

Section 8: DeFi and applications

DeFi (Decentralized Finance). A category of financial applications built on public blockchains, without traditional intermediaries. **Examples**: DEXs, lending protocols, derivatives, stablecoins, yield aggregators. **For Bitcoin Hyper, DeFi is one of the main target use cases.**

DEX (Decentralized Exchange). An exchange operated through smart contracts instead of through centralized entities. **Main models**: AMM (Automated Market Maker, e.g.: Uniswap), on-chain order book (e.g.: Serum), aggregators (e.g.: Jupiter).

AMM (Automated Market Maker). An exchange mechanism where the price is determined by a mathematical formula based on the liquidity ratios in the pools. **Examples**: Uniswap, Curve, Balancer.

Liquidity pool. A set of assets deposited in a smart contract that facilitates exchanges through an AMM. **Liquidity providers**: users who deposit assets in the pool and receive fees.

Lending protocol. A protocol that allows lending and borrowing assets in a decentralized way. **Examples**: Aave, Compound. **Typical operation**: users deposit collateral, can borrow other assets up to a certain loan-to-value ratio.

Liquidation. The automatic process where the position of a user who has borrowed is forcibly closed when the value of the collateral falls below critical thresholds. **Important for the stability of lending protocols.**

Stablecoin. A token designed to maintain stable value with respect to a reference asset (typically USD). **Types**: fiat-collateralized (USDC, USDT), crypto-collateralized (DAI), algorithmic (UST — failed).

Yield farming. A strategy of maximizing returns through active participation in multiple DeFi protocols. **Often includes**: liquidity provisioning, staking, participation in incentive programs.

TVL (Total Value Locked). The total value of assets locked in a protocol or ecosystem, typically expressed in USD. **Key metric**: it indicates the size and activity of the protocol. **For Bitcoin Hyper, TVL is one of the main indicators of the rollup's success.**

Oracle. A system that brings off-chain data (prices, events, etc.) on-chain in a verifiable way. **Important examples for Hyper**: Pyth Network (SVM oracles), Chainlink. **Importance**: without reliable oracles, many DeFi applications cannot work.

MEV (Maximum Extractable Value). Value that can be extracted through strategic ordering, inclusion, or exclusion of transactions. **Examples**: front-running, sandwich attacks, arbitrages. **For Bitcoin Hyper, MEV is an important consideration in the design of the decentralized sequencer**.

⁂

Section 9: Bitcoin Layer 2 sector concepts

Lightning Network. A Bitcoin Layer 2 for fast payments through bilateral payment channels. **Characteristics**: instant payments, low costs, optimized for pure payments. **Differences from Bitcoin Hyper**: Lightning is optimized for payments, Hyper for programmable smart contracts.

Stacks. A Bitcoin Layer 2 with its own blockchain, the Clarity language, and the Proof of Transfer mechanism. **Operational since 2021. Differences from Bitcoin Hyper**: Stacks has its own PoX consensus and the Clarity language; Hyper is a rollup with the SVM.

Clarity. Stacks' smart contract language, deliberately not Turing-complete for greater security. **Characteristics**: decidable, interpreted, secure by default.

Proof of Transfer (PoX). Stacks' consensus mechanism where miners transfer bitcoin to obtain the right to produce Stacks blocks; the stackers (those who lock STX) receive the transferred bitcoin.

Unique characteristic: it creates a bidirectional economic bond between Bitcoin and Stacks.

Rootstock (RSK). A Bitcoin Layer 2 in the form of a federated sidechain with complete EVM compatibility, activated through merge mining. **Operational since 2018**. **Differences from Bitcoin Hyper**: Rootstock is a federated sidechain with the EVM; Hyper is a rollup with the SVM.

Merge mining. A technique where Bitcoin miners can simultaneously produce blocks on another chain (e.g.: Rootstock), receiving rewards on both without additional cost.

Powpeg. Rootstock's federated bridge between native Bitcoin and RSK, managed by a federation of «pegnatori». **Custody model**: federated, multisignature with a typical 2/3 threshold.

Mintlayer. A Bitcoin Layer 2 focused on the tokenization of real-world assets (RWA), with BLS-DSA consensus and an extended UTXO model. **Operational since 2023**. **Differences from Bitcoin Hyper**: Mintlayer has a proprietary VM and a specialized focus on RWA.

BLS-DSA. Boneh-Lynn-Shacham digital signature aggregation, a cryptographic mechanism used by Mintlayer for efficient consensus with signature aggregation.

RWA (Real-World Assets). Real assets (real estate, commodities, stocks, debt) represented as tokens on blockchains. **A growing sector** that could significantly expand the use of Layer 2s.

Section 10: Operational and market terms

Mainnet. The main network of a blockchain project, where real value circulates. **Distinct from testnet** (a test network with non-real value) and devnet (a development network).

Testnet. The protocol's test network, technically identical to the mainnet but with tokens with no real value. **Use**: development, debugging, stress tests.

Devnet. The development network, typically more unstable than the testnet, for active experimentation by developers of the protocol and of applications. **For Bitcoin Hyper, the devnet has been operational since mid-2025**.

Throughput. The capacity to process transactions, typically expressed in transactions per second (TPS). **Native Bitcoin**: ~7 TPS. **Solana**: 50,000+ theoretical TPS. **For Bitcoin Hyper**: a target of thousands of TPS, similar to Solana.

Latency. The time between the sending of a transaction and its confirmation. **Native Bitcoin**: 10+ minutes. **Solana**: sub-second. **For Bitcoin Hyper**: a sub-second target for soft finality, hours for Bitcoin-grade hard finality.

Finality. The point at which a transaction is considered definitively confirmed and not reversible. **Important distinction**: soft finality (probabilistic) vs hard finality (definitive).

Soft finality. Probabilistic confirmation, where reversibility is theoretically possible but economically impracticable after a certain number of confirmations. **Bitcoin with 6 confirmations**: very strong soft finality. **For Bitcoin Hyper**: the sequencer provides immediate soft finality.

Hard finality. Definitive mathematical/economic confirmation, where reversibility is impossible or would require catastrophic attacks. **For Bitcoin Hyper**: reached after Bitcoin anchoring with sufficient confirmations.

Slippage. The difference between the expected price of a transaction and the price actually executed, typically due to market movements during execution.

FOMO (Fear Of Missing Out). A feeling of fear of missing an opportunity, which often leads to emotional rather than rational investment decisions. **To avoid**: investing because everyone else is doing it is a terrible strategy.

FUD (Fear, Uncertainty, Doubt). A tactic of spreading fear, uncertainty, and doubt to influence the perception of a project. **To avoid**: making decisions based only on FUD without independent verification.

Whale. A large holder of a crypto asset, typically with significant holdings that can influence the market. **For retail investors**: monitoring whale activity can provide indications, but should not be the sole basis of decisions.

HODL. A crypto-culture term for «holding» an asset without selling, regardless of volatility. **Origin**: a viral typo of «hold» that became a meme. **A long-term strategy** for investors convinced of the fundamentals.

Rug pull. A scam where the creators of a crypto project abandon it after having raised funds, leaving investors with worthless assets. **Red flags**: projects with an anonymous team, absent audits, unrealistic promises.

⁂

Section 11: Regulatory and compliance concepts

KYC (Know Your Customer). Customer identity verification procedures required in many jurisdictions for financial institutions and crypto exchanges.

AML (Anti-Money Laundering). Procedures to prevent money laundering, including transaction monitoring and reporting of suspicious activities.

Travel Rule. A regulation that requires transmitting information on the originator and beneficiary for transfers above certain thresholds between financial institutions. **A specific challenge for crypto**.

Security token. A crypto token classified as a «security» in specific jurisdictions, subject to more stringent regulations (registrations, restrictions on investors). **For $HYPER, the regulatory classification varies by jurisdiction and may evolve over time**.

Utility token. A crypto token designed for specific use in a system (fees, access to functionalities), classified as a non-security in many jurisdictions.

Regulated stablecoin. A stablecoin issued by a regulated entity, with compliance controls and verifiable collateral. **Examples**: USDC (Circle), GUSD (Gemini), PYUSD (PayPal).

FATF (Financial Action Task Force). An intergovernmental organization that establishes international standards for anti-money laundering. **Its recommendations influence global crypto regulations**.

SEC (Securities and Exchange Commission). The financial regulator of the United States. **Important for crypto because it has authority over the enforcement of the classification of security tokens**.

MiCA (Markets in Crypto-Assets). The European Union's regulatory framework for crypto-assets, in force since 2024. **Important for projects operating in the EU**.

⁂

Section 12: Analysis and evaluation concepts

Due diligence. A systematic and critical examination of a project before committing capital or resources. **Difference from «research»**: research is the gathering of information; due diligence is structured evaluation with specific frameworks.

Whitepaper. A document that describes a crypto project, typically including motivation, technical architecture, tokenomics, and roadmap. **For Bitcoin Hyper, there is an official whitepaper and numerous technical research posts**.

Roadmap. The chronological plan of development and milestones of a project. **To be evaluated with skepticism**: publicized timelines are often exceeded significantly.

Milestone. Specific and measurable objectives in the development of a project. **For Bitcoin Hyper, key milestones include**: the mainnet launch, published audits, institutional partnerships, progressive decentralization.

Burn rate. The speed at which a project consumes capital, typically for development and operations. **Important**: understanding the burn rate helps in evaluating the sustainability of the project.

Runway. How long a project can continue to operate before running out of capital, calculated as available capital divided by burn rate. **To monitor**: projects with a short runway may be forced into cuts or closure.

Network effect. The phenomenon whereby the value of a system increases faster than the number of its users. **Critical for Layer 2s**: without a network effect, even excellent technology fails to compete.

Path dependency. A characteristic of systems where the history of past decisions significantly influences future possibilities. **Important for Bitcoin Hyper**: technical choices made today limit possible future evolutions.

Lindy effect. The principle whereby the expected future longevity of a technology is proportional to its past longevity. **Bitcoin has a strong Lindy effect** after 17 years; new Layer 2s have yet to build it.

⁂

Section 13: Concepts specific to Bitcoin Hyper

Bitcoin Hyper. A Bitcoin Layer 2 designed as a rollup with the Solana Virtual Machine. **Distinctive characteristics**: SVM-compatibility, structural anchoring to Bitcoin, a path of progressive decentralization.

$HYPER. Bitcoin Hyper's native token. **Roles**: fee payment, operator incentives, governance, collateral, value-capture.

Canonical Bridge. Bitcoin Hyper's official bridge between native Bitcoin and the rollup. **A critical component** of the system's architecture.

Bitcoin Relay. A mechanism that brings information from the Bitcoin blockchain onto the rollup, allowing the rollup to react to events on Bitcoin. **An important component** for the Bitcoin-Hyper integration.

Hyper sequencer. Bitcoin Hyper's specific sequencer, initially centralized and run by the team, with a path of progressive decentralization.

Glimpse. A term used by the Hyper team to refer to the preview of the integrated ecosystem (wallet, explorer, staking, bridge) that users will see at the mainnet.

Global execution layer for Bitcoin. Bitcoin Hyper's long-term vision of becoming the reference platform for programmable applications on Bitcoin.

⁂

WHAT TO TAKE AWAY FROM THIS GLOSSARY

The sector's vocabulary is vast and continuously evolving. It is not realistic to expect to memorize all the terms in one go, and it is not even necessary. **What is important** is to understand the conceptual connections between the terms, to see how they organize into thematic families, and to return to the glossary when unclear terms are encountered.

For Bitcoin Hyper specifically, some terms are particularly important to master: **rollup, sequencer, Canonical Bridge, anchoring, fraud proof, validity proof, forced exit, SVM, account model, soft vs hard finality**. Without mastery of these concepts, reading the project's technical documentation and the comparisons with competitors becomes difficult.

The glossary is also a reflection of the complexity of the sector. Every term represents a concept developed to solve a specific problem, and understanding why it exists helps in understanding how it works. **Recommended approach**: when an unclear term is encountered, not only look up the definition but also understand the problem that the concept solves.

Appendix A closes here. We have presented a complete glossary of technical terms organized conceptually, with definitions that show the connections between the different terms. For the chronology of the Bitcoin Hyper project's updates, the reader may refer to the primary sources listed in the Bibliography, which provide a historical reference for those who want to understand the evolution of the project over time.

CRITICAL APPARATUS

Bibliography and References

Primary and secondary sources and online resources used in the writing

⁂

The apparatus that follows gathers the sources that fed the writing of this book, organized by type. It is not an exhaustive bibliography on the subject of Bitcoin Layer 2s — that would require a volume of its own — but an *operational selection* of what the reader can actually consult to explore further, verify, or contest the theses presented. Every reference was checked at the time of publication; the links may deteriorate over time, and in that case I suggest searching for the title of the document on search engines or on archive.org.

Primary sources · Bitcoin Hyper

The official documents of the project described in the book. They are the first reference to consult, but they should be read with the critical framework built in the text.

- Bitcoin Hyper, *Whitepaper v1.0*, 2025. Positioning document published by the team. Available at bitcoinhyper.com/whitepaper.
- Bitcoin Hyper, *Research Posts*, 2025–2026. Series of research posts on sequencing, ZK proofs, multi-decade scalability, anchoring. Updated at bitcoinhyper.com/research.
- Bitcoin Hyper, *Come Bitcoin Hyper rende più semplice l'accesso cross-chain* [How Bitcoin Hyper Makes Cross-Chain Access Easier], June 26, 2026. Positioning communication on cross-chain access published on the project's official channels.
- Bitcoin Hyper, *Tokenomics Public Disclosure*, 2025. Allocation of $HYPER, vesting schedule, governance. Verifiable on-chain through the vesting smart contracts.
- Bitcoin Hyper, *Devnet documentation*, 2025–2026. Technical documentation for developers. docs.bitcoinhyper.com.

Primary sources · Bitcoin and base protocols

- Nakamoto, Satoshi, *Bitcoin: A Peer-to-Peer Electronic Cash System*, October 2008. The founding whitepaper. Available at bitcoin.org/bitcoin.pdf.
- BIP 340, 341, 342 — *Taproot specifications*, 2020. The technical specifications of the Taproot upgrade activated in 2021.
- BIP 141 — *Segregated Witness*, 2015. The standard that quadrupled the effective capacity of Bitcoin blocks in 2017.
- Lamport, Leslie · Shostak, Robert · Pease, Marshall, *The Byzantine Generals Problem*, in «ACM Transactions on Programming Languages and Systems», vol. 4, no. 3, July 1982, pp. 382–401. The theoretical foundation of distributed consensus.

Primary sources · Lightning, Ethereum, and other Layer 2s

- Poon, Joseph · Dryja, Thaddeus, *The Bitcoin Lightning Network: Scalable Off-Chain Instant Payments*, draft 0.5.9.2, January 2016. lightning.network.
- Buterin, Vitalik, *A Next-Generation Smart Contract and Decentralized Application Platform*, November 2013. Ethereum's whitepaper.
- Buterin, Vitalik, *An Incomplete Guide to Rollups*, January 2021. At vitalik.eth.limo.
- Yakovenko, Anatoly, *Solana: A new architecture for a high performance blockchain*, 2017. Solana's whitepaper and the introduction of the Sealevel model.

- Al-Bassam, Mustafa · Sonnino, Alberto · Buterin, Vitalik, *Fraud and Data Availability Proofs: Maximising Light Client Security and Scaling Blockchains with Dishonest Majorities*, arXiv:1809.09044, 2018.
- Stacks team, *Proof of Transfer (PoX)*, 2020. Technical documentation of Stacks' consensus. docs.stacks.co.
- Rootstock Labs, *RSK Technical Whitepaper*, 2017. rootstock.io.

Critical readings

Books and articles that contributed to the formation of the analytical framework used in this work.

- Bier, Jonathan, *The Blocksize War: The battle over who controls Bitcoin's protocol rules*, independent edition, 2021. Historical and political reconstruction of the war over block size.
- Antonopoulos, Andreas, *Mastering Bitcoin: Programming the Open Blockchain*, O'Reilly, 2017 (3rd ed. 2023). Technical reference for understanding the Bitcoin protocol.
- Antonopoulos, Andreas, *The Internet of Money*, vols. I–III, Merkle Bloom, 2016–2019. For Bitcoin's philosophical-economic framework.
- Ammous, Saifedean, *The Bitcoin Standard*, Wiley, 2018 (It. trans. *Lo standard Bitcoin*, Bitcoin Italia Podcast, 2020). For the macroeconomic framework, although many theses require critical reading.
- Tapscott, Don & Alex, *Blockchain Revolution*, Portfolio Penguin, 2018 (It. trans. Franco Angeli). Historical, useful for context.

Useful online resources

Sites, dashboards, and tools that the reader can actively consult to verify metrics, monitor evolutions, and do independent due diligence.

- **L2BEAT** · l2beat.com — reference dashboard for TVL metrics, security, and decentralization status of Layer 2s (focused on Ethereum but includes some Bitcoin projects).
- **Blockstream Explorer** · blockstream.info — Bitcoin explorer with Liquid support and advanced search.
- **Mempool.space** · mempool.space — real-time visualization of the mempool, fees, and Bitcoin network metrics.
- **1ML** · 1ml.com — statistics and topology of the Lightning Network.
- **Hyper Explorer** · explorer.bitcoinhyper.com — Bitcoin Hyper's block explorer (devnet/testnet).
- **DefiLlama** · defillama.com — multi-chain TVL aggregator with sections dedicated to Layer 2s.
- **Bitcoin Optech** · bitcoinops.org — Bitcoin technical newsletter for operators, weekly, with coverage of protocol developments.
- **Bankless** · bankless.com — podcast and newsletter with good Layer 2 coverage (Ethereum-oriented, but useful as a methodological reference).
- **Sumsub, Veriff, Onfido** — KYC/AML providers for crypto pre-sales, covered in Volume II.

Normative and regulatory documents

- **Regulation (EU) 2023/1114 — MiCA** (Markets in Crypto-Assets). The European regulatory framework for crypto-assets, which entered into force in phases between June 2024 and December

2024. Official text at eur-lex.europa.eu.

- **SEC v. Ripple Labs**, 2020–2024. The United States legal case that influenced the interpretation of the Howey test applied to crypto tokens.
- **FATF Travel Rule**, Recommendation 16, 2019 and subsequent updates. International AML compliance standard for Virtual Asset Service Providers.
- **Banca d'Italia**, *Comunicazione sui crypto-asset*, various years. Available at bancaditalia.it.

Verification tools for due diligence

- **Etherscan, Blockchair, Mempool** — multi-chain explorers for verifying transactions and smart contracts.
- **GitHub** — direct verification of the project's repositories: number of contributors, commit frequency, presence of open critical issues, quality of the tests.
- **Snyk, GitGuardian** — automatic analysis of vulnerabilities in public repositories.
- **Trail of Bits, OpenZeppelin, Spearbit, ConsenSys Diligence** — reference crypto audit firms; look for their public reports on the projects you evaluate.
- **Immunefi** · immunefi.com — crypto bug bounty platform. The presence of a project on Immunefi with significant bounties is a positive signal of maturity.

Updated sources · July 2026

The most recent integrations (July 2026) rest on the sources that follow, gathered by type. They are complementary to the general bibliography, not a replacement for it.

Primary regulatory sources

- CNMV (Comisión Nacional del Mercado de Valores), *Advertencia al público sobre entidades no registradas*, warning of January 19, 2026. Direct URL to the original PDF: cnmv.es/webservices/verdocumento/ver?e=TFqk8fnW19d833w1qJGMcZqsmhmHlGKVzGKYDPXP7jQPj57IXgF7VdIcuAns0KKL. General section: cnmv.es/portal/Consultas/Consulta?id=14.
- Regulation (EU) 2023/1114 (MiCA / MiCAR), published on May 31, 2023. Official text at eur-lex.europa.eu.
- ESMA, public register of authorized CASPs: esma.europa.eu/document/list-authorised-crypto-asset-service-providers.
- Companies House UK, public company records: find-and-update.company-information.service.gov.uk. Malta Business Registry: mbr.mt. BVI Financial Services Commission: bvifsc.vg.

Audits and on-chain verifications

- Coinsult, *Bitcoin Hyper Audit Report*, May 2025: coinsult.net/projects/bitcoin-hyper.
- SpyWolf, *Security Audit Report — Bitcoin Hyper*: spywolf.co.
- Etherscan, record of Bitcoin Hyper's ERC-20 contract: the presale contract is verifiable on etherscan.io at the address declared by the project's team.

Independent chronicles and analyses of the project

- TheHolyCoins, *Spain CNMV Issues MiCA Warning on Bitcoin Hyper*, February 2026: theholycoins.com/news/spain-s-financial-regulator-cnmv-publishes-mica-warning-on-bitcoin-hyper-usdhyper-and-related.
- TheHolyCoins, *Bitcoin Hyper Presale Review*, March 2026: theholycoins.com/news/bitcoin-hyper-presale-review-is-the-bitcoin-layer-2-hyper-token-a-legit-project-or-a-scam.
- TheHolyCoins, *Finixio Network Exposed* series, parts 1–3, 2025–2026.
- Cryptonews, *Is Bitcoin Hyper a Scam or Legit?*, March 2026: cryptonews.com/cryptocurrency/is-bitcoin-hyper-a-scam-or-legit.
- 99Bitcoins, *$HYPER Analysis: Is Bitcoin Hyper a Legit L2 or Presale Risk?*, March 2026: 99bitcoins.com/cryptocurrency/is-bitcoin-hyper-legit-or-a-scam.
- CoinGabbar, *Bitcoin Hyper Presale Trends*, April 2026: coingabbar.com/en/crypto-currency-news/bitcoin-hyper-presale-hits-32m-q3-2026-mainnet-launch-plans.
- TradersUnion, *Is BITCOIN HYPER a Safe or Scam?*, April 2026: tradersunion.com/scam-or-safe/bitcoin-hyper-review.
- Trustpilot, page for Bitcoinhyper.com: trustpilot.com/review/bitcoinhyper.com (rating subject to change over time).

Layer 2 competitors, 2024–2026 generation

- Citrea: citrea.xyz · documentation: docs.citrea.xyz · repository: github.com/chainwayxyz/citrea.
- BitLayer: bitlayer.org · TVL dashboard: defillama.com/chain/Bitlayer.
- BOB (Build on Bitcoin): gobob.xyz · documentation: docs.gobob.xyz.
- Merlin Chain: merlinchain.io.
- Botanix Labs: botanixlabs.com · documentation: docs.botanixlabs.com.
- L2BEAT, dashboard of Layer 2 metrics and security: l2beat.com.
- DefiLlama, Bitcoin Sidechains category: defillama.com.

Temporal archives

- Internet Archive — Wayback Machine: web.archive.org. For the temporal snapshots of bitcoinhyper.com useful for documenting the trajectory of the staking APY and the evolutions of the presale page.

The Author and the Publisher

Michele Stefanelli is an Independent Financial Advisor, registered with the OCF Register, a member of NAFOP and AIAF, and the founder of MS Digital Asset Academy. Executive education at the Saïd Business School, University of Oxford. Over 35 years of experience between traditional finance and innovation, with a specialization in FinTech, blockchain, and digital assets.

For subsequent writings, updated analyses, errata, contacts, and for the public and continuously updated version of the work contained in this book:

- **michelestefanelli.com** — institutional site of MS Studio, home of the fee-only professional advisory practice.

- **bitcoinhyper.it** — independent editorial knowledge base of MS Digital Asset Academy. Public and free version of the research material at the base of this book: technical analyses, comparative sheets, glossary, structured due diligence, updated project status dashboard, blog, podcast. No paywall, no mandatory newsletter.
- **MS Digital Asset Academy** — editorial and research division of MS Studio dedicated to digital assets. Future publications of the *Due Diligence Cripto* series will be announced on the channels above.

Author's disclosure. The author has no economic or contractual relationships with Sentinum Ltd. (BVI), the issuer of $HYPER. Any direct positions in the projects cited are declared, when relevant, on the disclosure page of the site bitcoinhyper.it/disclaimer.

⁂

An honest bibliography is one that shows the reader not only what the author has read, but also where they can look for opinions different from their own. The sources listed above deliberately include both materials in favor of the rollup-on-Bitcoin thesis and critical materials. It is up to the reader to make their own use of them.

THE AUTHOR

Michele Stefanelli

Michele Stefanelli is an **Independent Financial Advisor**, registered with the Register kept by the OCF – Organismo di vigilanza e tenuta dell'Albo unico dei Consulenti Finanziari. He is a member of **NAFOP** – Associazione Italiana Consulenti Finanziari Indipendenti and of **AIAF** – Associazione Italiana per l'Analisi Finanziaria. He is the founder of **MS Digital Asset Academy**.

His professional activity sits at the crossroads of independent financial advisory, fintech, blockchain, digital assets, and artificial intelligence applied to financial markets. He has developed a particular focus on the new infrastructures of digital finance, with dedicated studies on Bitcoin, Layer 2 architectures, tokenization, and crypto-assets.

He complements his professional profile with executive education at the **Saïd Business School, University of Oxford**, dedicated to fintech, algorithmic trading, and the applications of generative and agentic AI in markets and decision-making processes.

Through his advisory, research, training, and educational activity, he accompanies investors, entrepreneurs, and professionals in understanding the transformations that are redefining global finance, adopting an approach that is independent, document-based, and oriented to due diligence and to the informed evaluation of risks.

Institutional site: michelestefanelli.com
MS Digital Asset Academy: msdigitalasset.com
Knowledge base: bitcoinhyper.it
YouTube: @MSDigitalAssetAcademy
Email: studio@michelestefanelli.com
Publisher: MS Digital Asset Academy

Updated as of July 2026

THE JOURNEY CONTINUES

Volume II

Competitive analysis, tokenomics, and operational strategy.

The comparison with the other Layer 2s, the tokenomics of $HYPER, the state of the ecosystem, the gaps between promise and whitepaper, the due diligence, and the pre-mainnet scenarios.

www.ingramcontent.com/pod-product-compliance
Lightning Source LLC
LaVergne TN
LVHW060015210926
848481LV00013B/3715